The United States and Pakistan, 1947–2000

An ADST-DACOR
Diplomats and Diplomacy Book

The United States and Pakistan, 1947–2000

Disenchanted Allies

DENNIS KUX

WOODROW WILSON CENTER PRESS
Washington, D.C.

THE JOHNS HOPKINS UNIVERSITY PRESS
Baltimore and London

EDITORIAL OFFICES

Woodrow Wilson Center Press
One Woodrow Wilson Plaza
1300 Pennsylvania Avenue, N.W.
Washington, D.C. 20004-3027
Telephone 202-691-4010
wwics.si.edu

ORDER FROM

The Johns Hopkins University Press
P.O. Box 50370
Baltimore, Maryland 21211
Telephone 1-800-537-5487
www.press.jhu.edu

Printed in the United States of America on acid-free paper ∞

24689731

Library of Congress Cataloging-in-Publications Data

Kux, Dennis, 1931-
The United States and Pakistan, 1947-2000: disenchanted allies / Dennis Kux.
p. cm. — (The ADST-DACOR diplomats and diplomacy series)
Includes bibliographical references and index.
ISBN 0-8018-6571-9 (hardcover : alk. paper)—ISBN 0-8018-6572-7 (pbk. : alk. paper)
1. United States—Foreign relations—Pakistan. 2. Pakistan—Foreign relations—United States. I. Title. II. Series.
E183.8.P18 K89 2001
327.7305491′09′045--dc21
00-013260

ABOUT THE CENTER

The Center is the living memorial of the United States of America to the nation's twenty-eighth president, Woodrow Wilson. Congress established the Woodrow Wilson Center in 1968 as an international institute for advanced study, "symbolizing and strengthening the fruitful relationship between the world of learning and the world of public affairs." The Center opened in 1970 under its own board of trustees.

In all its activities the Woodrow Wilson Center is a nonprofit, nonpartisan organization, supported financially by annual appropriations from the Congress, and by the contributions of foundations, corporations, and individuals. Conclusions or opinions expressed in Center publications and programs are those of the authors and speakers and do not necessarily reflect the views of the Center staff, fellows, trustees, advisory groups, or any individuals or organizations that provide financial support to the Center.

To Marie
with much love and gratitude
for her patience, encouragement, and interest
in South Asia

Contents

Foreword

The Association for Diplomatic Studies and Training (ADST) research center twice welcomed retired ambassador and career diplomat Dennis Kux as a research fellow working on U.S.-Pakistan relations. He is one among the many extraordinary men and women who, for the past 225 years, have represented the United States abroad under all kinds of circumstances. What they did and how and why they did it remain little known to their compatriots. In 1995, the ADST, together with Diplomatic and Consular Officers, Retired (DACOR), created the ADST-DACOR Diplomats and Diplomacy Series to increase public knowledge and appreciation of the involvement of American diplomats in world history. The series seeks to demystify diplomacy by telling the story of those who have conducted our foreign relations, as they saw them, lived them, and reported them. *The United States and Pakistan, 1947–2000: Disenchanted Allies,* the result of Ambassador Kux's extensive research, was enthusiastically adopted for inclusion in this series.

From the moment Pakistan gained its independence in 1947, its relations with the United States have careened between intimate partnership and enormous friction—reflecting the ups and downs of global and regional geopolitics and disparate national interests. Dennis Kux has written the first comprehensive history of this roller-coaster relationship from its inception to the present. A quintessential scholar-diplomat, Kux specialized in South Asia during much of his Foreign Service career and speaks both Urdu and Tamil. His acclaimed history of U.S.-India relations, *India and the United States: Estranged Democracies, 1941–1991,* was published in both countries. Work on this companion volume has taken him three times to Pakistan, where he had served first at the embassy in Karachi and ten years later in the new capital of Islamabad. He worked on South Asia in the State Department, lastly as country director for India. He also served in India and coedited the 1999 volume *India and Pakistan: The First Fifty Years.*

In *The United States and Pakistan, 1947–2000,* Kux combines scholarly research and analysis with his diplomat's understanding of what lies "between the lines" in official documents. Though the Cold War is over, Pakistan retains strategic importance for the United States, not least because of Pakistan's and India's festering enmity over Kashmir, their nuclear detonations, Pakistan's problematic links to Afghanistan, and its role in the Islamic world. Through extensive research, including more than 120 interviews with senior U.S. and Pakistani officials, and exercising scrupulous fairness, Dennis Kux gives a balanced history of a major diplomatic challenge.

EDWARD M. ROWELL, President
Association for Diplomatic Studies and Training
KENNETH N. ROGERS, JR., President
Diplomatic and Consular Officers, Retired

Acknowledgments

I am deeply grateful to the several institutions and many people who generously helped me during the five years I worked on *The United States and Pakistan,1947–2000: Disenchanted Allies.* Grants from the Fulbright Commission and the American Institute of Pakistan Studies permitted extended stays in Pakistan during 1995–96 and 1998. A fellowship at the Woodrow Wilson International Center for Scholars provided a home in 1996–97. The Association for Diplomatic Studies and Training and the Middle East Institute also generously offered friendly work settings in 1997–98 and 1999–2000. At various times during my research, I was lucky to have the help of excellent assistants: Jeff Kueter, then a graduate student at George Washington University, and Damon Daniels, David Abruzino, and Sohila Comninos, interns at the Wilson Center.

In gathering relevant U.S. government documents, the staffs at the National Archives, the Harry S. Truman, Dwight D. Eisenhower, John F. Kennedy, and Lyndon B. Johnson presidential libraries, and the Nixon Presidential Materials Project provided efficient and rapid help. I also received many newly declassified documents, mainly for the years since the Nixon administration, in response to Freedom of Information Act requests. In addition, I drew on official British records available at the Public Record Office in London, which shed much light on U.S.-Pakistan relations in the early years after independence.

On the Pakistani side, unfortunately, official documents were unavailable, except for minutes of cabinet meetings for August–December 1947. For this reason, interviews with more than fifty senior officials who played key roles in their country's dealings with the United States proved an indispensable resource. I owe special and deep appreciation to General K. M. Arif, Altaf Gauhar, Syeda Abida Hussein, Sahibzada Yaqub Khan, Sultan Mohammed Khan, Niaz Naik, Lt. Gen. Syed Refaqat, Abdul Sattar, and Agha Shahi, who patiently answered my many questions in multiple interviews. I also am sincerely thankful for the encouragement and assistance received from ambassadors Maleeha Lodhi and Riaz Khokar, who represented Pakistan in Washington while I was writing the book, and from Zamir Akram, deputy chief of mission at the Pakistan embassy for much of this time.

On the American side, interviews with more than sixty officials who dealt with Pakistan provided a valuable supplement to archival sources and were especially helpful in understanding events of recent years. Except for sessions with intelligence officers and discussions reviewing current developments, all interviews were on the record. Further useful information came from oral histories of officials who dealt with Pakistan, mostly from the extensive foreign affairs archive of the Association for Diplomatic Studies and Training. Ambassadors to Pakistan Thomas W. Simons, Jr., and William Milan and assistant secretaries of state for South Asia Robin Raphel and Karl F. Inderfurth offered much support and good cheer. I also want to thank Leonard Scensny and Walter Andersen of the State Department for their helpful response to my many calls for assistance.

After drafting the manuscript, I was extraordinarily fortunate that many individuals who are knowledgeable about U.S.-Pakistan relations were kind enough to review all or part of the text and give me their reactions. I am enormously grateful to Stephen P. Cohen, Sumit Ganguly, Robert Hathaway, Masud Khan, the late Paul Kreisberg, George Sherman, Sidney Sober, George Tanham, Thomas Thornton, Warren Unna, and Marvin Weinbaum, who patiently read the entire manuscript and provided many valuable comments. I am similarly indebted to Iqbal Akhund, Donald Camp, the late Peter Constable, Alan Eastham, Deane Hinton, Gen. Jehangir Karamat, Winston Lord, Robert Oakley, Nicholas Platt, Teresita and Howard Schaffer, Joseph J. Sisco, Ronald Spiers, Shirin Tahir-Kheli, and Eliza Van Hollen, who read chapters dealing with their personal involvement with U.S.-Pakistan relations and offered numerous useful suggestions.

Finally, I am much indebted for the efficient editorial assistance that I received from Joseph Brinley and Patricia Katayama of the Woodrow

Wilson Center Press, copyeditor Traci Nagle, and Margery Thompson of the Association for Diplomatic Studies and Training.

It is, in fact, hard for me to find appropriate words to express adequately my gratitude to all those who have aided me in producing this book. Their help and encouragement have clearly made *The United States and Pakistan, 1947–2000,* a far better and more accurate account of the relations between these disenchanted allies.

Introduction

The United States and Pakistan, 1947–2000: Disenchanted Allies ends a journey that started in November 1957 when I arrived in Karachi to begin my first diplomatic assignment. Pakistan was then America's "most allied ally in Asia," and relations were extremely cordial. During the two years I spent in Karachi, I became deeply interested in South Asia and decided to specialize in the region. A tour in India was followed by work on the subcontinent in the State Department. In 1969, I returned to Pakistan for a second assignment, this time in the new capital, Islamabad. By then, bilateral relations had soured. After the United States suspended aid during the 1965 India-Pakistan war, Pakistanis felt let down, even betrayed.

For me personally, the tour in Islamabad was professionally challenging and always interesting. For Pakistan, however, it was a time of national tragedy. Broad smiles over the first democratic elections in December 1970 turned to anguish after the military cracked down on East Pakistanis. Four months later, in July 1971, my assignment in Islamabad ended. My final task there was to serve as the unwitting control officer for Henry Kissinger's secret trip to China.

Back in Washington, I worked for five years on India and then spent the next decade dealing with other parts of the world, in the State Department and overseas. South Asia, however, was never far from my thoughts. In 1990 I became a fellow at the National Defense University in Washington in order to write a history of U.S-India relations. After retiring from the Foreign Service in the fall of 1994, I decided to try my hand at a companion history of U.S.-Pakistan relations. Although other authors have discussed periods and aspects of this relationship, none has written a comprehensive account. *Disenchanted Allies* tries to fill this void.

The task has proven more difficult and taken longer than preparing the history of U.S.-India relations. In contrast with the relatively stable, if estranged, relationship with India, American interaction with Pakistan has been intense and extraordinarily volatile. In the Eisenhower, Nixon, and Reagan years, the United States and Pakistan were allies or close partners. But at other times—during the Kennedy, Johnson, Carter, Bush, and Clinton presidencies—relations have been strained.

The unusual volatility has puzzled and frustrated both Americans and Pakistanis. I did not set out to find the reason for the turbulent relations, but as my work on *Disenchanted Allies* progressed, an answer began to take shape: It was not American fickleness or Pakistani stubbornness that explained the many ups and downs, but rather that U.S. and Pakistani interests and policies have been at odds almost as often as they have been in phase.

Pakistan has been and remains fixated on India. Although anticommunist, Karachi joined the U.S.-led alliance system in 1954–55 principally to strengthen itself against India. Pakistan's nuclear program, the source of enormous friction with the United States, has been motivated by the not unsurprising desire to have a deterrent against India's nuclear capability. Even Islamabad's wish for a friendly regime in Afghanistan is rooted in part in the hope of gaining "strategic depth" against India. Yet, except for President Nixon's "tilt" policy during the 1971 Bangladesh crisis, the United States has not been willing to take Pakistan's side against its larger neighbor. Despite estrangement, the United States has never seen India as an enemy.

During the four decades of the Cold War, U.S. interest in Pakistan waxed and waned as administrations judged that country to be helpful or harmful to American global aims. Since the disintegration of the Iron Curtain, relations have been burdened by continuing frictions over issues of nuclear proliferation and over Pakistan's handling of Islamic extremists, its backing of the Taliban in Afghanistan, and its support for the insurgency in Kashmir.

Disenchanted Allies tells the story of the political and security interaction between the two countries and discusses other aspects of the relationship, such as economic questions, mainly as they affect political-security ties. The book uses a chronological organization. It begins with a discussion of the pre-independence years and follows with chapters for each U.S. president since then, with two for the busy Eisenhower years, when the United States and Pakistan became allies. A final chapter draws conclusions.

Wherever possible, I have relied on primary sources or on interviews with persons who were or are directly involved with relations. Given my background as a State Department South Asia specialist, the wealth of American documents, and the paucity of Pakistani ones, the narrative inevitably is more U.S.-centered than I would have preferred. I have tried hard, nonetheless, to write a balanced history that presents the Pakistani, as well as the American, perspective. The willingness of retired Pakistani officials to share remembrances of their dealings with the United States has proven invaluable in helping me describe the rationale for Pakistan's actions and its perception of U.S. policies.

President Bill Clinton's March 25, 2000, stop in a Pakistan once more ruled by the military and his "tough love" approach underscored the complex range of bilateral issues. How Pakistan manages its troubled domestic political and economic scene, how it deals with the Taliban and other Islamic fundamentalists, and how it handles its tension-laden relations with India, vastly more dangerous since the two neighbors tested their nuclear weapons capabilities in May 1998, will have a decisive impact on U.S. interests in the subcontinent and beyond. As a narrative of past U.S.-Pakistan engagement, *Disenchanted Allies* will, I hope, prove useful to policymakers, scholars and students, business officials and journalists, and all in the general public who have an interest in America's relations with what President Clinton has called "one of the most dangerous parts of the world."

The United States and Pakistan, 1947–2000

1

The United States and the Pakistan Movement

On August 7, 1947, Mohammed Ali Jinnah flew from New Delhi to Karachi to take control of a nation about to be born: Pakistan. A vast but subdued throng greeted the leader of India's one hundred million Muslims at the airport, some fifteen miles from the heart of the city. "As the plane landed and came to a halt, shouts of 'Quaid-i-Azam Zindabad' (Long live the Great Leader) and 'Pakistan Zindabad' (Long live Pakistan) were raised by the crowd," American diplomat H. Gordon Minnigerode reported to the State Department.[1]

A three-mile-long procession drove the seventy-year-old Jinnah to Government House, a spacious colonial dwelling that until hours before had been the residence of the British governor of Sindh province. Its former occupant, Sir Francis Mudie, had shifted to Lahore to become the first governor of Pakistan's Punjab province. When Jinnah arrived at his new home, the green-and-white Muslim League emblem, soon to be the national flag of Pakistan, was unfurled on the flagstaff in place of the British Union Jack.[2]

Formerly a sleepy port city of 300,000 and the capital of the backwater province of Sindh, Karachi had doubled in population after it, rather than Lahore (the new country's largest city), was named as Pakistan's seat of government. Lahore was considered too close to India for comfort, with the border only a few miles away. As thousands of Muslim refugees swarmed into the new capital, most of the Hindu residents, formerly half of the population, fled in the other direction. Fortunately, Karachi was spared the savage communal riots that ripped apart the Punjab and created havoc and misery in Lahore, New Delhi, and elsewhere.

Jinnah was an unlikely father of a separate Muslim state. As an outstanding young lawyer in Bombay, he had been a vocal spokesperson for Hindu-Muslim unity. In 1916, he had presided over both the Muslim League, the main political voice for the Muslims of India, and the Indian National Congress, the preeminent nationalist, and predominantly Hindu, organization. Like Mohandas Gandhi, who led the Congress in the 1920s and 1930s, Jinnah was an ardent Indian nationalist. Unlike Gandhi, Jinnah eschewed populist mass politics, preferring the debates of the Central Legislative Assembly in Delhi.

Jinnah's lifestyle also made him an unusual leader of a movement for a separate Muslim homeland. He dressed immaculately in the most expensive British fashions and sported a monocle. In public, during the campaign for Pakistan, Jinnah wore Indian Muslim garb, including the black *karakul* cap that became his trademark, but in the privacy of his home would switch to Western dress. The Muslim League chief had married a non-Muslim and rarely entered a mosque. He was not comfortable speaking in Urdu, the lingua franca of Muslim India, and instead delivered his speeches in impeccable English with few traces of an Indian accent.

Until the late 1930s, Jinnah's political approach was that of strict constitutionalism. Only after elections in 1937 brought Congress Party governments to power in eight of the eleven provinces of British India did the Muslim League, which fared badly in the balloting, begin seriously to consider partition as its goal. Jinnah and other Muslim leaders feared that in an independent but undivided India the Muslim minority—one-quarter of the population—would not receive fair treatment from the Hindu majority.

In 1940, at Lahore, the League adopted partition as its goal and appealed for the support of the Muslim masses with the emotionally charged cry of "Islam in danger." Jinnah's single-minded, demanding, yet tactically brilliant leadership, in less than a decade, transformed the idea of Pakistan from the chimera of a handful to the reality of a new nation of seventy million people. As the Muslim League's popularity grew, Jinnah, its chief, was crowned "Quaid-i-Azam," or "Great Leader."

American journalist Phillips Talbot was in Karachi in August 1947 to report on India's and Pakistan's independence for the Chicago *Daily News*. Talbot, who would later serve as the assistant secretary of state for Near Eastern and South Asian affairs during the Kennedy administration, wrote,

> From the beginning the birth of Pakistan was Jinnah's show. While his ministers attended to details and worked at developing enthusiasm, he played his role with monarchial aloofness. As Governor General designate of Pakistan he installed himself in the local Government House, a new, ample building. The panoply of British governorships continued. The new resident kept the same police guard at night, the same impassive doorman, the same jeep and motorcycle escort when he drove in the official Humber. Though looking tired and far from well as he neared 71, Jinnah held a firm grip on the government reins.[3]

Pakistan's Independence Ceremonies

The evening of August 13, 1947, Jinnah and his younger sister, Fatima, his companion and confidante, hosted a reception at Government House for the British viceroy of India, Lord Mountbatten, and his wife Edwina, who had arrived from New Delhi earlier in the day. "The several thousands present passed down the receiving line to meet the elegant Viceroy, . . . the ever-gracious Lady Mountbatten, the unsmiling, impeccable Mr. Jinnah and the scarcely noticed Fatima," Talbot's wife, Mildred, wrote.[4] Shocked by his gaunt appearance, she described Jinnah as looking "like a walking, talking corpse."[5] Later that evening, the Jinnahs entertained the Mountbattens and some fifty guests. The only diplomats present, apart from British and the Indian high commissioners, were the chargé d'affaires of the newly established U.S. embassy, Charles Lewis, and the acting Chinese consul general.[6]

On the morning of August 14, 1947, the viceroy symbolically transferred power from the British Crown to the new dominion of Pakistan. The ceremony took place in the smallish chamber of the Sindh Provincial Assembly, which would become the home of Pakistan's Constituent Assembly. After Mountbatten read a message of friendship from King George VI, adding warm words of his own, the governor general–designate, in turn, pledged friendship between Pakistan and Great Britain. Jinnah, according to Mildred Talbot, "set the tone with his stiff, correct manner," which Mountbatten matched "detail for detail in controlled word and action."[7]

Once the ceremony ended, the two leaders rode back to Government House sitting side by side in the open horse-drawn state carriage. An assassination threat against Jinnah stretched nerves as the two passed exposed through the crowded city streets. During lunch, Mountbatten recalled Jinnah's touching his knee in a rare moment of humor to say wryly, "Thank God I was able to bring you back alive!"[8] As soon as the meal was over, Mountbatten flew back to New Delhi, where, at the strike of midnight, he proclaimed India's independence and was sworn in as its first governor-general. Mountbatten had hoped to become Pakistan's governor-general, as well, but Jinnah decided that he, not the last British viceroy, would occupy that position.

In contrast to joyous celebrations in New Delhi, Bombay, and other Indian cities, the mood in Pakistan's new capital remained subdued. "While there was [a] certain amount of jubilation in Karachi, the manifestations on the whole were restrained," American chargé Lewis cabled the State Department, adding that the Muslims of Sindh were perhaps not given to emotional displays and the city's Hindus could "hardly be expected to be in [a] jubilant mood over partition."[9] Still, Phillips Talbot sensed "an atmosphere of solid satisfaction at the creation of the Muslim state. This is what we've been waiting for, people seemed to be saying."[10]

The U.S. press, in reporting these ceremonies, stressed that the creation of independent India and Pakistan marked a major step toward the ending of European colonial rule in Asia. Although editorial comment was generally positive, paralleling friendly words of welcome from President Harry S. Truman and Secretary of State George C. Marshall, *Time,* the widely read national weekly newsmagazine, reflected the pro-India bias of its publisher, Henry Luce. The people of Karachi, *Time* commented, "did not welcome Pakistan with the wild enthusiasm that swept the new dominion of India. After all, Pakistan was the creation of one clever man, Jinnah; the difference between a slick political trick and a mass movement was apparent in the contrast between Karachi and New Delhi."[11]

The U.S. Attitude toward the Pakistan Movement

Turn the clock back seven years to March 1940, when the Muslim League, at its annual session in Lahore, formally adopted as its goal the partition of India into separate Hindu and Muslim states. Few Americans at the time were aware of the political grievances and concerns of India's largest minority community, its hundred million Muslims. In the late 1930s, as the two-nation theory—that British India should become two nations, Hindu India or Hindustan, and Muslim India or Pakistan—gained in popularity, there was little echo in the United States.

Although the India League actively lobbied liberal circles on behalf of the Indian National Congress, the Muslim League had no such organized group in the United States to voice its concerns about the future of the Muslim minority in post-British India.

American press coverage focused mainly on the Congress Party as the leading force for independence and on its principal leaders, Mahatma Gandhi and his designated heir, Jawaharlal Nehru, as the future rulers of free India.[12] Nonetheless, some journalists were reporting about the Muslim League. For example, in 1939, the *New York Times* ran a series of articles about the growing popularity of the League and Jinnah.[13] In his widely read book *Inside Asia,* foreign affairs writer John Gunther described Jinnah as one of the key leaders of the subcontinent.[14]

In 1940, the official American presence in India was limited to consular offices in Calcutta, Bombay, Madras, and Karachi. There was no U.S. diplomatic presence in New Delhi, India's capital. Any official dealings with the Indian government were handled in a cumbersome arrangement through the British Embassy in Washington or the American Embassy in London. Even though the U.S. officials stationed in India dealt mainly with consular and commercial matters, they followed political developments, sending in occasional reports or "dispatches," which reached Washington in diplomatic pouches via airmail. The Calcutta consulate general thus sent in a detailed report on the Muslim League's adoption of the Pakistan resolution on April 5, 1940. A year later, a more analytical dispatch commented perceptively that, although the call for "Pakistan might be postponed or put aside, it would be a great mistake to dismiss the Pakistan resolution as something of decreasing or no importance."[15]

After Pearl Harbor brought America into World War II, Washington began to pay far more attention to India. Just a month earlier, in November 1941, India and the United States had opened direct diplomatic relations. A U.S. mission began to function in New Delhi and an Indian agent-general began his work in Washington. In April 1942, President Franklin Roosevelt sent Louis Johnson, former assistant secretary of war, to head the Delhi mission as his "personal representative." As Japanese forces swept through Malaya and Burma and threatened to invade India, the British belatedly offered political concessions to the Indian nationalists to gain their cooperation in the war effort. Johnson worked feverishly, but unsuccessfully, to broker an agreement between British envoy Sir Stafford Cripps and Congress Party leaders. It was assumed that the Muslim League, which unlike the Congress had backed the Allied war effort, would support the British proposals. Ultimately the Cripps mission failed after Prime Minister Winston Churchill refused a meaningful wartime transfer of power to Indians. Mahatma Gandhi, still the most powerful voice in the Congress, had opposed the British plan, mainly because it left open the possible creation of Pakistan.[16]

An unhappy President Roosevelt sent a strongly worded cable to Churchill, blaming the mission's failure on "the British Government's unwillingness to concede to the Indians the right of self-government."[17] Roosevelt, however, felt that he could not press the British leader further without damaging the Allied war effort against the Axis powers. As the president told Interior Secretary Harold Ickes, "It would be playing with fire if the British Empire told me to mind my own business [about India]."[18]

In 1942 and 1943, a series of articles by Herbert Matthews of the *New York Times* chronicled the wartime rise in the Muslim League's popularity and the pivotal role that its leader would play in deciding India's future. In an October 4, 1942, article headlined "Jinnah Holds the Key to Peace in India," Matthews wrote, "Out of the throes of Indian travail a new figure has arisen and he holds in his hands more power for good or evil than any single Indian politician. It is that tall, thin, exasperatingly deliberate man who seems to be taking pleasure at keeping the world guessing—Mohammed Ali Jinnah. In his delicate hands lies the answer to the riddle: Can Hindus and Moslems agree?"[19]

The top U.S. leadership hoped that they would. President Roosevelt made clear his dislike of the idea of dividing India when British chargé d'affaires Sir Ronald Campbell lunched at the president's family home at Hyde Park, New York, in August 1942. The partition of India "sounded terrible" to American ears after the experience of the U.S. civil war, Roosevelt told the British envoy.[20] In India itself, veteran U.S. diplomat William Phillips, who had replaced Johnson as Roosevelt's personal representative, spent nearly four hours with Jinnah in early 1943 at the latter's home in New Delhi. Phillips found the Muslim League leader "brilliant" and was "attracted to him personally but not to his idea of severing India into separate nations."[21] Phillips later wrote prophetically in his memoirs, "The more I studied Mr. Jinnah's Pakistan, the less it appealed to me as the answer to India's communal problem, since to break India into two separate nations would weaken both and might open Pakistan, at least, to the designs of ambitious neighbors."[22]

As the war progressed, India became a major Allied supply base for sending military equipment to China and for preparing for the reconquest of Burma. Some 350,000 American troops were stationed in India, principally in quartermaster and engineer functions in Bengal and Assam in eastern India. Worried that nationalists might interpret the large U.S. military presence as a sign of political support for the British, an official statement issued on August 12, 1942, stressed that American forces were in India only to fight the war against the Axis.[23]

Even though U.S. diplomats avoided taking sides, they followed developments closely, keeping in touch with the major political groups, including the Muslim League. Among the most frequent caller on Jinnah was John Davies, Jr., a Foreign Service China specialist, who was serving as political adviser to Gen. Joseph W. Stilwell (better known as "Vinegar Joe"), the commander of the China-Burma-India theater. In his reports, Davies praised the Muslim League leader's acumen, commented on his vanity, but thought that Jinnah doubted that he would actually attain his goal of Pakistan, which seemed, initially at least, devised for bargaining purposes to gain political leverage for the Muslims.[24]

In fact, U.S. concerns about India related less to the nature of the postindependence government structure than to the willingness of the British to grant independence. In January 1945, at Phillips's prompting, the State Department publicly reaffirmed its support for a political settlement between the British, the Congress, and the League and offered to help the process along.[25] When Secretary of State Edward Stettinius met British foreign secretary Anthony Eden in April 1945, he urged Britain to move India toward self-rule. Stettinius told Eden that Allied "prestige in the Far East [will] be greatly improved whenever a solution to the problem of India is found." Eden's response was to express doubt that the Indian problem would be solved as long as Gandhi remained alive.[26]

Washington Supports a United India

In the July 1945 general elections, the British Labour Party trounced Churchill's conservatives. Given Labour's long-standing support for Indian independence, this issue was no longer in doubt. What remained in doubt was whether the British and the two principal Indian political groups could agree. The Indian National Congress wanted a united India. The Muslim League urged its division into two separate and independent states.

In the winter of 1945–46, elections in India for a constituent assembly greatly strengthened the League's hand when it won the vast majority of Muslim seats. In March 1946, London dispatched a three-person cabinet mission—Sir Stafford Cripps, Lord Pethick-Lawrence, and A. V. Alexander—in the hope that the trio could devise a plan to preserve the unity of India that was acceptable to both the Congress and the League. By this time, State Department South Asia specialists were becoming worried about developments. Loy Henderson, then head of the Office of Near Eastern and African Affairs, which had responsibility for the subcontinent, sent a memorandum to Undersecretary of State Dean Acheson urging him to take up India informally with Lord Halifax, the British ambassador and a former viceroy of India. "India is regarded in Asia as the acid test of the liberal professions of the Western powers," the Henderson memo stated. Failure to reach a satisfactory settlement would transform "a primarily British-Indian question" into one "of world interest." The memorandum expressed the hope that the British would move quickly to establish an interim government "without allowing any one group [i.e., the Muslim League] to veto this further constitutional progress."[27]

Implying a negative attitude toward Pakistan, the Henderson memo downplayed the significance of the League's sweep of Muslim seats in the Constituent Assembly, but played up the poorer performance of Jinnah's party in provincial elections, which enabled the Muslim League to form governments only in Sindh and Bengal, two of the five Muslim-majority provinces claimed for Pakistan.[28] Although there is no record of Acheson's having discussed India with Halifax, the Henderson memorandum is noteworthy as the only policy document that the author could find in the State Department archives during this critical period of political negotiations about the future of India.

If the State Department was cool toward the idea of Pakistan, some U.S. media commentary was positively hostile. The cover of the April 22, 1946, issue of *Time* pictured a grim-looking Jinnah and the caption, "His Moslem tiger wants to eat the Hindu cow." Commenting that "the Indian sun casts Jinnah's long thin shadow not only across the negotiations in Delhi but over India's future," *Time* acidly described the political rise of Jinnah as "a story of love of country and lust for power, a story that twists and turns like a bullock track in the hills."[29]

The American mission in New Delhi forcefully supported British efforts to maintain a united India. A U.S. diplomat, for example, made a point of cautioning Liaquat Ali Khan, Jinnah's chief lieutenant, that a continued hard-line attitude by the League on the cabinet mission plan would cost it America's sympathy.[30] Although it is unclear what impact the warning had, the Muslim League did agree to the British proposal for a united India with a weak central and strong regional governments. In so doing, Jinnah had played his cards skillfully, the U.S. mission reported to Washington: "[Jinnah's] greatest triumph would appear to lie in the fact that having been castigated both in India and abroad as an intransigent politician senselessly blocking India's road to independence, he is as of today, in a position to charge the Congress with obstructionism. . . . Mr. Jinnah may—for the time being—pose as a pious patriot and a benefactor of the Indian people.[31]

The agreement was short-lived. After Nehru publicly declared that the Congress Party might alter the cabinet mission plan after independence, the Muslim League withdrew its acceptance and refused to join a proposed interim government. Once more, India was deadlocked politically. Until then, Jinnah had been a stickler for constitutional niceties. He now changed tactics to call for demonstrations in favor of Pakistan on August 16, 1946, which he labeled "Deliverance Day." His appeal to the Muslim masses, already highly agitated by the bitterly partisan election campaign waged between the Congress and the League, stoked the embers of large-scale Hindu-Muslim violence.

Beginning with riots in Calcutta, communal disturbances slowly spread through other parts of India. The carnage was gruesome. The Calcutta consulate general reported police estimates of 2,000 dead; according to the India Office in London, the Calcutta disorders left 3,000 dead and 17,500 injured.[32] At the same time, the viceroy, Lord Wavell, proceeded to form the interim government without the participation of the League—even though he had promised Jinnah that he would not do so. The Muslim League leader and his colleagues were furious.

Disturbed by the rapidly deteriorating situation, the State Department became more active in backing British efforts to reach a political settlement. With China racked by civil war between U.S.-supported nationalists and their communist opponents, Washington wanted to avoid yet another major area of turmoil in Asia. On August 27, 1946, Acting

Secretary of State Dean Acheson declared that the United States offered its "best wishes" to the Indian interim government, expressed regret "that the Muslim League has not decided to participate," and hoped "that it may later find it possible to do so."[33] To bolster the interim government's prestige, Washington established full diplomatic relations with India, transforming the U.S. mission in New Delhi into an embassy, even though the British had not yet granted formal independence.[34] Henry Grady, a former assistant secretary of state and the leader of a 1942 wartime economic mission to India, was named the first U.S. ambassador to India.

On November 14, 1946, the initial official contact in Washington with the Muslim League took place. After failing to meet President Truman, M. A. H. Ispahani, a Calcutta businessman close to Jinnah, and later Pakistan's first ambassador to the United States, and Begum Shah Nawaz, a prominent Punjabi personality, spelled out the case for Pakistan to Acheson. The U.S. diplomat responded with a bland expression of thanks for the chance to hear the League's position but avoided taking a substantive stance.[35] Ispahani and Begum Shah Nawaz also participated in a *New York Herald Tribune* forum on the future of India and traveled throughout the United States to promote Pakistan among prominent Americans.[36]

The pair paid particular attention to the influential but anti-Pakistan weekly newsmagazines, *Time* and its companion, *Life,* lunching with senior editors and Clare Booth Luce, a prominent writer-journalist and wife of publisher Henry Luce. Reporting to Jinnah about the meeting, Ispahani urged him and Liaquat to give a good reception to the *Time-Life* South Asia correspondent. "I have learnt that sweet words and first impressions count a lot with Americans. They are inclined to quickly like or dislike an individual or organisation," the envoy wrote.[37] Over the years, Pakistanis would make a point of heeding Ispahani's advice in their dealings with Americans.

Increased U.S. Pressure on Congress and the League

Although the Muslim League eventually joined the interim government, the political deadlock remained unbroken and communal violence continue to rage. Hindu-Muslim disturbances seared eastern India and fresh disorders flared up in Bombay in September 1946. Fear of possible civil war in India and "perhaps at the same time a revolutionary war against the remnants of British power" spurred State Department regional specialists to recommend in late November 1946 stepped-up American pressure for an early agreement between the Muslim League and the Congress. Undersecretary Acheson gave his blessing even though he doubted "our chances for accomplishing very much were very good."[38]

As 1946 drew to a close, a frustrated British prime minister Clement Attlee summoned Nehru and Jinnah to London in a desperate attempt to break the impasse. In support of the effort, the State Department instructed the London embassy to "impress on Indian leaders . . . [the] deep interest" of the United States in the "successful conclusion [of the] talks."[39] In addition, Acheson, in a December 3, 1946, public statement, urged the major Indian political parties to accept the British cabinet mission's proposal.[40] In London, Chargé d'Affaires Waldemar Gallman was able to present the U.S. views to Jinnah at a lunch that they both attended. "During our talk," Gallman cabled, "Jinnah gave no evidence of thinking a solution of the present impasse might be worked out within a reasonable time. He did not seem disturbed by this, but seemed to view future developments coldly, calmly and in a very detached way."[41]

Although the London talks failed, the State Department continued to press for an agreement between the Congress and the League, instructing the New Delhi embassy to urge the Muslim League to cooperate with the Congress within the framework proposed by the British.[42] Embassy political officer Thomas Weil vainly argued the case for nearly two hours with Liaquat. Although Muslims had not given up on the cabinet mission proposal, Liaquat said, "as [a] result of Congress behavior [the] League was beginning to feel that perhaps [an] outright Pakistan would be [the] only means of obtaining their objectives."[43]

After a second discussion failed to move Liaquat, Vice Consul Joseph S. Sparks was instructed to see Jinnah in Karachi, where he was attending a meeting of the Muslim League leadership. Sparks was told to stress the "U.S. Government's deep concern [about the] serious deterioration [of the] Indian political situation; to state it is our impression that in view of [the] Congress['s] effort to accommodate itself to [the British government] and [the] League's interpretation of [the cabinet mission] plan, [the] U.S. public would be puzzled if [the] League now decline[s] [to] enter [the] Constituent Assembly; and to say [that the State Department] believes any halt in constitutional progress may well cause widespread chaos similar [to that in] China with world-wide repercussions."[44]

Jinnah received Sparks politely but spurned U.S. advice. "Tell your government," Jinnah said, that "we work towards the same ends but for God's sake not to be chloroformed by [a] meaningless Congress gesture made for purely propaganda effect." It was, Jinnah charged, the "same Congress tactics: propaganda to fool [the] world into believing [the] Congress had accepted [the British] Cabinet['s] December 6 statement and that only [the] League was at fault for not entering [the] Constituent Assembly when [the Congress] resolution is [a] statement of contradiction that in fact says nothing."[45]

Having failed to break the Congress-League deadlock, the Labour government decided drastic action was needed to pave the way for the British withdrawal from India and that Viceroy Wavell was not the man for the task. On February 20, 1947, the British ambassador in Washington, Lord Inverchapel, informed Secretary of State Marshall of the decision to grant India full independence in June 1948, with or without agreement about the future governmental structure, and to appoint Lord Louis Mountbatten, who had been the Allied commander in Southeast Asia during the war and was King George VI's cousin, as viceroy. Marshall made no comment other than noting that the United States had supported British efforts to find a satisfactory political solution in India.[46]

A few days later, on February 25, 1947, the State Department reiterated U.S. interest in Indian self-government and its support for the "persistent and sincere efforts of the British Government to bring the major Indian political parties together." The statement concluded with an only too accurate prediction: "The Indian internal crisis threatens to prevent India from making its rightful and honorable contribution to the maintenance of international peace and prosperity. An India torn by civil strife . . . could conceivably become the source of new international tensions in a world only beginning to grope its way back to peace."[47]

During this troubled period, U.S. diplomat Raymond Hare, who was slated to head up the State Department's South Asia division, spent two months in the subcontinent to learn firsthand about his new area of responsibility. During his travels, Hare had extended talks with all the top leaders, including Jinnah, whom he met for an hour and a half in New Delhi on May 1, 1947. The defiant Muslim League chief told the visitor that dividing the provinces of Bengal and Punjab (which Jinnah strongly opposed) would not "frighten" him into giving up Pakistan. Even if "driven into the Sind desert," he would insist on a sovereign state. Jinnah asserted that a positive decision for Pakistan would clear the communal atmosphere and reduce tensions, a position that U.S. diplomats did not share.[48]

Responding to Hare's query about the country's foreign policy, Jinnah said that Pakistan would be oriented toward the Muslim countries of the Middle East. Since they were weak, "Muslim countries would stand together against possible Russian aggression and would look to the U.S. for assistance." The League leader said that although he did not personally share the view, most Indian Muslims thought the United States was unfriendly. They had the impression that the U.S. press and many Americans were against Pakistan. This suspicion also fed on U.S. support for the Jewish position in the dispute over Palestine.[49]

By this time, the Congress Party was grudgingly moving toward acceptance of the partition of India. Mountbatten, the new viceroy, had also concluded that a united India was not possible. Fearing that further delay in granting independence would risk even greater chaos and communal bloodshed, Mountbatten won London's approval to advance the date by almost a year, to August 1947, and to accept the Muslim League's demand for Pakistan.

After obtaining the agreement of the unhappy Congress and the League—although delighted by partition, Jinnah was angry about receiving a "moth-eaten" Pakistan with only half of the provinces of Punjab and Bengal—the viceroy plunged the administration into a frenzied three-month preparation for splitting India into two separate and independent states. Moving the date forward a year made an orderly division of British India impossible. The decision fanned the flames of uncertainty and fear, especially in the Punjab, that triggered the tragic and bloody mass migration of millions of Hindus, Sikhs, and Muslims. Because of a lack of time, India and Pakistan became independent before the settlement of key issues, including the fate of the two largest princely states, Jammu and Kashmir and Hyderabad, and the division of financial and physical assets between the two successor states.

On June 10, 1947, the U.S. government welcomed the shotgun agreement the British had reached with the Congress and the League and expressed the hope that the partition accord would "bring [an] end to civil disorders in India and avoid further bloodshed." Curiously, the

State Department made no explicit reference to the decision to create Pakistan—as if the U.S. government was unwilling to accept this new fact. The statement commented only, "The future constitutional pattern is a matter to be determined by [the] Indian people themselves and whatever that pattern may be the U.S. Government looks forward to continuance of [the] friendliest relations with Indians of all communities and creeds."[50]

When Jinnah met Hare a second time on July 2, 1947, just six weeks before independence, the future leader of Pakistan, anxious for international acceptance of the new country, asked about U.S. diplomatic representation. Delhi embassy officer Howard Donovan, who accompanied Hare, replied stiffly that they were not authorized to discuss that question.[51] A few days earlier, Muslim League leader Yusuf Haroon had told Vice Consul Sparks in Karachi that Jinnah was eager to have a U.S. embassy as a means of strengthening Pakistan's ability to have an independent foreign policy, one not linked—as some wistfully hoped-with India's.[52] In a talk with Ambassador Grady, Mountbatten also urged the prompt establishment of an American embassy in Pakistan.[53]

In response to prodding by Grady, the State Department in a rather officious cable authorized discussion of the subject.[54] Grady then met Jinnah at the latter's New Delhi residence after the protocol-conscious Jinnah refused to call at the U.S. embassy. Pakistan's future governor-general advised that his country would act promptly to name an ambassador to Washington. "He was," Grady reported, "most cordial, expressed great admiration for the U.S. and said he was hopeful [the] U.S. would aid Pakistan in its many problems."[55]

During this period before Pakistan's and India's independence, reporting by U.S. diplomats assigned to India provided the State Department with a balanced assessment of the unfolding political drama. The telegrams and dispatches praised Jinnah's negotiating skills but implied that his original aim was not so much an independent Pakistan as a stronger political position for the Muslim minority within the framework of a united India. Indeed, U.S. diplomats believed that Gandhi, Nehru, and the Congress were as responsible for the creation of Pakistan as was Jinnah. An April 22, 1947, dispatch from the embassy in New Delhi commented, "The present unhappy situation is as much a result of Congress leaders' political ineptitude and lack of vision as of Mr. Jinnah's intransigence. Had Congress leaders put aside their fears regarding the effect of the Cabinet Mission plan on their party's position in Assam, the Punjab and the Northwest Frontier Province, Mr. Jinnah would not have been provided with a logical basis for the Muslim League's current stand, and India might today have been laying the ground-work for a united country instead of facing the prospect of Balkanization."[56]

Limited U.S. Interest in Pakistan and India

As the tone of the embassy dispatch implied, the U.S. attitude toward the creation of Pakistan had been unenthusiastic. During World War II, President Roosevelt and his personal envoy to India, William Phillips, expressed their dislike of the idea of partitioning British India. Later, after the British made clear their intention to grant independence, the United States supported London's efforts to maintain a united India. Despite the fact that America stood at the peak of its postwar power and prestige, the Muslim League disregarded U.S. advice—and so did the Indian National Congress.

In early 1947, as events in India were moving toward their climax, the major concerns of U.S. foreign-policy makers lay far from South Asia. The global struggle between the Soviet Union and the United States was hardening into the Cold War. In February 1947—the same month that Britain advised America of its decision to grant India independence in 1948—financially strapped London also informed Washington that it could no longer help Greece and Turkey against the communist threat. In a monumental national security decision, President Truman decided that the United States would take up the burden. On March 12, 1947, the president spelled out the policy, known as the Truman Doctrine, and sought congressional funds for aid to Greece and Turkey to counter communism.

Three months later, on June 5, 1947, Secretary of State Marshall announced another key policy initiative: U.S. willingness to help European economic recovery, the program that soon became known as the Marshall Plan. In the summer of 1947, Washington was also concerned about events in the Middle East, where a beleaguered Britain was unable to satisfy either Arab inhabitants of Palestine or Jewish immigrants demanding a separate homeland. A further source of anxiety that same summer was the civil war raging in China, where U.S.-supported Nationalists were steadily losing ground to their communist foes.

Given concerns about crises elsewhere, Washington was content to let the British worry about the states emerging from their Indian empire. The principal anxiety was that continuing Hindu-Muslim differences might spark even more intense violence and lead to broader political instability in Asia. The United States simply did not perceive major interests in the subcontinent. In part, this was explained by the fact that the region stood apart from the Cold War struggle with the Soviet Union, which was already dominating U.S. foreign policy. Moscow regarded both India and Pakistan as Western pawns and showed little inclination to establish friendly ties with either country. Even if Washington had few explicit policy aims regarding Pakistan, the fulsome expressions of goodwill on August 14, 1947, underscored that the United States looked forward to amicable relations with the new state.

2

Truman: Friends, Not Allies

The new nation of seventy million people faced enormous problems in 1947, not the least of which was caused by Pakistan's unusual geography. A thousand miles of hostile Indian territory separated the eastern wing, initially called East Bengal and later named East Pakistan, from the west, where the Punjab, the Northwest Frontier Province, Sindh, and Baluchistan were located. Although India inherited New Delhi, the impressive capital of the British Raj, and strong administrative institutions, Pakistan had to build its central government infrastructure and national institutions from scratch.

As governor-general, Mohammed Ali Jinnah wielded decisive power from August 1947 until his health failed in the spring of 1948. Liaquat Ali Khan, as prime minister, had charge of the day-to-day functioning of the new government. His easygoing, gregarious manner contrasted with Jinnah's austere demeanor. If Jinnah was the brains and strategist of the Muslim League, Liaquat was its heart and chief political operator. He was affectionately called "Quaid-i-Millat," or "Leader of the people." Although born in the Punjab, Liaquat had lived in the United Provinces (since renamed Uttar Pradesh), where he served for over a decade in the provincial legislature.

The composition of the cabinet, in which Liaquat also held the defense portfolio, balanced Pakistan's provinces and refugee population. The substantial role of former officials from the British Raj reflected the limited depth of administrative and political talent in the Muslim League hierarchy. The finance minister was Ghulam Mohammed, a capable and strong-willed former finance minister of Hyderabad. Chaudhri Mohammed Ali, a senior civil servant in British India, became secretary-general of the new government. Jinnah appointed Sir Zafrullah

Khan, a distinguished jurist from Lahore who had represented India in China during World War II, as foreign minister.

The Ministry of Foreign Affairs was fortunate to find a home in a spacious residence vacated by a fleeing Hindu in Clifton, a pleasant part of Karachi near the Arabian Sea. M. A. Ikramullah, a Bengali and an accomplished former member of the prestigious Indian Civil Service of the Raj, became foreign secretary and senior career official. Initially, the ministry staff consisted of just six officers: Ikramullah, two other Pakistanis, and three Englishmen. The ministry had a few desks, but not a single typewriter nor any records. Agha Hilaly, one of the two Pakistani officers and later ambassador to the United States, recalled having to buy office supplies from a downtown Karachi stationery store so that the ministry could commence business.[1]

In reporting to Washington, U.S. diplomats painted a gloomy picture of Pakistan's early months. On October 2, 1947, the recently established Lahore consulate general cabled the State Department, "Five refugee trains [were] attacked [in] this province, [and] six in east Punjab [in India], resulting in over 2,000 Muslim dead, 1,500 wounded and 1,000 non-Muslim dead, 800 wounded, not including abductions on either side."[2] At the end of the month, the Karachi embassy reported "wholesale rioting and anarchy in the Punjab," serious disturbances in Quetta (the chief city of thinly populated Baluchistan), along with the influx of refugees and "their appalling stories of murder and atrocities which served to inflame the minds of the masses whether Muslims, Hindus or Sikhs with a sense of grievance and a not unnatural desire for revenge."[3] Summing up the situation, the embassy commented, "The difficulties with which the new Dominion government of Pakistan was confronted in August were increased manifold in September and assumed such proportions as to threaten the very existence of the new state."[4] A month after independence, 40 percent of the central government staff was still stranded in New Delhi because communal disturbances had disrupted rail transportation.[5] In order to fly the officials to Karachi, Pakistan had to charter some twenty commercial aircraft.[6]

In the eastern wing, where the communal situation was less tense, a considerable Hindu minority, perhaps 10 percent of the population, stayed on. Setting up the provincial administration in Dacca, however, formerly a backwater city of modest importance, was almost as formidable a task as establishing the central government in Karachi, especially in the absence of capable local leadership. According to U.S. diplomat Thomas W. Simons, Sr., East Bengal chief minister Khwaja Nazimuddin was "accepted by all as a good and honest man, but one who lacks intellectual capacity to grasp the essentials and the will to execute policies that are needed."[7]

Pakistan's Foreign Policy

Even though foreign affairs did not play a significant role in the struggle for Pakistan, the outlines of the new country's policies quickly emerged. Relations with India overshadowed everything else. Pakistan's traumatic birth would have made the India-Pakistan relationship difficult and complex under the best of circumstances. Dividing British India's financial and physical assets, settling refugee property claims, deciding how to distribute vital irrigation water, demarcating borders, establishing ground rules for economic interaction, and above all, overcoming the emotional bitterness caused by partition were thorny and intractable tasks. The suffering and pain—physical, financial, and psychological—of millions of refugees who fled their homes for an uncertain future made establishing a modus vivendi harder. Perhaps more normal, if not friendly, ties might have evolved had the dispute over the princely state of Jammu and Kashmir not provided a chronic flash point to embitter relations between India and Pakistan.

Relations with another neighbor, Afghanistan, immediately soured after the Kabul government opposed Pakistan's entry into the United Nations. The Afghans further upset the Pakistanis by voicing the hope that "the natural and legal rights of freedom of the Northwest Frontier people and the free tribes along the borders may also be established."[8] Furthermore, they supported the call for "Pushtunistan," an independent state for the Pathans to be carved out of Pakistan's Northwest Frontier Province, and questioned the validity of the frontier between Afghanistan and Pakistan—the so-called Durand Line, named after the British official who drew the boundary in the 1890s. The border split the ethnic Pathans between Pakistan and Afghanistan, where they were the largest, dominant ethnic group. The new government in Karachi, though annoyed, regarded trouble with Kabul as manageable. Pakistan had greater military and economic potential than its landlocked neighbor, which depended on transit routes through Pakistan for most of its access to the rest of the world.

The Muslim League's emphasis on Islam in the struggle for Pakistan ensured that solidarity with other Muslim countries would stand high on the foreign policy agenda. Jinnah had frequently criticized Western policy toward Palestine. In 1948, Pakistan vocally opposed the creation of Israel. Foreign Minister Zafrullah Khan soon became the acknowledged spokesperson for the Arab cause at the United Nations.

Pakistan, like India, favored an early end to Western colonial rule throughout the Middle East and Asia, and opposed apartheid in South Africa.[9] But Karachi pursued these aims in a quieter fashion than did India: Pakistan's leaders and diplomats were not given to public sermonizing nor did they seek a leadership role in the anticolonialist cause.

In the Cold War, Pakistan leaned toward the West. During a September 7, 1947, cabinet meeting, Jinnah plainly spelled out his views: "Pakistan [is] a democracy and communism [does] not flourish in the soil of Islam. It [is] clear therefore that our interests [lie] more with the two great democratic countries, namely, the U.K. and the U.S.A., rather than with Russia."[10] From the start, therefore, Pakistan's orientation differed from that of India, which sought the middle ground of neutrality.

Practical considerations bolstered Pakistan's pro-Western orientation. The financially strapped country badly needed help and was not bashful about seeking it from the United States. Barely two weeks after Pakistan's independence, Finance Minister Ghulam Mohammed sounded out Chargé d'Affaires Charles Lewis regarding possible aid.[11] In a September 11, 1947, cabinet meeting, Jinnah outlined Pakistan's case—in effect, a Cold War version of the "Great Game" between imperial Russia and British India. "The safety of the North West Frontier [is] of world concern and not merely an internal matter for Pakistan alone," Jinnah stated. He had reason to believe that the Russians were behind the Afghan call for Pushtunistan and were trying to stir up fresh communal troubles in both India and Pakistan. "In this connection," Jinnah added, "it [is] significant to note that Russia alone of all the great countries has not sent a congratulatory message on the birth of Pakistan."[12]

Soon after, Jinnah dispatched Mir Laik Ali, a former economic adviser to Hyderabad and a close associate of the finance minister, to Washington, where M. A. H. Ispahani was settling in as Pakistan's first ambassador. Mir Laik's daunting assignment was to obtain a $2 billion loan to meet his country's economic development and defense needs over the coming five years.[13] Such a mammoth and unrealistic request had no chance of acceptance. Moreover, it revealed the limited understanding that Jinnah and his colleagues had of the United States and its willingness to assume new and expensive engagements in South Asia. Washington's attention was fixed on Europe, the Middle East, and China; South Asia remained on the periphery of the U.S. worldview. On December 17, 1947, Acting Secretary of State Robert Lovett responded with a polite, but near total turndown. In the end, Pakistan received a $10 million relief grant from the War Assets Administration, or .5 percent of its request.[14]

When news of the rebuff reached Karachi, a dejected Ghulam Mohammed and an unhappy Zafrullah Khan poured out their grief to Lewis. The foreign minister declared that the "well-known friendship of Pakistan toward the U.S. and Pakistan's obvious antipathy to the Russian ideology would seem to justify serious consideration by the U.S. Government of the defense requirements of Pakistan."[15] Less than a decade later, Washington would find this rationale persuasive.

The Kashmir Dispute

Jammu and Kashmir, the largest of the 564 Indian princely states, had a Hindu ruler, or maharajah, an 80 percent Muslim population, and a strategic location in the mountainous northernmost tip of the subcontinent. The beauty and agreeable climate of the state's central valley, known as the Vale of Kashmir, had attracted the Mughal emperors and later provided the British with respite from the scorching summer heat of the plains of northern India. When the temperature in New Delhi soared to around 115 degrees in May and June each year, the British flocked to the lovely lakes near Srinagar, Kashmir's capital, where the peaks of the Himalayas provided a magnificent mountain backdrop.

Under the ground rules that the viceroy, Lord Mountbatten, had spelled out in May 1947, the Indian princely states theoretically would regain their full independence after the termination of the Raj. The princes, however, were strongly urged to join either India or Pakistan after taking into account their geographic location and the composition of their population. In view of Kashmir's large Muslim majority and the fact that the state's transportation and economic links were entirely with Pakistan, it was expected that the state would accede to Pakistan. The Hindu maharajah, however, who ruled Kashmir as a despot, hesitated and took no decision before India and Pakistan became independent in August.

Within the state, the maharajah had jailed leaders of the two major political groups, the conservative Muslim Conference, which favored joining Pakistan, and the leftist National Conference, which had close links with the Indian National Congress. The charismatic head of the National Conference, Sheikh Mohammed Abdullah, was Kashmir's most popular political figure. By fall 1947, Hindu-Muslim communal violence in neighboring Punjab had spilled over the borders. Reports that the maharajah's militia was forcing out Muslims touched off an uprising in the western part of the state by Muslim Indian army veterans. In October 1947, the rebels proclaimed the state of Azad (Free) Kashmir and sought to overthrow the maharajah. Some 2,000 armed Pathan tribesmen, who had been trucked in from Pakistan's Northwest Frontier Province, crossed the border to join the Azad Kashmir forces. Their goal was to capture the capital city of Srinagar and the surrounding Vale, the political heart of Kashmir.

The state militia's resistance quickly collapsed and the Pathans advanced toward Srinagar, looting and pillaging as they proceeded. The panicked maharajah fled his capital on October 26, 1947, and sought New Delhi's help. That same day, he signed an instrument of accession to India after agreeing to turn over the state administration to Sheikh Abdullah. In accepting this accession, the Indian government indicated that Kashmir's ultimate fate would be decided by a plebiscite to be held after the raiders were driven out and the fighting ended. With their advance slowed by pillaging, the Pathan tribesmen had reached the edge of the Vale by October 26, 1947, but failed to capture the vital airfield. As there were no overland transportation links with India, the airfield was the only possible entry point for Indian military help. The day after the accession, on October 27, 1947, New Delhi was able to fly in troops, who soon cleared the valley of the Pathan intruders.

The extent of official Pakistani involvement in these events has long been disputed. The British high commissioner in Karachi, Sir Lawrence Grafftey-Smith, who was arguably the best-informed foreign observed, told BBC correspondent A. R. Stimson that he found no proof that Pakistan's central government had planned the incursion. However, he believed it was "likely that individual Pakistan officials up to the level of District Commissioner [in Peshawar] did back the raiders by furnishing them with petrol, trucks, etc."[16] The U.K. Foreign Office made a similar assessment in a January 1948 message to its diplomatic missions: Pakistani authorities in the Northwest Frontier Province "no doubt" helped the tribals "with respect of supplies and transport . . . and the Pakistan Government did not attempt to stop [the] incursion. They may have known in advance what was intended but there is no evidence that it occurred on their initiative."[17]

After India and Pakistan were unable to resolve the dispute through bilateral discussions, Indian Prime Minister Jawaharlal Nehru agreed to Governor-General Mountbatten's suggestion that India bring the Kashmir issue to the United Nations (UN) Security Council.[18] Senior British officials—Commonwealth Relations Secretary Philip Noel-Baker, UN Representative Sir Alexander Cadogan, and Lord Hasting (Pug) Ismay, formerly Mountbatten's chief of staff—met Acting Secretary of State Lovett in Washington in January 1948, before the start of Security Council deliberations on Kashmir. They urged America to step forward and take the lead; Britain's doing so, they argued, would suggest the reimposition on the Raj. Although the visitors alluded darkly to a potential "holocaust," an unmoved Lovett, they reported to London, stressed, "how very difficult it was for the United States delegation to play the part which we suggested."[19] Lovett declared that the United States "is spread very thinly in its present commitments." He also expressed concern that U.S. involvement might attract Soviet interest, making it harder to solve the Kashmir dispute.[20]

When the Security Council met on Kashmir in early 1948, American diplomats followed the British lead in trying to reach a satisfactory solution. The UN deliberations revolved around four interrelated issues: the control of the Kashmir administration during the plebiscite (Pakistan wanted this in UN hands; India insisted that Sheikh Abdullah remain in charge); the nature and pace of the withdrawal of Indian and Azad Kashmir forces; India's desire to label Pakistan an aggressor; and Pakistan's wish to condemn its overall treatment by India. Zafrullah Khan proved a highly effective advocate for his country and succeeded in focusing the Security Council's attention on the future of Kashmir rather than on the narrower question of the Pathan tribal invaders.

During the UN session, Sheikh Abdullah, who served on the Indian delegation, met with Warren Austin, the U.S. representative to the UN and a respected former Republican senator from Vermont. Austin believed that Abdullah's main aim during their talk was to suggest a third alternative for Kashmir, beyond joining India or Pakistan: independence. "[I] gave Abdullah no encouragement on this line," Austin cabled the State Department, "when he left he understood very well where we stood.[21] Like India and Pakistan, neither Washington nor London favored an independent Kashmir. Apart from worry about further Balkanization of British India, there was concern that Kashmir's political and economic weakness, as well as its strategic location, would invite communist interference and fuel further regional instability.

By March 1948, the Security Council had settled on a draft resolution proposed by China. India, but not Pakistan, favored the proposal because it left Sheikh Abdullah in office during the plebiscite. In conveying his views to the U.S. embassy, Jinnah stressed that a fair plebiscite was impossible if Sheikh Abdullah, "a Congress Quisling," remained in power.[22] The governor-general went on to "beg" the United States not to be misled by British claims that "they knew the situation better than we did."[23]

In the end, the United States joined Britain, Belgium, Canada, and China to support a modified formulation. The Security Council unanimously adopted the resolution on April 21, 1948. Neither India nor Pakistan was happy.[24] In Karachi, where the reaction was particularly negative, Prime Minister Liaquat Ali Khan declared that the Kashmir resolution "showed complete lack of understanding [of] Oriental psychology, [and] that as long as Abdullah remained in charge [of the] Kashmir Government [the] populace would not dare risk voting against him."[25] In view of this initially hostile reaction, it is ironic that insistence on implementing the April 21, 1948, resolution has become an icon of Pakistan's policy in the succeeding years. Meanwhile, with the stalemate unresolved, the stage was set for the de facto partition of Kashmir and the prolonged dispute between India and Pakistan over the state's final status.

The First U.S. Ambassador to Pakistan

Paul Alling, a career diplomat and previously deputy chief of the State Department's Near Eastern affairs division, arrived in Karachi early in 1948 as the first U.S. ambassador to Pakistan. Accompanied by the small embassy diplomatic staff, Alling presented his credentials on February 26, 1948. The reception at Government House recalled "the pomp and circumstance with which the British governed India," David Newsom, then an embassy junior officer, wrote to his mother in California. After the Americans proceeded through the teak-paneled entry hall, they walked up the staircase to the governor-general's reception room. Two "resplendent guards" stood at attention, each wearing "a jacket with silver epaulets and a patch of brilliant ribbon over the left chest . . . a turban of gold cloth, streaked with silver strips. The picture was completed by the lance with a red and white pennant which each carried."[26]

Jinnah, who was standing when the Americans entered the room, appeared healthy: Newsom wrote, "His 71 years are apparent only when he is speaking in a low, rather tired voice." The governor-general was dressed in his traditional public garb, a long, high-collared black frock coat and white trousers, and wore the familiar *karakul* fur cap. After Alling finished reading a message from President Harry S. Truman, "Jinnah adjusted a monocle to his right eye and, in a very low voice, . . . read the reply." The ceremony's one humorous moment occurred, according to Newsom, when "Mr. Jinnah lost his place in his speech and the monocle fell from his eye. He adjusted it again, but apparently got it in backward. It was necessary to adjust it still a third time before he could proceed."[27]

Three weeks later, Alling and his wife had tea with Jinnah and his sister, Fatima, at their beach cottage on the Arabian Sea, a few miles from Karachi. During the afternoon, the U.S. envoy and Pakistan's leader had a wide-ranging discussion as they walked together along the sandy beach. When Alling expressed America's hope for friendly India-Pakistan relations, Jinnah replied that "nothing was nearer to his heart. What he sincerely wished was an association similar to that between the United States and Canada." Jinnah said that he had told Nehru, Gandhi, and others that "Pakistan desired a defensive understanding with India on a military level . . . with no time limit, similar perhaps to [the U.S.] arrangements with Canada." On Kashmir, the governor-general alleged that India and Mountbatten had been less than fair. He was firmly convinced that Pakistan was the victim of a conspiracy.[28]

The afternoon's only off note came when Alling responded negatively to Jinnah's expression of interest in having Flagstaff, his house in Karachi, become the ambassador's residence. The embassy, Alling replied, had already obtained another property for the ambassador and Flagstaff would be too large for more junior staff. "Mr. Jinnah and his sister were disappointed," Alling reported. "[T]hey would have liked particularly to have their house become the residence of the American Ambassador." In spite of rumors of Jinnah's poor health, Alling found him "perfectly sound in mind and body" and able "to enjoy a brisk walk of a couple of miles which we took along the beach."[29] In fact, both Jinnah and Alling would soon fall fatally ill: Jinnah died that fall from tuberculosis; Alling was medically evacuated with cancer later in the year and died in the United States.

For the small embassy staff, life in the new capital was exhilarating and challenging, Newsom and fellow junior officer Harold Josef recalled. Protocol was informal; government leaders, including Liaquat, invited even junior officers to social functions. The gregarious prime minister enjoyed entertaining at his home, at times asking American guests to remain for late-night jazz sessions, during which Liaquat enthusiastically beat the drums. In Pakistan's early days, the American diplomats admired the small band of overworked, highly motivated, and idealistic civil servants who struggled to establish their new country. It was hard for the embassy staff not to empathize with the Pakistanis and their view of the troubles with India over Kashmir and other issues.[30]

On September 11, 1948, Jinnah died. After falling seriously ill with tuberculosis in the spring of 1948, Jinnah had left humid Karachi for the cooler mountain air of Ziarat, a resort at an altitude of 7,000 feet in Baluchistan. Pakistani officials pretended that the governor-general remained in active charge of affairs. Although Liaquat told the British high commissioner that Jinnah was "keeping normal health," his absence from Karachi during the celebrations of the first anniversary of independence in August 1948 made it clear that something was very wrong.[31]

Early in September, the doctors transferred the ailing leader to Quetta, the capital of Baluchistan, and then on September 11, 1948, flew him to Karachi. Jinnah was so weak that he had to be carried on a stretcher and transported in an ambulance to and from the aircraft. He reached Government House in late afternoon, the trip made worse when the ambulance broke down on the way to the city from the airport. The governor-general was immediately put to bed, and during the night, Jinnah took his last breath.[32]

Although not unexpected, Jinnah's death was an enormous blow. His towering prestige, intellectual acumen, and incorruptibility were assets that Pakistan sorely missed as it struggled to establish an identity and overcome staggering problems. Liaquat, who became the dominant political figure after Jinnah's death, decided to remain as prime minister.

Nazimuddin, whose tenure as chief minister of East Bengal had not altered his image as a decent but amiable lightweight, became the new governor-general.

Although Liaquat was a more human figure than the aloof and distant Jinnah, he did not possess the Quaid-i-Azam's authority or decisiveness. As a refugee from India, Liaquat also lacked a regional political base in Pakistan. The U.S. embassy correctly predicted that he would have trouble managing the increasingly unruly Muslim League, the nation's only significant political party. An umbrella organization, the League encompassed a broad spectrum that included quarrelsome rural grandees from the Punjab and Sindh, disgruntled refugee leaders from India, ambitious Muslim clerics, and squabbling Bengali politicians.[33] Only the demand for partition had unified the League. Once Pakistan was achieved, the party began to unravel in the face of mounting infighting, bickering, and the lack of programmatic goals.

When Jinnah's passing was reported in the American press, *Time* magazine remained as unfriendly toward him as it had been during his life. A September 28, 1948, story titled "That Man" read, "Out of the travail of 400 million in the Indian subcontinent have come two symbols—a man of love and a man of hate. Last winter the man of non-violence, Gandhi, died violently at the hands of an assassin. Last week the man of hate, Mohammed Ali Jinnah, at 71, died a natural death in Karachi, capital of the state he had founded."[34]

Generally, the American media coverage about Pakistan continued to reflect skepticism about the country's viability. On the first anniversary of its independence, a *New York Times* editorial stated, "[t]he record of the first year gives promise that . . . the future of India (ultimately a reunited one, we hope) will be better than its past."[35] A Reuters report speculated whether Jinnah's death would weaken Pakistan's determination to maintain partition.[36]

Kashmir: Cease-Fire but No Settlement

During 1948, the UN worked hard to achieve a cease-fire and lay the groundwork for a plebiscite in Kashmir. After the United States reluctantly agreed to become a member of the UN Commission for India and Pakistan (UNCIP), the U.S. representative on the commission, ambassador to Burma Klahr Huddle, found "little to choose" between the Indians and the Pakistanis. Prime Minister Nehru, in Huddle's view, adopted a "self-righteous intransigent stand," while Foreign Minister Zafrullah Khan's "attitude toward [the] Commission has been patronizing and approaching arrogance."[37] Although India eventually accepted the UNCIP proposals, Pakistan added so many qualifications that the UN team regarded Karachi's response as rejection.[38]

Charles Lewis, who had become chargé d'affaires again after Ambassador Alling fell ill and was evacuated, stoutly defended Pakistan's action. His dispatches of September 10 and 24, 1948, expressed little faith in UNCIP's ability "to suppress or control Indian perfidy."[39] They were good examples of the Foreign Service malady called "localitis," when an embassy becomes so identified with its host country's point of view that its reporting loses objectivity. Although there is no record of Washington's reaction, the State Department could not have been impressed with Lewis's special pleading. U.S. policy was to end the threat that the Kashmir dispute posed to peace, not to take sides between India and Pakistan or to pass judgment about who was to blame.

One month later, in October 1948, Liaquat met Secretary of State Marshall during the UN General Assembly session, held that year in Paris. In the highest-level bilateral discussions since Pakistan's independence, Liaquat outlined the problems his country faced, stressed that it was "unthinkable that Pakistan could fall prey to communism since [communism was] against Islam," and urged the United States to provide economic help for Pakistan and the nations of the Middle East as it had for Europe. Liaquat described India's attitude toward Pakistan as "hostile." He asserted that Pakistan wanted peace, but would fight if India persisted in being aggressive. The prime minister thought the Kashmir problem could be solved by a plebiscite, "however, there must be no coercive forces present."

In response, Marshall said he was pleased to learn of Pakistan's concern about communism, commenting (with an eye toward India-Pakistan differences) that one way nations outside the "police state" orbit could strengthen themselves was to settle disputes quickly and peacefully. He hoped that the "Kashmir question could be settled in conformity with UN principles." The secretary parried the call for economic aid, urging Pakistan to seek private capital.[40]

Following the meeting with Liaquat and a similar session with Nehru, Marshall expressed little optimism about the prospects for a Kashmir settlement in discussing the issue with Sir Alexander Cadogan, the British UN representative. The secretary commented that although both Nehru and Liaquat had stressed "the need for stability, they did not seem to be willing to suit action to their words."[41] With Marshall as secretary of state, the United States continued to work in close harness with the British on the Kashmir issue, "without breaking away from our carefully considered neutral path" between India and Pakistan.[42]

On December 11, 1948, after reaching a consensus on cease-fire arrangements and on the appointment of a high-level plebiscite administrator,[43] UNCIP forwarded its proposal to Karachi and New Delhi on a take-it-or-leave-it basis.[44] This time both countries accepted the UN plan. A cease-fire took effect in Kashmir on January 1, 1949. Each side remained in physical control of the areas it was occupying. The Security Council endorsed the UNCIP proposals and reaffirmed the call for a plebiscite. Half a century later, with a few adjustments, the same line still separates the parts of Kashmir held by India and Pakistan.

Several factors explained why Karachi accepted cease-fire proposals similar to those it had rejected just four months earlier. First, the departure of Jinnah from the scene had badly shaken the nation's self-confidence. Second, India's forcible seizure of the former princely state of Hyderabad on September 13, 1948, just two days after Jinnah's death, had stirred genuine anxiety that Pakistan might be the next target. Fearing an attack, Liaquat sounded alarm bells several times during the fall of 1948 that the Indians were about to invade. (As in Kashmir, the ruler of Hyderabad had balked at accession and flirted with independence. Unlike Kashmir, Hyderabad had a Muslim ruler, the fabulously wealthy but miserly nizam, and a majority-Hindu population. The fact that it was physically surrounded by India sealed Hyderabad's fate once New Delhi decided to use force to resolve the problem.)[45] Finally, the U.S. willingness to have an American serve as the plebiscite administrator encouraged the Pakistanis to accept the UNCIP proposals. Karachi was eager to maximize the American involvement, especially as it sensed that the British Labour government favored India.

In March 1949, UN Secretary Trygve Lie appointed Adm. Chester Nimitz, who had commanded American naval forces in the Pacific during World War II, as the administrator of the Kashmir plebiscite. George McGhee, who had become the first assistant secretary of state for Near Eastern, South Asian, and African affairs in a departmental reorganization,[46] took credit in an interview for the Nimitz appointment. A former Texas oil man, McGhee had become acquainted with the admiral during the war and thought that Nimitz's solid reputation and quiet personal style would enable him to deal effectively with Indian and Pakistani leaders.[47]

When the guns stopped firing in Kashmir on January 1, 1949, UNCIP was optimistic about an early agreement on the withdrawal of forces. Meanwhile, Nimitz waited in New York for the accord to be finalized before shifting to South Asia to conduct the voting. But it shortly became apparent that reaching an agreement would not be easy. India started raising a variety of problems, including its desire to disarm and disband all Azad Kashmiri forces and to challenge Pakistan's continued control over Gilgit and Hunza, two small, isolated, but strategic territories in northern Kashmir that had joined Pakistan on their own initiative in August 1947.

After struggling without success for six months, UNCIP proposed that India and Pakistan submit their differences to arbitration. President Truman endorsed the idea in personal appeals to Liaquat and Nehru and urged a parallel approach by British prime minister Clement Attlee. London agreed, undoubtedly pleased that Washington was taking a high-level initiative on Kashmir.[48] Truman's message to Liaquat was to the point: "I am sure you will agree that peace and cooperation between your country and India are essential to the continuance of social and political progress on the subcontinent. The Kashmir dispute is the greatest threat to such peace and cooperation. My Government is therefore deeply interested in an early settlement of this dispute. . . . In the interest of your own nation and in the interest of the world community, I urge you to accept the recommendation for arbitration of truce terms."[49]

Liaquat agreed to arbitration. The prime minister replied to Truman on September 8, 1949, "Had the proposal not hinged around the eminent personality of Fleet Admiral Chester W. Nimitz and had it not been so emphatically sponsored by the President of the United States my government would have felt considerable hesitation in accepting it. . . ."[50] Nehru, however, turned Truman down. Although India's prime minister agreed that Kashmir was "a cause of acute tension," he claimed that the basic problem was the anti-Indian attitude of the Pakistani leadership. Resorting to what Americans regarded as legalistic quibbling, Nehru claimed that he was not opposed to arbitration, but found the proposal insufficiently "precise and defined."[51]

A week later, a disappointed Dean Acheson, who had succeeded Marshall as secretary of state in 1949, conferred with Foreign Minister Zafrullah Khan. Pakistan's top diplomat had by then won the respect of

U.S. interlocutors as an eloquent and balanced spokesman for his country. Zafrullah expressed fear that India's resistance to the plebiscite would lead to an interminable delay, greatly increasing pressures on the Pakistani government to take rash action. "This Government," the secretary of state replied, "shared Pakistan's concern in this matter. . . . We were very pleased over Pakistan's acceptance of the arbitration proposal and greatly disappointed by the reply we had received from India."[52]

The episode marked an important milestone in the U.S. perception of the Kashmir dispute. Until then, the Americans found little to choose between the conduct of India and Pakistan. But the view altered as India spurned a series of proposals to remove impediments to the plebiscite: in 1949, the Truman-Attlee call for arbitration; at Christmas, further ideas offered by the UN Security Council president, Canada's Gen. Andrew McNaughton; in 1950, proposals by Australia's Sir Owen Dixon; and in 1951–52, suggestions from America's Dr. Frank Graham.

At the time, only a small group of State Department officials dealt with the Kashmir issue: Secretary Acheson, Assistant Secretary McGhee, UN affairs officer Howard Meyers, South Asian Affairs Director Burt Mathews, and Frank Collins from the Department of State's South Asia office. Meyers recalled that they gradually became convinced that India preferred to maintain and, if possible, make permanent the status quo rather than to settle the dispute on less favorable terms.[53] The perception also grew that Prime Minister Nehru, given his family roots as a member of the Kashmiri Brahmin community, was the principal barrier to a settlement. "Nehru was the stumbling block," McGhee commented. "If he had cooperated, the Kashmir problem could have easily been solved."[54]

Liaquat Visits America, but Not the Soviet Union

In mid-1949, Truman invited Nehru to pay a state visit to the United States, the first by a South Asian leader. When Liaquat did not receive a similar invitation, his pride was hurt and he felt snubbed. The prime minister's political standing had already slumped because of criticism that his relatively moderate approach toward India and his pro-Western stance had not produced results on Kashmir. The failure of the U.S. government to invite Liaquat further damaged his prestige.

In an unexpected counterpunch, the Pakistani leader elicited an invitation to visit the Soviet Union.[55] Given that relations between Moscow and Karachi were cold and that neither country had established an embassy in the other's capital, the development caused considerable surprise. On the Pakistani side, the groundwork was laid by Raja Ghazanfar Ali, a freewheeling Muslim League politician, who as ambassador to Iran had become friendly with his Soviet counterpart. When Liaquat passed through Tehran in late May 1949, he met Soviet chargé d'affaires Ali Aliev at dinner and voiced an interest in visiting his country. An official invitation quickly was transmitted through Ghazanfar Ali in Tehran on June 2, 1949. Five days later, Liaquat formally accepted the invitation using the Tehran channel.[56]

The reaction in Karachi was enthusiastic; Pakistanis saw the Soviet visit as a way to show the West not to take their country for granted. The invitation was a major political coup, especially as the Soviets had yet to invite Prime Minister Nehru. Liaquat was eager to go to Moscow even though he had few illusions that Pakistan's relations with the Soviet Union would become close. In London, British officials reacted with reasonable calm. In Karachi, however, an agitated High Commissioner Grafftey-Smith told Zafrullah Khan that the visit would "create doubts in the mind of the British and American public" without helping Pakistan.[57]

From Washington, Ambassador Ispahani sent a syrupy letter on September 7, 1949, to the prime minister, calling the proposed Soviet trip "a masterpiece in strategy" that had greatly increased American interest in Pakistan.[58] The invitation from Moscow, in fact, had received Washington's attention. The desirability of offsetting the impact of Liaquat's anticipated travel to the Soviet Union, along with balancing Nehru's state visit to the United States, were the main arguments that Assistant Secretary McGhee used successfully to request an invitation for the Pakistani leader. Truman gave his final approval on November 17, 1949, and a month later, McGhee personally presented the invitation to the prime minister during the first trip of an assistant secretary of state to the subcontinent.[59]

By then, the Soviet trip had gone off the rails. Conventional wisdom in Pakistan has attributed this change of heart in Moscow to supposed annoyance that Liaquat had succumbed to pressures from pro-Westerners in the cabinet, such as Ghulam Mohammed, to travel to the United States before going to the Soviet Union. The available evidence does not bear this out and instead suggests that the Soviets had shifted their position before Truman had approved inviting Liaquat to the United States.[60]

After the Pakistanis initially suggested that Liaquat arrive in Moscow on August 20, 1949, the Soviets proposed that he get there on August 15. The Pakistanis countered that this was physically impossible because the prime minister had to be present at Pakistan's independence day celebrations the day before, on August 14. The Soviets then suggested a two-month delay and eventually agreed to an early November arrival date. They also insisted on having resident envoys in place before the visit, but delayed giving agrément for the Pakistani ambassador until October 28 and failed to nominate a Soviet envoy to Pakistan.[61] At the end of October 1949, a perplexed Foreign Secretary Ikramullah confided to British high commissioner Grafftey-Smith that Moscow was dragging its feet on the trip and had even allowed the prime minister's passport to languish three weeks at the Soviet Embassy in New Delhi.[62]

Although at this point Liaquat reportedly was still eager to go and prepared to travel on short notice, Moscow continued to delay matters and eventually indicated that the visit was indefinitely postponed. The Pakistanis never received a convincing explanation for the Soviet cancellation of Liaquat's trip. The timing of events, however, indicates that the reason was something other than Soviet irritation over the American invitation to Liaquat.[63] Although the Soviets eventually nominated an envoy to Pakistan, relations remained distant until 1954 and then became frigid after Pakistan joined the Western alliance system. It was not until 1965, when President Ayub Khan traveled to Moscow, that a Pakistani head of government actually visited the Soviet Union.

In March 1950, a month before Liaquat was due to arrive in the United States, a major outbreak of Hindu-Muslim violence in East Bengal triggered a potentially explosive crisis in India-Pakistan relations. As tensions rose, a concerned Truman, then vacationing in Key West, Florida, telephoned Acheson to suggest that he send a message to encourage Liaquat and Nehru to find a way to resolve the problem.[64] With American and British diplomats playing a helpful behind-the-scenes role, the Indian and Pakistani leaders were able to ease tensions by reaching an agreement to improve treatment of minorities.

To prepare Truman for Liaquat's May 1950 visit, the State Department sent the White House a forty-one-page briefing memorandum that offered a candid and comprehensive snapshot of bilateral relations and U.S. policy toward Pakistan on the eve of the Korean War:

—Liaquat was well disposed toward the United States and "Western ways" but unable to "express openly his desire for such an alignment because of strong local opinion which still considers western nations 'imperialistic.' "

—Although bilateral relations were basically friendly, they "have not . . . been without irritation and resentment. Our Palestine policy occasioned widespread press criticism and demonstrations in Pakistan. We have been criticized for too great leniency toward India in the Kashmir dispute and for favoring India at the expense of Pakistan."

—Pakistan had received very little economic or military help from the United States. Its economic requests thus far had "seemed impracticable" and "because of our existing heavy commitments to supply military equipment to other parts of the world which are faced with a greater potential threat of external aggression than Pakistan we shall not be able in the near future to make available to Pakistan any large quantity of such equipment."

—"The entire South Asian region is of relatively secondary importance to the United States from a military point of view," although Pakistan might have value in the event of a war with the Soviet Union as a place from which U.S. aircraft could operate. "However, this should not be openly stressed since it negates our oft-expressed interest in helping the region for economic reasons."[65]

On the afternoon of May 3, 1950, Truman and most of the cabinet were on hand to greet Liaquat and his wife at Washington's National Airport. That evening, the president hosted a formal state dinner at Blair House, where the Trumans were living during the renovation of the White House. Liaquat kept busy the next two days with usual state-visit activities: separate—and apparently identical—addresses to the Senate and the House of Representatives, a press conference at the National Press Club, wreath-laying at the tomb of the unknown soldier, a visit to George Washington's home at Mount Vernon, a dinner hosted by the secretary of state, and a reception given by Ambassador Ispahani.

Substantively, Liaquat's schedule in Washington was light. There was apparently no separate business meeting with President Truman. A session between Acheson and Liaquat scheduled for after the state dinner did not take place because the State Department protocol officer strangely failed to inform the Pakistanis.[66] In fact, the prime minister's only substantive meeting seems to have been at the Pentagon with Secretary of Defense Louis Johnson and Chairman of the Joint Chiefs of Staff Gen. Omar Bradley. When the Pakistani leader reiterated his country's interest in obtaining arms, this was merely noted by the American side.[67]

Liaquat's basic approach during the trip was that of a goodwill salesman. It was not a Cold War–oriented visit. The prime minister tried to explain Pakistan to Americans, to emphasize his country's interest in U.S. economic aid and business investment, and to underscore its support for democratic principles. Although Liaquat maintained Pakistan's interest in receiving military equipment, he did not stress the subject or urge closer security ties with the United States during public appearances.[68] His flip response to a question at the National Press Club, however, stirred media interest in the security issue. When a reporter asked how large a standing army the prime minister wanted, Liaquat quipped that this depended on "this great country of yours. . . . If your country will guarantee our territorial integrity, I will not keep any army at all."[69]

Two weeks later, a tragic explosion in South Amboy, New Jersey, triggered further attention to the arms question. On May 20, 1950, longshoremen were in the process of unloading 467 tons of explosives—antitank and antipersonnel mines purchased for the Pakistani army and cases of dynamite bought for Afghanistan—from twelve railroad freight cars. The explosives were to be reloaded into four lighters for ferrying to a freighter in the harbor that was scheduled to transport the cargo to Karachi. Suddenly, the matériel blew up, creating an enormous roar. The noise and shock were so great that some South Amboy citizens panicked, believing their city had come under foreign attack. The devastating blast left 4 people dead, 31 missing, and 312 injured. Although the cause of the explosion was never fully established, it was assumed to have been an accident.[70]

During the three-week trip, Liaquat made a positive impression in Washington and in other cities he visited around the United States. The British embassy reported to London that Pakistan's prime minister came across as appealing, low-key, and straightforward.[71] George McGhee, who spent considerable time with the visitor and his outgoing wife, considered Liaquat a friend and "a man we could do business with."[72] In contrast, McGhee was put off by Prime Minister Nehru,

Prime Minister Liaquat Ali Khan and President Harry Truman exchange official greetings at National Airport, Washington, D.C., May 1950. (Courtesy of the Harry S. Truman Library.)

whom he found "vague and shifty," quite apart from his dislike of Nehru's neutralist foreign policy.[73]

The U.S. press covered Liaquat's trip in a friendly manner. The *New York Times* praised the prime minister's commitment to democracy in his address to the Congress as "heart-warming."[74] But the press demonstrated far less interest than in the earlier visit by the better-known Nehru. "Mr. Liaquat Ali Khan probably learnt more about America than Americans learnt about Pakistan," the British embassy reported. The extent of ignorance about the subcontinent, the embassy wryly noted, was underscored during a lunch in Los Angeles when a California businessman asked Liaquat "whether the blank space between the two parts of Pakistan as shown on the menu card was Africa."[75]

The prime minister was still in the United States, receiving medical treatment for goiter in Boston, when North Korea sent its troops across

At Blair House, Washington, D.C., May 1950, left to right: Begum M. A. H. Ispahani, Prime Minister Liaquat, First Lady Bess Truman, Secretary of State Dean Acheson, Begum Liaquat Ali Khan, Ambassador M. A. H. Ispahani, Margaret Truman, President Truman. (Courtesy of the Harry S. Truman Library.)

the thirty-eighth parallel on June 25, 1950. Liaquat fully endorsed the U.S. decision to invoke the UN collective security system against the North Korean invasion. After Egypt abstained in UN Security Council voting, Pakistan backed the U.S. position in démarches to other countries of the Middle East and South Asia. An appreciative Acheson thanked Ambassador Ispahani for "Pakistan's support of the Security Council's resolution of June 27" and its "very useful" willingness to approach Arab states on the Korean issue.[76]

But when Washington sought more tangible help on Korea, Karachi was less forthcoming. During the summer of 1950, Liaquat's government wrestled with a request that Pakistan dispatch troops to join UN forces. Although the United States agreed to equip a Pakistani contingent, the leadership hesitated and ultimately decided to reject the request. While voicing his continued support for the UN effort, Liaquat stressed that, as long as Pakistan felt threatened by India, he could not commit his country's limited security resources for other causes. A year later, in May 1951, the United States approached Pakistan again about sending forces to Korea. Liaquat responded that his country was ready to commit a full division, but the "U.S. must give him a commitment that will assure his people."[77] Ambassador Avra Warren, a crusty professional diplomat who had arrived in Karachi in early 1950 to replace the long-departed Paul Alling, urged the State Department to agree.[78] Washington thought otherwise, believing that acceding to the Pakistani request would alienate India and Afghanistan and limit U.S. freedom of action in Asia. A rather officious reply expressed annoyance about having to bargain on "issues not related to Korea for fulfillment of [the Pakistani government's] responsibility under the UN charter to provide help to deter aggression."[79]

In fact, Liaquat had limited room for maneuver. In the absence of a firm U.S. security guarantee against India, there was broad opposition to committing forces to Korea at a time when the Kashmir problem remained unresolved and tensions with India were high.[80] Although Pakistan, under Liaquat's leadership, was pro-Western, he was unwilling to align his country fully with the United States and its allies against the communists unless Washington guaranteed Pakistan's security against India. This was a step that the Truman administration was not ready to take.

Stalemate on Kashmir

While Liaquat was visiting the United States in May 1950, Sir Owen Dixon, a distinguished Australian jurist, was undertaking another UN effort to solve the Kashmir dispute. Even though Dixon probably came closer to success than anyone else before or after, in the end he too failed. After shuttling back and forth between Karachi and New Delhi in the blistering late-May heat, Dixon concluded that a statewide plebiscite was no longer a feasible approach. Instead, he fixed on an idea initially put forward by Sir Girja Shankar Bajpai, secretary-general of India's Ministry of External Affairs. The proposal was for India and Pakistan to keep the portions of Kashmir that they controlled, except for the Vale, where a plebiscite or some other arrangement, possibly partition, would settle matters. After considerable difficulty, Dixon gained the agreement of Liaquat and his cabinet colleagues in Karachi.

A suspicious Liaquat insisted that Dixon obtain Nehru's word that he would not oppose the idea out of hand.[81] Hopeful that he had a solution, Dixon traveled to New Delhi to meet Nehru. But India's prime minister rejected the proposal, which he claimed was not suitable for Kashmir. Dixon's mission was over.[82]

The U.S. embassies in Karachi and New Delhi differed in their assessment of what the United Nations should do next. From New Delhi, Ambassador Loy Henderson, who had succeeded Henry Grady, thought it should continue the effort to seek a settlement and leave Sheikh Abdullah in place as long as the plebiscite administrator believed the Kashmiri leader was supporting a fair vote. From Karachi, Warren, who showed far more "localitis" than Henderson, echoed official Pakistani views in vehemently opposing giving "Abdullah's stooge government the slightest possibility of bringing pressure on the local population either before or during the balloting."[83]

To succeed Dixon as the UN's Kashmir negotiator, Washington first proposed Ralph Bunche, a UN undersecretary-general and the highest-ranking African American then in public service. After Pakistan rejected Bunche as "too devoted to Nehru as [a] champion of colored races," the choice fell on Dr. Frank Graham, who had earned an excellent reputation in dealing with the 1949 Indonesia dispute. By this time, Howard Meyers, one of the small group of State Department officials who dealt with Kashmir, recalled that Washington no longer expected an agreement and instead adopted the tactic of engaging the parties in ongoing diplomatic discussions as a means of reducing the chances of a conflict.[84]

Graham, in fact, made little substantive progress after he took up the assignment. Following discussions in India in September 1951, he was pessimistic in debriefing Ambassador Henderson: "After [a] long talk with Nehru . . . [Graham] has almost come to the conclusion that it is useless for his mission to remain longer in South Asia."[85] Graham eventually reported on his lack of progress to the Security Council on October 16, 1951.

That same day, Liaquat was assassinated while addressing a public meeting in Rawalpindi, in the northern Punjab. The assassin, an Afghan political refugee and former paid informer for the British, was immediately killed by the angry crowd. His motive has never been satisfactorily clarified. Apart from blaming the police and local authorities for bungling their security responsibilities, the official inquiry failed to develop a plausible explanation for the murder, although it concluded that the Afghan government was not behind the assassination.

Liaquat's death was a disaster for Pakistan, depriving the still-wobbly nation of its one truly popular national leader. Even though Liaquat had had to put down an attempted military coup earlier in 1951 and faced growing dissidence within the Muslim League, which was beginning to fragment as a political party, he remained Pakistan's dominant public figure. At home and abroad, he was regarded as a leader of moderation, good sense, and integrity.

The shaken Pakistani leadership moved quickly to name Governor-General Nazimuddin as the new prime minister. Finance Minister Ghulam Mohammed became governor-general. The State Department found the appointments "reassuring," since both were seen as pro-Western and "men of moderation," but questioned whether Nazimuddin would "have the strength to resist growing popular pressure" to take direct action in the wake of continued failure to reach a Kashmir settlement.[86] Although the new prime minister did not act rashly despite continued frustration about Kashmir, he proved to be a weak and indecisive leader.

Meanwhile, Graham plodded ahead. His strategy was to seek points of agreement and to narrow the differences to three areas: the ratio of troops to remain in Kashmir, the period of time for the demilitarization process, and the date for the plebiscite administrator to start his work. Although Graham doubted the Indians could block the plebiscite once Nimitz was on the ground in Kashmir, he told Ernest Gross of the U.S. mission to the UN in December 1951 that he found "little tendency on the part of the Indians to agree to any reasonable proposition."[87]

Up until the beginning of 1952, the Kashmir dispute remained largely outside the scope of the Cold War. In keeping with its cool and distant relations with both India and Pakistan, the Soviet Union had steered clear of the issue in UN deliberations. Signaling a significant policy shift in January 1952, however, Jacob Malik, the Soviet representative to the United Nations, tore into Graham's report to the Security Council. He blasted the envoy as a U.S.-U.K. "secret agent" and charged that the West "intended to transform Kashmir and Pakistan into [a] military springboard against the U.S.S.R. and new China."[88]

With Graham's efforts going nowhere, the Pakistanis were becoming even more downcast. An unhappy Foreign Minister Zafrullah Khan told Ambassador Warren in April 1952 that "[h]is colleagues [were] disposed to believe that Graham [was] an old man of the sea with his legs locked around the neck of Kashmir and [would] never let go."[89] A month later, Karachi was even more unhappy when Nimitz decided to resign as plebiscite administrator after having sat idle for three years in New York. In a call on Acting Secretary of State David Bruce, Nimitz commented, "No mediation effort in Kashmir [is] going to succeed as long as Mr. Nehru maintain[s] his present unstatesmanlike attitude."[90]

In June 1952, when it looked as if the Kashmir discussions had reached a dead end, Prime Minister Nazimuddin informed Warren that Pakistan was ready to break the deadlock by offering a major concession on the question of troop withdrawal ratios. Chester Bowles, who had succeeded Henderson as ambassador to India, happened to be passing through Karachi, and Warren arranged for him to meet Nazimuddin to discuss the issue. An upbeat Bowles cabled Washington after the session: "It is difficult to see how Nehru can turn down this proposal."[91] A delighted State Department responded that it was "gratified at [the Pakistani government's] willingness [to] offer concessions in [the] hope [of] achieving demilitarization and [the] entrance into office of [the plebiscite administrator] and regards [the Pakistani] proposal as [a] statesmanlike act."[92] But Nehru turned Bowles down. The Indian leader refused to budge from his previous position on the troop issue, asserting that "ratios were not the way to approach the problem since this implied [the Pakistanis] had definite rights in Kashmir which [the] Indians had consistently denied."[93]

Despite this setback, Graham soldiered on through a round of India-Pakistan ministerial talks in Geneva, Switzerland, in the fall of 1952. After these failed to advance matters, Washington and London readied a new draft UN resolution that drew sharp fire from Bowles, by then on his way out after the defeat of the Democrats in the November 1952 U.S. presidential elections. Assistant Secretary of State for UN Affairs John Hickerson and Henry Byroade, who had replaced McGhee as assistant secretary of state for Near Eastern, South Asian, and African affairs in late 1951, rebuffed Bowles in a November 20, 1952 cable that reaffirmed "our basic policy of attempting [to] help both parties without siding with either." Summing up the U.S. government's view after five frustrating years of wrestling with the Kashmir problem, Hickerson and Byroade cabled, "[The Department of State] considers Nehru [the] key figure in [the] settlement [of the] Kashmir issue. Until he is willing [to] make some agreement there of course can be none. When he indicates a sincere desire to make [a] settlement it probably will follow."[94]

Trouble with Afghanistan: The Pushtunistan Issue

The State Department also worried about festering trouble with Afghanistan. After Pakistan gained independence, the Kabul regime voted against Pakistan's admission to the UN, periodically stirred the pot with complaints about Pakistan's treatment of Pathans, and raised the irredentist cry of "Pushtunistan." The majority of Afghanistan's population, including King Zahir and the ruling clan, were ethnic Pathans, but were called Pashtuns to distinguish them from their brethren across the border in the Northwest Frontier Province. The Pakistanis were basically disdainful of the Afghans and perceived their complaints as motivated in part by the ruling Afghan elite's desire to deflect criticism from their own country's economic backwardness, and in part by Indian machinations. Paradoxically, Pakistan had successfully reversed the long-standing British policy of stationing troops in the Pathan tribal areas. Jinnah had withdrawn the military, believing correctly that Muslim rather than British rulers could win the allegiance of the tribals.[95]

What stirred concern in Washington was that the Soviet Union, sitting to the north of landlocked Afghanistan, might provide an alternative route for Afghan trade as well as other support if the Pakistanis reacted by blocking the transit of Afghan goods. The Truman administration's anxiety mounted after the Korean War increased fear of a more aggressive Soviet posture. Even though Pakistan opposed third-party involvement in its dispute with Afghanistan, the State Department launched a diplomatic initiative in November 1950, offering to assist Kabul and Karachi as an "informal go-between."[96] Perhaps worried that they had bitten off more than they could chew, the Afghans accepted the U.S. proposal. Pakistan reacted coolly. When Zafrullah Khan and Secretary-General of the Pakistani government Chaudhri Mohammed Ali met Assistant Secretary McGhee at the State Department in mid-November 1950, they asserted that the U.S. suggestion would lead only "to interminable discussions with no chance of solving the basic problem," which was Afghanistan's refusal to accept the Durand Line that the British had imposed in the 1890s. The next day, the Pakistanis vainly urged Acheson and McGhee to go beyond informal acceptance of the Durand Line to recognize it officially as the border.[97]

Returning to Washington in January 1951, Chaudhri Mohammed Ali told McGhee that, unless the United States formally recognized the frontier, the talks would fail, because "those blackmailers" from Kabul would raise the question of Pashtun independence.[98] After Warren, once more supporting the Pakistani view, urged U.S. recognition of the frontier, McGhee received Acheson's blessing to maintain the U.S. position. The assistant secretary argued—incorrectly, it turned out—that Karachi "may be amenable to initiating talks on the basis we have suggested" if the State Department stood firm. A month later, when Zafrullah Khan asked Acheson directly about recognition of the Durand Line, the secretary of state responded, "My views remain unchanged."[99]

An activist by nature, McGhee continued to press for talks between Kabul and Karachi. During his second visit to South Asia in March 1951, he tried—but failed—to get the two sides together. In Kabul, the assistant secretary warned that "this [Pushtunistan] problem, as all others, must be considered in light of the expansionist policy of Soviet Russia which had no hesitancy in taking advantage of the power vacuums in Asia as well as in Europe."[100] In Karachi, McGhee thought that he had obtained Liaquat's agreement for talks,[101] but there was disagreement on a key point. McGhee wanted the Afghans to be free to raise Pushtunistan. The Pakistanis refused, since they regarded this issue as a purely domestic matter and none of Kabul's business.[102]

Although the State Department attempted to keep the idea of talks alive, it finally gave up in November 1951, deciding that there was nothing further to be gained from pursuing the initiative.[103] Nonetheless, Washington would continue to worry that chronic friction between Pakistan and Afghanistan might permit the Soviet Union to gain predominant influence in Kabul. Later, the Eisenhower and Kennedy administrations, like Truman's, would try their hand at reducing tensions—with equal lack of success.

Military Aid and Middle East Defense

As Pakistan scrambled to constitute its defense forces, the new nation could draw on a proud tradition of military service in the western districts of the Punjab and a large pool of qualified soldiers—the Punjabi Muslims had been a backbone of the British Indian army. What the new nation lacked was military equipment and the industrial plant to produce arms and munitions. The constant fear of India propelled Pakistan to commit a major part of governmental outlays to defense expenditures, starting with the initial budget in 1948.

In searching abroad for arms and equipment, Pakistan turned primarily to Britain, the traditional supplier for the Indian army, and secondarily to the United States, which had provided equipment during World War II. Washington responded coolly; it wanted London to shoulder responsibility for South Asian security and to remain Pakistan's and India's principal source of arms, equipment, and training. Any U.S. role was initially envisioned as a modest supplement to British efforts. At the time, the United States offered neither India nor Pakistan grant assistance or financial credits. All arms had to be purchased for cash, either commercially or through the U.S. military procurement system.

The rejection of Pakistan's startlingly large request in the fall of 1947 for $510 million of military aid was therefore no surprise. Although some sales were approved, in March 1948 President Truman embargoed arms exports to both India and Pakistan because of the fighting in Kashmir.[104] In spite of the fact that the embargo was lifted in 1949 after the cease-fire took effect, the Pentagon was slow to meet Pakistani arms requests. There was no political objection; Pakistan was considered a "friendly country." The problem was a shortage of equipment and Pakistan's low strategic priority.

The new country was not without supporters, however. An articulate military attaché in Karachi, Lt. Col. Nathaniel Hoskott, argued forcefully—even during the Kashmir war embargo—for a more positive attitude. Believing that Pakistani airfields could be important in the event of war with the Soviets, Hoskott feared the West might lose their use if it continued to ignore Karachi's requests for arms.[105] In Washington, Pakistani diplomats also stressed their country's military value in a war with the Soviets. In this vein, a October 18, 1948, diplomatic note from the Pakistani embassy to the State Department declared, "The strategic importance of Pakistan from an international point of view cannot be overlooked or treated lightly. In a period of emergency, Pakistan can form a base both for military and air operations."[106]

Yet the Pakistanis received little satisfaction. Even a visit to Washington by Defense Secretary Iskander Mirza in the summer of 1949 and support by Assistant Secretary McGhee for early release of spare parts requested by the Pakistanis did not help matters much.[107] A graduate of the prestigious British military academy Sandhurst and a British Indian army officer, Mirza had been the first Indian to serve in the elite Indian Political Service that managed relations between the British Raj and Indian princely states, as well as dealings with strategically sensitive regions such as the unruly Pathan tribal belt. Mirza would become the key figure in the Pakistani political scene after he succeeded Ghulam Mohammed as governor-general in 1955.

In May 1950, when Liaquat made his state visit to the United States, the military supply situation remained basically unchanged, notwithstanding the publicity generated by the explosion of munitions in South Amboy harbor. Karachi's subsequent refusal to send troops to fight with the UN in Korea hardly bettered its prospects for receiving U.S. arms.

American interest in Pakistan, however, grew after the Korean War stirred concern about a more aggressive Soviet posture in areas such as the Middle East. The oil-rich and strategically vital region was militarily weak and politically unstable—a tempting target, so Washington and London thought, for Moscow. When allied strategists considered ways to bolster the security of the unstable area, some believed Pakistan could become a significant source of troops. British conservatives, particularly old India hands like Sir Olaf Caroe, a former governor of the Northwest Frontier Province, argued in favor of using South Asians to help defend the Middle East—as the British had done in the days of the Empire. Since Nehru had removed India from consideration through his policy of neutralism, Pakistan became a natural place to look.[108]

British defense planners developed the idea of a Middle East Defense Organization (MEDO), a British-led military group to be headquartered in Egypt with mainly Arab members, but perhaps including Pakistan. When the British raised the possibility with Liaquat in January 1951, he stated bluntly that his country could not participate in MEDO until the Kashmir dispute was settled.[109] A month later, British officials told visiting State Department South Asia director Donald Kennedy that Kashmir remained "the main barrier": "Until this question was out of the way, little could be done to bring Pakistan into the Western alliance."[110]

U.S. ambassadors to South Asian countries, meeting with Assistant Secretary McGhee in Ceylon in February 1951, favored the idea of Pakistani participation in the defense of the Middle East, but similarly doubted that this would be feasible unless there was a settlement with India.[111] Stopping in London on his way back to Washington, McGhee argued that the challenge was to find a formula that would meet Pakistan's price—"insurance against attack from India"—without undermining relations with New Delhi.[112] British officials were skeptical that this was possible. In the summer of 1951, the British embassy in Washington reported that officials at the State Department, although still interested in Pakistani association with MEDO, "have so far been completely stumped by the question of working out" the difficulties.[113]

Planning for MEDO proceeded to the point that the British, the French, and the Americans, in October 1951, put the idea to Egypt, which was seen as the key to the alliance. Viewing MEDO more as a vehicle for prolonging British imperialism than for deterring the Soviets, the Egyptians flatly rejected the proposal.[114] Even though British and American policy planners continued periodically to talk about MEDO, the proposed alliance, as originally conceived, was effectively dead after Cairo turned it down.

Pakistani Arms Missions to Washington

In the fall of 1951, former foreign secretary Ikramullah led a mission to Washington to seek arms. While meeting with McGhee on October 18—just two days after Prime Minister Liaquat was assassinated—the Pakistani diplomat said that his instructions were to procure as much military equipment as he could "as a gift, under a loan arrangement, or by outright purchase." Putting Ikramullah off, McGhee said that the United States "was already heavily committed to supply military equipment for several parts of the world, especially for the armies in Korea."

After McGhee asserted that "Pakistan had made the mistake of not sending troops to Korea," Ikramullah retorted that, "[f]aced with a hostile neighbor, Pakistan could do no other than it did. . . . Now Pakistan was taking the initiative and putting forth its requirements. It was ready to hear what the U.S. wanted of Pakistan."[115] Later that day, the Pakistani envoy stressed this point in talking with South Asian affairs director Kennedy: "The time [is] past for words; Pakistan want[s] action. If America want[s] a commitment on the Middle East it should ask for this. . . . You must make up your mind about Pakistan."[116] When the envoy saw Secretary Acheson on October 21, he received friendly words, but no arms.[117]

A month later, Foreign Minister Zafrullah Khan met with Acheson to probe what U.S. officials meant when they had told Ikramullah, "The Pakistanis must make up their minds where their country stood in case of trouble." The secretary of state responded: "I presumed that the persons asking these questions had in mind that arms were scarce, that we had many demands upon us, and that we wished to have some idea how useful arms would be to the general cause if sold or transferred to Pakistan. . . . We knew that Pakistan would say that what it could do would be very much affected by its relations with India."[118] In short, the Truman administration's reaction to Pakistan's willingness to help in the defense of the Middle East remained one of wariness, lest arming Pakistan ensnare the United States in India-Pakistan disputes.

In late 1951, Henry Byroade replaced McGhee as regional assistant secretary of state. A West Pointer and the youngest brigadier general in the U.S. Army during World War II, Byroade had firsthand experience in South Asia, having spent part of the war building airfields in eastern India. In 1946, he served as General Marshall's chief of staff during the ill-fated China mission. He transferred to the State Department to head German affairs after Marshall became secretary of state in 1947.[119]

Byroade shared McGhee's interest in using Pakistani troops in the defense of the Middle East, but was skeptical about the feasibility of MEDO. "The British didn't seem to realize that the concept, with a British commander, belonged to the colonial age. We never said no, but just let the idea die by itself," Byroade commented.[120] Gradually, the assistant secretary came around to the concept of protecting the Persian Gulf from the north, rather than from the Suez Canal. A student of maps, Byroade thought that a defense arrangement extending from Turkey to Pakistan—a geographic arc of Muslim, but mainly non-Arab, states—bolstered by small amounts of military assistance from the United States, would help stabilize the region and make it less vulnerable to Soviet inroads.[121] At Byroade's urging, the State and Defense Departments considered the Middle East defense problem in June 1952. In the meeting, General Bradley, chairman of the Joint Chiefs of Staff, declared, "I don't know how far we could get with Pakistan until the Kashmir problem has been solved. If we give Pakistan military aid we will find ourselves in trouble with India."[122]

A month later, in July 1952, the Pakistanis were again in Washington seeking arms. Carrying a letter from Prime Minister Nazimuddin,

Mir Laik Ali led the team as he had in 1947, but on this occasion as adviser to the Ministry of Defense. The Pakistani envoy met with Secretary of State Acheson and Secretary of Defense Lovett to request $200 million worth of aircraft, tanks, anti-tank weapons, and artillery. Pakistan proposed to pay $15 million a year over three years and sought credits to cover the remaining $155 million. Lovett responded only that the Defense Department would look into the matter. Acheson listened politely, but similarly made no commitment.[123]

In August 1952, Byroade officially advised Mir Laik that the United States could not meet the requests. There was then no legal basis for the United States to provide concessional arms sales and credits to Pakistan. To avoid any possible misunderstanding in Karachi, and also to ensure that Avra Warren, by then regarded as thoroughly pro-Pakistani, understood the message, the State Department instructed the ambassador to deliver an aide-mémoire conveying the gist of what Byroade had told Mir Laik. In December 1952, after Dwight Eisenhower had been elected president but before he took office, Mir Laik saw Byroade again. Once more, the assistant secretary of state responded negatively to the arms request, stating, "We had thought about the problem but had very few answers; that we were still faced with the same basic obstacles that prevented positive action earlier in the year."[124]

As British planners continued to ponder Middle East defense during 1952, they developed a more modest proposal. Instead of a full-fledged military alliance, MEDO was transformed into a planning body with its headquarters in Cyprus, then still a British colony.[125] Because London's internal review dragged on for six months, the British were not ready to inform the State Department about the new plan until mid-November 1952.[126] South Asia chief Kennedy, a supporter of arms for Pakistan, responded enthusiastically on a personal basis and a few days later, conveyed a positive official response. "The Department of State is pleased with this proposal and," Kennedy added, "if circumstances make it appropriate, would be prepared to support the UK in this approach."[127]

When the British took soundings about the revised MEDO among other prospective members, however, the reactions were unenthusiastic and the idea petered out. The French noted that Pakistan was farther from the Middle East than was Greece, which was not being invited to participate. The Turks expressed concern about the Indian and Afghan reaction.[128] The British high commissioner in Karachi advised that

Pakistan would be welcome to join when the planning organization took shape, but he did not solicit an immediate response. In India, the reaction was sharp although somewhat muted by the fact that the revised MEDO was only a military planning body.

Bowles, near the end of his tenure as ambassador to India, fired off a strong but uncharacteristically short telegram opposing the idea of including Pakistan in MEDO.[129] The State Department sent a calming reply to the effect that no approach had been made to the Pakistanis.[130] Donald Kennedy, however, told the British, "Bowles would soon be out anyway," adding that, in his view, the pluses of helping the Pakistanis militarily outweighed the minuses.[131]

During a November 28, 1952, meeting of State and Defense Department officials, Byroade addressed the issue directly: Pakistan would probably join an anticommunist alliance if the United States were willing to provide enough military equipment. This would be a positive development but would run into the Kashmir issue and India. Sooner or later, Byroade declared, Washington might have to meet this question head on.[132]

As the curtain rang down on the Truman administration, the question of arms to Pakistan thus remained up in the air. Only days before leaving office in January 1953, the secretary of state reassured an anxious Indian ambassador G. L. Mehta that press speculation about military aid was incorrect. The Pakistanis, Acheson said, had not been approached to join MEDO, which was still in the discussion stage. Some thought that the Pakistanis could help in Middle East defense, the secretary told Mehta, but others were more concerned about the effect on India.[133]

Friends, Not Allies

With Truman in the White House, the United States sought good relations with both Pakistan and India and tried to avoid taking sides between the two countries. The principal American interest in the subcontinent was in solving the Kashmir dispute in order to prevent further instability in South Asia. The memory of the communal horrors of 1946 and 1947 remained vividly in the collective mind. Since the Soviet Union kept largely aloof from the region, Cold War considerations were not the major factor in U.S. policy, except with regard to Pakistan's troubles with Afghanistan.

Still, officials in Washington preferred Pakistan's pro-Western foreign policy to the approach of neutralist India, despite Karachi's refusal to send troops to Korea. Americans found Pakistani leaders—Liaquat Ali Khan, Ghulam Mohammed, and Zafrullah Khan—more agreeable and easier to deal with than their Indian counterparts. Truman, Acheson, and McGhee considered Jawaharlal Nehru prickly and difficult and regarded his chief foreign affairs aide, Krishna Menon, as obnoxious and procommunist. Nonetheless, recognizing the geopolitical realities of the subcontinent, the Truman administration held back from establishing a security relationship with Pakistan lest this antagonize larger and more important India.

For its part, under the leadership of Muslim League politicians—Mohammed Ali Jinnah, Liaquat Ali Khan, and Khwaja Nazimuddin—Pakistan adopted a pro-Western orientation without aligning itself firmly with the Western camp. The burning problem for Pakistan was not the Cold War with the communist bloc, but its own struggle with India, particularly the festering dispute over Kashmir. Regarding Britain as a declining power, Pakistan made establishing closer security links with the United States its top priority. Although Karachi received little satisfaction in this effort, it persisted in wooing the Americans. The Pakistanis, as Dean Acheson put it, "were always asking us for arms and I was always holding them off."[134] After Dwight Eisenhower replaced Harry Truman in the White House and John Foster Dulles became secretary of state, this attitude would change.

3

Eisenhower I: America's Most Allied Ally in Asia

In January 1953, Dwight Eisenhower became the first Republican president of the United States in twenty years. During the election, he promised a tougher national security policy with greater reliance on collective security pacts to contain the Soviet bloc. Although South Asia was not the focus of special attention during the campaign, Republican rhetoric stirred hopes in Pakistan that the quest for U.S. military aid might at last bear fruit.

Eisenhower's selection of John Foster Dulles as secretary of state was also heartening news in Karachi. A prominent New York lawyer, Dulles had been foreign policy adviser to two-time Republican presidential candidate Thomas E. Dewey, had served on several U.S. delegations to the United Nations, and had negotiated the Japanese peace treaty at the end of World War II. The new secretary combined a passion for foreign affairs and strong streak of Calvinist morality that reflected his family background. The maternal side had produced two secretaries of state—grandfather John W. Foster in the 1880s and uncle Robert Lansing, who served under Woodrow Wilson. On the paternal side, Dulles's father and grandfather had been Presbyterian ministers, his grandfather a missionary in British India.

Dulles had no firsthand knowledge of South Asia, however, and prior to 1953 had apparently read only two books about the subcontinent. One was *Life in India,* a mid-Victorian paean to the virtues of British colonial rule; the author was Rev. John Welsh Dulles, the new secretary's grandfather. The other book was Jawaharlal Nehru's *Glimpses of World History,* which the future Indian prime minister had written for his daughter, Indira, from jail during the 1930s.[1] Nehru's agnostic and socialist views can hardly have impressed the profoundly religious and deeply anticommunist Dulles.

By the time he became secretary of state, Dulles had already formed an unfavorable impression of India and a favorable one of Pakistan. He found Nehru's neutralist foreign policy naive, if not unprincipled, and much preferred Pakistan's anticommunist orientation. During a January 1947 address to the National Publishers' Association in New York, Dulles had expressed concern about alleged communist influence in the Indian interim government.[2] He later told Henry Villard of the State Department that his encounters with Krishna Menon at the United Nations had led to this view.[3] The new secretary was the first of many Americans to be put off by the acerbic tongue and far-left views of Nehru's principal foreign policy adviser.

After Truman had appointed Dulles as negotiator of the peace treaty with Japan, Nehru had further irritated the future secretary of state by refusing either to participate in the negotiations or to sign the treaty.[4] In contrast, Pakistan's foreign minister, Zafrullah Khan, had won much favor by helping to corral Asian support for the peace accord and by glowingly praising the effort at the treaty-signing conference in San Francisco.[5]

In January 1953, shortly before Eisenhower entered the White House, the *New York Times* reported that the new secretary intended to visit India and Pakistan and elsewhere in Asia "to determine to what extent their Governments are ready to cooperate in the new Administration's plans for a coordinated defense against Communist aggression in the Far East."[6] Commenting editorially, the *Times* warmly praised Pakistan—then a favorite of America's most influential newspaper. "The Pakistanis are developing an Eastern area of substantial strength that can be vital to the whole of the free world," the *Times* wrote. "If Mr. Dulles can bring about closer ties with this great young Asian state, he will have made an additional contribution to the cause of peace."[7]

It was not Pakistan's "substantial strength" but rather its economic weakness that was on display when Zafrullah Khan strode into the State Department on January 23, 1953, to request emergency wheat shipments in order to avert a grave food shortage.[8] Assistant Secretary of State for Near Eastern, South Asian, and African Affairs Henry Byroade, who had managed to survive a rough transition from the Democrats to the Republicans, urged the new secretary of state to support a positive response.[9]

Dulles agreed and his memorandum to President Eisenhower stressed the importance of helping Pakistan, quite apart from the food shortage. "The political situation in Pakistan is confused and precarious," the secretary wrote. "[A]ny public evidence that the President and other leaders of the United States government are sympathetic to this problem could have an important effect in stabilizing this situation."[10] After Eisenhower formally sought emergency assistance, Congress rapidly approved food aid legislation, which the president was able to sign into law on June 25, 1953—just two weeks after he had submitted the request. The contrast between the smooth and quick agreement on wheat aid for Pakistan and the protracted wrangling over a 1951 wheat loan for India was striking.

The political trouble in Pakistan to which Dulles referred related to the dismissal of Prime Minister Khwaja Nazimuddin by Governor-General Ghulam Mohammed on April 17, 1953. This action was constitutionally questionable, since Nazimuddin continued to have majority support in the Constituent Assembly, which also served as Pakistan's parliament.[11] A domineering, opinionated Punjabi, Ghulam Mohammed had emerged as the country's strongest political figure after Liaquat Ali Khan's assassination in October 1951. The forceful governor-general overshadowed the ineffective and indecisive Nazimuddin, who, as head of the Muslim League and prime minister, should in theory have been Pakistan's top leader.[12] On the emotional issue of the role of religion in Pakistan, Nazimuddin had upset the supporters of a secular state by catering to pro-Islamic sentiments in deliberations regarding a statement of basic principles for Pakistan's constitution—still not drafted six years after independence. The final straw came when Nazimuddin floundered in the face of serious riots in Lahore in March 1953. The target of the disorders was the unorthodox Ahmadiyah sect of Islam, whose most prominent member was Zafrullah Khan.[13]

Ghulam Mohammed appointed another Bengali, Mohammed Ali Bogra, as the new prime minister. An amiable, second-tier Muslim League politician, Bogra was serving as ambassador to Washington at the time and had previously been envoy to Burma and to Canada. Apart from coming from East Bengal, Bogra's main assets were his friendly relations with the Americans and the improbability that he would challenge the leadership. The Karachi embassy reported that Nazimuddin's dismissal "was planned and accomplished" by Ghulam Mohammed, Mirza, and Gen. Mohammed Ayub Khan, the commander of the Pakistani army. Praising Nazimuddin's ouster as a "God-given" act, Ayub told Lahore consul general Raleigh Gibson that "he had worked hard to have something along this line accomplished."[14]

Washington, where the pro-American Bogra was popular, greeted the change positively. An internal State Department memorandum applauded the new prime minister as "energetic [and] progressive-minded" and predicted an increased likelihood of "a more active and determined approach to the solution of internal political and economic problems."[15] This view reflected the Karachi embassy's assessment that the move "represents a victory [for] those elements rejecting reactionary religious influence and desiring strong assertive and more effective central government" and a "welcome gain as far as U.S. interests are concerned."[16] What the embassy failed to note was that Nazimuddin's dismissal marked an important step toward the demise of popular government and the control of the central government by the predominantly West Pakistani civil service and military leadership.

U.S. Arms Aid to Pakistan

A month later, in May 1953, Dulles visited India and Pakistan as part of the first trip to the Middle East and South Asia by a secretary of state. Before arriving in New Delhi, stops in Arab capitals had convinced the secretary that there was little hope for creating a Middle East Defense Organization (MEDO). In India, the talks between Dulles and Prime Minister Nehru, which touched on China, the Korean War, and broader Cold War issues, confirmed the secretary's skepticism about the Indian leader's neutralist approach. In dealing with possible U.S. military assistance to Pakistan—the subject of greatest concern to the Indians—Dulles told Nehru with lawyer-like but misleading precision that the United States had "no present plans that would bring it into a military relationship with Pakistan which could reasonably be looked at as unneutral regarding India."[17]

The secretary of state's next stop was Karachi. Unlike his hosts in New Delhi, the Pakistanis were eager to impress the visitor with their warm hospitality when his plane touched down on May 23, 1953. Dulles was the first of many senior U.S. officials chilled by their reception in India and charmed by their welcome in Pakistan. At the Karachi airport, the smartly turned-out cavalry honor guard made a great impression. So did the fact that the Pakistanis, unlike the Indians, said the things that

Dulles wanted to hear about the dangers of communism. Ghulam Mohammed, Bogra, Zafrullah Khan, and Ayub Khan, in their meetings with Dulles, all stressed their allegiance to the anticommunist cause and emphasized Pakistan's desire to join the free world's defense team.

In his typically direct manner, Ayub Khan told Dulles that the United States "should not be afraid to openly aid those countries which have expressed a willingness, and even desire, to cooperate." The handsome and well-built soldier, who looked as if he had walked off the set of a Hollywood production of *Lives of the Bengal Lancers,* made an excellent impression on Americans. A Pathan, Ayub came from a village in the Northwest Frontier Province near the Punjab border. He was the product of two decades as an officer in the British Indian army and of his own modest family background—his father had been a noncommissioned officer. Ayub's strategic assessment of Pakistan's situation, a copy of which the general gave Dulles, was in the tradition of the nineteenth-century "Great Game" between Britain and Russia. The threat was the possibility of a massive Soviet invasion through the mountain passes of Central Asia aimed at reaching the warm waters of the Arabian Sea. The proposed response was an expanded Pakistani army properly equipped for the task of blocking the Soviets.[18]

Speaking enthusiastically of the "potential both in manpower and bases that is available in Pakistan," Ayub declared, Pakistan "under the present Government is extremely anxious to cooperate with the United States." To allay U.S. concerns about the impact on India, Ayub asserted, "If Pakistan were strengthened by United States economic and military aid, it would result in India dropping its present intransigent attitude [on Kashmir]."[19] Although there is no official U.S. record of any formal meeting between Ghulam Mohammed and Dulles, the governor-general summoned Lt. Col. Stephen J. Meade, a member of the secretary's party and a former defense attaché to Pakistan, for a private talk, during which Ghulam Mohammed "pledged" that no U.S. military aid would ever be used against India. He also asserted that Pakistan would be willing to come to India's aid if it were attacked.[20]

The stop in Karachi turned Dulles's head. Two days later, he cabled enthusiastically from Turkey,

> Genuine feeling of friendship encountered in Pakistan exceeded to a marked degree that encountered in any country previously visited on this trip. Was impressed with the spirit and appearance of what we saw of [the] armed forces and their leaders. Have [a] feeling Pakistan is one country that has [the] moral courage

> to do its part [in] resisting communism. . . . Believe Pakistan would be a cooperative member of any defense scheme that may emerge in the Middle East and that we need not await formal defense arrangements as [a] condition to some military assistance to Pakistan.[21]

When the secretary returned to Washington, he continued his praise. On June 1, 1953, Dulles told the National Security Council (NSC) that "Pakistan was a potential strong point for us" and declared that he was "tremendously impressed by the martial and religious qualities of the Pakistanis." In contrast, Dulles described India's Prime Minister Nehru as an "utterly impractical statesman."[22]

That evening, in a nationwide radio and television report about the trip, the secretary of state advanced the idea of a northern-tier defense arrangement as a substitute for MEDO in bolstering Middle East security. Stating that the Arab nations were absorbed by their disputes with Israel, Britain, and France, Dulles said, "There is more concern where the Soviet Union is near. In general, the northern tier of nations shows awareness of the danger."[23] Dulles had given his blessing for the northern tier after Byroade had discussed the idea during a day's rest stop near Istanbul at the end of the three-week-long trip.[24] The comments in Dulles's radio and television address amounted to a trial balloon for the concept.

In closed congressional hearings on June 2 and 3, 1953, Dulles was euphoric about the Pakistanis. "I believe," he testified before the House Foreign Affairs Committee, "those fellows are going to fight any communist invasion with their bare fists if they have to."[25] In the same vein, the secretary told the Senate Foreign Relations Committee, "The lancers that they have were fellows that had to be 6 feet 2 inches to be qualified and they sat there on these great big horses, and were out of this world."[26] When the NSC met on July 6, 1953, to consider Middle East defense policy, Dulles reiterated his belief that MEDO was impractical and urged support for the northern-tier concept.[27] The NSC agreed and adopted a revised policy statement (NSC 155/1) on July 14, 1953.[28]

Yet Assistant Secretary Byroade planned no early action on the northern tier and was content to let matters sit for a while. There were obvious problems with the proposed arrangement. Any military aid agreement with Pakistan would cause trouble with India. Iran, where the shah had only recently reclaimed power with the help of the Central Intelligence Agency (CIA), remained unstable. Under the nationalist leadership of Gamal Abdel Nasser, Egypt was likely to oppose the northern tier vehemently, especially if it included rival Iraq. Nor was it clear how much interest Turkey would show in the arrangement. Moreover, as the Eisenhower administration's defense policy was aimed at reducing, not increasing, military spending, the Defense Department had shown little interest in the northern tier and had undertaken no preliminary planning regarding the still-nebulous concept. Byroade believed that the United States should support the security group with a modest amount of arms aid—in the case of Pakistan, perhaps $20 million.[29]

Dulles's June 3 speech, nonetheless, was music to Pakistani ears. Although both Liaquat and Nazimuddin had sought U.S. arms, neither had been willing to commit fully to the Western camp in the absence of a security guarantee against India. Pakistan's new rulers had no such hesitations about taking sides in the Cold War in return for military and economic assistance. Even if Washington remained unwilling to give Pakistan a commitment against India, Karachi believed that the expected arms aid would substantially bolster the country's security.

If Byroade was content to let the northern-tier concept simmer, Ayub was not. Along with his mentor, Mirza, the army chief was the prime mover behind the quest for U.S. military aid. His professional mission was to modernize and expand the Pakistani military. In view of the country's weak finances, U.S. help was the only feasible way to achieve this goal. In September 1953, the general took matters into his own hands, transforming a routine trip to the United States to inspect army facilities into a campaign for a positive decision on the arms issue. One day during his visit, Ayub stormed into Byroade's office in the State Department, frustrated by his inability to get a firm answer on arms aid from the Americans. "For Christ's sake," Byroade recalled Ayub's saying, "I didn't come here to look at barracks. Our army can be your army if you want us. But let's make a decision."[30]

Official Washington, whether Congress, the Pentagon, the CIA, or the State Department, liked Ayub. His handsome and imposing physical presence and clipped Sandhurst manners conveyed the impression that, in signing up Pakistan, the United States would be enlisting the successor to the British Indian army in the effort to counter the perceived threat from the Soviet Union to the Middle East. When Ayub called on Dulles on September 30, 1953, the secretary of state assured the visitor that he personally supported arms aid for Pakistan regardless of the Indian reaction, but cautioned that the issue had yet to be put for decision to President Eisenhower.[31] Gen. Walter B. Smith, Dulles's deputy and Eisenhower's wartime chief of staff, told the Pakistani army commander that even though there was as yet no definitive answer, the top levels of the U.S. government were "approaching the problem with a desire to work out a program of military assistance to Pakistan."[32]

Not content with this positive outlook and despite Byroade's warning against premature publicity,[33] Ayub and his colleagues told James Callahan, the *New York Times* correspondent in Karachi, that "formal discussions between the United States and Pakistan looking to a military alliance are expected" after an upcoming visit to the United States by Ghulam Mohammed.[34] The purpose of the governor-general's trip, in fact, was to receive medical treatment in Boston for a stroke that had impaired his mobility and rendered his speech almost unintelligible.

Ghulam Mohammed nevertheless traveled to Washington on November 12, 1953, to meet with Dulles, Secretary of Defense Charles Wilson, and Eisenhower. When Ghulam Mohammed discussed arms aid with Eisenhower, he expressed the hope that "the answer would be affirmative" but cautioned about "an adverse reaction in India." If the United States did decide to give arms aid to Pakistan, the governor-general urged, the president should implement the policy "wholeheartedly," since a "half-hearted follow-through would place his country in an extremely awkward position."[35]

In India, media speculation generated by the *New York Times* article and Ghulam Mohammed's trip triggered an uproar. Prime Minister Nehru warned Washington and Karachi that it would be "a matter of grave consequence to us . . . if vast armies are built up in Pakistan with the aid of American money."[36] He told the chief ministers of India's states that U.S. arms for Pakistan would bring the Cold War to the region and have "very far reaching consequences on the whole structure of things in South Asia, and especially in India and Pakistan."[37] Speaking in Bangalore, the prime minister described the arms proposal in extreme terms as "a step not only towards war, even world war, but a step which will bring war right to our doors."[38]

Taking note of Nehru's "disagreeable statements," Eisenhower sent Dulles a perceptive note about the problems of dealing with India and Pakistan on November 16, 1953. "Dear Foster," the president wrote, "This is one area of the world where, even more than most cases, emotion rather than reason seems to dictate policy. I know you will be watchful to see that we do not create antagonism unnecessarily." In his

President Dwight Eisenhower and Secretary of State John Foster Dulles meet with Governor-General Ghulam Mohammed at the White House, November 1953. (Courtesy of the Dwight D. Eisenhower Library.)

reply, Dulles commented, also perceptively, that "this . . . is another of those situations like Trieste and Israel where emotion rules and where it is difficult to help one without making an enemy of the other."[39]

The tumult in India, which included stormy anti-American demonstrations, prompted a query by *Washington Post* diplomatic correspondent Chalmers Roberts at Eisenhower's November 18, 1953, press conference. The president tried to calm the waters with a typically opaque answer: "While the matter was not discussed in detail when the Governor General came to see him, the fact is the Administration's effort would be to produce a friendship with that entire subcontinent and not with just one group."[40] A few days later, however, the president grumbled in private to *New York Times* columnist C. L. Sulzberger. "Pakistan wants to help the cause of the United States and the Western powers," Eisenhower said, but India and Afghanistan were objecting. Although the Afghans were concerned that the Russians might use U.S. military aid to Pakistan as an excuse to move against them, "Nehru and his tribe" were just being "a nuisance."[41]

Indeed, India was not the only country upset by the possibility of U.S. arms aid to Pakistan. Given the strained relations with Pakistan over the disputed frontier and Kabul's support for "Pushtunistan," Afghanistan was also worried. Ambassador Mohammed Kabir Ludin told Secretary Dulles on January 4, 1954, that his country feared that if Pakistan received U.S. military assistance, this would make the "Afghan position re Pakistan weaker" and might create a "power vacuum" in Afghanistan that a "foreign ideology" [i.e., communism] could exploit. "In essence," the State Department cabled the Kabul embassy, "[the] Afghan attitude as explained by Ludin was not one of protesting U.S. military aid to Pakistan but of saying in effect: Don't forget Afghanistan."[42]

The British, whom the State Department had informed only belatedly of what was being considered, also weighed in negatively. The Republican administration, however, was far less concerned than their Democratic predecessor had been about British views regarding their former Indian empire. After Foreign Secretary Anthony Eden voiced London's doubts when he and Dulles met in Bermuda on December 7, 1953, the secretary confirmed that the United States "definitely" wished to help Pakistan but said that Washington had not yet decided what arms it would give. Expressing annoyance at Nehru's reaction, Dulles commented testily that India did not have "the right not only to remain neutral herself but to prevent other countries from lining up with the West."[43]

In early December 1953, Vice President Richard Nixon visited New Delhi and Karachi during a seventeen-nation Asia trip. The vice president departed from the Indian capital with an even more negative view of the prime minister than had Dulles. In his memoirs, Nixon described Nehru as "the least friendly leader" that he had met in Asia.[44] Like Dulles, the vice president gained a highly favorable impression of Pakistan. In Nixon's talks in Karachi, which focused on the arms issue, Ghulam Mohammed told the visitor, "Were the U.S. not to grant aid now, especially in view of all the publicity, it would be like taking a poor girl for a walk and then walking out on her, leaving her only with a bad name." The governor-general downplayed the potential for trouble with India if Washington gave arms to Pakistan, predicting that the difficulties would "blow over in three or four months."[45]

The Karachi embassy report on Nixon's discussions posed the policy judgment that the U.S. government needed to make: "Are [the] advantages of Pakistan's contribution to Middle East defense as [an] active participating free world partner outweighed by the adverse reaction in India?" Not surprisingly, the new U.S. ambassador to Pakistan, Horace Hildreth, answered the question affirmatively.[46] A genial former governor of Maine and a Republican political appointee, Hildreth had quickly become a strong supporter of arms assistance to Pakistan.

If anything, the vice president was even more in favor of providing military equipment to the Pakistanis. After returning to Washington, he spoke out forcefully on December 24, 1953, in briefing the NSC about his Asia trip. "Pakistan," Nixon declared, "is a country I would like to do everything for. The people have less complexes than the Indians. . . . It will be disastrous if the Pakistan aid does not go through. This may force out the Prime Minister [of Pakistan], but it isn't going to force the people toward Communism."[47]

President Eisenhower formally took up the issue on January 4, 1954, in a meeting with Secretary Dulles, Secretary of Defense Wilson, and Foreign Operations Administrator Harold Stassen. According to Dulles's account, the president "agreed in principle to our proceeding with military aid to Pakistan, subject, however, to our capacity to present this in a reasonable way, which would allay apprehensions of reasonable people that we were trying to help Pakistan against India."[48] Ten days later, on January 14, 1954, when Dulles received the final go-ahead from Eisenhower, the president again focused on India. He directed that "every possible public and private means at our disposal be used to ease the effects of our action on India." During the meeting, Dulles spoke less about what the United States would gain from giving Pakistan military assistance than about what it would lose by failing to proceed in the face of Nehru's strident public criticism.[49]

With little apparent consideration about Pakistan's specific role in the defense of the Middle East, Eisenhower thus gave his blessing to a policy decision that would shape U.S. relations with India and Pakistan for the next three and a half decades. Essentially, the administration concluded, as Dana Adams Schmidt wrote in the February 14, 1954, *New York Times,* "that the importance of bringing in Pakistan on the defense of the Middle East is greater than the importance of preserving pleasant relations with Mr. Nehru."[50] In late January 1953, Dulles informed Eden when they met in Berlin that India's attitude had made it impossible for the United States to back down. "If the Indians had used the diplomatic channel for their representations and made less noise," the secretary said, "reconsideration would have been possible. Now that they had held public meetings, etc., the United States could not give way" on military aid to Pakistan.[51]

What explained the failure of the Eisenhower administration to examine more systematically whether and how Pakistan, in fact, would be able to bolster Middle East defense? In part, the reason was that the northern-tier concept remained vague and was more political-psychological than military in character.[52] In part, it was Dulles's own vision of Middle East defense, which appeared to be a mid-twentieth-century update of British imperial strategy. For over a century, London had relied on the British Indian army, backed by the might of the British Empire, to provide the bulwark against the threat perceived from Russia. Similarly, Dulles seemed to think that the Pakistani army (along with the military of North Atlantic Treaty Organization ally Turkey), backed by the might of the United States, would be able to serve as the bulwark against the Soviet threat.[53] Another factor explaining the lack of a more rigorous policy review was bureaucratic. The northern-tier concept was promoted mainly by Dulles and Byroade, with scant Defense Department involvement. With the Eisenhower administration seeking to reduce military spending, the Pentagon was not looking for new tasks and missions and showed little enthusiasm about the idea of providing arms to Pakistan.

The United States was not seeking to build up Pakistan as a balance against India in South Asia, as many Indians have alleged, even though some Republican conservatives favored this approach. Richard Nixon, for instance, viewed military aid to Pakistan as a way to marginalize Nehru. According to Byroade, though, Nixon did not play a significant role in the decision to arm Pakistan. The decision, he insisted, was inspired by the desire to enhance the defense of the Middle East, not to balance off India. Byroade did not believe that the small amount of arms aid being contemplated—perhaps $20–30 million—would upset the South Asia power balance or enable Pakistan to become a credible military threat to India.[54]

After the January 14, 1953, green light from Eisenhower, events moved rapidly. With encouragement from Washington, Pakistan and Turkey negotiated a bilateral treaty for military, economic, and cultural cooperation, a relatively bland affair that was announced on February 19,

1954. This first step toward the broader northern-tier arrangement provided the supposed rationale for Pakistan to seek arms from the United States. On February 22, 1954, Karachi submitted a formal request for U.S. military help without specifying the nature or amount of assistance. Two days later, Eisenhower responded positively and George Allen, the U.S. ambassador to India, delivered a letter of explanation to Nehru. On February 25, 1954, the administration released the text of this letter and an accompanying policy statement. In this, Eisenhower pledged that "if our aid to any country, including Pakistan, is misused and directed against another in aggression, I will undertake immediately, in accordance with my constitutional authority, appropriate action both within and without the United Nations to thwart such aggression."[55] Neither the letter nor the policy statement, however, calmed India's furious response to the U.S. decision to arm Pakistan.

On the whole, political circles and the media in the United States responded positively. Leading the way, the *New York Times* called arms aid to Pakistan "realistic, rational and feasible."[56] Still, some influential papers, including the *Washington Post* and the *St. Louis Post-Dispatch,* opposed the move along with a small number of liberal Democrats, most prominently former ambassador to India Chester Bowles, Representative Emanuel Celler (D-N.Y.), and Senator J. William Fulbright (D-Ark.). These opponents stressed that it was unwise to upset larger and more important India by giving arms to Pakistan.

In Karachi, Prime Minister Bogra exuberantly welcomed the decision, declaring, "Pakistan today enters what promises to be a glorious chapter in its history. . . . United States military aid will enable Pakistan to achieve adequate defensive strength without the country having to assume an otherwise increasing burden on its economy."[57] The prime minister went on to pledge that the aid would not be used in "any act of aggression against any nation" and to deny that Pakistan had either offered or the United States requested any bases or other military facilities.[58]

Ayub and others in the ruling group regarded the U.S. action as a tremendous boost for Pakistan's security. The move was generally welcomed in political circles, although leftists in East Bengal and intellectuals from both eastern and western wings were unhappy about the abandonment of an independent foreign policy. By aligning itself with the West, Pakistan soon earned an outpouring of brickbats from the Soviet Union, China, and neutralist countries such as Egypt, not to speak of the barrage of emotionally charged criticism from India. For

Pakistan's rulers, this was an affordable price for signing up with the United States. Previously, the country felt psychologically isolated and militarily threatened by its stronger neighbor. Even if Pakistan had not obtained a security guarantee, it had acquired a military-assistance relationship with the most powerful country and leader of the free world.

Kashmir: Dim Prospects for Settlement

When the Eisenhower administration settled into office in the early months of 1953, the Kashmir dispute between India and Pakistan was not forgotten. Secretary Dulles agreed with the recommendation from Byroade and Assistant Secretary of State for UN Affairs John Hickerson to seek Eisenhower's approval for a fresh effort toward a settlement, this time outside the UN framework. The plan was to send a high-level emissary, Paul Hoffman, the respected president of the Ford Foundation and the former administrator of the Marshall Plan, quietly to South Asia to urge the two countries to start bilateral talks. Moreover, Dulles agreed that solving the dispute through a division or partition of Kashmir seemed a more promising approach than continuing to urge a plebiscite. Dividing the state "is the only solution that seems to have practical possibilities," the secretary's March 24, 1953, memorandum to the president stated.[59] In approving the Hoffman mission, Eisenhower expressed his personal concern about Kashmir. "Our world simply cannot afford an outbreak of hostilities between these two countries," he wrote on Dulles's memo, "and I would risk a great deal to prevent such an eventuality."[60]

When Hoffman traveled to South Asia in April 1953, he had positive meetings with Nehru and Bogra, who both accepted the idea of India-Pakistan bilateral talks on Kashmir. The Pakistani prime minister, who had been in office less than two weeks, impressed Hoffman as someone who "can be counted upon to negotiate in good faith, to go more than half way, in fact, in trying to work out a settlement." After returning to the United States, Hoffman wrote Dulles that the two prime ministers were going to persist in bilateral negotiations until they reached a settlement.[61] This was, unfortunately, an overly optimistic assessment.

A month later, the secretary of state raised the Kashmir issue in New Delhi during his May 1953 trip to the region. Not surprisingly, Nehru readily agreed with Dulles that partition might be a better way to solve the problem than a plebiscite. The Indian leader suggested that the cease-fire line, with minor modifications, would provide a reasonable basis for dividing the state.[62] This has remained the unofficial Indian position ever since.

In Karachi, when Dulles took up the Kashmir question, he encountered strong opposition to the idea of dropping the plebiscite and partitioning the state as a way to settle the dispute. "We have no right to make a settlement not acceptable to the Kashmiri people," Bogra asserted. Recalling the troubled plebiscites in Europe after World War I, Dulles countered, "Reliance on the will of the people [is] a noble principle but . . . it [is] sometimes difficult to carry out . . . in an atmosphere of mistrust with opportunities to whip up violent emotions on both sides."[63] Foreign Minister Zafrullah Khan, who also opposed abandoning the plebiscite, offered no alternative ideas, but predicted—only too accurately—that until Kashmir was settled, "there [would] be no peace in this part of the world."[64]

In the face of Pakistan's opposition, Dulles did not press the proposal to drop the plebiscite and partition the state. Nor did the State Department pursue the Kashmir issue with much vigor after the secretary returned to Washington. For example, no senior-level follow-up to Paul Hoffman's mission was sent when India-Pakistan bilateral discussions began in Karachi in July 1953.

The initial round of talks had a positive tone, but produced nothing tangible. Before the next round took place, the ouster of Sheikh Abdullah as the head of the Kashmir state government badly muddied the waters. After Abdullah had begun talking publicly about independence, he was deposed and arrested by his deputy, Bakshi Ghulam Mohammed. In spite of the fact that this triggered major protests in Pakistan, Bogra proceeded to Delhi for a second round of talks. Surprisingly, he and Nehru agreed to name a new Kashmir plebiscite administrator by April 1954—a step the Indians had previously resisted.

Progress was short-lived, however. India refused to have an American succeed Adm. Chester Nimitz as plebiscite administrator, something the Pakistanis wanted. Nehru was also angered when Pakistan was the only member of the British Commonwealth to oppose Indian participation in the UN political conference on Korea. New Delhi was further upset when the Pakistani press, contrary to the agreement reached during the Bogra-Nehru talks, resumed strident attacks on India. The final derailment came with the U.S. decision to provide arms to Pakistan. After Nehru warned that this step would affect the Kashmir issue,

Bogra countered that Pakistan's enhanced military strength would improve, not set back, the prospects for a settlement.[65] But the Indian prime minister was as good as his word. Following the announcement of the arms accord, the Indian position on Kashmir hardened. The bilateral talks collapsed. New Delhi soon ruled out a plebiscite, asserting that the election of a constituent assembly in Kashmir in 1953 had served this purpose and further balloting was unnecessary.

Political, Arms Aid, and Economic Woes

Despite the Karachi embassy's upbeat appraisal of the impact of the governmental changeover in April 1953 that had seen the ouster of Nazimuddin and the appointment of Bogra as prime minister, Pakistan continued to wobble politically. A year later, in March 1954, provincial elections in East Bengal decimated the Muslim League, which won only 10 assembly seats to the victorious opposition United Front's 223. Although the United Front opposed the military aid accord with the United States, foreign policy was not a major issue in the elections. Voting turned on massive Bengali dissatisfaction over the East's treatment by the West Pakistan-dominated central government and the weak performance of the ruling Muslim League. The United Front, an unstable coalition of several parties, held power for less than three months. After riots at East Bengal's largest jute mill took 400 lives and the province's chief minister, Fazlul Huq, told the *New York Times* that "independence" was "one of the first things to be taken up by my ministry,"[66] the central government dismissed the provincial government and imposed direct rule. Defense Secretary Mirza, who had gained a reputation as one of Pakistan's most effective administrators, was appointed governor of East Bengal and charged with restoring order. He promptly arrested numerous alleged communists and other left-wingers whom he blamed for the troubles. After several months, the United Front split and a new provincial government took office in Dacca. Meanwhile, in Karachi, the election defeat in East Bengal badly weakened the position of the Muslim League in the Constituent Assembly.

The U.S.-Pakistan arms relationship also got off to a rocky start. The Pakistani leadership and Ambassador Hildreth were stunned when a military survey team led by Brig. Gen. Harry F. Meyers arrived in Karachi in late March to advise that Washington was considering a one-time arms package of just $29.5 million. A perplexed Hildreth cabled that he assumed a "continuing defense build-up of Pakistan was an integral part" of the northern-tier defense concept and was "consequently astonished [to] find [the] survey team thinking of [a] one-shot operation."[67] In a calming reply, the State Department said that long-term funding would be available, but cautioned that working out the details of the arms program would take time.[68]

A classified letter that Deputy Assistant Secretary of State Jack Jernegan sent Hildreth on April 22, 1954, shed light on the problem. In spite of Eisenhower's approval of the military aid, the Pentagon bureaucracy was dragging its feet, Jernegan advised, and the survey team's instructions to propose a $29.5 million program reflected this attitude. But Jernegan expressed confidence that "we will be able to follow through with the Pakistan program in a manner which will convince even the doubters that the United States supports its friends."[69] Dulles had pushed through the arms aid accord without significant input from the Defense Department. Charged with its implementation, an unenthusiastic Pentagon was trying to get by with a modest program.

The bureaucratic wheels, nonetheless, continued to turn. On May 19, 1954, Pakistan and the United States signed a mutual defense assistance agreement. This accord provided the legal basis for military aid and was the first formal bilateral security connection between the two countries. Still, no agreement on the nature or scope of military assistance had been reached when Brig. Gen. William T. Sexton arrived in the summer of 1954 to head the newly established U.S. Military Advisory Group. After Sexton was unable to promise more than $30 million in aid, the Pakistanis quickly and loudly began to voice their dissatisfaction. As Professor Robert McMahon descriptively put it, "A gaping chasm existed between the free-flowing dollars that Pakistani military officers and bureaucrats conjured up as their just reward for open alignment with the West and the modest dollar figures contemplated by Washington planners."[70]

In the United States in August 1954, Syed Amjad Ali, Pakistan's new and affable ambassador to Washington, who had previously dealt with economic matters at the UN and had helped orchestrate the successful approval of emergency wheat aid, told Jernegan that a "dejected" and "broken hearted" Ayub had said that "if Pakistan was to get no more than Sexton indicated in the nature of military assistance, it would be better for Pakistan not to be involved in a defense arrangement with the United States."[71] At about the same time, Pakistan's acting foreign secretary, Agha Hilaly, warned U.S. embassy officials in Karachi that "if [the] military aid program became known as [a] mere token, . . . disillusionment within Pakistan would threaten [the] present government which had staked [its] future on this bold decisive step."[72]

Two months earlier, in June 1954, Zafrullah Khan had traveled once more to Washington with his "beggar's bowl" to seek additional economic help. Pakistan, he explained to Stassen, was suffering from a steep decline in the prices of its main exports, jute and cotton, which accounted for roughly two-thirds of its foreign exchange earnings, and desperately needed $100 million in additional help.[73] To assess the situation, the Eisenhower administration dispatched a special study mission led by business executive H. J. Heinz II. Its sober report confirmed that America's new friend was in terrible economic shape and would require substantial and sustained financial assistance to achieve meaningful growth.[74]

Uncertainty over U.S. military and economic assistance continued until the fall of 1954, when a high-powered Pakistani team that included Bogra, Ayub, and Chaudhri Mohammed Ali traveled to Washington. In a meeting with Dulles, Bogra complained that if Pakistan were to receive only $30 million in aid for the "responsibilities" it was assuming in the Middle East and Southeast Asia, he would be "derided." The secretary of state countered tartly that he "thought Pakistan had undertaken its anti-communist stand because it was right, not just to make itself eligible for certain sums of dollar aid."[75]

In spite of the private discord about aid levels, the British embassy reported that Washington greeted the Pakistanis as staunch allies. According to the embassy, Bogra, who met with business executives in New York, received an honorary degree from Columbia University, and hunted elk in Wyoming, received "a welcome far greater and more sincere than is normally given a foreign Premier." In turn, the Pakistani prime minister "lost no opportunity" to express "the admiration of his countrymen and himself for all things American."[76]

By the time Bogra met Eisenhower, Pakistani anxieties had been eased. The U.S. administration had put together a more generous and comprehensive aid package for America's new protégé. Washington decided to increase economic help to $105.9 million for the current fiscal year ($75.6 million in commodity assistance, $5.3 million in technical assistance, and $25 million in defense support that could be used for economic development purposes). U.S. officials also presented the

President Eisenhower greets Prime Minister Mohammed Ali Bogra at the White House, October 1954. (Courtesy of the Dwight D. Eisenhower Library.)

visitors a secret aide-mémoire that boosted the level of military aid to $50 million for the coming fiscal year and established specific program goals. The aide-mémoire committed the United States to equip 4 army infantry and 1.5 armored divisions, to provide modern aircraft for 6 air force squadrons, and to supply 12 vessels for the navy. The estimated cost of this program was $171 million.[77]

At the same time that Washington was facing up to Pakistan's healthy appetite for assistance, it was deciding how to respond to a request for military aid by Afghanistan. When that country's foreign minister, Prince Naim, met Dulles in October 1954, the Afghan stressed his country's desire for U.S. arms, expressed deep anxiety about Soviet intentions, and voiced an interest in joining the northern-tier security arrangement. The secretary of state responded negatively, reflecting State Department views that it was not wise for Kabul to join the incipient defense group or to receive U.S. military assistance.[78] In December 1954, Dulles handed Ambassador Ludin an aide-mémoire elaborating this position. The U.S. government, the document explained, believed that American military help "would create problems" for Afghanistan "which would not be offset by the strength such aid might create."[79]

U.S. archival evidence suggests that in turning the Afghans down, Washington was concerned primarily with the possible Soviet reaction rather than with the Pakistani response. Assistant Secretary Byroade told Ludin that "a U.S.-Afghan military aid program might provoke a very strong Soviet reaction. The consequences might be very serious for Afghanistan, and the interests of neither of our countries would be served thereby." Byroade also stressed that the United States had extremely limited military aid funds and "could not embark on a large program for Afghanistan."[80]

The Afghans, of course, did not give up their quest for arms and, a year after the turndown by the Americans, accepted military assistance from the Soviets. By deciding not to aid Kabul, Washington thus inadvertently opened the door for Moscow to establish a military aid relationship with Kabul. For two decades, Soviet influence in the Afghan military establishment grew, culminating in the seizure of power by the communists in 1978. With the benefit of hindsight, a more positive response to the Afghan arms request in 1954 would have served U.S. national interests and conceivably might have averted the catastrophe that engulfed Afghanistan in the 1980s and 1990s.

The Most Allied Ally in Asia: SEATO and the Baghdad Pact

Karachi's alignment with the United States quickly manifested itself on the international scene, where Pakistani diplomats became vocal supporters of the Western cause. In Colombo, Ceylon, during the April 1954 meeting of the countries of South Asia, Burma, and Indonesia, the Pakistanis joined the Ceylonese in pressing successfully for the gathering to criticize communist imperialism as well as Western colonialism. "We can rid ourselves of colonialism," Prime Minister Bogra declared, "but any country that is overrun by communism may be lost forever."[81]

A year later, in April 1955, during the Afro-Asian summit in Bandung, Indonesia, Bogra again insisted that Western imperialism should not be singled out for criticism.

Interestingly, at Bandung, Bogra pointedly distinguished between the policies of the Soviet Union and those of China. Although the Pakistani leader called the Russians "imperialists," he urged that the conferees not apply this label to the Chinese. When Bogra met Premier Zhou Enlai, the Pakistani explained that his country wanted good relations with Beijing, notwithstanding the security arrangement with the United States. Following the talks, the Chinese leader commented, "We achieved a mutual understanding although we are still against military treaties."[82] At a time of friendly relations between India and China, Pakistani diplomacy thus sought to limit the damage that joining the Western camp would cause in the relations with its giant northern neighbor.

Although Washington's fear of Soviet expansion into the Middle East had spurred military aid for Pakistan, the first regional anticommunist alliance that Karachi joined was the Southeast Asia Treaty Organization (SEATO). The origins of SEATO lay in the desire of Secretary Dulles and the British to establish some sort of defense system to bolster Southeast Asia against further communist inroads after the defeat of the French in Indochina.[83]

When the idea of Pakistan's joining SEATO arose, the State Department initially expressed skepticism.[84] After Amjad Ali advised that he was urging Karachi to become a member of the proposed pact, Deputy Assistant Secretary of State Jernegan questioned the wisdom of this decision, since no other South Asian states were likely to join.[85] Shortly before the preparatory conference for the pact at Manila, the British took the initiative to invite South Asian countries to attend. When only the Pakistanis accepted, Secretary Dulles reluctantly agreed to their participation.[86]

Pakistan's key aim at Manila was to have the SEATO shield include aggression from all quarters, not just from communist states.[87] Despite Zafrullah Khan's best efforts, Dulles refused to agree and even added an explicit reservation to the treaty to make clear that SEATO would deal only with communist aggression.[88] The secretary later told the British that he had no interest in embroiling the new alliance in India-Pakistan disputes.[89]

Although Zafrullah Khan was supposed to seek further instructions if he failed to get satisfaction on Pakistan's desire that SEATO protect it against attack by India, he proceeded to initial the draft treaty without consulting Karachi. After his deputy, Hilaly, argued against this step, Zafrullah Khan cabled that he was acting on his own and offered to resign if the government disavowed him.[90]

When the foreign minister returned home, General Ayub, the army chief who by this time had also become defense minister, did not see how SEATO would help Pakistan. Zafrullah argued that even if the treaty did not give Pakistan security against an attack by India, the country would be better off with the Americans if it joined SEATO. The fact that the foreign minister had initialed the draft treaty made it difficult, in any case, for Pakistan not to accede without appearing to back away from its pro-U.S. policy. In the end, in January 1955, the cabinet formally ratified Pakistan's membership in SEATO.

The seven-country pact was a strange affair. For one thing, only two non-white Southeast Asian countries—the Philippines and Thailand—became members. Its value was largely symbolic and political. SEATO signaled the intent of the signatories to oppose with force further communist incursions in the region, but did not commit them to do so. In contrast to the North Atlantic Treaty, the SEATO document provided no automatic military commitment. Indeed, this fact helped the SEATO treaty sail through the U.S. Senate on February 1, 1955, with only a single negative vote.

SEATO was not without critics, however, including Walter Lippmann, America's most influential foreign affairs columnist. When he encountered Dulles at a Washington dinner party shortly after the Manila conference, Lippmann quizzed the secretary about the benefits of the new alliance.

> "Look Walter," Dulles replied, "I've got to get some real fighting men into the south of Asia. The only Asians who can really fight are the Pakistanis. That's why we need them in the Alliance. We could never get along without the Gurkas [sic]."
>
> "But Foster," Lippmann countered, "the Gurkas aren't Pakistanis, they're Indians." [In fact, the Gurkhas are from Nepal and serve in both the British and Indian armies.]
>
> "Well," responded Dulles, unperturbed by such details, "they may not be Pakistanis but they're Moslems."
>
> "No, I'm afraid they're not Moslems, either; they're Hindus," Lippmann stated.
>
> "No matter," the secretary of state retorted and proceeded to lecture Lippmann for half an hour on the virtues of SEATO in stemming communism in Asia.[91]

The northern-tier defense arrangement, which had prompted U.S. interest in providing military aid to Pakistan, became more tangible on

February 24, 1955, after Iraq and Turkey initialed a defense pact in Baghdad. Working closely with the British, the pro-Western Iraqi regime of Nuri Said took the initiative in pressing for the agreement, a step that made Washington uneasy because of the bitter rivalry within the Arab world between the Iraqi leader and Egypt's Nasser. Britain decided to join as a way to maintain air bases in Iraq; the new pact provided a replacement for the unpopular Anglo-Iraqi Treaty of 1930. Foreign Secretary Eden stated frankly in his memoirs, "Our purpose [in joining the pact] was very simple. I think by so doing we have strengthened our influence and our voice throughout the Middle East."[92]

The United States decided not to become a full member of the Baghdad Pact and opted for observer status. Two factors prompted Washington's action to pull back from the northern-tier security group that Dulles had originally advanced on his return from the Middle East in May 1953. The first was the worry that becoming a full pact member would worsen U.S. relations with nationalist and neutralist Egypt, which vociferously opposed the Baghdad Pact as a new form of imperialism. The second concern was that the alliance might take on an anti-Israel coloration and run afoul of potent U.S. domestic political support for Israel.[93]

The Pakistanis, especially Ayub Khan, wondered if it made sense to join the pact after the Americans decided to stay out. Turkish prime minister Adnan Menderes and Nuri Said, however, convinced the reluctant Pakistani general that the pact would entail no new obligations for his country. Nevertheless, the government in Karachi still delayed taking the final step. When Moscow vaulted over the northern tier by sending arms to Egypt via Czechoslovakia, the United States renewed its support for the pact. After the Americans urged Pakistan to complete the accession process, the cabinet formally approved membership on September 25, 1955. Karachi hedged the step, however, by stating that the action implied no commitment that would detract from Pakistan's defense capabilities or involve the country in a military engagement relating to Turkey's membership in NATO.[94]

In October 1955, Iran became the fourth regional country to join the Baghdad Pact, its membership geographically completing the northern tier. The United States indicated that it would establish close political and military liaison with the pact, but reaffirmed its decision not to become a full member.[95] The first meeting of the alliance took place in Baghdad on November 20, 1955. The regional members sent their prime ministers and Britain its foreign secretary, Harold Macmillan. The United States, participating as an observer, was represented by Ambassador to Iraq Waldemar Gallman. Throughout the twenty-four-year life of the Baghdad Pact and its successor, the Central Treaty Organization (CENTO), America maintained this detached posture: it worked actively in the organization and various committees and served as the pact's major element, without ever formally joining the alliance.

In the end, neither the Baghdad Pact nor SEATO amounted to much militarily. Specific pact forces never were designated nor were unified command structures created. Nonetheless, becoming a member of the two security organizations had important consequences for Pakistan. Joining the Baghdad Pact and SEATO gave Karachi a strengthened claim on U.S. resources and, in turn, the United States acquired an even larger stake in Pakistan's well-being. As Ayub put it in his autobiography, *Friends Not Masters,* Pakistan had become America's "most allied ally in Asia."[96]

Another benefit to Pakistan was the regular contact and interaction between Pakistani civilian and military officials and their counterparts from the other pact members and the United States. Both SEATO and the Baghdad Pact developed elaborate committee structures and held numerous meetings and conferences. The most significant of these were high-level annual gatherings attended by foreign ministers, defense ministers, military chiefs of staff, and other senior officials.

On the negative side, membership in SEATO and the Baghdad Pact earned Pakistan the special ire of the Soviet Union and a further barrage of brickbats from India. What hurt more psychologically was the stinging criticism that Pakistan received from Egypt and other Arab states, who favored a neutralist stance and were opposed to anything that smacked of a revival of Western imperialism.

More Political Turmoil in Pakistan

Meanwhile, against the background of these major Pakistani incursions into the world of Cold War diplomacy, political instability at home continued without letup. On October 21, 1954, as Prime Minister Bogra was winding up his trip to the United States and getting ready to travel to Canada, Governor-General Ghulam Mohammed ordered him to return immediately to Karachi. The governor-general was furious at Bogra, who, a month earlier, had cooperated in a maneuver by ex-prime minister Khwaja Nazimuddin and disgruntled Muslim League members of the Constituent Assembly to cut Ghulam Mohammed down to size by approving a substantial reduction in his powers.

Not willing to accept defeat, the governor-general struck back, apparently taking only Defense Secretary Mirza into his confidence to ensure the support of the Pakistani military. When Bogra arrived in Karachi, he was driven to Ghulam Mohammed's residence, where the angry governor-general, who was sick in bed, muttered that he was going to fire the prime minister, to proclaim a national emergency, and to suspend the Constituent Assembly.

Accepting the advice of Mirza "not to disturb foreign and especially American opinion more than could be avoided,"[97] he finally agreed to allow Bogra to remain in office. The prime minister then tamely followed orders to dismiss the assembly and reconstitute the cabinet. Chaudhri Mohammed Ali continued as finance minister, Mirza was named home minister (in charge of internal security), and Ayub, in an unusual move that was one of the first public signals of the political clout of the army, became the defense minister while also remaining as the army commander. The political crisis caused Mirza to miss the marriage of his son in Cumberland, Maine; the bride was the daughter of Ambassador Hildreth.

The publicly stated reason for Ghulam Mohammed's action—this time without any constitutional basis, since the Constituent Assembly itself was the source of popular sovereignty in Pakistan—was that the body had become unrepresentative of public sentiments after the rout of the Muslim League in the March 1954 East Bengal elections. The governor-general's real purpose was to reassert his own power and that of the civil service-military leadership over the politicians. *Time* magazine summed up events in its usual snappy fashion, but four years prematurely: "Bloodlessly, Pakistan changed from an unstable pro-Western democracy to a more stable pro-Western military dictatorship."[98]

Shaken by its ally's continuing political instability, the State Department took solace that the crisis "did not seem likely to bring about a change in Pakistan's policy of cooperation with the U.S."[99] Despite the fact that Pakistan had become a virtual client state, desperately dependent on Washington's economic and military largesse, the United States tried, at the official level, to steer clear of the troubles that wracked the political scene. Thus in March 1955, the State Department turned Hildreth down when he sought permission to speak frankly with Mirza about the country's domestic woes. The State Department doubted that U.S. advice "could contribute significantly to [an] improvement [in the] fundamentals [of the] situation." However, it did authorize the envoy to tell Mirza that "U.S. and world opinion would react favorably to developments pointing toward return [to a] democratic constitutional structure."[100]

Unofficially, however, Washington was less hesitant about passing on advice. The CIA arranged for a well-known political scientist, Dr. Charles Burton Marshall, to spend two years in Pakistan as a "constitutional adviser." In addition to providing help to the Pakistanis in drafting their constitution, Marshall's mission was to "try by precept and example to help Pakistani leaders settle down and establish a smoother government." Marshall had easy access to the top leadership, which was aware that the CIA, not the Dearborn Foundation, a cover organization for which he ostensibly worked, was his true employer.[101]

As the governor-general's health deteriorated during 1955, Mirza emerged as Pakistan's most powerful figure. When Ghulam Mohammed began to show signs of mental instability in August 1955, Mirza became acting governor-general. He formally assumed that office after Ghulam Mohammed resigned for health reasons two months later. The new governor-general impressed people with his quick intelligence and decisiveness: Mirza's relative by marriage, Ambassador Hildreth, thought of him as a "selfless patriot." But his reputation for intrigue made other Americans less charitable in their appraisal. Marshall, for one, regarded Mirza as a "buccaneer." Outspokenly pro-Western, the new governor-general strongly supported the alliance with the United States. At the same time, he held his own country's politicians in contempt and made no effort to hide his belief that Pakistan would be better off under authoritarian rule.[102]

Despite its political instability, the Pakistani government pressed ahead with a series of major domestic measures. The four western provinces were combined into a single administrative entity called West Pakistan, designed to counterbalance more populous East Bengal, which was renamed East Pakistan. The provincial assemblies elected members of a new Constituent Assembly in which the Muslim League, reflecting its collapse in the east, held a minority of twenty-five of the eighty seats. The Awami (People's) League, led by Husein Shaheed Suhrawardy, and the United Front shared the seats elected from East Pakistan. Chief minister of Bengal in 1946–47, Suhrawardy was a small, pudgy man with a lively mind and parliamentary skills rare in Pakistan. He looked rather like a Bengali version of Fiorello LaGuardia, New York City's flamboyant mayor of the 1930s and 1940s, or like modern-day Hollywood movie star Danny DeVito.

Suhrawardy's ambition to become Pakistan's prime minister was frustrated by Mirza, who disliked and distrusted the Bengali politician. Mirza instead named Chaudhri Mohammed Ali to fill the post in September 1955. Although an outstanding civil servant and an effective finance minister, Chaudhri Mohammed Ali had neither the stomach nor the skill for political intrigue needed to be an effective prime minister. He succeeded, nonetheless, in gaining approval for a constitution. Eight and a half years after the country's founding, on March 23, 1956, the Islamic Republic of Pakistan came into being with Mirza as its president.

More Trouble with Afghanistan

In 1955, Pakistan's relations with Afghanistan deteriorated badly after the Kabul government vehemently opposed the decision to integrate the Northwest Frontier Province, where the Pathan ethnic group dominated, into the new province of West Pakistan. In March 1955, Afghan mobs, presumably instigated by the regime, sacked the Pakistani embassy in Kabul and attacked consulates in Kandahar and Jalalabad. Karachi's response—a retaliatory attack on the Afghan consulate in Peshawar and a threat to shut the borders—gave rise to anxiety in Washington.

Closing the frontier "would result very shortly in near strangulation [of] Afghan economic life," an anxious State Department cabled the U.S. embassy in Karachi, and would cause "the Afghans [to] turn inevitably to [the] Soviets." The State Department feared that the Soviets "may be eager for [an] opportunity [to] end Afghanistan's historical buffer status."[103] When Pakistan nonetheless embargoed Afghan goods, Secretary of State Dulles personally approved instructions that Hildreth tell Pakistan's prime minister that the United States did not believe the Soviets were unwilling or unable to take advantage of the crisis.[104] Fortunately, diplomacy prevailed. Tempers eventually subsided and more normal relations gradually resumed between Kabul and Karachi. In September 1955, Pakistan's flag was again raised at its embassy and consulates, and the Afghan emblem flew once more over its consulates in Pakistan.[105]

In November 1955, the regional power equation significantly altered after Moscow thrust itself vigorously onto the South Asian scene. Soviet leaders Nikita Khrushchev and Nikolai Bulganin paid a highly publicized visit to India in late 1955 during which they endorsed New Delhi's position on Kashmir. When they stopped off in neighboring Afghanistan, the Soviet leaders announced Moscow's backing for the Afghans on Pushtunistan, pledged $100 million in economic aid—a mammoth sum given the size of the Afghan economy—and offered military assistance. A gloomy U.S. embassy in Kabul concluded, "for all intents and purposes Afghanistan has become [a] complete economic satellite of [the] USSR."[106]

Dulles was not ready to give up on Afghanistan, however. The secretary bluntly questioned Pakistan's Afghan policy when he met Chaudhri Mohammed Ali during a SEATO meeting in Karachi in March 1956. Pakistan's approach, Dulles asserted, "would probably make certain that a bad result would ensue." The secretary added that "he did not believe in quitting a case like this . . . [and] wanted a program to save Afghanistan from Soviet control."[107]

Dulles pressed these views two days later during a session with Mirza, who favored a tough line toward Kabul. "It [does] not make much sense," the secretary of state declared, "to just sit around doing nothing and let Afghanistan pass by default into the control of the Soviets." Mirza replied that although he favored the removal of hard-line Afghan prime minister Sardar Mohammed Daoud, who had revived the Pushtunistan issue, he would withhold judgment until he paid an official visit to Kabul to "find out what the situation was and what prospects there might be."[108]

After the trip went well, Mirza concurred with U.S. proposals to improve facilities to transport goods to Afghanistan from the port of Karachi. Initially, Daoud was lukewarm in his response to this proposal, contending that the transit question was a secondary issue and would not resolve itself until the larger political question of "Pushtunistan" was settled. In the end, however, Daoud agreed to explore U.S. suggestions, which envisaged establishing a transit zone in Karachi, providing special rolling stock for the Afghan trade, building short railway spurs into Afghanistan from the existing railheads at the border towns of Chaman and Landhi Kotal, and improving roads and warehouse facilities inside Afghanistan. The cost, to be borne by the United States, would be about $30 million.[109]

Back in Washington, when the NSC considered Afghanistan in May 1956, President Eisenhower questioned whether the United States could compete with the Soviets in the economic arena. "Nationalism and the Moslem religion," he commented perceptively, "[are] the only real influences in Afghanistan on which we [can] base our hopes."[110]

Further Trouble over Arms Aid

The U.S.-Pakistan military aid relationship continued to be troubled even though the October 1954 aide-mémoire provided comprehensive and specific program goals. After visiting Pakistan, Adm. Arthur Radford, the chairman of the Joint Chiefs of Staff (JCS), told a January 1955 State Department-JCS meeting that although Ayub Khan received lots of assurances from Washington, "there was general confusion" among U.S. government agencies in Karachi "about how to implement the program." Radford remained high on Pakistan as "a potential ally of great importance" with "a trained armed force which no other friendly power can match."[111]

A month later, Assistant Secretary of Defense for International Security Affairs Struve Hensel came away from Pakistan with a very different view. A troubled Hensel wrote, "No member of the Country Team had any clear idea of the part Pakistan was expected to play in the defense of the Middle East. . . . At the same time, it seems quite clear that Pakistan regards the Indian threat as much more serious to Pakistan than the Russian or Communist China threats."[112] Hensel urged the Pentagon to develop a plan "to outline the military role expected of Pakistan and permit us all to move in that direction."[113]

In March 1955, the Joint Strategic Plans Committee completed such a study for the JCS. The northern-tier concept, the U.S. military planners concluded, would not "result in any significant reduction of the area's vulnerability." Because of Pakistan's intrinsic weakness, the study indicated that Karachi was unlikely to deploy forces beyond its borders for the foreseeable future.[114] Thus, a year after the United States had decided to give arms aid to Pakistan to bolster Middle East defense, the Pentagon found that the concept had little military validity because a significant Pakistani contribution to the defense of the Middle East was unlikely. Despite this frank admission, the decision to help Pakistan was history and could hardly be reversed without major political embarrassment and loss of face for the United States.

Meanwhile, the Karachi embassy began to second Pakistani complaints about the slow flow of arms aid. Failure to maintain the schedule for implementing the 1954 aide-mémoire, a joint cable from the State, military aid, foreign aid, and United States Information Service elements of the embassy warned, could shake the ruling group. "[Members of this group] took Pakistan boldly into [the] free world camp," the message sternly asserted, ". . . and their position in Pakistan depends in considerable measure on [the program's] success."[115] Although the State and Defense Departments assured the embassy that there was no slowdown, Ambassador Hildreth remained unhappy, asserting in an August 26, 1955, telegram that delivery projections "seem to amount to a repudiation of a written commitment."[116]

In September 1955, the envoy's protests became sharper: either the embassy did not understand U.S. policy toward Pakistan or Washington had a "different appreciation of facts here and actions required to achieve policy objectives."[117] Although the JCS admitted in answer that "the hastily conceived figure" for the Pakistani force objectives spelled out in the October 1954 aide-mémoire was wrong and a more realistic total was $301.1 million,[118] the Pentagon insisted that the $171 million figure, not the force goals, governed the U.S. commitment.

The Pakistanis stridently objected, claiming that the force targets, not the cost estimates, should determine the U.S. military aid program. Ayub was particularly upset. Since the Pakistani army had the most to lose, his prestige was at stake. Talking with Ernest Fisk, the consul general in Lahore, Ayub warned that there would be much criticism in the Constituent Assembly that "you can't trust the Americans." Ayub claimed that he was "personally in a bad position" since he had shrugged off naysayers over the arms agreement by arguing that U.S. commitments were firm.[119]

Ayub went beyond American diplomats to make sure that Washington knew how unhappy he was. He confronted visiting member of Congress Clement Zablocki (D-Wisc.) with the charge that the United States was guilty of bad faith. He also wrote a stinging letter to Admiral Radford and then shared its contents on a "non attribution" basis with *New York Times* correspondent James Callahan.[120] In Washington, where the ruckus stirred concern over potentially negative political fallout, the State Department took up the Pakistani cause. Undersecretary of State Herbert Hoover, Jr., wrote the Defense Department that if Ayub's view gained acceptance, "we would have suffered a serious setback in terms of our objectives in Middle East defense and in the political stability of Pakistan."[121]

In the end, the Pentagon buckled and agreed that force-level goals, not the figure of $171 million, would determine the parameters of the program. Assistant Secretary of Defense for International Security Affairs Gordon Gray wrote Hoover in December 1955 that the United States would be able "to assure Ayub that Americans can, in fact, be trusted."[122] In January 1956, when Admiral Radford visited Pakistan again, an outwardly contrite Ayub apologized for having aired the U.S.-Pakistan dispute in the press.[123]

With dissatisfaction fanned by grumbling about slow military aid deliveries, complaints about alignment with the West, as Ayub predicted, had begun to mount in the assembly. The critics could correctly claim that Pakistan had little to show in the form of either military equipment to bolster the country's security or greater support for its positions on Kashmir or Pushtunistan. Quite the contrary, on these issues, Khrushchev had boisterously backed India and Afghanistan. If Pakistan wanted to join the free-world camp, Moscow had shown that it could make life difficult for the new U.S. ally.

At the March 1956 SEATO meeting, East Pakistani politician Hamidul Haq Choudhury, who had become foreign minister after Zafrullah Khan was elected a judge on the International Court of Justice, pressed hard for greater U.S. support on Kashmir. Dulles tread warily, offering only continued backing for the implementation of the 1948 Security Council resolution.[124] The Pakistanis fared better on Pushtunistan. Reacting to Khrushchev's backing for the Afghan claim, SEATO expressed its support for Pakistan's international borders. In the process, the United States officially recognized the British-imposed Durand Line as the frontier between Pakistan and Afghanistan.

After the SEATO conference, the secretary headed to India, where he faced a barrage of criticism over U.S. arms aid to Pakistan as well as his support for the Portuguese position regarding Goa, the small colonial enclave in western India still held as a colony by Portugal. In a heated press conference in New Delhi, Dulles stoutly defended American policy. His statement went beyond the carefully crafted language of Eisenhower's February 1954 letter to Nehru: "I think there can be every confidence on the part of India that there will be no use of those armaments in any aggressive way against India. Certainly Pakistan knows that if that should happen, there would be a quick end to its relations with the

United States. On the contrary, under the principles of the United Nations charter, the United States would be supporting India if it became the victim of any armed aggression."[125]

During the visit, the secretary of state had extensive private talks with Prime Minister Nehru about global and regional issues. The most important result was to deepen Dulles's awareness of India's anxieties about Pakistan. He cabled President Eisenhower: "The one distinct impression I gained is their almost pathological fear of Pakistan. . . . I do not think we can alter our Pakistan relationship which is of great value, but I do think we must handle it in ways which will give maximum assurance to India that our military aid will only be used for purely defensive purposes."[126]

Suhrawardy and Suez

In September 1956, Prime Minister Chaudhri Mohammed Ali resigned, worn down by political infighting. President Mirza unhappily agreed to appoint Suhrawardy as prime minister, making no secret of his reluctance to do so.[127] The president told Hildreth and acting UK high commissioner Morrice James that he would back the new prime minister as long as Suhrawardy did not meddle with foreign policy or the military. When Hildreth commented that Suhrawardy had criticized previous governments as "very inept, negligent and stupid in not explaining the foreign policy to the people and pointing out the reasons and advantages for it and that he intended to correct this," Mirza tartly responded, "Well, when is he going to start?"[128]

With Mirza as president and Suhrawardy as prime minister, Pakistan had two strong personalities leading the government for the first time since Jinnah and Liaquat had left the scene. But unlike the country's founders, the new leadership team had conflicting approaches. Schooled in the Indian Political Service tradition of manipulating truculent Pathan tribals, Mirza used similar techniques in dealing with Pakistani politicians. The new prime minister, on the other hand, was the country's most agile operator in the give-and-take of the subcontinent's version of democratic politics. Unlike Mirza, Suhrawardy at heart believed in democracy. His politically shaky base in East Pakistan and his dependence on uncertain partners in West Pakistan, however, weakened his position.

Almost immediately after becoming prime minister, Suhrawardy faced a major crisis over the November 1956 British-French-Israeli attack on Egypt. The public reaction in Pakistan toward the British and French action was stormy. In Karachi, mobs attacked the British high commission. In Lahore, some three hundred thousand angry demonstrators protested against the invasion. The press stridently urged the government to quit the Western camp and the British Commonwealth. Suhrawardy wobbled at first and then, stiffened by Mirza, who worked closely with the British, refused to break with Pakistan's Baghdad Pact allies.[129] "I refuse to be isolated. We must have friends," Suhrawardy argued.[130]

After the United States opposed the attack on Egypt, Suhrawardy's stance became politically more palatable. Still, his action widened the breach between Pakistan and Egypt and other neutralist Arab states. The Soviet Union's crushing of the Hungarian uprising coincided with the attack on Egypt. Unlike the Suez crisis in the Muslim Middle East, Moscow's invasion of an East European satellite state with which Pakistan had limited ties caused few political ripples in Karachi. But, in contrast to India, Pakistan took a firm anti-Soviet stance in the deliberations on Hungary at the United Nations.

Eisenhower: "It Was a Terrible Error"

As the Eisenhower administration's first term was drawing to its close, a June 1956 National Intelligence Estimate (NIE) painted a gloomy picture of Pakistan's prospects and expressed doubt as to whether America's shaky ally could provide meaningful assistance in the defense of the Middle East.[131] Paralleling the pessimistic NIE assessment was an interagency review of foreign military aid programs headed by Undersecretary of State for Economic Affairs Herbert Prochnow, a Chicago banker. The study revealed that fulfilling the October 1954 arms aid commitment to Pakistan would cost $505 million—almost three times the original estimate of $171 million. The report also found that Pakistan would need more than $100 million a year in ongoing U.S. assistance just to maintain the force structure. Although the ideal solution would be to reduce the size of the Pakistani military, Prochnow recognized that this was impossible without great political embarrassment for the United States.[132]

On January 3, 1957, almost three years to the day after Eisenhower had given the green light for U.S. military aid for Pakistan, the NSC reviewed the issue anew as it considered a revised South Asia policy paper (NSC 5701). When the question of how the intention to provide a small amount of arms aid in 1954 had ballooned into a $500 million financial commitment came up for discussion, an exasperated president criticized "our tendency to rush out and seek allies" as not very sensible. "We had decided some time ago that we wanted Pakistan as a military ally. Obviously it had proved costly to achieve this objective. In point of fact we were doing practically nothing for Pakistan except in the form of military aid. This was the worst kind of a plan and decision we could have made. It was a terrible error, but now we seem hopelessly involved in it."[133]

Eisenhower confessed that "he did not quite know what to do about Pakistan." Cutting the military aid program "might have severe repercussions on our relations" and "might even destroy the Baghdad Pact." When the president asked whether "a skilled hand" might not induce the Pakistanis themselves to reduce military aid, Undersecretary of State Robert Murphy, sitting in for Dulles, said, with diplomatic finesse, that this "was exactly what the State Department would like to do."[134] It would not prove an easy task.

Divergent Aims

When Eisenhower became president in 1953, U.S. policy emphasized strengthening the collective security cordon around the communist bloc. In the case of South Asia, this meant enlisting an only too willing Pakistan as a partner in bolstering the defense of the Middle East. Even though Washington realized that the move would strain relations with larger India, the step was deemed worthwhile. But the United States and Pakistan entered into the alliance for different and ultimately conflicting reasons. Despite its anticommunist orientation, Pakistan remained at heart concerned about the threat from India rather than any menace from the communists. In contrast, the United States saw the security accord as directed strictly against the communist threat and was wary of becoming entangled in Pakistan's dispute with India.

By January 1957, the end of Eisenhower's first term, these fundamentally divergent aims were apparent in both Karachi and Washington, even if U.S. and Pakistani leaders preferred to sweep their differences under the rug. Although Washington was aware that the original rationale for military aid for Pakistan was flawed and that even with U.S. help Karachi was unlikely to boost Middle East defense, the clock could not be turned back. A frustrated Eisenhower might blow up within the classified confines of an NSC meeting, but the U.S. government remained warm in its public praise of Pakistan as a firm and faithful ally. Similarly, despite the fact that Ayub Khan might complain about slow U.S. arms deliveries and other Pakistanis might grumble about Pakistan's having joined the Western camp, the leadership in Karachi remained committed to the course it had chosen as the best means of improving Pakistan's security against India.

4

Eisenhower II: Ike Likes Ayub

In his second inaugural address on January 24, 1957, President Eisenhower signaled his concern that communism would prove attractive to newly independent nations unless they enjoyed more rapid economic development. "New forces and new nations [are] stirring across the earth," the president declared. To counter the Soviets more effectively, Eisenhower asked for a substantial increase in foreign assistance, arguing that this was in the U.S. national interest.[1] In practice, these views of the president translated into a new focus for U.S. policy toward South Asia, one that placed greater emphasis during Eisenhower's second term on bolstering India's economic development than on strengthening Pakistan's defense forces.

The change was gradual, but still unsettling to Karachi, which began to complain that the United States was favoring neutralist India over ally Pakistan. Unhappiness over alignment with the West, already strong in intellectual circles, gained ground in Karachi. Rival India basked in international prominence as the leader of the emerging nonaligned bloc, courted by both the United States and the Soviet Union. In contrast, a number of Middle Eastern Muslim countries disdainfully regarded Pakistan as a U.S. camp follower that had bartered its foreign policy independence for a pot of American arms.

On the other hand, the inflow of U.S. security and economic aid pleased senior military and civilian officials. Although assistance programs had started slowly, by 1957 Pakistan was receiving significant amounts of defense equipment and training, along with substantial economic aid. As the United States implemented the comprehensive military aid program spelled out in the October 1954 aide-mémoire, Pakistan's armed forces were boosted across the board. Patton tanks, modern artillery, howitzers, and state-of-the-art communications and transportation equipment greatly enhanced the army's power and mobility. The arrival of F-86 jet fighter squadrons created a regionally potent air force. Numerous U.S. military teams visited Pakistan and greatly enhanced its military training. Large numbers of Pakistanis also received specialized training at military schools in the United States.

According to retired senior Pakistani army and air force officers, access to U.S. equipment, training, and doctrine gradually reshaped Pakistan's military posture. No longer were its armed forces poorly equipped with World War II hand-me-downs and strong on morale and tradition but little else. The country was acquiring an impressive capability, numerically inferior to India's, but superior in equipment and training. For the first time, Pakistan could mount a credible defense against the threat it perceived from its larger neighbor.[2]

Improvement of the Pakistani economy was slower. The continuing depressed price of cotton and jute, the county's principal exports and foreign-exchange earners, was one problem. Lack of progress in production of food grains was another. Even though the Punjab had been the breadbasket of British India, Pakistan was unable to feed itself and grew increasingly dependent on food imports from America. Indeed, U.S. assistance had become indispensable in keeping the economy afloat. In addition to a substantial official U.S. aid presence, private American assistance groups began to have a significant impact on economic policy formulation. Harvard University's Development Advisory Service, for example, worked closely with Pakistan's planning commission in shaping the country's development plans.[3] In contrast to India, which followed a socialist approach, Pakistan placed greater emphasis on the role of the private sector and market forces, in line with U.S. advice.

Suhrawardy as Prime Minister, 1956–1957

As Eisenhower's second term began, the politically incompatible couple of President Iskander Mirza and Prime Minister H. S. Suhrawardy seemed to be managing their marriage of convenience. Despite chronic political intrigue and infighting in both East and West Pakistan, the UK high commission in Karachi was optimistic—as long as Mirza and Suhrawardy worked in harness—that the prime minister could "mould events into the democratic pattern in which he genuinely believes."

There was hope that the domestic situation would remain stable long enough for Pakistan finally to go to the polls in a national election scheduled for March 1958, more than a decade after independence.[4]

Placing considerable emphasis on improving Pakistan's international standing, Suhrawardy continued the effort to minimize tensions with China—this despite active membership in the anticommunist Baghdad Pact and SEATO. In late 1956, he exchanged well-publicized official visits with China's premier, Zhou Enlai. Pakistan's prime minister told Sir Gilbert Laithwaite, who headed the Commonwealth Relations Office in London, that he cultivated ties with China as a means of holding Indian ambitions in East Pakistan "in check." At the same time, Suhrawardy was careful to keep the level of official warmth with Beijing within limits acceptable to the United States. The prime minister made a point of passing reports of his dealings with the Chinese to Washington via Charles Burton Marshall, the American who was privately advising the Pakistani government.[5]

As always, however, India remained at the top of the foreign policy agenda. Frustrated by the lack of progress toward a Kashmir settlement, Suhrawardy and Foreign Minister Feroz Khan Noon, a veteran Punjabi politician, informed Ambassador Horace Hildreth in January 1957 that Pakistan planned to take the Kashmir problem back to the UN Security Council. At a minimum, they asked that the United States voice its support for a plebiscite. "Anything less than staunch reaffirmation of support for [the] plebiscite would be shattering to Pakistani-U.S. relations," the prime minister warned Hildreth.[6] A week later in New York, Noon increased the pressure, informing U.S. Representative to the UN Henry Cabot Lodge that he "would resign if the U.S. did not give Pakistan firm support on Kashmir."[7]

Washington approached the UN session without enthusiasm. The State Department realized that renewed consideration of Kashmir would create fresh difficulties with India at a time when bilateral relations were improving (after cordial talks between Nehru and Eisenhower in December 1956). Few, however, anticipated the fiery two-day debate that featured Krishna Menon's vitriolic defense of India's position and his acid criticism of Pakistan and the United States. Americans from President Eisenhower on down took a particular aversion to Nehru's closest foreign policy adviser. They disliked Menon's anti-U.S. views and were put off by the unpleasant and aggressive manner in which he pressed Indian positions.[8] In the end, after a Soviet veto blocked one resolution, the Security Council agreed to send its president, Sweden's Gunnar Jarring, to South Asia to explore what might be done about Kashmir.[9] Jarring's pessimistic report provided little to nourish Pakistani hopes for early progress toward a settlement.

Suhrawardy kept his word that he would publicly defend Pakistan's alliance with the West. In spite of considerable political risk after his unpopular handling of the Suez crisis, the prime minister took the initiative to hold a foreign policy debate in the National Assembly in February 1957—the only occasion that Pakistan's parliament formally considered the pro-Western policy.

The heart of Suhrawardy's case was the question he posed to critics: Could Pakistan be neutral? "In the face of so many dangers, Pakistan [can]not afford this," the prime minister answered. "India [is] able to order and pay for arms on a large scale. . . . Pakistan [can]not do so and must therefore turn to others for her defense."[10]

Praising the Baghdad Pact and SEATO, Suhrawardy urged the National Assembly to affirm that "the two pacts were to Pakistan's benefit and had yielded fruitful results."[11] On February 25, 1957, the eighty-member assembly endorsed the foreign policy by a 40-2 vote. Abstention by the opposition United Front and Muslim League weakened the impact of the victory, but the only negative votes were cast by two leftists, one from East Pakistan and the other, Mian Iftakharuddin, a wealthy Lahorite and founder of the influential and, at the time, leftist *Pakistan Times.*

In July 1957, Suhrawardy embarked on an extensive foreign trip, including a three-week official visit to the United States. During a stopover in London before going on to America, he met privately with Nehru and British Prime Minister Harold Macmillan. The Indian and Pakistani leaders agreed, when Macmillan pressed them for a practical way to deal with the Kashmir problem, that the only feasible answer lay in direct negotiations and some form of partition. But both Nehru and Suhrawardy said that they could not state this publicly for domestic political reasons.[12]

Suhrawardy's visit to the United States, Secretary of State Dulles told Eisenhower, provided the administration an opportunity to boost the standing of the person who "probably represents the best hope for the achievement of primary United States objectives in Pakistan—the development of a stable, popularly based government friendly toward the United States and aware of the Communist threat."[13] For Suhrawardy, in addition to generating positive publicity back home, the trip to America offered a chance to lay out Pakistan's complaints about India, to seek increased economic aid, and to request earlier delivery than planned of B-57 bombers for the Pakistani air force.

When the prime minister met U.S. leaders in July 1957, he was friendly but feisty. He voiced Pakistan's complaints about Kashmir and expressed fear that India would divert water from the extensive network of irrigation canals that tapped the Indus River and its tributaries. After partition had split this large irrigation system, most of the canal head works remained in India, whereas most of the irrigated land lay in Pakistan. Since New Delhi had the power to turn Pakistani Punjab into a near-desert, the issue had enormous consequences. The fact that India was talking of developing new irrigation projects in the state of Rajasthan deepened the concern of the Pakistanis. Although the World Bank had been conducting negotiations with the two countries for a

Prime Minister Husein Shaheed Suhrawardy, President Dwight Eisenhower, and Secretary of State John Foster Dulles meet at the White House, July 1957. (Courtesy of the Dwight D. Eisenhower Library.)

number of years, it had yet to obtain their agreement on a mutually satisfactory settlement.

When the secretary of state received Suhrawardy on July 10, 1957, Dulles commented pointedly that some Middle Eastern states were spending too much on arms and neglecting economic development—his remarks reflecting the concerns already expressed publicly in Eisenhower's inaugural address. The prime minister quickly countered that Pakistan did not fall into this category. His country, Suhrawardy asserted, was being reasonable, but India's negative attitude made it impossible to reduce spending on arms.[14]

Although the American interlocutors listened politely to the visitor, they made no promises that the United States would adopt a tougher line toward New Delhi. The U.S. officials also did not respond positively to the Pakistani prime minister's request for early delivery of B-57 bombers under the military aid program.[15] Dulles, however, warmly praised Suhrawardy's efforts to defuse bilateral tensions with Afghanistan. Unlike Mirza, the prime minister favored trying to get the Afghans "on our side."[16]

Although official U.S. records on the issue remain closed, the most significant event during Suhrawardy's visit may have been his informing Eisenhower of his government's agreement for the United States to establish a secret U.S. intelligence facility in Pakistan and permission for U-2 aircraft to fly from Pakistan.[17] Formal negotiations on the facility began after Suhrawardy left office and were not completed until early 1959. It was then announced that Pakistan would grant the U.S. Air Force a ten-year lease to set up a "communications facility" at Badaber, ten miles from Peshawar, the capital of the Northwest Frontier Province, and just an hour's drive from the Khyber Pass and the frontier with Afghanistan.[18]

In fact, the air force communications station was the cover for a major communications intercept operation run by the National Security Agency (NSA), the semi-secret organization responsible for collecting communications and electronic intelligence. Because of its proximity to Soviet Central Asia, Badaber was an excellent place from which to monitor signals from Soviet missile test sites and to intercept other sensitive communications. The Badaber facility became an important link in the chain of electronic listening posts that U.S. intelligence agencies established around the borders of the Soviet Union in the top-priority effort to gain knowledge and understanding of Russian military capabilities.

Pakistan also agreed that the CIA could use the Pakistani air force's portion of the Peshawar airport as a takeoff point for flights over the Soviet Union by U-2 aircraft. Developed by the CIA and nicknamed the "spy in the sky," the sleek U-2 supposedly could fly higher than the maximum range of Soviet air defenses. The sophisticated craft, which made its first overflight of the Soviet Union on July 4, 1956, was filled with special cameras that could produce unique photography of Soviet military installations and equipment. The photo intelligence gathered by the U-2 had vital strategic importance in the years before the United States developed space satellites. Pakistan thus joined Norway, West Germany, Japan, and Turkey as countries that offered landing and take-off facilities for the super-secret aircraft.

Karachi's willingness to host these key U.S. intelligence operations substantially increased the value of the security relationship for Washington. Until then, Pakistan had gained far more than the United States had from the alliance. When Pakistan agreed to Badaber and U-2 flights, the Americans received in return something that they judged to be of great importance for U.S. national security.

When Suhrawardy stopped again in London on his way home at the end of July 1957, he gave Prime Minister Macmillan a glowing account of the American trip. "[Suhrawardy] was the cynosure of every eye and the darling of the people. . . . The President and Mr. Dulles made much of him," Macmillan recorded dryly.[19] But when the prime minister arrived back in Karachi, he found little to cheer about. His base of support in East Pakistan remained shaky. In West Pakistan, his partners in the Republican Party, an unstable collection of provincial notables who had quit the Muslim League at the urging of Mirza, withdrew their support because of differences over provincial administrative arrangements and voting procedures in West Pakistan. With Mirza playing an unhelpful behind-the-scenes role, Suhrawardy lost his majority in the National Assembly in October 1957 and resigned. I. I. Chundrigar, a colorless Muslim League politician originally from Bombay whom President Mirza appointed as the new head of government, lasted only a few weeks before he was replaced by Feroz Khan Noon. A wealthy Punjabi with large land holdings, Noon was representative of what Pakistanis call "the feudals." On paper, he had impressive qualifications. Before independence, Noon had served as a minister in the Punjab government and had represented India in London during World War II. Like many other Punjabi feudals, Noon jumped to the Muslim League only late in the day, in 1946. He held several high-level posts in Pakistan—governor of East Bengal, chief minister of the Punjab, and foreign minister—before becoming prime minister. Regarded as a gentlemanly lightweight, Noon had a penchant for speaking impulsively in public without thinking through the consequences of his words. This would shortly cause trouble for U.S.-Pakistan relations.

"The Present Military Program Is Based on a Hoax"

Ambassador Hildreth left Pakistan in the summer of 1957 to run unsuccessfully for a U.S. Senate seat from Maine. His replacement was James Langley, a New Hampshire newspaper publisher and friend of Eisenhower's chief of staff, Sherman Adams. Apart from being a New Englander and a Republican political appointee, Langley had little in common with his predecessor. The gregarious, easygoing Hildreth was outspoken in his affection for Pakistan. Moreover, the marriage of Hildreth's daughter to Mirza's son provided an unusual family link. In contrast, Jules Bassin, a senior U.S. embassy officer at the time, recalled that the taciturn and aloof Langley never felt at home in Karachi.[20] Unlike Hildreth, he also quickly became skeptical about whether the security links with Pakistan made much sense.

In a frank December 1957 letter to William Rountree, the intelligent but bland bureaucrat who had become assistant secretary of state for the Near East, South Asia, and Africa, Langley wrote, "I wonder if we have not collectively developed certain generalizations about Pakistan and then proceeded to accept them as gospel truth without sufficient periodical scrutiny. . . . The situation of strength which we have accepted as synonymous with Pakistan has too large a component of wishful thinking. . . . [It is] not too difficult to make a rather convincing case that the present military program is based on a hoax, the hoax being that it is related to the Soviet threat."[21] Urging U.S. policymakers to consider the subcontinent as a whole, Langley argued, "We cannot afford to participate or close our eyes to an arms race between India and Pakistan." His hope—similar to that which Eisenhower had expressed during the January 1957 National Security Council discussion—was that Pakistan would agree to cap military spending without upsetting the bilateral relationship.[22] Washington gave Langley the green light to try. In turn, President Mirza agreed to receive a technical team from the Pentagon to review U.S. military assistance and to begin planning for what would follow after the fulfillment of the October 1954 aide-mémoire.[23]

Had Mirza and his colleagues been able to read Langley's letter to Rountree, they would have been even unhappier than they already were about the trend of events in late 1957 and early 1958. First, there was no progress on Kashmir. When Dr. Frank Graham returned to South Asia for a second attempt to solve the dispute at the bidding of the UN Security Council, he ran into a stone wall with the Indians. Second, the Pakistanis were becoming increasingly irritated by the steady rise in U.S. economic assistance to India. The refrain that nonaligned India was being treated better than ally Pakistan was becoming shriller and more insistent. Third, Karachi claimed—since money was fungible—that larger inflows of foreign aid from the United States and other countries, including the Soviet Union, enabled New Delhi to buy more military equipment and thereby increase the security threat that Pakistan faced. Indian purchases of Canberra bombers and Centurion tanks from Great Britain were cited as evidence.

Against this background, Washington's reluctance to advance the delivery date of B-57 bombers, a U.S. version of the Canberra, was particularly upsetting. As Pakistani frustration mounted, Prime Minister Noon's penchant for impulsive remarks caused a bilateral fracas. Speaking extemporaneously during a March 8, 1958, National Assembly debate, Noon charged that Western economic aid was funding India's military expansion and warned that he would change Pakistan's foreign policy unless there was progress in solving Kashmir. To loud cheers, the prime minister threatened, "We will break all pacts in the world and shake hands with those whom we have made our enemies for the sake of others."[24]

Noon's emotional outburst raised hackles in Washington, where criticism of arms aid to Pakistan, especially by liberal Democrats in Congress, was on the rise. To smooth things over, Mirza decided to send a high-level team—Finance Minister Amjad Ali, the well-regarded former ambassador to the United States; army chief Ayub Khan; and air force chief Asghar Khan—to the United States. Their mission, Mirza told Langley, was to try to "undo the great damage they believed Noon's March 8 speech had done to Pakistan's image in the United States" and also to press the case for earlier delivery of the B-57s.[25]

When the group arrived in Washington, Amjad Ali reassured Dulles, Rountree, and others that Pakistan was not going to jump off the alliance wagon. Noon made "snap judgments—some good, some bad—and often his frankness and bluntness work[ed] against the interest" he supported, Amjad Ali told U.S. officials. In an April 30, 1958, meeting with the visitors, the secretary of state showed that his affection for Pakistan remained undiminished. Dulles, who was ailing from the cancer that eventually took his life, declared that U.S. "feelings for Pakistan were, in a sense, totally different from those for India. . . . The basic relationship with India was intellectual in contrast to its relationship with Pakistan which came from the heart."[26]

Assistant Secretary Rountree, in his low-key style, complained to Amjad Ali that "statements by Pakistan leaders to the effect that their military buildup was vis-à-vis India" made it harder for the administration "to justify programs which it wished to carry on in Pakistan." The United States, Rountree emphasized, was not providing Pakistan with military aid to fight India.[27] Despite the admonition, Ayub and Asghar Khan frankly told Defense Department officials that Pakistan wanted the bombers to meet the threat from India. Acting as if he had not heard these words, Assistant Secretary of Defense Mansfield Sprague responded that any bombers would be part of common support against communism, not India.[28]

While in Washington, Ayub Khan also met with CIA Director Allen Dulles (the brother of Secretary of State John Foster Dulles), played golf with Joint Chiefs of Staff chairman Gen. Nathan Twining and retired general Omar Bradley, and was the guest of the Joint Chiefs at lunch. On these occasions, Ayub pressed his warnings about the threat posed by India and presumably also discussed the U-2 flights and the proposed intelligence facility. According to Ayub's account of the discussions, the CIA director and the military chiefs were friendly listeners. Allen Dulles reportedly said that he would "do all he [could] on Pakistan's behalf." General Twining commented that he did not "understand" the policy toward India and felt "there were still too many communists in the State Department." The Joint Chiefs of Staff, Ayub recalled, "were sympathetic to [Pakistan's] requirements and [would] do what they [could] to support [Pakistan's] demands."[29]

In the end, Ayub and Asghar Khan left Washington satisfied after the Americans agreed to an accelerated delivery schedule for the B-57s. Although available U.S. government documents do not shed light on what caused the change, it is reasonable to assume that Pakistan's willingness to permit sensitive intelligence facilities on its territory helped explain the U.S. decision.

At about this time, Washington decided to seek a way out of the policy bind with India and Pakistan by persuading the two countries to reduce tensions. This desire, as well as Ambassador Langley's admonitions about fueling a regional arms race and parallel concerns expressed by Ellsworth Bunker, the highly respected U.S. ambassador to India, led the United States to launch an ambitious regional policy initiative. The basic idea, developed by State Department South Asia specialists during the winter of 1957–58, was to put the major sources of India-Pakistan tensions—Kashmir, the Indus waters dispute, and the arms race—into a single negotiating basket. The hope was that large-scale American aid would provide sufficient leverage so that a U.S. mediator could advance solutions for all three problems. The view on Kashmir was that "any reasonable solution" was acceptable, whether a plebiscite, partition, or some other arrangement. Regarding the Indus waters dispute, Washington backed ongoing negotiations under the aegis of the World Bank and was, in principle, ready to help fund new construction projects that an agreement might envisage. To prevent a further India-Pakistan arms race, the proposal sought agreement by the two countries to freeze the levels of their military forces.[30]

Interagency deliberations regarding the package plan brought to the surface significant policy differences between the State and Defense Departments. Although agreement was eventually reached, the two departments, in effect, had reversed their positions on arms aid for Pakistan. In 1954, the State Department had been strongly supportive and the Pentagon lukewarm. By 1958, the State Department was skeptical whereas the Pentagon had become a staunch advocate of military assistance to Pakistan. Quite apart from the value of the intelligence facilities and the regional security pacts, senior U.S. military officers had formed friendly ties with Pakistani counterparts, whom they liked personally and respected professionally. At least on paper, the U.S. military also took more seriously than State Department regional specialists the role that Pakistan might play within the Baghdad Pact.

In this vein, Gen. Lyman Lemnitzer and Adm. Arleigh Burke told their State Department counterparts during a January 10, 1958, meeting, that "[t]hey would not wish any reduction of Pakistan forces as a result of pressure from the U.S." Lemnitzer added, "In light of the current threat against the Baghdad Pact nations, . . . the level of

Pakistan forces [is] essential."[31] Assistant Secretary of Defense Sprague wrote Rountree later in the month that "present or planned Pakistani forces in themselves should not pose a serious military threat to India's national security."[32]

When President Eisenhower received the package plan from Secretary Dulles in April 1958, he reacted enthusiastically. The president told Dulles that he was "all for" the idea and ready to help personally. "There is no inconvenience at which I would balk," Eisenhower indicated. "For example, I'd be ready to welcome and entertain the Prime Ministers simultaneously—I would even go out there."[33]

On May 16, 1958, Ambassador Langley presented the U.S. initiative to President Mirza and Prime Minister Noon. "We accept the President's proposal" was their immediate and positive response. Noon dictated Pakistan's agreement on the spot.[34] In New Delhi, Ambassador Ellsworth Bunker fared less well with India's prime minister. When Bunker talked with Nehru, who was about to leave for a vacation in the Himalayas, the Indian leader questioned whether the politically wobbly Pakistani government would be able to undertake serious negotiations and commented that he did not see much hope as long as Pakistanis continued "their attitude of hate" toward India.[35] After returning from his vacation, Nehru sent Eisenhower a lengthy letter that said in effect, "Thank you, but no thank you."[36]

Martial Law

As Pakistan's political situation continued to be extremely unstable, Ambassador Langley worried that President Mirza would carry out his frequently voiced threat to impose a dictatorship. In January 1958, the envoy had sought Washington's permission to tell Pakistan's president "on a personal basis" that the "sooner elections [could] be held . . . the better." The State Department turned down the idea as too interventionist, cabling starchily that the U.S. government "must as a matter of principle avoid any semblance [of] tutelage of [the] Pakistani leadership." Langley was, however, authorized to voice "his concern that another disruptive political crisis at this time would be unfortunate."[37]

Even though no crisis occurred in early 1958, voting for the National Assembly was postponed for yet another year, until early 1959. Having no faith in the democratic process, Mirza and other members of Pakistan's ruling elite were uneasy about the outcome of an election.

The contrast with India, which had held its second democratic election in early 1957, did not enhance Pakistan's standing in Washington.

The Noon government staggered on during 1958, although both the East and West Pakistani provincial governments were in near-constant turmoil. In May 1958—just as the United States launched its unsuccessful package plan initiative—the Karachi embassy sent in a stream of reports that Mirza was thinking of imposing a dictatorship. This time, the State Department responded strongly, instructing Langley to caution Pakistan's president against scuttling the democratic political process.[38] On this occasion, Mirza stayed his hand.

During the summer of 1958, turbulence in the Middle East shook both Washington and Karachi. In July 1958, a bloody nationalist revolution overthrew the pro-Western regime in Iraq. Brig. Abdul Qasim seized power there, killing both the young king and Prime Minister Nuri Said, the prime mover behind the Baghdad Pact. Adopting a rabidly anti-Western policy, Qasim withdrew Iraq from the anticommunist alliance. Worried about spreading instability in the Middle East, the United States sent troops to Lebanon to stabilize the internal situation in that country. To justify this step, President Eisenhower invoked the Joint Congressional Resolution on the Middle East of 1957, which authorized intervention in the face of actual or threatened communist aggression. When shaken Baghdad Pact leaders assembled in London without Iraq for their annual ministerial meeting, Turkey, Iran, and Pakistan pressed the United States to join the organization. Dulles opposed such a move, but telephoned Eisenhower that it was necessary "to make some kind of declaration of intentions and purposes toward the three countries" to steady their nerves. In seeking concurrence on the text, the secretary told the president that he did not expect congressional difficulties since the proposed language "did not go beyond the Middle East Resolution."[39]

After Eisenhower gave his approval, the London declaration was issued on July 28, 1958, affirming that the United States would increase its cooperation with the pact members "for their security and defense" and would "promptly enter into negotiations designed to give effect to this co-operation."[40] Although shaken, the Baghdad Pact survived the Iraqi revolution and was transformed into the Central Treaty Organization (CENTO), with its headquarters in Ankara. As a result of the London declaration, negotiations began on new and identical bilateral security accords between the United States and the three CENTO regional members.

The summer of 1958 saw further political turmoil in Pakistan. In the West, the Muslim League was reviving under the leadership of Khan Abdul Qayyum Khan, the forceful former chief minister of the Northwest Frontier Province and a bitter foe of Iskander Mirza. In well-attended political rallies, Qayyum vociferously criticized Pakistan's alliance with the West, called for the re-establishment of four provinces in West Pakistan, and urged greater emphasis on Islam. Defying a central government ban, the Muslim League leader pressed ahead with plans for a large paramilitary force.[41] In East Pakistan, strife between factions in the provincial assembly in Dacca became physical. The climax came on September 21, 1958, when Shahed Ali, the deputy speaker of the assembly, died after he was hit on the head with an inkwell thrown during a melee in the legislative chambers.[42]

These events proved the last straw. Backed by army commander Ayub Khan, Mirza decided to act. On October 4, 1958, he informed Langley that martial law would be proclaimed within the week.[43] According to Mirza, the army had been pressing him to take this step for a year, but he had argued that the "politicians must be permitted to make asses of themselves" before he moved. Analyzing the political situation in an October 5, 1958, cable, the U.S. embassy predicted correctly that the public was unlikely to oppose the coup, even though Mirza's personal prestige had slumped because of his reputation for political intrigue.[44]

The State Department reacted to Mirza's alert by trying to head off the coup. Langley was instructed to inform Pakistan's president that, in the U.S. view, there was insufficient cause for abandoning the democratic path. The cable, which Assistant Secretary Rountree approved, stated, "While in some instances democracies have had to depart temporarily from basic principles upon which their institutions are founded (but only as a last resort and then only to protect those institutions in the long run), we do not have evidence to show this stage has been reached in Pakistan."[45] If Mirza refused to back down, Langley was to tell him that the U.S. government hoped the "interval of restricted rule would be as short as necessary to preserve democracy in Pakistan and to ensure [the] conditions under which free elections, already scheduled, may be held."[46]

Brushing aside Langley's private, but official, objection, Mirza proclaimed martial law on October 7, 1958, abrogated the 1956 constitution, and suspended political activity. When the coup was announced, Karachi remained quiet. The author, then serving as a junior economic officer at the U.S. embassy, recalls neither violence nor disturbances and relatively few signs of military presence in the streets of Karachi. The British high commission reported, "If this morning's newspapers did not all of them carry the president's proclamation under very large headlines one would hardly realize that anything had happened."[47] The initial public reaction was one of general relief. Pakistanis widely believed that the politicians had run the country into the ground. The army and its commander, Gen. Ayub Khan, who initially shared power with Mirza, enjoyed a reputation for integrity and efficiency. The average Pakistani hoped that a period of military rule would turn things around. Despite the U.S. effort to avert the coup, President Eisenhower and Secretary Dulles responded with understanding to Mirza's letters explaining the imposition of martial law. Although emphasizing the American interest in a return of constitutional government, Dulles wrote, "The changes which have occurred do not alter in any respect the close ties which exist between our two countries."[48]

The Mirza-Ayub duumvirate lasted less than a month. After Ayub received reports that the president was intriguing with the military and was reluctant to accept a role of "elder statesman," the army commander decided that Mirza would have to go.[49] Unceremoniously, three senior generals "obtained" the president's resignation during the night of October 27, 1958. He was held in custody for a few days in Quetta, the isolated capital of Baluchistan some five hundred miles away, and then bustled into exile in Great Britain on a commercial airline flight. Ambassador Langley was the only diplomat to bid Mirza farewell at the Karachi airport. He and Australian high commissioner Maj. Gen. W. J. Cawthorne, had Ayub's blessing to see the former president off, but through a mix-up, Cawthorne missed the departure.

Ayub Khan, Pakistan's first military dictator, had gained a considerable reputation in his seven years as army commander-in-chief as a well-qualified professional, a highly competent administrator, and as a person who got things done. He quickly settled in as Pakistan's president and chief martial law administrator. Tackling issues with military-like order, his martial law regime established a series of commissions to study major problems and then implemented most of their recommendations, which called for moderate reform measures.[50] A number of civil servants charged with corruption were fired; some politicians were barred from political activity; and prominent black marketeers were arrested. There was a general sense of satisfaction in Pakistan about the early days of the Ayub regime, a feeling that the country, at last, was getting down to the serious business of nation-building.

Ayub's vision of governance, in effect, called for a return to the benevolent despotism of the British Raj. In his autobiography, *Friends Not Masters,* the Pakistani leader spoke candidly of his disdain for the politicians who had ruled after the death of Liaquat Ali Khan and his belief, shared with Mirza and many former British Indian officials, that Pakistan was not ready for Western-style democracy. Ayub wielded executive authority like the British viceroy, leaving the details of administration in the hands of the civil service. The army remained in the background. Ayub made a nominal bow to the principles of Islam but wanted Pakistan to be a secular state. Political life would gradually be reintroduced through indirect elections on the basis of limited suffrage, with direct participation expanding as the population became more literate and better educated.[51]

Ayub's Foreign Policy: At First, No Change

Four days after the ouster of Mirza, Pakistan's new president received best wishes from U.S. Chargée d'Affaires Ridgway Knight. Ayub accepted these and a friendly letter from Defense Secretary Neil McElroy, who had just visited Pakistan, as something to be expected from such "warm friends as the U.S., but welcome nonetheless." Ayub assured Knight, "Recent developments have, if anything, strengthened Pakistan's faithfulness to its alliances. Pakistan is more than ever on the side of the free people of the West. Continuance [of] U.S. aid is [a] matter of life and death to Pakistan."[52]

As foreign minister, Ayub appointed Manzur Qadir, a prominent Lahore lawyer, who had little experience with international affairs and spent much of his time working on a new constitution. Completing the negotiations for a bilateral security agreement begun after the July 1958 London declaration was an early order of business for the new foreign minister. At first, Qadir surprised U.S. officials by indicating that he was reluctant to proceed further since the proposed accord appeared largely cosmetic. In an unusual remark—considering that Pakistan was under martial law—Qadir told Knight that he was concerned about public opinion, which "was deeply opposed to Pakistan 'satelliteship' to [the] U.S., while an uncommitted India receives favors from the U.S."[53]

Two days later, the foreign minister reversed his position, presumably after consulting Ayub. Were the Pakistanis alone, Qadir stated, he would not have gone forward with the agreement, since the "text would give nothing new to Pakistan and because of internal policy reasons." Pakistan was, however, not alone: Iran, in particular, was eager to conclude a bilateral accord. Moreover, Pakistan's refusal would suggest disunity within the alliance and give the Soviet Union a psychological victory.[54]

The U.S.-Pakistan bilateral security agreement was signed on March 5, 1959. It was an executive agreement, which unlike a treaty, did not require approval by the U.S. Senate. The operative language in Article I committed the United States, in the case of aggression against Pakistan, to "take such appropriate action, including the use of armed forces, as may be mutually agreed upon." This commitment, however, was tied to situations envisaged under the Joint Congressional Resolution on the Middle East of 1957—i.e., to instances of communist aggression.[55] The 1959 agreement did not commit the United States to come to Pakistan's aid against an attack by India—the commitment that Pakistan really wanted. Foreign Minister Qadir was accurate in claiming that the accord gave "nothing new," since Pakistan already had a U.S. commitment against communist aggression under SEATO.

Although there was nothing secret about the 1959 U.S.-Pakistan accord, a layperson might well have misread the text as offering a more open-ended pledge of U.S. help. This was exactly what many Pakistanis did, either failing to understand or simply ignoring the fact that the 1959 agreement restricted the U.S. commitment to aid Pakistan to instances of communist aggression. As a consequence, it has become conventional wisdom among Pakistanis that the United States "betrayed" its ally in Pakistan's 1965 war with India when Lyndon Johnson not only refused to come to Pakistan's aid but suspended military and economic aid. With little success, U.S. officials over the years have tried to convince Pakistanis that the 1959 agreement was limited to aggression by the communists and did not provide a guarantee of help against India.

Initially, Ayub was hopeful that he could patch things up with India, enabling the two countries to cooperate in defending the subcontinent against potential foes. From a military standpoint, Ayub argued, tensions between the two countries and their deployment of troops against each other weakened both against external threats.[56] His proposal for a joint India-Pakistan defense, made on April 24, 1959, harked back to

British desires at the time of partition that the two countries would work together on security matters. The idea also closely paralleled American hopes for a cooperative India-Pakistan security relationship. As Sino-Indian tensions had gradually mounted over disputed territory in the Himalayas, the possibility of actual fighting between India and China no longer seemed so remote.

Nehru, however, firmly rebuffed the Pakistani leader, stating in parliament on May 4, 1959, "We do not want to have a common defense policy which is almost some kind of military alliance—I do not understand against whom people talk about common defense policies."[57] Earlier, the Indian prime minister had undiplomatically characterized Ayub's seizure of power in Pakistan as "naked military dictatorship."[58] In any case, even had Nehru responded more positively, an agreement would have been difficult. Pakistan's new leader had been careful to condition joint defense on a settlement of the Kashmir and Indus waters disputes. He made clear that unless these problems were resolved, India-Pakistan military cooperation was not feasible.

A More Hopeful Outlook

After the military government took hold in Karachi, the outlook for Pakistan began to brighten. Officials in Washington thought that Ayub might succeed in bringing stability to their wobbly ally. The army takeover in Pakistan, moreover, did not appear as an isolated instance but as part of a broader pattern of weak, postcolonial democratic governments giving way to military regimes. (Within one month of Pakistan's coup, Burma and Sudan also experienced military takeovers.)

In May 1959, a U.S. National Intelligence Estimate (NIE) titled "The Outlook for Pakistan" summed up Ayub's initial six months in office as "so far, so good." The analysis did not foresee any major change in Pakistan's foreign policy but predicted (correctly) that Ayub would be more confident than his predecessors and less likely to seek or take advice from Washington. Regarding China, whose relations with India had deteriorated after the 1959 revolt in Tibet, the NIE expressed doubt that Pakistan would expand its ties. Quite the contrary, the NIE asserted (incorrectly) that events in the Himalayas would make the Pakistanis more wary of the Chinese.[59]

On the economic side, the policies of Finance Minister Mohammed Shoaib, who had returned to Karachi from a senior post at the World

Bank, impressed U.S. officials. Under his leadership, Pakistan's economic situation began to improve. Even if American aid remained the major source of external financing for Pakistan's development program, the future seemed less bleak.

Further grounds for optimism came as a result of progress in the World Bank-led negotiations over the Indus waters dispute. Building on an idea put forward in 1951 by former Tennessee Valley Authority head David Lilienthal, the World Bank proposed that the existing irrigation system be divided into two entirely separate and independent canal networks. Under the bank's plan, India would have the full use of the three eastern rivers that flowed through the Punjab: the Ravi, the Beas, and the Sutlej. Pakistan would have complete use of the three western rivers: the Jhelum, the Chenab, and the Indus. Construction of new dams, canals, and other irrigation works would ensure that neither country lost irrigation water in the process.

During the April 30, 1959, National Security Council meeting, Undersecretary of State Douglas Dillon was upbeat about the possibility of an Indus waters settlement.[60] A member of a prominent New York banking family, former ambassador to France, and former undersecretary of state for economic affairs, Dillon had moved into the number two position at the State Department after Eisenhower appointed Christian Herter to succeed the dying John Foster Dulles. Dillon sought and received the president's formal approval for the United States to provide half of the $1 billion needed for new construction projects envisaged under the Indus waters accord. A pleased Eisenhower described the proposed expenditure as "one of our more worthwhile projects."[61]

Should Pakistan Receive F-104s?

In May 1959, a fresh arms supply issue arose after the Pakistanis asked for supersonic F-104 fighter aircraft. In justifying the request, Ayub stressed the problems that the U.S. intelligence facility at Badaber had caused for Pakistan. He told Ambassador Langley that the Soviet Union, China, and India, despite public denials, suspected that "the unit is an actual or potential launching site for missiles." Foreign overflights of Pakistani territory had substantially increased and his country, Ayub asserted, needed the F-104s to counter this new threat.[62]

The initial U.S. reaction was negative. Although Assistant Secretary Rountree made clear that the United States planned to continue military aid after the 1954 commitment was fulfilled, he poured cold water on the idea of Pakistan's receiving supersonic F-104s. This aircraft, he argued, would be costly, be hard for the Pakistani air force to absorb, and probably cause New Delhi to seek a weapons system with similar capabilities, triggering a new round of India-Pakistan arms competition.[63]

On the heels of the F-104 rebuff, testimony a month later during June 1959 congressional hearings by Dillon, Secretary of Defense McElroy, and Air Force Chief of Staff Gen. Thomas White, implying that Pakistan had too large a military establishment, angered Ayub. In a stiff public rejoinder, Pakistan's president fired back: The "general feeling in [the] minds of influential people in [the] United States that Pakistan is keeping forces in excess [of] its requirements . . . is totally erroneous and based on an incorrect appreciation of [the] military requirements of Pakistan."[64]

About to complete his assignment in Karachi, Ambassador Langley sourly cabled that the congressional testimony and Ayub's reply once again underscored the need to clarify what the United States expected of Pakistan.[65] In fact, when Langley had complained a year earlier about Washington's failure to spell out this out, Dillon had replied candidly: "The military role and value of the Pakistan army was dubious at best. In retrospect, it now appears clear that the military program in Pakistan was launched as a political measure designed to induce Pakistan to join regional security pacts. From a purely military standpoint, maintaining large armed forces in Pakistan cannot be justified."[66] Dillon expressed a similar view during a July 30, 1959, briefing session for Rountree, who had been designated to succeed Langley in Karachi.[67]

In the early months of 1959, policy differences between the State and Defense Departments made it difficult for an interagency working group to agree on a new arms-supply policy for the period after the completion of the program contained in the October 1954 aide-mémoire. By the time Rountree was packing his bags to leave for Pakistan in mid-1959, a bureaucratic compromise was cobbled together. With a bow to the State Department, the new arms-supply policy called for a serious effort to get Pakistan to moderate its demands for military aid and to place priority on economic development. To satisfy the Pentagon, the new policy endorsed continued military aid "to protect U.S. investment in Pakistan" and to maintain the military forces developed as a result of U.S. help with "some modernization of equipment."[68] The key operational question was how to define "some modernization." In typically opaque officialese, the interagency document stated, "In recognition of the need to maintain the excellence of the military units in Pakistan which we now support, it is our intention to provide military assistance to Pakistan which would logically include some modernization of equipment. This, however, should proceed in an orderly and gradual manner as a result of natural attrition and take into account absorptive capacity as well as financial limitations."[69]

For Karachi, this ambiguous formulation was far more welcome than the growing clamor on Capitol Hill against military aid to Pakistan and in favor of increased economic aid for India. This view was especially strong among the Democrats, who scored a thumping victory in the 1958 congressional elections. Concern about both issues was at the top of Pakistani ambassador Aziz Ahmed's agenda when he met with Dillon on July 31, 1959. Ayub had sent Ahmed, a senior civil servant and former officer of the Indian Civil Service under the Raj, to head the embassy in Washington shortly after assuming power. In discussing the military aid issue with Dillon, Ahmed employed more than a little hyperbole in asserting that the security threat in Asia was even graver than the threat to the peace caused by recent Soviet pressures over Berlin. Regarding economic aid to India, the envoy said that he was "perturbed" that Vice President Richard Nixon had joined Senator John F. Kennedy as a keynote speaker at a major conference to generate support for helping India's economic development.[70]

Dillon countered that even though the United States was increasing economic aid for India, Pakistan was receiving two or three times more assistance per capita than its neighbor. Washington was neither ignoring nor neglecting Pakistan, Dillon emphasized. The undersecretary stressed that pressure to reduce military assistance was rising in Congress. It was hard, Dillon asserted, to argue that aid to Vietnam, Korea, or Taiwan could be reduced, so "Pakistan was left as the only country which could provide a target for possible cuts."[71]

Eisenhower Visits Pakistan

Despite increasing frictions, both Washington and Karachi maintained the public posture that the two countries were warm friends and sturdy allies. This was underscored in December 1959 when Dwight Eisenhower became the first U.S. president to visit Pakistan. Earlier, in the fall of 1959, Ayub Khan had announced measures designed to move his country slowly toward greater public participation in government. He established a system of local councils, called "basic democracies," elected by universal suffrage. In turn, the eighty thousand "basic democrats" became a national electoral college that would select a national assembly in 1962 and elect a president in 1965.

Ayub also decided to shift the seat of government from Karachi. A new capital, which was to be named Islamabad, would be built 800 miles north of Karachi, and about 15 miles away from the city of Rawalpindi, at the edge of the Margalla Hills, the first foothills of the Himalayas. Apart from a healthier climate and a strategically less exposed location, the new capital would enable Ayub to keep an eye on the army, his ultimate source of power, which had its headquarters in Rawalpindi. Ayub himself moved back into his old home in Rawalpindi, the commander-in-chief's residence, which continued to house Pakistani presidents until a new official mansion in Islamabad was completed in the late 1970s.

Over the next decade, the Pakistani government gradually shifted from Karachi as Islamabad took shape. Foreign embassies were among the last to move, not until the late 1960s. In the meantime, the Americans opened a small embassy office in 1960 in the cool hill station of Murree, six thousand feet above sea level; later they opened a larger one in Rawalpindi. With Ayub spending much of his time in the north—he intensely disliked Karachi—Ambassador Rountree and his successor, Walter McConaughy, found themselves shuttling back and forth between Pakistan's old and new capitals during this transition period.

When President Eisenhower left the United States for a three-week trip to South Asia and Europe in December 1959, he flew for the first time in Air Force One, the specially configured Boeing 707 jet aircraft that enabled the president to cover far greater distances in comfort than he could in propeller-driven aircraft. Even though Eisenhower wrote in his memoirs that India was the magnet that drew him to the subcontinent,[72] the president did not neglect U.S. ally Pakistan. When Air Force One landed at Karachi airport in mid-afternoon on December 7, 1959, the president was welcomed by a beaming Ayub Khan. The first visit to Pakistan by a serving U.S. president, especially one as popular as Eisenhower, was a major event.[73] The two leaders drove the fifteen miles into downtown Karachi cheered by 750,000 flag-waving Pakistanis. They then shifted into an open horse-drawn state carriage for the final, mile-long ride through jammed city streets to reach Ayub's official residence.[74]

In wide-ranging talks that afternoon and the next day, the Pakistani leader painted a gloomy picture of the region's security. Ayub doubted that any change in Soviet strategy was in the offing and urged America not to lower its guard. The Soviets were trying to penetrate Afghanistan and the Chinese were building air bases near the region. In time, Ayub feared, Afghanistan would pose a "grave threat to us all" and India might collapse. To meet this danger, the Pakistani leader stressed the view that India and his country needed to cooperate. It "would be fatal," he declared, "if India and Pakistan should remain enemies. They [have] a common interest in the defense of the subcontinent." Above all, Ayub

Presidents Eisenhower and Mohammed Ayub Khan confer with aides during Eisenhower's visit to Karachi, December 1959. Seated on the left side of the table are, left to right, Foreign Minister Manzur Qadir, President Ayub, and Finance Minister Mohammed Shoaib. Across the table are, right to left, Ambassador to Pakistan William Rountree, President Eisenhower, and Undersecretary of State Robert Murphy. (Courtesy of the Dwight D. Eisenhower Library.)

emphasized, this required settlement of the Kashmir dispute. "A plebiscite was fine," according to him, "but, if that is not possible, he was willing to consider any alternative" that ensured Pakistan, India, and the people of Kashmir "a stake in the area."[75]

The Pakistani president urged the United States to use its "tremendous influence" on India to help find a Kashmir solution. "Massive" U.S. economic aid to India, Ayub argued, would be "disastrous" for Pakistan in the absence of a settlement. Economic aid simply permitted India to divert other funds for arms. "Nehru still want[s] Pakistan to remain weak while India builds its strength," Ayub claimed. Eisenhower responded that he would talk about these matters in New Delhi but did not intend to negotiate on Kashmir. Although "he could do little more than urge Nehru to get together with Pakistan to try to work out the problem," Eisenhower said that he "saw great value in finding some way of finding a solution."[76]

Ayub used the discussion of the Middle East as the framework in which to press for additional military assistance. When the Pakistani leader praised CENTO as a "shield" for the region and mentioned his desire for additional U.S. military equipment, Eisenhower responded that "these problems were very much in mind" and that "in Pakistan and Turkey we had sturdy allies." In justifying the need for more U.S. arms help, Ayub emphasized the threat from China—rather ironic in view of subsequent close Sino-Pakistani security ties. "If Pakistan, for example," Ayub warned, "did not receive American support it was inevitable that the Chinese sooner or later would get it, as well as India." In this context, Ayub raised the F-104 issue and stressed his strong desire that Pakistan receive the supersonic fighter. Eisenhower promised that he would review the issue and "give the matter further thought."[77]

With regard to neighboring Afghanistan, Pakistan's president painted a bleak picture. Using a briefing map, he pointed to roads the Soviets were building "solely for their own strategic purpose."[78] The leadership in Kabul, especially Prime Minister Daoud, Ayub asserted, thought the Soviets would win the Cold War and therefore sought Moscow's friendship. Soviet aid had become so significant that the Russians had virtually taken over Afghanistan. Although Daoud hoped to receive U.S. aid, Ayub, in keeping with his hard-line view, urged Eisenhower to tell the Afghans, "We believe you have gone beyond the point of no return and unless you recover our support will be ended." Eisenhower responded that the U.S. appraisal of the situation was less gloomy. The president hoped that it would be possible "to try to do something" when he visited Afghanistan after his stay in Pakistan.[79]

In addition to intensive official talks, Eisenhower had a busy time in Karachi. He greeted the two-thousand-strong American community at Rountree's residence, briefly watched a cricket match between Pakistan and Australia, attended a civic reception, and accompanied Ayub on a helicopter ride over the Korangi refugee colony. One of the martial law regime's proudest accomplishments, Korangi was the site of some thirty thousand small but adequate concrete homes built to house about a hundred thousand refugees from India, who had been languishing for a decade in squalid camps scattered around the city.[80]

From Karachi, Eisenhower flew to Kabul for a round of talks with Afghan leaders and that evening traveled to New Delhi to begin his four-day visit to India. In Afghanistan, Eisenhower found Daoud stubborn, parochial, and distrustful of the Pakistanis, but not "dumb," as Ayub had called him. Daoud, the president concluded, felt the risk with the Soviets was "worthwhile taking" to exploit the "Russian willingness to assist Afghanistan's economy and build up a military force."[81] Later in the trip, when Eisenhower met Francisco Franco in Madrid, he told the Spanish leader that Afghanistan wanted to remain neutral but he didn't "see how this can be done" given the extent of Soviet aid.[82] In reviewing the stop in Kabul with congressional leaders after returning to Washington, the president was less pessimistic, commenting that "the Afghans are a tough and independent people."[83]

The high point of the South Asia trip came during Eisenhower's stay in India, where he received a tumultuous welcome and had extensive talks with Prime Minister Nehru. During these, Nehru suggested that if Ayub agreed to a "no-war" declaration, he would be less concerned about U.S. arms aid to Pakistan. Eisenhower promptly instructed Rountree to put the proposal to Ayub, stressing "the great opportunity this could give [Ayub] for the modernization of his army."[84] As Rountree anticipated—since Nehru had proposed the no-war pledge in the past—Ayub rejected the suggestion. The Pakistani leader, according to Rountree's cabled report, stated, "The effect . . . would be for the Pakistan public to assume that Pakistan had handed Kashmir to India on a silver platter" unless the no-war pact included a mechanism to address the dispute.[85]

Eisenhower's trip to South Asia proved a great public relations success. Even if the president was unable to get India and Pakistan together on the no-war pact, the visit simultaneously strengthened U.S. relations with the two antagonists, no mean achievement. Eisenhower was wildly cheered by massive crowds wherever he went. The people of South Asia clearly "liked Ike." In the case of Pakistan, although Eisenhower and Ayub differed in their assessments regarding India and Afghanistan, the two shared a similar perception of the communist threat and appeared very comfortable in dealing with each other. For his part, Ayub respected fellow soldier Eisenhower as the victorious Allied commander in Europe in World War II, the North Atlantic Treaty Organization's first chief, and the leader of the postwar Western alliance.

Eisenhower, in turn, gained a positive impression of Ayub. "So while some of our starry-eyed and academic types of liberals criticized General Ayub when he seized power by a military coup," he told Franco, "one can see everywhere in Pakistan improvements and a quite happy attitude."[86] In his memoirs, Eisenhower described Ayub as "an agreeable, intelligent and persuasive gentleman." He liked the Pakistani leader's candor and found him "pleasant and modest, but incisive—characteristics that gave an aura of credibility to his avowed purpose of steadily developing healthy democratic institutions in his country."[87]

In their discussions, however, the two leaders did not seriously address the future of U.S.-Pakistani military cooperation after the end of the initial phase of the partnership. The Pakistani request for the F-104s would not go away, despite muffled resistance from the Eisenhower administration.

F-104s, the U-2, and Indus Waters

Further review of the F-104 request during January and February of 1960 did not change Washington's mind, at least at first. Ambassador Rountree was informed that the new policy of "limited modernization" ruled out providing Pakistan with the supersonic aircraft.[88] But before the envoy received formal instructions to convey this final "no," the U.S. government was to make a 180-degree turn on the issue. This change of heart caught the Washington working-level bureaucracy completely by surprise.

State Department Pakistan desk officer William Spengler recalled going home on a Friday evening assuming that the telegram that he and his colleagues at the State and Defense Departments had cleared, definitively rejecting the F-104s, was on its way to the U.S. embassy in

Pakistan. But when he came to work the following Monday morning, an astonished Spengler found that the outgoing telegram had approved—not disapproved—the supply of F-104s.[89] Rountree, the March 3, 1960, cable instructed, was to tell Ayub that the favorable decision to "provide F-104s [was] based on Pakistan's special military requirements."[90] Understandably pleased with the news, Ayub asked the ambassador to convey his great appreciation to President Eisenhower, whose personal interest, Ayub presumed, had led to the change of heart.[91]

The relevant documents remain classified, yet from other sources and events occurring at the time we can put together what appears to have happened in the upper councils of the U.S. government. In rejecting Pakistan's long-standing F-104 request as contrary to the new arms-supply guidelines, Spengler and his colleagues were unaware of the key, although highly secret, Cold War links with Pakistan—the use of the Peshawar airport for U-2 flights and the true function of the Badaber facility. But the senior echelons of the U.S. government were aware and almost certainly concluded that providing the F-104s was the price the United States had to pay for Pakistan's cooperation, in spite of the action's inconsistency with the new arms policy and the inevitable repercussions the move would have on relations with India.

If receiving the F-104s pleased Ayub, the U-2 episode that was soon to follow was a far less happy affair. On May 7, 1960, as leaders of the United States, the Soviet Union, France, and Great Britain were about to gather for a long-awaited summit in Paris, Washington announced that a weather reconnaissance aircraft was lost after straying over the Soviet Union. Soviet leader Nikita Khrushchev countered with a thunderbolt: The Russians had shot down a U.S. spy plane and captured its pilot, Gary Powers. Addressing a meeting of the Supreme Soviet in Moscow, Khrushchev dramatically revealed the details of the U-2 flight. "We warn those countries," Khrushchev threatened, "that make their territory available for launching planes with anti-Soviet intentions: Do not play with fire, gentlemen! The governments of Turkey, Pakistan and Norway must be clearly aware that they are accomplices in this flight."[92] Increasing the pressure, Khrushchev cornered the Pakistani ambassador during a Czech national day reception on May 9, 1960. The Soviet party boss asked loudly, "Where is this place Peshawar? We have circled it in red on our maps."[93] In the future, Khrushchev continued, "if any American plane is allowed to use

Peshawar as a base of operations against the Soviet Union, we will retaliate immediately."[94]

After first denying the charge, Eisenhower then made a clean breast and assumed responsibility for the U-2 flight. The world learned that Gary Powers had taken off from Pakistan to fly across the Soviet Union and land in Norway after photographing defense installations. When Ayub, who happened to be in London, was informed of events by the CIA station chief, he shrugged his shoulders and said that he had expected this would happen at some point.[95] In line with a prearranged understanding, State Department spokesperson Lincoln White asserted that the United States had used Pakistan's territory for the flights without its permission or knowledge. In turn, the Pakistan government "protested" the U-2 flight which it said was not authorized.[96]

Confronted with shrill and public Soviet threats, Ayub needed to do more than shrug his shoulders. Trying to reassure his fellow citizens, he declared, "These harsh things have to be faced. If such a thing comes, Pakistan will not be alone."[97] The country, nonetheless, was shaken by Moscow's threats. Ayub himself aired some of these concerns in a June 27, 1960, interview with Paul Grimes of the *New York Times*. Voicing doubts about U.S. steadiness under pressure, Pakistan's president stated that America "appears cumbersome, sluggish and a clumsy juggernaut."[98]

The U-2 episode brought home to Pakistanis that alignment with the United States entailed risks and dangers as well as the benefits of military and economic aid. In his typically cautious manner, Ayub began to take some steps to reduce the possibilities of friction with neighboring China and to try to establish less-tense relations with the Soviet Union. In late 1959, even before the U-2 problem arose, Ayub had signaled to Beijing his interest in demarcating the several-hundred-mile-long Sino-Pakistani border in northern Kashmir. The Pakistani leader hoped to avoid India's experience of tensions over conflicting frontier claims. At first, the Chinese turned a deaf ear and made no response to Ayub's initiative.[99]

Eisenhower's term in the White House ended on a more positive note than the U-2 episode, after the World Bank was able to gain Indian and Pakistani agreement on the Indus waters accord. A beaming U.S. president began his September 7, 1960, press conference declaring, "In a very depressing world picture that we so often see there is one bright spot that seems to me worthy of mention and that is the settling of the

Indus River Water problem between India and Pakistan."[100] On September 19, 1960, Nehru formally signed the waters agreement in Karachi with Ayub and World Bank Vice President William Iliff, who had been the principal negotiator in the decade-long effort to resolve the dispute. The settlement called for construction of a series of new dams and canals to ensure that neither India nor Pakistan lost valuable irrigation water and both gained improved dam and canal facilities. The United States confirmed its willingness to provide half of the necessary funding.

Exit Eisenhower

When Dwight Eisenhower left the White House in January 1961, he was happy that U.S. ally Pakistan appeared to be getting on its feet under Ayub Khan and was beginning to make tangible economic progress. Pakistan also was moving, if slowly and gradually, from a military dictatorship toward the establishment of a more open political system. Although the Pakistanis remained extremely unhappy about growing U.S. support for India's economic development, the U.S.-Pakistan bilateral relationship seemed solid.

The Americans were continuing a substantial economic and arms aid program, including the promised provision of the controversial F-104 fighters. Despite the U-2 episode, Pakistan appeared to be a reliable member of the anticommunist team. U.S.-India relations had also become increasingly friendly during Eisenhower's second term, as they improved from the low point reached following the decision to enter into an alliance relationship with Pakistan.

On the surface, the Eisenhower administration had achieved the long-standing American goal of having good relations with both India and Pakistan. But in spite of appearances, the quicksands on which the security ties with Pakistan were based would become apparent during the presidency of Eisenhower's successor. The response of John F. Kennedy to the 1962 Sino-Indian border conflict would unhinge the U.S.-Pakistan partnership.

5

Kennedy: Alliance Troubles

Pakistan closely followed the 1960 U.S. presidential elections. Karachi considered former vice president Richard Nixon, the Republican candidate, a friend and feared that John F. Kennedy, his Democratic challenger, would accelerate the policy shift toward India begun during President Eisenhower's second term. As a senator from Massachusetts, Kennedy had sharply criticized John Foster Dulles's penchant for military pacts with Third World states. In an influential October 1957 *Foreign Affairs* article and a well-publicized March 25, 1958, Senate speech, Kennedy supported more cooperative relations with the nations of the "uncommitted world" and called for a major boost in economic assistance to India.[1] A resolution endorsing increased aid for India, jointly sponsored by Kennedy and Senator John Sherman Cooper (R-Ky.), a former ambassador to New Delhi, was adopted by the Senate in 1958 and by both houses of Congress in 1959.

After Kennedy became president, Pakistan had more tangible grounds for concern. In his State of the Union address to Congress on January 30, 1961, Kennedy lauded the "soaring idealism" of Jawaharlal Nehru, whom he praised as one of the great leaders of the twentieth century.[2] The new administration's foreign policy and diplomatic appointees were unusually knowledgeable about South Asia and, Karachi feared, biased toward India. Secretary of State Dean Rusk had served in the subcontinent during World War II and had dealt with the Kashmir issue during the Truman administration. As Rusk's deputy Kennedy named outspokenly pro-Indian Chester Bowles, former ambassador to New Delhi and a leading Democratic Party liberal. The assistant secretary for the Near East and South Asia was Phillips Talbot, the scholar-journalist who had reported on Pakistan's and India's independence for the *Chicago Daily News* in 1947 and had later written his Ph.D. thesis on the Kashmir dispute.[3]

As ambassador to India, Kennedy appointed his personal friend and prominent Harvard economist John Kenneth Galbraith. At the same time, he let William Rountree, the competent but bland career Foreign Service officer, stay on as envoy to Pakistan for over a year before replacing him with another low-key career diplomat, China specialist Walter McConaughy. Robert Komer, a hard-charging former Central Intelligence Agency (CIA) analyst, handled South Asia for a reorganized, less structured, but more potent National Security Council (NSC) staff led by National Security Adviser McGeorge Bundy, another former Harvard professor. Komer favored closer ties with India and believed that the Eisenhower administration had blundered in providing military assistance to Pakistan.[4]

Kennedy himself remained interested and involved in South Asia throughout his presidency. Whereas Eisenhower, who also had paid considerable attention to the subcontinent, usually dealt at the level of high policy, Kennedy liked to plunge into the details. Reflecting his personal style, the new president frequently bypassed the normal bureaucratic chain of command to telephone State Department specialists, such as Talbot and his deputy, James P. Grant, to discuss current issues.[5] Kennedy held numerous operational sessions on the region with senior advisers from the NSC, the Departments of State and Defense, and the CIA. The door to the Oval Office was open to visitors from India and Pakistan, as well as to their ambassadors in Washington.

Worried about a further shift in U.S. policy, President Ayub Khan sent his respected finance minister, Mohammed Shoaib, to Washington within weeks of Kennedy's taking office.[6] On March 7, 1961, Shoaib presented the new president a short but pointed message from Ayub reaffirming that Pakistan's "destiny lies in friendship with the United States."[7] Kennedy responded positively and, ever curious, peppered the visitor with questions about Afghanistan, Iran, India, Pakistan's relations with China and the Soviet Union, and its economic development plans.[8]

Two weeks later, Democratic Party elder Averell Harriman, whom Kennedy had appointed as a roving ambassador, met Ayub in Karachi. Pakistan's president praised the new American administration, saying that he hoped it would redress the slippage in U.S. leadership during the final Eisenhower years (the Bay of Pigs disaster had yet to occur).

Although Ayub added that he did not oppose Kennedy's desire for better relations with nonaligned countries, such as India, he urged Washington to "maintain [the] distinction between [the nonaligned] and allies." Ayub stressed that the "focal point of Pakistan's policy continued to be friendship with" the United States but indicated that he was trying to establish more normal relations with China and also with the Soviet Union. The border talks with China that Pakistan had proposed, the Pakistani president stated, were intended to avoid trouble along the undemarcated frontier, not to embarrass India.[9]

Ever since the U-2 incident, Ayub had been edging cautiously to increase Pakistan's maneuvering space in the field of foreign policy and to reduce its near total dependence on the United States. Within the cabinet, the strongest advocate of this approach was young Zulfikar Ali Bhutto, appointed in 1958 as a token representative from the province of Sindh, where he belonged to a wealthy landowning family. Educated at the University of California at Berkeley and at Oxford, Bhutto soon won the president's favor as one of the cabinet's most intelligent, articulate, and energetic members. He served creditably in a series of ministerial posts—in the Ministries of Commerce and Industry, Natural Resources, and Information—but Bhutto's passion was for foreign policy and his immediate ambition was to succeed Manzur Qadir, who wanted to return to his law practice. In cabinet deliberations, Bhutto argued that Pakistan's interests would be served by the country's being less slavishly pro-American and also contended that better relations with Moscow and Beijing would improve Karachi's bargaining position vis-à-vis Washington.

The leader of the "U.S. lobby" was Finance Minister Shoaib. Since Pakistan's economic future heavily depended on continued and, if possible, increased U.S. aid, Shoaib thought that foreign policy initiatives likely to antagonize the Americans, such as the proposal to invite the Soviets to explore for oil and gas in Pakistan, were a mistake. Although Ayub genuinely valued close ties with Washington and realized the essential role played by U.S. aid in Pakistan's economic development, he ultimately gave Bhutto, then the natural resources minister, the green light to try to negotiate energy agreements with Moscow, a move that made Washington uneasy and was strongly opposed by Shoaib and his supporters within the bureaucracy.[10] Later in 1961, Ayub agreed to another of Bhutto's suggestions: that Pakistan shift its vote at the United

Nations to support seating the Chinese communists in the place of the Chinese nationalists, an action that would greatly upset President Kennedy.[11]

Johnson Visits Pakistan; Ayub Comes to Washington

In May 1961, Vice President Lyndon Johnson stopped in Karachi during a goodwill trip through Asia. To the bewilderment of Pakistani officials accustomed to the conservative British style, Johnson acted as if he were on an election campaign swing through Texas. Doffing his coat and tie, he stopped his motorcade several times during the drive into the city from the airport to wade into the crowd and shake hands with dumbfounded onlookers. His most publicized encounter was with a camel driver named Bashir Ahmed, who readily accepted the vice president's invitation to "come and see us in America."[12]

In Johnson's talks with Ayub, and even in the public welcome, bilateral policy differences were evident. Pakistan's president argued forcefully that the large U.S. economic aid program and India's troubles with China gave the Americans leverage to force Nehru to the bargaining table on Kashmir. Johnson responded that Pakistan's president "attributed to us a capacity to influence Nehru that [Johnson] was not sure we had."[13] At a public reception Karachi Municipal Corporation chairman H. M. Habibullah, who spoke in Urdu, gave vent to mounting Pakistani unhappiness by caustically criticizing U.S. policy on Kashmir and India. More in keeping with the diplomatic pablum normally dispensed on such occasions, the vice president ignored these barbs to voice pride that "the commitments of our alliances will be fully honored on both sides."[14]

Despite the substantive discord, Johnson was taken with Ayub. In his report to Kennedy about the trip, he lauded Ayub as "the singularly most impressive and, in his way, responsible head of state encountered on the trip." The vice president recommended that the U.S. "military should see how to improve the effectiveness and achieve modernization of Pakistan's army." He gave Ayub credit for wishing "to resolve the Kashmir dispute to release Indian and Pakistani troops to deter the Chinese rather than each other."[15]

With regard to economic assistance, the new administration appeared lukewarm about Pakistan, in contrast to the early decision to substantially boost assistance to India to $1 billion annually. When the Pakistan

Vice President Lyndon B. Johnson shakes hands with camel driver Bashir Ahmed during Johnson's visit to Karachi, May 1961. (Courtesy of the Lyndon Baines Johnson Library.)

aid consortium organized by the World Bank met for the first time on June 5–7, 1961, the United States pledged only $150 million. The other major donors, Germany and Britain, made little more than token offers of $25 and $19.6 million, respectively, only a tenth of the amount they had put on the table at the earlier India aid consortium. To console a downcast Finance Minister Shoaib, George Ball, the Chicago lawyer who had become undersecretary of state for economic affairs, advised that the United States was ready to increase its aid if other countries were willing to boost their assistance. Ball said that he hoped for better results at a second consortium session scheduled for later in the year.[16]

In July 1961, Ayub paid his first official visit to the United States as president of Pakistan. In keeping with his no-nonsense style, he sent a series of warning shots across Kennedy's bow before departing from Karachi. Defining Pakistani feelings toward the United States as "not so much anger as disappointment," Ayub warned about re-examining membership in the Southeast Asia Treaty Organization (SEATO) in an interview with Associated Press correspondent Jim Becker. "Can it be the United States is abandoning its good friends for people who may not prove such good friends?" he pointedly asked the journalist.[17]

When Pakistan's president passed through London, he stressed these concerns in talking with Prime Minister Harold Macmillan. Ayub said

President John F. Kennedy and President Mohammed Ayub Khan en route to the White House, July 1961. (Courtesy of the John F. Kennedy Library.)

that he did not understand why the Americans "who were giving so much money to India could not create an area of stability in the subcontinent." In the future, he cautioned the British leader, Pakistan might be forced leave the Western alliances unless the troubles with India were settled. Although Ayub was confident that he could manage things domestically in the short term, after political life resumed in 1962 under a new constitution, he felt, "the pressure of public opinion on him would be irresistible."[18] Ayub was presumably exaggerating in the expectation that Macmillan would pass on the message to Washington, but in time his gloomy prognosis proved to be not far off the mark.

On the defensive because of the Bay of Pigs fiasco and an unsuccessful Vienna summit with the Soviets, the Kennedy administration wanted the Ayub visit to be a success. The U.S. president's welcoming remarks at Andrews Air Force Base on July 11, 1961, were notably warmer than the visitor's. Kennedy even went so far as to laud

President Ayub receives a bust of George Washington from the head of the Mount Vernon Ladies Association just before the state dinner at Mount Vernon, July 1961. (Courtesy of the John F. Kennedy Library.)

Pakistan's nonexistent help during the Korean War. To provide a special cachet, the U.S. president hosted a glittering dinner for Ayub at Mount Vernon. This was the first time that George Washington's home had been used to fete a foreign head of state.[19] Ironically, Pakistani ambassador Aziz Ahmed was initially upset over the idea of the state dinner's not being at the White House. According to Phillips Talbot, it took much persuasion to convince the reluctant envoy that a function at Mount Vernon would generate much greater interest and publicity than a normal White House affair.[20]

Along with the Mount Vernon dinner, a public high point of Ayub's stay in Washington was his address before a friendly joint session of Congress.[21] Speaking forcefully and with undiplomatic bluntness, Pakistan's president cautioned the legislators not to grow weary of giving foreign aid: "I would like to suggest that you had better not get tired at this point." To conclude his speech, Ayub stressed Pakistan's reliability as an ally. "If there is real trouble," he declared, "there is no other country in Asia where you will be able to even put your foot in. The only people who will stand by you are the people of Pakistan."[22]

In extensive private discussions, Ayub hammered away at the threat his country faced from India. Although Kennedy agreed to support Pakistan on Kashmir at the United Nations if upcoming talks with Nehru failed to advance prospects of a settlement, the U.S. president refused to use economic assistance to India as a lever on Kashmir. America did not give aid, Kennedy said, in the expectation of getting "Nehru's support on the items that were vital to" the United States, but because it was in everyone's interest that India not collapse. A disappointed Ayub countered that Nehru "had to come to the U.S. He had no maneuverability left. . . . Why could the U.S. not see that?"[23]

Worried by reports that the Kennedy administration was thinking of giving military assistance to India, Ayub warned that this "would force his country out of the pacts and alliances and everything."[24] Kennedy denied that he was considering this, adding that he would talk with Ayub if he ever thought of providing arms to the Indians. The memorandum of the conversation, drafted by Assistant Secretary Talbot, stated, "If, sometime a situation, such as impending war with China, should arise that would cause the Indians to come to the U.S. for military aid, we would talk with Pakistan and see what was the best course of action. However, there was no intention now to give India military aid. If there should be a change in U.S. policy, President Kennedy would talk with President Ayub first."[25] (Unsurprisingly, Kennedy's failure to consult with Ayub before giving arms to India in November 1962 deeply offended the Pakistani leader.)

The two presidents sharply disagreed about Chinese representation at the United Nations. When Foreign Minister Qadir advised that Pakistan would be changing its position to vote in favor of seating the communists in the upcoming session of the UN General Assembly, Kennedy was extremely unhappy. Losing the China vote at the United Nations would be "terrible," he declared. Showing great sensitivity to the long-standing Republican Party charge that the Democrats had "lost China," the president, with more than a little exaggeration, called this problem "the most important issue in our generation in the U.S."[26]

Ayub found more sympathy in discussing bilateral economic aid. Kennedy confirmed that the United States was ready to increase substantially its assistance pledge at the next World Bank Pakistan consortium session. The U.S. Agency for International Development (AID) subsequently offered $500 million over a two-year period. After Ayub explained how poor drainage in West Pakistani irrigation systems was causing great damage and reducing agricultural production, Kennedy said that he would send experts to see what could be done.[27] A high-level team visited Pakistan and prepared a comprehensive plan to attack the problem. AID then played a major role in funding a large-scale and generally successful project to improve the irrigation system.

Ayub's trip was a considerable success. In Washington and other places that he visited, including an overnight stay at Vice President Lyndon Johnson's ranch in Texas, the Pakistani leader firmed up his country's credentials as a loyal, if demanding, ally. Even though critical of aspects of U.S. policy, Ayub made "a favourable impression on the president, the administration, the public and the press," the British embassy reported to London, adding that his "frank, forceful manner and breezy no nonsense attitude" went over well.[28] Assistant Secretary Talbot echoed this view, commenting that Ayub had convinced Kennedy that he was not just concerned about India but was sincerely interested in promoting his country's economic development.[29]

The Indians, as often has been the case, helped Pakistan's standing with the Americans. Veteran U.S. baiter Krishna Menon, India's defense minister since 1957, continued to hurl verbal barbs at Washington throughout this period. Although much less offensive than the vitriolic Menon, Nehru himself proved unwilling to cooperate to any marked extent with the Kennedy administration in dealing with critical issues like Southeast Asia, nuclear testing, or the status of Berlin. When the Indian prime minister paid a much-anticipated visit to the United States in November 1961, Kennedy and others found him listless and often noncommunicative. Washington's disappointment about India's seizure by force of the Portuguese colonial enclave of Goa in December 1961 provided a further indirect boost for Pakistan.[30]

If Ayub impressed Kennedy and his colleagues, Pakistan's president was less taken with his U.S. counterpart. Ayub had been able to talk with Eisenhower as one soldier to another and greatly respected him as America's foremost World War II commander, whose worldview Ayub basically shared. It was much less so with Kennedy. Ayub found the young president unsure of his grasp, lonely, and "surrounded by too many theoreticians."[31] Kennedy's handling of the Bay of Pigs episode seemed weak and hesitant to the no-nonsense Pakistani. Most of all, the U.S. president's interest in bettering relations with India set Ayub's teeth on edge.

Fresh Trouble over Afghanistan and Kashmir

During the state visit, Pakistan's president also discussed his country's troubled relations with Afghanistan. Ayub told Kennedy that he held the ruling family, other than the king himself, in contempt. Asserting that the Kabul regime had mortgaged its future to the Soviets, Ayub urged the United States to adopt a tough line. Like Eisenhower, Kennedy did not agree, arguing that this approach would only push the Afghans closer to the Soviet camp.[32]

Fresh and serious trouble arose in the fall of 1961 as a result of cross-border raids into Pakistan by Afghan tribesmen. Ayub responded by shutting Afghanistan's consulates and trade offices in Peshawar and Quetta, which, he charged, had become centers of subversion. In retaliation, Kabul broke off diplomatic relations, closed the border, and suspended transit trade with Pakistan.[33] These moves effectively cut landlocked Afghanistan off from most of the world, leaving it dependent on transportation links with the Soviet Union, except for extremely limited access through Iran.

In keeping with the activist spirit of his New Frontier, Kennedy offered U.S. good offices to Afghanistan's King Zahir and to Ayub and dispatched veteran diplomat Livingston Merchant, ambassador to Canada and former assistant secretary of state for Far Eastern affairs, as a special envoy.[34] During a meeting with Merchant before he left for South Asia, Kennedy realistically judged the problem "difficult and complicated."[35] That did not, however, deter him from trying to tackle it.

When Merchant arrived in Pakistan, President Ayub said that although he was willing to reopen the Afghan trade offices, he would not allow the consulates back. He urged the American diplomat to "beat some sense into [the] bloody minds of the Afghan Royal family." In Kabul, Prime Minister Sardar Mohammed Daoud, the king's cousin, denied that the Afghans were, in effect, blockading themselves, but refused to budge on trade unless Pakistan agreed to reopen the Afghan consulates. As neither side backed down, Merchant returned to Washington empty-handed. Even though he criticized Ayub's approach, Merchant found it difficult to exert "what Pak[istanis] would regard as excessive pressure" on "an ally which is staunch and now cooperates in an area vital to our own security [referring to the Badaber intelligence facility]."[36]

The year 1962 saw major institutional changes in Pakistan. On March 1, Ayub lifted martial law and promulgated a new constitution, which he described as "a blending of democracy with discipline." The basic law gave the president strong executive powers and established a weak national legislature. During the martial law years, 1958–62, Ayub had shown himself as a confident and steady leader. He would become more hesitant and less comfortable, even though he retained the preponderance of power, under the new constitution. After pressure built up, Ayub reluctantly agreed to permit political parties and then became the head of the reconstituted Pakistan Muslim League, the progovernment grouping.[37]

One of the party's deputy leaders was Bhutto, who proved far more skillful and adept at the game of politics than was Ayub. Although frustrated in his ambition of becoming foreign minister (the president named former prime minister Mohammed Ali Bogra to succeed Qadir), Bhutto was gaining popularity as strongly nationalist, fiercely anti-India, increasingly critical of the United States, and in favor of closer ties with China. At the same time, the young Sindhi politician was careful to cultivate cordial relations with Ayub. When the president asked for advice on how to ensure that he remained securely senior in rank to other army generals, Bhutto cleverly suggested that Ayub appoint himself a field marshal. Calling the idea "brilliant," General Mohammed Ayub Khan became Field Marshal Mohammed Ayub Khan.[38]

Meanwhile as 1962 began, the Kennedy administration for the first time had to deal with the nettlesome Kashmir problem. After Nehru had refused to budge on the issue when he and Kennedy met in November 1961, Pakistan decided to raise Kashmir once more in the UN Security Council. Washington faced the unpleasant prospect of an acrimonious debate that was sure to cause fresh friction with the Indians, especially as Kennedy had agreed to support Pakistan. In the hope of sidestepping the problem, the administration proposed that former World Bank president Eugene Black serve as a mediator.[39] In theory, Black was a good choice. Thanks to the bank's role in promoting economic development and in the successful negotiation of the Indus waters treaty, he was familiar with India-Pakistan issues and enjoyed good rapport with the leaders of the two countries.

Ayub readily accepted Black as a mediator. Nehru, however, rejected the proposal.[40] As a result, in mid-1962, Kashmir was again on the agenda of the Security Council. At U.S. urging and with the support of Pakistan, Ireland introduced a mildly worded resolution that called on India and Pakistan to enter into direct negotiations. In the face of a fierce diplomatic onslaught by India's Krishna Menon, no other country was willing to cosponsor the resolution. When even Dublin began to get cold feet, it took a personal telephone call from Kennedy to the Irish ambassador in Washington to put things back on track. The UN debate predictably led nowhere. At India's behest, the Soviet Union vetoed the resolution on June 22, 1962. The United States had, however, kept its promise to support the Pakistanis.[41]

Ayub also achieved a measure of satisfaction on his proposal for border negotiations with the Chinese. After Pakistan switched its vote on the China representation question in the 1961 UN session, Beijing agreed to commence bilateral talks. Since the area of Pakistan that bordered China was part of disputed Kashmir, New Delhi criticized both the Chinese and the Pakistanis for starting discussions about territory that India claimed as its own. Negotiations began in Beijing in May 1962 but made no progress. The respective Chinese and Pakistani border claims were far apart. Neither side was ready at this point to put a serious counterproposal on the table.[42]

In Washington, Kennedy's underlying skepticism about the Pakistan security relationship surfaced during a June 19, 1962, meeting with advisers about another upsetting South Asia problem: the possible procurement of Soviet MiG fighter aircraft by the Indian air force, a proposal strongly backed by Defense Minister Krishna Menon. During the discussion, Kennedy ruled out offering F-104 jet fighters to India as a substitute for MiGs because of certain Pakistani and likely U.S. congressional opposition and made clear that he was "dubious about giving more jets to the Pakistanis regardless of what happened."

When George McGhee, whom Dean Rusk had brought back to the State Department, proposed that the United States guarantee Pakistan's security against India if the West supplied jet fighters to New Delhi, Kennedy rejected the idea. He told his advisers that he was "extremely reluctant" to give any new commitments to Pakistan. Deputy Assistant Secretary of State James Grant, who was sitting in for his boss, Phillips Talbot, commented, "Our main objective in supplying such security reassurances to Pakistan was to forestall their 'doing something' to our Peshawar [Badaber] facilities in retaliation for what they regarded as pro-India U.S. actions." Kennedy was unmoved.[43]

Further Kennedy-Ayub Talks

The U.S. president met a second time with Ayub Khan in the fall of 1962 when the Pakistani leader came to the United States to attend the UN session. Accompanied by aides, the two leaders talked for several hours on September 24, 1962, at Hammersmith Farm, Jacqueline Kennedy's family home in Newport, Rhode Island. Ayub reiterated his familiar refrain that large-scale U.S. economic aid to India posed a security threat to Pakistan by permitting New Delhi to divert resources to build up its military and to adopt a "tougher, more unyielding attitude toward Pakistan on Kashmir." Kennedy once more refused to use economic assistance as a lever to press India to negotiate on Kashmir. Withholding aid would not only undermine India's prospects, the U.S. president declared, "but might be seriously prejudicial to the security and stability of the entire subcontinent."[44]

For his part, Kennedy zeroed in on Afghanistan, where relations with Pakistan remained strained; the border between the two countries continued to be closed. Stressing his concern about growing Soviet influence in Kabul, the American chief executive commented, "The break with Pakistan had accelerated the adverse trend." As pessimistic as ever about Afghanistan, Ayub responded that the prospects in Kabul were bleak as long as the current leaders remained in power. In order to reduce Afghan dependence on the Soviets, Kennedy offered to finance the extension of railway lines from Pakistan into Afghanistan and urged the temporary reopening of Afghan trade offices. Ayub was agreeable to a cross-border rail link near Quetta but had doubts about the need or feasibility of one near Peshawar.[45]

After Ayub showed reluctance to allow the return of Afghan officials to Pakistan, Kennedy countered: if America could control communist consulates in New York, he failed to see how "with various safeguards" a small Afghan consulate in Peshawar "could create serious difficulties, or threaten Pakistan security." Kennedy urged Ayub to view the issue "from a broad standpoint, bearing in mind the very large stakes involved." The Pakistani president finally agreed "rather reluctantly" to consider allowing the Afghan "tentacles" across the border and to a meeting between Pakistani and Afghan foreign ministers in New York.[46]

Following the talk with Kennedy, Ayub traveled to Washington to meet other U.S. government leaders. He also found time for a well-publicized afternoon of horseback riding with Jacqueline Kennedy in the rolling hills near the president's weekend home in Middleburg, Virginia. Mrs. Kennedy made a point of riding Sardar, the handsome stallion that Ayub had presented her during the first lady's highly successful goodwill trip to South Asia earlier in the year.

By the autumn of 1962, U.S.-Pakistan relations had attained a somewhat unsteady equilibrium. Although the Kennedy administration's increased attention and economic aid to India continued to annoy Ayub, he kept his upset within bounds. Indeed, the complaint that American aid to India was harming Pakistan proved a helpful lever in prying more economic assistance out of Washington. After the unpromising beginning at the Pakistan consortium's June 1961 meeting, the level of pledges had risen dramatically, from $320 million to $945 million. The United States played a key role in pressing other countries to increase their assistance programs.[47]

Military aid to Pakistan was also continuing at a level of about $50 million annually, in line with the arms policy adopted in 1959 by the Eisenhower administration. In the United States, Pakistan's and Ayub's prestige remained high, especially on Capitol Hill and among the U.S. military and intelligence communities. Talbot commented that no one in the administration was interested in losing the Badaber communications intercept facility, which U.S. intelligence officials continued to consider of great value.[48]

President Ayub and First Lady Jacqueline Kennedy stand beside Sardar, the horse that Ayub gave to Mrs. Kennedy, Middleburg, Virginia, September 1962. (Courtesy of the John F. Kennedy Library.)

Bilateral relations might have remained in balance had it not been for the Sino-Indian clash in the Himalayas in October–November 1962. Although the fighting caught observers by surprise, trouble between India and China had been brewing for several years. The Sino-Indian friendship of the mid-1950s had dissolved after New Delhi and Beijing began an acrimonious dispute over exactly where their Himalayan borders lay. Once Nehru acknowledged in 1959 that armed clashes had taken place, Indian public opinion demanded that he vigorously defend New Delhi's frontier claims. The Tibetan revolt and the flight of the Dalai Lama to India, also in 1959, had intensified frictions. In late

1961, New Delhi imprudently adopted a "forward policy," establishing military posts behind Chinese positions in the mountains. Although Beijing initially did not react, after July 1962 Chinese forces stiffened their posture along the disputed borders.

The Sino-Indian Border War

On October 12, 1962, in offhand remarks to reporters, Nehru stated, "Our instructions are to free our territory. I cannot fix the date [when that will happen]; that is entirely for the Army."[49] A week later, it was China that fixed the date when its forces attacked along the disputed frontier. After Indian military posts rapidly collapsed, the political effect in New Delhi was shattering: Krishna Menon was fired as defense minister; India put out feelers for Western military aid; nonalignment seemed in shreds.

The Himalayan border war coincided with the Cuban missile crisis, the tensest moment of the Cold War. Despite the fact that President Kennedy and top advisers were preoccupied with the nuclear confrontation with the Soviet Union, South Asia specialists focused quickly on the policy implications of the Sino-Indian conflict. Always fast off the mark, NSC staff member Robert Komer saw "a golden opportunity for a major gain in our relations with India." He urged a positive response to Indian feelers for arms aid and pressure on Ayub to provide reassurances to New Delhi so that the latter would feel secure in shifting its military resources to the conflict with China.[50] On October 26, 1962, Deputy National Security Adviser Carl Kaysen sought Kennedy's blessing to provide military assistance to India if requested and to urge Ayub to make a significant gesture, "for example, breaking off in a public way his own negotiations with the Chinese about the border."[51]

That same day, halfway around the globe, Ambassador McConaughy urged Ayub to make "a positive gesture of sympathy and restraint" toward India. Even a private assurance against "any . . . diversionary move" by the Pakistani government, the U.S. envoy asserted, would make the Indians "more tractable and flexible" on Kashmir. Ayub "testily" assured the ambassador that Pakistan would do nothing to hamper the Indians, but flatly rejected sending a message to Nehru as not "helpful or necessary." Making clear that he had little sympathy for the Indians, whom he thought had acted rashly and unwisely, Pakistan's president said that, as a military man, he did not believe the Chinese were mounting a major campaign, since winter snows would soon block the mountains. In turn, Ayub urged the United States to take advantage of the situation to press the Indians to settle the Kashmir dispute.[52]

In rebuffing McConaughy's suggestion that he show some sympathy to the Indians, Ayub was reflecting Pakistani public opinion. Far from having understanding for India's plight, Pakistanis were delighted by the bloody nose that the Chinese had administered their foes. If anything, Ayub's information adviser Altaf Gauhar recalled, the Pakistani chief was under pressure to exploit India's difficulties to his country's advantage by launching a military attack against Kashmir.[53]

After meeting McConaughy, Ayub headed north into the Himalayas to visit the isolated and mountainous state of Hunza, along the disputed frontier with China. On October 27, 1962, Kennedy sent a message to inform Ayub of his decision to provide military assistance to India. This communication assessed the Chinese threat as major and urged Ayub to tell Nehru "that he can count on Pakistan's taking no action on the frontiers to alarm India." The State Department further instructed McConaughy to suggest that Pakistan adjourn the border talks with China and tone down pro-Chinese coverage in the Pakistani press. The telegram stated sternly that, as in the Cuban missile crisis, "We expect our allies . . . will do all they can to meet the Communist challenge."[54]

Although McConaughy tried to deliver Kennedy's letter in person to distant Hunza, Ayub, perhaps sensing the contents, told Foreign Minister Bogra to receive the message in Rawalpindi. For Pakistan, the key passage, and the red flag, was word of the decision to provide India with military aid. In the desire to respond rapidly to New Delhi's plea for help, the top echelon of the U.S. administration had overlooked Kennedy's promise to consult with Ayub before taking such a step.[55] Even though Pakistani opposition would not have changed Kennedy's mind, his failure to consult the Pakistani "deeply offended" Ayub, a Pathan with a strong belief in the value of a personal pledge. Ambassador McConaughy believed that the Pakistani leader never forgave Kennedy for not keeping his word.[56]

A week later, after Ayub returned from the mountains, he discussed the proposed reply to Kennedy with the U.S. envoy. The message, Ayub stated, would reaffirm his belief that China's military aims were limited, would complain about the U.S. president's failure to consult, especially as the "situation which has arisen is exactly that envisaged in [the] understanding as calling for advance consultation," and would reject with "obvious personal hurt" pressure to make a gesture toward India. Pakistan's leader said that he interpreted this as a "demonstration [that the] U.S. [was] not sympathetic with, nor understanding of [the Pakistani] position and essential interests."[57]

In an effort to reduce the damage and after receiving authorization from Washington, McConaughy "formally reiterated to Ayub our past . . . assurances of our assistance in [the] event [of] aggression against Pakistan from India . . . and handed him an aide-mémoire to that effect."[58] The aide-mémoire stated, "The Government of the United States of America reaffirms its previous assurances to the Government of Pakistan that it will come to Pakistan's assistance in the event of aggression from India.[59] A pleased Ayub responded, "It would be helpful if the assurances were made public." Two weeks later, the State Department released a watered-down version of the aide-mémoire, which mirrored the pledge that President Eisenhower had given India when he announced U.S. arms assistance for Pakistan in 1954.[60] Even though Pakistan had privately received the assurance of U.S. help against an Indian attack that it had vainly sought from the Eisenhower administration, the pledge, especially when coupled with the weaker public statement, failed to allay the emotionally negative reaction to the decision to provide military aid to India.

The response to Kennedy, which Ambassador Aziz Ahmed delivered on November 12, 1962, was tough. Turning to the U.S. request for Pakistani assurances to India, Ayub wrote, "I am surprised that such a request is being made to us. . . . No, Mr. President, the answer to this problem lies elsewhere. It lies in creating a situation whereby we are free from the Indian threat, and the Indians are free from any apprehensions about us. This can only be done if there is a settlement of the question of Kashmir." Ayub termed "regrettable" the lack of consultation "in light of the promise that [Kennedy had been] good enough to make." Regarding the U.S. promise that arms supplied to India would not be used against Pakistan, Ayub wrote with a touch of sarcasm, "This is very generous of you, but knowing the sort of people we are dealing with, whose history is a continuous tale of broken pledges . . . the arms now being obtained by India from you for use against China will undoubtedly be used against us at the very first opportunity."[61] Despite the letter's harsh tone, Kennedy responded in a measured way to Ahmed: "We understand the problem of Kashmir. Possibly out of this will come some settlement. [I] can also understand Ayub's feeling that what is happening to India is [the] result of its own foolish policies. On the other hand, [the] U.S. cannot stand by idly while China tries to expand its power in Asia."

The Pakistani ambassador emphasized that the entire political spectrum in Pakistan was opposed to U.S. military aid to India and to offering New Delhi any assurances. Kennedy countered that the "question of assurances is [a] matter for Pakistani decision, but [the] U.S. is interested in stopping the advance of Communism in Asia."[62]

Although the Kennedy administration realized that it was in for a tough time with Pakistan, Washington underestimated how tough it would be. U.S. officials thought the troubles could be weathered, believing that American military and economic aid was too important for Pakistan to risk a crisis over military aid to India. As Komer wrote in a November 12, 1962, memo to Kennedy. "The Pakistani[s] are going through a genuine emotional crisis. . . . Whether Pakistan moves from words to action depends on whether it is willing to risk its relationship with the U.S. Ayub probably isn't, but he may be a prisoner of Pak[istani] public emotions in this case. I am convinced, however, [that] in the last analysis the Pak[istanis] will realize that they get far too much from their U.S. tie to be able to do without it."[63]

For several weeks, there was a lull in the fighting between India and China in the border region. This ended abruptly on November 14, 1962, when the Chinese struck again. Brushing aside Indian resistance, Chinese forces advanced rapidly toward the plains of Assam. On November 19, 1962, near panic reigned in New Delhi as much of eastern India seemed vulnerable to the Chinese. That day Nehru wrote Kennedy to request direct and substantial military help. He asked for two squadrons of B-47 bombers and for accelerated training for Indian pilots so they could use the aircraft to bomb the Chinese in Tibet. The prime minister further requested that the U.S. Air Force send twelve squadrons of supersonic fighters manned by American crews to protect Indian cities and installations against possible Chinese air attacks. Describing the situation as "really desperate" and dropping any pretense of nonalignment, Nehru expressed confidence that "your great country will in this hour of trial help us in our fight for survival and for the survival of freedom and independence in this sub-Continent as well as the rest of Asia."[64]

Before President Kennedy had time to decide how to reply to Nehru's startling request, the Chinese unexpectedly announced a cease-fire and withdrew their forces to roughly the frontier line that Beijing had earlier proposed as a compromise settlement. The action was a shrewd move, underscoring that China's aims in the border conflict were, in fact, limited—as Ayub had asserted. But all this was not clear at the time. Kennedy decided to send a high-level team headed by Averell Harriman to the subcontinent. The British dispatched a parallel mission led by Commonwealth Relations Secretary Duncan Sandys. In contrast to Dulles and Eisenhower, Kennedy and Rusk cooperated closely with the British regarding India and Pakistan. For its part, London was eager for a chance to demonstrate that Britain still had a significant international role to play after the Suez debacle.

As Harriman's plane was winging its way toward the subcontinent, Pakistan's National Assembly was holding a closed-door session on the South Asia situation. According to press reports, Ayub took a hard line on India, telling the parliamentarians on November 21, 1963, that the threat from "Hindu imperialism" was greater than that from international communism. Even though he hinted at a foreign policy shift and downplayed the significance of the Central Treaty Organization (CENTO) and SEATO, the Pakistani president reportedly balanced this by expressing appreciation for American military and economic aid.[65]

Signaling the importance that he attached to the mission, Kennedy sent personal instructions. "I do not want to push Ayub so hard to get his back up," the president cabled Harriman, but the latter should make clear that Kennedy could no longer disregard a basic U.S.-Pakistan difference about what the alliance meant. America would proceed to help India. Pakistan should accept that fact. The United States was ready to do all it could to bring about India-Pakistan reconciliation, but Ayub needed to help. Regarding China, Pakistan "must realize that there are certain limits which should not be overstepped if a fruitful Pak-U.S. relationship can continue."[66]

Negotiations on Kashmir

When Harriman and Sandys met Ayub Khan on November 28, 1962, after they had talked with Nehru in New Delhi, the Pakistani leader readily agreed to Kashmir negotiations with India. In the discussions, he also appeared to agree that a plebiscite was not the best way to settle the dispute and that Pakistan could not expect to receive all of the Kashmir Valley.[67] The next evening, Harriman and Ayub met alone while Sandys was in New Delhi to talk further with Nehru. In discussing Kashmir, Ayub commented that he "understood that any fair settlement would be unpopular in both countries." When Harriman brought up the subject of Pakistan's relations with China and warned against a nonaggression pact, about which the Americans had heard rumors, Ayub replied, "It was unthinkable for him to do such a thing."[68]

Meanwhile, Nehru nearly scuttled the negotiations before they started by stating in the Indian parliament on November 30, 1962, that any change in the status of Kashmir would be "very bad for the people there." After Sandys hurriedly flew back to New Delhi, he persuaded Nehru to issue a clarification denying that he was imposing any conditions on the talks.[69] Harriman's trip report to Kennedy, however, was gloomy about the prospects for success. The trouble, Harriman wrote, was that terms for a settlement acceptable to Pakistan were unacceptable to India.[70] On December 3, 1962, when Harriman reviewed his trip with the NSC Executive Committee, he appraised the chances of successful Kashmir negotiations as "quite remote."[71]

Despite this unpromising outlook, Kennedy agreed to engage U.S. influence in support of the talks. In effect, he accepted the view of Assistant Secretary Talbot that the Sino-Indian conflict had sufficiently shaken the subcontinent to offer some chance for a Kashmir settlement. Failure to reach an accord, Talbot believed, would ensure that India and Pakistan would remain enemies for decades to come.[72] The fact that the risk of failure was high did not deter the Kennedy administration, with its activist, can-do frame of mind.

Just before the Kashmir talks got under way, the president sent letters of encouragement to Ayub and Nehru. Neither's response was encouraging. Ayub reiterated his view that Washington should use arms aid as a lever to press for Indian concessions.[73] In an even less upbeat reply, Nehru wrote, "To give up the valley to Pakistan, or to countenance its internationalization [poses] political and strategic problems for India which [render] such solutions impossible."[74]

On December 20, 1962, Kennedy and British Prime Minister Harold Macmillan discussed South Asia during their meetings in Bermuda and agreed to provide $120 million of "emergency" military aid to India to equip six mountain divisions to face the short-term threat from China. In discussing South Asia, Macmillan was more critical of India and showed greater concern about Pakistan than did Kennedy. The prime minister said he was worried: "We support the people who are troublesome, such as Nehru and Krishna Menon, and abandon the people who support us. . . [It will] be dangerous if we let Ayub feel we are abandoning him."[75] Although Kennedy allowed others to do most of the talking, he intervened pointedly when Sandys expressed concern about the "disastrous effect" on Pakistan should the West aid India and the Kashmir talks fail. Disagreeing, the president countered, "What would be so disastrous if the Pak[istanis] left CENTO? . . . What do we get from Pakistan? In return for the protection of our alliance and our assistance what do they do for us?"[76]

After the U.S.-UK talks, Kennedy once more wrote to Ayub, describing the India military aid package as "reasonable but frugal." Although the aid was "not made contingent on a Kashmir settlement," Kennedy said, "any one-sided intransigence on Kashmir" would be "a factor in determining the extent and pace" of future assistance.[77] When Ambassador McConaughy presented the message, Ayub suggested that New Delhi's conduct during the Kashmir talks would determine his ultimate reaction to U.S. arms aid to India.[78] Ayub's subsequent written response to Kennedy's letter was more pointed. Even though Western aid to India might appear "frugal," the Pakistani leader wrote, it was "sufficiently massive" to alter the strategic balance in the region and "to aggravate the danger to our security."[79]

In place of the seriously ill foreign minister, Mohammed Ali Bogra, Ayub named Bhutto to lead the Pakistani delegation for the Kashmir talks. Nehru, who was his own foreign minister, dispatched Railway Minister Swaran Singh to head the Indian team. On December 26, 1962, the day before the negotiations were slated to start in Rawalpindi, it was Pakistan's turn to upset things with the surprise announcement that it had reached a border agreement with China.

According to Pakistani diplomat Agha Shahi, at the time in charge of China at the Foreign Ministry and later his country's foreign secretary and foreign minister, the border negotiations had stalled almost immediately after they had begun in Beijing in May 1962. When a study of the available records suggested that neither Pakistan nor China had a strong legal or historical basis to support any particular boundary claim, Shahi proposed to his superiors that Pakistan seek what seemed the most rational frontier—the watershed of the Karakoram Range—and also try to obtain five hundred square miles beyond the watershed that the people of Hunza traditionally had used for salt and grazing land. Foreign Minister Bogra and President Ayub gave their blessing to the idea and in December 1962—after the Sino-Indian border war had ended—Pakistan's ambassador to China put the proposal on the table. According to Shahi, Chinese Foreign Minister Chen Yi and Premier Zhou Enlai agreed on the understanding that the Pakistanis were making a firm and final offer, not just bargaining. The Chinese, according to Shahi, later admitted that they also "didn't know where the boundary is because no claim is conclusive."[80]

In territorial terms, the border accord was a good bargain for Pakistan. Politically also, despite certain troubles with the Americans, the agreement was extremely appealing. It resolved a potentially troublesome frontier dispute, showed up the Indians, and marked a significant breakthrough in the effort to improve relations with Beijing. For their part, the Chinese were undoubtedly happy to concede a small amount of territory in return for better relations with the Pakistanis. Indeed, in his eagerness to court Ayub, Zhou Enlai went further, offering a nonaggression pact and a modest amount of economic aid. According to Shahi, Pakistan decided against accepting either proposal since they were "all the time very conscious of the American reaction and did not wish to infuriate" Washington.[81]

Washington was, nonetheless, infuriated. U.S. officials feared that the accord would badly damage, if not wreck, the Kashmir talks. They were also angry that Pakistan had disregarded warnings about consorting with China. The Indians were livid. When Ayub claimed that the Chinese had tricked him by timing the announcement of the border agreement to sour the atmosphere for the Kashmir talks, the British and the Americans—but not the Indians—were willing to accept this explanation.[82]

Despite the uproar caused by the Pakistan-China border accord, the Kashmir talks began on schedule. During the initial round in Rawalpindi, both sides reiterated their traditional positions. Ambassador McConaughy and his British counterpart, High Commissioner Sir Morrice James, kept in close touch with each other and with the two delegations but did not directly participate in the talks. This pattern continued throughout the six rounds of negotiations as they moved from Indian to Pakistani cities and back again over the next five months.

In early January 1963, McConaughy had the opportunity to talk extensively with Ayub during a hunting weekend at Bhutto's estate in rural Sindh. A tough cable from the State Department instructed the U.S. envoy to tell Ayub, "Recent Pak[istani] actions have come perilously close to trafficking with [the] enemy" and "hardly comported with what we expect in time of trial from [a] hitherto tried and true ally such as Pakistan."[83] Ayub countered that he understood "to some extent" U.S. concerns and assured McConaughy that nothing else was being considered with Beijing. For good measure, Pakistan's president added that he had no use for the "damned Chinese."[84]

The second round of talks, in New Delhi on January 16–19, 1963, proved the most substantive session of the negotiations. The two delegations seriously discussed the basis for drawing an international boundary through Kashmir. As guiding principles, the Pakistanis recommended the character of the population, security considerations, and the control of river headwaters. The Indians objected to the first point, which they feared would lead to a resurgence of Hindu-Muslim communal troubles. In the end, the two sides were able to agree on a confidential joint statement of principles calling for an international boundary line through the state. They could not, however, agree how the line should be drawn.[85]

To keep the pressure on, Washington decided to send a series of senior officials to India and Pakistan. The first traveler was Assistant Secretary of State Talbot, who met Ayub on February 1, 1963. When they talked, Talbot found that Pakistan's position had stiffened against partition. "Division of [the] Vale would be [a] crime against the inhabitants," Ayub told his American visitor.[86] The assistant secretary also met with Bhutto, who had finally achieved his ambition to become foreign minister after Bogra died on January 24, 1963. Bhutto said that partitioning the valley was "suicidal" and declared that it would be "preferable [to] wait for [the] future rather than accept a settlement with dishonor."[87]

Despite the rebuff, American and British diplomats in Rawalpindi and New Delhi advised the Indians and Pakistanis that dividing the valley seemed the best way to resolve the dispute. Nehru reacted sourly, saying it would "surely be bad to divide such a small and economically and culturally homogenous area."[88] Bhutto remained equally negative, but indicated that Pakistan could accept the division of Kashmir to the north and south but not the partition of the valley.[89]

When the two sides met for the third round in Karachi, February 8–10, 1963, the Indians put on the table some modest territorial concessions to adjust the cease-fire line. Pakistan's disappointing counterproposal was to allot India only a sliver of territory in Jammu (which had a largely Hindu population) and to claim all of the valley and also all of Ladakh, the northeastern part of Kashmir, where the Indians and Chinese had clashed militarily over a disputed boundary. Although Bhutto later indicated that the offer was only an opening gambit, it took brisk U.S. and UK intervention to get the "embittered" Indians to agree to a fourth round of talks in Calcutta in March 1963.[90]

American officials mainly blamed Pakistan for the floundering negotiations. When President Kennedy met with advisers on February 21, 1963, Talbot remained hopeful that the game was not up but stressed that Pakistan needed to do more. "If Pakistan doesn't come through with a better compromise offer," Kennedy commented with a touch of sarcasm, "it will probably try to blackmail us into holding off on aid to India." After Talbot outlined a U.S.-UK proposal for a joint India-Pakistan presence in the valley and partition for the rest of Kashmir, he sought the president's approval to step up U.S. involvement. "We were asking permission," Secretary Rusk interjected, "to get in from up to our ankles to up to our knees." Kennedy agreed.[91]

The next day, the announcement that Foreign Minister Bhutto would be flying to Beijing to sign the border agreement further angered the Indians and upset the Americans. Rusk called in Ambassador Aziz Ahmed to complain about the Bhutto trip and also about Pakistan's poor territorial offer during the Karachi round of talks. The secretary stated bluntly, "From a strictly U.S. national point of view, we do not care what sort of a solution is arrived at in Kashmir." If the negotiations were to fail because of Pakistan, Rusk warned, "the sympathy that Pakistan has enjoyed from other governments on Kashmir in the United Nations and elsewhere would be dissipated."[92]

On the eve of the fourth round, McConaughy delivered yet another presidential letter to Ayub. In this, Kennedy urged that Pakistan put forward "a far more forthcoming and realistic position." The president went on to echo Rusk's warning that if the opportunity to solve Kashmir were lost, "it would seem almost inevitable that the issue would, for all practical purposes, be settled on the basis of the status quo."[93] In talking with McConaughy, Ayub readily agreed that Pakistan's proposal was unrealistic. Surprisingly, he even termed it "damn nonsense."[94] But the Calcutta round on March 12–14, 1963, made no progress. The Indian side complained bitterly about Pakistan's border agreement with China. In turn, notwithstanding Ayub's and Bhutto's comments, Pakistan failed to improve on the territorial proposal made during the Karachi round.[95] When President Kennedy reviewed the negotiations on April 1, 1963, he expressed increasing pessimism that they could be salvaged. He nonetheless approved the release of a U.S.-UK paper outlining "elements of a settlement":

—Giving both India and Pakistan a "substantial position in the Vale";
—Ensuring access through the Vale for defense to the north and east (i.e., India's defense of Ladakh);
—Ensuring Pakistan's interest in the headwaters of the Chenab River;
—Ensuring some local self-rule in the Vale and free movement of people to India and Pakistan; and
—Enhancing economic development efforts.[96]

Events soon showed that Kennedy's pessimism was warranted. On April 15, 1963, in "the most unadorned conversation I have had with Nehru," Ambassador Galbraith tackled the future of the valley head on. "Once or twice [Nehru] got very angry, shouted and pounded the table but in the end calmed down," the envoy cabled. When Galbraith raised Kashmir again with Nehru on April 20, 1963, the prime minister took a hard line against partitioning the valley and stressed the desire to keep the talks going, but did not suggest any improvement in the Indian brief.[97]

After U.S. and British diplomats produced the "elements" paper, New Delhi vociferously claimed that this step had upset the pace of negotiations and implied that the concept had been worked out with Karachi behind the backs of the Indians. Through a bureaucratic mix-up, the Pakistanis had received the paper from British and U.S. diplomats before the Indians had.[98] In a sharp letter to Kennedy, Nehru wrote on April 21, 1963, "I am convinced that these ill-considered and ill-conceived initiatives, however well-intentioned they may be, have at least for the present made it impossible to reach any settlement on this rather involved and complicated question."[99] Galbraith cabled that India's prime minister would have found some other escape route if the "elements" paper had not surfaced. "Nehru," the ambassador commented, "is unquestionably angry, in part at my pressure, much more at the fact that I have translated his vague talk of wanting a settlement into firm concessions he doesn't want to make."[100]

Predictably, the talks remained deadlocked during the fifth round, in Karachi. The Indians sat on their hands. The Pakistanis once more failed to improve on their third-round territorial offer. The only thing on which the two sides could agree was that they both opposed the U.S.-UK idea of partitioning the valley. Although the negotiations were effectively over, the two sides agreed to a sixth round, mainly because Dean Rusk and Duncan Sandys would be visiting South Asia in early May.[101]

Having concluded that chances for a Kashmir settlement were "almost nil," Kennedy instructed Rusk to tell Ayub that the United States was going ahead with arms aid to India and would not tie this to progress in the Kashmir talks. When Kennedy asked whether this would mean the loss of the Badaber intelligence facility, the secretary of state replied that it would be "rough." Summing up his thinking, the president commented, "Let's not be penny wise about India; let's not get them in a position where they feel that they can't cope with the [Chinese communists] and the Pak[istanis] on top of their other problems."[102]

In meetings with visitors from India, Kennedy was frank in discussing the Pakistan problem. When Defense Production Minister T. T. Krishnamachari called at the White House, the president told him, "We [have] real problems with the Pak[istanis]. We [have] important intelligence relations with them, and we [do] not want the Pak[istanis] in a moment of violence to destroy CENTO and SEATO."[103] Kennedy explained to Indian president Dr. S. Radhakrishnan that the United States desired "to help India both economically and militarily and that we want a point short of causing a real crisis with Pakistan." The U.S. goal, Kennedy said, was to "give India more security without heavy costs in terms of our relations with Pakistan."[104]

Rusk's talk with Ayub made clear how hard it would be to achieve this aim. After the meeting, the secretary of state cabled that the "[e]ntire conversation was marked by [Ayub's] deep fear, distrust and hatred of India and especially the Brahmin Nehru whom he regards as an evil and dangerous man." Regarding U.S. arms to India, Ayub expressed more concern about future assistance than the aid that had already been given and did not appear interested in U.S. security assurances. Since he could not be sure of persuading others to meet his country's security needs, Pakistanis preferred to "do it themselves."[105] Later, after Rusk returned to Washington, he commented, "We cannot rely on Pakistan to act rationally and in what we might think would be in its own interest."[106]

The trouble was exactly that: what the United States thought was in Pakistan's interest and Pakistan's own perception of its interests fundamentally differed. Kennedy saw India as a potential partner in containing China. Pakistan regarded India as the major threat to its own security. The United States perceived China as its major foe in Asia. Ayub saw China as a potential partner against India. American and Pakistani policies were on a collision course.

On May 15–16, 1963, the sixth and final round of Kashmir talks took place in New Delhi. The Indians rejected a Pakistani proposal to internationalize the valley for six months followed by a plebiscite and, in turn, suggested that the two countries agree not to use force to change the status quo in Kashmir. The Pakistanis rejected this proposal while stressing that they too believed in a peaceful settlement.[107]

As an epilogue, the idea of mediation emerged from the Rusk-Sandys discussions in New Delhi. Although India in the past had rejected this approach—most recently in January 1962, when Nehru turned down Kennedy's suggestion to have Eugene Black serve as a mediator—on this occasion its prime minister accepted the idea in principle. Ayub and Bhutto were less than enthused, however. An annoyed State Department instructed McConaughy to tell the Pakistanis that if they rejected mediation, "We do not see how we can help [them] any further in altering [the] status quo [on Kashmir]; we cannot subordinate our strategic interests in Asia to [the] settlement of Kashmir." Foreign Minister Bhutto eventually accepted, but imposed conditions that the Indians were certain to reject. After further futile discussion, the State Department dropped the mediation proposal.[108]

Meanwhile, in Washington, the July 9, 1963, farewell call on Kennedy by Aziz Ahmed saw an undiplomatically blunt exchange. Ahmed, who was returning to Pakistan to become Bhutto's foreign secretary, complained that America was proceeding with long-term military aid to India despite the fact that the Chinese threat was receding and there was no Kashmir settlement. This action, the ambassador asserted, was imperiling Pakistan's security. The president disagreed, arguing that the United States was taking Pakistan's interests into account and giving much less aid than India wanted. Pressure had not worked with India on Kashmir, but, he recalled, it had also not worked with Pakistan on Afghanistan. Kennedy then spoke sharply about Pakistan's move toward China and the barrage of anti-U.S. commentary in the Pakistani press: "[The] Pak[istanis] display little appreciation of this primary concern of ours and instead apparently feel impelled to move towards [Communist China] and away from us because [of] Pak[istani] concern about India. In [the] last few months [the] Pak[istani] press has exceeded all but [Communist China] in its attacks on us. One would gather from [the] Pak[istani] press, which is closer to [the government of Pakistan] than [the American press is] to [the U.S. government], that [the] U.S. was enemy number one."[109] As the meeting ended, the president urged Ahmed to "bear in mind that [the] U.S. has one basic interest—prevention of control over Europe by [the] USSR or Asia by [Communist China]. Pakistan should understand this outlook since it accepted [the] responsibilities of [an] alliance with us."[110]

Pakistan's actions soon made clear the widening gap between the two allies. On July 17, 1963, Bhutto raised eyebrows in a National Assembly debate by asserting that an attack by India on Pakistan would involve the "largest state in Asia." The hawkish foreign minister refused to elaborate, but observers assumed that if not bravado, the statement signaled some sort of defense understanding with China.[111]

The most immediate problem, however, related to establishing civil aviation links between Pakistan and China. With Bhutto's blessing, Air Marshal Nur Khan, the head of Pakistan's national carrier, Pakistan International Airline (PIA), took the initiative to explore the possibility of providing commercial air service to China, a move that would breach a Western ban. According to Nur Khan, the Chinese initially proposed a link between Dacca and Kunming, similar to the World War II "over-the-hump" flights across the Himalayas. He rejected this as not viable commercially and suggested instead that PIA fly from Dacca to major Chinese cities—Shanghai, Canton, and Beijing. After listening to Nur Khan's proposal, Zhou Enlai said that he would approve PIA flights to Shanghai and Canton, but not to Beijing. He also agreed that the Pakistanis could help upgrade Chinese airports, which Nur Khan described as "quite primitive" and twenty years behind the times. Following extended and heated internal debate within the Pakistani government, Ayub gave his blessing to the proposal.[112]

Despite Washington's vehement protest that the aviation accord marked "an unfortunate breach of free world solidarity," Pakistan signed the agreement with China on August 29, 1963. The Kennedy administration responded by imposing a tangible sanction against Pakistan for the first time, postponing indefinitely a $4.3 million AID loan to build a new airport at Dacca, from which PIA planned to fly to China.[113] Considering the depth of concern that the U.S. administration had voiced about Pakistan's relationship with China, this was a modest punishment. Of even more direct concern in Washington was word that the Pakistanis had halted negotiations for a proposed expansion of the communications intercept facility at Badaber. During a July 31, 1963, NSC meeting, a worried CIA director John McCone urged that something be done promptly—for example, sending a high-level emissary to talk with Ayub. A few days later, Kennedy accepted the idea and decided to dispatch George Ball, who had succeeded Chester Bowles as the undersecretary of state, for in-depth discussions with the Pakistani leader.[114]

The Ball Mission

On August 12, 1963, Kennedy met with Ball, Rusk, and top officials from the Departments of State and Defense and the CIA to review the undersecretary's brief. Ball said that he would try to reassure Ayub that U.S. assurances to help Pakistan in case of an Indian attack were credible. He saw an Indian Ocean Task Force, joint military exercises and planning, and pre-positioning of military equipment as ways to allay Pakistani concerns about U.S. reliability. There was disagreement over what Ayub really wanted: Assistant Secretary Talbot felt he was less interested in assurances than in America's not helping India militarily; Averell Harriman said that the "nub of the problem was how to convince Ayub we mean what we say."

Kennedy himself doubted that Ayub feared India militarily. He thought that the Pakistani leader wanted to use the United States to press India over Kashmir, but "we couldn't give this to him." The president continued, "We [aren't] getting much from the Pakistani either. About all the alliance [is] worth to us [are] the intelligence facilities." A skeptical Kennedy wondered what Ball would be able to achieve: "We know each other's arguments, so the best we can do is remind them we don't like the [Chinese communists], get them to call off their distasteful press campaign and tell them that Peshawar is vital to us so that if they don't play ball, we will give our aid to someone else." The president commented that he "understood Ayub's arguments and could see his point of view. As seen by the Pakistani, India was a threat to their interests. However, we were right too in our position so the best we could get was a standoff."[115]

Reiterating his doubts that Ayub was genuinely worried about the Indian threat, Kennedy thought the Pakistani leader was concerned about losing "the capability to attack India or at least get his way vis-à-vis India." Nor did the president believe the Indians would seriously consider attacking Pakistan, a move that would cost them $1 billion in economic aid. When Rusk interjected that the United States would "nuke"

India if it attacked Pakistan—a truly astounding statement—Kennedy disagreed, saying that America was unlikely to use nuclear weapons except in a crisis with the Soviets.[116]

During three days of talks in Pakistan, September 3–6, 1963, Undersecretary Ball had ample time for detailed review of U.S.-Pakistan relations. In the final session, Ayub delivered a prepared statement that accurately summed up the conflicting U.S. and Pakistani positions. Because of the increased threat from India caused by U.S. aid, Ayub declared, "[i]t has become imperative for Pakistan to bring down its political and military liabilities within its means." Pakistan, he continued, would therefore "normalize our relations with as many of our neighbors as possible." In addition to the approach to China, he hoped to do something with the Soviet Union, and also with Afghanistan. Pakistan's president rejected Ball's proposals for an enhanced U.S. military presence, saying that such a presence was "useless" unless directed against the threat from India. The undersecretary responded that the United States "had given Pakistan straightforward assurances on coming to its aid if it should be attacked from any source."

When Ball expressed concern about talk of Pakistan's normalizing relations with the Soviet Union and China, Ayub countered that his country had "cause for complaint against its friend [i.e., the United States]. . . . Pakistan's interests [have] been hurt and its security jeopardized against all reason and logic." As the meeting ended, Ayub warned, "Should U.S. policy change, and should we seek to squeeze Pakistan, there would be difficulties. Pakistan may be poor, but it is proud. Pakistan is not stupid, however, and not in a hurry to lose its best friend." To conclude, Ayub said that he was not urging a radical change in U.S. policy, but wanted to put a "safety limitation on our assistance to India."[117]

A cable that Ball sent from Lisbon summed up his gloomy assessment: Fear that India wanted to destroy it "is the central obsessive basis of [the Pakistani government's] policy." U.S. military aid to India, in Ayub's view, had upset the balance, which at least had permitted West Pakistan to be defended. "Frustration and despair translate into a sense of bitterness and betrayal," since the Pakistanis saw the shift in the military balance the result of the action of their "best friend." If the present course continued, the undersecretary predicted "a gradual erosion of our influence with Pakistan, with mounting pressures for Pakistan to move in the general direction of neutralism."[118] Events over the next few years would show that Ball had accurately read the situation.

During a September 9, 1963, meeting with Kennedy to review the trip, Ball covered much of the same ground. The only good news that he brought back concerned the intelligence facility at Badaber. Ayub had agreed that the expansion could go ahead, since he conceded that he had given CIA director McCone "two-thirds of a commitment."[119]

"One of Our More Difficult Problems"

A few days later, during a September 12, 1963, press conference, President Kennedy succinctly summed up the U.S. policy dilemma in South Asia. "I can tell you that there's nothing that has occupied our attention more . . . over the last nine months," the president said. Although the United States wanted to help India against the Chinese, "everything we give to India adversely affects the balance of power with Pakistan . . . so we are dealing with a very complicated problem because the hostility between them is so deep." The United States had hoped for a Kashmir settlement, Kennedy continued, "but Kashmir is further from being settled today that it was six months ago. So we're trying to balance off what is one of our more difficult problems."[120]

In October 1963, Foreign Minister Bhutto, whom Washington by then considered an unhelpful hawk on India, pro-Chinese, and anti-American, met at the White House with Kennedy, Ball, and Harriman. The talk broke no new ground, although Bhutto accepted the president's suggestion that General Maxwell Taylor, chairman of the Joint Chiefs of Staff, visit Pakistan to examine "the measures which we could take that might tend to reassure Pakistan about our support in the event of an attack on it by India."[121]

By the time General Taylor traveled to Pakistan in December 1963, Kennedy was dead, and Lyndon B. Johnson had become president of the United States. At the time of Kennedy's assassination, the U.S.-Pakistan alliance was beginning to unravel. Kennedy was bent on providing long-term military aid to India and seemed willing to accept the consequences in terms of further trouble with Pakistan. In turn, Ayub did not want to lose U.S. assistance, but seemed set on moving toward friendlier relations with China, an action Washington regarded as contrary to U.S. interests and Pakistan's alliance obligations.

Kennedy was willing to accept Ayub's contention that U.S. military aid to India hurt Pakistan's security interests. His successor, Lyndon Johnson, would show less understanding of Pakistani sensitivities.

6

Johnson: The Alliance Unravels

One of Lyndon Johnson's first tasks as president was to receive the more than one hundred heads of state and other foreign dignitaries who attended John F. Kennedy's funeral on November 25, 1963. After Mass at St. Matthew's Cathedral in downtown Washington, the new president met with each visitor for a few minutes in the State Department's diplomatic reception rooms and later had more extended meetings with heads of state and government but not with lesser-ranking visitors.

Reflecting his negative attitude toward the late president, Ayub Khan chose not to represent Pakistan at Kennedy's funeral and sent Foreign Minister Zulfikar Ali Bhutto.[1] This proved a costly mistake. By not coming himself, Pakistan's president lost the chance to re-establish personal ties with Lyndon Johnson and to talk through the problems in U.S.-Pakistan relations with the new president. Instead, Bhutto got into a testy argument with Johnson that further aggravated the bilateral relationship.

When Johnson and Bhutto met at the State Department after the Kennedy funeral, the president asked the foreign minister to convey greetings to "his friend President Ayub who was one of the ablest men he had ever met." Johnson said that, as he had watched Sardar, the horse that Ayub had given Jacqueline Kennedy, walk behind the fallen president's hearse in the funeral procession, he had been "thinking a good deal about Pakistan on [that] day of sorrow."

Bhutto advised that Ayub had asked him to convey an important personal message. When Johnson asked what it was, to his surprise the foreign minister responded that he had not brought the communication with him, but would like a separate meeting in order to deliver it. Johnson commented on how crowded his own schedule was, but Bhutto stressed his willingness to wait as long as necessary, saying that Ayub regarded the message as extremely important.[2] Given the tremendous pressures during his first days in the White House, Johnson rebuffed several requests from National Security Adviser McGeorge Bundy before he finally agreed to receive Bhutto again on November 29, 1963.

Before the meeting, Undersecretary of State George Ball, who "deeply distrusted" Pakistan's foreign minister, told the president that Bhutto had "persistently undercut" U.S. interests.[3] After the Pakistani was ushered into the Oval Office, he handed the president a short message expressing Ayub's warmest wishes, but containing nothing of substance that required the separate meeting. Following a few pleasantries, Bhutto assumed the session was over and got up to leave. An annoyed Johnson brusquely told him to sit down and launched into a heated discussion of U.S.-Pakistan difficulties. The United States, the new president declared, was "indeed a friend of Pakistan and would continue to be one if Pakistan would let [it]." The foreign minister, however, should know that there would be a serious public relations problem if Pakistan continued to build up its relations with the Chinese. Bhutto responded that the Pakistani government had its own public relations problem; he could not describe "the intensity of feelings about India." Admitting the dangers regarding China, Bhutto said that "Pakistan could be trusted to handle them." When he asserted that China's appetite was for Southeast Asia, not India, the president sharply interjected: "It is you who are going to sit down to eat with the Chinese Communists." A flustered foreign minister countered that U.S. actions to strengthen India were pushing Pakistan "to the wall."[4]

As he left the White House after the meeting, Bhutto was visibly shaken and complained to Ball about his "discourteous reception." That evening, when Assistant Secretary of State Phillips Talbot saw the foreign minister off at the airport, Bhutto remained deeply upset and seemed convinced that there was a "wild man" in the White House from whom Pakistan could expect little. "It was a bad start for the new administration's dealings with Pakistan," Talbot later commented.[5]

Paradoxically, Johnson liked Ayub, whom he had met in Karachi and had hosted at his Texas ranch in 1961. The new president was also unsympathetic to his predecessor's desire to shift the policy focus from Pakistan to India. National Security Council (NSC) staff member Robert Komer remembered Johnson's having asked him during a vice presidential trip, "Why is it that Jack Kennedy and you India lovers in the State Department are so Godammed ornery to my friend Ayub?"[6]

Aware of Johnson's attitude, Komer attempted unsuccessfully to convince Bundy to press for approval of the long-term military assistance package for India that had been readied for presidential consideration just before Kennedy died. Komer argued, "We may lose a real opportunity [unless we get Johnson to sign on] while he is still carrying out the Kennedy policy."[7] Instead, the issue was deferred and Johnson asked Gen. Maxwell Taylor, chairman of the Joint Chiefs of Staff, who was already scheduled to travel to South Asia, to make recommendations about military aid after he visited the subcontinent.

When Taylor met Ayub in December 1963, the two soldiers covered much the same ground that George Ball had gone over three months earlier. Ayub explained his dilemma: "Pakistan was facing a tragic predicament in which loyalty to our own country is coming into increasing conflict with loyalty to our friends."[8] The United States was genuinely concerned about Pakistan's security, Taylor replied. He proposed joint military exercises and pre-positioning equipment as a way to demonstrate U.S. capacity to deploy forces for Pakistan's defense against attack from all sides, including India.

The key problems, Pakistan's president stressed, were that U.S. arms to India were increasing the threat to Pakistan, and that his country should be able to deter by itself any attack. When Taylor said this was beyond Pakistan's capability, Ayub insisted that his country must be able to defend itself rather to rely on someone else. As events in other parts of the world might prevent the United States from fulfilling its assurances, Pakistan needed to have the capacity to withstand an attack on its own.[9] Ayub was also skeptical about Taylor's suggestion of a possible U.S. naval task force in the Indian Ocean; in Ayub's view, Pakistan's military problems involved the army and the air force, not the navy. The task force idea sounded to the president like a "military gimmick" that smaller nations would see as "a revival of gunboat diplomacy."[10]

In line with his instructions, Taylor chided Ayub about the "unfortunate nature" of an upcoming visit by Chinese premier Zhou Enlai. Ayub responded that the trip signified nothing more than Pakistan's desire to normalize relations with a neighbor. More generally, Taylor expressed his "deep regret" over bilateral troubles and asked why the United States and Pakistan could not accept their honest difference over military aid to India, "cease the recriminations which have been souring our relations and move forward toward common objectives."[11]

After returning to Washington, Taylor recommended that the United States "give due recognition to Ayub's case and . . . strengthen Pak[istani] confidence and good will without appearing to succumb to querulous complaining." He proposed a five-year military aid program, including additional supersonic aircraft—provided the Pakistanis showed "a wholehearted change of attitude toward CENTO [the Central Treaty Organization], SEATO [the Southeast Asia Treaty Organization]and the U.S." Despite Ayub's emotional opposition to U.S. military aid to India, Taylor believed that the Pakistani president "is swallowing hard, [but] it is going down."[12] Events would soon show that his assessment was overly optimistic.

Relations Sour

In February 1964, President Johnson gave the green light for "austere minimum" five-year military aid programs for Pakistan and India. He did not, however, authorize U.S. officials to mention funding levels; he asked that Pakistan first develop its own plans on which Washington could comment, and he wanted arms aid linked to "satisfactory performance" of Pakistan's alliance obligations. Johnson deferred any discussions of aid specifics until after an assessment of the Zhou Enlai visit.[13] In the new president's first important decision about Pakistan, he thus signaled a tougher stance than Kennedy probably would have adopted.

The Pakistanis were careful to avoid overdoing the official welcome given to the Chinese leader when he arrived in Karachi on February 18, 1964. Zhou was greeted by Finance Minister Mohammed Shoaib, the cabinet member regarded as closest to Washington, and not by Bhutto, who as foreign minister would normally have welcomed a visiting premier. There was, nonetheless, an emotional outpouring of public warmth for the Chinese leader, whose country had gained enormous popularity in Pakistan through its military victory over India in the 1962 border war. For their part, the Chinese diligently continued to woo the Pakistanis. During the visit, Zhou announced an important policy shift on Kashmir to support Pakistan's long-standing call for a plebiscite to solve the dispute.[14] In mid-1964, the Chinese took an additional step toward closer ties, providing Pakistan a $60 million interest-free loan.[15]

In May 1964, President Johnson finally approved a long-term military aid program for India that provided for about $50 million worth of grant aid annually along with a similar amount in credit sales. Largely out of concern for the Pakistanis, the program did not include the weapons system that the Indians most wanted and that Pakistan already had received: F-104 supersonic aircraft. Despite this, news of the arms package caused a uproar in Pakistan. Concluding that Washington had ignored Pakistan's interests by entering into a long-term arrangement with "enemy" India, Ayub blasted U.S. foreign policy in an interview published in the June 23, 1964, London *Daily Mail.* "Today American policy is based on opportunism and is devoid of moral quality," the president intemperately charged. "Pakistan deeply regrets that although she has fulfilled all her commitments, she has been let down by politicians she regarded as friends."[16]

Foreign Minister Bhutto was equally biting in a June 22, 1964, speech before the National Assembly. Alleging "utter disregard" by the United States of Pakistani interests, he declared, "The time has come for Pakistan to undertake a reappraisal of its foreign policy and to review her political and military commitments." The United States "had to choose" between "a system of alliances and betrayal of allies," Bhutto told the assembly.[17]

The Pakistani attacks stung Johnson. His feelings showed when he met Pakistani ambassador Ghulam Ahmed (the older brother of former envoy Aziz Ahmed) on July 7, 1964, to receive a letter from Ayub complaining about arms aid to India. In the letter, Pakistan's president asserted that the U.S. action had upset the balance of power in the subcontinent and had eroded his country's ability to meet its obligations to its allies. Johnson interrupted Ahmed to ask if this explained Pakistan's failure to respond to U.S. requests for assistance in prosecuting the Vietnam War, which was rapidly becoming the top U.S. foreign policy priority. The president commented angrily that he "had been shocked by Ayub's silence" and did not share the view that "because the United States had helped India, Pakistan should ignore its alliance obligations." Johnson sternly asked the ambassador to carry a message to Ayub: "In light of the way President Ayub seemed to feel, [Johnson] guessed we were coming to a point where we would all have to reevaluate the condition of our relationship. This troubled him deeply because there were no people for whom he had greater regard than for the Pakistani people."[18]

On a less contentious and more personal note, Johnson queried Ahmed for news about "my camel driver" [referring to Bashir Ahmed, whom Johnson had met in Karachi and who had visited the United States at Johnson's invitation]. The ambassador noted that he was driving a truck rather than a camel and doing very well. Johnson instructed Assistant Secretary Talbot to give him a report on Bashir Ahmed's welfare.[19]

When Ambassador Walter McConaughy met President Johnson the following week, the still-upset president brushed aside the envoy's suggestion that Ayub be invited to Washington for a thorough discussion of bilateral difficulties. Instead, Johnson instructed the ambassador to convey his "considerable distress" about the attention Pakistan was paying to a country (China) that posed "a grave threat" to U.S. interests in Vietnam and to underscore his displeasure regarding Ayub's unwillingness to send troops to Vietnam. Pakistan, in Johnson's view, should "at least show [its] flag."[20]

As relations drifted downward during the fall and winter of 1964–65, both the United States and Pakistan held presidential elections. On November 3, 1964, Johnson gained a landslide victory over Barry Goldwater, his conservative Republican opponent, winning 61 percent of the popular vote. Two months later, on January 2, 1965, in Pakistan's first presidential election, Ayub defeated a surprisingly strong bid by Fatima Jinnah, the Quaid-i-Azam's sister, who ran as the combined opposition candidate. Even with the vigorous support of the civil administration and indirect balloting, Ayub won only 64 per cent of the 80,000 electoral college votes. He lost the city of Karachi and came close to being defeated in East Pakistan. The election showed that, although respected, Ayub had failed to gain the affection of his people. His regime rested more on the power of the army and the bureaucracy than on the president's personal popularity.

The Pakistani public, nonetheless, enthusiastically supported the altered foreign policy stance that he had adopted after Washington's decision to provide military aid to India. Pakistanis applauded Ayub's downplaying of the alliance with the Americans and development of friendly ties with China.[21] Although foreign policy was not an important election campaign issue, both the opposition and the government found it useful to criticize the United States. The opposition chastised Ayub for having nurtured the alliance with America. The president's supporters accused Washington of funneling funds into Fatima Jinnah's campaign coffers.[22]

After their election victories, the two presidents set about pursuing their chosen—and ultimately conflicting—foreign policy paths.

Johnson's aim was that, as a quid pro quo for continued large-scale U.S. aid, Pakistan once again become a "good ally"—i.e., go slow on further improvement in relations with China, hopefully support the rapidly expanding U.S. involvement in Vietnam, and rein in criticism of the United States in the Pakistani media. Johnson also agreed to invite Ayub to visit Washington for talks in April 1965.

Ayub's goal—to gain U.S. understanding for improved Sino-Pakistani relations—was a key part of his ambitious strategy of trying to maintain good relations with Washington while developing friendlier relations with Beijing and also with Moscow. The complex maneuvering to achieve this, Ayub wrote in his memoirs, "would be like walking on a triangular tightrope."[23] The Pakistani president hoped that official visits planned for early 1965, to Beijing in March and in April to Moscow (the first trip there by a Pakistani leader), and then to Washington, would show that he could manage the diplomatic high-wire act. When asked during a foreign policy briefing for senior officials whether Pakistan could survive as a small country "in the position of a lamb between the lions," Ayub denied that Pakistan was "a lamb" and asserted self-assuredly that "he knew how to live peacefully among the lions by setting one lion against another." He said that Pakistan would remain in CENTO and SEATO and yet have good relations with China and the Soviet Union.[24]

Johnson Upsets the Triangular Tightrope

Ayub's traverse of the triangular tightrope got off to a promising start in Beijing, where he received the most enthusiastic welcome that the communist regime had ever accorded a foreign leader.[25] Although Ayub was careful in discussing the war in Vietnam publicly—aware that Washington was closely monitoring his words—the joint communiqué's support for "national independence movements and struggles against imperialism and all forms of colonialism in Asia and Africa"[26] came close to toeing the Chinese line. Nor was the U.S. government amused when Foreign Minister Chen Yi told the press that Ayub had offered to serve as a go-between in establishing relations between China and Turkey, a close ally of both the United States and Pakistan.[27]

The second leg of the triangle was Moscow. Reflecting the cooler temperature of Pakistani-Soviet relations, no cheering crowds greeted Ayub on the drive in from the airport. The initial round of meetings was stiff and formal. After the Soviets criticized Pakistan's alliance with the United States, Ayub criticized Soviet military aid to India and the Soviet stance on Kashmir. As the talks proceeded, the mood improved. Conceding that the Soviets had a basis to complain about Pakistan's ties with Washington, Ayub said, "These pacts are dead but we are not in a position to bury them." If the Soviets were worried about U.S. bases in Pakistan and the Pakistanis were concerned about the Soviet veto on Kashmir, Ayub suggested, "[t]he matter could be negotiated and the two sides could come to a reasonable solution." He assured the Soviet leaders that Pakistan would not serve as an instrument of U.S. policy in South Asia. Although the Soviets did not immediately alter their policy, Ayub appeared to have softened Moscow's view of Pakistan as a U.S. lackey.[28]

But the glow from these diplomatic forays suddenly dimmed. Just days before Ayub was due to arrive in Washington on April 15, 1965, Johnson abruptly put off the Pakistani president's visit. His message stated, "I have in fact reluctantly come to the view that this month is not a good time for the two of us to meet in Washington. Your visit at this time would focus public attention on the differences between Pakistan and the United States policy toward Communist China. This I fear might gravely affect our ability to assist your Government in the economic and defense programs on which you are embarked."[29]

Johnson's action was triggered by his anger at Canadian prime minister Lester Pearson, who had criticized U.S. Vietnam policy after talks at the White House. An embarrassed U.S. chief executive wanted to avoid hosting other visitors who might make unflattering comments or stir trouble about Vietnam. Because of Pakistan's cozying up to China and its unhelpful Vietnam stance, Johnson decided to put off Ayub. As an afterthought, he also postponed a visit scheduled for June 1965 by India's prime minister, Lal Bahadur Shastri.[30]

Despite the fact that the cancellation, according to Ayub confidante Altaf Gauhar, "was like a bombshell which shattered Ayub's whole game plan,"[31] the Pakistani president gritted his teeth and put on the best public face. His task was eased when the Indians reacted with loud public indignation about the treatment that Shastri had received from Johnson. Komer advised the president, "Disinviting Ayub seems to have shaken him (though the Indian stink about disinviting Shastri too softens the blow and mutes the lesson)."[32] Johnson's brusque treatment of the two leaders stirred deep resentment and resulted in a de facto break in high-level communications between the United States and both Pakistan and India just as a crisis was beginning to brew in South Asia.

In mid-April 1965, Indian and Pakistani army units clashed in the Rann of Kutch, a disputed tidal mud flat off the Arabian Sea. Pakistan claimed that the desolate and uninhabited area was a landlocked "sea" and that therefore the international boundary ran through the middle of the Rann. New Delhi argued that the Rann was a marsh and totally within Indian territory.[33] After the Indians decided to take physical possession of the entire area by stationing troops on the northern side of the Rann, the Pakistanis responded militarily. Fighting quickly escalated to a brigade-size engagement. On April 18, 1965, the Indians decided to withdraw their forces rather than risk having them cut off when the Rann flooded during the rainy season.[34] Upon the withdrawal, morale soared in Rawalpindi and slumped in New Delhi. It was one thing for the Indian army to be drubbed by the Chinese in the Himalayas, but quite another to receive a bloody nose from the Pakistanis.

Its relations strained with both countries, Washington took a back seat to London in diplomatic efforts to end the conflict. In June 1965, the protagonists agreed to Britain's suggestion that an arbitration panel resolve the disputed border claims. That the Indians accepted the idea was surprising, because New Delhi had consistently refused arbitration as a means of settling aspects of the Kashmir dispute.[35] The United States was worried that the fighting in the Rann of Kutch might spread and also was concerned about Pakistan's use of U.S.-supplied military equipment, in violation of the ground rules of the 1954 defense agreement under which the aid was provided. When the Indians complained officially about this, Secretary of State Dean Rusk dodged the issue, trying to focus New Delhi's attention on stopping the fighting and preventing a spread of the conflict.[36]

By the spring of 1965, Johnson was also souring on the large-scale economic aid programs to India and Pakistan—which Kennedy had strongly supported. The president felt edgy about allocating roughly a third of U.S. economic assistance funds to South Asia, shared widespread congressional criticism of foreign aid, and was increasingly concerned that although India was doing poorly economically, its leaders took U.S. aid for granted "regardless of what they did or how effectively they used it."[37]

In the case of aid to Pakistan, Johnson's problem was political. Indeed, the country's economic performance was strong and there was broad satisfaction with its use of foreign aid. Gross national product (GNP) had risen from $8.5 billion in fiscal year 1963 to $10.1 billion in fiscal year 1965, an impressive 9.4 percent annual rate of increase.[38] For the five years ending in June 1965, GNP had also risen at an average annual rate of 5.2 percent. The World Bank and the Agency for International Development (AID) warmly praised the economic policies followed by Ayub and Shoaib. The United States was providing roughly $400 million in assistance annually—$200 million in economic aid, $160 million in food aid, and $40 million in military assistance. This amounted to half of the foreign assistance that Pakistan was receiving.

As Johnson pondered what to do, a memorandum from Komer summed up the situation: "Our immediate problem is how to keep Pakistan from leaning so far toward [Beijing] that Congress cuts off U.S. aid. We may lose Pakistan, unless we can convince Ayub that he can't have his cake and eat it too. Pakistan's still desperate need for U.S. aid gives us real leverage. . . . Our dilemma is that U.S. economic aid is making Pakistan a real success story, so we hate to cut back for political reasons (but the Pak[istanis] would hate it too)."[39]

On April 21, 1965, Johnson decided on a tougher approach, imposing a de facto freeze on assistance to India and Pakistan until "a new contract" was worked out. The president held up future aid commitments, required White House approval for all pending decisions, and withdrew AID's authority to make informal commitments in advance of congressional approval of funding.[40] In a June 9, 1965, meeting with Secretary of State Rusk, Defense Secretary McNamara, National Security Adviser Bundy, Undersecretary of State for Economic Affairs Thomas Mann, AID Administrator David Bell, and NSC staff member Komer, the president agreed to release loans already approved but said that he personally would approve all new aid decisions until Congress passed the fiscal year 1966 aid bill.

In the case of Pakistan, Johnson also asked "what U.S. pledge, if any" should be put on the table at the World Bank–sponsored consortium session scheduled for late July 1965. Bell commented that U.S. unwillingness to increase aid would be strong medicine, especially as Pakistan's economic performance warranted a larger U.S. aid pledge.[41] Since the consortium session would set the stage for Pakistan's ambitious third five-year plan, the donors' meeting would have great importance.

Unaware of Johnson's intentions, an upbeat Shoaib and his staff were in Washington during June 1965, shaping an optimistic development program with World Bank and AID counterparts.[42] Sustainable growth seemed a real possibility, a vast improvement from Pakistan's desperate straits of the mid-1950s, just a decade before. The planners hoped to double development expenditures to $10.9 billion during the coming five years and targeted an annual growth rate of 6.5 percent. Although the third five-year plan would continue to emphasize private-sector development, it would also promote increased agricultural production and pay far more attention to population control, health, and education—areas where Pakistan's performance remained weak.[43] Despite the strain in the bilateral political-security relationship, the economic ties seemed as strong as ever when the finance minister and his colleagues flew home from Washington.[44]

The Pakistani economic team, however, did not know that Lyndon Johnson was about to make sure that Ayub Khan could no longer take U.S. economic aid for granted. On June 30, 1965, he instructed Ambassador McConaughy to tell Shoaib that the U.S. government wanted a two-month postponement of the consortium meeting in order to permit congressional action before an aid pledge "and in view of certain other problems which we would be prepared to discuss with [the government of Pakistan] should it wish."[45] Although Johnson hid behind the alleged congressional problem, "the postponement was designed to show Ayub," NSC staff member Harold Saunders wrote, "that American aid was far from automatic, and to be a forceful reminder that his relations with Communist China and other U.S.-Pakistani difficulties could endanger his nation's economy."[46]

Contrary to White House hopes, the Pakistanis "took the news very hard" and "made the postponement a major public issue."[47] In a speech in the National Assembly on June 13, 1965, Bhutto stated, "We are willing to hold a discourse and dialogue with the United States of America and to tell them how we are the aggrieved party and how, in spite of these aggravations, in spite of these grievous injuries, we have not abandoned our friendship with them." The next day, addressing a June 14, 1965, Muslim League gathering, Ayub charged, "The U.S. has always acted in a manner that [is] prejudicial to Pakistan's interests in the context of Indo-Pakistani relations." The president declared that Pakistan would not agree to any U.S. demand that would incur the hostility of

China or the Soviet Union. But he ended his remarks on a calmer note, saying, "Pakistan [cannot] afford a big political mistake. It must face the situation with courage and be rational in its approach." Pakistan's government-controlled press ran banner headlines: "Freedom, Honor, Not for Barter" and "We Won't Yield to Pressure."[48]

In line with his stiff public reaction, Ayub refused to take up the U.S. suggestion that he send Shoaib to Washington or come himself to discuss "the certain other problems." Instead of bowing to Johnson's pressure tactics, Ayub chose to sit tight. He was a proud Pathan, and U.S. arm-twisting did not elicit the desired response. As Washington waited to see whether Pakistan would bend, officials fretted about the harm being done to U.S. economic objectives. Komer commented that although Ayub was putting himself "out on a limb," he had "also created a dilemma for us." What would the U.S. government do in September if the Pakistanis failed to respond and Congress approved the AID bill? Komer asked.[49] The first casualty as a result of the consortium postponement was Pakistan's liberal commodity import policy, which, in the absence of an assured aid flow, Shoaib reluctantly curtailed. Bell wanted to save it, but told Rusk he could not recommend an interim commodity loan in view of Pakistan's "belligerent and provocative response" to the consortium postponement.[50]

The 1965 India-Pakistan War

Unknown to U.S. officials, developments were brewing in Pakistan that rendered moot the question of a U.S. pledge at the consortium meeting. In late 1964, after Ayub had authorized the foreign office, the army, and the intelligence services to draw up a plan to "defreeze" the Kashmir situation, a secret cell chaired by Foreign Secretary Aziz Ahmed had come into being.[51] Reflecting the hawkish views of Foreign Minister Bhutto, the group pressed Ayub to adopt an aggressive strategy. Alarmed by Indian moves in December 1964 to complete Kashmir's political integration into India, the hard-liners argued that Pakistan needed to act quickly before Kashmir became just another Indian state and the world forgot about the problem.

Emboldened by the then-fashionable concept of wars of national liberation, especially after the success of the Algerians in their struggle against the French, the cell recommended a somewhat similar strategy in Kashmir. The bold proposal called for covertly infiltrating a large number of men from the Pakistan-controlled portion of Kashmir (called Azad Kashmir, or "Free Kashmir") to carry out widespread acts of sabotage and arson in the part of Kashmir that India controlled. The aim was to ignite the flame of what the hawks believed was an incipient revolutionary situation in the Kashmir Valley. A presumed harsh Indian military response, the Pakistani hawks believed, would spark further trouble inside Kashmir, anger Muslim opinion throughout the world, and provide an excuse for the Pakistani army to intervene in southern Kashmir to cut off Indian forces in the north. Bhutto, Ahmed, and other cell members assumed that, as the situation deteriorated, the United States and the international community would not sit still but would intervene to force serious negotiations over the disputed state.

Ever since its 1962 war with China, India had seemed a much-diminished country, and it was against this background that the Kashmir cell thought the strategy made sense. Nehru's successor, the diminutive and frail Shastri, appeared to be a weak leader. Militarily, India's reputation stood at its nadir after the defeat by the Chinese and the poor showing in the Rann of Kutch encounter. Strengthened by a decade of U.S. military assistance and training, the Pakistani military appeared the equal of India's larger but less well equipped forces. New Delhi, however, had embarked on a major defense buildup after the Chinese debacle. Given India's far larger economic base, it was only a matter of time until Pakistan would lose its military advantage. As Bhutto wrote Ayub in May 1965, the current "relative superiority of the military forces of Pakistan in terms of quality and equipment" was in danger of being overtaken as India's defense buildup progressed.[52]

When the Kashmir cell first put its proposal to Ayub in February 1965, he flatly rejected the idea. "Who authorized the Foreign Office and the ISI [Inter-Services Intelligence Directorate] to draw up such a plan?" the president asked. "All I asked them was to keep the situation in Kashmir under review. They can't force a campaign of military action on the Government."[53] Despite this firm "No," the Kashmir cell did not give up and continued to press the president to accept the plan. After India's poor showing in the Rann of Kutch, the usually cautious Ayub gave the green light on May 13, 1965.[54]

The goal of Operation Gibraltar, as the proposal was called, was to "defreeze the Kashmir problem, weaken Indian resolve, and bring [India] to the conference table without provoking a general war."[55] But the proposal was seriously flawed. First, the belief that the Kashmiris would rise in support of the intruders was a leap of faith not justified by any solid intelligence. Second, the assumption that Shastri would limit India's military response to Kashmir and not strike across the international boundary in the Punjab to relieve pressure to the north was a bad misreading of Indian intentions. Third, puffed up by their victory in the Rann of Kutch, the Pakistanis mistakenly believed that India's forces would prove no match militarily. Finally, the hawks wrongly concluded that the United States and other countries would engage themselves to force a Kashmir settlement rather than permit an India-Pakistan conflict.

Operation Gibraltar began on August 5–6, 1965. In short order, the Indians gained the upper hand. Even though the intruders were able to cause a certain amount of disorder and disruption, few Kashmiris cooperated and Indian security forces were able to capture many of the infiltrators. It was clear by late August that Operation Gibraltar was failing. Although Ayub could have cut his losses, he unwisely decided to up the ante by trying to cut off the Indian military in Kashmir. On August 31, Pakistan sent a large armored force, including several dozen U.S.-supplied Patton tanks, across the cease-fire line in southern Kashmir toward Akhnur, strategically located on the road to Srinagar that was the sole access to the valley from India. By capturing Akhnur, Pakistan would cut off Indian troops in Kashmir. Komer alerted President Johnson that "having failed to spark a 'war of liberation' via a Kashmiri uprising, [the Pakistanis] may now feel they've got to enter the lists directly to forestall a humiliating failure."[56]

When UN Secretary-General U Thant urged a halt in hostilities, Secretary Rusk called in the Indian and Pakistani ambassadors to second the appeal. As the scope of the fighting broadened, both countries charged that the other was using American-supplied equipment, contrary to U.S. stipulations that this not be permitted. Meanwhile, Johnson decided, "given existing strains in our relations with both parties, . . . not to engage in direct pressure on either Pak[istanis] or Indians for time being, but to place primary reliance on [the] UN."[57] In his September 4, 1965, response to a message from Ayub, the U.S. president urged Pakistan to accept U Thant's call for an end to the fighting.[58]

On September 6, 1965, the conflict became a full-scale war. India struck across the international border in the Punjab to relieve pressure on Kashmir, sending several divisions toward Lahore, which lay only fourteen miles from the frontier. Ayub and Bhutto met with McConaughy that same morning to inform him officially of the Indian attack and to plead for U.S. support. Presenting the U.S. envoy an aide-mémoire, the president called on the United States to take immediate action under the 1959 U.S.-Pakistan bilateral agreement and the November 5, 1962, aide-mémoire. The Pakistani communication stated, "As Pakistan has become a victim of naked aggression by armed attack on the part of India, the Government of Pakistan requests the Government of the United States to act immediately to suppress and vacate the aggression." Even though Ayub did not deny that Pakistan had organized the infiltration into Kashmir and was using U.S.-supplied equipment, the president still asked for support. When McConaughy stressed the role of the UN, Ayub countered, "You are on trial. You cannot hedge or hide from this obligation."[59]

The same morning, an angry, "almost hysterical" Pakistani army commander, Gen. Mohammed Musa, speaking with the U.S. military assistance chief, Maj. Gen. Robert Burns, condemned America for providing military aid to India. Musa said that his country had "burned her bridges" in accepting U.S. military assistance and was now paying the price.[60] During a press conference at midnight on September 5, an emotional Foreign Minister Bhutto declared that Pakistan expected "not only moral and diplomatic but tangible military support from allies and associates." The future course of Pakistan's relations with all countries of the world "would depend on [the] attitude they took in the present crisis," Bhutto stated.[61] In effect, Pakistan's stance was that stirring the pot in Kashmir—and even sending infiltrators across the cease-fire line—was acceptable, but India's attack across the international frontier was "naked aggression" and an act of war.

Washington did not see things the same way. In the face of a "volcanic" reaction in the U.S. Congress, the Johnson administration announced on September 8, 1965, that it was suspending military and economic aid to both India and Pakistan.[62] U Thant flew off to South Asia the same day in a vain effort to get the two parties to stop the fighting. The fact that the Soviet Union, in the wake of the Ayub visit and during a period of reduced tensions with the United States, was at the time not following a totally pro-India stance made it possible for the UN to play a meaningful role in trying to stop the war.

On September 9, 1965, McConaughy and Bhutto argued heatedly after the U.S. envoy formally advised that Washington was embargoing arms shipments. Bhutto vehemently charged that this action would not further the prospects for peace. Washington was rewarding Indian aggression, he stated, and badly treating an ally dependent on U.S. military equipment. Charging India with "naked aggression," the foreign minister said, "It is our honor we have to safeguard." McConaughy retorted, "Was this realized when guerrilla operations were started in Kashmir? . . . It was a fateful decision you took to plan, organize, and support the Mujahid [freedom-fighter] operations." Bhutto denied that Pakistan had planned the operations and called the movement a "purely Kashmiri affair."[63] The following day, when McConaughy gave Bhutto the text of the congressional resolution, the foreign minister termed the U.S. decision to stop aid as "one which [if] adhered to, would mean that Pak[istani]-U.S. relations could not be the same again. . . . [T]he decision [was] not an act of an ally and not even that of a neutral."[64]

McConaughy had a less heated conversation with Ayub, also on September 10, 1965, during which the envoy conveyed the official response to Pakistan's request for U.S. help. McConaughy asserted that the United States was implementing its assurances to Pakistan by supporting U Thant's peace efforts. Washington considered India's attack across the international border a most serious development, but noted that Pakistan had triggered the crisis by infiltrating large numbers across the cease-fire line in Kashmir.[65]

The war front in the Punjab witnessed some of the largest tank battles since World War II. After a series of fierce armor attacks and counterattacks, Indian and Pakistani forces bogged down in hard but indecisive combat on the outskirts of Lahore and further to the north near the city of Sialkot. According to Altaf Gauhar, Ayub Khan realized on September 11, 1965, that "for Pakistan the war was over" after a major counteroffensive south of Lahore ran out of steam. In view of the losses Pakistani forces had suffered and growing shortages of ammunition and other supplies, the president knew it was only a matter of time until his military would be defeated.[66] Until mid-September, the Pakistani media had reported the war as a series of sweeping victories and major Indian defeats. The tone then subtly began to shift from the need to continue the fighting "to a discussion of how peace can be brought about."[67] During a September 15, 1965, press conference, Ayub took up this theme, appealing for U.S. intervention to end the war.[68]

Lyndon Johnson, however, refused to bite. In a September 17, 1965, meeting with top advisers, the president declared, "We cannot get involved in unilateral approaches" and insisted on continuing to back UN peace efforts. "I made up my mind last April we simply were out of business with Ayub and Shastri until we sign a contract," Johnson told Rusk, McNamara, and the others present. "We are now in a position to tell them to quit fighting or else we will do no more business with them."[69] Although U.S. intelligence did not think Chinese military intervention likely, the Americans, the British, and the Soviets redoubled efforts to bring about an end to the conflict.

According to Altaf Gauhar, Ayub and Bhutto flew secretly to Beijing to meet with Premier Zhou Enlai the night of September 19–20, 1965, and returned twenty-four hours later. Zhou reportedly told the Pakistanis that the Chinese were prepared to help by maintaining pressure on India in the Himalayas "for as long as necessary." The Chinese leader stressed that Pakistan "must keep up the fighting even if [its troops] have to withdraw to the hills," but Ayub was not psychologically ready for a prolonged guerrilla war. It was simply not within the ken of the Sandhurst-trained Pakistani leader to consider retreating to the hills to fight against the Indians as the Chinese communists had in their struggle against the nationalists.[70] As Altaf Gauhar put it, "Neither Ayub nor Bhutto were prepared for this. The whole Foreign Office strategy was designed as a quick-fix to force the Indians to the negotiating table. Ayub had never foreseen the possibility of the Indians surviving a couple of hard knocks, and Bhutto had never envisaged a long drawn out people's war."[71]

After returning from China, Ayub reportedly wavered between continuing the struggle or throwing in the towel in response to pressure from Washington, London, Moscow, and his own military. The best the United States would offer in pressing Pakistan to accept a cease-fire was to agree to the need for a Kashmir settlement. Johnson refused to commit to any particular solution and at the same time warned Ayub that he would assume collusion if Pakistan rejected the cease-fire and the Chinese moved militarily against India.[72]

In the end, Ayub gave way, sending Bhutto to New York to attend the Security Council deliberations. In a fiery speech, the foreign minister suggested that Pakistan would continue to fight unless it got its way on Kashmir and gave no indication that his country was about to throw in the sponge. Then, just before the cease-fire deadline, he dramatically pulled a cable from his pocket to announce Pakistan's acceptance.[73] If the performance did not impress those sitting in the Security Council chamber, the foreign minister's remarks won wide applause in West Pakistan.

Ayub's own address to the nation was less successful. Trying to make the best of a bad situation, the president called the cease-fire an "end to the firing" not an "end to the fighting." The talk caused widespread unhappiness in West Pakistan, where the cease-fire triggered a psychological backlash among a people led to believe that Pakistan was winning the war. East Pakistan, which felt totally exposed and defenseless during the seventeen-day conflict, welcomed the news.[74]

The 1965 war proved a disaster for Pakistan and for Ayub. Although neither India nor Pakistan gained a decisive military advantage, India won simply by not losing. In the wake of the war, Bhutto might talk with bravado but could not realistically expect New Delhi to give ground on Kashmir or expect the rest of the world to exert itself after Pakistan had tried and failed to resolve the issue through the use of force.

The conflict also set back Pakistan's economic development. Quite apart from the suspension of U.S. aid and a further postponement of the World Bank consortium meeting because of the war, Finance Minister Shoaib found it necessary to divert funds to make up for substantial combat losses. Moreover, the war gravely jeopardized the relationship with the United States, previously the source of half of Pakistan's economic aid and its main military arms supplier.

For Ayub personally, the blow was in its way as heavy as the one that Nehru had suffered from the Sino-Indian war, even if this was less immediately apparent. Before the war, Pakistan's leader was considered a major international figure; after Nehru's death in May 1964, Ayub had become South Asia's most prominent and impressive leader. In less than a decade, he had guided Pakistan from the status of a near basket case onto the road of sustained growth. Ayub appeared to be managing a stable, if not very democratic, political system. Rather like Charles de Gaulle, with whom he was sometimes compared, Ayub had thumbed his nose at the United States without totally fraying alliance links and had succeeded in establishing friendly ties with China, the main U.S. foe in Asia. The 1965 war changed all this. As Altaf Gauhar wrote, "[Ayub] seemed to have lost all power of decision. He continued to agonize over his own mistakes. . . . He knew that Gibraltar was his decision. Others might have used their positions to mislead him but there was no one in the Foreign Office or [General Headquarters] who could have forced him to act against his judgment."[75]

In the wake of the conflict, U.S. prestige in Pakistan slumped to "an all-time low," Komer advised Johnson. Even though the United States considered the suspension of aid justified, since Operation Gibraltar had touched off the fighting, Pakistanis felt bitterly let down and betrayed by their ally. After the war ended, the government-controlled media continued to fuel anti-U.S. and pro-Chinese sentiments.[76] "Bitterness toward the U.S. is deep-seated," a State Department research memorandum declared.[77]

Internationally, it was the Soviet Union, not the United States, that offered its good offices to try to patch things up between India and Pakistan, proposing to host peace talks at Tashkent. Ayub at first rejected the idea, but in November 1965 he reluctantly agreed. The Pakistani leader was disturbed that the British and the Americans seemed to be allowing the Soviets, India's long-time friends, to step forward as the peacemaker for the subcontinent. Since opposing communist involvement in the region had been the principal goal of U.S. South Asia policy, it was a startling development that Washington actively supported the Soviet initiative for peace talks at Tashkent. Secretary of State Dean Rusk explained: "We encouraged the Russians to go ahead with the Tashkent idea, because we felt we had nothing to lose. If they succeeded in bringing about any detente at Tashkent, then there would be more peace on the subcontinent and we would gain from that fact. If the Russians failed at Tashkent, at least the Russians would have the experience of some of the frustration that we had for twenty years in trying to sort out things between India and Pakistan."[78]

Ayub Visits Washington: "Pathetic and Sad"

Ayub visited Washington on December 14–16, 1965. Shortly before the Pakistani leader's arrival, the White House summed up U.S. thinking for the press. In order to resume aid, President Johnson wanted "to be sure that peace has returned between India and Pakistan." It was disappointing, according to the press spokesperson, that "Pak[istani] foreign policy has made it increasingly difficult to defend such massive aid before Congress just at a time when that aid was really beginning to show results." Regarding China, he said, "[T]he U.S. cannot cavil at normal Pak[istani] relations . . . but it can hardly be expected to support—however indirectly—any . . . alignment [between the Pakistanis and the Chinese intended] to squeeze India."[79]

When the two leaders met—their first face-to-face encounter since July 1961—Ayub was a chastened and diminished figure. After they

President Mohammed Ayub Khan gets the "LBJ treatment" from President Lyndon B. Johnson at the White House state dinner, December 1965. (Courtesy of the Lyndon B. Johnson Library.)

talked alone, Johnson praised the visitor before assembled U.S. and Pakistani advisers, declaring, "Our people must be friends, we must find out what went wrong and erase it and we are going to do just that." The U.S. president said that "[h]e was proud of the association between America and Pakistan, and especially of President Ayub, one of [the] truly great leaders [of that time]."[80]

Responding with "no warmth at all" and "almost as a formality," Ayub expressed affection for Johnson. Admitting that there had been differences between the two countries, he said he did not want to blame America because it could be argued the world had changed and the security pacts had lost their relevance.[81] In a muted tone, Ayub gave his perspective about the "drift" in U.S.-Pakistan relations. India's military buildup, he declared, was directed mainly against Pakistan, not against China. He urged, almost plaintively, that the United States remain active in South Asia. "A gesture towards settling Indo-Pak[istani] disputes would be enormously appreciated."[82]

During a second meeting alone, Johnson urged Ayub to do his best on Kashmir at Tashkent. If that failed, the United States would try to

President Johnson leans in to talk with President Ayub (at left) during the White House state dinner, December 1965. Foreign Minister Zulfikar Ali Bhutto is on Ayub's left. (Courtesy of the Lyndon B. Johnson Library.)

help, the U.S. president said, but Ayub should "not be under any illusion" that Washington could force a settlement. Turning to Vietnam, Johnson stated that although he would not "ask" Pakistan to send troops, he would like to have them there under the umbrella of SEATO.

Ayub remained preoccupied with India. "I know you won't believe it," he declared, "but those Indians are going to gobble us up." Johnson replied that if the Indians tried, the United States would stop them. At the same time, he stressed that Pakistan could not tell the United States how it should handle India. "We give India food or anything else we want. Our India policy is our business." Expressing understanding, Ayub asked Johnson, "What if the Indians try to knock us off?" "We would not let them," was Johnson's reply. Ayub said that was all he wanted to know. He was not seeking economic or military aid at this point, only the reassurance "you have given me."

On China, the U.S. president flatly told Ayub that if Pakistan wanted close relations with the United States, "there could be no serious relationship with China." But, Johnson added, he "understood certain relationships just as a wife could understand a Saturday night fling by her husband so long as she was the wife." Ayub said that his country's "first obligation was to the United States and there were no [security] agreements of any kind with China." Presumably to boost the visitor's sagging morale, Johnson emphasized "how close he felt to Ayub, his fear, his problems. . . . [Johnson] would no more think about injuring Lady Bird than he would Ayub."[83]

When the two leaders rejoined their advisers, Johnson summarized the discussion and expressed his regret that the visit had not taken place "a year or two earlier." Johnson said that he "had made clear to President Ayub that if the Pakistani people are in danger of being gobbled up the United States would be there just as [it is] in Vietnam. President Ayub had come asking for nothing but was going away with everything—with our friendship, our confidence, and our trust."[84]

Ayub was far less effusive, saying that he "wished the United States had felt the same way a few months ago when Pakistan's life was being threatened."[85] Although Pakistan could not dictate U.S. policy toward India, America should "understand our difficulties and our position. . . . Let us hope we get more comfort in [the] future out of our alliance with the U.S.."[86] A downcast Ayub departed from Washington, according to Altaf Gauhar, disappointed by Johnson's reluctance to reengage U.S. influence in South Asia and his willingness to leave peacemaking to the Soviets.[87] For his part, Johnson found the Pakistani president "much chastened . . . subdued, pathetic and sad. . . . He had gone on an adventure and been licked."[88]

Tashkent and After

At the Tashkent conference, in the first week of January 1966, Ayub reluctantly agreed to sign the Soviet-brokered declaration when pressed to the wall by Premier Alexei Kosygin. The accord simply returned the situation in South Asia to where it had been before the war. Pakistan failed to achieve its main aim: a self-executing mechanism to solve the Kashmir dispute. When Indian prime minister Shastri died of a heart attack just hours after signing the Tashkent declaration, the Soviet-sponsored peace deliberations came to a tragic end.

Although the India-Pakistan accord pleased the United States, the reaction in Pakistan was sour. To a public brainwashed by media reports of glowing military victories, Ayub's failure to make progress toward a Kashmir solution and his acceptance of the status quo ante were hard medicine. Given the meager results, people asked why Pakistan had shed the blood of so many of its young men against India. Especially in West Pakistan, where anti-Indian and anti-U.S. feelings remained at a fever pitch, the public increasingly blamed Ayub for failing to reap the fruits of Pakistan's supposed victory.

The most prominent figure to turn against the Tashkent declaration was Foreign Minister Bhutto. Ironically, although the intellectual father of Operation Gibraltar, Bhutto was able to absolve himself of responsibility for the consequences of the war. The foreign minister spread the word that if Ayub had heeded his advice and not bowed to Western pressures for a cease-fire, Pakistan would have prevailed militarily. Over the course of several months, Bhutto adroitly transformed himself from Ayub's loyal lieutenant into his acerbic critic.

In Washington, an ever-upbeat Komer advised Lyndon Johnson that the talks with Ayub had halted the downward trend in U.S.-Pakistan relations and that developments were moving in the right direction: "Ayub made clear that he regarded us as his ally and would not tie [Pakistan] up with China, in return for [Johnson's] promise that we would not let India gobble up Pakistan. The game is by no means over, and could be upset if Bhutto got rid of Ayub rather than vice versa. . . . But the odds are favorable if we resume aid just fast enough to convince the Pak[istanis] that full resumption is in the cards if they behave, yet . . . slowly enough to force Ayub to match it with performance."[89]

A month later, on February 15, 1966, Johnson used the occasion of a stop in Pakistan by Vice President Hubert Humphrey during an Asia trip to turn the economic aid tap back on. Humphrey informed Ayub that the United States was prepared to provide a $50 million commodity loan, to start negotiations on food aid, and to relax the ban on arms transfers to permit some commercial and credit sales of nonlethal military equipment.[90] Yet doubts persisted about Ayub's relations with China, especially after a state visit for China's President Liu Shaoqi was scheduled for late March 1966.

Just before the Chinese leader's arrival, Ambassador McConaughy expressed U.S. regrets about Pakistan's receiving Liu "at a time of international bad behavior by the [Chinese]" and expressed the hope that the public welcome would be kept within bounds. Ayub answered testily that public enthusiasm for the Chinese must be expected: "After all, [the Chinese] came to our aid with unconditional offers of assistance when our national existence was at stake. That our people cannot forget."[91] As a sop to the Americans, however, Ayub dispatched Bhutto to attend CENTO and SEATO ministerial meetings, which the foreign minister had pointedly skipped in the previous year.

Washington found Ayub's balancing act sufficiently ambiguous that it held back from giving the green light for a full resumption of economic aid and rebuffed a proposed visit to the United States by Finance Minister Shoaib. In mid-April 1966, the finance minister came anyway. In economic terms, the argument for helping Pakistan's development remained strong. Despite the fact that the Indo-Pakistani war had caused a 20 percent shortfall in Islamabad's budget for the year, the deficiency could be made up if U.S. aid were resumed in the near future. The Johnson administration had to ask itself whether it was wise to further crimp Pakistan's growth—and a possible foreign-assistance success story—by continuing to go slowly on resuming aid. In addition to economic damage, the U.S. stance was further hurting Ayub's political position, already weakened by the war and the outcome of Tashkent.

In Washington, Shoaib sought an early resumption of commodity lending, additional food aid, and approval for a long-pending steel-mill project proposed for Karachi. Apart from the status of the steel mill as a sign of economic modernization, the proposal was sensitive because the United States had muscled out a lower-cost German steel proposal with the promise of U.S. aid in 1961. Since then, consideration of the project had dragged on inconclusively because of additional, time-consuming feasibility studies and a funding dispute between the Export-Import Bank and AID. When Shoaib met with Walt Rostow, who had replaced Bundy as Johnson's national security adviser, the Pakistani argued forcefully—but with some exaggeration—that the steel mill was "the biggest single thing we could do to restore U.S.-Pakistan relations."

The finance minister also stressed his country's willingness to act reasonably with India. Shoaib said Pakistan was ready to export natural gas to India, to cooperate in an international effort to develop the waters of the Ganges-Brahmaputra basin, and to work with the World Bank in negotiating a mutual arms-expenditure ceiling. To meet U.S. concerns that higher defense spending would reduce development outlays, Shoaib said that any additional spending on arms would be funded by special taxes, not by tapping the development budget.[92] After discussion with Rusk and Rostow, Johnson responded positively. He approved

$140 million of commodity aid, or roughly the prewar level, and the negotiation of a food aid program. Regarding the steel mill, the president said that if the bilateral political climate remained satisfactory, he was in principle willing to approve the project later in the year.[93]

With the renewed flow of U.S. aid funds and a reasonably successful consortium meeting, the outlook for the Pakistani economy brightened. U.S. experts saw the prospect of an early breakthrough in food-grain production if the higher level of assistance were sustained. Pakistan seemed posed for a genuine leap forward—the green revolution—through improved seeds, better use of fertilizers and water, and agricultural marketing and policy reforms.

Although Shoaib succeeded in getting the U.S. aid tap turned back on, he did not have long to enjoy this success. In the summer of 1966, Ayub dropped Bhutto as foreign minister, a move that greatly pleased Washington, and then balanced this and upset Washington by letting his finance minister go. Shoaib's departure, however, did not portend a change in economic policy: his less well known successor, M. I. Uquali, continued Shoaib's free-market policies, although he lacked his predecessor's prestige and close ties with the Americans. After Ayub dropped Shoaib, the latter returned quietly to a senior post at the World Bank.

In contrast, Bhutto's departure was anything but quiet. A large crowd of supporters cheered the former foreign minister when he left for Europe "on sick leave." After returning to Pakistan in the fall of 1966, he launched the Pakistan Peoples Party, an anti-Ayub political movement that espoused populist economic policies and a pro-China, anti-U.S., and anti-India foreign policy. That Bhutto had genuine political charisma soon became clear. His emotional yet articulate speeches drew large, cheering crowds, and a wide spectrum of nonestablishment opinion in West Pakistan found his message appealing.

April 1967: A New U.S. Arms Supply Policy

Resuming U.S. military aid to Pakistan proved a much more controversial issue than restarting economic aid. As soon as Washington and Rawalpindi were again on speaking terms, Ayub began to press for equipment and spares to make up for the major losses suffered during the war. Since the United States had provided almost all of Pakistan's military equipment, the September 1965 arms suspension had hit

Islamabad far harder than it did New Delhi. India had received relatively little from the United States, had a growing domestic defense industry, and received substantial military help from the Soviet Union.

In March 1966, Johnson approved a modest easing of the arms embargo to permit Pakistan to obtain "nonlethal" equipment. To avoid criticism that he was fueling further conflict between India and Pakistan, the export of "lethal" items—i.e., tanks, fighter aircraft, artillery, etc.—continued to be barred. Even though the U.S. intention was to "relieve some of the pressures" on Ayub to turn to the Chinese for military equipment,[94] the measure did not help much in terms of replenishing war losses. China, in fact, stepped in to replace the United States as Pakistan's main arms supplier, providing substantial amounts of equipment, including MiG-19 fighter aircraft and T-54 tanks.

In a further sign of interest in rebuilding relations, Johnson replaced career diplomat Walter McConaughy in mid-1966 with a Texas political friend, Eugene Murphy Locke, who had direct access to the president. Locke's instructions from Johnson were to "keep President Ayub happy."[95] Soon after arriving in Pakistan, the new ambassador became embroiled in a heated debate over arms policy with Chester Bowles, whom Johnson had retained as U.S. envoy to India. At dispute was whether to provide Pakistan with $8 million worth of spare parts for lethal equipment. When Locke argued that the United States should be forthcoming "to maximize the chances of improving our position in Pakistan and to limit that of Communist China,"[96] Bowles countered that this would wreck the chances for India-Pakistan arms limitations and severely damage U.S.-India relations.[97]

Despite the fact that Locke sharply criticized Bowles in private messages to Johnson[98] and warned in a September 27, 1966, embassy cable, "[W]e are losing our chips in Pakistan by our indecision,"[99] the president proved unwilling in the end to increase the flow of arms to any substantial degree. This foot-dragging reflected the lower priority for India and Pakistan after their 1965 war, Washington's reluctance to resume an extensive military supply with either country, and Johnson's absorption with the war in Vietnam. In fact, in early 1967, Johnson sent Locke to Saigon as deputy ambassador after less than a year in Pakistan. During that short tenure, however, Locke was able to take some of the chill out of relations, establishing warm ties with Ayub and convincing him that Locke was "a friend . . . when it came to dealing with Washington."[100]

Consideration of the issue of South Asia arms policy dragged on for nearly a year, until April 1967. Johnson then finally decided that the United States would sell spare parts for previously supplied U.S. equipment but would not provide financial credits or grant military assistance. The door remained closed against the export of tanks, fighter and bomber aircraft, and artillery to Pakistan.[101] Although Ayub was pleased to receive spare parts to help maintain U.S.-origin equipment, the April 1967 policy meant a far more restrictive and narrower military supply relationship with the United States.

Neither Pakistan nor India was happy with the policy. Dissatisfied with the narrowness of the supply pipeline, the Pakistanis charged that they continued to be let down badly by their supposed ally. The Indians were even louder in their criticism—ironically, since, relatively speaking, they had the most to gain from the new approach. New Delhi, however, feared that the April 1967 decision marked only a first step toward rebuilding the U.S.-Pakistan security relationship. Pakistan more accurately understood that it could no longer count on America for more than marginal military support.[102]

After a decade of heavy engagement in South Asian security issues, the Johnson administration essentially gave up in frustration and was willing to accept a more passive role in the competition with the Soviet Union and China for influence in the region. Under the 1967 arms supply policy, the United States kept its hand in play, but just barely. Nonetheless, Johnson still hoped to better relations with Pakistan if this were possible without paying too high a price. On December 22, 1967, the president met Ayub briefly at Karachi airport en route home from a trip to Vietnam. In addition to agreeing to help Pakistan with additional supplies of vegetable oil and wheat, Johnson said that he would explore the possibility of replacing aging World War II–vintage Sherman tanks with more modern Patton tanks.[103]

During the remainder of Johnson's term in the White House, according to James Spain, then in charge of Pakistan at the State Department, U.S. officials scoured the globe trying to locate tanks that could be transferred to Pakistan, since the arms policy ruled out sending them from the United States. At first, Belgium, Italy, and Germany were ready to oblige, but they pulled back mainly for domestic political reasons. Turkey was possible source, but it expected to receive more in return than Washington was willing to provide. In the end, the search for the tanks proved fruitless.[104]

Presidents Johnson and Ayub confer at the Karachi airport, December 1967. (Courtesy of the Lyndon B. Johnson Library.)

Pakistan's response to the more restrictive U.S. arms supply policy was not long in coming. When Ayub paid a second visit to the Soviet Union in late 1967 and Prime Minister Kosygin traveled to Pakistan in April 1968, a bargain was struck. In an effort to offset Chinese influence in Pakistan and to further reduce the U.S. position, the Soviets offered Ayub expanded economic aid and, for the first time, some military equipment.[105] In return, Ayub decided not to extend the lease of the U.S. communications intercept facility at Badaber, which was due to expire in 1969. Had Ayub not acted, the lease would have automatically been renewed for another ten years.[106] Washington was unhappy to lose Badaber but accepted that this was a not unnatural consequence of events. In any case, after U.S. space satellites capable of intercepting Soviet communications had become operational in the mid-1960s, the Badaber facility had been reduced in importance. A memo from Acting Secretary of State Nicholas Katzenbach advised Johnson that the loss of Badaber did not represent a major setback to U.S. intelligence capabilities.[107]

Even though Pakistan nominally remained a U.S. ally in 1969, Ayub, in effect, had completed the shift to neutralism that George Ball foresaw after his September 1963 talks. Nowhere was this more apparent than in the contrast between Pakistan's reaction to the Soviet military crackdown in 1956 in Hungary and its response to the similar Soviet action in 1968 in Czechoslovakia. In the case of Hungary, Pakistan, then the United States's "most allied ally in Asia," vehemently criticized Moscow's action. Twelve years later, Pakistan adopted a quite different stance during the UN deliberations. Pakistan's UN ambassador, Agha Shahi, abstained on the anti-Soviet resolution. A State Department intelligence note described his statement on Czechoslovakia as just "short of obvious alignment with the Soviets."[108]

Ayub in Political Trouble

Domestically, Ayub Khan never fully recovered from the consequences of the 1965 war. In East Pakistan, the sense of helplessness and insecurity during the conflict fanned long-standing Bengali grievances against West Pakistan, sparking the call for far greater political and economic autonomy embodied in the "Six Points" program of the Awami League. Leading the cry was Sheikh Mujibur Rahman, a rising and popular Bengali politician who had assumed the party's leadership after the death of H. S. Suhrawardy in 1963. Mujibur Rahman's arrest on charges of conspiring with the Indians made him a hero in East Pakistan. In West Pakistan, Ayub's former protégé Bhutto had artfully moved into a position of leadership among the political opposition. His Pakistan Peoples Party lambasted Ayub for giving too much away at Tashkent, for failing to continue the struggle for Kashmir, and for failing to pursue economic policies that benefited the poor masses.

Setbacks to the economy as a result of both the 1965 war and poor monsoons had sparked criticism that only a new and wealthy capitalist class was reaping the gains from Ayub's free-enterprise policies. The president's no-nonsense secularist approach had angered pro-Islamic elements. His disdain for democracy had earned the enmity of lawyers, students, and intellectuals. After nine years of rule by Ayub, corruption was again becoming a way of life in Pakistan. Particularly damaging was the widespread belief that Ayub's eldest son, Gauhar Ayub, fattened his wallet by taking advantage of the family name.

The shakiness of the Pakistani president's position became more evident in early 1968 after a severe case of pneumonia effectively sidelined Ayub for several months. Having removed Bhutto and other potential rivals, the president stood alone. During his illness, according to Altaf Gauhar, the government ran largely on inertia.[109] Having never succeeded in winning the affection of his people—as a more charismatic leader might have—foreign and economic policy setbacks cost Ayub their respect. His illness revealed that he was far more vulnerable than imagined.

In a serious public relations blunder, the regime launched a major publicity campaign to celebrate ten years of Ayub's presidency as the "Decade of Development." Opponents took to the streets in protest. With a new round of elections slated for 1970, opposition politicians clamored that the indirect voting system be scrapped in favor of universal suffrage. After anti-Ayub demonstrations rocked major cities, the government made matters worse by arresting Bhutto and other opposition leaders. Weakened by his illness, Ayub responded sluggishly to his opponents. He showed little of his old pep or snap. As the Johnson administration ended in January 1969, Ayub was beginning to totter.

A Notional Alliance

The Johnson years witnessed a fundamental shift in U.S.-Pakistan relations. When Johnson became president after Kennedy's assassination, relations were at a "standoff" over U.S. military aid to India and Pakistan's flirtation with China. In his rough-hewn Texan fashion, Johnson twisted Ayub's arm to limit Pakistan's relationship with Beijing as the price for continued large-scale economic aid. When the pressure tactics failed and Pakistan and India went to war over Kashmir in 1965, Johnson largely gave up on Pakistan. With the Vietnam War at its peak, the United States lost interest in the subcontinent. By the time Johnson left office in January 1969, the alliance was over in all but name and the United States was no longer trying to serve as South Asia's security manager. Even though Washington continued to provide substantial economic assistance, it had drastically restricted the military supply relationship.

A proud Pathan, Ayub had refused to give up his country's new friendship with China to satisfy the Americans, who he felt had threatened Pakistan's security by agreeing to long-term military aid to India.

But an overconfident Pakistani president made a major misjudgment in concluding that he could have a warm relationship with China and still maintain intimate security ties with the United States. With Lyndon Johnson as president, this was not possible.

After the United States not only refused to help against India during the 1965 war but suspended aid, the Pakistanis felt betrayed. As the alliance relationship shriveled, the one substantial quid pro quo that Pakistan had provided the Americans—the Badaber intelligence facility—became a casualty. For all practical purposes, the U.S.-Pakistan alliance had become a notional affair by the time Pakistan's old friend Richard Nixon defeated Vice President Hubert Humphrey in the 1968 presidential elections.

7

Nixon: The Tilt

Pakistan had greatly changed during the eight years since Richard Nixon had ended his term as vice president in January 1961. At that time, President Ayub Khan was considered a valued ally who was doing a creditable, if not very democratic, job of managing his country. In January 1969, when Nixon became president, Ayub's regime was crumbling.

To maintain order in the streets against antigovernment demonstrators, the Pakistani president found it necessary to deploy the army in Karachi, Lahore, Dacca, and other major cities.[1] Ayub's willingness to negotiate with opposition leaders, not to run in the 1970 elections, and to shift from a presidential to a parliamentary system failed to restore calm.[2]

Although Ayub wanted the military to intervene, his service chiefs were reluctant and pressed the president to work out a political settlement. Ayub tried but failed to reach agreement with key opposition leaders, including Awami League chief Sheikh Mujibur Rahman, whom Ayub had reluctantly released from a prison term for charges of conspiring with India. The principal stumbling block in the negotiations was the extent of autonomy that East Pakistan would enjoy—which was the issue that in 1971 would lead to the breakup of the country.

With no agreement in sight, a tired and dejected Ayub resigned on March 25, 1969, handing power over to Army chief Gen. Mohammed Yahya Khan. In his farewell radio address, the once-proud Ayub declared, "I cannot preside over the destruction of my country."[3] Yahya then proclaimed martial law and abrogated the 1962 constitution.

Martial Law Once More

Unlike in 1958, the Pakistani military did not have an action plan when it assumed power in 1969. Fun-loving, easygoing Yahya Khan was a striking contrast to sober, serious, and hard-working Ayub. In another departure from Ayub's example, Yahya ruled as first among equals, in effect sharing power with his senior colleagues. Although the tragic events of 1971 would reveal Yahya as sadly out of his depth, his initial months as president seemed promising. The country quickly appeared to return to normal. Economic life resumed. Even though Yahya banned public meetings, he did not jail the politicians, who were quietly content to let the dust settle.

U.S.-Pakistan relations had dramatically deteriorated during the Kennedy and Johnson administrations. Despite the fact that the United States remained Pakistan's largest source of economic aid, it no longer provided security assistance. CENTO and SEATO had become largely paper alliances. Pakistanis deeply resented the treatment received during the 1965 war and firmly believed that they had been betrayed by the Americans. But when Richard Nixon moved into the White House, Islamabad had reason to hope for better days.

An old friend of Pakistan, Nixon had visited the country five times, twice as vice president and three times after he left that office. Ayub had wisely given Nixon a red-carpet welcome during his travels as a private citizen. In contrast, the Indians received him with the minimum courtesy consistent with protocol.[4] As president-elect, Nixon wrote to foreign leaders urging them to maintain direct contact with him after he occupied the Oval Office. In his letter to Ayub, Nixon added a personal note, "I shall always be grateful for the courtesies extended to me on my visits to Pakistan."[5]

As Nixon settled into the presidency, he nonetheless continued the South Asia policy that he inherited, "except to adopt a somewhat warmer tone toward Pakistan," according to Henry Kissinger, the Harvard professor whom Nixon had named as his national security adviser. "Our policy objective on the subcontinent was, quite simply, to avoid adding another complication to our agenda," Kissinger wrote in his memoirs.[6] In Asia, the administration's major goal was to disengage U.S. military forces from Vietnam without appearing to lose the war. Nixon's solution was the gradual withdrawal of American troops and the shift of the military burden to South Vietnamese forces—the policy of "Vietnamization."

A brief visit to South Asia in May 1969 by the new secretary of state, William Rogers, provided the Nixon administration's first high-level contact with the Yahya regime. During Rogers's stop in Lahore, on May 24, 1969, Pakistan's new leader sounded an old refrain, pressing the visitor to ease U.S. restrictions on the supply of arms. Rogers's comments to the press that administration proposals would "go a long way to meeting Pakistan's requirements" were soothing words to his hosts.[7]

Yahya's main focus lay on domestic affairs. To reduce discontent, he announced a number of popular changes, including an increased share of development spending for East Pakistan and the redivision of West Pakistan into four separate provinces. He also lifted the ban on political activity and announced that national elections would be held in 1970.[8] At the same time, Yahya accepted Bengali demands that National Assembly seats be allocated on the basis of one man, one vote—i.e., population rather than parity between East and West Pakistan—thereby assuring a majority for the more populous east. The one key issue that he did not address was the extent of provincial autonomy, the issue on which Ayub and Mujib had been unable to agree and which would become the major dispute once more with East Pakistan after the 1970 elections.

The inexperience of Pakistan's new president in handling foreign affairs soon became apparent. In May 1969, Soviet premier Alexei Kosygin paid his second visit within a year to Pakistan, this time presumably to size up the post-Ayub leadership.[9] At immediate issue was a proposal by Kosygin to open up transit trade across Pakistan and Afghanistan to permit increased economic activity between the Soviet Union and South Asia. Although Yahya readily agreed with this proposal, he had to back off in the face of stiff opposition from the foreign ministry and his military colleagues. The plan would have risked involving Pakistan in an anti-Chinese grouping—the Sino-Soviet split was then at its height after the March 1969 border clashes between the two powers—and would have meant renewed trade with India, which had been banned by Islamabad since the 1965 war.[10] The episode revealed a major weakness of Yahya's: his tendency to act before thinking through the consequences.

In June 1969, when Pakistan's president paid an official visit to Moscow, he probed about additional Soviet military assistance. Kosygin stressed that Pakistan could not "be on friendly terms at the same time with China and with the Soviet Union."[11] If Islamabad wanted more Soviet arms aid, it would have to distance itself from Beijing. This was a step that Yahya and his colleagues were unwilling to take.[12] Given New Delhi's increasing unhappiness about the Soviets' sending arms to Pakistan and Yahya's unwillingness to reduce ties with Beijing, Moscow decided to revert to a more pro-India stance. Although the Russians delivered the arms that they had previously promised, they made no further military supply commitments to Pakistan.

Nixon Seeks Yahya's Help

Just as the Soviets were refocusing their South Asia policy, Richard Nixon became the second serving U.S. president to visit the subcontinent. In mid-summer 1969, he stopped for a day each in India and Pakistan during a tour that included six Asian countries and Romania.

Presidents Richard Nixon and Yahya Khan watch ceremonies in Lahore, August 1969. (Courtesy of the Nixon Presidential Materials Project.)

After New Delhi's 110-degree heat, Lahore, where it was only 100 degrees, seemed almost comfortable. In contrast to the lower temperature, the official welcome in Lahore was markedly warmer than the reception in New Delhi the day before. After Air Force One touched down, Yahya praised the U.S. president as "an old friend" of Pakistan. In replying, Nixon spoke of his intention "to restore a relationship of friendship based on mutual trust." As far as the public and the bureaucracy were aware, the main issue that the leaders discussed was the U.S. arms-supply policy. The press was told that the administration would be making a decision on this question later in the year.[13]

Vastly more important, but a closely guarded secret, was Nixon's request for Yahya's help in opening up relations between the United States and China. The U.S. president asked that Yahya tell Pakistan's friends in Beijing that Nixon did not believe Asia could "move forward" without China and would not be party to Soviet efforts to isolate the Chinese.[14] Yahya was initially reluctant to become involved, according to Pakistani ambassador to Washington Agha Hilaly, but in the end agreed to raise the subject with the Chinese leadership.[15]

Nixon's request marked the beginning of two years of secret diplomacy between Washington, Islamabad, and Beijing that would culminate in Kissinger's stunning visit to China in July 1971. Ironically, the friendly relationship that Islamabad had developed with Beijing, which the Kennedy and Johnson administrations considered Pakistan's major sin, became its cardinal virtue when Nixon looked for ways to communicate with the Chinese.

The opening to China was an essential element in Nixon's strategy of creating a new global balance of power. His aim was to bring China into the family of nations—reversing two decades of U.S. efforts to isolate Beijing—and to use an improved U.S.-Chinese relationship as a lever with Moscow to press for U.S.-Soviet détente. In contrast to this global "Great Game," South Asia per se had limited importance to the new administration. Only 1 of the 85 pages of the administration's 1970 report to Congress on foreign policy and 3 of the 125 pages in the 1971 report were devoted to the subcontinent. In the latter, the president summed up U.S. policy goals as promoting economic development, addressing humanitarian concerns, and encouraging India and Pakistan to settle their differences. U.S. strategic concerns, Nixon declared, were limited to seeing that neither China nor the Soviet Union gained a dominant position on the subcontinent. Indicating U.S. acceptance of

India's nonalignment and Pakistan's altered foreign policy stance, the report stated, "We have no desire to press on them a closer relationship than their own interest leads them to desire."[16]

On February 22, 1970, Yahya sent word to the White House through Ambassador Hilaly that the Chinese had responded positively to Nixon's overture. The White House reply, which was sent via the Pakistanis, suggested that the two countries seek a more suitable vehicle for bilateral discussions than the stylized dialogue that U.S. and Chinese diplomats had conducted at meetings in Warsaw for nearly two decades. A similar message was passed to Beijing through the Romanians. At this juncture, according to Kissinger, the administration had a "slight preference" for the Pakistani channel, mainly because the fact that Romania was a communist state could complicate matters.[17]

In keeping with the "somewhat warmer tone toward Pakistan," Nixon decided to make a gesture in the area of arms supply. Recognizing that any loosening of the ban on transfers of lethal weapons would disturb the Indians, the bureaucracy pondered for nearly a year over what the gesture would contain and how the package would be presented. It was not until shortly before October 25, 1970, when Yahya was scheduled to attend a White House dinner celebrating the twenty-fifth anniversary of the United Nations, that the U.S. government made up its collective mind. The decision, announced on October 8, 1970, was for a "one-time exception" to permit Pakistan to procure about $50 million worth of replacement aircraft and some three hundred armored personnel carriers. Islamabad welcomed the decision; New Delhi was upset.[18]

While in Washington to attend the UN anniversary dinner, Yahya also met privately with Nixon and Kissinger. The *New York Times* reported that they talked about U.S. military and economic aid to Pakistan and China's relations with Asia.[19] Only a few people, not including Secretary of State Rogers, knew that Nixon had reiterated his interest in better U.S.-China relations. As Yahya was scheduled to visit Beijing the following month, Nixon asked him to tell his hosts in Beijing that the United States regarded rapprochement as "essential," would not join a "condominium" against China, and would be prepared to send a high-level envoy for secret discussions.[20]

At this point, the U.S. ambassador to Pakistan, Joseph Farland, was not informed about Pakistan's role in the exchanges with China. A Republican political appointee, Washington lawyer, and onetime Federal Bureau of Investigation agent, Farland had gained diplomatic experience as ambassador to Panama and to the Dominican Republican during the Eisenhower administration. He was not personally close to Nixon, who gave him no special instructions regarding the assignment to Pakistan when Farland called on the president before departing for Islamabad in late 1969.[21]

Pakistan's First General Elections

During the October 1970 White House meeting with Yahya, Kissinger inquired about the prospects for the elections that were to take place two months later. Pakistan's president replied confidently that numerous political parties would win seats, that there would be quarrels between them, and that he would remain the arbiter of his country's politics.[22] On December 7, 1970, the voters of Pakistan proved Yahya to be a poor political pundit. In East Pakistan, Mujib and his Awami League, campaigning for full regional autonomy, won a nearly total sweep. They gained 160 of 162 seats to obtain an absolute majority in the 300-seat assembly. In West Pakistan, former foreign minister Zulfikar Ali Bhutto's Pakistan Peoples Party (PPP) emerged as the surprise victor. Running on a populist program of "bread, clothing, and shelter," Bhutto gained 81 seats to win a clear majority in the western wing.

Mujib's victory was expected, but not its extent. What turned the anticipated landslide into a political volcano was the central government's sluggish response to a devastating cyclone and tidal wave that killed an estimated two hundred thousand people in East Pakistan. Not until after foreign disaster aid started pouring in did the Pakistani central government mount a substantial relief effort. For the Bengalis, the lackadaisical attitude toward their enormous human tragedy was the final straw.

The day after Pakistan's elections, on December 8, 1970, Ambassador Hilaly delivered another positive message from Chinese premier Zhou Enlai to the White House. In it, Zhou stated that "a special envoy of President Nixon would be most welcome. . . . The United States knows that Pakistan is a great friend of China and therefore we attach great importance to the message."[23]

Yahya had received the text from the Chinese ambassador in Islamabad. He then wrote out the message in longhand for dispatch to Hilaly by a special courier. In keeping with Yahya's instructions, the ambassador read the message to Kissinger but did not leave a copy. The national security adviser wrote down the text himself. Kissinger later gave Hilaly a typed response, which the courier carried back to Islamabad for delivery to the Chinese ambassador. This unusual procedure—designed to minimize the risk of leaks—was followed throughout the secret exchanges. When Kissinger asked Hilaly not to mention these messages to anyone, including Secretary of State Rogers, the ambassador found the request "bizarre," but complied.[24]

During the four months between the December 1970 elections and the March 1971 army crackdown in the east, joy in Pakistan over the country's first democratic elections dissipated. After the three key leaders—Yahya, Mujib, and Bhutto—failed to agree on a constitutional arrangement, a political impasse developed.[25] The heart of the problem remained how to reconcile Bengali demands for autonomy with the survival of a united Pakistan. Although Mujib had told Yahya before the elections that his demands for provincial autonomy were negotiable, the extent of the electoral sweep made the Awami League leader the prisoner of Bengali hard-liners who wanted independence. Instead of compromising, Mujib stonewalled, refusing to travel to Islamabad for political discussions and insisting that Yahya meet with him in Dacca. Bhutto, who was the cleverest but also the most opportunistic of the three key leaders, pressed the military not to yield to Awami League demands after Mujib spurned a power-sharing arrangement with the West Pakistani election winner.

Despite the stalemate, Yahya announced that the assembly would meet on March 3, 1971. Playing the spoiler, Bhutto then declared that he would boycott the session unless Mujib agreed to settle major constitutional issues beforehand. When Mujib refused and Bhutto threatened a general strike in West Pakistan, Yahya postponed the meeting. In the face of a fierce reaction and paralyzing strikes in East Pakistan, however, a vacillating Yahya reversed himself and agreed to convene the assembly later in March. Mujib, however, threatened that he would not attend unless Yahya ended martial law and transferred political power to the Awami League majority.

In this confused and tense atmosphere, Pakistan's president arrived in Dacca on March 15, 1971, supposedly for further negotiations. Professor Golam Wahid Choudhury, a Bengali who served in Yahya's cabinet, described the situation as being "like giving oxygen to a dying patient when the doctors have declared him a lost case."[26] The talks, surprisingly, seemed to be making progress, even as rumors spread that they were simply a charade to permit the Pakistani army to complete its buildup before cracking down in the east. In Lahore, for example, veteran West Pakistani politician Mumtaz Daultana approached the American consulate general to warn that army intervention was imminent and to urge that the United States press Yahya to continue trying for a settlement. Ambassador Farland proposed to Washington on March 10, 1971, that he convey U.S. hopes for a satisfactory resolution of the political crisis. Two days later, the State Department approved his doing so.[27]

On March 23, 1971, normally celebrated as Pakistan Day, the Awami League ruled the streets of Dacca and raised the banner of Bangladesh throughout the city. The green-and-white Pakistani flag flew only in a few places, such as the president's house and the military cantonment. That morning, in what turned out to be the final negotiating session, the Awami League formally rejected the government's proposal and presented its own draft constitution. This called for a "Confederation of Pakistan" that left the central government with negligible powers. The next day, as the crisis atmosphere mounted, the State Department instructed Farland to avoid any further involvement in the political situation. "We do not believe we can play [a] useful role as [a] middleman or mediator in [an] essentially Pakistan[i] domestic concern," the cable stated.[28] By then, outside intervention had become irrelevant, for the Pakistani army had decided to resolve matters by the use of force.

The Army Cracks Down

Yahya departed from Dacca unannounced during the afternoon of March 25, 1971. At 1 A.M. the following day, the Pakistani army implemented its plan to crush the Awami League and its supporters. Broadcasting from Karachi that night, Yahya called Mujib a traitor, blamed him for the crisis, and banned the Awami League. Although the army was able to arrest Mujib at his home, most other Awami League leaders managed to flee. At first, there was considerable confusion about events. The military imposed a news blackout, confining the several dozen foreign journalists to Dacca's Intercontinental Hotel. The journalists were expelled the next day after the army seized their notes and film.[29]

Although the foreign press reported widespread shooting and tracer rounds lighting up the Dacca skies,[30] only gradually did a picture of the Pakistani army's bloody repression of the Bengalis emerge. In its classified cables, the Dacca consulate general reported that "the Pakistani military forces were on a reign of terror. They were systematically seeking out and killing Awami League leaders and members, including student leaders and university faculty."[31] Consul General Archer Blood urged the U.S. government to express shock at events in the east. Although not going as far as Blood, the embassy in Islamabad recommended that the administration voice its deep concern but try "not to make developments a contentious international political issue." Washington decided to hold off taking a position, saying that it wanted to await further developments.[32]

Within a few days, the State Department accepted Blood's recommendation to evacuate some seven hundred American citizens from East Pakistan, leaving only twenty members of the consulate staff in Dacca. Despite the fact that the U.S. Air Force was ready to transport the evacuees to Bangkok, only an hour's flight away, the Pakistani government insisted that they first fly from Dacca to Karachi in Pakistan International Airlines (PIA) aircraft before leaving the country. Although unhappy about this demand, Ambassador Farland agreed in order to avoid further delay. What Farland did not know and what infuriated the evacuees was that the PIA planes were returning to Karachi after ferrying Pakistani soldiers to Dacca to reinforce the military in the east.[33]

In Washington, Rogers deplored the suffering caused by the civil strife but refused to get drawn into what he termed "an internal Pakistan matter."[34] As evacuees began to relate harrowing tales of army killings of Bengali civilians, the reluctance of the Nixon administration to condemn the Pakistani action began to draw sharp criticism. An April 7, 1971, editorial in the *New York Times* declared, "Washington's persistent silence on recent events in Pakistan is increasingly incomprehensible in light of eye witness evidence that the Pakistani Army has engaged in indiscriminate slaughter."[35]

The silence was particularly incomprehensible to the staff remaining at the Dacca consulate general. Angered by events on the ground and their government's refusal to speak out, they sent a collective "dissent channel" telegram to the State Department.[36] The Dacca dissent argued that the United States had no major national security interests at stake and, therefore, in keeping with traditional American support for human rights and self-determination, should condemn the military's repression of East Pakistan.

When Ambassador Farland saw Dacca's telegram, he shrugged his shoulders.[37] The reaction of the White House and top levels of the State Department was less laid back. According to Kissinger, Nixon reportedly ordered that Blood be transferred; Secretary Rogers "found it 'outrageous' that his diplomats were writing petitions rather than reports."[38] Blood had given the cable a low classification of "limited official use." The next day the State Department reclassified the message as "secret—nodis" (a far higher security classification with stringently controlled and extremely limited distribution). Nonetheless, official Washington and the media soon became aware that the Dacca staff was up in arms about the U.S. government's silence over events in East Pakistan.

What only a handful of officials knew, not including Rogers, was the pivotal role that Yahya Khan was playing in Nixon's efforts to open a dialogue with China. Just as the Pakistani army was in the process of making the country an international pariah by its brutal repression of East Pakistani aspirations, the secret Washington-Islamabad-Beijing exchanges were nearing their climax.

On April 27, 1971, Hilaly read Kissinger a key message from Zhou Enlai in which Zhou confirmed Chinese willingness to receive a secret U.S. envoy. Zhou proposed that the logistics and modalities of the visit be worked out "through the good offices of President Yahya Khan."[39] Two weeks later, Kissinger handed Hilaly the reply, which stated that he would lead the secret mission and agreed to work out the arrangements through Yahya.[40] On June 2, 1971, Hilaly conveyed Zhou's proposal that Kissinger travel to China in mid-June. Nixon's reply suggested that the trip take place a month later in order to avoid stirring up media speculation about a sudden Kissinger visit to Asia.[41]

The only two officials in the Islamabad embassy aware of the secret trip were Farland and the Central Intelligence Agency's station chief. They had been called back to Washington in May 1971 and instructed to work out a cover plan directly with Yahya. After various alternatives were considered, it was agreed that Kissinger would stop in Pakistan during an Asia trip and travel to Beijing in a PIA jetliner while supposedly resting in the mountains after a feigned attack of dysentery.[42]

The secrecy surrounding the China trip prevented the White House from revealing to officials dealing with South Asia the most important reason for its refusal to criticize Yahya about events in East Pakistan. The best explanation Kissinger could offer was to refer obliquely to "Nixon's special relationship with Yahya" and to say the president "does not want to be in the position where he can be accused of having encouraged the split-up of Pakistan."[43] This approach did not sit well with most Democrats and some Republicans in Congress. They interpreted Nixon's silence as a further example of his administration's disregard for human rights. Typical of the public criticism was a *New York Times* editorial lambasting Nixon for "following a dangerously shortsighted policy."[44]

In contrast to America's hands-off stance, neither the Soviet Union nor China remained silent. A week after the army crackdown, on April 2, 1971, Soviet President Nikolai Podgorny publicly urged Yahya to take "immediate measures so as to put an end to bloodshed and repressions against the population of East Pakistan." Despite this criticism, however, Moscow continued its economic assistance and delivery of military supplies promised earlier to Pakistan.[45] China was predictably more supportive, publicly backing the Pakistanis "in their just struggle to safeguard State Sovereignty and national independence."[46] Later, however, Pakistan's foreign secretary, Sultan Khan, recalled that Zhou Enlai had privately urged a greater effort toward political normalization with the eastern wing and never "held out any possibility of coming to Pakistan's aid with her armed forces."[47]

In the United States, public attention turned to the Pakistani army's use of U.S.-supplied military equipment in the suppression of the Bengalis. The Senate Foreign Relations Committee voted unanimously for an immediate and complete cutoff of arms transfers. Revelation that the U.S. government had been selling ammunition to Pakistan as a "nonlethal" item provided further embarrassment.[48] Even though the White House tightly controlled foreign policy, Kissinger and his National Security Council (NSC) staff could not manage all the details. After the White House failed to respond to a recommendation to suspend arms exports to Pakistan as a way to allay critics, the State Department went ahead to impose what it thought was a complete ban.[49]

Thus press revelations in June 1971 that arms exports to Pakistan were, in fact, continuing provided fresh embarrassment. These reports sparked stinging criticism by Senator Edward Kennedy (D-Mass.) and by India, whose foreign minister had been informed in Washington that all arms shipments had stopped.[50] What happened was not duplicity, as Kennedy, the media, and the Indians alleged, but an administrative snafu. When the State Department suspended issuance of export licenses, it did not realize that the Pentagon was continuing to allow the Pakistanis to ship out of the country equipment that they had taken custody of under earlier licenses.[51]

Although Nixon refused to agree to stop economic aid, he eventually endorsed the ban on arms exports. In approving it, Nixon added a personal note: "To all hands. Don't squeeze Yahya at this time."[52] The Pakistani leader, however, further tarnished his country's already dreadful image by refusing to accept emergency humanitarian aid. In rejecting assistance, Yahya termed press reports about human suffering in East Pakistan "highly exaggerated—if not altogether tendentious."[53] The trickle of those fleeing East Pakistan into India had become a torrent, with the number of refugees estimated at 1.5 million.[54]

As a sign of his stance regarding Pakistan, Nixon received M. M. Ahmed, a special envoy from Yahya and his top economic adviser, at the White House on May 10, 1971. Calling the Pakistani leader "a good friend," the president said he could "understand the anguish of the decisions which he had to make." Nixon commented that he was not going to tell Pakistan how to work out its political difficulties. "Attitudes in Congress had to be taken into account and could restrict our ability to help. . . . But, we would not do anything to complicate the situation for President Yahya or to embarrass him."[55] The Pakistani dictator could not have asked for much more.

In keeping with Nixon's instructions, the United States in July 1971 refused to join other members of the World Bank's Pakistan consortium in suspending economic aid. After visiting Pakistan, World Bank vice president Peter Cargill had recommended that renewed assistance "would serve little purpose" in view of the chaotic conditions in East Pakistan. When Cargill's report leaked to the press, pressure increased on the Nixon administration to suspend aid.[56] Only after a normally docile House Foreign Affairs Committee voted on July 15, 1971, to bar all assistance to Pakistan did the administration give way, announcing that aid was being held in abeyance pending a "clarification" of the East Pakistan situation.[57]

Kissinger's Secret Trip to China

On July 9, 1971, Henry Kissinger arrived in Islamabad for a supposed one-day visit during a tour of Asian capitals.[58] Although Deputy Chief of Mission Sidney Sober would normally have been in charge of Kissinger's stop, Ambassador Farland had insisted that he take previously planned out-of-country leave. This was ostensibly to give the hardworking Sober a well-deserved holiday, but in fact was intended to ensure his absence. Farland designated the author, then acting embassy political counselor, to replace Sober as the control officer for the visit. I had fewer high-level Pakistani contacts and was less likely to become aware of Kissinger's true mission.

Planning for the visit proceeded normally. A full schedule of embassy briefings and meetings with Yahya and other senior Pakistani officials filled the supposed one-day stay. When Kissinger and his party, which included NSC aide Harold Saunders, arrived from New Delhi, Foreign Secretary Sultan Khan was on hand to welcome Nixon's national security adviser. During the drive in from the airport, Saunders mentioned that Kissinger was not feeling well and was suffering from a mild case of "Delhi belly."

During the afternoon, Kissinger discussed the East Pakistan crisis with the embassy staff. When he asked about the chances for a war between India and Pakistan, I said, "About one in three." After his talks in New Delhi, Kissinger responded, the odds seemed to him to be more like "two in three." Later in the day, Kissinger and Farland met Yahya and had dinner with him. Kissinger wrote in his memoirs that in discussing East Pakistan, the Pakistani leader "was oblivious to his perils and unprepared to face necessities." Kissinger concluded that Yahya "did not believe India might be planning war; if so, [Yahya and other Pakistani generals] were convinced they could win."[59]

At about midnight, Farland and Saunders showed up at my home. Kissinger's stomach trouble had become much worse and he could not carry on with the planned schedule, they said. Yahya had suggested that he rest for a day or two in the nearby 8,000-foot mountain resort of Nathiagali. Kissinger had agreed and also had gone along with Yahya's "wacky" idea that he arrive in Nathiagali in time to see the sun rise over the Himalayan peaks. This meant that he had to depart by 4 A.M. Farland, the Kissinger party, and Sultan Khan planned to accompany him to Nathiagali, leaving Saunders behind to deal with any important cables. I said that I would be at the state guest house, where Kissinger was staying, at 3:30 A.M. to make sure everyone left in good order. Saunders and Farland insisted that this was not necessary. I disagreed, saying this was part of a control officer's responsibility. After Farland still insisted, I acquiesced, frankly happy to get a full night's sleep.

The party, indeed, left the guest house at 4 A.M. Farland and Sultan Khan drove up to Nathiagali; Kissinger and his NSC aides, however, headed for the Islamabad airport, where they boarded a PIA jet and took off for Beijing. The crew was not told who the passengers were.[60] The next day, some in the embassy were skeptical about Kissinger's "illness" and there were rumors that he was holding secret talks. That evening at a party, Associated Press correspondent Arnold Zeitlin, the sole resident American journalist, asked me about the rumors. I replied fliply, "You're right, Kissinger is off to China for secret talks with Zhou Enlai." Zeitlin's eyes lit up, but they dimmed when I said it was only a joke.

The following afternoon, Kissinger was scheduled to return from Nathiagali at 2 P.M. and depart shortly thereafter. I was on hand at the guest house to make sure that all the arrangements were in order. At the scheduled time, Farland and Sultan Khan appeared, but not Kissinger. Their explanation was that his car had turned off the road in the town of Murree, presumably for some souvenir shopping, and was delayed. In fact, the PIA plane had left Beijing later than planned and had failed to inform Islamabad. In about half an hour, Kissinger appeared, full of smiles and seemingly recovered from his stomach ailment.

Before flying off to Europe in his U.S. Air Force jet, Kissinger paid a brief farewell call on Yahya, whom he filled in on the Beijing trip. Among other things, Kissinger said that the Chinese had indicated they would intervene militarily if India attacked East Pakistan. A few days later, when Sultan Khan received the Chinese ambassador's version of the Beijing talks, the Pakistani diplomat concluded that Kissinger had misinterpreted Zhou's remark that "China would not be an idle spectator" if India invaded Pakistan as meaning that China's help would go beyond rhetoric and political backing.[61]

On July 15, 1971, President Nixon announced Kissinger's trip to China and his own planned visit there. The news was a political bombshell that caught the world totally by surprise. That Nixon, who had made his name in politics as a hard-line anticommunist, would take the initiative to seek normalization of relations with China was stunning news. Kissinger's secret mission lent an added touch of drama. Few people were more surprised than the author, by then en route to the United States for home leave.

Tensions Mount with India

Meanwhile, relations between India and Pakistan had deteriorated badly. Even though India did not recognize the Bangladesh government-in-exile established in Calcutta, New Delhi trained and armed Bengali

President Nixon and National Security Adviser Henry Kissinger thank Pakistani ambassador Agha Hilaly for his help in the opening to China, July 1971. (Courtesy of the Nixon Presidential Materials Project.)

ex–Pakistani army members, the so-called Mukhti Bahini, to mount an insurgency. East Pakistan was ideal terrain for guerrilla warfare: it had poor ground communications, ample river and water channels, and a nearby safe haven across the border in India. Even though the Mukhti Bahini were unable to hold territory, they moved in and out of the province virtually at will, making life miserable for the Pakistani military. After a lull, the refugee exodus resumed during the summer months and included a substantial portion of East Pakistan's ten million Hindus, whom the Pakistani army harshly prodded to leave. Soon, over five million refugees had fled, posing a tremendous burden on India.

When Kissinger briefed the NSC after his return to Washington, his assessment was that India seemed "bent on war" and that Yahya lacked "the imagination to solve the political problems in time to prevent an Indian assault." He recommended that the United States aim for an "evolution that would lead to eventual independence for East Pakistan," even though he doubted this was likely "to happen in time to head off an Indian attack." Nixon agreed that Pakistan should be pressed to do the maximum to encourage the return of the refugees in the hope of lessening the chances of war.[62]

In late July 1971, Yahya finally agreed to permit UN supervision of relief and resettlement efforts, reversing his former position. It was then India's turn to stonewall. New Delhi refused to accept UN operations on its side of the border, effectively scuttling the relief plan. Indian prime minister Indira Gandhi, who insisted on the return of all the refugees, was suspicious that UN relief programs might encourage the refugees to remain in India.[63]

The possibility of war preoccupied Nixon when he thanked Ambassador Farland on July 28, 1971, for his role in the China initiative. An India-Pakistan conflict, Nixon said, had "its intrinsic tragedy" but also "could disrupt . . . our policy toward China."[64] By this time, policy differences between the White House, the State Department, and elsewhere in the bureaucracy over the handling of the East Pakistan crisis had sharpened. When Maurice Williams, deputy administrator of AID and the former chief of the AID mission in Pakistan, proposed in a White House meeting on July 31, 1971, that the United States press for a reduced army role in civil administration in the east to facilitate the relief effort, Kissinger exploded. "The President always says to tilt toward Pakistan, but every proposal I get is in the opposite direction. Sometimes, I think I am in a nut house," he shouted.[65] Six months later, the word "tilt" would become the symbol of U.S. policy during the East Pakistan crisis, after a journalist published classified transcripts of crisis-management meetings on South Asia.

Meanwhile, sympathy about the plight of the millions of Bengali refugees and criticism of Nixon administration policy continued to mount in the United States. Forty thousand people attended two sold-out concerts at the beginning of August in New York City's Madison Square Garden to raise funds for the Bengali refugees. The Beatles, Bob Dylan, and India's Ravi Shankar performed for the enthusiastic crowd, lambasted Nixon, and called for an independent Bangladesh.[66]

On August 3, 1971, the House of Representatives voted to suspend all assistance to Pakistan. Nonetheless, the president defended his refusal to cut off aid at a press conference the next day. "The most constructive role we can play is to continue our economic assistance," Nixon declared, "to influence the course of events in a way that will deal with the problem of hunger in East Pakistan, which would reduce the refugee flow into India and which will, we trust, in the future look toward a viable political settlement." The president ruled out "public pressure" on Pakistan as "totally counterproductive."[67]

Four days later, Nixon sent a handwritten letter to Yahya to express his appreciation for his help in facilitating the opening to China. "Through this personal note I want to you to know," the president wrote, "that without your personal assistance the profound breakthrough in relations between the USA and the [Peoples Republic of China] would never have been accomplished. . . . Those who want a more peaceful world in the generations to come will be forever in your debt."[68] The note followed more formal, official thank-you letters to Yahya from Nixon and Kissinger that had been sent ten days earlier.[69]

At this point, Indira Gandhi sprung her own surprise, signing a friendship treaty with the Soviet Union on August 9, 1971. Although short of a formal alliance, the accord provided for bilateral consultations in the event of crises and pledged that neither country would support a third party against the other. With the threat of war increasing, Nehru's daughter was willing to depart from the principles of nonalignment—although she denied that she was doing so. The Indo-Soviet treaty provided a riposte to what many Indians feared was an emerging U.S.-China-Pakistan entente. But Kissinger's assertion in *White House Years* that "with the treaty, Moscow threw a lighted match into a powder keg"[70] appears a considerable exaggeration. The Soviets remained fairly cautious in dealing with the crisis until Indira Gandhi's visit to Moscow at the end of September 1971. Only after she rebuffed pressure for a peaceful solution did the Kremlin provide the full political support and additional military supplies for which the Indians had been pressing.[71]

"Anything—All We Can" to Prevent War

On August 11, 1971, Nixon discussed South Asia in cold-blooded realpolitik terms with members of the Senior Review Group, the interagency policy committee that Kissinger chaired. The president told the officials that the U.S. aim must be to do "anything—all we can to restrain" those who want war. If war came, "the new China relationship would be imperiled, probably beyond repair, and we would have a 'very sticky problem' with the USSR." Although he "held no brief for what President Yahya has done," the United States, Nixon stressed, "must not—cannot—allow India to use the refugees as a pretext for breaking up Pakistan." The president added that "[breaking up Pakistan] is what he might want to do if he were in New Delhi." Continuing his comments, Nixon stated, "It is not our job to determine the political future of Pakistan" nor should the United States measure its relationship with Pakistan by Islamabad's conduct in East Pakistan. "By that criterion," he said, "we would cut off relations with every Communist country in the world."[72]

In considering what to do with Pakistan, Kissinger chimed in sarcastically that asking Yahya "to deal with the Awami Leaguers in Calcutta is like asking Abraham Lincoln to deal with Jefferson Davis." Nixon nonetheless agreed that Deputy AID Administrator Williams could pass on some American ideas to ease the crisis when he met Yahya during a planned visit to Pakistan to review the refugee relief effort. Nixon also indicated his agreement for Ambassador Farland to make 'private' suggestions to Yahya, "such as not shooting Mujib."[73]

The slim prospects for a political settlement became slimmer when, on that same day, a court began try Mujib in secret for "waging war against Pakistan."[74] Word of the trial widened the gap between the White House and the bureaucracy, especially State Department regional specialists who viewed the crisis as a South Asian struggle rather than one involving the global balance of power (the Nixon-Kissinger view). Regional specialists also doubted that the White House strategy would work: they were skeptical that Yahya would be willing to agree to political accommodation on terms acceptable to the Bengalis. A week later, an assessment that Kissinger sent Nixon urged continued focus on famine and refugee help. Regarding China, the national security adviser wrote, "It is important that they not feel that we are lining up with India and the USSR against them. That is why for the moment it is important that we stay one step behind the Soviets in India, although over the longer run, we have no interest in writing off 600 million Indians and Bengalis."[75]

When Maurice Williams met Yahya Khan on August 19, 1971, his most important suggestion—that a Bengali civilian replace Gen. Tikka Khan as governor of East Pakistan—was considered so sensitive that it was mentioned neither in Williams's instructions nor in the cable report of the meeting. To ensure that Yahya was forewarned, Williams had previewed his presentation with economic adviser M. M. Ahmed.

The meeting started inauspiciously. After Williams handed over a letter from Nixon, Pakistan's president threw it unopened across the room and began to "curse a blue streak" for more than ten minutes. Having vented his frustration, Yahya, Williams recalled, then calmed down and welcomed the visitor as "a friend of Pakistan." Yahya listened to what Williams had to say and in the end accepted most of what was proposed, including the recall of Tikka Khan.[76] When Williams subsequently traveled to Dacca, he found that the general lived up to his reputation as a cold and heartless personality.[77]

Although Yahya agreed to a gradual reversion to civilian rule in the east, as U.S. officials had recommended, he acted in a half-hearted manner. Most Awami Leaguers continued to be banned from participation in political life. Despite the fact that Dr. A. M. Malik, a Bengali politician and former minister of labor, became the governor, the Pakistani army still wielded effective power in East Pakistan. When Williams visited Pakistan two months later in October 1971, top civil servants M. M. Ahmed and Ghulam Ishaq Khan advised him that the army was operating largely on its own in the east with Yahya's role increasingly limited to dealing with foreigners, "including managing the U.S. relationship." Maj. Gen. Farman Ali, the military's civil affairs adviser in East Pakistan, also acknowledged to Williams that the army was following a policy of "terror and reprisal" to counter the insurgents.[78] Kissinger sent Williams's trip report, which he termed "disturbing," to President Nixon.

Yahya eventually agreed not to execute Mujib and gave his blessing for talks between U.S. diplomats in Calcutta and the Bangladesh government-in-exile. Yet he refused to consider direct negotiations with banned Awami Leaguers or with Mujib.[79] On the question of dealing with Mujib—according to Sultan Khan—Yahya's consistent stance was, "I am not going to talk to that traitor!" Nor would Yahya permit an Awami League delegation from Calcutta to meet with Mujib.[80] After first agreeing that Ambassador Farland could talk with Mujib's defense lawyer, Yahya later torpedoed the idea, to Farland's annoyance.[81]

Christopher Van Hollen, the State Department's senior South Asia expert, recalled that even though "almost to a person, the US officials working on South Asia were convinced the White House strategy would not work," Nixon and Kissinger persisted.[82] The approach formed the heart of their presentation to Indira Gandhi when she visited Washington on November 4–5, 1971. The president expressed confidence that a satisfactory political settlement could be worked out if India gave the United States enough time. Skeptical about the prospects, not trusting Nixon's bona fides, and having decided by then to use force to solve the problem, Mrs. Gandhi remained silent. The Nixon-Gandhi talks were a dialogue of the deaf.[83]

Ten days later, when Pakistani foreign secretary Sultan Khan followed in Mrs. Gandhi's footsteps to Washington, he received a considerably friendlier welcome. Among other things, Kissinger reviewed with the Pakistani envoy secret, and illegal, efforts—approved by President Nixon but undertaken without the knowledge of the State Department—to encourage other countries to meet Pakistan's pressing need for military spare parts and aircraft. Because of the Nixon administration's own ban on arms transfers, the United States was prohibited from helping Pakistan either directly or by approving transfer of U.S. equipment from other countries. When Kissinger took Sultan Khan to the

National Security Adviser Kissinger introduces Pakistani foreign secretary Sultan Mohammed Khan to President Nixon at the White House, November 1971. (Courtesy of the Nixon Presidential Materials Project.)

Oval Office for a courtesy call, the visitor recalled that President Nixon was "solicitous about Yahya" and "conveyed feelings of understanding about the problems facing [Pakistan]."[84]

By this time, ample signs indicated that a military showdown was approaching. As the *New York Times* put it, there was "a smell of war in the air."[85] Both India and Pakistan were amassing troops along their borders. Guerrilla attacks against the Pakistani military in the east were increasing. After November 22, 1971, Indian troops supporting the Bengali insurgents became more aggressive, physically occupying territory across the border.[86] The White House saw this action, in effect, as the start of war by India and redoubled its diplomatic efforts to avert an all-out conflict. On November 22, 1971, the Chinese passed a message through Gen. Vernon Walters, the U.S. defense attaché in Paris, that urged Washington to "exert its influence to prevent the further deterioration of the situation." The next day, Kissinger, accompanied by UN representative George Bush, met secretly in New York with Huang Hua, China's UN ambassador, to review how the United States and China could deal with the East Pakistan issue in the United Nations. Kissinger outlined U.S. diplomatic démarches and discussed possible UN moves. After Kissinger quipped, "This violates every security rule," Deputy National Security Adviser Alexander Haig briefed the Chinese on the U.S. intelligence appraisal of the military situation in East Pakistan.[87]

The Third India-Pakistan War

India, according to army chief Gen. Sam Manekshaw, had planned to begin the general assault against East Pakistan on December 4, 1971.[88] To New Delhi's pleasant surprise, however, Yahya Khan removed the onus of India's having to strike first by launching air attacks from West Pakistan on December 3, 1971.[89] Indira Gandhi immediately reacted by giving the green light for the planned attack against East Pakistan. India also countered militarily in the west, but in a far more limited fashion.[90] Indian forces advanced steadily in the east toward their objective—the capital city of Dacca. In the west, despite some hard fighting, a standoff developed. Although the war was going largely according to Indian plans, Yahya Khan continued to exude an unrealistic air of confidence that the United States or China would come to his rescue, Sultan Khan later recalled.[91]

Once the conflict began, diplomatic action shifted to the UN Security Council, where the Soviet Union employed its veto to block U.S.-backed calls for a cease-fire. In Washington, in a December 4, 1971, press background information presentation, Assistant Secretary of State Joseph Sisco set the pro-Pakistan tone of the U.S. reaction. Although "the crisis in its initial stage was not really of Indian making . . . India bears the major responsibility for the broader hostilities which have ensued," Sisco stated.[92] At the United Nations, Bush, who worked closely with his Pakistani counterpart, Agha Shahi, fingered India as "the major aggressor."[93] Interviewed on December 6, 1971, by CBS News, Bush repeated the charge: "There's quite clear aggression. It's obviously quite clear." That same day, the State Department announced that it was freezing $87.6 million in development assistance to India.[94]

The effort to obtain a cease-fire moved to the UN General Assembly after the Soviets vetoed the Security Council resolution. By an overwhelming 104-11 vote, with 10 abstentions, the assembly called for a halt in fighting and pullback of forces—i.e., withdrawal of Indian forces from East Pakistan. Apart from Bhutan, only Soviet bloc countries supported India. Even for a popular cause like Bangladesh, India's sending troops across an international border was not an action that nation-states were willing to condone.

The same day, Kissinger, briefing the press on a nonattribution basis, denied that the Nixon administration was "anti-Indian" and asserted that New Delhi had not given the administration enough time to reach a political solution and had resorted to military action without adequate cause. In a spirited hour-long exchange with journalists, he conceded that there had been little concrete progress toward a political settlement.[95] A few days later, Senator Barry Goldwater (R-Ariz.) publicly revealed the identity of the briefer.

Saving West Pakistan?

By this time the White House had accepted that the situation in East Pakistan was hopeless. After a CIA intelligence source reported that India would continue the war in the west "until the Pakistani army and air force were wiped out" and India gained control of more of Kashmir, Nixon's and Kissinger's attention turned to the west.[96] Although CIA and State Department officials played down the intelligence report's significance, the president and his national security adviser seized on it as hard evidence that India was out to crush West Pakistan. Stepping up the diplomatic pressure, Kissinger called in Indian ambassador L. K. Jha to warn against such a course. Nixon used a December 9, 1971, meeting with a surprised Soviet agriculture minister Vladimir Matskevich, who knew little about South Asia and thought he had been invited for a courtesy call, to convey his concerns to Moscow. Nixon asked Matskevich to tell Communist Party secretary Leonid Brezhnev, "a great cloud hangs over US-Soviet relations" that can "poison the whole new relationship between the US and USSR." The president warned, "if the Indians continue their military operations [against West Pakistan], we must inevitably look toward a confrontation between the Soviet Union and the United States. The Soviet Union has a treaty with India; we have one with Pakistan."[97]

The following day, on December 10, 1971, Undersecretary of State John Irwin asked for official assurances from Jha that "India had no intention of taking any territory, including any part of Azad Kashmir [the portion of Kashmir controlled by Pakistan]." Jha assured Irwin that India had no intention of taking West Pakistani territory, but could not give a certain answer about Azad Kashmir and said that he would have to query New Delhi.[98] Not satisfied with the response, Nixon kept up the pressure, informing Soviet chargé d'affaires Yuri Vorontsov that Washington would honor the November 1962 pledge to aid Pakistan against an attack by India. To underscore this threat, Nixon ordered the nuclear aircraft carrier *Enterprise* to proceed toward the Bay of Bengal.[99] The *Enterprise*'s mission was ostensibly to be available to evacuate U.S. personnel from East Pakistan, but in fact, Kissinger declared, was intended "to give emphasis to our warnings against an attack on West Pakistan."[100]

Kissinger met that same evening secretly in New York with Huang Hua to brief him on the steps the Nixon administration had taken to help Pakistan and to coordinate U.S. and Chinese action at the UN. Although barred by law from providing military help to Pakistan or permitting other countries to give American equipment, Kissinger told Hua that the administration had told Jordan, Iran, and Saudi Arabia and would tell Turkey that Washington would "protest" but would "understand" their sending military help to Pakistan. The Pakistani army in the east was destroyed, Kissinger stated, and would run out of fuel in the west in a couple of weeks. He painted a dire picture of Pakistan's plight: "The immediate objective must be to prevent an attack on the

West Pakistan army by India. We are afraid that if nothing is done to stop it, East Pakistan will become a Bhutan and West Pakistan will become a Nepal."[101]

Huang sharply criticized the Indians and the Soviets, indicating that he would promptly report the conversation to Zhou Enlai. Kissinger commented, "When I asked for this meeting, I did so to suggest Chinese military help to Pakistan, to be quite honest." He stressed that the United States was not looking for a way out but "for coordinating positive steps. . . . We have particular affection for Pakistan because we feel they helped reestablish contact between the People's Republic and the United States."[102]

At the same time, Kissinger urged Yahya to hold on in the east a while longer. "The U.S. has now sent [the] strongest possible demarche to [the] Soviets suggesting cease-fire and negotiations," the national security adviser cabled, adding that the U.S. Seventh Fleet was on the move but would not reach the area for two days. When Sultan Khan woke Yahya at 4 A.M. to read him Kissinger's message, the president "felt buoyed up" and urged Dacca to hold out for another thirty-six hours because of "very important military and diplomatic moves." According to Sultan Khan, Yahya was like a "drowning man [who] grasps at any straw."[103]

On morning of December 12, 1971, Nixon met in the Oval Office with Kissinger and Haig just before flying to the Azores to confer with French president Georges Pompidou. Deciding that the Indian response regarding West Pakistan was inadequate, Nixon sent his first-ever message to Brezhnev over the joint U.S.-Soviet hotline. He sternly warned the Soviet leader, "Time is of the essence to avoid consequences neither of us want."[104]

As the president and Kissinger were preparing to leave for the Azores, Huang asked to see the Americans in New York. In his memoirs, Kissinger expressed surprise about the Chinese taking the "unprecedented" initiative in a seeking the meeting. "We guessed," he wrote, "that they were coming to the military assistance of Pakistan." Since the White House believed that the Soviets would intervene to help India, a Sino-Soviet showdown seemed possible. President Nixon then decided that the United States would not stand idly by if the Soviets threatened China and would act in support of Beijing.[105]

Kissinger guessed wrong about China's intentions. The message, which Huang conveyed to Haig in New York on the afternoon of

December 12, 1971, was that Beijing was prepared to accept a cease-fire, not that it was going to intervene militarily against India.[106] Although Kissinger misread Chinese intentions, the Indians and the Pakistanis, and presumably the Soviets, knew that China was not going to send their forces in support of Pakistan. When Yahya had dispatched Bhutto to Beijing in early November 1971, he received no indication that the Chinese would change their position and intervene militarily.[107] From their intelligence sources, the Indians were also aware of Chinese intentions, and presumably so were the Soviets.[108]

A Threat to the Balance of Power

During wide-ranging talks on December 13, 1971, in the Azores, Nixon and Pompidou devoted time to the South Asia crisis. Speaking "in greatest confidence," Nixon stated, "Our strategy [is] to create enough pressure on India and the USSR so they [will] not pursue the war to its ultimate consequences. . . . [I]f India and the Soviet Union succeed in destroying Pakistan as a military and political entity, this can only have a devastating effect in encouraging the USSR to use the same tactics elsewhere. . . . This would very definitely change the balance of power in Asia. . . . A victory of India over Pakistan [would be] the same as a victory of the Soviet Union over China."[109] Kissinger, who was also present, told the French leader that India seemed bent on making "the rest of Pakistan non-viable." U.S. policy was to "protest" events in East Pakistan but "to prevent the destruction of West Pakistan."[110]

Pompidou's comments reflected a different view of the crisis, which the French leader described as a South Asian affair rather than one involving the global balance of power. Yahya had been wrong in not seeking a political settlement in the east, Pompidou stated. "West Pakistan would have lost a part of its authority in the East. Now it [has] none," he commented. At the end of the discussion about South Asia, Nixon reiterated his view of the importance of maintaining the balance of power in the subcontinent.[111]

Meanwhile, Indian troops continued to tighten the noose around Dacca, advancing on the capital from all sides. When the Indian military began a general assault on December 14, 1971, Gens. Farman Ali and A. A. K. Niazi, the Pakistani army commander in the east, asked U.S. consul general Herbert Spivack to transmit a surrender proposal to New Delhi, as the Pakistanis lacked direct communication with the

Indians. Nazi said that he had full authority for his action and no reference to Yahya was necessary. Before authorizing delivery of the message, Washington nonetheless instructed Farland to get Yahya's blessing.

Speaking on the president's behalf, Sultan Khan said the message could be passed to the Indians and also to Zulfikar Ali Bhutto, whom Yahya had appointed deputy prime minister and sent to New York for the UN deliberations. A nervous Washington still insisted on explicit word from Yahya. When this was received, the State Department decided against passing the message to the Indians directly and asked Bhutto to do so. Only after he flatly refused were U.S. officials in New York and New Delhi authorized to convey the surrender proposal to the Indians.[112] Washington's hesitation delayed the end of the war by a day.

During December 15, 1971, Security Council deliberations, Bhutto put on one of his more melodramatic performances. In a fiery forty-minute speech, he castigated the British and French as "opportunists," called the Soviet representative "Tsar Malik," and charged that Indian foreign minister Swaran Singh had hands "full of blood." At the same time, he thanked the United States for "its stand on principle" and expressed appreciation for China's help. As he ended his speech, Bhutto ripped up his notes and, with tears streaming down his cheeks, declared, "I will not be a party to legalizing aggression." He then stormed out of the Security Council chambers.[113]

Pakistan Defeated; Bhutto Replaces Yahya

The next afternoon, Lt. Gen. Jagjit Singh Aurora, the Indian commander in the east, arrived in Dacca to receive General Nazi's formal surrender. That night, a triumphant Indira Gandhi proposed a cease-fire in the west to take effect twenty-four hours later. When Yahya accepted, the war ended.

Before returning to Pakistan, Bhutto met with President Nixon at the White House and Secretary Rogers at the State Department on December 18, 1971. Bhutto told the president that Pakistan was "completely in the debt of the United States during the recent trying days." Although he had been called a "Yankee hater," Bhutto stressed that he now wanted good relations. Nixon responded that the United States would do "all within its power" to help Pakistan. Because of congressional attitudes, this would be mainly in the form of economic and humanitarian assistance, since "military assistance was . . . a more difficult problem."[114] When Bhutto called on the secretary of state, he similarly assured Rogers that his days of U.S.-bashing were over and that Pakistan badly wanted U.S. support and friendship.[115]

On December 20, 1971, Yahya resigned in the face of serious unrest within the military and designated Bhutto, just back from the United States, as Pakistan's new president and chief martial law administrator. The victor in the west in the December 1970 elections assumed charge of a psychologically shattered nation that had lost more than half its population and its entire eastern wing. The vaunted Pakistani army had suffered a humiliating defeat. Some 93,000 soldiers were Indian prisoners of war.

The South Asia crisis faded briefly from the Washington radar screen only to return with a vengeance after journalist Jack Anderson started publishing minutes of secret Washington Special Action Group (WSAG) meetings on the East Pakistan crisis. These made clear that far from being even-handed, Nixon wanted a "tilt" toward Pakistan throughout the crisis. At one point Kissinger commented that he was receiving "hell every hour" from the president because the U.S. government was not doing enough against the Indians.[116] The investigation soon revealed that the source of the leak was a Navy yeoman assigned to the Joint Chiefs of Staff liaison office at the NSC. During an earlier assignment in the naval attaché's office in the New Delhi embassy, the yeoman had become acquainted with Anderson's parents. After returning to the United States, the yeoman later met and became friendly with Anderson himself. Incensed by U.S. policy during the crisis, he passed copies of minutes of sensitive WSAG meetings to the journalist.

Potentially even more embarrassing for the Nixon administration was the realization that the yeoman was copying sensitive White House documents for the information of Adm. Thomas Moorer, chairman of the Joint Chiefs of Staff. Rather than deal with a nasty scandal, the White House hushed up the affair, transferred the yeoman to a pleasant assignment in Oregon, and reappointed Admiral Moorer to a second term as JCS chairman.[117]

Stung by the criticism of U.S. policy during the crisis, twelve pages of the 1972 "Report to the Congress on United States Foreign Policy" were devoted to South Asia. In this section, the president reiterated that Indira Gandhi had refused to allow sufficient time for a peaceful resolution of the crisis and claimed that U.S. pressure had reduced the chances that India would dismember West Pakistan.[118] Nixon went further in his memoirs, taking credit for having pressured the Soviets into deterring India from attacking in the west.[119] Kissinger was even less modest, claiming in his memoirs that U.S. diplomacy saved "a major American initiative of fundamental importance to the global balance of power" (i.e., the opening to China) and alleging that the "very structure of international order was endangered by the naked recourse to force by a Soviet partner."[120]

It is hard to agree with these claims. Far from a victory, U.S. diplomacy suffered an embarrassing setback in the 1971 crisis. Nixon's response to the East Pakistan crisis—pressing Yahya to make political concessions—was, as Maurice Williams put it, a reasonable approach, but "too little, too late."[121] When war came, moreover, the White House's flawed reading of India's intentions toward West Pakistan almost succeeded in transforming a regional war into a great-power showdown. Senior Pakistani officials, such as UN representative Agha Shahi, Ambassador to the United States Agha Hilaly (Shahi's older brother), and Foreign Secretary Sultan Khan, while crediting Nixon for doing what he could to help Pakistan in the face of strong domestic opposition, did not share the Nixon-Kissinger view that India intended to crush West Pakistan after its victory in the east. Like U.S. regional specialists, they believed that India's ambitions were limited to the establishment of Bangladesh and the humiliation of Pakistan.[122]

The impact of Nixon's "tilt" was, in fact, quite marginal on events in South Asia during the crisis. There is little evidence that U.S. pressures or advice significantly affected either India's or Pakistan's actions. In the final analysis, it was Yahya's tragic blunder of trying to resolve the East Pakistani political problem by suppressing Bengali aspirations that, as Indian defense policy analyst K. Subrahmanyam put it, presented India with "an opportunity the like of which will never come again."[123] Although Nixon's actions may have influenced Chinese thinking, specialists like the Brookings Institution's Raymond Garthoff are skeptical, believing that Beijing had sufficient desire for détente with the United States to not be terribly upset had Washington tilted less toward Pakistan.[124]

Continued Good Relations

After the war ended, South Asia once more became an area of secondary foreign policy concern for the United States. In February 1972,

Nixon enjoyed a personal and political triumph when he visited China. As the president had hoped, the trip opened a new era in Sino-U.S. relations and improved the U.S. position relative to the Soviet Union in the global balance of power.

In Pakistan, however, national morale was at a low point after the Bangladesh disaster. In working to restore the self-confidence of his depressed people, Bhutto enjoyed his finest hour, displaying enormous energy and leadership talents of a high order. In a whirl of domestic activity, he moved to implement much of his Pakistan Peoples Party's economic program, announcing new land reforms, nationalizing a number of industries and banks, and promising educational and other reform measures. At the same time, he began work on a new constitution to provide a firmer footing for civilian and democratic government.

Bhutto also acted vigorously in the international arena. To refurbish ties with the Muslim Middle East, he rapidly visited eight countries in January 1972.[125] He reaffirmed Pakistan's close ties with key supporter China during a trip to Beijing. To strengthen the country's nonaligned credentials and undoubtedly to please the Chinese, Bhutto withdrew Pakistan from SEATO and established diplomatic relations with North Vietnam and North Korea. He tackled the tougher task of trying to mend fences with Moscow, but had only modest success in restoring more normal relations.[126]

Richard Nixon's positive attitude toward Pakistan did not end with the end of the Bangladesh crisis. The administration tried to be as supportive as possible, but as Kissinger advised Sultan Khan, whom Bhutto had sent to Washington as his ambassador, Pakistan's poor public image and related congressional opposition limited the president's ability to help, especially with regard to the supply of arms.[127] Less-controversial economic aid was quickly resumed. A $30 million commodity aid agreement was signed on March 18, 1972.[128] Three months later, Chargé d'Affaires Sober announced $60 million in long-term loans for industrial raw materials and spare parts and the full resumption of economic assistance.[129]

For his part, Bhutto continued to value good relations with the United States and refrained from the anti-U.S. rhetoric which had been his hallmark as foreign minister and opposition leader in the 1960s. In an interview with *New York Times* roving correspondent C. L. Sulzberger, the Pakistani president praised the U.S. role in the 1971 crisis, crediting a "firm ultimatum" from Washington as responsible for Soviet pressure on Indians to accept a cease-fire. "If there had been no U.S. intervention," India would have attacked West Pakistan, he asserted.[130]

India remained Bhutto's main foreign policy concern. With Indira Gandhi at the peak of her power, Bhutto played a weak diplomatic hand with skill when the two met in late June 1972 at Simla, the 6,000-foot hill station and the former summer capital of British India. After several days of tough bargaining, Pakistan agreed, as India had long sought, to settle all disputes peacefully and bilaterally, including that over Kashmir. According to what Indira Gandhi told the Indian delegation, Bhutto also expressed willingness to settle the Kashmir dispute on the basis of the status quo, with the line of control becoming the border, but added that he needed time to gain political acceptance for this. Bhutto said nothing about this to the Pakistani delegation.[131]

In return, India agreed to return 5,139 square miles of Pakistani territory seized during the war. The ninety-three thousand Pakistani prisoners of war, however, were not released; in effect India continued to hold them hostage for Bhutto's recognition of Bangladesh, an action he was, as yet, unwilling to take. The United States welcomed the Simla agreement "as an important step toward establishing a durable peace in South Asia."[132] Following the agreement, the formal U.S. stance on the Kashmir dispute shifted. Although previously the United States had supported the 1948 and 1949 UN resolutions calling for a plebiscite, after Simla Washington indicated that any settlement that India and Pakistan worked out would be acceptable.[133]

Secretary of the Treasury John Connally, who was close to Nixon, visited India and Pakistan during a round-the-world trip immediately after the Simla conference. When Connally called on Bhutto on July 6, 1972, the Pakistani leader lauded Nixon and expressed confidence that he would defeat George McGovern in the upcoming presidential elections. Pakistan badly needed help, Bhutto stressed, including military aid, but he would not press for this until after the U.S. elections. Connally found the Pakistani president "enormously upset about the Indians," whom he said "were going to try to use every device they could, including duplicity, to solve their problems at Pakistan's expense."[134] For his part, the treasury secretary assured the Pakistanis, "The end of that crisis does not mean the end of that friendship. We want to continue as friends and be of what help we can."[135]

After Nixon's landslide re-election in November 1972, Bhutto became edgy when Washington took no early action to ease arms-supply restrictions. But in March 1973, he felt better after Nixon released $24 million worth of military equipment blocked since 1971 and reinstated the 1967 arms-supply policy. This action enabled Pakistan to procure nonlethal equipment and spare parts for weapons that the United States previously had supplied.[136]

During April 1973, Pakistan's National Assembly adopted a new and democratic constitution that appeared to set the country on the path of representative government. Sober played a helpful behind-the-scenes role in encouraging opposition parties and the government to work out their differences. Bhutto personally thanked the U.S. diplomat for his assistance, as did leaders of the opposition.[137] The adoption of the 1973 constitution marked one of the rare times in Pakistan's history that there was broad consensus on a major domestic political issue. The new constitution changed Pakistan from a presidential to a parliamentary system, and the National Assembly elected Bhutto as prime minister on August 12, 1973.

When he arrived at the White House for a state visit a month later, on September 19, 1973, Bhutto's prestige had never been higher. In warmly greeting the visitor, Nixon declared, "The independence and integrity of Pakistan is a cornerstone of American foreign policy." The formulation aptly captured the Nixon administration's positive attitude. In talks at the White House, Bhutto made the case for lifting all remaining restrictions on arms transfers but showed understanding for Nixon's continuing difficulty in overcoming congressional opposition.

The prime minister also sought U.S. help to construct a new port at Gwadar, on the Arabian Sea coast of thinly populated Baluchistan, and said that the U.S. Navy could use the facility. Although Nixon responded that he would have the proposal examined carefully, his NSC briefing paper indicated no "great interest in having a naval facility in Baluchistan," which would stir up the Soviets, the Indians, and the Afghans "without greatly contributing to US interests."[138] The administration took no action on the proposal, which Premier Zhou Enlai strongly seconded when Kissinger visited China in November 1973.[139] Subsequently, the U.S. Navy built a base for Indian Ocean operations on the politically less sensitive, British-owned Diego Garcia atoll.

To help meet an unexpected requirement for food imports caused by unusually severe floods in the Indus River valley, the Nixon administration agreed to provide Pakistan with one hundred thousand tons of wheat worth $24 million, to grant an $18 million AID loan, and to seek

President Nixon confers with Prime Minister Zulfikar Ali Bhutto at the White House, September 1973. (Courtesy of the Nixon Presidential Materials Project.)

a further $40–50 million rehabilitation loan, in addition to providing other food commodities. Except for the short-term food problem, Pakistan's economic prospects, in fact, seemed much improved without the burden of the poorer eastern wing.

Accustomed to the fiery, U.S.-baiting foreign minister Bhutto of the 1960s, Washington found Prime Minister Bhutto of the 1970s more accomplished, more subdued, and more statesmanlike. In assessing his visit to Washington, the State Department cabled, "Bhutto displayed [an] air of confidence and maturity clearly designed to build [the] public image of Pakistan as [a] reliable and responsible friend of [the] United States."[140]

During the prime minister's stay in Washington, Nixon named veteran diplomat Henry Byroade as ambassador to Pakistan. Kissinger, whom Nixon had by then appointed secretary of state, asked Byroade to take the assignment with one main aim—to complete the process of lifting the arms embargo. After the envoy had spent enough time in Pakistan to speak authoritatively about the country, Kissinger wanted him to return to Washington to lay the groundwork with Congress for removing the decade-long ban on the export of weapons to Pakistan.[141] Ironically, two decades earlier, in 1953, when Byroade was serving as assistant secretary of state for the Near East, South Asia, and Africa, he had been the key promoter of the idea of U.S. military aid for Pakistan. Before the new ambassador arrived on the scene, Kissinger underscored close U.S.-Pakistan links by stopping in Islamabad on his way to China in November 1973. The telegram reporting the discussions between him and Bhutto indicated that they had dealt principally with Middle East peace negotiations and U.S.-Soviet détente efforts.[142]

In February 1974, Pakistan finally recognized Bangladesh and Sheikh Mujibur Rahman flew to Lahore to participate in a glittering thirty-seven-nation summit of Islamic countries under the aegis of the Organization of Islamic Conference (OIC). In an accord brokered by several Muslim states, Bangladesh agreed to drop war crimes trials in return for diplomatic recognition by Pakistan.[143] India had earlier released all the Pakistani prisoners of war except for 195 suspected by the Bengalis of war crimes.

The Lahore gathering proved a foreign policy triumph for Bhutto, who aspired to become a leading Third World figure. With the first generation of postcolonial leaders—Jawaharlal Nehru of India, Sukarno of Indonesia, Gamal Abdel Nasser of Egypt, and Kwame Nkrumah of Ghana—all off the stage, Pakistan's articulate prime minister hoped to carve out a larger international role for himself by serving as a major spokesperson for Africa and Asia. Although India was able to bar Pakistan's entry into the Nonaligned Movement because of its continued membership in CENTO, the OIC provided Bhutto with an attractive alternative platform to pursue his ambitions.

India Explodes a Nuclear Device

Three months later, on May 8, 1974, India shook the global scene by detonating an underground nuclear device at the Pokharan test site in the Rajasthani desert. Although New Delhi called the explosion "peaceful" and said it was not pursuing a nuclear weapons program, the action greatly agitated nonproliferation supporters in the United States and elsewhere. If a poor country like India could make a bomb, they feared, other holdouts from the 1968 nuclear Nonproliferation Treaty, especially Pakistan, might well try to follow suit.

Indeed, no country was more shaken by the Indian nuclear test than Pakistan. Prime Minister Bhutto called the explosion "a fateful development" and vowed that his country would not be blackmailed. Taking scant comfort in Indira Gandhi's assurances of peaceful intentions, the prime minister pledged that Pakistan would press ahead with its own nuclear program but said that it would not seek to explode a device.[144] Given Pakistan's limited technical capability, U.S. experts interpreted Bhutto's remarks largely as psychological bravado to bolster morale in the face of the Indian test. What Washington did not know was that in May 1972, two years before India had exploded its bomb, Bhutto had told a gathering of Pakistani scientists in the Punjabi city of Multan that he wanted them to start work on developing a nuclear weapons capability, which, he declared, the country needed to ensure its security against India.[145]

Bhutto had, in fact, consistently supported the idea of Pakistan's acquiring nuclear weapons. On March 11, 1965, he told the Manchester *Guardian* that Pakistan would "eat grass" if necessary to match any nuclear capability that India developed.[146] As foreign minister in 1966, Bhutto had strongly supported a proposal to procure a nuclear fuel reprocessing plant from the French as a building block toward developing a nuclear explosive capability. After the Finance and even Defense Ministries opposed the idea, Ayub Khan, who was in any case unenthusiastic, let the matter drop.[147] Three years later, when he was out of office and opposing Ayub, Bhutto emphasized in his book *The Myth of Independence* his belief that it was important for Pakistan to develop a nuclear capability to ensure that it did not fall behind India.[148]

At the time Bhutto instructed Pakistani scientists to begin work on a nuclear program, the country's technical capability was extremely limited. According to Pakistani atomic energy chairman Munir Ahmed Khan, the nuclear program did not, in fact, get under way in earnest until after the 1974 Indian test.[149] Once Washington became aware that Pakistan's nuclear ambitions were not mere rhetoric, thwarting Islamabad's attempt to match India would become a top policy goal—and the principal source of bilateral friction between the United States and Pakistan—for the remaining years of the twentieth century.

Three months to the day after the Indian test, on August 8, 1974, the Nixon presidency came to an abrupt and premature end. Rather than face impeachment for his conduct in the Watergate affair, Nixon became the first and only U.S. president to resign from office. Pakistan sincerely and deeply regretted his departure from the White House. The people of Pakistan, a sad Prime Minister Bhutto declared on learning of Richard Nixon's resignation, would always be grateful for his support for the country's independence and territorial integrity during the 1971 crisis.[150]

Years of Tumult

The Nixon years in the White House, marked a tumultuous and tragic time for Pakistan. Once seemingly invincible, Ayub Khan tumbled from power. His successor, Yahya Khan, lacked the acumen to manage his country's delicate political situation and blundered in using force to try to crush East Pakistani aspirations. Accepting Bengali demands would probably have resulted in splitting the country peacefully; rejecting them ended in India's humiliating dismemberment of Pakistan in the December 1971 war.

A shrunken Pakistan's new leader, Zulfikar Ali Bhutto, restored his country's morale and international standing after the 1971 debacle. Despite his earlier "Yankee-baiting," Bhutto shifted gears and sought friendly relations with the United States after taking over his country's leadership. But relations with China and the Muslim world—not those with the United States—had become the main pillars of Pakistan's foreign policy.

For the United States, the Nixon years were also tumultuous, overshadowed by the Watergate drama that ultimately drove the president from office. In foreign policy, they saw the successful opening of relations with China, the development of détente with the Soviet Union, the withdrawal of U.S. military forces from Vietnam, the 1973 Arab-Israeli War, and the ensuing oil crisis. During 1971, the coincidence of the East Pakistan crisis and Nixon's China initiative unexpectedly placed South Asia at the center of foreign policy concerns. Tilting toward Pakistan, Nixon sought to protect the opening to China and to prevent what he feared would be a major Soviet gain in the balance of power in Asia. A fundamental misread of the India-Pakistan situation, Nixon's tilt had

8

Ford: Enter the Nuclear Issue

In 1973, Richard Nixon appointed Gerald Ford, the Republican leader in the House of Representatives, as vice president after Spiro Agnew resigned rather than face prosecution on charges of corruption. A year later, when Nixon himself resigned, Ford became the first president in U.S. history not elected by the people. On assuming office, his main task was to move the nation beyond the trauma of Watergate. Relaxed and quietly self-confident, the new chief executive soothed rattled nerves and revived the country's confidence. Although few had previously considered "good old Gerry" of presidential timber, Ford earned the nation's thanks for restoring a sense of dignity and calm during his two and a half years in the White House.

In dealing with foreign relations, the new president relied heavily on the expertise of Henry Kissinger, whom he retained as secretary of state. By this time, Kissinger had become the superstar of U.S. foreign policy, gaining global recognition for his dexterous "shuttle diplomacy" in the Middle East and winning a Nobel Prize for his role in the peace negotiations with North Vietnam. The Ford administration's immediate focus lay on the consequences of the 1973 Arab-Israeli War and the consequent oil embargo, the growing weakness of the government of South Vietnam, the future of détente with Moscow, and management of the fledgling relationship with Beijing. South Asia was not an area of major concern.

In October 1974, the peripatetic Kissinger sandwiched a week in the subcontinent between a visit to Moscow and travel to the Middle East. In Pakistan, Prime Minister Zulfikar Ali Bhutto remained preoccupied with the continuing American embargo against weapon transfers to his country. In private and public, he asserted that Pakistan needed to enhance its security, especially after India's nuclear test, New Delhi's acquisition of large amounts of Soviet weaponry, and its "swallowing up" of the Himalayan kingdom of Sikkim.[1] To encourage a positive U.S. response, Bhutto implied that sufficient conventional forces might deter him from seeking nuclear weapons. "If security interests are satisfied, if people feel secure and if they feel they will not be subject to aggression, they [will] not want to squander away limited resources in [the nuclear] direction," he told the *New York Times* in an October 10, 1974, interview.[2]

Ambassador Henry Byroade, who had developed a particularly friendly relationship with the prime minister, had cabled Washington in late September that the arms issue was "a touchstone of bilateral U.S.-Pak[istan] ties." The envoy had warned that the Pakistanis would become "disillusioned if the discussions do not lead to reasonably prompt action."[3] Reminiscent of his advocacy of the "northern-tier" concept two decades before while he was assistant secretary of state for the Near East and South Asia, Byroade described Pakistan and Iran as the eastern anchors of U.S. interests in the Middle East.[4] But lingering memories of Pakistan's conduct in 1971 fueled congressional opposition to lifting the embargo, particularly among Democrats. A possible negative reaction by India to arms supplies to Pakistan was less of a concern now, though: India's May 1974 nuclear test had substantially eroded New Delhi's standing in Washington.[5]

Kissinger arrived in Islamabad on October 31, 1974, after three days in New Delhi, where, in a major address, he had described India as the preeminent power in the region.[6] Although the Indians were happy to hear such words, especially from Kissinger, the Pakistanis worried about their import. To calm nerves in Islamabad, the secretary instructed Byroade to stress that press attention about his favoring better U.S.-India relations "did not detract from the importance we attach to our relations with Pakistan."[7]

When Bhutto, Kissinger, and their senior aides met, the prime minister did not belabor the arms-supply issue, raising it primarily in the context of strengthening Pakistan so it could feel more confident about seeking better relations with India: "It was not that Pakistan wanted toys. . . . Pakistan sought sufficient arms to permit it to defend itself." At the same time, Bhutto remained highly critical of India, saying that "Pakistan had cause to be worried."[8]

Although Kissinger made no commitment about lifting the arms embargo when aides were present, Bhutto's upbeat comments to the press suggested the secretary was more forthcoming during private talks: "[We have had] very useful discussions. I'm very happy." Asked about the embargo, Bhutto replied fliply, "Results don't come instantaneously. We are not going to a cafeteria to order a hamburger."[9] The prime minister had additional cause for satisfaction, as Kissinger advised that President Ford would be happy to receive the Pakistani leader in Washington. Bhutto had been pressing for an invitation, for he was eager to establish personal contact with the new U.S. president.[10]

Old Issues and New: Arms and Nuclear Weapons

When Bhutto arrived in Washington on February 4, 1975, his main aim was to achieve the final lifting of the arms embargo. After Byroade's soundings had confirmed that the mood on Capitol Hill was favorable,

President Gerald Ford and Prime Minister Zulfikar Ali Bhutto meet in the Oval Office, February 1975. From the left, Foreign Minister Aziz Ahmed, Prime Minister Bhutto, President Ford, Secretary of State Henry Kissinger, and Ambassador Sahibzada Yaqub Khan (Courtesy of the Gerald R. Ford Library).

the administration advised Bhutto privately that it would remove the ban but wanted to delay the public announcement in order to permit additional consultation with congressional leaders. Talking with the press, the president and the secretary of state signaled the likelihood of a positive decision. Ford stated that he was giving "active consideration" to removing the restrictions. Kissinger commented that Pakistan was "an ally which is in the curious position of being subject to an American embargo."[11]

On February 24, 1975, Washington officially announced that it was removing all limitations on arms transfers to Pakistan (and India), ending the embargo that Lyndon Johnson had imposed almost ten years before during the two countries' 1965 war over Kashmir. To dampen possible congressional criticism and the Indian reaction, the new policy envisaged only cash sales and ruled out military assistance grants or concessional sales—which had been the mainstay of arms aid to Pakistan in the 1950s and 1960s. The Ford administration also decided that, initially at least, sales would be limited to defensive weapons.[12] The congressional and press reaction was mild. Although the *New York Times* criticized the decision as "a stimulus to an arms race," the *Washington Post* praised the move as marking "a maturing in American dealings" with the South Asia region.[13]

Because Pakistan had experienced an extremely poor wheat crop that year, Bhutto also asked for significant amounts of food aid from the United States. In line with the administration's friendly approach, Washington agreed to provide four hundred thousand tons of wheat, worth about $65 million, and $78 million of development loans. Although still substantial, U.S. economic aid was becoming relatively less significant for the Pakistani economy. Bhutto's persistent wooing of fellow Muslim states in the Persian Gulf had begun to pay off. Oil-producing friends such as Saudi Arabia and Iran promised some $400 million in economic and financial assistance.

By the time Bhutto visited Washington, U.S. officials were becoming concerned about Pakistan's ambitions to match India's nuclear capability. An important indicator that something of this nature was under way was Pakistan's revival of discussions with the French about purchase of a nuclear fuel reprocessing plant.[14] Since the reprocessing plant's capacity was greatly in excess of the fuel requirements of the Karachi nuclear reactor and other projected power projects, U.S. specialists worried that it was intended to provide the plutonium needed for a nuclear weapons program. In a State Department briefing paper for the Bhutto visit, Alfred (Roy) Atherton, who had succeeded Joseph Sisco as assistant secretary of state for the Near East and South Asia, advised Kissinger, "The [government of Pakistan] is trying to develop an independent nuclear fuel cycle and the technical skills that would make the nuclear explosion option feasible."[15] In turn, the secretary's briefing memorandum to President Ford stated, "There is now considerable evidence that Pakistan is embarked on a program that could in time give it the option to duplicate India's nuclear explosion of last May."[16]

Although neither Kissinger nor Ford took up the issue directly with Bhutto, the secretary of state agreed that it could be raised at a lower level. Accordingly, the State Department's country director for Pakistan, Peter Constable, told Iqbal Riza, the chargé d'affaires at the Pakistani embassy, that the United States hoped that lifting the arms embargo would encourage Pakistan not to pursue "the politically risky and costly development of nuclear explosives."[17] The démarche had little impact: a short while later, the Pakistanis completed negotiations with the French and signed a contract for the reprocessing plant.[18]

1975–76: Mostly Positive Developments

During 1975, the political landscape in South Asia changed dramatically. In Bangladesh, disgruntled military officers assassinated President Mujibur Rahman at his home in Dacca and seized power. Maj. Gen. Ziaur Rahman, a hero of the 1971 battle for independence, shortly ousted the killers of Mujib to establish a military-backed regime. In India, after political discontent had mounted and a court order had voided her election to parliament, Prime Minister Indira Gandhi had persuaded the president to approve "emergency" powers that permitted her to arrest opposition leaders, gag the press, and impose authoritarian rule. At year's end, Sri Lanka and Pakistan were the only democratic states in the region.

By this time also, the key U.S. partners in western Asia—Saudi Arabia and Iran—had emerged with vastly increased economic wealth following the success of the oil producers' cartel in boosting petroleum prices. The shah of Iran, in particular, wanted to play an expanded regional role. With U.S. support, he mounted an ambitious effort to counter Soviet influence in Afghanistan. Through promises of lavish economic aid, the shah sought to entice Afghan president Sardar Mohammed Daoud from his close embrace of Moscow. (In the mid-1960s, Daoud had been pushed out of the prime ministership by his cousin, King Zahir. In July 1973, however, with the help of leftist military officers, Daoud had seized power from the king and had abolished the monarchy.)

A hard-line Afghan nationalist, Daoud soon revived the dormant Pushtunistan dispute with Pakistan and fanned smoldering tribal unrest in Pakistan's Baluchistan province, where Bhutto had felt it necessary to employ the military to suppress the tribals. In retaliation against Kabul, Islamabad secretly recruited conservative, pro-Islamic opponents of Daoud to mount an insurgency against his regime. Maj. Gen. Nasrullah Babar, the head of Pakistan's paramilitary Frontier Scouts, who was close to Bhutto and, later, to Bhutto's daughter, Benazir, organized and directed the covert anti-Daoud operation.[19] The insurgents, who included later Afghan mujahideen leaders such as Islamic radical Gulbuddin Hekmatyar, were able to accomplish little against the Kabul regime, however.[20]

Economically and psychologically, Pakistan by 1976 was back on its feet, seemingly recovered from the trauma of 1971. When Bhutto reversed field on economic policy to drop support for "Islamic socialism," the economy perked up and its gross national product began to grow at an annual rate of 5 percent. A billion dollars in aid and credits from the Middle Eastern oil-producing countries and Iran were important pluses. "We supported the Middle East long before their oil made everyone their suitors. Now we are getting some rewards for that support," a Pakistani official told the *New York Times* in January 1976.[21]

The only domestic trouble was largely of Bhutto's own making. The prime minister increasingly was acting more like a feudal autocrat than a democratic political leader. Showing growing intolerance with those who opposed him, Bhutto cracked down hard on critics within his own Pakistan Peoples Party (PPP). He also jailed senior opposition leaders from Baluchistan and the Northwest Frontier Province.

In managing Pakistan's foreign relations, Bhutto's performance was more successful, as he made a number of moves to broaden Pakistan's options in the changing regional environment. Despite his antipathy toward India, Bhutto restored relations to their level before the 1965 war. Supporting the shah's efforts to wean Afghan president Daoud away from the Soviets, he worked to reduce tensions with Kabul. The prime minister nurtured the relationship with China and flirted with the idea of establishing closer ties with North Korea after a visit to Pyongyang. Finally, Bhutto continued to signal interest in a meaningful improvement in bilateral ties with the Soviet Union.

An August 1976 State Department analysis of Pakistan's foreign policy commented, "Bhutto has been trying to compensate for Pakistan's relative political, military and economic weakness by conciliating his neighbors, hedging his bets with the regional and world powers, and by trying to play a larger than life role on the world scene."[22] That same month, in an article in *Pakistan Horizon,* Bhutto described his foreign policy as "balanced bilateralism."[23]

Nuclear Troubles with Washington

Anxiety among nonproliferation supporters that other countries would try to follow India's example increased after the French and the West Germans signed contracts with Pakistan, Brazil, and Argentina that could facilitate their acquiring nuclear explosive capabilities. Credible intelligence reports also pointed to the development of research reactors by South Korea and Taiwan that could similarly enable these states to move toward nuclear weapons.

In the case of Pakistan, U.S. concerns focused on the nuclear fuel reprocessing plant contract with France and on a facility to produce heavy water, which Pakistan hoped to obtain from West Germany. The contract with the French made little sense to U.S. specialists except as part of a broader program to develop a nuclear weapons capability[24] The contract with West Germany for the supply of a heavy-water production facility, another important element in the nuclear fuel cycle, was also troubling.

The Ford administration's policy response, adopted as the U.S. presidential election campaign began to heat up in 1976, was to tighten export controls on sensitive items for states, such as Pakistan, that had not signed the nuclear Nonproliferation Treaty (NPT) and were unwilling to allow international inspection of all their nuclear facilities, so-called full-scope safeguards. Using muscular diplomacy, Washington succeeded in derailing suspect projects in Argentina, Brazil, South Korea, and Taiwan—but not in Pakistan. Although the West Germans were willing to drop their heavy-water project, the French refused to back away from the contract for the reprocessing plant.

In February 1976, Kissinger raised the issue directly with Bhutto during a meeting in New York. The secretary of state suggested that Pakistan defer the nuclear project to allow time to explore setting up an international nuclear fuel reprocessing facility. Washington was seeking the shah's approval to locate such a facility in Iran, which, unlike Pakistan, had signed the NPT.[25] A month later, in March 1976, President Ford seconded Kissinger's request in a letter to Bhutto that asked Pakistan to forgo plans for acquiring reprocessing and heavy-water capabilities until a clear need existed and alternatives were fully examined.[26] The Pakistani leader refused to either postpone or cancel the projects.[27]

In a further bid to persuade Bhutto to drop the nuclear option, Kissinger traveled to Pakistan in August 1976, his third trip there as secretary of state. As the secretary's aircraft winged its way across Europe and the Middle East toward South Asia, reporters were told in no uncertain terms of U.S. opposition to the French reprocessing project. Despite strict International Atomic Energy Agency safeguards, State Department sources said that the plant raised "concern that Pakistan was trying to match India by exploding a nuclear device of its own."[28] With the Democrats sharply criticizing the administration's nonproliferation policy, especially its relaxed reaction to the Indian test, Kissinger and Ford were under pressure to demonstrate that they were doing everything possible to prevent Pakistan from continuing its effort to match India's nuclear capability.[29]

Kissinger's strategy was a combination of carrots and sticks. The carrots came in an offer of 110 A-7 attack bombers, which the Pakistani air force badly wanted to improve its strike capability against India. If "a successful resolution of the reprocessing issue" could be brought about, Kissinger indicated that congressional approval for the A-7s seemed likely.[30] The sticks were not any direct threat, but the prospect that the Democrats, who were favored to win the upcoming presidential election, would adopt a tougher nonproliferation approach and might make an example of Pakistan.

At an official dinner on the evening of Kissinger's arrival in Lahore, the prime minister and the secretary of state bantered about the nuclear issue in their toasts. Bhutto declared, "[Lahore] is our reprocessing center, and we cannot in any way curb the reprocessing center of Pakistan." Kissinger replied that governments must constantly review their policies, "to reprocess themselves" and decide "what is worth reprocessing."[31]

When the two leaders met the next day in the company of senior aides, the discussion roamed the globe with considerable frankness, touching on South Asia, China, the Middle East, and Korea. The nuclear issue was left for a private session. Talking about India, Bhutto doubted that Indira Gandhi's emergency was wise: "In a wobbly parliamentary democracy, there was some sublimation and some chance for people to feel involved. . . . But this totalitarian system is artificial. . . . Those who praise it show a myopic approach."[32] It was unfortunate for Pakistan, and for Bhutto himself, that he failed to follow this comment in ruling his own country.

Regarding North Korea (the Pakistani leader had raised eyebrows in Washington with his friendly trip to Pyongyang) the secretary stated that, from Pakistan's viewpoint, "it was an intelligent move . . . so we didn't raise any question." Kissinger added, reflecting his realpolitik approach to foreign policy, that he had never "raised the question about [Pakistan's] sincerity. I don't think it has meaning for nations. I assume a nation does something for its own interest. In 1971, the U.S. and China, for their own reasons, had compatible policies. With North Korea, that compatibility isn't there."[33]

When they met alone, the secretary told the prime minister that he ran the risk of far harsher treatment should Jimmy Carter and the Democrats win the 1976 elections.[34] As part of the process of tightening up nuclear policy, Congress had adopted amendments to sections 669 and 670 of the foreign assistance act proposed by Senators John Glenn (D-Ohio) and Stuart Symington (D-Mo.) to bar assistance to non-NPT signatories that imported uranium-enrichment or nuclear fuel reprocessing technology. Warning that Pakistan might face an economic aid cutoff under the new legislation, Kissinger urged the prime minister to accept the Ford administration's proposal: a substantial conventional arms package, including the potent A-7s, if Pakistan agreed to forgo the nuclear fuel reprocessing plant.[35]

Despite good personal relations and genuine mutual respect, the secretary of state was unable to sway the prime minister. Notwithstanding Nixon's 1971 tilt and the friendly attitude of the Ford administration toward Pakistan, U.S. influence was limited. Following the shock of Washington's aid cutoff during the 1965 war, neither Bhutto nor other senior Pakistani officials were willing to place their country's security against India in American hands, especially after India had acquired a nuclear capability. The Pakistanis firmly believed that their only sure defense against their vastly larger neighbor lay in acquiring a nuclear explosive capability to match India's.

When Bhutto discussed the U.S. proposal with his senior security advisers, all of them, including air force chief Zulfikar Ali Khan, urged the prime minister not to bend on the nuclear question. Bhutto agreed and turned Kissinger down.[36] Robert Oakley, who was on the trip as a National Security Council staff member, commented that both the Pakistanis and the Americans surprised each other by their strong stands. The intensity with which Kissinger pursued the nuclear question surprised his Pakistani hosts. Bhutto's refusal to give ground in return for a substantial U.S. conventional arms package, in turn, surprised the Americans.[37]

Unbeknownst to the United States, Pakistan had by this time secretly embarked on a parallel and technically more difficult route toward a nuclear explosive capability. A Pakistani metallurgist, Abdul Qadeer Khan, had gained detailed knowledge of the highly sensitive and complex ultracentrifuge uranium-enrichment process while working in the Netherlands. In late 1975, Bhutto had placed A. Q. Khan in charge of a high-powered secret effort to produce enriched uranium for nuclear weapons.[38]

The Pakistanis, according to Munir Ahmed Khan, set about purchasing equipment from suppliers in France, Britain, Belgium, and West Germany. At first, they made little effort to cover their tracks. Although European countries and the United States had tightened export controls on sensitive items as part of the tougher nuclear policy after the Indian test, Khan explained that the Pakistanis were able to circumvent restrictions by procuring individual components and parts of sensitive equipment rather than purchasing entire units.[39]

Compatibility, Except on the Nuclear Issue

For Pakistan, the Ford years saw further steps by Bhutto to reorient foreign and security policy away from the triangular tightrope that Ayub Khan had pursued in the mid-1960s to a sturdier structure resting on three main pillars. The first, and most important, was the intimate relationship with Beijing. Ever since the 1965 war with India, China had replaced the United States as Pakistan's principal source of military equipment and its main security blanket against India.

The second pillar was the relationship with the United States. Despite Bhutto's vociferous criticism of U.S. policy during the 1960s, he reversed field after gaining power in December 1971 and—as he told President Nixon—pursued a friendly relationship with Washington. Even if the United States did not provide military aid and seemed a less formidable power after Watergate and the defeat in Vietnam, Bhutto believed good ties with America were in Pakistan's national interest. The United States continued to provide substantial economic aid and, after lifting the arms embargo, sold Pakistan significant amounts of military equipment. Nonetheless, many Pakistanis continued to harbor a deep grievance against the treatment received from Washington during and after the 1965 war. Some also felt, without much justification, that the United States could have done more to help Pakistan against India during the 1971 crisis in East Pakistan.

The third foreign policy pillar was the greatly strengthened relationship with fellow Muslim states of the Middle East. Bhutto breathed new life and substance into this long-held Pakistani aspiration, which the country's earlier pro-Western orientation had impeded. Stronger links with the Arab states and Iran not only helped Pakistan firm up its Islamic credentials but resulted in substantial financial assistance from wealthy oil producers and the inflow of remittances from several million Pakistanis who found work in the booming Persian Gulf states.

Bhutto also sought a fourth pillar, still not fully realized: membership in the Nonaligned Movement (NAM) and, more generally, an expanded role for Pakistan in the Third World. Although India was able to block Pakistan's formal joining of the NAM because of Islamabad's continued membership in CENTO, Bhutto found it possible to use the Organization of Islamic Conference as a platform for pressing his worldview on a wider international stage.

From the U.S. perspective, the two and a half years of Gerald Ford's presidency saw a continuation of Nixon's policy of warm relations toward Pakistan. Even though Islamabad had left SEATO in 1972 and remained only a nominal member of CENTO, the Ford administration considered Pakistan a good friend and ally. Still, lingering congressional antipathy because of Pakistan's conduct in 1971 delayed lifting the decade-old embargo on lethal arms transfers until February 1975. Moreover, when President Ford removed the restrictions, he was unable to renew the intimate pre-1965 security relationship.

9

Carter: The Low Point

Zulfikar Ali Bhutto had reason to be uneasy about Jimmy Carter's arrival in the White House. Ford's defeat meant the departure of Secretary of State Henry Kissinger, with whom the prime minister had developed a close working relationship, and of the Pakistan-friendly Republicans. Islamabad worried that the policies that Carter had advocated during the election campaign—a tougher nuclear nonproliferation stance, a more restrictive approach to arms transfers to nations of the developing world, and a greater emphasis on human rights—would not augur well for U.S.-Pakistan relations. A further concern was that Carter might feel a special affinity for India, where his mother had served as a sixty-year-old Peace Corps volunteer.[1]

On January 7, 1977, perhaps with an eye on Washington, Bhutto announced general elections in March, almost a year earlier than constitutionally necessary. With Indira Gandhi's dictatorship seemingly firmly in place in India—she had yet to announce her own elections and lift the state of emergency she had declared in 1975—and military rule in Bangladesh, Pakistan appeared, relatively speaking, a South Asian democratic strong point. But things soon went very wrong.

Initially, the American embassy in Islamabad predicted that Bhutto and his Pakistan Peoples Party (PPP) would win the balloting in an easy walkover. Following a field trip, political officer Arnold Raphel, who would become the U.S. ambassador to Pakistan a decade later, described the elections as a "non-event."[2] But after nine opposition parties forged an anti-Bhutto coalition called the Pakistan National Alliance (PNA) and began to draw massive crowds, observers concluded that the race would be closer than expected, even though they still thought that the PPP would win a respectable victory.[3]

During his five years at Pakistan's helm, Bhutto had retained an emotional hold on the poor masses who had voted overwhelmingly for him in the 1970 elections. At the same time, however, he had made many enemies. The nationalization of major industries during his first two years in office had upset business circles. An ill-considered decision to take over several thousand wheat-milling, rice-husking, and cotton-ginning units in July 1976 had angered small-business owners and traders. The left—intellectuals, students, and trade unionists—felt betrayed by Bhutto's shift to more conservative economic policies and by his growing collaboration with feudal landlords, Pakistan's traditional power brokers. Bhutto's increasingly authoritarian personal style and often high-handed way of dealing with political opponents had also alienated many.[4]

On election night, March 7, 1977, the prime minister invited his friend Ambassador Henry Byroade to watch the results on television. Byroade recalled, "[Bhutto] was losing in Karachi. He was losing in Peshawar. Then the Punjab numbers started coming in and guys who were absolute thugs won by 99 per cent. . . . Then [Bhutto] became absolutely quiet and started drinking heavily, calling Lahore [in the Punjab] and he said, 'What are you guys doing?' . . . I saw Bhutto at 8 the next morning, and he wasn't himself. He hadn't had any sleep, obviously drinking. He was just sad."[5]

It was a far bigger PPP sweep than anyone had anticipated. The final tally gave Bhutto's party 155 out of 200 National Assembly seats, including 107 of 115 in the Punjab. If the results saddened the prime minister, they enraged the opposition, which screamed that widespread rigging had ensured the PPP landslide. In a matter of days, PNA supporters filled the streets of major cities with antigovernment demonstrations. As the protests grew in intensity, it became clear that Bhutto was in trouble. To dampen the disturbances, he imposed limited martial law in Karachi, Lahore, and Hyderabad, ordering the army to back up the police.[6]

The deployment of the military put the spotlight on its leader, Gen. Mohammed Zia ul-Haq. In 1975, Bhutto had selected Zia over six more-senior generals to become chief of army staff, presumably because he appeared to be a personally servile and politically unambitious professional. Born in the part of eastern Punjab that had remained with India at independence, Zia came from a middle-class family with a strong religious background. He had won plaudits while assigned to the Pakistani training mission in Jordan when Arab radicals threatened

King Hussein's position in 1970. Zia later flattered Bhutto and attracted favorable attention as the commander of the army corps headquartered in Multan.

If Ayub Khan looked like a Bengal lancer, Zia appeared more like a character from "Monty Python's Flying Circus" or a caricature of British movie comedian Terry Thomas. Of medium height and stocky, the army chief's most prominent features were his slicked-down hair parted in the middle and his black moustache. In public, Bhutto treated Zia with near contempt, making him the butt of ridicule on social occasions as "his monkey general." Whatever his inner thoughts, Zia outwardly accepted the prime minister's taunts with an ever-present smile and expressions of appreciation for "your such kind attentions, sir."[7]

After Bhutto had to call on the military to help maintain order, however, the equation changed. Although always polite and seemingly respectful, the army chief began to assert himself more forcefully. Making clear that he and his fellow generals had little stomach for employing soldiers to put down their fellow citizens, Zia pressed Bhutto to reach a political settlement with the opposition.[8]

The United States Trying to Do Bhutto In?

As Bhutto's domestic situation worsened, he received an unexpected rebuke from the Carter administration. On April 21, 1977, the State Department announced that it was blocking the export of $68 thousand worth of tear gas on the grounds that this would signal U.S. support for a "repressive regime" and be contrary to the administration's human rights policy.[9] Since tear gas, regarded as more humane than bullets for crowd control, was not considered a sensitive export commodity, the move amounted to a public slap.[10] The incident stirred Bhutto's suspicions about U.S. intentions, while the PNA opposition praised the action as a "source of great strength."[11]

Intercepts of telephone conversations between U.S. diplomats further fueled the prime minister's suspicion that America was trying to do him in. After a journalist informed Robert Moore, the consul general in Karachi, that Bhutto had been forcibly detained at a reception, Moore telephoned Political Counselor Howard Schaffer in Islamabad. Assuming that the telephone line was tapped, the consul general paraphrased his message.[12] Moore called Schaffer again after learning that the story about Bhutto's detention was incorrect. Once more trying to disguise his comments, the consul general said, "My source tells me the party is over."[13]

Perhaps misunderstanding the intercepted conversations, Bhutto decided to play the "U.S. interference" card in the increasingly tense battle with the PNA opposition. During an emotional address in the National Assembly on April 28, 1977, the prime minister charged that the United States was financing a "vast, colossal, huge international conspiracy" to oust him from power. Bhutto alleged that Washington was punishing him for opposing U.S. Vietnam policy, for backing the Arab cause against Israel, and for refusing to bow to Washington's pressure on the nuclear reprocessing issue. To climax the speech, he referred to the Moore-Schaffer phone conversations. "The party's over, the party's over. He's gone," Bhutto declared. "Well, gentlemen," the prime minister added to loud cheers, "The party is not over!"[14]

U.S. officials were not amused. In Islamabad, the embassy lodged an official protest at the foreign ministry. In Washington, the State Department publicly denied the charges and Cyrus Vance, Carter's secretary of state, sent a "fairly stern but conciliatory" rejoinder.[15] Peter Constable, at the time the chargé d'affaires at the embassy in Islamabad, recalled, "Bhutto, being a real political rogue and rascal, went out in an open jeep around Rawalpindi and had all his supporters out in the streets and he was waving this letter from Secretary Vance, saying that the Americans had apologized to him. Of course, it wasn't an apology at all, and then we got the Department to release the text."[16]

After the attacks on the United States appeared to gain him little political advantage, the prime minister backed off, calling Constable to his house to explore ways to restore a more normal relationship. Bhutto claimed that he had evidence of interference but did not produce any when Constable asked for specifics. It was nonetheless agreed that Secretary Vance would meet with Foreign Minister Aziz Ahmed in Paris to discuss the problem.[17]

When the two ministers met on May 31, 1977, Aziz Ahmed told Vance—much as he had told President Kennedy in 1963—that the United States had let down "its faithful ally" Pakistan. Like Bhutto, however, the foreign minister failed to provide any specifics to back up the charges of U.S. interference. Indeed, Pakistan's intelligence services had been unable to produce anything concrete when pressed by the Pakistani government for evidence of U.S. support for the opposition PNA.[18]

In talking with Aziz Ahmed, Vance denied that the United States was trying to oust Bhutto and speculated that the charges might be the result of an anti-U.S. "disinformation" campaign. Adopting his usual gentlemanly approach, Vance expressed a desire for friendlier bilateral relations, saying, "We should try to put the past behind us." Aziz Ahmed agreed and stated that he would explore ways to dampen the anti-U.S. atmosphere when he returned home. In line with Vance's accommodating stance, the United States continued to provide arms to Pakistan—the secretary characterized the tear gas episode as a "special case."[19] Ironically, on April 28, 1977, the very day that Bhutto had blasted America for "colossal" interference, the U.S. Navy transferred two destroyers to Pakistan under a long-term loan arrangement.[20]

The improvement in relations proved short-lived. In line with its policy to de-emphasize arms transfers to the developing world, the Carter administration withdrew the offer of 110 A-7 attack aircraft that had remained on the table when Gerald Ford departed the White House. To make matters worse, the State Department failed to inform the Pakistanis of the action, which they learned of from the media. The fact that the press spoke of concern about India's reaction as a major reason for the decision further irked the Pakistanis.[21] The U.S. embassy in Islamabad warned that the episode gave "the strong impression, regardless of how fortuitous or false it is, that we have decided we can no longer do business with Bhutto and we are punishing Pakistan."[22]

Meanwhile, as the deadlock between Bhutto and his political opponents hardened, Saudi Arabia tried to mediate between the two sides, an indication of the growing importance of the oil-rich Saudis in Pakistani politics. The Saudis were able to get serious negotiations under way but had difficulty in firming up a compromise agreement for new elections in the fall of 1977. In dealing with the Saudis, Bhutto seemed to be looking over his shoulder, still nervous about foreign interference. At one point, the prime minister charged that the Soviets were "massively" interfering in Pakistan. When the Saudi ambassador queried how this squared with his allegations about the United States, an ever-glib Bhutto responded that Washington was trying to "weaken" Pakistan, and that Moscow wanted to "dismember" the country.[23]

On June 17, 1977, the prime minister flew to Saudi Arabia to thank King Khalid for his help in arranging what then seemed to be a viable agreement with the opposition. Bhutto told the Saudi monarch that he blamed both Moscow and Washington for his domestic troubles but believed the Americans were more responsible than the Russians. Bhutto recalled Kissinger's warning that Carter would make an example of Pakistan because of the nuclear issue and claimed to have "ample proof" that the Americans had funneled money and advice to his opponents.[24]

By this time, Pakistan's military chiefs were becoming worried about maintaining troop morale in the face of ongoing political instability. Zia and the corps commanders emphasized their wish that Bhutto reach an early accord with the opposition to end the unrest. At the same time, they readied a contingency plan called Operation Fair Play, which envisaged a military takeover to prevent a total breakdown of law and order.[25]

As July 1977 began, political negotiations were continuing almost nonstop. Although the PPP and the PNA seemed tantalizingly close to an accord, mutual suspicions hindered their bringing an agreement to closure. During this time of extreme tension, career diplomat and China specialist Arthur Hummel arrived in Islamabad to succeed Henry Byroade as ambassador. With the traditional July 4 American Independence Day celebration at hand, an awkward problem arose: according to Pakistani protocol, the prime minister could not attend the American function—a midday reception for top officials and diplomats—unless he had previously received the new ambassador. The frenetic pace of political negotiations had made it difficult for Bhutto to find the time to receive Hummel. It was not until 2 A.M. on July 4 that the prime minister was finally able to meet with Hummel. The envoy recalled having a "reasonably friendly discussion," during which Bhutto said that he wanted to be on good terms with the United States once the political troubles ended.[26] Having satisfied the niceties of protocol, the prime minister arrived at the ambassador's residence ten hours later to attend the July 4th party. According to Hummel, Bhutto "made his presence very conspicuous by talking with the Soviet ambassador the whole time."[27] At one point during the reception, Arnold Raphel approached General Zia, with whom he was on friendly terms, to ask if he would like to greet Bhutto. The army chief answered somewhat stiffly that "[i]t wasn't necessary." He similarly brushed off Raphel's suggestion that they inspect the U.S. military attaché's airplane the following day—something that the army chief had previously expressed an interest in doing. Zia told Raphel that he would be "very busy" on July 5.[28]

The Army Ousts Bhutto

What would keep Zia "very busy" soon became apparent. The army chief informed his senior colleagues shortly after 6:30 P.M. that Operation Fair Play would be implemented that night, since "the government and the PNA have agreed to disagree."[29] Shortly after midnight on July 5, 1977, just twelve hours after the American reception, the military took power for the third time since Pakistan gained independence, and for the first time ousted an elected government. Zia imposed martial law and placed Bhutto, other senior leaders of the PPP, and top figures of the opposition PNA under house arrest. The general personally called Bhutto to say, "I'm sorry, Sir, I had to do it. . . . But in ninety days I'll hold new elections. You'll be elected Prime Minister again, of course, Sir, and I'll be saluting you."[30]

It is possible that General Zia initially expected to maintain martial law for only a short period and to hold new elections after the country cooled down. It is also possible that Zia, a vastly more cunning and ambitious individual than his self-effacing manner suggested, never intended an early return to civilian rule. Whatever his true thoughts, Zia announced that the military did not plan to remain in power for long and would hold fresh elections in the fall of 1977.

On July 15, 1977, Zia called on Bhutto, who was then being held in a comfortable government rest house in the 6,000-foot, fir-tree-covered hill station of Murree, just an hour's drive from Islamabad. Acting as if he were still running the country, Bhutto imprudently chastised Zia for imposing martial law and reminded him that the 1973 constitution called for the death penalty for anyone trying to overthrow the government.[31] The general listened politely, said that he had intervened reluctantly, would remain neutral, and would hold fair elections, after which he would "revert to the barracks leaving the field free to you to manage the affairs of state as you consider appropriate."[32]

Two weeks later, when Zia released the former prime minister and the other political prisoners from custody, it looked as though the generals genuinely intended to rule the country for only a brief period. If so, the public's tumultuous reception for Bhutto jolted their thinking. Once free, the ex–prime minister sharply criticized the imposition of martial law[33] and demonstrated that his popularity with the masses remained undiminished. A wildly enthusiastic reception welcomed Bhutto in Karachi. In Lahore, the city's largest-ever crowd turned out to greet him. It seemed likely that the PPP would win the upcoming elections.

Although Zia and his colleagues may not have planned to retain power, the likelihood of a Bhutto victory undoubtedly helped convince them to stay on. Given the ex-prime minister's criticism of the military's action, his track record for vindictiveness in dealing with opponents, and the provisions of the 1973 constitution, the generals must have realized that they could expect harsh treatment should Bhutto regain power. The martial law regime then rapidly assembled a battery of legal charges against Bhutto, maintaining that it was taken aback by evidence found in official files of criminal abuse of power. The purpose was clear: to remove Bhutto from the political stage.[34]

On September 3, 1977, the ex–prime minister was arrested on charges of murder and "other high crimes." Although M. A. Kasuri, a Punjabi politician who had fallen out with Bhutto, was allegedly the intended victim of the murder, it was Kasuri's father who, in fact, had been shot to death in an ambush. Solicitous about the U.S. reaction, Zia made a point of informing Ambassador Hummel personally. During their meeting, the general reiterated that he would shortly hold elections and expressed the hope that these would result in the formation of "a reasonably stable government."[35] For the next nineteen months, Bhutto's fate preoccupied the political life of Pakistan.

On October 1, 1977, only eighteen days before elections were supposed to take place, Zia postponed the balloting. He set no new date. Pakistan then settled into its longest stretch of martial law, which lasted for eight years, until December 31, 1985. Unlike during the two earlier periods of martial law, the constitution was suspended but not abrogated. However, as chief martial law administrator, chief of army staff, and after September 1978, president,[36] General Zia had total control of the reins of power.

U.S.-Pakistan Relations Skid

By this time, U.S.-Pakistan relations were skidding downward. After the stunning election victory of the Janata Party and the end to Indira Gandhi's authoritarian emergency, India was once more the world's largest democracy. When Zia became his country's military dictator, the India-Pakistan contrast was even more marked. With its emphasis on promoting democracy and human rights, the Carter administration looked on India with favor and on Pakistan with concern. In keeping with the views of Carter's national security adviser, Zbigniew Brzezinski, Washington was also trying to strengthen relationships with "regional influentials." In South Asia, that meant India, not Pakistan. In July 1977, Jimmy Carter welcomed India's new prime minister, Morarji Desai, to the White House. On January 1, 1978, Carter became the third U.S. president to pay an official visit to India. Unlike Eisenhower and Nixon, he did not stop in Pakistan.[37]

In dealing with foreign affairs, Zia basically followed Bhutto's approach, but in a less flamboyant manner. Aziz Ahmed, who was regarded as too close to the former prime minister, was dropped as foreign minister. Agha Shahi, the accomplished career diplomat who had been serving as foreign secretary, became his successor, with the title of "foreign affairs adviser."

Nor did Zia alter course on the nuclear issue. When State Department nuclear specialist Joseph Nye visited Islamabad in September 1977, he brought only sticks after Washington had withdrawn the principal carrot—the offer to sell A-7 attack bombers. Nye warned the Pakistanis that if they persisted with the French fuel reprocessing project, the United States would have to cut off economic assistance under the Glenn amendment to the foreign assistance act. This amendment barred U.S. aid to countries that had not signed the nuclear Nonproliferation Treaty (NPT) but that imported nuclear fuel reprocessing technology.[38] The fact that Pakistan had agreed to special international safeguards made little impression on U.S. nuclear specialists; they continued to be convinced that Islamabad wanted the reprocessing facility in order to be able to match India's nuclear explosive capability.

Zia informed Nye that his country intended to proceed with the project. Quite apart from strategic considerations, Pakistan's military dictator had little choice on a issue that had become charged with nationalist pride. After Zia refused to bend, the U.S. government proceeded to suspend economic assistance. With aid levels running at about $50 million annually, considerably less than during the halcyon days of the early 1960s, the economic blow was not enormous. Washington, in any case, continued a substantial food aid program that the Glenn amendment did not bar. The political blow was nonetheless sharp. The cooling of U.S.-Pakistan ties paralleled the warming trend in the U.S.-India relationship.

Although the Carter administration failed to dissuade Islamabad, it fared better in Paris. After French president Valéry Giscard d'Estaing dropped Gaullist Jacques Chirac as prime minister, Paris decided to shift its policy and informed Washington that it would not be unhappy if the reprocessing-plant project were terminated.[39] To put a better face on things, the French proposed a technical modification called "co-processing" that would permit production of fuel usable in a nuclear power reactor but not in making a bomb.[40] When French nuclear expert Andre Jacomet visited Pakistan in February 1978, Zia rejected the suggested alternative. At this point, Jacomet recalled, the French became "convinced Pakistan wanted the atomic bomb" and decided definitively to back out of the contract.[41]

For Washington, the French action appeared to mark an important nonproliferation victory and to remove the major source of friction in bilateral relations with Pakistan. A pleased State Department announced that the United States would be resuming economic aid and seeking $69 million for the coming fiscal year's program.[42] But the smiles did not last long. U.S. officials soon became aware that Pakistan was secretly pursuing a parallel, but technically more difficult, path toward a bomb: the uranium-enrichment process.[43] In the spring of 1978, Western governments realized that something was amiss after the British discovered that the Pakistanis were trying to purchase "inverters," a key component for enriching uranium.[44] A parliamentary question put the issue in the public domain in July 1978. In the fall, the British imposed export controls on "inverters."[45]

As intelligence about the secret program mounted, Ambassador Hummel decided on a direct approach with Zia: to lay out what the United States knew about Pakistan's clandestine effort to produce enriched uranium. After hearing Hummel out, Zia responded with a straight face, "That's absolutely ridiculous. Your information is incorrect. We have to clear this up. Tell me any place in Pakistan you want to send your experts and I will let them come and see." The ambassador was skeptical that Zia would follow through. He was right.[46]

Bhutto Dies on the Gallows

Meanwhile, on March 18, 1978, the Lahore high court found Bhutto guilty of murder and sentenced him to death. The court's decision triggered calls for clemency from many foreign leaders, including President

Jimmy Carter.[47] An unmoved Zia told British television that he had so far granted none of seventy appeals for clemency that had been presented to him and saw no special reason to intervene in Bhutto's case.[48] After the former prime minister decided to appeal his conviction to the Supreme Court of Pakistan, the legal process continued for the rest of the year. On December 18, 1978, Bhutto began four dramatic days in court to argue his own appeal. Although "haggard and pale" after months in prison, according to a cabled report from the embassy in Islamabad, the former prime minister delivered an articulate and eloquent defense that called "not for mercy or clemency but for justice."[49]

While Bhutto's fate was consuming Pakistanis, in neighboring Iran the curtain was falling on America's longtime ally, the shah. In the face of antigovernment riots during the fall and early winter of 1978–79, his regime crumbled. After the monarch went into exile in January 1979, Shi'ite fundamentalist leader Ayatollah Ruhollah Khomeini made a triumphal entry into Tehran to launch the Iranian revolution. Although the Pakistani leadership had no great love for the shah, whose imperial pretensions they found grating, nor much respect for the martial qualities of the U.S.-trained and -equipped Iranian military, the failure of the Carter administration to support more effectively a major U.S. ally took Islamabad aback. Earlier, the Pakistanis had also been surprised by Washington's restrained reaction to the April 1978 coup d'état in Kabul that ousted President Sardar Mohammed Daoud and brought the communists to power in Afghanistan.[50]

When the revolutionary Iranian government announced it was withdrawing from CENTO, Pakistan quickly followed suit. Foreign Affairs Adviser Agha Shahi told the press that the alliance had "lost its meaning with the withdrawal of Iran but [Pakistan] had been moving independently to that position" anyway.[51] Although Shahi had previously urged Zia to leave the alliance so that India could no longer use CENTO membership as an excuse to block Pakistan's joining the Nonaligned Movement (NAM), Zia preferred to avoid adding to his difficulties with the Americans.[52] After Pakistan quit CENTO, it was officially accepted into the NAM at the group's 1979 summit in Cuba. Once Iran and Pakistan withdrew from CENTO, that alliance formally disbanded.

On February 2, 1979, the Supreme Court of Pakistan rejected Bhutto's appeal by a single vote. That same day, Ambassador Hummel delivered another request for clemency from President Carter.[53] On

March 1, 1979, the U.S. House of Representatives added its voice, adopting a resolution that urged Zia to spare Bhutto's life. Despite these pleas and numerous others, Zia told the press that he saw "no justification to use his prerogative [to grant clemency] against the decisions" of the courts. He characterized the Bhutto trial as "a pure and simple criminal case" that has "nothing to do with politics." At the same time, the Pakistani president reiterated that he would soon announce a date for the long-promised elections.[54] During March, Zia received a third message from Carter, along with similar appeals for clemency from the pope, UN Secretary-General Kurt Waldheim, and leaders of the Soviet Union, Saudi Arabia, France, and many other nations. Zia took no action.

On the morning of April 4, 1979, Bhutto was hanged.[55] Although Hummel had pressed for clemency in keeping with Washington's instructions, his private assessment was that Zia had little practical choice. It was either Bhutto or Zia. "Although I did everything I was told with fervor, if I had been in Zia's shoes," Hummel commented, "I would not have wanted a live Bhutto in some prison from which he could escape at any time or be sprung."[56]

In assessing Zulfikar Ali Bhutto, it is hard to disagree with the judgment of Sir Morrice James, the British high commissioner to Pakistan in the mid-1960s, that the Pakistani leader was "a Lucifer, a flawed angel."[57] Bhutto combined great intelligence, personal charm, a keen grasp of international affairs, and a genuine flair for politics. After Jinnah and Liaquat Ali Khan, he was by far Pakistan's most gifted and charismatic political leader. But his negative qualities were also formidable. In the end, the clumsy and unnecessary rigging of the 1977 elections triggered his downfall. Instead of providing Pakistan with stable and enlightened leadership, Bhutto died on the gallows, beloved by the masses to whom he had promised "bread, clothing, and shelter" and reviled by others as an unprincipled demagogue.

Further Nuclear Troubles

On April 6, 1979, just two days after Bhutto's execution, the State Department confirmed that the United States had once more suspended aid to Pakistan because of the nuclear program. Washington had hoped to avoid publicizing the reimposition of sanctions but felt obligated to make the action public because of media leaks.[58] Given the proximity to Bhutto's hanging, some observers in Pakistan assumed that the United States was punishing Zia for spurning Carter's appeals for clemency. Pakistan's president knew that this was not the case.

A month earlier, after the U.S. intelligence community had concluded that Pakistan was covertly pursuing the enriched-uranium path toward a nuclear explosive capability, Deputy Secretary of State Warren Christopher had stopped in Islamabad during a trip abroad to alert Zia to the possible renewed suspension of aid. Christopher had advised that the United States would have to take this action pursuant to the Symington amendment to the foreign assistance act unless President Carter received "reliable assurances" that Pakistan was not seeking a nuclear weapon. Zia promptly "assured" Christopher that the program was "entirely peaceful" but refused to rule out a "peaceful" nuclear test and was unwilling to accept international safeguards on Pakistan's nuclear facilities. The Carter administration found Zia's response inadequate and suspended economic aid a second time. In the hope of minimizing the damage to bilateral relations, at first no announcement was made of the action.[59]

Blaming the renewed imposition of sanctions on "Zionist circles,"[60] the Pakistanis were especially rankled that Washington had taken no action against India, which had actually exploded a nuclear device. Far from punishing New Delhi, the Carter administration—to the annoyance of Islamabad—was engaged in a strenuous and politically costly battle to continue the supply of enriched-uranium fuel for the nuclear power reactors at Tarapur, near Bombay. As a top-level Pakistani put it, "If the United States had applied sanctions against the Indians, we would not have minded so much. We could understand U.S. favoritism toward Israel as a special case, but not the refusal to sanction India while hitting so hard at Pakistan."[61]

In discussions with visiting Americans, Pakistani officials regularly insisted—much as Zia had "assured" Christopher—that the nuclear program was entirely peaceful. For example, in August 1979, Foreign Affairs Adviser Shahi told visiting member of Congress Lester Wolff (D-N.Y.) that Pakistan had "no intention to make a bomb" and pursued a peaceful program in order to gain knowledge of nuclear energy for electric power generation. Shahi labeled press reports that Libya and other Arab countries were funding the program to make an "Islamic bomb" as "pure fantasy."[62] In similar vein, General Zia told the *New York Times* in September 1979, "Pakistan is not making a bomb.

Pakistan is not in a position to make a bomb and has no intention of making a bomb." The president claimed that the enriched uranium program was designed to produce nuclear fuel for electric power. "If we do not get an alternative source of energy," Zia stated, "Pakistan will choke in the next few years."[63]

As the Carter administration explored ways to derail Pakistan's nuclear program, an interagency group led by arms-control expert Gerard Smith found few promising avenues. When the *New York Times* reported that the Smith group had considered, along with other possibilities, the option of destroying Pakistan's nuclear capability by an attack on the Kahuta uranium-enrichment facility, the story caused an uproar in Islamabad. A categorical State Department denial failed to calm the waters.[64]

Two months earlier, in June 1979, Pakistan's extreme sensitivity about the Kahuta facility had caused an embarrassing diplomatic incident. Two diplomats from the French embassy in Islamabad, the ambassador and the first secretary, were driving in the vicinity of Kahuta after a meeting of European Community envoys. Although their car was traveling on a public road and was not in a restricted area, two vehicles suddenly blocked their path. Six Pakistanis then pulled the diplomats from their car and beat them severely. The first secretary, Jean Forlot, told the U.S. embassy that he assumed the Pakistani government organized the attack to scare people away from the area around the nuclear facility.[65]

In October 1979, Shahi traveled to Washington for a further round of discussions. After the communist takeover in Afghanistan and the fall of the shah in Iran, the Pakistanis hoped that the Americans would show greater sensitivity to the altered security environment in the region and dwell less heavily on the nuclear issue. But Shahi perceived little change in the U.S. stance. Although the Carter administration recognized the desirability of improving ties with Pakistan, Shahi found that the Americans were unwilling to soft pedal the nuclear issue and continued to regard Zia's military dictatorship with distaste, especially after Bhutto's execution.[66]

To aggravate matters, while his envoy was in Washington, Pakistan's president announced an indefinite postponement of elections. The State Department responded sternly that the action "deeply disappointed" the United States.[67] The Carter administration was also leery about Zia's efforts to gain greater domestic legitimacy through his policy of

Islamization. In the process, Zia substituted traditional Koranic punishments for Western legal norms, promoted religious schools (*madrassas*), and establish a special *sharia* (Islamic law) court to ensure that Pakistan's laws were consistent with the Koran. Zia also cooperated with conservative religious parties, such as the Jamaat-i-Islami, which earlier governments had regarded with distaste.

But Pakistan's nuclear program, not its domestic political scene or events in the region, dominated Shahi's talks in Washington. Secretary Vance asked for three commitments: first, that Pakistan not transfer nuclear technology to other countries; second, that it open its nuclear facilities to international inspection; and third, that it not test a nuclear device. Shahi gave Vance satisfaction only on the first item. He said that Pakistan would refuse to permit inspection of Kahuta and other nuclear installations unless India similarly opened its nuclear facilities to inspection. On the question of testing, the envoy stated that Pakistan "had not yet reached that stage" and would review the pros and cons after it attained the necessary capability to explode a device.[68]

At one point, Vance said that he wanted to speak alone with Shahi in his private office. To the Pakistani visitor's surprise, he found nuclear expert Gerard Smith already present there. Smith promptly began to hammer away about the dangers that nuclear proliferation posed for Pakistan: "Don't you know you are entering the valley of death? Do you think you are enhancing your security by what you are doing? The Indians are far ahead of you. They can utterly destroy you." Taken aback, Shahi countered that he did not have to be a nuclear expert to understand that "the value of a nuclear capability lies in its possession, not in its use."[69]

Despite these bilateral frictions, U.S.-Pakistan relations improved in one sensitive area: that of intelligence cooperation. After losing electronic listening posts in Iran because of the revolution, U.S. officials approached Zia about collaboration in the collection of communications intelligence. After the president agreed to cooperate, the Central Intelligence Agency (CIA) provided technical assistance and equipment to improve Pakistan's electronic intercept capabilities. U.S. intelligence agencies received the data collected by these installations but did not station American specialists in Pakistan.[70] Although far more limited in scope than the arrangement for Badaber, which was a large and entirely U.S.-manned facility, the accord nonetheless marked a significant development in the bilateral relationship.

In July 1979, President Carter also approved a small covert-assistance program for Afghans opposing the communist government in Kabul. The CIA worked with its Pakistani counterpart, the Inter-Services Intelligence Directorate (ISI), to channel aid to the fledgling Afghan resistance movement. This aid built on the covert capability that Pakistan had earlier developed against the Daoud government. After Zia seized power, direction of the covert assistance passed from the Frontier Scouts to the ISI,[71] whose chief, Lt. Gen. Akhtar Rahman Khan, was a close confidant of Zia.

The covert U.S. help involved propaganda support and nonmilitary assistance but did not include arms or ammunition. According to Robert Gates, a later director of the CIA, the funding level was modest—less than $1 million.[72] Although small, the CIA-ISI effort was the seed from which the vastly larger and ultimately successful Afghan covert program grew. Despite the strain in other facets of the relationship, growing cooperation between intelligence agencies signaled Zia's interest in maintaining Pakistan's links with the United States and Washington's reciprocal willingness to work with Pakistan when it suited U.S. interests, notwithstanding the two governments' substantial differences, especially over nuclear issues.

The Burning of the U.S. Embassy

The sacking of the U.S. embassy in Islamabad brought the bilateral relationship to its lowest point ever.[73]

After rumors spread that Israel and the United States had had a hand in the seizure of the Grand Mosque in Mecca, the holiest religious site for Muslims, anti-American disturbances flared in many parts of the Islamic world. None was as violent as the outburst in Islamabad. At noon on November 21, 1979, several hundred irate students from nearby Quaid-i-Azam University arrived in buses and started demonstrating in front of the American embassy compound, located in the sparsely populated diplomatic enclave about three miles from the university. After talking with embassy officers, the demonstrators seemed satisfied, climbed back into the buses, and drove off. Ambassador Hummel and Deputy Chief of Mission Barrington King, who were both at their homes for lunch, were informed that the disturbance was over.

In fact, it was only beginning. Within a few minutes, the vehicles turned around and returned, accompanied by many other buses and trucks. A far larger and nastier crowd, thought to number several thousand, swirled around the embassy compound. In an ugly mood, the rioters brushed aside a thin protective police cordon and began to batter away at the compound gates. As the mob became angrier, the embassy staff urgently phoned for help from Hummel, King, and the Pakistani Ministry of Foreign Affairs. In accordance with an emergency plan, those inside the main embassy building—American and Pakistani employees and *Time* correspondent Marcia Gauger, who was having lunch with Political Counselor Herbert Hagerty—gradually retreated toward the steel-shielded communications vault. One hundred thirty-seven people had taken shelter inside the vault when the heavy metal doors swung shut at 1:40 P.M.

After the surging demonstrators broke down the compound gates, they went on a rampage, smashing everything in sight. The mob wrecked some eighty cars in the parking lot and set the main embassy building on fire with gasoline drained from the vehicles. As flames seared the paint off the walls and smoke seeped through the corridors, the temperature inside the vault rose dangerously. Even though some armed rioters had clambered onto the embassy roof and attempted to fire weapons down into the vault, the morale of those trapped inside remained intact. There was no panic. The staff remained in telephone contact with Hummel and with the State Department in Washington. The fact that an embassy security guard, Cpl. Stephen Crowley of the U.S. Marine Corps, had died from gunshot wounds sustained on the roof, was kept from the others.

The trapped embassy officials assumed that rescuers would soon be on the scene; getting a relief force to the compound did not seem a difficult task. Military barracks, President Zia's residence, and the Pakistani army headquarters were all located in Rawalpindi, less than fifteen miles from the embassy and at most a half-hour drive, mainly on a four-lane highway. Yet despite repeated pleas from Hummel, calls from Shahi at the foreign office, and even a "very impassioned" telephone call from Jimmy Carter to President Zia, it took nearly four hours for the Pakistani military to arrive at the compound.

According to Zia's chief of staff, Gen. K. M. Arif, and the Pakistani government's press spokesperson, Maj. Gen. Mujibur Rehman, the authorities had been caught by surprise and were unprepared for the attack on the embassy. At the time the riot had begun, much of the government's security apparatus was tied up shadowing Zia, who was cycling through the streets of Rawalpindi on a public relations tour to promote the use of bicycles. The Punjabi provincial authorities, responsible for protecting embassies, failed to call for assistance from the army when the rioters overwhelmed the police cordon. Arif said that he first had learned of the attack through frantic calls from Hummel and Shahi.

After Zia's top aide became aware of what was happening, he ordered two helicopters to fly to the embassy to get a better fix on the situation and, if possible, to help in rescuing the staff. Smoke from the burning compound obscured the pilots' vision, however, and they were unsure whether the embassy roof could hold the weight of their helicopters. It was not until 5:30 P.M., almost four hours after the door of the communications vault had shut, that a Pakistani army unit reached the compound. By then, as dusk set in, the crisis was over. Having failed to break into the vault, the demonstrators had gradually melted away. The shaken embassy staff was already safe. Many had taken refuge in the adjacent compound of the British high commission.

The mob's departure was a godsend. With the heat in the vault becoming unbearable, those inside had decided to escape onto the roof rather than suffocate. Had the armed demonstrators still been present, the attempt might have ended in bloody carnage. Nonetheless, the tragedy took four lives. In addition to Corporal Crowley, Chief Warrant Officer Bryant Ellis of the defense attaché's office and two Pakistani employees of the embassy had died after they were unable to reach the safety of the vault. The compound was a charred ruin. It looked as if a battle had raged over the terrain. The mob had left little in its wake.

The next day, the State Department commandeered Pan American Airways aircraft to evacuate all dependents and nonessential personnel from Islamabad. Zia conveyed his regrets and apologies to Carter in a phone conversation during which the U.S. president—to the annoyance of the Islamabad embassy staff—thanked the Pakistani army for its help.[74] After accepting responsibility for their failure to protect the embassy, the Pakistanis in time handed over a check to Hummel for the $23 million that the U.S. government said was needed to rebuild the main embassy building.[75]

Although Pakistani officials attributed the slow reaction to bureaucratic snarls, lack of preparedness, and plain incompetence, the less charitable views of U.S. officials on the scene appear closer to the mark. Some Americans thought that the Pakistanis were hesitant about intervening lest the rumors of U.S. involvement in Mecca prove true. Others felt that the Pakistanis found it not a bad idea to let the Americans "sweat a bit." Still others believed that Pakistani intelligence had instigated the embassy demonstration (U.S. facilities in Rawalpindi, Lahore, and Karachi were also attacked), which then had gotten out of hand.

In the wake of the incident, U.S. relations with Pakistan, according to National Security Council staff member Thomas Thornton, were "about as bad as with any country in the world, except perhaps Albania or North Korea."[76]

The Soviet Military Intervention in Afghanistan

Just a little more than four weeks later, on Christmas Eve 1979, the Soviet Army marched into Afghanistan to oust headstrong Hafizullah Amin and install the more pliable Babrak Karmal as the country's president. The Soviet action shook the globe. The Carter administration's quest for détente abruptly ended, and the chill of the Cold War returned. The U.S. attitude toward Pakistan, as Thornton put it, "[o]vernight, literally, . . . changed dramatically."[77] When the president telephoned Zia that day, his tone and message differed drastically from those of the conversation the two had had a month before. The United States, Jimmy Carter told his Pakistani counterpart, reaffirmed the 1959 bilateral security agreement against communist aggression and offered to bolster Pakistan's security. With Soviet soldiers at the Khyber Pass, the traditional gateway for invasions of South Asia, Pakistan had become a "front line" state.[78]

Moscow's action also shocked the Pakistanis, who probably never fully believed their frequent predictions about the likelihood of a Soviet takeover of Afghanistan. Quite apart from Pakistan's strategic interests, the de facto seizure of the neighboring Muslim state deeply offended Zia's sense of Islamic brotherhood. Although Islamabad had been very unhappy over the communist coup d'état in Kabul in 1978, the Afghan regime that conducted the coup was, at least, an indigenous Afghan affair with which Zia was prepared to deal. Indeed, a December 1979 snowstorm in Kabul had forced a last-minute postponement of a meeting between Hafizullah Amin and Agha Shahi. Before their get-together could be rescheduled, the Soviets had killed Amin and put Babrak Karmal in his place.

When the Soviet ambassador called on Zia to request Pakistan's "understanding" of events, Shahi recalled, the envoy stated that Soviet forces had entered Afghanistan in a limited manner for a limited period of time at the invitation of the Kabul government. To Zia's query, "Which government, Mr. Ambassador, invited you in?" the ambassador replied, "Babrak Karmal's." The president said that he would think the matter over and, showing his usual courtesy toward visitors, personally accompanied the diplomat to his car.[79]

Before deciding how to respond, Zia consulted with senior military officers, the foreign office, provincial governors, and a range of other advisers. According to Arif, the president received conflicting advice. A minority of doves, including some in the military, argued that "Pakistan was too small and weak to challenge Moscow. It would be a dangerous game for Pakistan to take on the Big Bear. The Soviet Union was not only a great power, but was near by."[80]

A contrary view held that Afghanistan itself was not sufficiently important to be the real Soviet target: in keeping with lore of the Great Game, the Soviets were after Pakistan or Iran, or perhaps access to the Arabian Sea. Whatever the case, it was better to oppose the Soviets in Afghanistan. Without such opposition, Pakistan's turn could be next. For his part, Shahi commented, "It's aggression and an invasion and we have to take a stand."[81] Had Babrak actually asked the Soviets in, Pakistan would have had no basis for opposing the action. Babrak Karmal, however, had no authority and was not even in Afghanistan when he supposedly issued the invitation.

The Pakistanis conceded that opposing the Soviets ran significant risks: Moscow might refuel the insurgency in Baluchistan and could stir trouble elsewhere inside Pakistan. At the same time, they doubted that the Soviets would actually invade, since Moscow would fear a U.S. military response. Moreover, Shahi believed that the Soviet action would stir vocal and widespread opposition, especially in the Muslim world, as a blatant violation of the UN Charter. It would be possible, he thought, to mount a major diplomatic counterattack against Moscow.[82]

After taking his soundings, Zia decided on the line of action that he would consistently follow. Pakistan would oppose the Soviet action publicly, would provide shelter for Afghan refugees, would offer public support for the resistance, and would provide clandestine military assistance to the insurgents while denying that it was doing so.[83] Arif, who agreed with Zia, elaborated: "We felt very acutely . . . that if we do not react to what happens in Afghanistan it will be our turn tomorrow. Even if we were on a weak wicket, should we wait and let

Afghanistan be crushed and then wait for our turn to be crushed or should we act now, accept the wrath of the Polar Bear and, at least, if we have to go down, go down fighting. We thought this was our moral obligation. Better to fight in Afghanistan than let it go down and fight in your own country."[84]

In line with Zia's decision, the Pakistani Foreign Ministry prepared a formal reply to the Soviet démarche. Perhaps misled by Zia's noncommittal reaction and personal courtesy, the Soviet ambassador was, Shahi recalled, so stunned by the stiff tone of the aide-mémoire that he at first refused to accept the document as the Pakistani government's official word.[85]

In Washington, the Carter administration reacted strongly to the Soviet action, which the U.S. president believed was a major and qualitative change in Russian behavior. The United States embargoed wheat sales, boycotted the Olympic games scheduled to be held in Moscow in the summer of 1980, and withdrew the second Strategic Arms Limitation Treaty from consideration by the Senate. Bolstering Pakistan's security was an important element of the American response. In a January 4, 1980, speech dealing with Afghanistan, President Carter stated, "We will provide military equipment, food and other assistance to help Pakistan defend its independence and national security against the seriously increased threat from the north."[86]

After the president's phone call to Zia, the administration moved to flesh out the offer of support. In the State Department, Assistant Secretary for the Near East and South Asia Harold H. Saunders reviewed possible help in a memorandum sent on New Years Day 1980 to Secretary of State Vance, proposing a budget request to Congress for $150 million in aid and credits for Pakistan, consideration of debt relief—which Islamabad wanted—and a waiver of the legislation barring economic and military aid because of the nuclear program. Even though Saunders commented that the Pakistanis would find this "an inadequate basis for a closer, more supportive relationship," the assistant secretary argued for "caution" because of the expected negative Indian reaction to U.S. provision to Pakistan of high-performance aircraft, such as the potent F-16 fighter-bomber, or tanks "which the Pakistanis want and will try to make our response the litmus test of our resolve."[87] Apart from concern about the Indians, Deputy Assistant Secretary of State for South Asia Jane Coon and Thornton recalled that budgetary restraints deterred administration planners from proposing higher levels of assistance.[88]

Well aware of his vastly improved bargaining position, President Zia proved reluctant to agree to vague promises and wanted to know specifically what Washington had in mind. Reflecting bruised feelings about his dealings with the Americans, Zia told journalists, "We have had bitter experiences with U.S. aid in the past."[89] Pakistan's president rebuffed an initiative to send Warren Christopher to Islamabad and instead proposed that Shahi, who would be attending the UN General Assembly's special session on Afghanistan, visit Washington. In the UN debate, where the Soviets found themselves on the defensive, Pakistan took a leading role in organizing Muslim countries and other members of the NAM. In the end, the General Assembly condemned the Soviet action by an overwhelming 104-18 vote with 14 abstentions. Apart from the communist bloc, the only major country not to vote against the Soviets was India.

Before the Pakistani diplomat arrived in Washington, U.S. officials accurately recognized Pakistan's key concern: "Whether the credibility and magnitude of U.S. support is sufficient to offset the real danger of Soviet intimidation as well as the potential damage of close association with the U.S. to their nonaligned and Islamic credentials."[90] In discussions with Hummel in Islamabad, Shahi had signaled that his country wanted to strengthen U.S. security guarantees by replacing the 1959 executive agreement with a formal treaty, as well as a substantial economic and military aid program.[91]

The U.S. approach, which was spelled out during Shahi's two meetings with Vance and a White House session with President Carter, had four principal points:

1. To make "the costs to the Soviet Union of [the Afghan] operation high enough so that Soviet leaders will be deterred from thoughts of similar adventures in the future";
2. To maintain in place the 1959 executive agreement which "provides a sound basis" for "cooperating against the threat from the north" (Although Vance rejected a treaty, he was willing to seek a congressional vote affirming the 1959 agreement);
3. To offer Pakistan $400 million of military and economic aid over the coming two years (President Carter, however, specifically turned down providing advanced F-16 aircraft, which the Pakistanis had requested); and

4. To maintain U.S. concerns about Pakistan's nuclear program even though the administration planned to seek authority from Congress to waive sanctions. (Willingness to resume assistance "should not be construed," Vance's brief declared, "to mean any lessening of the importance the U.S. attaches to nuclear non-proliferation.")[92]

Only on the first point—making the Soviets pay as a high a price as possible—was there a real meeting of the minds. On the question of security guarantees, Shahi accepted that a vote by Congress approving the 1959 agreement would mark a step forward, even if it was not as good as a treaty commitment. But he found the U.S. position inadequate with regard to both assistance and the nuclear question.

"Peanuts!"

The fact that details of the U.S. aid offer soon appeared in the press, along with the implication that Pakistan would accept, irritated Zia, who was still making up his mind. During a January 13, 1980, press conference, the Pakistani leader insisted that Washington was going to have to "prove its credibility and durability" as an ally before Pakistan accepted U.S. aid.[93] The next day, on January 14, 1980, the State Department nonetheless released specifics of the assistance package, emphasizing that $400 million would be the U.S. share of a broader international effort to bolster Pakistan's security.[94]

Annoyed at having his hand forced and dissatisfied with the aid offer, Zia dismissed the proposal as "peanuts" when he talked with journalists on January 18, 1980. "I have not heard it officially," he said, "but if it is true what has been in the press then it is terribly disappointing. Pakistan will not buy its security for $400 million." This amount, Zia continued, "will buy greater animosity from the Soviet Union which is now much more influential in this region than the United States."[95] A few days later, Shahi phrased the rejection more diplomatically, telling the *Washington Post*, "The assistance must be commensurate with the size of the threat."[96]

Although Brzezinski, Jimmy Carter's national security adviser, recalled that Zia's "peanuts" statement irked President Carter, the administration proceeded as if it would in time reach agreement with the

Pakistanis. The State Department called Zia's remark "a quibble" and continued discussions with Congress to obtain additional aid funding and necessary waivers of nuclear sanctions.[97] Talking on the television news program *Meet the Press* on January 20, 1980, Carter stated, "We have reconfirmed our 1959 commitment to Pakistan. We are committed to consult with Pakistan and to take whatever action is necessary—under the constitutional guidelines that I have to follow as president of our country—to protect the security of Pakistan, involving military force if necessary."[98]

In his State of the Union message three days later, the president spelled out the "Carter Doctrine," the new policy under which a Soviet attack against the Persian Gulf would be regarded as an attack on U.S. vital interests. He reaffirmed the security commitment to Pakistan, declaring, "The United States will take action—consistent with our laws—to assist Pakistan resist any outside aggression."[99]

Not accepting "peanuts" as the final answer, but not greatly increasing the aid offer, Brzezinski and Christopher flew to Islamabad in the hope of obtaining a "yes" from Zia. Originally, Christopher was to lead the mission, but Brzezinski joined the party to underscore Carter's desire for an agreement. In assessing the chances, State Department officials thought that ultimately "Pakistan, after complaining and with continuing reservations, will accept our assistance." They believed the language in the State of the Union message would "help allay Pakistani concerns regarding the depth of our resolve and the durability of our commitment."[100]

But the talks in Pakistan, which included an emotionally charged and much-publicized visit by Brzezinski to the Khyber Pass, where he was photographed peering down the sights of a Kalashnikov AK-47 automatic weapon, failed. When the discussions began, Brzezinski tried to flatter Zia, saying "I see you are a Pole not a Czech" (a reference that Zia may or may not have understood).[101] After the discussion got down to specifics, the Pakistanis were disappointed to learn that the U.S. aid offer was only slightly more forthcoming—Brzezinski suggested that the two-year figure could be "close to $500 million."[102] Nor were their concerns allayed by the U.S. team's explanation that the two-year program was only a first installment and that more would be available in later years.[103]

The Pakistanis were also were put off by Brzezinski's deference to Christopher, who in his dry, lawyer-like manner argued that an executive agreement would provide as good a security commitment as a treaty, which he admitted Congress would not be willing to approve. In Pakistani eyes, the stress that the American visitors placed on speedy action because of congressional budget deadlines hardly improved matters. Perhaps most important, however, was the U.S. unwillingness to extend the security commitment to an attack by India.[104]

At the end of the first day of talks, after Zia and his advisers concluded that the U.S. position was not good enough, the Pakistani president telephoned Carter to say that the discussions had failed to bridge the gap between the two sides.[105] The visiting Americans, even experienced South Asia hands Coon and Thornton, were surprised and puzzled by Zia's rebuff.[106]

Despite the fact that Washington tried to put on the best face, the turndown marked an embarrassing diplomatic setback. When the administration continued discussions with Congress regarding the aid package, the Pakistanis went public in their rejection of the U.S. offer. In a March 5, 1980, speech, Shahi declared that his country was not interested in the $400 million proposal and "specifically disassociated itself from any U.S. initiatives to introduce the relevant legislation in the U.S. Congress."[107] Driving the final nail into the coffin, Shahi added, "It was felt on our side that acceptance of the U.S. offer, unless substantially modified, would detract from rather than enhance our security."[108] At the same time, both Zia and Shahi declared that even though Pakistan was no longer seeking military aid from the United States, it was interested in economic assistance and especially in debt relief.[109]

After the United States pressed other nations, with some success, to increase their help for Pakistan as a "central element" in the West's response to the Soviet occupation of Afghanistan, the absence of a U.S. aid program was awkward, to put it mildly. Trying to make the best of the situation, the Carter administration supported a generous debt-rescheduling package, even though the action ran counter to traditional U.S. policy to agree to rescheduling only in the event of imminent default.[110]

Covert Cooperation

Things were not entirely negative, however. Despite the lack of agreement on military and economic aid, intelligence cooperation on Afghanistan between the CIA and the ISI expanded. Just four days after the Soviet intervention, on December 29, 1979, Jimmy Carter approved a broader covert action program that instructed the CIA to provide military weapons and ammunition in addition to nonlethal supplies and support for the Afghan anticommunist resistance fighters, who soon became widely known as mujahideen, or freedom fighters.[111] Brzezinski discussed the idea of a larger covert effort with Zia when he visited Islamabad in February 1980 and then persuaded the Saudis to match the U.S. contribution to the insurgency dollar for dollar.[112]

Although still modest in size compared with the program of the later 1980s, covert assistance for Afghanistan "expanded to include all levels of military support for the mujahideen."[113] The operational ground rules worked out at this time continued during the Reagan presidency. At Pakistan's insistence, the CIA funneled all aid through the ISI, which in turn handed over supplies to the Afghans. In order to strengthen its control over the mujahideen, the ISI limited the distribution of arms and other aid to "recognized" resistance groups, most of which were headquartered in the Pakistani city of Peshawar, an hour's drive from the Khyber Pass and the border with Afghanistan. The Pakistanis further insisted that the CIA not deal directly with the mujahideen, but only through the ISI. This, the Pakistanis felt, would further improve their control and also prevent the CIA from establishing a large and quasi-independent presence in Pakistan.

In order to maintain "plausible deniability"—to make it difficult for the Soviets to show tangible evidence of U.S. involvement—the CIA supplied only types of weapons and equipment that were also used by the Soviets or their East European satellite countries, or items, such as World War I–vintage Lee-Enfield rifles, that were commonly available in Afghanistan. No arms or equipment made in the United States or typically associated with the West were provided to the mujahideen.[114]

When commenting publicly about reports of aid to the resistance, the Pakistanis followed a disciplined approach: they flatly denied that they were providing military supplies to the Afghan fighters or serving as a staging area or a channel for other countries to provide equipment. For example, Shahi declared in a March 5, 1980, speech, "Let it be stated categorically that Pakistan is determined not to allow itself to become a conduit for the flow of arms into Afghanistan."[115] Pakistan maintained that its help was limited to food and shelter for Afghan refugees but did not deny that it politically supported the resistance. If queried about the source of the mujahideen's arms, Pakistani sources and the insurgents themselves claimed that they captured the weapons from the notoriously feckless Afghan army.

After the start of the Soviet military intervention, Afghan nationalist sentiment and the cry of "Islam in danger" provided fertile ground for armed resistance. Efforts by the Kabul regime to modernize and secularize Afghan society along communist lines and to reduce the role of traditional Islam had already sparked substantial opposition, especially in deeply religious and conservative rural areas. By the end of January 1980, an estimated four hundred thousand Afghans had fled to Pakistan, and the number of refugees was rapidly increasing: it would eventually reach three million people. Given the high level of motivation, the Afghan warrior tradition, and the virtually open frontier between Afghanistan and Pakistan, it was relatively easy to recruit fighters for the resistance from the burgeoning refugee camps located close to the border in the Northwest Frontier Province and Baluchistan.

Nevertheless, in 1980, few Americans or Pakistanis thought that the Afghans would be able to mount an insurgency capable of holding Soviet forces at bay. U.S. Soviet specialists, in particular, believed the Russians would be able to contain the resistance movement. Officials with direct experience in Afghanistan had a higher opinion of the capability of the resistance, however, and felt that it might make life difficult for the Soviets.[116]

Zia Welcomed at the White House

During 1980, Jimmy Carter's final year in office, the Iran hostage crisis consumed the White House, the State Department, and the American public. The embarrassing failure of a hostage-rescue mission in April 1980 strengthened the world's impression of declining U.S. power. As part of the Carter administration's effort to counter this perception, Washington continued to seek a broader security relationship with Pakistan to buttress covert CIA-ISI ties.

On October 3, 1980, after Zia attended the UN General Assembly in New York, Carter invited him to the White House. Their meeting began with a review of Zia's unsuccessful efforts, on behalf of the Organization of Islamic Conference, to end the Iran-Iraq War, which had begun in mid-1980. Discussion then turned to other subjects, including Afghanistan.[117]

Smiles despite "peanuts": Presidents Jimmy Carter and Mohammed Zia ul-Haq at the White House, October 1980. (Courtesy of the Jimmy Carter Library.)

Having concluded by then that Republican challenger Ronald Reagan would win the upcoming presidential election, the Pakistanis decided that they would not take the initiative in bringing up the question of security assistance. If Carter won, they reasoned that any offer that he had previously made would remain on the table. If Reagan were the victor—as the Pakistanis expected—any proposal made by Carter would be meaningless. In fact, in preparing for the meeting, Carter, overriding the State Department, had decided to reverse his position on the F-16s and to offer the aircraft to Zia.

As the time allotted for the session was about to run out and as Zia had said nothing about security assistance, Carter brought up the subject. When he informed Zia and Arif (who was present, as was Brzezinski), of his willingness to include the high-performance F-16s in an arms aid package,[118] Zia casually replied that the matter could wait, since Carter was undoubtedly extremely busy with the presidential campaign.[119]

As he walked out of the White House, Pakistan's military dictator could feel great satisfaction. Since Moscow's intervention in Afghanistan, Zia was no longer a near-pariah because of his human rights record, his nuclear policies, and the execution of Bhutto. Instead, Zia found himself courted by the Americans, the West Europeans, and the Arabs, not to speak of Pakistan's Chinese friends, as a bulwark against the Soviet threat. Even though Washington and Islamabad had been unable to work out a mutually satisfactory security and economic aid package, Zia could look forward to brighter days in dealing with the United States after Ronald Reagan defeated Jimmy Carter in the November 1980 presidential elections.

10

Reagan: Partners Again

Ronald Reagan took the oath of office on the steps of the U.S. Capitol on January 21, 1981, a cold but clear winter day in Washington. The incoming president had promised higher defense expenditures and a more vigorous foreign policy in response to Soviet advances in the Third World. High on the new administration's national security agenda was forging a closer relationship with Pakistan. Regarding the former ally as a potentially key partner in opposing the Soviet military presence in Afghanistan, Reagan and his top foreign policy aides, Secretary of State Alexander Haig, Director of Central Intelligence William Casey, and Secretary of Defense Caspar Weinberger, believed that Pakistan deserved far more U.S. support than Carter had offered. Even before taking office, the secretary of state–designate had signaled to the Pakistani embassy's chargé d'affaires, Najmuddin Sheikh, that relations were going to improve. "I know we have had problems, but these are going to change," Haig told Sheikh at a diplomatic reception.[1]

When Ambassador Arthur Hummel sent the new secretary of state a cable urging a greater aid effort, Haig called the envoy back to Washington and instructed him to help put together a bigger assistance program.[2] Avoiding Carter administration missteps, the Reagan team at the Departments of State and Defense assembled a \$3.2 billion, five-year proposal that President Mohammed Zia ul-Haq was unlikely to dismiss as "peanuts." In March 1981, Hummel returned to Islamabad to review the package privately with the Pakistani leadership—a contrast to the highly public diplomacy of the year before. As spelled out in a memorandum from Assistant Secretary of State for the Near East and South Asia Nicholas Veliotes, the U.S. purpose was straightforward: to "give Pakistan confidence in our commitment to its security and provide us reciprocal benefits in terms of our regional interests."[3] In other words, Washington was trading military and economic aid for Pakistan's co-operation in opposing the Soviet presence in Afghanistan.

Establishing A New U.S.-Pakistan Partnership

Although the Pakistanis responded positively to the package Hummel brought back, Agha Shahi, whom Zia had named foreign minister, emphasized his country's unwillingness to take any step that would undercut its recently achieved nonaligned status. He stressed to Hummel that Pakistan would not grant military bases to the United States, even though Washington had not asked for any. Zia was optimistic about reaching an agreement, but given Pakistan's past difficulties with the Americans, he wanted to make sure both sides understood exactly what the relationship involved. Accordingly, the president instructed Shahi and General K. M. Arif, who were heading to Washington for further discussions in April 1981, not to get into the details of the assistance package until they had reached a satisfactory understanding on the issues of concern to Pakistan.[4]

First came the nuclear problem, which had bedeviled relations during the Carter years. When Shahi and Arif bluntly told Haig that Pakistan would not compromise on its program, the secretary of state responded that the issue need not become the centerpiece of the U.S.-Pakistan relationship. But, Haig warned the Pakistanis, if Islamabad were to detonate a nuclear device the reaction in the U.S. Congress would make it difficult to cooperate with Pakistan in the way that the Reagan administration hoped.[5] Deputy Assistant Secretary of State Jane Coon, the State Department's senior South Asia specialist, sensed that there was, in effect, a tacit understanding that the Reagan administration could live with Pakistan's nuclear program as long as Islamabad did not explode a bomb.[6]

The second issue of concern to the Pakistanis was U.S. policy toward human rights and the restoration of democracy. Carter administration criticism on both counts had stung the military regime in Islamabad, which wanted to be sure that the Reagan administration did not continue this type of fault-finding. Arif told Haig, "We would not like to hear from you the type of government we should have." The secretary of state replied, "General, your internal situation is your problem."[7]

Third came the ground rules for U.S. covert assistance to the Afghan resistance. The Pakistanis insisted, and the Americans agreed, on maintaining the modus operandi established during 1979 and 1980. The Central Intelligence Agency would serve as the quartermaster, to supply arms, equipment, and munitions for the mujahideen, funneling supplies through Pakistan's Inter-Services Intelligence Directorate (ISI). The Americans would train Pakistanis in the use of weapons and equipment, and the ISI, in turn, would instruct the Afghan resistance fighters. The CIA reconfirmed its earlier agreement not to deal directly with the mujahideen, but to arrange all contacts through the ISI.[8]

The fourth issue related to U.S. security assurances to Pakistan. Although Zia had sought a treaty commitment from Carter, he did not press for this in 1981. "When Reagan came in," Arif explained, "we found a dramatic change in the U.S. attitude toward our region, [and toward] the 'polar bear' and the 'Evil Empire.'"[9] Given the altered atmosphere, the Pakistanis no longer felt it necessary to seek a security guarantee beyond what was already embodied in the 1959 bilateral agreement: a pledge of U.S. help against a communist attack.

After the talks, a smiling Shahi told the press, "I believe we have moved forward in developing a Pakistan-American friendship on a durable basis."[10] The foreign minister added, "The previous Carter administration offer did not carry for us credibility in a U.S.-Pakistan relationship commensurate . . . [with] what we considered to be the magnitude of the threat."[11] Although protracted, and at times difficult, negotiations were needed to reach full agreement on the aid package, Pakistan was basically happy with what that the Reagan administration had proposed, a $3.2 billion, multi-year commitment equally divided between economic and military assistance.

In mid-1981, Haig's close aide, State Department Counselor, Robert "Bud" McFarlane, traveled to Islamabad. Zia surprised the American visitor and upset Shahi by querying, "Why don't you ask us to grant bases?" Taken aback, McFarlane responded that it would be "inconceivable" for the United States to seek military bases in Pakistan.[12] Although the foreign minister did not know if Zia was serious—Pakistan's president had a habit of making offhand offers to Americans and then not following up—his remarks agitated Shahi.

The veteran diplomat feared that Zia and his fellow generals would be willing to jettison Pakistan's nonaligned status for a revived alliance with Washington. Indeed, at Shahi's insistence, the arms package was modified to substitute commercial loan rates for concessional financing terms. The latter, the foreign minister argued, were given only to U.S. allies.[13] Although his point was off the mark, the Americans went along with the request, offsetting the higher financing cost for arms by increasing the amount of concessional lending in the economic assistance package. In addition to his concern about Zia's views, the foreign minister sensed that U.S. officials were ill at ease in working with him after chronic friction and prickly dealings during the Carter administration. This was indeed the case.[14]

F-16s and the Nuclear Issue

Despite reaching overall agreement on the new relationship, all was not smooth sailing. Problems developed over the inclusion of forty F-16 fighter-bombers in the military aid package. Before 1981, the United States had agreed to supply the state-of-the-art, nuclear-capable F-16 only to NATO allies and Japan. The high-performance aircraft was still in the initial production phase, with projected deliveries to U.S. forces not yet completed. As a result, both the U.S. Air Force and the Office of Management and Budget were unhappy about Pakistan's receiving the F-16s and tried to remove them from the arms package. In the end, however, the Reagan administration decided to go ahead with the deal, since the Pakistanis had made clear they regarded the F-16 transaction as "a test of American earnest[ness]."[15]

Further trouble arose over delivery dates and avionics. Tough bargaining in Washington and a hurried visit to Islamabad by Undersecretary of State for Security Affairs James Buckley were required before the agreement could be announced on September 14, 1981.[16] By juggling schedules for other recipients, Washington arranged for Pakistan to receive its first F-16 in twelve rather than the forty-three months earlier proposed. The Pentagon also agreed to equip the fighter-bombers with more advanced avionics after the Pakistanis balked at the initial proposal. Zia and his colleagues knew they had a strong bargaining position, hung tough, and, in the end, got what they wanted.[17]

Some U.S. officials, including Ambassador Ronald Spiers, who succeeded Hummel as U.S. ambassador in Islamabad in late 1981, regarded the F-16s as "an unnecessary luxury." Spiers believed the Pakistanis were unwise to allot such a large share of security aid for the fighter-bomber.[18] According to General Arif, Islamabad had two principal reasons for pressing for the F-16s. First, the Pakistani military had concluded that the army could absorb the entire aid package and still not remedy major equipment deficiencies. But by using the bulk of the funds to acquire forty F-16s, the Pakistani air force could gain a capability that would last a generation and "give us a slight edge over India and what forces there are in Afghanistan."

The second reason, Arif emphasized, was psychological. The F-16s would "signal to the people of Pakistan that we have done something to improve our defense capability" and could "give a damn good fight" against the Soviets.[19] Spiers agreed that the F-16s provided a great boost for Pakistani morale. "The acquisition of the aircraft," the U.S. envoy commented, "became a symbol of national virility. The whole issue caught the imagination of the Pakistani public."[20]

Nor did the nuclear issue go away on Capitol Hill, where nonproliferation supporters were strong. Only after a difficult fight, the Senate Foreign Relations Committee, on May 13, 1981, voted 10-7 to approve a six-year waiver for the sanctions that barred assistance to Pakistan. Although congressional authorization of the multiyear package seemed assured, the process of navigating the legislative hurdles would delay approval until the end of the year. To emphasize congressional concern about nonproliferation, Representative Stephen Solarz (D-N.Y.) gained acceptance of an amendment that would cut off aid to any country that exploded a nuclear device.[21] When the Senate approved a similar amendment, the "tacit" understanding about Pakistan's not testing became a legal requirement for U.S. aid.

For its part, the Reagan administration was openly skeptical about the effectiveness of sanctions in deterring Pakistan from the nuclear path. Testifying before the House Foreign Affairs Committee, Deputy Assistant Secretary Coon declared in April 1981, "We certainly cannot claim . . . [that sanctions] have been successful. . . . [O]ur interests would be better served by addressing the underlying security concerns of countries such as Pakistan and by developing more useful and cooperative relations which could engage us with them in a positive fashion."[22]

Undersecretary of State Buckley similarly stressed the positive impact of arms aid in responding to a *New York Times* op-ed broadside by Carnegie Endowment Asia specialist Selig Harrison, a frequent critic of Reagan's South Asia policy. In his August 5, 1981, letter to the editor, Buckley stated that the administration hoped to address "the underlying sources of insecurity that prompt a nation like Pakistan to seek a nuclear capability in the first place" through the supply of conventional arms.[23]

At this stage, U.S. intelligence on Pakistan's progress toward the bomb remained "rudimentary," according to Spiers. "It was very clear that there was a group in Pakistan that was working towards the development of a nuclear capability," the envoy stated, "but we didn't know how far it had advanced." Apart from a lack of concrete evidence about where the Pakistani nuclear program stood, Spiers also believed that the U.S. assessment in the early 1980s was influenced by skepticism "that the Pak[istanis] could actually achieve the capability."[24]

The Covert War

From the day William Casey walked into CIA headquarters in Langley, Virginia, he enthusiastically supported the covert war in Afghanistan. A veteran of the Office of Strategic Services, the World War II predecessor of the CIA, Casey had become wealthy on Wall Street, held senior economic posts during the Nixon and Ford administrations, and, in the 1980 election, served as national campaign manager for the victorious Ronald Reagan. His reward was to become America's spymaster. The new CIA director had direct access to the president, who, in an unprecedented move, appointed Casey a full member of the cabinet, giving the CIA chief an important voice in national security policy.

Support for the Afghan insurgency, for Casey, Alexander Haig, and others at the top levels of the administration, was a key part of what came to be known as the "Reagan Doctrine"—the strategy of confronting and trying to reverse the rising Soviet tide in Afghanistan, Central America, Africa, and elsewhere in the Third World. For his part, Spiers believed that it was important that the Soviets not conclude that they could intervene as they had in Afghanistan without paying a substantial price.[25] At the working level at the CIA, helping the Afghan resistance had a narrower purpose: "The aim of the program was to cause pain. It was revenge after the series of U.S. defeats in Vietnam, Angola, the Horn of Africa, etc. It was payback time," a senior U.S. intelligence officer stated.[26]

In line with Casey's desire to increase the pressure on the Soviets, his instructions in late 1981 to the newly assigned Islamabad chief of station were to do everything possible "to grow the war." Accordingly, the CIA officer regularly urged Lt. Gen. Akhtar Rahman Khan, the director-general of the ISI, to agree to increase the amount of arms and equipment supplied to the mujahideen.[27] When Akhtar, who routinely sought Zia's approval on all significant issues relating to Afghanistan, raised the question, Pakistan's president responded that he too wanted to keep the pressure on the Soviets but felt it was essential to "calibrate" the level of pressure carefully in order not to provoke major Soviet retaliation. Zia would add that he wanted "to keep the pot boiling, but not have it boil over."[28]

In early 1982, Casey paid his first visit to Islamabad; he would return there regularly until the onset of his fatal illness in late 1986. Zia and Casey turned out to be soul mates, sharing a strong anticommunism and a common perception of an aggressive Soviet Union that should be countered as forcefully as feasible.[29] Zia gave Casey—as he did most senior American visitors—his "red template" briefing. On a map of central Asia, the Pakistani leader would place a triangular red template covering much of southern Afghanistan. The tip of the template lay at the junction of Afghanistan, Iran, and Pakistan in Baluchistan and pointed directly at the Arabian Sea, some 350 miles away. This briefing graphically suggested that the driving force behind Moscow's strategy in Afghanistan was the "traditional" Russian push southward toward the Arabian Sea.[30] An adroit manipulator, Zia knew how to appeal to the anti-Soviet predilections of his American visitors.

The covert program did not immediately expand after the Reagan administration took office, but grew gradually as the mujahideen's ability to absorb weapons increased and their operational capability improved. At the time, the CIA spent about $30 million annually on the program. Saudi Arabia, where Casey regularly stopped after his visits to Pakistan, contributed an equal sum. Other countries provided smaller amounts of aid. A complex CIA logistics operation arranged for clandestine procurement of Soviet-type weapons and ammunition from East European countries and elsewhere, for equipment purchases from China, and even for the manufacture of weapons in ordnance factories that the Soviets had set up in Egypt before President Anwar Sadat broke off the two countries' close relationship in 1971.

Most of the supplies arrived by sea at the port of Karachi, where the ISI took possession from the CIA. The bulk was then transported by rail to northern Pakistan to a military supply depot called Ojiri Camp, located near the Rawalpindi-Islamabad airport. At Ojiri, the ISI broke down the shipments into smaller lots for onward movement by truck to mini-depots near Peshawar. A small share of the items arriving in Karachi was sent by rail to another logistics depot near Quetta in Baluchistan.

The ISI distributed the supplies among the "recognized" guerrilla groups. Originally, these numbered about forty, but in 1982, in order to strengthen Pakistani control, the ISI forced the mujahideen to consolidate into seven resistance groups, all headquartered in Peshawar. Representatives of these factions transported the supplies, often by mule caravan, over the mountains into Afghanistan, where they eventually reached the fighters.[31]

Contrary to the general impression, the CIA did not maintain a large permanent staff in Pakistan for the Afghan program. At first, the station chief managed the effort alone. Later, one assistant was added. Numerous specialists, however, were assigned on a temporary basis to instruct Pakistani trainers in the use of the equipment, to address logistics problems, and to provide intelligence to help the ISI in planning mujahideen operations inside Afghanistan. Sophisticated technical collection systems—satellite photography and communication intercepts—gave U.S. intelligence agencies a good grasp of Soviet operations and tactics in Afghanistan and, to a lesser extent, an ability to track resistance activities.[32]

Initially, Pakistan and the United States were largely successful in keeping the covert program out of the public domain. After the Shahi visit to Washington in April 1981, for example, the *Washington Post* reported that there were "no signs that Pakistan is prepared to take on the role as conduit for increased U.S. and Western military aid to rebel forces fighting in Afghanistan."[33] Discussing the issue in May 1981, the foreign minister told the press that the United States understood Pakistan's "policy of refusing to act as a conduit for arms" for rebels in Afghanistan and had not pressed him on this point.[34]

Afghanistan Negotiations Start; Yaqub Replaces Shahi

In the United Nations, Pakistan rather than the United States took the lead in successfully mobilizing support on the Afghan issue, especially among Muslim and nonaligned countries. The Pakistani leadership on this issue prevented the question from being considered solely in the framework of the Cold War. One hundred four countries voted in favor of the resolution condemning the invasion of Afghanistan in the

January 1980 special session. The number rose to 111 in the regular General Assembly gathering in the fall of 1980. A year later, in 1981, the resolution garnered the support of 116 states. Again it was the Pakistanis, with Shahi playing a leading role, who urged UN Secretary-General Kurt Waldheim to initiate peace talks. Despite a lack of interest in Moscow and Kabul, indifference in Washington, and difficulties in engaging the revolutionary Iranian authorities, a process got under way that culminated seven years later in the Geneva accords of April 1988.[35]

Javier Pérez de Cuellar initially headed the UN negotiating team. After Pérez de Cuellar's election as UN secretary-general in 1982, Diego Cordovez, an ebullient Ecuadoran diplomat, became the head of the UN Afghanistan negotiators. Shuttling back and forth between Moscow, Kabul, Islamabad, and Tehran, Cordovez was able to establish a modus operandi that permitted a first round of talks in Geneva in June 1982. As Pakistan refused to recognize the legitimacy of the Babrak Karmal regime in Kabul, he met separately with the Pakistani and Afghan delegations in "proximity" talks. Cordovez traveled to Moscow and Tehran to keep the Soviets and Iranians informed about the progress of these discussions.

For its part, Moscow stressed that the withdrawal of the Soviet army was not negotiable and that the sole issue was how to end "outside interference" in Afghanistan, as covert help to the resistance movement was euphemistically described. At this stage, the United States did not participate in the Geneva talks and relied on briefings by the Pakistanis and Cordovez to stay abreast. The seven mujahideen groups in Peshawar also had no direct role and showed great antipathy toward the negotiations. While their communist enemies met with Cordovez, the mujahideen had to rely on the Pakistanis to represent their interests.

In February 1982, Shahi decided to retire as foreign minister, citing medical problems. Although these were genuine enough, the veteran Pakistani diplomat basically felt out of tune with Zia. The foreign minister supported Pakistan's Afghan policy and the re-establishment of security ties with the United States but had more faith than the president in diplomacy as a means for reaching an Afghan settlement. He also remained uneasy that Zia and his fellow generals would undercut Pakistan's nonaligned status by getting too close to the Americans.[36]

To replace Shahi as foreign minister, Zia appointed Sahibzada Yaqub Khan, a retired lieutenant general, who had gained an excellent reputation as ambassador to France, the United States, and the Soviet Union during the 1970s. Yaqub's military career had ended abruptly in March 1971 when he resigned as governor of East Pakistan in opposition to Yahya Khan's proposed crackdown on the Awami League. Although this action ran counter to the Pakistani army's tradition of rigid discipline, Zia, who at one point had worked for Yaqub, valued his keen intellect, grasp for geopolitical issues, and considerable access to international leaders (acquired in the course of his diplomatic assignments).

The new foreign minister felt comfortable in dealing with Americans, who in turn were impressed by Yaqub's ability to analyze complex foreign policy issues in a highly articulate manner.[37] During his ambassadorial tour in the United States, he had also won much praise for his role in helping to defuse a dangerous March 1977 hostage crisis in Washington involving Afro-American Muslim extremists. Yaqub had less faith than Shahi in the utility of multilateral organizations, such as the nonaligned movement or the United Nations, as vehicles to further Pakistan's national interests. He believed that after Pakistan had committed itself to overt and covert opposition to the Soviet superpower in Afghanistan, his nation's security depended on strengthened ties with Washington.[38]

After Yaqub became foreign minister, Zia established a high-level "cell" to coordinate Pakistan's tricky balancing act in Afghanistan. Apart from the president, regular members included Yaqub, Finance Minister Ghulam Ishaq Khan, ISI chief Akhtar Rahman Khan, top Zia aide Gen. Arif, and Foreign Secretary Niaz Naik. Others took part in deliberations, depending on the topic under discussion. Predictably, the main policy difference related to the proper mix of diplomacy and force and was between the foreign ministry and the ISI. Zia would sometimes support Yaqub and, on other occasions, would back Akhtar Rahman. Despite the fact that the president was a dictator, he welcomed frank discussion and free give-and-take, even though he reserved the right to make the final decision on issues. Until 1986, when Zia began to share power with a prime minister, the Afghan cell proved a highly effective vehicle for policy coordination.[39]

On the U.S. side, there was less coordination on Afghanistan, which lay essentially in the hands of the CIA. Casey dealt directly on major policy issues with the secretaries of state and defense and the national security adviser. Lower echelons at the State Department and the Pentagon were usually not consulted. In Pakistan, the CIA station chief managed the program, keeping Ambassador Spiers and his successors,

Deane Hinton and Arnold Raphel, generally informed. Others in the embassy were usually not involved. As Richard Murphy, assistant secretary of state for the Near East and South Asia from 1984 until the end of the Reagan administration, put it, "It was CIA's war, not State's."[40]

Zia Visits the United States

By late 1982, the United States and Pakistan appeared to have evolved a new and, for the time being, happy partnership. Washington was providing Islamabad with $600 million a year in military and economic aid—only Israel, Egypt, and Turkey received more assistance. In return, the United States was able, with Pakistani cooperation and matching funds from Saudi Arabia, to fuel the growing resistance against the Soviet military presence in Afghanistan. At the same time, the Reagan administration hoped that closer security links would influence Pakistan's leadership to desist from—or at least go slow on—the nuclear program. In keeping with the 1981 Shahi-Haig discussions, the United States refrained from commenting on Zia's handling of Pakistan's domestic political scene.[41]

For Pakistan, the renewal of intimate ties with the Americans provided a major security and economic boost. The surge of foreign aid helped revive a lagging economy and initiated a decade of substantial growth. The Pakistani military acquired large amounts of badly needed equipment. For Zia personally, the Afghan war meant a new lease on life politically, enormously strengthening his previously shaky position. Both Western and Muslim countries applauded the president and his country for standing up to the Soviets and for sheltering three million refugees who had fled Afghanistan for the Northwest Frontier Province and Baluchistan.

Yet U.S.-Pakistan ties in the 1980s differed from the alliance of the late 1950s and early 1960s. During the Afghan war, the Americans and the Pakistanis were partners, not allies. Their relationship was a marriage of convenience. Still, in contrast to the ultimately conflicting motivations of the CENTO-SEATO years, the two countries shared a strong common purpose in opposing the Soviet presence in Afghanistan. Nevertheless, the Pakistanis had no illusions that the United States would support them against India, and U.S. concerns about the nuclear issue kept simmering just below the surface.

President Ronald Reagan receives President Mohammed Zia ul-Haq at the White House, December 1982. (Courtesy of the Ronald Reagan Library.)

Zia's December 1982 state visit to the United States reflected the refurbished bilateral relationship. The Reagan administration went out of its way to welcome Pakistan's president and to applaud the role he was playing in the Afghan conflict. To counter criticism of harsh handling of the political opposition and the lack of a free press, as Howard Schaffer, then the deputy assistant secretary of state for South Asia, recalled, U.S. officials stressed Zia's willingness to provide a home for several million Afghan refugees despite the considerable burden and real danger this posed.[42] Afghan aircraft periodically bombed areas near the border where the mujahideen were active. Terrorist bombs exploded frequently in Peshawar and other places where Afghan refugee camps were located in the Northwest Frontier Province and Baluchistan.

On December 6, Zia met with Secretary of State George Shultz, who had succeeded Haig in mid-1982. Shultz's briefing paper recommended that he warn Pakistan's president that "the nuclear weapons program could seriously undermine U.S.-Pakistan relations" and that he also mention the U.S. interest in improved human rights in Pakistan.[43] How far the secretary of state followed the brief is unclear, since the report of his one-on-one meeting with Zia remains classified. After U.S. and

Pakistani advisers joined the discussion, the secretary expressed the hope that the United States and Pakistan would build a bilateral relationship that "grows over time and is strong enough to survive disagreements and problems which inevitably occur." Replying more realistically if less diplomatically, Zia said that the two countries were a "union of unequals" and "incompatible" in terms of culture, geography, and national power, even though they had strong common interests. When Shultz raised U.S. concerns about increased production and trafficking of narcotics in Pakistan, Zia was quick to request help in dealing with the drug problem.[44]

At the White House on December 7, Zia and Reagan met alone for twenty minutes in the Oval Office before joining their senior advisers in the cabinet room for another hour of talks. In their private session, Reagan raised U.S. concerns about the Pakistani nuclear program.[45] (Later in the day, a White House spokesperson declared, "We accept that the President of Pakistan is telling us the truth" in assuring Reagan that the nuclear program is strictly "for peaceful purposes.")[46] The discussion in the cabinet room focused mainly on Soviet prospects and intentions in Afghanistan and on the recent meetings that Zia, Shultz, and Vice President George Bush had had with the new Soviet leader, Yuri Andropov, at the funeral of Leonid Brezhnev. When U.S. attorney general William French Smith brought up the increase in narcotics trafficking, Zia responded, "Pakistan [is] determined to solve this problem." Among other topics covered were the Middle East, Iran, and China. When the conversation turned to India, Zia said that he was "doing his best" to improve relations but, given close Indo-Soviet ties, it would be "impossible to pull India too far from the Soviet network."[47]

Skilled at public relations, an ever-smiling and amiable Zia handled himself adroitly on Capitol Hill and with the press during his stay. Although Afghanistan was the main focus of questions, Pakistan's president kept his cool in the face of often-hostile queries regarding Pakistan's nuclear program and its human rights record. Meeting with members of the Senate Foreign Relations Committee, he repeated "very emphatically," according to Senator Charles Mathias (R-Md.), that Pakistan was not seeking a nuclear weapon. Zia further assured the senators that he was moving toward a more democratic system—but gave no timetable. At the National Press Club, Pakistan's president stoutly defended his failure to hold elections; before departing for the United States he had once more put them off.[48] He also rebutted criticism of his human rights record. "We have a constitutional government. It is a civilized government. We are not a bunch of clowns," Zia briskly told journalists.[49]

No Breakthrough at Geneva

Despite pessimism about the prospects for the Afghan peace talks, Cordovez kept chipping away during 1982. In time, he succeeded in gaining agreement on the major elements of an accord: withdrawal of Soviet forces, cessation of external support for the resistance, international guarantees, and agreed procedures for the return home of Afghan refugees. In informal discussions with Soviet diplomats and Foreign Minister Yaqub, Cordovez linked the timetable for the withdrawal of Soviet troops from Afghanistan—Pakistan's key demand—with a Pakistani pledge to end "outside interference"—the Soviet Union's key wish.[50]

As 1983 began, a somewhat more positive tone from Soviet Communist Party general secretary Yuri Andropov appeared to brighten the prospects for an agreement.[51] A good meeting with Andropov[52] and a further round of talks in Geneva led Cordovez to speak, with typical optimism, about "substantial progress . . . in all areas."[53] On May 11, 1983, he painted an even rosier picture, telling the press that a settlement was "95 per cent ready."[54] Although Yaqub and Zia were more cautious, they too spoke of "signs" that Moscow might be willing to withdraw Soviet forces and to install a government in Kabul less objectionable to Pakistan and to the Afghan resistance.[55]

Cordovez visited Washington on February 22, 1983, and, after prompting by Ambassador Spiers, was cordially received by top State Department officials. Although the Americans continued to be skeptical about the outlook for the Geneva negotiations, they were willing to give Cordovez a chance. Undersecretary of State for Political Affairs Lawrence Eagleburger insisted that the United States was not trying "to bleed" the Soviets and wanted an accord that genuinely resulted in Afghan self-determination. As a sign of support for the Geneva talks, Secretary Shultz wrote Soviet foreign minister Andrei Gromyko to endorse Cordovez's efforts.[56]

Despite the fact that U.S. officials did not believe that the Soviets were prepared to withdraw from Afghanistan—except on their own terms—conservative supporters of the mujahideen on Capitol Hill worried about a "UN sellout" and campaigned for increased U.S. covert assistance for the resistance. Indeed, the Afghan cause, by this time, had won widespread support across the U.S. political spectrum. The story of the ragtag resistance standing up to the powerful Red Army in defense of its homeland caught the American public's imagination. In the Senate, liberal Paul Tsongas (D-Mass.) headed a large congressional caucus that pressed the Reagan administration to boost funding for the mujahideen.

Their supporters need not have worried. When Yaqub traveled to Moscow in June 1983 to test the waters before the next round of talks at Geneva, the dour Gromyko dashed any prospects for an early settlement. The Soviet foreign minister reverted to the previous Kremlin line that the Red Army had entered Afghanistan in response to the Kabul government's request and that its departure was not a subject for negotiation. According to Yaqub, Gromyko stressed that the sole issue at Geneva was to arrange for an end to Pakistan's support for the resistance, which he compared to lending your house "to bandits to fire on the neighbors."[57]

The reason for the hardened Soviet position was unclear, according to Yaqub. He thought that it was possible that Andropov's serious illness had given hard-liners like Gromyko the chance to reimpose their views. Cordovez's aggressively optimistic tactics may have resulted in Moscow's and Islamabad's gaining a faulty understanding of each other's positions.[58] Some observers, such as journalist and author Selig Harrison, regarded the episode as a missed opportunity and blamed the setback on pressure from U.S., mujahideen, and ISI hawks.[59] Pakistani diplomat Riaz Mohammed Khan seems closer to the mark in his account of the negotiations: after the Soviets toughened their position in the Gromyko-Yaqub talks, "the elusive opportunity [for peace] disappeared before it had matured."[60]

Zia was, in any case, less hopeful than Yaqub about the prospects for an early agreement on Afghanistan. He periodically said that the negotiations were going to be a *"lamba chakkar"* (a long haul). Although the Pakistani president did not want to break off the talks, Yaqub sensed that he regarded them as a sideshow to the main effort of maintaining military pressure on the Soviets.[61] During a July 1983 dinner in Islamabad for Shultz, who was visiting Pakistan, Akhtar Rahman, who normally said little on such occasions, reacted sharply to a suggestion by Yaqub that the return of the former Afghan monarch, King Zahir, might facilitate a peace settlement. The ISI chief declared with much emotion that the Soviets were never going to leave Afghanistan. When Schaffer, who was accompanying Shultz, asked Zia what he thought, the president responded, "I think it would be a miracle if they leave Afghanistan."[62]

Shultz, Weinberger, and Bush Visit Pakistan

Shultz's sojourn in Pakistan was far happier than the last visit there by a secretary of state had been: Henry Kissinger's unsuccessful 1976 effort to convince Bhutto to drop the nuclear program. Shultz praised his hosts for providing a home for three million refugees, expressed U.S. willingness to continue a large Afghan aid program, and, in a lower key, voiced continuing American worries about the nuclear program. In turn, the Pakistanis vowed to maintain the struggle to free Afghanistan, thanked the United States for its help, and reiterated that they were not seeking a nuclear weapon.[63] Assistant Secretary of State Veliotes described the Pakistan stop as a "love in."[64] In cables to the White House about the visit, Shultz lauded Zia as "a capable and impressive leader" and described Yaqub as "one of the most impressive and articulate foreign ministers now in office."[65]

In what would become a ritual for senior U.S. visitors, Shultz traveled to Peshawar to meet with refugees. "Fellow fighters for freedom, we are with you," the secretary of state told a cheering crowd of Afghans.[66] "George Shultz, who is really a quite emotional person despite his stone face, got carried away when he visited the Afghan tribals near Peshawar. I thought he was going to grab a gun and run off into Afghanistan," Veliotes commented about the World War II Marine veteran.[67]

A few months later, in the fall of 1983, Secretary of Defense Caspar Weinberger followed in Shultz's footsteps, conferring with Zia and then traveling to Peshawar to hail the refugees. Weinberger told a group of applauding Afghan tribals, "I want you to know that you are not alone. You will have our support until you regain the freedom that is rightfully yours."[68] The defense secretary lauded Pakistan as a key U.S. ally in opposing the presumed Soviet push toward the Arabian Sea. "[Pakistan has] a strong military, and we're trying to strengthen it all the more," Weinberger stated. In line with the Reagan administration's hands-off approach regarding Pakistan's domestic political scene, Weinberger dodged press questions about Zia's repression of large-scale anti-government unrest in the province of Sindh.[69]

In May 1984, Vice President George Bush joined the procession of top-level U.S. visitors to Pakistan. "Your visit," his State Department brief read, "will both symbolize and further solidify the strong relationship with Pakistan we have successfully developed over the past three years, a major Administration objective and accomplishment."[70] Cheering Afghan tribals greeted Bush near Peshawar along what the *Washington Post* called a "well-worn VIP path . . . through the harsh hills to the Khyber Pass for a peek across the border into Soviet-controlled Afghanistan."[71] The vice president responded by praising the Afghans and "their indomitable spirit of freedom" which, he declared, has "earned the admiration of free men everywhere."[72]

Bush and Zia discussed the nuclear issue during lunch in Murree, where they had fled the scorching 105-degree heat of Islamabad. Pakistan's president assured the U.S. vice president, as he had other Americans, that the nuclear program was strictly peaceful. As long as he was head of state, Zia stated, Pakistan would have no intention of acquiring a nuclear device. "You have my personal assurance," the

Vice President George Bush and President Zia meet in Islamabad, May 1984. (Courtesy of the George Bush Presidential Library.)

Pakistani leader declared. After thanking Zia for his assurance, Bush stressed that exploding a device, violating safeguards, or reprocessing plutonium would pose a "very difficult" problem for the Reagan administration. The nuclear question, the vice president emphasized, remained a highly sensitive issue in the United States.[73]

Deadlock in Afghanistan

As Americans, especially members of Congress, trooped through Islamabad and Peshawar, they regarded the Pakistanis as good people, but their heroes were the Afghans who were holding the vaunted Red Army to a draw with little more than basic infantry weapons. The "freedom fighters" awed the visitors with their grit and determination. Rather like the British in 1940, their message was, "Give us the guns and we will do the job." A CIA station chief recalled that he never heard the tribals, despite heavy casualties and severe suffering, describe their situation as "hopeless."[74]

By mid-1984, it had become evident that a standoff was developing in Afghanistan. According to Veliotes, "We began to see a Vietnam pattern starting to establish itself. The Russians would take an area, then the mujahideen would move back in as soon as they left. . . . Optimism gradually grew as we saw the staying power of the Afghans and saw signs of Russian losses."[75] The CIA chief of station grew increasingly confident that the Soviets could not succeed in Afghanistan. He reached this conclusion not because of the human and matériel losses the Soviet military was sustaining, but because "the Afghans were bloodthirsty and cruel fighters who simply refused to give up."[76]

Unless the Soviets significantly increased their military strength above the roughly one hundred thousand troops that they maintained in Afghanistan, U.S. specialists doubted that they could suppress the insurgents. But at the same time, it seemed unrealistic to expect that the mujahideen "by themselves can drive the Soviet army out of Afghanistan."[77] The Soviets were able to control urban areas and their military bases, and to keep the country's major transportation routes open. The resistance, however, held sway over much of the countryside. Despite their splintered and fractious leadership, the mujahideen were also able to attack the Red Army almost anywhere. Yaqub summed up the situation when he met Shultz in Washington in fall 1984: "The Soviet war effort in Afghanistan is marked by ineptitude, incompetence, and erosion of morale. After four and a half years, they have not learned how to fight in Afghanistan, and they have not won over the Afghans to their side."[78]

Increasingly enthusiastic about the prospects in Afghanistan, CIA director Casey was eager to up the ante. He kept pressing his chief of station to convince the Pakistanis that the scope of the conflict could be expanded without risking major retaliation from the Russians. When Casey put this view directly to Zia, the Pakistani leader responded that since they did not know what the limit was, they should keep raising the heat, but do so carefully.[79]

As the temperature rose, combined U.S.-Saudi spending on the covert aid program ballooned from $60 million in 1981 to $400 million in 1984. Saudi Arabia continued to cover half the costs, matching the U.S. contribution. Unlike controversial covert aid for the contras in Nicaragua, congressional budget approval for the Afghan program was never a problem. By 1984, a band of enthusiastic Afghan hawks, most notably Representatives Charles Wilson (D-Texas) and William McCollum (R-Fla.), and Senators Gordon Humphrey (R-N.H.) and Orrin Hatch (R-Utah), led a vocal and emotional chorus of congressional supporters. Their criticism was that the CIA was doing too little, not too much.

Two aspects of Afghan covert aid became especially controversial, however. The first was alleged corruption: the charge that ISI personnel were diverting a substantial portion of the supplies either for personal gain or for official Pakistani uses. CIA officers conceded some misuse but claimed that clandestine intelligence sources and other indicators, such as black-market prices for weapons, suggested that most supplies were reaching the mujahideen.[80] Critics scoffed at the CIA's response and similar denials by Pakistani authorities as a whitewash and cover-up for substantial fraud. Where the truth lay was not clear.

More contentious and, in the long run, politically far more significant, was the way in which the Pakistanis parceled out arms and equipment to the seven recognized resistance groups.[81] The ISI gave by far the largest share to fundamentalist factions that wanted Afghanistan to become a conservative Islamic state, an approach that echoed Zia's own, only partially successful, effort to impose Islamic norms on Pakistan. The ISI showed special favor to Gulbuddin Hekmatyar, an outspoken and vehemently anti-American Islamic radical with whom Pakistan had had a covert relationship since the mid-1970s.

The Pakistanis justified their division of the arms pie on the grounds that the fundamentalists earned the lion's share by doing most of the fighting in Afghanistan. Given U.S. dependence on the ISI to wage the insurgency, CIA officials believed that it was not wise to challenge the Pakistanis on this issue. They also felt that the differences between the seven groups were overdrawn. As a former CIA Pakistan station chief put it, "They were all brutal, fierce, bloodthirsty, and basically fundamentalist. There were no Thomas Jeffersons on a white horse among the Afghan resistance leaders."[82]

Sitting in the policy driver's seat in Washington, the CIA brushed aside the views of critics, such as State Department Afghan specialist Eliza Van Hollen, who argued that the fact that Islamic extremists received most of the arms resulted in their attracting the bulk of the fighters. There was also little apparent CIA concern that the ability of the fundamentalists to hand out weapons gave them a potent form of political patronage, strengthening their standing and weakening that of more moderate Afghan groups.[83]

The Pressler Amendment

Despite the primacy of the Afghan war in Washington, the nuclear issue refused to go away. By early 1984, nonproliferation supporters in Congress had become deeply worried by intelligence reports increasingly at odds with the "peaceful" assurances Zia regularly offered American visitors. An April 4, 1984, story in the Urdu-language daily *Nawai-i-Waqt,* quoting nuclear scientist Abdul Qadeer Khan as claiming that Pakistan had succeeded in enriching uranium to weapons grade, stirred further anxiety.[84] In a hard-hitting statement, Senator Alan Cranston (D-Calif.) asserted on June 20, 1984, that Pakistan was pressing ahead with a program that would soon be capable of producing "several nuclear weapons per year." Cranston chastised the State Department for "obscuring, withholding or downright misrepresenting the facts" about the Pakistani nuclear program.[85] Congressional misgivings increased after three Pakistani nationals were indicted in Houston, Texas, in July 1984 for trying illegally to export equipment useful for a weapons program. The Houston indictment came on the heels of the conviction in Canada of two other Pakistanis for seeking illegally to export U.S.-origin nuclear-related items.[86]

As congressional apprehension mounted, the Reagan administration felt that a word of warning was called for. Accordingly, the president cautioned Zia in a September 12, 1984, letter that there would be "serious consequences" should Pakistan enrich uranium beyond the 5 percent level. (This level of enrichment was sufficient to produce nuclear fuel for power reactors but was still insufficient to make a bomb). "I am determined to work strenuously to continue our various programs of close and productive cooperation with Pakistan," Reagan wrote. "[H]owever, I must reiterate my deep concern that the nuclear issue may undermine all that we are trying to achieve and the considerable progress we have made so far."[87] He received a noncommittal reply from Zia, which Yaqub delivered in mid-November 1984.[88]

That same month, the presence of Shultz and Zia at the funeral of assassinated Indian prime minister Indira Gandhi provided a chance for further high-level discussion of the nuclear question. When Shultz, seconded by Senate majority leader Howard Baker (R-Tenn.), raised the subject, Zia responded, "We support [your] non-proliferation policy, and we implement it. But the difference for us is happening around here

President Reagan confers with Foreign Minister Sahibzada Yaqub Khan at the White House, November 1984. (Courtesy of the Ronald Reagan Library.)

[i.e., India]." Asked directly by Senator Daniel Patrick Moynihan (D-N.Y.), a former ambassador to India, whether Pakistan had a bomb, Zia replied, "We are nowhere near it. We have no intention of making such a weapon. We renounce making such a weapon."[89]

Congressional suspicions that Zia was not telling the truth, however, caused growing disquiet as the Reagan administration geared up to seek approval for a second and slightly larger multiyear military and economic aid program for Pakistan—a six year package worth $4 billion. Senator John Glenn (D-Ohio), one of the most vocal nonproliferation proponents, argued that the sanctions waiver approved in 1981 had removed all restraints on Islamabad's developing a nuclear weapon as long as it did not explode a device. To impose a higher barrier, Glenn proposed an amendment to the foreign assistance act that would require the president to certify annually that Pakistan neither possessed nor was developing a nuclear weapon for aid to continue.[90]

The Senate Foreign Relations Committee initially approved Glenn's proposal, but in the face of strong pressure from the Reagan administration it backed off to a milder version requiring an annual certification that Pakistan did not possess a nuclear device and that U.S. assistance was advancing nonproliferation goals.[91] Although the administration was unable to obtain a waiver, the revised amendment seemed safe enough. Quite apart from Zia's "assurances," U.S. intelligence did not believe the Pakistanis were that close to achieving a nuclear explosive capability. After agreement on the substitute language, the White House arranged for Senator Larry Pressler (R-S.D.)—who ironically had not been previously involved in the Pakistan nuclear question—to sponsor the amendment.

When U.S. officials discussed the issue with the Pakistanis, they characterized the Pressler amendment as a way to avert more damaging legislation, not as a device for cutting off assistance. The fact that the amendment was country-specific and thus discriminatory was not at the time deemed to be a problem by the Pakistanis, although Islamabad complained loudly about this after sanctions were imposed in 1990. Indeed, Pakistani officials seemed to regard the Pressler amendment as an internal U.S. affair, part of the executive branch's management of its nuclear problem with Congress, rather than something that Pakistan should be concerned about.[92]

The Reagan administration also accepted an amendment to the foreign assistance act submitted by Representative Solarz barring aid to any country whose government entities illegally imported nuclear technology from the United States. Irritated by indications that Pakistan was doing just that, Solarz wanted to send a warning to Islamabad to stop violating U.S. law. Unlike the Pressler amendment, the Solarz amendment included a presidential waiver.[93]

In November 1985, Reagan met with Zia and Indian prime minister Rajiv Gandhi in New York City, where they were attending the UN General Assembly's fortieth-anniversary session. The focus of the Reagan-Zia session was to emphasize U.S. hopes for better India-Pakistan relations.[94] In a separate meeting alone with Zia, National Security Adviser McFarlane took up the nuclear problem. McFarlane said that he could "understand" why Pakistan felt it needed a nuclear deterrent but warned about the growing congressional pressures for sanctions that had resulted in the Pressler amendment. Whatever Pakistan did in its program, McFarlane cautioned, it should not achieve a nuclear weapon or test a device. Pakistan's president did not respond with his usual bland assurances that the program was "purely peaceful." Instead, he said that Pakistan had a minimum nuclear program necessitated by its security environment. No leader of Pakistan, he stated, could shut that program down without compromising the country's security. Zia added, however, that the program would not reach the point where it would "embarrass" U.S.-Pakistan relations[95]—a pet phrase, almost a mantra, that Zia used in talking with U.S. officials about the nuclear program.

A shrewd judge of how far he could push the Americans on the nuclear issue, Zia calculated that occasional trouble over clandestine procurement of nuclear-related equipment—any link with the Pakistani government could be denied—and even enriching uranium to weapons grade, would not breach the "embarrassment" barrier. Zia assumed correctly that Washington would give the struggle against the Soviets in Afghanistan a higher priority than his country's nuclear program. As long as Pakistan did not explode a device, Zia believed, the Reagan administration would find some way to avoid undercutting the struggle against the Red Army by imposing nuclear sanctions against Pakistan. Moreover, Pakistan's president did not foresee an early end to the Afghan war[96]—a view that U.S. officials shared.

The fact that the nuclear program was the CIA's top collection target in Pakistan caused friction in the otherwise amicable working relationship between the chief of station and the director-general of the ISI.

"Are you trying to sabotage our effort by sending in all these lies?" Akhtar Rahman asked tartly after the *Washington Post* ran a story about the nuclear program, citing U.S. intelligence sources. At first, in talking with the station chief, the ISI chief routinely denied that Pakistan was seeking a weapons capability. But after Zia briefed him on the program, Akhtar Rahman changed his approach. "Let's not discuss this issue any further," he told the CIA officer, who was only too happy to put the subject aside.[97]

Somehow the U.S. government thought that showing Zia intelligence data on the nuclear program would influence the Pakistani leader to back off. Peripatetic and multilingual U.S. envoy Gen. Vernon (Dick) Walters, who had served as deputy director of the CIA during the Watergate years, traveled to Pakistan several times to discuss the nuclear program. During one visit, Walters showed the president a blueprint design that the CIA had obtained of the Pakistani bomb.[98] Ambassador Spiers recalled that the drawing looked like something from a science-fiction magazine. On another occasion, when Walters showed Zia a satellite photograph of the Kahuta facility, Pakistan's president commented, "This can't be a nuclear installation. Maybe it is a goat shed."[99] In fact, the Pakistanis found the briefings rather bizarre. Munir Ahmed Khan, the chairman of Pakistan's Atomic Energy Commission, told the author that the "show and tell" exercises had no effect on the nuclear program, except to alert Pakistani officials about what the Americans knew.[100]

1985: Change in Pakistan and the Soviet Union

The year 1985 saw major changes in both Pakistan and the Soviet Union. Following seven years of martial law, Zia took a step toward more representative government in the face of severe political unrest in Sindh and the army's dislike of having to assume police functions. Although the Reagan administration had not pressed Zia, congressional Democrats had vocally criticized his regime's human rights record and the lack of democracy in his country.

In February 1985, after a referendum "approved" Zia's performance and "elected" him president for another five years, Pakistanis voted for a National Assembly for the first time since the aborted 1977 elections.[101] Although eleven opposition parties urged a boycott of the polls, a respectable 52 percent of eligible voters cast their ballots. The results were hardly a stirring vote of confidence for Zia: five of nine members of his cabinet who contested the elections were defeated.[102]

One month later, Zia opened up the political process a bit more when he appointed Mohammed Khan Junejo, a little-known politician from Sindh, as prime minister. To Zia's unpleasant surprise, Junejo refused to be a pliant front man and insisted on acting like a prime minister. After Junejo pressed on the issue, Zia agreed to lift martial law on December 31, 1985. The democratic 1973 constitution was reinstated as the country's supreme law. At Zia's insistence, however, an eighth amendment was adopted that made the president, not the prime minister, the ultimate wielder of power.[103]

In the Soviet Union, 1985 also saw important political change. Conservative septuagenarian Konstantin Chernenko, who had succeeded Yuri Andropov as Communist Party leader, died and was replaced by Mikhail Gorbachev. The new general secretary was almost two decades younger than his three predecessors and brought renewed verve and energy to Soviet policy after an extended period of drift. As events would soon show, Gorbachev was intent on introducing radical change in the hope of modernizing Soviet society. In the case of Afghanistan, he initially showed few signs of a policy shift. Quite the contrary, when hardliners claimed that, by applying a little more pressure, the Soviets could gain the upper hand, Gorbachev agreed to an intensified military effort.[104]

Despite this, Shultz sensed that there might be a change regarding Afghanistan after the November 1985 U.S.-Soviet summit in Geneva. The secretary of state told NBC News that Gorbachev had "some interesting and a little different kind of things to say."[105] A month later, on December 13, 1985, the United States formally engaged itself in the Geneva peace process by declaring that it was willing to serve as a guarantor power to the accords. Tucked into a speech before the World Affairs Council of Washington, the statement by Deputy Secretary of State John Whitehead, which National Security Council staff member Donald Fortier had cleared, triggered vociferous opposition from conservatives who feared a sellout of the mujahideen. The State Department defended the step, arguing that it put the Soviets on the defensive diplomatically and that, in any case, the Geneva negotiations were unlikely to achieve concrete results.[106]

On February 26, 1986, Gorbachev signaled a shift in the Soviet attitude toward Afghanistan more concretely, telling the Twenty-seventh

Congress of the Soviet Communist Party that the war had become "a bleeding wound."[107] A month later, in March 1986, the Kabul regime finally offered a timetable for the withdrawal of the Soviet military. Although there was an enormous gap between the four-year schedule that Kabul proposed and the three to four months that Pakistan wanted, the Afghan move set in train the process of more serious bargaining at Geneva.[108]

1986: Change in Afghanistan

On the ground in Afghanistan, the Soviets appeared to be making headway through improved and more aggressive tactics, especially greater use of helicopter gunships. The mujahideen lacked an adequate defense against these helicopters and were beginning to suffer as the Soviets pressed gunship attacks. When resistance leaders sought to obtain the U.S.-made Stinger missile, a light but sophisticated anti-aircraft weapon, their congressional friends vigorously pressed the case with the Reagan administration. They argued that the mujahideen's need was greater than any trouble breaching the fiction of U.S. noninvolvement in Afghanistan might cause with the Soviets. Moscow, they said, was well aware of the U.S. role, which by then had become an open secret.

At first, Zia was reluctant to have the Afghans receive Stingers. When pressed by mujahideen backer Orrin Hatch, however, Pakistan's president asked that the weapon be supplied.[109] After considerable internal debate, the Reagan administration agreed, overriding Defense Department and intelligence community concerns about "leakage" of the Stingers into the hands of terrorists and the possibility that the Soviets could copy the technology through reverse engineering.[110] In September 1986, the Stinger claimed its first helicopter victim; thereafter, Soviet losses mounted substantially. Helicopter pilots became more cautious, reducing the effectiveness of the gunships. Morale soared among the mujahideen. In retrospect, the introduction of the Stinger proved a major turning point in the Afghan struggle.[111]

In mid-1986, when Bill Casey gave instruction to the officer assigned to take over as the chief of station in Islamabad, the CIA director no longer talked just of causing pain for the Soviets by "growing the war." He emphatically ordered the new station chief to do everything possible to increase the military pressure on the Soviets in Afghanistan and "to win the war."[112] In the same spirit, the Congress approved doubling the level of U.S. funding for the covert program from $300 million to $600 million annually. With Saudi Arabia's matching contribution, this meant that by the end of 1986 more than $1 billion a year in supplies was being pumped into Pakistan for the insurgents. This was enough, according to a senior CIA official, to arm some four hundred thousand Afghan resistance fighters.[113]

As the Soviets appeared increasingly bogged down and unable to gain the upper hand in Afghanistan, observers began to think that Moscow might actually decide to pull out. After a visit to Islamabad by Soviet diplomats, Zia told Diego Cordovez that "a miracle" might be possible.[114] During another round of talks in March 1987, the Pakistanis and the Afghans substantially narrowed the gap between their respective timetables for the withdrawal of Soviet troops. The Afghans reduced the period for the Red Army's departure from four years to eighteen months. Yaqub increased the time that Pakistan was willing to accept from four to seven months. Cordovez, who had by then reached agreement on less-contentious elements of an Afghan accord, "sensed the negotiations had finally acquired needed credibility and respectability."[115]

When Zia had begun Pakistan's support for the mujahideen, his aim had been to reduce the likelihood that Moscow would push further south. As a Soviet withdrawal became a real possibility, Zia's ambitions expanded. Victory by the resistance, he believed, could produce for the first time since 1947 an Afghan regime genuinely friendly to Pakistan, which in turn would enable Pakistan to gain "strategic depth" against India, long a goal of Pakistani military planners. Moreover, Zia hoped that the new government in Kabul would reflect his own Islamic leanings far more than any previous Afghan regime had, and far more than the Pakistani president had been able to impose on his own country.[116]

Junejo Visits Washington; More Nuclear Trouble

In July 1986, Prime Minister Junejo visited the United States, providing the Reagan administration a chance to applaud Pakistan's more open political system and to reaffirm the bilateral partnership. The most tangible sign was U.S. willingness to provide $4.02 billion worth of aid over the next six years. While the earlier multiyear assistance package (1981–86) had been equally divided between military and economic assistance, at Zia's suggestion, 57 percent of the new six-year commitment (1987–93)

President Reagan meets with Prime Minister Mohammed Khan Junejo at the White House, July 1986. (Courtesy of the Ronald Reagan Library.)

would be for development aid and only 43 percent for security assistance.[117] The Junejo visit also offered yet another opportunity for U.S. officials to stress the importance of Pakistani "restraint on the nuclear issue if [the United States is] to be able to continue [its] multi-year program of economic and security assistance."[118]

The prime minister, in fact, had little voice in the management of the nuclear program. In talking with Americans, he hewed strictly to the official line that it was "purely for peaceful purposes." In a meeting at the *Washington Post,* however, Junejo wandered off the reservation when he "confirmed" that Pakistan would not enrich uranium beyond the 5 percent level mentioned in Reagan's September 1984 letter.[119] Zia, himself, was always careful to avoid making an explicit commitment on the level of enrichment, falling back on his mantra, "We won't embarrass our friends."

In October 1986, President Reagan certified for the first time under the Pressler amendment that Pakistan did not possess a nuclear device and that American aid "reduces significantly" the risk that Pakistan would acquire one. A few days later, Washington was jarred by leaked intelligence reports indicating that Pakistan had tested a triggering device for a nuclear weapon and had enriched uranium to weapons grade. The press quoted an anonymous U.S. official as saying that Pakistan was only "two screwdriver turns" away from possessing a fully assembled weapon.[120] Still, according to Undersecretary of State for Political Affairs Michael Armacost (the key State Department official dealing with Afghanistan), there was enough doubt in the intelligence community to enable the administration to avoid imposing sanctions under the Pressler amendment: "There was no smoking gun and the fact of differences among the intelligence analysts pointed to the uncertainty."[121]

In January 1987, tensions between India and Pakistan suddenly rose after India began to conduct its largest-ever military maneuvers in the deserts of Rajasthan, near the border with Pakistan. Concerned that the maneuvers, called Operation Brasstacks, might be a cover for an actual invasion, the Pakistani military strengthened its own positions near the frontier. Tensions rapidly mounted between the two foes. The crisis eased after the two sides began diplomatic talks. Zia himself lowered the temperature by making a point of attending an India-Pakistan cricket match at Bangalore.[122]

When the Brasstacks crisis was at its peak at the end of January 1987, the head of Pakistan's secret uranium-enrichment program, Abdul Qadeer Khan, who rarely appeared in public view, told Kuldip Nayar, a visiting Indian journalist, that Pakistan had achieved a nuclear weapon capability.[123] "They told us Pakistan could never produce the bomb," Nayar quoted A. Q. Khan as saying, "and doubted my capabilities, but they know we have done it." A. Q. Khan added, "The word 'peaceful' associated with a nuclear program is humbug."[124]

When the report appeared in the *Observer* (London) on March 1, 1987, it created a sensation even though the Pakistani nuclear scientist quickly claimed he was misquoted and had only spoken briefly with the Indian journalist about a wedding invitation.[125] Apparently, Mushahid Hussain, then editor of the daily newspaper *The Muslim,* and a decade later minister of information for Prime Minister Nawaz Sharif, had arranged the get-together without official blessing, presumably as a way to exert psychological pressure on India.

Zia was angry about being upstaged by A. Q. Khan, whom Pakistan's president regarded as politically naive and a publicity-seeker. According to Zia's top aide, Lt. Gen. Refaqat and others, the president gave the scientist a dressing-down and saw to it that Mushahid lost his job.[126] A month later, Zia himself confirmed the gist of what A. Q. Khan had said, telling *Time* magazine, "You can write today that Pakistan can build a bomb whenever it wishes."[127] The response in Washington, according to Pakistan's ambassador, Jamshed Marker, was what he regarded as "an aye and a wink." At the same time, U.S. officials urged in the strongest possible terms that Islamabad avoid stirring up any further trouble on the nuclear front.[128]

Zia was also unhappy about a warning in mid-February 1987 by U.S. ambassador to Pakistan Deane Hinton. In an address before the Pakistani Institute of Strategic Studies, Hinton had stated that some aspects of the nuclear effort were "inconsistent" with a peaceful program and urged Pakistan to sign the nuclear Nonproliferation Treaty. Angry about Hinton's public chiding, a government spokesman said, "Pakistan will not be browbeaten or cajoled."[129]

On July 15, 1987, a serious new problem arose on the nuclear front. The Federal Bureau of Investigation (FBI) arrested a Pakistan-born Canadian citizen named Arshad ("Archie") Pervez in Philadelphia in a sting operation. Pervez was charged with trying to arrange for the illegal export of highly specialized "maraging" steel, which is used in making atomic bomb casings.[130] At one point during the sting operation, Pervez had informed the FBI agent masquerading as a businessman that the special steel was intended for Pakistan's nuclear program.[131] Although the authorities in Islamabad immediately denied any involvement, the impact on Capitol Hill was highly negative. An annoyed House Foreign Affairs Committee chairman Dante Fascell (D-Fla.) called for the suspension of aid to Pakistan until the situation was clarified.

To make matters worse, two days later, two Americans and a Hong Kong national were indicted in Sacramento, California, for illegally exporting to Pakistan sophisticated instruments and advanced computer items used in making a nuclear weapon.[132] In a damage-control exercise, Undersecretary Armacost flew to Islamabad, where the Pakistani government labeled the Pervez incident a "rogue affair" and promised to cooperate in its investigation. The Pakistanis, however, rebuffed Armacost's request to permit inspection of Kahuta and other nuclear facilities.[133]

On September 21, 1987, President Reagan met again with Prime Minister Junejo, this time in New York during the annual UN General Assembly. "I have to certify on the nuclear program and you have to make it possible for me to do so," Ambassador Marker recalled the president's telling the prime minister.[134] As a sign of increased concern about Pakistan's nuclear activities, Congress in the fall of 1987 had allowed the six-year waiver of sanctions to expire, temporarily halting new commitments of aid. It was not until December 17, 1987, that the waiver authority was reinstated; this time, however, the waiver was granted for only two and a half years, not the six years that the administration had sought.

That same day, the president issued the required Pressler amendment certification for the second time. Threading the eye of the needle carefully, Reagan's letter to House Speaker Jim Wright (D-Texas) stated that the finding rested on the "statutory standard as legislated by Congress" of whether Pakistan "possesses a nuclear explosive device, not whether Pakistan is attempting to develop or has developed various relevant capacities."[135]

Ironically, also on December 17, 1987, a jury in the U.S. District Court in Philadelphia found Archie Pervez guilty. The Reagan administration found itself in a corner, because the investigation had revealed that the illegal export was intended for use in Pakistan's nuclear program. The provisions of the Solarz amendment called for suspension of aid.[136]

Faced with this prospect, Reagan used his waiver authority, citing U.S. national interests as the reason for not imposing sanctions against Pakistan.[137] Defending the action, as well as the earlier Pressler certification, Deputy Assistant Secretary of State for South Asia Robert Peck argued—by this time unconvincingly—that quite apart from the harmful impact on the Afghan war effort of suspending aid, imposing sanctions "would make it significantly more likely that Pakistan would proceed to acquire nuclear weapons."[138]

The End Game at Geneva

Some months earlier, in September 1987, Soviet Foreign Minister Eduard Shevardnadze had advised Secretary of State Shultz privately that Soviet troops would leave Afghanistan within a year.[139] During the December 1987 U.S.-Soviet summit in Washington, Gorbachev publicly announced that Soviet troops would leave over a twelve-month period after agreement was reached on ending external aid to the mujahideen. He no longer insisted on a political settlement as a condition for the departure of Soviet forces. The road seemed open for an agreement, but as the withdrawal of the Soviet army from Afghanistan became more likely, U.S. and Pakistani interests began to diverge. According to Armacost, "Our main interest was getting the Russians out. Afghanistan, as such, was remote from major U.S. concerns. The United States was not much interested in the internal Afghan setup and did not have much capacity to understand this."[140] In contrast, the Pakistanis, especially President Zia, regarded the nature of the government in Kabul of major importance. According to Arnold Raphel, who had succeeded Hinton as U.S. ambassador in 1987, the United States focused on the Soviet withdrawal "while Zia and the ISI . . . felt that after eight years of war Pakistan was entitled to run its own show in Kabul.[141]

To complicate matters, Pakistan's policy began to lose coherence just as the endgame of the Geneva negotiations commenced. Friction between Zia and Junejo led to the resignation of the suave and experienced Yaqub Khan, who had stepped down in the fall of 1987 rather than have his deputy, Zain Noorani, a Junejo supporter, head Pakistan's delegation to the UN General Assembly; upon Yaqub's departure, Noorani, who possessed scant foreign affairs experience, became foreign minister. Although Zia had previously orchestrated Afghan policy, he was forced to work with the Junejo-dominated foreign ministry, which did not always see things the president's way. Zia grew increasingly frustrated as developments began to slip out of his control.[142]

At this point, Pakistan's president threw a spanner in the works by threatening not to sign the Geneva accords unless there was a political settlement in Kabul. The action reversed Pakistan's long-standing position that the only major issue to be negotiated at Geneva was the timetable for the departure of Soviet troops. Although conventional wisdom held that the communist regime, headed by Najibullah Khan, who had replaced Babrak Karmal in 1986, would quickly collapse after the Soviet military departed, Zia was not so sure, according to Refaqat. In a strictly intra-Afghan struggle, Zia was uncertain whether the fractious mujahideen would gain the upper hand and did not think that Najibullah would simply fade away. Zia expected that, instead, Najibullah would fight hard to retain power. Under these circumstances, Zia hoped to force a political settlement while the superpowers were still engaged.[143]

Neither Moscow nor Washington agreed. In a mid-February 1988 trip to Islamabad, Soviet diplomat Yuri Vorontsov rebuffed the Pakistani president in what Refaqat called "the toughest meeting he had ever attended." Vorontsov warned Zia of "unpredictable consequences if a unilateral withdrawal is forced upon us."[144] When Armacost visited Islamabad a short time later, he adopted a similar, if less brusque, position. The Americans, Armacost made clear, were unwilling to delay the signing of the Geneva accords until an interim Afghan government was agreed upon. Secretary of State Shultz termed this as "desirable" but something that the Afghans themselves had to decide.[145]

Nor did Zia have domestic political support on the issue. Junejo favored an early agreement at Geneva and, over Zia's objection, convened an all-parties meeting in early March 1988 to discuss the issue. The gathering endorsed Pakistan's support for the mujahideen, but not a delay in the Soviet withdrawal from Afghanistan.[146] To complicate matters further, Zia found little common ground for a possible compromise between the mujahideen leadership in Peshawar and the Kabul regime,[147] with which he was in secret contact through American business magnate Armand Hammer.[148] When the mujahideen leadership met with Cordovez, they flatly rejected the Geneva accords, stressing their intention to take power in Kabul on their own. Faced with a wall of opposition, an unhappy Zia backed down.[149]

The second problem that nearly derailed the settlement concerned the supply of arms to the mujahideen after the Geneva accords went into effect. The Soviets had made clear that they would continue to provide military help to the Kabul regime, and the Geneva accords did not bar their doing so. The agreement, however, required Pakistan to stop helping the mujahideen thirty days after Soviet forces completed their pullout from Afghanistan. By becoming a guarantor to the Geneva accords, the United States had also implicitly agreed to end its own covert assistance for the mujahideen.

As the prospect for agreement at Geneva increased, the Peshawar resistance leaders and their conservative American friends focused on the import of Moscow's maintaining the supply of weapons to the Afghan regime while Washington and Pakistan stopped sending arms to the mujahideen. Senator Gordon Humphrey (R-N.H.), Representative Charles Wilson (D-Texas), and other mujahideen backers accused the State Department of making preemptive concessions and charged that the White House had been lax.[150]

It turned out that they had a powerful ally: Ronald Reagan. Profoundly sympathetic to the mujahideen cause, the president, perhaps unaware that he was changing his own administration's position, told a television interviewer on December 3, 1987, that he had no intention of stopping arms aid after the Soviet pullout: "I don't think we could do anything of that kind. . . . You can't suddenly disarm [the mujahideen] and leave them prey to the other government. . . . No, the people of Afghanistan must be assured of the right of all of them to participate in establishing the government they want, and that requires more than getting [Soviet] forces out of there."[151]

Shultz and Armacost had a extraordinarily difficult time in selling the president's position to their Soviet counterparts, who argued with justification that the Americans were backing away from an earlier commitment to halt arms aid. It required lengthy and extremely hard bargaining before the Soviets reluctantly agreed that, notwithstanding the terms of the Geneva agreement, both sides could continue to supply arms to their friends—so-called "positive symmetry"—or, alternatively, could terminate assistance—so called "negative symmetry."[152]

The Reagan administration was very concerned, nonetheless, that Pakistan would find itself in the awkward and embarrassing position of violating its obligations under the Geneva accords if it continued to send arms to the resistance. Telephone calls between Washington and Islamabad eased the worry. First, Prime Minister Junejo told Secretary Shultz that Pakistan concurred in the U.S.-Soviet understanding. Then Zia called Reagan to reassure him about the matter. When the U.S. president asked how Zia would respond to charges that Pakistan was violating the Geneva accords, Zia answered, "They would just lie about it. We've been denying our activities there for eight years. Muslims have the right to lie in a good cause."[153] To be absolutely sure about the Pakistani position, U.S. Defense Secretary Frank Carlucci also took up the issue during a visit to Islamabad. In his reporting telegram Carlucci said that when he asked Zia what he would tell the Soviets, the president responded, "I'll lie to them like I have been lying to them for the past ten years." Carlucci reportedly added, "Just as he has been lying to us about the nuclear business."[154]

On April 10, 1988, only four days before the accords were signed at Geneva, a gigantic explosion rocked Islamabad and Rawalpindi. The ISI munitions-storage depot located at Ojiri Camp near the airport blew up, raining rockets, artillery shells, and mortar rounds down on the two cities. More than one hundred people died and eleven hundred were wounded. Shrapnel remnants were found in the wall of the American embassy compound, more than ten miles away. It was as if Pakistan's capital area had become a war zone.[155]

The reaction was one of shock and panic. Zia initially suspected sabotage by the Afghans or Soviets. "It couldn't have been anything else but sabotage, a very effective act of sabotage," he declared.[156] As the government investigated the tragedy—the results of the inquiry were not made public—it became clear that accidental mishandling of munitions rather than sabotage had caused the explosion. After a worker loading mortar shells onto a truck dropped a defective round, it exploded and in turn ignited other rounds stacked nearby. Fire broke out and spread like a chain reaction through the depot, triggering the explosions that destroyed the camp's mammoth stock of munitions.[157]

Because the CIA had been accelerating shipments to bolster the mujahideen's capabilities for the period after the signing of the Geneva accords, Ojiri was packed with eight thousand tons of artillery shells, mortar rounds, and other munitions valued, Ambassador Raphel told Foreign Secretary Abdul Sattar, at between $120 and $130 million.[158] After a worried Zia instructed Ambassador Marker in Washington to ask William Webster, Casey's successor as CIA director, to do everything possible to replenish the losses so the ISI could continue to pump the maximum amount of arms into Afghanistan, the U.S. government mounted a massive resupply operation to replenish the lost ammunition stocks.[159]

On April 14, 1988, Shevardnadze, Shultz, Noorani, and Afghan envoy Abdul Wakil separately signed the Geneva accords under the approving eye of UN Secretary General Pérez de Cuellar. The mood remained somber throughout the signing ceremonies. The four delegations never came together. As Riaz Khan wrote, "There were no smiles and little celebration."[160] Still the agreements marked a major milestone in the winding down of the Cold War. For the first time since the Austrian State Treaty of 1955, the Soviet Union had withdrawn its military forces from territory under its control.

In Pakistan, the investigation into the Ojiri tragedy quickly became entangled in the friction between Junejo and Zia. Politically, the most damaging question was not why the explosion happened but why the ISI had failed to relocate the munitions depot to a safer place. Using the incident as a tool to attack Zia and the military, Junejo wanted to fire both Akhtar Rahman, who in 1987 had become chairman of the

Pakistani joint chiefs of staff, and his replacement as ISI director-general, Lt. Gen. Hamid Gul. Zia wanted to calm the waters and shield his colleagues from public censure and, according to Refaqat, was furious with Junejo.[161]

Taking no one into his confidence until the last moment, the president struck back on May 29, 1988. Invoking the eighth amendment to the 1973 constitution, Zia dismissed Junejo and the National Assembly on grounds of corruption and failing to maintain law and order. The president then named himself prime minister, reappointed Yaqub as foreign minister, and announced new elections for November 1988. In Washington, the reaction was very negative, although Reagan administration officials tried to put the best face on developments.[162]

Whether Zia would, in fact, hold elections became the subject of intense debate. The president himself seemed uncertain how to deal with the situation that he had created. The master juggler and shrewd tactician seemed to have lost his touch. A sense of drift and uncertainty hung over Islamabad.

Zia Dies

Less than three months later, on August 17, 1988, Zia, Raphel, Akhtar Rahman, U.S. defense representative Brig. Gen. Herbert Wasson, and senior Pakistani officers flew to Bahawalpur in southern Punjab to observe firing tests by the M-1 Abrams tank, which was being considered for Pakistan's armored units. After the demonstration, Raphel and Wasson, who had flown to Bahawalpur in a U.S. military aircraft, accepted Zia's invitation to return to the capital in the president's C-130. About ten minutes after takeoff, the usually reliable Pakistani air force plane, one of several at Zia's disposal, began to flounder and then crashed. All thirty-two people on board died. The pilot gave no indication of trouble over the radio, although just before the crash, the control tower heard a voice asking what was wrong.

Zia's death was an enormous shock. The man who had ruled Pakistan for eleven years, pressing his campaign of Islamization, facing down the Soviets on Afghanistan, and facing down the Americans on the nuclear program, was suddenly gone. With the Soviet withdrawal from Afghanistan only partly accomplished, Washington worried about a leadership void and serious instability in Pakistan. A sad Shultz led the official U.S. delegation to the funeral to pay homage to the dead leader's role in the victory over the Soviets in Afghanistan. As the new U.S. ambassador to Pakistan, Shultz left behind Robert Oakley, a senior diplomat who had served as ambassador to Zaire and Somalia and was responsible at the time of Raphel's death for the Middle East and South Asia on the National Security Council staff. Such a rapid appointment was unusual, but the Reagan administration wanted an activist presence quickly on the ground. As Oakley put it, "They wanted to do it in a hurry because they didn't want to allow any time to go by lest the time create uncertainty about our commitment. . . . The situation was very unsettled in Pakistan."[163]

In accordance with the provisions of Pakistan's 1973 constitution, Ghulam Ishaq Khan, president of the senate, became acting president on Zia's death. A conservative civil servant from the Northwest Frontier Province, Ghulam Ishaq had occupied senior posts under Presidents Ayub, Bhutto, and Zia. The acting president first asked Gen. Mirza Aslam Beg, who as head of the army was Pakistan's ultimate arbiter of power, what his wishes were. When Beg answered that he thought the country should follow the democratic path, plans for elections in the fall of 1988 went forward.[164]

Among Oakley's initial tasks was to oversee the investigation of the C-130 crash. The envoy and the acting president agreed on a joint U.S. and Pakistani inquiry, which found insufficient evidence to support any explanation firmly. The report ended, nonetheless, with conflicting Pakistani and American views. In the absence of hard evidence of mechanical failure, the Pakistani investigators concluded that sabotage was the probable cause. In contrast, the U.S. team, not finding credible evidence for sabotage, concluded that a mechanical failure probably led to the crash.[165] The U.S. and Pakistani authorities released a thirty-page summary in late 1988, which Oakley said accurately reflected the full two-hundred-page report, which remains classified. The fact that the FBI did not participate in the joint investigation raised suspicions about a cover-up in Pakistan and also on Capitol Hill. Because of congressional pressure, the FBI some months later conducted a separate inquiry, which reportedly reached similarly inconclusive findings about why the plane crashed.[166]

A decade later, the cause of the tragedy remained a mystery. U.S. government officials familiar with events, on the whole continue to believe that the C-130 went down because of some unexplained mechanical failure. Many senior Pakistanis remain convinced that the plane was sabotaged. Some saw the hand of the Soviet spy agency (the KGB); others blamed the Afghan secret service (the Khad); still others India's spy agency (the Research and Analysis Wing, or RAW); and some even thought that the CIA was behind the crash, despite the fact that Raphel and Wasson were killed along with Zia.

Benazir Bhutto Becomes Prime Minister

The 1988 Pakistani election was a popularity contest between the heirs of two people in the grave: Zia and the man he hanged, Zulfikar Ali Bhutto. Zia's standard-bearer was Nawaz Sharif, an affable Punjabi businessman whom the military had previously installed as chief minister of Punjab, Pakistan's largest province. Sharif's father had made a fortune parlaying a small business into the country's largest steel-rolling mill. Bhutto's standard bearer was his daughter, thirty-three-year-old Benazir, who had returned from exile in 1986 to a tumultuous welcome. Leading her father's Pakistan Peoples Party (PPP), Benazir Bhutto proved a formidable and charismatic campaigner, drawing enormous crowds as she traveled around the country. Like her father, she had received a college education in the United States—at Radcliffe rather than the University of California—and then had gone on to study in England at Oxford.

When the votes were counted, the PPP had won a narrow victory over the Islamic Alliance, the conservative pro-Zia coalition of Sharif's Pakistan Muslim League and smaller allies. With the active support of the ISI, Nawaz Sharif fared better than anticipated and won the important Punjabi provincial elections. Oakley and other U.S. officials had pressed for fair elections and, after the results were in, had urged the military to agree to Benazir Bhutto's assuming office. Assistant Secretary of Defense for International Security Affairs Richard Armitage and Assistant Secretary of State for the Near East and South Asia Richard Murphy visited Pakistan to stress the U.S. interest in seeing that Pakistan followed democratic ground rules. According to Armitage, the military leadership said that it was ready to accept Benazir Bhutto as long as she did not meddle with promotions and other internal military matters. Oakley indicated that there was a further understanding that she would not become heavily involved with Afghanistan and the nuclear question.[167]

As the new democratic Pakistani government settled in, the reins of power that Zia had held in his own hands until 1986 were uneasily shared by what became known as the "troika"—the president, the prime minister, and the chief of army staff. Ghulam Ishaq, as president, theoretically held ultimate power because of the eighth amendment to the 1973 constitution. As the democratically elected prime minister, Benazir Bhutto had political legitimacy. But the decisive word—in view of the army's powerful position in Pakistan—rested with General Beg.

Shortly before Reagan left the White House, he certified for a third time under the Pressler amendment that Pakistan did not possess a nuclear weapon. But his transmittal letter to Speaker Wright warned that the status of the Pakistani program might make it difficult to issue another certification.[168]

Despite this danger signal about the nuclear program, Reagan could end his presidency satisfied about developments in South Asia. In Afghanistan, the U.S.-backed mujahideen had outfought the Soviets, who were in the process of withdrawing their forces as agreed at Geneva. The collapse of Najibullah's communist regime in Kabul after the last Soviet soldier left Afghanistan in February 1989 was widely anticipated. Pakistan itself had seen a relatively smooth transition from Zia's dictatorship to Benazir Bhutto's democratically elected government. Although Washington and Islamabad recognized that Pakistan's strategic importance to the United States would inevitably decline after the Soviet pullout from Afghanistan, and the nuclear problem would become harder to manage, outgoing Reagan administration officials and the Pakistani leadership had reasonable grounds to look forward to continued close and friendly bilateral ties under the incoming president, George Bush. Events would prove this optimism misplaced.

11

Bush: The Partnership Collapses

As George Bush moved into the White House in January 1989, the Cold War was winding down. Mikhail Gorbachev was pressing ahead with domestic reform and seeking improved relations with Washington. One after another, the Soviet satellites in Eastern Europe were shedding their communist rulers. The Iron Curtain was crumbling. U.S.-Soviet conflicts in the Third World, in Central America, Angola, the Horn of Africa, and Afghanistan were moving toward settlements favorable to Washington. The foreign policy focus of the incoming U.S. administration lay on these dramatic events that were fundamentally altering the global balance of power.

President Bush appointed James Baker, a personal friend and Washington insider, as his secretary of state. Although Baker had served as White House chief of staff and treasury secretary during the Reagan administration, he lacked the empathy that his predecessor, George Shultz, had developed for Pakistan as the main U.S. partner in the struggle against the Soviets in Afghanistan. One of Baker's initial acts, on his first day as secretary of state, was to close the embassy in Kabul, which had remained open throughout the 1980s despite U.S. covert aid to the mujahideen. Although mainly spurred by concern that American diplomats might be in physical danger during the anticipated collapse of the communist regime, the decision would deprive Washington of a useful listening post, as well as a possible point of contact with the Afghan government, after the Soviet military completed its withdrawal.[1]

A few months earlier, in mid-1988, the U.S. Congress, spurred by Senator Gordon Humphrey (R-N.H.), had mandated the appointment of an ambassador to the Peshawar-based mujahideen to boost their image and prestige. After low-key diplomat Maurice Ealum served briefly in the post, the activism of his successor, Peter Tomsen, resulted in a more visible State Department presence on Afghan matters just as the departure of Soviet troops was moving intra-Afghan politics to center stage.

Friction quickly developed between Tomsen and the CIA, which disliked his involvement in an area that, until the final stages of the Geneva negotiations, had been a CIA preserve. Tomsen also ran afoul of Pakistan's Inter-Services Intelligence Directorate (ISI) by criticizing its support for Pashtun fundamentalist Gulbuddin Hekmatyar and urging increased help to moderates like Ahmed Shah Masood, a Tajik who had displeased Pakistani intelligence by insisting on maintaining operational independence.[2]

Pakistan's Afghan policy had become far less cohesive by this time. Previously, President Zia ul-Haq provided a strategic vision, resolved internal differences and, moreover, had the confidence of the mujahideen. Following his death, there were many voices, but as Benazir Bhutto's national security adviser, Iqbal Akhund, put it, "no one" was in charge of policy.[3] The ISI, which continued to have operational control of the war, had the major say. Its flamboyant, pro-Islamic leader, Lt. Gen. Hamid Gul, continued to back Hekmatyar and other fundamentalists as Pakistan's best bets for obtaining a friendly regime in Kabul and the longed-for "strategic depth." In contrast, Yaqub Khan, whom Benazir Bhutto had reappointed as foreign minister, questioned whether Hekmatyar or other Peshawar-based fundamentalists would remain pro-Pakistani after taking Kabul.

Yaqub also favored more serious exploration of a transitional role for the former Afghan monarch, King Zahir, as did Tomsen.[4] Both the mujahideen ideologues and their ISI patrons were against recalling the monarch, someone over whom they would have little control. A number of the resistance leaders had strongly opposed the king's reforms in the 1960s. The Pakistanis blamed Zahir and his fellow Mohammadzai clan members for the many years of Pakistani-Afghan tensions over the Pushtunistan issue and remained uneasy about his long-standing friendly relations with India. In any case, the septuagenarian ex-king was himself hesitant about returning to his turbulent homeland after fifteen years of comfortable exile in the outskirts of Rome.[5] In the end, the ISI was able to have its way in continued backing for more fundamentalist leaders such as Hekmatyar as the expected victory over communist leader Najibullah Khan loomed nearer.

Soviets Leave Afghanistan, but Communists Remain

A month before the last Soviet soldier departed in February 1989, Soviet foreign minister Eduard Shevardnadze visited Islamabad and urged the Pakistanis to support a compromise political settlement in Kabul. Benazir Bhutto said that she favored this idea but could do nothing in the face of opposition from President Ghulam Ishaq Khan and hardliners in the ISI and the army.[6] Confident that the Najibullah regime would collapse once the Red Army completed its withdrawal, they saw little need for negotiations about the future Afghan government. For their part, the mujahideen refused to meet with the Soviet foreign minister and opposed any power-sharing arrangement in Kabul that included the communists.[7] Sharing the conventional wisdom that Najibullah would quickly fall after the Russians left, the Bush administration in Washington saw neither need nor reason to support a compromise opposed by the mujahideen. The conservative mujahideen supporters in Congress strongly backed this position, urging no truck with the communists.[8]

The fact that the Peshawar-based resistance groups had agreed, at long last, to form an Afghan Interim Government (AIG), a broadly based body that, in theory, was supposed to include Shi'a groups and some noncommunist supporters of Najibullah, was regarded as a major advance toward forming a new Afghan government. But the development proved more impressive on paper than in reality. Feuding and infighting among mujahideen leaders continued unabated. Neither Afghan Shi'a groups nor supporters of the Kabul regime ever joined the AIG.[9]

On February 15, 1989, Lt. Gen. Boris Gromov strode north across the bridge spanning the Amu Dar'ya River, the frontier between Afghanistan and the Soviet Union, to terminate Moscow's ill-fated, nine-year military adventure. Like the British before them, the Soviets had little to show for their attempt to tame the unruly Afghans. Some fifteen thousand Soviet soldiers died in the effort to prop up the unpopular communist regime.

To follow up the Soviet departure, Hamid Gul strongly urged early diplomatic recognition of the AIG as the legitimate Afghan government to hasten the disintegration of the Najibullah regime. In the Pakistani government's restructured Afghan cell, co-chaired by Iqbal Akhund and Yaqub, the foreign minister countered that the AIG first needed to capture and hold a significant city, such as Jalalabad, Afghanistan's fourth-largest urban area, located some forty miles from the Khyber Pass. The AIG, Yaqub said, had to demonstrate that it was a real government, "not just some Johnnies riding around Peshawar in Mercedes." Ambassador Robert Oakley agreed and indicated that the United States would follow Pakistan's lead on the issue of recognition.[10]

At a March 6, 1989, meeting of the Afghan cell, at which Oakley was present—a sign of his high-profile style—Benazir Bhutto decided to follow the course advocated by Yaqub and to withhold recognition until the AIG captured Jalalabad. Although Hamid Gul had repeatedly predicted the city's imminent fall, he was more hesitant on this occasion, saying he preferred attrition to a frontal attack. The ISI chief, nonetheless, said that Jalalabad could be taken in a week "if the government was prepared to allow for a certain degree of bloodshed."[11] Recalling sarcastically the many times that Hamid Gul had promised that Jalalabad would fall like a ripe apple into her lap, the prime minister ordered him to have the mujahideen attack Jalalabad.[12] Thus, a major Afghan war decision was taken by the Pakistanis with no Afghans present, but with the U.S. ambassador looking on.

The battle for Jalalabad began in a promising fashion, but the mujahideen soon became bogged down. Fighters of different factions failed to coordinate their efforts, frequently fought among themselves, and showed little skill in attacking fixed defensive positions. Afghan government troops also put up a tougher fight than expected. They were able to keep open the key supply route when the mujahideen failed to interdict the road between Jalalabad and Kabul. Before long, it was clear that the early capture of Jalalabad was beyond the capability of the AIG forces.[13] The question of diplomatic recognition no longer arose.

As the mujahideen's march toward early victory stalled, it became clear that the regime in Kabul was not going to crumble after the Red Army left. As George Bush and his national security adviser Brent Scowcroft admitted in their book, *A World Transformed,* the conventional wisdom on the staying power of Najibullah had proven wrong.[14] One important consequence of this misreading of the Afghan scene was a lack of clarity in U.S. policy. For its part, after the Soviets left, the CIA wanted to wash its hands of Afghanistan. Anticipating an early end to the war, the State Department and the Agency for International Development (AID) wanted to shift covert action funds to the economic rehabilitation of Afghanistan. In the end, strong congressional support for the mujahideen, still regarded as "anticommunist knights in armor," helped sway the Bush administration to maintain the arms pipeline, especially as the Soviets were still providing military help to Najibullah.[15]

With the benefit of hindsight, Oakley and others admit that the United States made a mistake in continuing to support the largely ISI-driven Pakistani policy on Afghanistan and in failing to shift gears sooner after the Soviet pullout. As former assistant secretary of defense for international security affairs Richard Armitage commented, "We drifted too long in 1989 and failed to understand the independent role that the ISI was playing."[16]

Nuclear Understanding?

If frustrations were increasing over Afghanistan, nuclear developments appeared more promising. After Zia's death, the chief of army staff, Gen. Mirza Aslam Beg, and President Ghulam Ishaq Khan had charge of the nuclear program. Benazir Bhutto initially was not involved, but she asserted that after a briefing by a visiting CIA team in December 1988, she was able to "push her way" into the policy circle with the two other members of the troika.[17]

Ronald Reagan's final certification of Pakistan under the Pressler amendment and a separate letter from president-elect Bush had put the Pakistanis on notice that they stood on the edge of sanctions. A visit to the United States by General Beg in early 1989 offered U.S. officials an opportunity to address the issue directly. At Oakley's suggestion, Gen. Colin Powell, the outgoing Reagan administration national security adviser, and his successor, Scowcroft, had separate meetings with Beg to explain the U.S. position as one general speaking to another. Scowcroft recalled warning Beg, "You have to realize that the administration's hands are tied on the nuclear issue. President Bush [will] certify as long as he [can] under the Pressler amendment, but he [will] not lie. Pakistan [stands] very close to the line."[18]

In February 1989, Bush met Benazir Bhutto in Tokyo, where both were attending the funeral of Emperor Hirohito. The president, who was much impressed by the Pakistani prime minister, reviewed the nuclear issue along lines similar to those that Scowcroft used when he talked with Beg. Benazir Bhutto assured Bush that Pakistan understood U.S. concerns.[19]

In so many words, the president was signaling his desire to continue the close security relationship with Pakistan, provided Islamabad froze the nuclear program. At the same time, the U.S. leadership was making clear that, with the departure of Soviet troops from Afghanistan and the winding down of the Cold War, the policy dynamic on the nuclear issue had changed. The reasons for not imposing sanctions on Pakistan would carry far less weight and pressure from nonproliferation supporters in Congress would become stronger. In Islamabad, Ambassador Oakley bluntly warned the members of the troika, "If you take any action on the nuclear program and you go past that line . . . [Bush] will blow the whistle and invoke Pressler."[20]

After Beg returned home, U.S. intelligence reported that the Pakistanis had stopped the production of weapons-grade uranium, which was regarded as the most troublesome part of the nuclear program. According to Benazir Bhutto, Pakistan had what amounted to a nuclear understanding with the United States, one which she regarded as highly favorable: Her country could keep its existing nuclear capability and continue to receive military and economic aid.[21] Although denying any understanding with Washington, Beg said that Islamabad could safely suspend production of enriched uranium because it already had enough for the deterrent. Beg and Benazir Bhutto maintained that, by 1989, Pakistan had already developed a nuclear explosive capability.[22]

On May 31, 1989, just days before Benazir Bhutto was due to depart for an official visit to the United States, the prime minister removed Hamid Gul from his position as director-general of the ISI. Although observers thought that this might foreshadow a shift on Afghan policy,[23] the intelligence chief's departure was unrelated to differences over Afghanistan. He was fired after Bhutto learned that Hamid Gul was conspiring with the political opposition to oust her from power.[24] Reflecting the political clout of the military—and also Bhutto's relative weakness—Hamid Gul received another prestigious post as one of the Pakistani army's corps commanders and was not retired.

President George Bush talks with Prime Minister Benazir Bhutto at the White House, June 1989. (Courtesy of the George Bush Presidential Library.)

Prime Minister Benazir Bhutto, President Bush, First Lady Barbara Bush, and Azif Zardari (Benazir Bhutto's husband) at a White House state dinner, June 1989. (Courtesy of the George Bush Presidential Library.)

Benazir Bhutto Charms Washington; Stumbles at Home

When Pakistan's prime minister arrived in Washington on June 5, 1989, the thirty-five-year-old Radcliffe graduate was warmly greeted as a symbol of her country's transition from dictatorship to democracy. Articulate, attractive, and charismatic, Benazir Bhutto had a star quality about her. Both Republicans, who occupied the White House, and Democrats, who controlled both houses of Congress, were happy to welcome a political leader who genuinely seemed to like the United States and was the first female head of government in a Muslim country.

The prime minister confronted the nettlesome nuclear issue head on in her address before a joint session of Congress. "Speaking for Pakistan," she told the applauding legislators with seeming sincerity but little truth, "I can declare that we do not possess, nor do we intend to make, a nuclear device. This is our policy."[25] U.S. officials doubted that she was part of the nuclear decision-making process, but, according to Benazir Bhutto, the three members of the troika had carefully scripted how she would play the issue during her public appearances in the United States and in her private talks with President Bush and other U.S. leaders.[26]

The prime minister's successful visit appeared to seal close and friendly U.S.-Pakistan relations in the post–Cold War period. In the wake of the goodwill that she generated, intelligence reports that Islamabad was no longer enriching uranium to weapons grade, and a desire to bolster Pakistan's fledgling democracy, George Bush confirmed that the United States would sell Pakistan an additional sixty F-16 fighter-bombers and would continue the large military and economic aid program, then running at close to $600 million annually.

The president also issued the required annual Pressler amendment certification to permit aid to continue. According to Richard Haass, then the National Security Council's staff member for South Asia, the decision on Pressler "was a close run thing." Even if evidence about whether Pakistan actually "possessed" a nuclear weapon remained ambiguous, the status of the program did not appear to have changed since the Pressler amendment certification of a year before. The Pakistanis seemed to have heeded U.S. warnings about not advancing the development of their nuclear capability.[27]

If Benazir Bhutto won plaudits abroad, at home she was proving less successful. As one Western diplomat told the *New York Times,* "Benazir has had trouble making the transition from the scrappy fighter against political oppression to acting like a Prime Minister."[28] She was an indifferent manager, would frequently change her mind on issues, and at times seemed more concerned about her right to rule than the substance of governance. Widely believed allegations of corruption involving her husband, Asif Zardari, further tarnished her reputation.

Bhutto's dealings with the two other members of the troika also became strained. Although their relationship had begun reasonably amicably, there was little affection between the daughter of Zulfikar Ali Bhutto and veteran technocrat Ghulam Ishaq, a close associate of President Zia, who had executed her father and put her in prison.[29] The Pakistani military, for its part, mistrusted the prime minister and had supported her opponent, Nawaz Sharif, in the 1988 elections. Although she was initially on good personal terms with General Beg—indeed, it was the chief of army staff's refusal to take power on Zia's death that set the stage for the 1988 election—their relations gradually soured.

One source of friction was the prime minister's attempt to involve herself in military personnel matters in the summer of 1989 by removing Adm. Iftikhar Ahmed Sirohey as the chairman of the joint chiefs of staff.[30] Despite the impressive title, in fact, this post carried little authority in Pakistan. Oakley, who had established what he called a "very frank relationship" with Benazir Bhutto, cautioned her that trying to oust Sirohey would help efforts by the opposition to turn the military against her. A headstrong prime minister insisted that it was her right to remove Sirohey.[31] Even though she eventually backed off, the episode frayed her ties with Beg, who suspected that Benazir Bhutto wanted to get rid of him as well.

While this was taking place, Senate Foreign Relations Committee chairman Claiborne Pell (D-R.I.) visited Islamabad. Pell, who had become an admirer of Benazir Bhutto when she was in exile, spoke frankly: "I hope you reign as long as Queen Victoria, but at the rate you are going, since you don't seem interested in compromise or consensus, I don't think you are going to make it through to the end of the year."[32] Indeed, by the beginning of 1990, the prime minister was in deep political trouble and the Pakistani government was in disarray. As her relationship with Beg and Ghulam Ishaq deteriorated, it was not clear who was running the country, or even whether anyone was in charge. In the face of this uncertainty, Oakley developed the habit of passing important messages to all three troika members to make sure that the word got through.[33]

Meanwhile, in Afghanistan, the shortcomings of the mujahideen—their propensity for bloody infighting, their inability to forge a common front, and their lackluster military performance against the Najibullah regime—prompted renewed but still unsuccessful diplomatic efforts to work out a political compromise. Eager for the return home of the more than three million Afghan refugees living in Pakistan, Benazir Bhutto favored some sort of accommodation. She remained politically too weak, however, to break with the mujahideen and their ISI backers.

During a January 1990 visit to Pakistan, Undersecretary of State for Political Affairs Robert Kimmitt, who had replaced Michael Armacost as the top State Department official dealing with Afghanistan, found it hard to define a possible solution. When he met the mujahideen leaders in Peshawar, they complained bitterly about alleged bad treatment by the United States and maintained their hard line against a compromise with Najibullah. In Islamabad, the Pakistanis painted a far more optimistic picture of mujahideen prospects for defeating the Najibullah regime than the Americans thought was justified. In keeping with the policy of avoiding substantive contact with the communist government and in the absence of an official presence in Kabul, the American visitor had no discussions with the Najibullah regime, which stubbornly clung to power.[34]

The Kashmir Insurgency

About the time that the Soviets were withdrawing their troops from Afghanistan, the long-smoldering dispute between India and Pakistan over Kashmir unexpectedly became more active and dangerous. This development soured the improvement in India-Pakistan relations that had occurred after Benazir Bhutto took office and established good personal relations with India's prime minister, Rajiv Gandhi. Interference by New Delhi in Kashmiri politics after the death of Sheikh Mohammed Abdullah in 1982 had already upset disaffected Kashmiri Muslim youth. Until New Delhi's flagrant manipulation of the 1987 state elections, however, alienated young Kashmiris had largely been willing to express dissatisfaction with Indian rule peacefully. But after the 1987 elections, they began to adopt more violent protest tactics.

These gave birth to the insurgency that wracked Kashmir and raised India-Pakistan tensions throughout the decade of the 1990s.[35]

On December 8, 1989, members of the Jammu and Kashmir Liberation Front, a major dissident group, kidnapped Rubaiya Sayeed, the daughter of India's home minister, Mufti Mohammed Sayeed, a Kashmiri Muslim. After the Kashmiri state government effectively collapsed in the face of ensuing statewide disturbances, New Delhi imposed direct rule. As the insurgency became more violent, security forces responded harshly. Far from weakening the dissidents, India's heavy-handed tactics helped to radicalize the insurgents.

Although Pakistan did not start the uprising in Kashmir, the temptation to fan the flames was too great for Islamabad to resist. Using guerrilla-warfare expertise gained during the Afghan war, Pakistan's ISI began to provide active backing for Kashmiri Muslim insurgents. The support, supply, and training system that had been developed for the war in Afghanistan was redirected to aid the Kashmiri struggle against Indian rule. Quite apart from providing a means to support self-determination for Kashmir—long at the core of Pakistan's foreign policy—helping the insurgency was also regarded as a fit way to pay India back for its support of the East Pakistani independence movement and the dismemberment of Pakistan in 1971.

Frustrated by its inability to put down the uprising, New Delhi strengthened its security forces in Kashmir and blamed Pakistan for the troubles. As India continued to build up its military and paramilitary presence, artillery and mortar exchanges became more frequent and intense across the previously quiet line of control, the de facto but porous frontier separating the Indian- and Pakistani-held parts of Kashmir. In early 1990, unusually large-scale Indian military deployments and parallel Pakistani troop movements caused a sharp rise in tension between the two countries. India's prime minister, V. P. Singh, who had defeated Rajiv Gandhi in the 1989 elections, raised the temperature further by publicly speaking of the possibility of an India-Pakistan war.

In New Delhi and Islamabad, Ambassadors William Clark and Robert Oakley became concerned about the possibility of conflict between the two neighbors.[36] In Washington, Undersecretary of State Kimmitt warned of a "growing risk of miscalculation which could lead events to spin dangerously out of control."[37] What especially worried the Americans was that a new India-Pakistan war might involve the use of nuclear weapons. Although New Delhi had not exploded a nuclear device since its 1974 test, U.S. experts assumed that India in the intervening fifteen years had developed a weapons capability. They also believed that Pakistan's program had reached the point where Islamabad could quickly take the final step of assembling a nuclear device.

The Gates Mission

In an exercise of preventive diplomacy, President Bush sent his deputy national security adviser, Robert Gates, to South Asia in May 1990.[38] Gates cautioned Pakistani and Indian leaders against the use of force and proposed a series of confidence-building measures to reduce the risk of conflict. In his talks in Islamabad, he stressed the firm U.S. view that India would soundly defeat Pakistan in any military clash.[39] Gates also expressed concern about Pakistan's active support of the insurgency in Kashmir, stressing that the United States regarded this as an extremely dangerous activity. The flat denial by Pakistani officials that they were helping the Kashmiri resistance "was not a confidence builder" with the visitors.[40]

The threat of an India-Pakistan war receded and the two countries agreed on their own to undertake a number of confidence-building measures. These included setting up hot lines and arranging for advanced notice regarding troop movements. In retrospect, it is not clear how threatening the situation actually was, but almost certainly investigative journalist Seymour Hersh was wrong in claiming in his March 29, 1993, *New Yorker* article, "On The Nuclear Edge," that Pakistan was readying a nuclear strike.[41]

Significantly, the Gates mission received a friendlier welcome in India than in Pakistan—the first time this had happened since the Carter administration and a signal of the rapidly changing climate in U.S.-Pakistan relations. Ghulam Ishaq, by nature quite formal, was stiff during the discussions and Beg was at times "accusatory and confrontational."[42] Gates's tough words about ISI support for the Kashmiri insurgency were one reason for the cool reception in Islamabad. The warning that Gates delivered about the Pakistani nuclear program was another.

By May 1990, U.S. intelligence analysts had concluded that Pakistan had taken the final step toward "possession" of a nuclear weapon by machining uranium metal into bomb cores. Washington no longer had any doubts that Pakistan had crossed the line.[43] When Gates raised the issue with the president and the army chief of staff, they vehemently disagreed, asserting that Pakistan's nuclear capability had not changed from the previous year. Unless Pakistan melted down the bomb cores that it had produced, the visitor warned, Bush would not be able to issue the Pressler amendment certification needed to permit the continued flow of military and economic aid.[44] When the Pakistanis denied that they had "crossed the line," Foreign Minister Yaqub recalled Gates's commenting, "If it waddles like a duck, if it quacks like a duck, then maybe it is a duck."[45]

Benazir Bhutto, the Pakistani leader most adept in dealing with the Americans, was traveling in the Middle East and did not meet Gates. U.S. officials believed that she tried to avoid talking with Gates, but she has said that this was not the case.[46] When the prime minister returned home, Ambassador Oakley laid out the problem and cautioned her that Pakistan was "committing suicide" so far as relations with the United States were concerned—unless it agreed to roll back its nuclear capability. The envoy was similarly frank in separate conversations with Ghulam Ishaq and Beg. Apart from denying that Pakistan had advanced the program, the response was one of disbelief that the Americans would actually implement draconian Pressler amendment sanctions.

By this time, the relations between Benazir Bhutto and the other two troika members had badly deteriorated. Neither the army chief of staff nor the president were talking with the prime minister. As Oakley put it, "There was no way the three of them could come together to address this issue. . . . They kept hoping that it wasn't going to happen. . . . They were in a state of denial. So I kept putting it in front of them and nothing ever happened."[47]

The political storm cloud that had been gathering over the prime minister's head finally burst on August 6, 1990. Invoking the eighth amendment to the constitution, which Zia had adopted in 1985 to ensure presidential supremacy, Ghulam Ishaq dismissed Benazir Bhutto, dissolved the National Assembly, and called for new elections on October 24, 1990. The president charged the prime minister with corruption, nepotism, and other acts "in contravention of the Constitution and the law." The principal target for corruption charges was not Benazir herself, but her husband, who allegedly had made large sums of money through exploiting his wife's position.[48]

In Washington, the State Department called Benazir Bhutto's dismissal "an internal matter for the people of Pakistan to decide" but warned about "any action" that would upset the democratic process. Democratic members of Congress, who were friendly to the prime minister, were more critical. Senator Daniel Patrick Moynihan (D-N.Y.), chairman of the Senate Foreign Relations Committee's Near East and South Asia Subcommittee, said that the action "would surely strain U.S.-Pakistan relations."[49]

On August 2, 1990, just four days before Ghulam Ishaq removed Benazir Bhutto from office, Iraq seized Kuwait to touch off the Persian Gulf crisis. After Saddam Hussein defied the UN Security Council's call for him to withdraw, the United States commenced a military buildup in Saudi Arabia and sought the active support of other nations in forming an anti-Saddam coalition. On August 13, 1990, the caretaker government in Islamabad decided to back the coalition, announcing that Pakistan was prepared to send troops to help defend Saudi Arabia, long a close friend and a major source of financial aid. Among those endorsing the decision was the chief of army staff, Aslam Beg.[50]

The Pressler Axe Falls

Just as the Bush administration was coming to grips with the Persian Gulf crisis, it had to decide what to do about the Pressler amendment certification for Pakistan. The facts were no longer in doubt. With one voice, the intelligence community told the president that Pakistan "possessed" a nuclear device. George Bush had scant wiggle room to avoid imposing sanctions. After "hedging and fussing" as long as possible, the president reluctantly accepted the interagency recommendation that he not issue the certification. According to Scowcroft, Bush was "genuinely sad" about taking the action but felt that his hands were tied.[51] When Oakley returned to Islamabad from home leave in mid-September 1990, he carried a presidential letter informing the Pakistanis of the decision.[52]

After October 1, 1990, passed without the certification, the $564 million economic and military aid program approved for fiscal year 1991 was frozen. At the time, Pakistan was the third-highest recipient of U.S. aid; only Israel and Egypt received more assistance. Although Jimmy Carter had twice suspended aid, George Bush's action hurt much more and had substantially greater impact. The loss of nearly

$300 million of arms and other military supplies a year was a heavy blow to Pakistan's defense establishment. All U.S. military assistance and government-to-government transfers of weapons and equipment were halted in their tracks. Caught in the ban were the F-16 aircraft that Pakistan had purchased from the General Dynamics Corporation. The U.S. government refused to permit the Pakistanis to take possession of the planes, which ended up in storage at Davis-Monthan Air Force Base, near Tucson, Arizona. Although the U.S.-Pakistani military-to-military relationship was more limited and less intimate than during the alliance years of the 1950s and 1960s, it had, nonetheless, become substantial, especially the links between the two air forces.

Pressler sanctions had a less immediate impact on economic development, since they barred only new assistance commitments. AID was able to continue to implement programs that were already under way and to disburse funds from roughly $1 billion still in the pipeline. Nonetheless, this action had considerable negative effect. During the 1980s, along with remittances from workers abroad, a surge of foreign aid led by the Americans greatly benefited Pakistan. Although the country enjoyed competent, if conservative, economic management during the Zia years, after 1988, popularly elected governments proved less disciplined financial managers. The loss of U.S. aid and the policy rigor that the Americans demanded added significantly to the problems that were beginning to weaken the Pakistani economy.[53]

The Bush administration made a half-hearted attempt to delay sanctions in order to give the government that Pakistanis would elect in October 1990 a chance to deal with the nuclear problem. When the State Department floated the idea on Capitol Hill, the reaction was negative. Opposition by administration critics such as Senators John Glenn (D-Ohio) and Alan Cranston (D-Calif.) was to be expected, but even Republicans were against the idea. As Senator William Cohen (R-Maine) declared, "If we lower our [nuclear] standards again, who is going to take the standard seriously?" The administration backed off.[54]

In mid-October 1990, Yaqub Khan, who stayed on as foreign minister in the caretaker government, flew to Washington in the hope of finding some way of getting around Pressler sanctions. When he met with Secretary of State Baker, Yaqub offered to freeze Pakistan's nuclear program if the United States lifted the sanctions. Baker replied that this was not good enough. In order for the president to make the required

Pressler amendment certification, Pakistan had to destroy its nuclear bomb cores and "roll back its capability to the other side of the line." The secretary of state added that, "as a lawyer," he had been uneasy about the certification in 1989 and could not recommend it be issued again unless Pakistan accepted U.S. conditions. When Yaqub declared that a rollback was not possible, the die was cast. The foreign minister found Baker cold and lacking in sympathy for his country.[55]

The reaction in Islamabad to the imposition of sanctions was one of disbelief, shock, and anger. The Americans had threatened frequently that trouble lay ahead but in the end had always found a way to avoid punishing Pakistan. Although warned explicitly in 1990 that the Pressler axe was going to fall, the Pakistanis had not expected that the United States would actually carry through with the threat. The free press in Pakistan bitterly denounced the U.S. action as unfair, anti-Islamic, and discriminatory. Pakistanis were particularly incensed that Pressler amendment sanctions penalized only their country and did not punish India, which had actually exploded a nuclear device in 1974. They charged that the United States had once more—as in 1965—proved to be a "fickle friend." Observers commented acidly, "With the Afghan War over, the United States no longer need[s] Pakistan. You Americans have discarded us like a piece of used Kleenex."[56]

The secrecy that surrounded Pakistan's nuclear program and U.S. intelligence efforts to learn its status make it difficult to know with certainty what actually happened in 1990. U.S. officials were firmly convinced that Pakistan had relaunched the program and had taken the final step toward "possessing" a bomb by machining uranium metal into nuclear weapon cores,[57] thereby disregarding Washington's warnings and its own pledges. The Americans admit that Pakistan may have had the capability earlier than 1990 but stress that the intelligence community reach a definitive conclusion only in 1990.[58]

Most Pakistanis assert that the bomb capability had been achieved by 1988 and that Islamabad had therefore not violated any understanding with the United States or crossed any new lines in 1990. As Benazir Bhutto put it, "We had both the nuclear capability and American aid. Why would we upset the bargain?"[59] In the Pakistani view, the United States had moved the nuclear goalposts in 1990 by replacing "Stay where you are" with the tougher requirement of "Roll back your nuclear capability" through the destruction of bomb cores. General Beg expressed a view that most senior Pakistanis shared: with the Afghan war over the United States no longer needed to look the other way on the nuclear issue, and it let the Pressler axe fall.[60]

Conceivably, the Pakistanis were simply dissembling and, as the Americans alleged, had reactivated the program to machine bomb cores in 1990. It is also possible that the capability was achieved earlier (as Pakistanis claim) but that U.S. analysts did not reach a firm conclusion about this until 1990. Since the intelligence community assessments were based on information collected clandestinely rather than firsthand knowledge, such a time lag is not implausible.

Whatever the actual facts, the imposition of Pressler sanctions marked a major benchmark in U.S.-Pakistan relations. The action effectively ruptured the bilateral security partnership that had flourished during the 1980s. Although the links would almost certainly have weakened after the end of the Cold War, there would not have been such a sudden and near-total break. Both economic and military aid programs would have continued, probably at reduced levels of funding. The Bush administration, Brent Scowcroft stressed, wanted to maintain a friendly relationship with Pakistan, regretted having to impose sanctions, but felt its hand was forced.[61]

Nawaz Sharif Takes Charge

As the Pressler sanctions began to bite, Pakistan was once more engaged in a heated election. To some extent, the bitter 1990 campaign was a rerun of the 1988 contest between the heirs of Zulfikar Bhutto and Zia. This time Zia's man, Nawaz Sharif, and his Pakistan Muslim League–led coalition won handily with the backing of the ISI and much of Pakistani officialdom. In the campaign, Sharif charged that Benazir Bhutto, in addition to being corrupt and incompetent, had sold out to American nuclear "imperialism, blackmail and exploitation." When Oakley, in a speech to the Asia Society in Washington, D.C., asserted that Benazir was being singled out for corruption while others were being overlooked, he was pejoratively dubbed "the Viceroy."[62] After the votes were counted, Bhutto's PPP won only 45 seats in the National Assembly, while Sharif's coalition elected 105 members. Although foreign observers found a substantial number of election irregularities, the State Department judged that the polling was "generally fair." In Oakley's view, the Muslim League had won because its supporters had worked harder and were better organized at the grass roots than the PPP.[63]

Soft-spoken, forty-one-year-old Sharif was a new type of political leader. He represented the rising Punjabi urban classes rather than traditional rural landlord elites like the Bhuttos. Sharif's policies were more pro-business than Benazir Bhutto's and were closer to those of Islamic groups, in line with the views of his political godfather, Zia ul-Haq.

Shortly after the new prime minister took office, right-wing religious parties and more conservative members of the ruling coalition pressed for a change in Pakistan's anti-Saddam policy in the Persian Gulf crisis. Although Sharif initially expressed doubts about the approach, he eventually accepted the Foreign Ministry view that it was in Pakistan's best interest to oppose Saddam. Iraq, the ministry pointed out, was a longtime friend of India and had never supported Pakistan on Kashmir. Saudi Arabia, on the other hand, was an intimate friend and an important source of financial aid. The policy would please the Americans and perhaps facilitate an easing of Pressler amendment sanctions. During internal discussions, Beg did not object to maintaining Pakistan's support for the anti-Saddam coalition.[64]

It therefore came as a total surprise when the chief of army staff advocated the opposite position in an address to officers on January 28, 1991. In his talk—during the height of the U.S. bombing campaign against Iraq—Beg expressed sympathy for Saddam, criticized Saudi Arabia for toeing the U.S. line, and charged that the Gulf War was part of "Zionist" strategy.[65] A day or two later, the chief of army staff publicly repeated these views, making it clear that he was at odds with his government's position.[66] With the backing of the president, Sharif put his foot down. Although the prime minister did not dismiss Beg, he ordered him to stay in line with official policy. The chief's senior army colleagues did not share his pro-Iraq views and supported Sharif's stance.[67] Public opinion, however, was with Beg. An opinion poll taken in Pakistan on January 19, 1991, revealed "overwhelming" support for Saddam.[68]

Given the politically powerful position of the chief of army staff and his key role in the nuclear program, Beg's support for the Iraqis raised eyebrows in Washington and hardly eased the already difficult task of trying to find a mutually satisfactory solution to the Pressler problem.[69] According to Oakley, Beg had by then demonstrated that he was erratic and heavily influenced by Iranian thinking. In early 1990, for example,

Beg, who was a member of the Shi'a community, returned from a visit to Tehran convinced that Iran's support would enable Pakistan to win a war with India. When Oakley offered a briefing on Iranian capabilities by U.S. regional commander Gen. Norman Schwarzkopf, Beg brushed off the U.S. envoy, saying that the Americans would never tell him the truth about Iran.[70]

Nuclear Standoff

Within the Bush administration, few were happy about the Pakistan sanctions. The Pentagon was especially sorry about the rupture in cooperative-security ties. The U.S. military liked its Pakistani counterparts and was unhappy with the strain in relations. Despite Beg's pro-Saddam stance, many in the Defense Department and elsewhere in the Bush administration thought that Islamabad could play a helpful role in support of U.S. interests in the Persian Gulf and regarded Pakistan as a force for moderation in the Islamic world.

At immediate issue in 1991 was whether the Pakistanis would continue to pay for the stranded F-16s. In part to help the financially troubled General Dynamics Corporation, with whom Pakistan had contracted to purchase the aircraft, the Pentagon urged Islamabad not to stop payments—even though deliveries were frozen by the Pressler amendment. Defense Department officials asserted that nonpayment would breach the F-16 contract and make it harder to gain congressional support for an easing or lifting of Pressler sanctions. After considering various options, including invoking a penalty clause to avoid further payments, Pakistan followed the Pentagon's advice. As a result, even though the F-16s remained mothballed on the western desert sands of Arizona, the U.S. supplier received an additional several hundred million dollars before Pakistan finally suspended disbursements in 1993.[71]

Although privately angry about American sanctions, the Sharif government reacted in a subdued public manner. It saw little gain from any further strain in relations with the United States, which remained a partner in the struggle against the communists in Afghanistan. It still hoped that the breach with Washington would be temporary and that some way could be found to resume U.S. aid. In June 1991, the prime minister sent Akram Zaki, the secretary-general of the foreign ministry, to

Washington to test the waters about a possible settlement of the nuclear issue. Zaki brought no change in the Pakistani position, reiterating that Islamabad was willing to stop production of enriched uranium and weapon cores but was unwilling to destroy its existing cores. As the U.S. stance remained unaltered, sanctions continued.[72]

At the same time, to improve Pakistan's overall image, Islamabad unveiled an ambitious diplomatic initiative calling for a five-power conference to consider a ban on nuclear weapons in South Asia. The proposed conferees were the United States, the Soviet Union, China, India, and Pakistan. Washington showed interest in the idea. New Delhi, however, was upset by the inclusion of China. India's rejection of the proposal rendered it moot.[73]

In November 1991, Undersecretary of State for Security Affairs Reginald Bartholomew traveled to Islamabad to continue the nuclear dialogue. Ghulam Ishaq, who served as the principal Pakistani spokesperson on the nuclear issue, and not Nawaz Sharif, presented the visitor with a methodical and labored recitation of the correspondence between the two governments regarding the nuclear issue. This history, according to Pakistan's president, showed that the United States did not have a legitimate basis for imposing sanctions in 1990. Ghulam Ishaq urged Washington to show more understanding for his country's security situation and find some way around legislative barriers.[74]

An unimpressed Bartholomew replied that it was Pakistan that was out of line with U.S. laws. "We can't change our policies. You have to change yours," the undersecretary bluntly declared. Finding that the discussion was not leading anywhere, Bartholomew stood up, said, "Thank you for your time, Mr. President," and walked out of the room. The Pakistanis were taken aback by the abrupt end of the meeting. "What did I say that was wrong?" a red-faced Ghulam Ishaq asked, slumping back into his chair.[75] The next day, after consulting Sharif, Foreign Secretary Shahryar Khan met with the undersecretary to try to smooth things over. More polished and suave than the president, Shahryar told Bartholomew that the Pakistanis accepted that there was a difference of views over the nuclear issue but felt that the United States was trying to bully them.[76]

The impasse between Islamabad and Washington continued. As then-journalist Maleeha Lodhi wrote in November 1991, "The U.S. reading of the Pressler Amendment and what it required Pakistan to do had not changed. . . . For their part, Pakistani officials insisted that the country's [nuclear] programme remained within the limits set by Pressler."[77]

In early 1992, Shahryar tried a new and different approach during a visit to Washington: to come straight with the Americans. In a meeting with *Washington Post* staff members, the foreign secretary stated on the record that Pakistan had the capability to make a nuclear bomb. Pakistan possessed, he declared, "elements which, if put together, would become a device." He explained that his purpose in being frank was to "avoid credibility gaps" caused by earlier Pakistani statements.[78] Although Shahryar's candor impressed U.S. officials, it did not lead to a change in sanctions policy.

When Abida Hussein, a prominent Pakistan Muslim League politician, arrived in Washington to become her country's envoy in 1992, she heard much pleasant talk about the importance of bettering U.S.-Pakistan relations and finding some way to ease Pressler amendment sanctions. But the new ambassador soon concluded that the words were essentially diplomatic soft-soap with little substance behind them. Her personal assessment was that in the post–Cold War era the United States "had about as much interest in Pakistan as Pakistan had in the

Ambassador Abida Hussein presents her credentials to President Bush, March 1992. (Courtesy of the George Bush Presidential Library.)

Maldives." Ambassador Hussein found it difficult to get the leadership in Islamabad to accept this unpleasant reality.[79]

Kashmir and Afghanistan

The nuclear issue was not the only serious bilateral problem in the early 1990s. Soon after Abida Hussein's arrival in Washington, Undersecretary of State for Political Affairs Arnold Kanter warned that if Pakistan continued its covert help for the Kashmiri insurgency, it ran the risk of being declared a country officially supporting terrorism. "If you get hit with this on top of Pressler, that will end the U.S.-Pakistan relationship," Kanter stated bluntly.[80] His comments were based on credible intelligence reports that the ISI was continuing to provide direct assistance to the anti-India insurgents, in some cases training and supplying Kashmiri Muslims and infiltrating them across the line of control, and in other instances enabling mujahideen veterans of the Afghan struggle to join in the uprising against Indian rule in Kashmir.

For Nicholas Platt, who replaced Oakley as U.S. ambassador in Islamabad in late 1991, the terrorism problem stood at the top of his agenda, along with the nuclear problem. "I raised this issue at every level from the prime minister on down," Platt stated. Initially, the Pakistanis denied that the ISI was involved and claimed that "there are private institutions and private people that may be doing this but not us." The Pakistani government, the response went—much as it had in the case of the Afghan war—was offering only political and moral support for the Kashmiri insurgency. Later, according to Platt, officials acknowledged that the ISI had been providing more concrete help but claimed that this had stopped.[81]

According to Shahryar, the foreign office and the ISI disagreed about how to respond to U.S. pressure. The foreign office stressed the consequences of failing to heed U.S. warnings; the ISI favored continuing direct support for the Kashmiri insurgents and expressed skepticism that Washington would actually designate Pakistan a "terrorist state." In the end, Sharif sided with the foreign office and reined in the ISI enough for Pakistan to avoid being tagged a state sponsor of terrorism, along with "rogue states" such as Libya, North Korea, and Iran.[82]

Meanwhile, the war in Afghanistan was dragging on with no apparent end in sight. Racked by internal infighting and increasingly split along ethnic lines, the mujahideen remained unable to oust Najibullah from power. Shortly before ending his assignment, Oakley summed up the situation in an interview: "Unfortunately [a] lack of . . . cohesion [in the Afghan resistance] on the political side has been matched in recent months by similar disarray on the military side with the overall result that [Najibullah] and his supporters emerge relatively stronger and more secure while the supporters of the Resistance lose interest."[83]

In September 1991, the United States and the Soviet Union finally agreed that they would both stop the supply of military equipment to Afghanistan. The accord reached between Secretary of State Baker and Foreign Minister Shevardnadze rang down the curtain on one of the last remaining U.S.-Soviet Cold War confrontations. With this action, Washington effectively washed its hands of Afghanistan, which became a second- or third-tier foreign policy issue. As one top State Department official told then–Pakistan country director John Holzman, "Afghanistan is no longer on our radar screen."[84]

Shortly thereafter, the disintegration of the Soviet Union following a failed coup against Gorbachev radically reshaped the region's geopolitical landscape. Kazakhstan, Uzbekistan, Kyrgyzstan, Tajikistan, and Turkmenistan, the five Central Asian Soviet republics, suddenly became independent nations. Although they remained largely dependent on economic links with Moscow, the new states sought ties with their neighbors to the south, which in turn, and in varying degrees, vied for influence in the fledgling countries. Afghanistan gained importance as a potentially important corridor for trade and other links between South and Central Asia—but only if peace could be restored so that commerce could flow freely.

In Kabul, the sudden demise of the Soviet Union undermined the Najibullah regime. The government collapsed in April 1992 after Interior Minister Gen. Abdul Rashid Dostum, an Uzbek, deserted to the anticommunist cause. Twelve days later, the mujahideen marched triumphantly into Kabul. But the euphoria of victory was short-lived: Afghanistan's new leaders proved incapable of forming a viable government. In an arrangement brokered by the Pakistanis, the ISI's favored Pashtun, Gulbuddin Hekmatyar, became prime minister, in theory sharing power with two Tajik mujahideen leaders, Professor Burhanuddin Rabbani, who became president, and Ahmed Shah Masood, the defense minister. Hekmatyar, however, refused to join the coalition and instead launched fierce rocket attacks on Kabul against his supposed partners.[85]

Najibullah's fall thus did not usher in an era of peace. It sadly began a new phase of what would become an Afghan civil war in which rival factions, divided mainly along ethnic lines—Pashtuns in the south, Uzbek and Tajik in the north, and the Shi'a Hazara in the center—battled each other. The United Nations continued to sustain a large relief and humanitarian aid program and tried with scant success to promote a peace settlement. Disappointed by the turn of events, Pakistan for a time gave up its efforts to control events in Afghanistan and backed the UN peacemakers. Content with a secondary role, the United States limited its activities to providing humanitarian aid and verbal support for the United Nations.

U.S. Arms and Chinese Missiles

On the U.S.-Pakistan bilateral front, Sharif still hoped that things could somehow be patched up with Washington and that the United States would resume military and economic aid. Neither the prime minister nor opposition leader Benazir Bhutto saw gain in risking even worse relations with the victor in the Cold War, especially after the disintegration of the Soviet Union left the United States as the sole remaining superpower. With relations with India seriously strained over the Kashmiri insurgency and continued uncertainty regarding the future of Afghanistan, the uneasy leadership in Islamabad yearned for renewed ties with Washington. To avoid further trouble with the Americans, the prime minister was willing to risk domestic discontent with pro-Islamic groups by blocking a march across the line of control by militant Islamic supporters of the anti-India uprising.[86]

Nor was the Bush administration with its "more in sorrow than anger" attitude about sanctions totally hard-nosed toward Pakistan. In a policy decision that could have gone either way, Washington had decided to allow Islamabad to purchase military equipment on a commercial basis, notwithstanding the Pressler amendment. During fiscal year 1991, for example, the State Department had approved licenses for $120 million worth of arms sales, largely for the export of spare parts for the F-16 aircraft that Pakistan had received before sanctions were imposed. Defending the policy in a February 1992 congressional hearing, Secretary of State Baker said that the State Department had concluded that arms sales did not violate the Pressler amendment, which explicitly barred only government-financed transfers of equipment and made no specific reference to commercial transactions. The Bush administration stuck to its guns despite sharp criticism by Senator Pell and Representative Stephen Solarz, chairman of the House Foreign Affairs Committee's Asia subcommittee, who called the policy "inconsistent with the spirit if not the letter of the law."[87]

About this time, a new bilateral problem developed over Pakistan's desire to match India's growing missile capability. After the failure of Islamabad's own efforts to develop missiles indigenously, Pakistan turned for help to its old friend, China. To the dismay of Washington, Beijing obliged. Early in 1991, U.S. intelligence picked up indications that China might be providing Pakistan with medium-range, mobile M-11 missile launchers. Such a transaction, U.S. officials charged, would be contrary to the ground rules of the Missile Technology Control Regime (MTCR), an international effort to prevent the spread of delivery systems for nuclear weapons. Even though China was not a party to the MTCR, U.S. law imposed sanctions on countries that violated MTCR standards, which prohibited export of missiles capable of delivering a payload of more than 500 kilograms over a distance greater than 300 kilometers.

After China disregarded U.S. warnings and shipped the launchers to Pakistan, Washington proceeded to impose sanctions, blacklisting the Chinese and Pakistani entities involved in the transaction.[88] Unlike the Pressler amendment, MTCR legislation gave the president flexibility in the type of punishment that could be imposed. After Baker obtained what he thought was agreement by the Chinese to abide by MTCR ground rules, Washington lifted the sanctions in February 1992.[89]

The problem did not go away, however. In the waning days of the Bush administration, in December 1992, after Bill Clinton had won the November presidential elections, U.S. intelligence detected that the Chinese had, in fact, provided the Pakistanis with M-11 missiles as well as launchers. Beijing disputed that the M-11s violated MTCR guidelines, claiming that their range was slightly under the 300-kilometer limit. Although U.S. officials disagreed with the Chinese, the Bush administration decided not to take any action before leaving office and passed the decision about whether to impose new and more drastic sanctions to the incoming administration.[90] By this time, the missile issue had moved beyond the parameters of U.S.-Pakistan relations to become embroiled in the emotionally charged U.S. domestic political debate over relations with China after the bloody crackdown in 1989 on the prodemocracy demonstrators in Beijing's Tiananmen Square.

When George Bush left office in 1993, the glue of the Cold War and the common struggle against the Soviet occupation of Afghanistan no longer cemented U.S.-Pakistan ties. In the absence of other significant shared national interests, bilateral differences were all too apparent. For Washington, Pakistan had not only lost strategic importance but had become a nuclear troublemaker and a source of regional instability. For Islamabad, the imposition of Pressler amendment nuclear sanctions and the turnaround in U.S. policy once more were seen as evidence that the United States was fickle, unreliable, and not a true friend of Pakistan.

12

Clinton: Living with a Nuclear Pakistan

The election of Governor Bill Clinton of Arkansas as president brought little cheer to Islamabad. To the Pakistanis, the incoming Democratic administration looked liked warmed-over Jimmy Carter. The new president's emphasis on nuclear nonproliferation, human rights, and democracy had a familiar ring. And his secretary of state was the same Warren Christopher who, as the number two official in Jimmy Carter's State Department, had sternly lectured Islamabad on the dangers of nuclear proliferation. To underscore the negative, during Christopher's January 16, 1993, Senate confirmation hearings, the secretary-designate inexplicably coupled Pakistan with Burma as a country where free elections and greater human rights were needed.[1]

Nor did the creation of a Bureau of South Asian Affairs in the State Department greatly please the Pakistanis. New Delhi had long sought this reorganization, complaining that the Middle East got all the attention and South Asia and India were left languishing in the wings of the Bureau of Near Eastern and South Asian Affairs. An influential congressional friend of India, Rep. Stephen Solarz (D-N.Y.), took up the cause and eventually won approval for a separate bureau, over the opposition of the State Department.[2] Clinton's nominee as the new bureau's assistant secretary was career diplomat Robin Raphel. Junior in rank for the job, she was serving as political counselor at the New Delhi embassy when nominated.[3] As a result of the lengthy security clearance and Senate confirmation processes, Raphel did not assume her new duties until the fall of 1993.

Meanwhile, the Clinton administration took up where its predecessor had left off on the terrorism issue. In the Bush administration's waning days, renewed reports of the involvement of Pakistan's

Inter-Services Intelligence Directorate (ISI) with groups involved in the Kashmiri insurgency had landed Pakistan on the terrorism "watch list." The new director of central intelligence, James Woolsey, took a hard line, warning publicly that Pakistan stood "on the brink."[4] What especially disturbed Washington was the realization that Pakistan was harboring hundreds of young Islamic extremists, graduates of guerrilla training camps set up during the Afghan war and located near Peshawar or just over the border in Afghanistan. The camps had become breeding grounds for a generation of militant fundamentalists. Camp graduates, who included numerous Arabs as well as Pakistanis, not only fought the communists in Afghanistan and the Indians in Kashmir but maintained close links with terrorists throughout the Islamic world. For example, an extremist Egyptian faction sent a fax from Peshawar to deny involvement in the bombing of New York's World Trade Center.[5]

In April 1993, Prime Minister Nawaz Sharif, worried by the possibility that Pakistan might end up on the terrorist list, sent the secretary-general of the Foreign Ministry, Akram Zaki, to assure the Americans that he would put the lid on the extremists.[6] Secretary of State Christopher warned Zaki that the United States expected "action" to curb groups engaging in "terrorism." To back up his assurances, Sharif cracked down on Arab extremists within Pakistan, although many of them simply shifted across the border into Afghanistan. The prime minister also replaced ISI director-general Lt. Gen. Javed Nasir, "a maverick identified with religious extremists" and a strong backer of ISI involvement in Kashmir.[7]

Direct ISI support for the insurgents tapered off, but retired military intelligence personnel and Afghan mujahideen working through the Jamaat-i-Islami and other extremist groups with close ties to the ISI provided "privatized" help to the Kashmiri dissidents. Even though the change was to some extent cosmetic, it proved sufficient for the State Department not to take the extreme step of pinning the "terrorist state" label on Pakistan.[8]

Lamenting the turn of events, Foreign Secretary Shahryar Khan commented ruefully to the *Washington Post,* "We fought the Afghan War for 14 years, and now people who were committed to our side are suddenly seen as villains and branded as terrorists."[9] For the Americans, the mujahideen freedom fighters in the struggle against the Red Army in Afghanistan had, in effect, become terrorists after they joined the Kashmiri insurgents in their struggle against India. For the Pakistanis, however, backing the Kashmiri quest for self-determination was as just a cause as was the struggle of the Afghans to oust the Red Army from their homeland.

In spite of the fact that the U.S. decision, as journalist and later ambassador to Washington Maleeha Lodhi wrote, removed "the noose of terror,"[10] the Clinton administration did Islamabad no favors in enforcing Pressler amendment sanctions. Washington insisted on the return of six aging frigates leased to Pakistan, which had provided the bulk of the navy's firepower. Although the U.S. Navy intended to scrap the vessels, American officials were adamant that Pakistan give back the frigates and even insisted that it pay for their transit to Singapore, where the ships were broken up for scrap.[11]

By 1993, the economic aid pipeline had also run dry. Since Pressler sanctions barred any new assistance commitments, this put the United States, long Pakistan's major source of development help, out of the aid business. Because the Pressler amendment did not bar humanitarian help, private U.S. charities, such as CARE (Cooperative for American Relief Everywhere) and Catholic Relief Service, continued to distribute modest amounts of food aid. The Pressler amendment also permitted assistance to counter the narcotics problem. Thus, the United States was able to maintain an antidrug program that provided about $2 million annually to the Pakistanis.

Indeed, one of most negative byproducts of the Afghan war was the surge in the production, traffic, and use of illegal drugs. During the war years, the lucrative cultivation of opium poppies had shifted from Afghanistan to remoter parts of the rugged Pathan tribal belt of the Northwest Frontier Province, an area where the central government's control was traditionally weak. By the early 1990s, Pakistan was producing an estimated one-fifth of the heroin consumed in the United States. Domestic addiction, which before the Afghan war had been minor, had become a serious social malady in Pakistan. In 1988, the United Nations estimated that the country had more than a million addicts. Five years later, in 1993, the UN estimate put the number of addicts at 1.7 million, or nearly 1.5 percent of Pakistan's population.[12]

Prior Pakistani prime ministers—Zia, Benazir Bhutto, and Nawaz Sharif—had all responded positively to U.S. and UN pressures to address the narcotics problem. But Islamabad was better at promising action than at implementing antidrug programs. In 1993, the Pakistan

Narcotics Control Board was so starved for funds that it was five years behind in reimbursing some officials. The telephone company had disconnected its phone lines because of nonpayment of bills by the cash-strapped control board.[13] The enormous potential for financial gain from the illegal drug trade led to widespread bribery of officials. Given lax anticorruption standards in Pakistan, profits from drug trafficking flowed into many pockets. The massive influx of high-powered weaponry during the Afghan war provided further yeast for narcotics trafficking—in addition to fueling the rise of violence in Pakistan.

Nawaz Sharif Out; Benazir Bhutto Back

By early 1993, Sharif had served more than two years as prime minister. His record was mixed: he had carried out a number of reforms to liberalize the economy, but his reputation as a can-do leader was tarnished by reports of widespread corruption and a penchant for flashy but questionable schemes, such as making thousands of small, imported taxicabs available at below-market prices. The prime minister and President Ghulam Ishaq Khan, both staunch conservatives who had worked closely with Zia, were natural political allies. Nonetheless, they managed to entangle themselves in a messy quarrel triggered by Sharif's attempt to trim the presidency's powers.[14]

The upshot of their brawl was that, on April 19, 1993, the president dismissed the prime minister for corruption and maladministration. It was a repeat performance of his removal of Benazir Bhutto two and a half years before. But a month later, in May 1993, the Supreme Court of Pakistan, in an unprecedented judgment, overturned the president's action and restored Sharif as prime minister. The two leaders then battled publicly until the army intervened to force them both to resign on July 19, 1993. Moen Quereshi, a retired World Bank vice president, who had lived outside Pakistan for many years, was named head of a caretaker government to hold office until new elections took place in October 1993.[15]

Quereshi surprised the country by adopting a series of anti-corruption measures and economic reforms. When his government publicly named defaulters on loans of more than one million rupees (approximately $35 thousand), both Benazir Bhutto and Sharif were on the list. The authorities revealed that Benazir Bhutto had given friends and supporters land worth $160 million and Sharif had awarded a more modest $6.6 million. Quereshi put a stop to the lavish imported-taxicab scheme, devalued the Pakistani rupee, gave the State Bank of Pakistan greater independence, and introduced the first income tax on the "feudals"—the large landlords who continued to dominate rural Punjab and Sindh. The caretaker government stopped payments to the General Dynamics Corporation for the F-16s that were still stored in Arizona, their shipment blocked by Pressler amendment sanctions. During Quereshi's three months in office, Pakistan's foreign exchange reserves rose from $180 million to $448 million and the economy began to move in a more positive direction.[16]

At about this time, the Clinton administration had to address the M-11 missile issue that George Bush had left unresolved. Candidate Clinton had lambasted Bush for being too gentle with Beijing over human rights abuses and missile exports to countries such as Pakistan. Once president, however, Clinton shifted ground, supporting dialogue and engagement with China and the extension of most-favored-nation (MFN) trade status. Still, it was difficult for Clinton to duck the awkward question of how to deal with China's sending M-11 missile components and technology to Pakistan, the focus of much congressional attention and criticism.[17]

In July 1993, Secretary of State Christopher warned Chinese foreign minister Qian Qichen, when they met in Singapore, that Beijing might face sanctions because of the missile exports. The Chinese responded that the reports were a "fabrication," denying that they had violated their promise to abide by the rules of the Missile Technology Control Regime (MTCR).[18] The State Department concluded otherwise and, a month later, on August 25, 1993, imposed a major trade sanction—a two-year ban on U.S. exports to China affecting nearly $1 billion worth of military-related goods, electronics, aircraft, and space systems. In addition to aggravating relations with Beijing, the sanctions hurt important American business interests, especially high-technology companies, which faced the loss of substantial sales to China.[19]

For their part, Pakistani authorities admitted that they had received M-11 missiles from China but claimed that the weapons did not exceed the limits imposed by the MTCR—i.e., a range of not more than 300 kilometers and a carrying capacity of no more than 500 kilos.[20] Along with sanctions against China, the United States imposed parallel restrictions on high-technology exports to Pakistan, but these restrictions had little economic impact. In fact, Pakistan was largely a bystander in the M-11 missile controversy, which Washington addressed almost entirely in the context of U.S.-China relations.[21]

On October 6, 1993, in Pakistan's third election in five years, the voters returned Benazir Bhutto to power. Although the majority her Pakistan Peoples Party (PPP) won in the National Assembly depended on a smaller coalition partner, Bhutto was able to strengthen her position through the election of Farooq Leghari, a longtime PPP stalwart, as president. To protect against opposition charges that she would buckle under U.S. pressure on the nuclear issue or relations with India, she quickly declared, "[R]olling back the nuclear program is not feasible. . . . The nuclear program is linked with the Jammu and Kashmir issue. There cannot be peace in the region without the peaceful resolution of the Kashmir issue."[22]

Pakistan's foreign policy and security environment had deteriorated badly in the five years since Benazir Bhutto had first assumed the office in the fall of 1988. Although relations with China, now Pakistan's closest friend, remained intact, the Afghan war partnership with the United States had withered. Relations with India, which had seemed so promising when Benazir Bhutto and Rajiv Gandhi first met in 1988, were once more tense as a consequence of Pakistan's support for the Kashmiri insurgency. Indeed, one unhelpful consequence of Pakistani democracy was that Bhutto and Sharif regularly outbid each other in demonstrating their toughness against India.

Pakistan had also failed to harvest the expected rewards of the collapse of the communist regime in Afghanistan. Islamabad's hope for a friendly, if not subservient, government in Kabul remained an unfulfilled goal. Relations with the Tajik-dominated Burhanuddin Rabbani government had become strained because of continued ISI support for Pashtun Gulbuddin Hekmatyar, and also because of Rabbani's overtures to India. Hekmatyar's rocket attacks on Kabul caused more damage and civilian casualties than the Afghan capital had suffered during the ten years of the anti-Soviet insurgency. Continued turmoil in Afghanistan also frustrated Pakistan's hope of gaining significant economic benefits from the opening up of trade and economic relations with the newly independent Central Asian republics. To make matters worse, most Afghan refugees remained in Pakistan, unwilling to return to their impoverished and war-torn homeland.

In March 1994, the Clinton administration launched an ill-fated nuclear nonproliferation initiative, announcing its willingness to seek congressional approval to deliver the embargoed F-16s if Pakistan agreed to cap its nuclear program and accept what Americans described as "nonintrusive" verification. In spite of its rhetoric about a more vigorous nuclear nonproliferation policy, the Clinton administration was, in effect, shelving the unrealistic goal of rolling back the Pakistani capability and signaling its willingness to live with a freeze in the program—something that the Pakistanis had previously offered. The rub came in the U.S. desire to be sure that the program was, in fact, frozen. Although Washington spoke of "nonintrusive" verification, the procedures involved physical inspection of nuclear facilities in addition to monitoring by cameras and other technical devices.[23]

The nuclear proposal ran into trouble even before Deputy Secretary of State Strobe Talbott flew to South Asia in April 1994 to seek Pakistani assent and Indian understanding. After details of the initiative were leaked to the press by Senator Larry Pressler (R-S.D.) before the administration had completed its soundings with Congress, Islamabad, and New Delhi,[24] Indian-Americans and their congressional friends vociferously opposed the release of the F-16s. On the Pakistani side, the chief of army staff, Gen. Abdul Waheed, who was visiting the United States, made clear his opposition. The army chief declared that the military would not "bargain away Pakistan's nuclear programme for F-16s or anything else." Were the country's political leadership willing to compromise, the army would certainly make its views known, Waheed declared threateningly.[25] Given the political power of the military, the statement sounded the death knell for the U.S. initiative.

In any case, after India reacted sourly, the proposal was doomed in Pakistan, even if the army had responded positively. Traditionally, Islamabad had refused to agree to nonproliferation measures unless India also accepted them. Benazir Bhutto told Talbott, "If we are unilaterally pressed for the capping, it will be discriminatory and Pakistan will not agree to it."[26]

Relations Improve

Despite the continuing standoff on the nuclear issue, bilateral relations began to improve. One reason was the attitude of Robin Raphel. Before setting off on her first official visit to the subcontinent in the fall of 1993, Raphel pleased Islamabad and raised hackles in New Delhi when she told journalists that the United States had never accepted the accession of Kashmir to India. Notwithstanding State Department "clarification" of Raphel's statement, the Indian press began to lambaste the assistant secretary, a phenomenon that continued without letup during her four years in office.

Raphel thought that Pakistan remained a potentially useful friend for the United States and a force for moderation in the Muslim world. She was also skeptical of how far U.S.-India relations would improve—despite a friendly May 1994 visit to Washington by Prime Minister Narasimha Rao. The cold shoulder that the assistant secretary received during her visits to New Delhi and the persistent attacks against her in the Indian media hardly improved Raphel's attitude. In contrast, the Pakistanis regularly rolled out the red carpet whenever the assistant secretary visited Islamabad.

Even though the top echelons of the Christopher-led State Department showed only limited interest in South Asia beyond the nonproliferation issue, one senior official who shared Raphel's desire for better relations with Pakistan was Secretary of Defense William Perry. The Pentagon remained unhappy about the break in ties and sought ways to rebuild the relationship. Like Raphel, the U.S. military considered Pakistan a longtime friend, a potentially helpful partner in western Asia and the Middle East, and an important source of forces for burgeoning UN peacekeeping missions. The Pakistani army had sent six thousand troops to Somalia. Three thousand Pakistani soldiers took part in the peacekeeping effort in Bosnia.

When Perry visited Islamabad in January 1995, he was the first U.S. official in several years to suggest any steps to rebuild security cooperation. The secretary of defense proposed reviving the Pakistan-U.S. Consultative Group, which had been established during the Afghan war as a vehicle for senior military-to-military discussions. Even though Perry doubted that Congress would lift the Pressler amendment sanctions, he told the media, "I intend to press on, to make the most I can of the security relations between the United States and Pakistan. . . . I want to try to make things better."[27] In her own public comments during Perry's visit, Benazir Bhutto focused on the F-16 issue: "We want either the planes or our money back," she told Perry. "We think this is all very unfair."[28] Adept at dealing with Americans, the prime minister sensed that many U.S. officials were uncomfortable with the F-16 situation and accepted the Pakistani complaint as justified.

Raphel found another ally in Senator Hank Brown (R-Colo.), who became chairman of the Senate Foreign Relations Committee's South Asia subcommittee after the Republican sweep in the 1994 congressional elections. Brown told the author that he supported good U.S.-India relations, but that a trip to the subcontinent had convinced him that the draconian sanctions against Pakistan were damaging U.S. interests. He recalled being particularly annoyed during a press conference in Islamabad when Pressler, who was also on the trip, defended the sanctions in terms of preventing an "Islamic bomb."[29]

Brown initially proposed easing sanctions by lifting the ban on economic assistance and releasing all military equipment frozen in the United States, including the F-16s. But he dropped the F-16s after he concluded that their inclusion would doom the effort to ease sanctions.[30] Despite unhappiness in the arms control community, the Clinton administration agreed to back the proposal. The fact that Brown was a Republican made the initiative politically more palatable.

In February 1995, Pakistan won applause in Washington through its cooperation in the arrest of Ramsi Yusuf, an Islamic militant believed to be the mastermind behind the February 26, 1993, terrorist bombing of New York's World Trade Center that killed six and injured more than a thousand people. After Yusuf was spotted in the Philippines, he fled to Pakistan and was hiding in a seedy rooming house in Islamabad when he was seized. The Pakistanis permitted U.S. law enforcement officers to join the raiding party and rapidly approved an extradition request, permitting the Federal Bureau of Investigation to fly Yusuf back to the United States to stand trial.[31]

The murder of two Americans working at the Karachi consulate general on March 8, 1995, was less helpful to Pakistan's image. The death of the officials dramatized the violence that racked the country's largest city. Ethnic rivalries between native Sindhis and the *muhajir* community (refugees from India and their descendants, who made up the majority of Karachi's population), as well as bloody infighting within the *muhajir* community, took more than a thousand lives during 1994.[32] Since Karachi was Pakistan's commercial hub, the site of much of its industry, and its only port, instability there dealt a serious blow to the national economy. The violence in Karachi was symptomatic of the widespread upswing in lawlessness that followed the massive influx of weapons during the Afghan war. The disturbing phenomenon became known as the "Kalashnikov culture," after the nickname for the standard weapon of the mujahideen, the Soviet AK-47.

In April 1995, Benazir Bhutto paid her second official visit to Washington and, according to a senior U.S. official, "once more made a good impression on Americans."[33] During the stay, the prime minister's focus was on gaining support for the release of the F-16s and a relaxation of Pressler amendment sanctions. Pakistan, she declared at the Johns Hopkins School of Advanced International Studies, has "honored our contract with America. We want America to honor its contract with us."[34] President Clinton readily accepted her argument about the F-16s: "I don't think it is right for us to keep the money and the equipment. That is not right, and I am going to try to find a resolution to it."[35]

When the prime minister pressed for the release of the F-16s, Clinton responded that Congress would not agree unless Pakistan gave something in return—for example, permitting inspection of nuclear facilities. Benazir Bhutto said that this was not possible but argued that if the administration made the effort, it could carry the day on Capitol Hill. When the president disagreed, there was little the Pakistanis could do.[36]

Brown Amendment Adopted

After the prime minister left Washington, the battle over Senator Brown's desire to ease the Pressler amendment sanctions began in earnest. Although the amendment to the foreign assistance act that Brown offered maintained the ban on U.S. government arms assistance and transfers, it gave the green light for renewed economic assistance, loan guarantees by the Overseas Private Investment Corporation, and Export-Import Bank lending. It also permitted Pakistan to take possession of the military equipment frozen in the United States, except for the F-16s, and allowed the resumption of training of Pakistani military personnel.[37] Even if Congress was unwilling to appropriate funds to repay Pakistan for the stranded F-16s, it agreed that the airplanes could be sold elsewhere and the proceeds used to reimburse Islamabad.[38]

In the Senate, Brown and administration supporters—mainly the Defense Department and the State Department's South Asia bureau—battled a vocal opposition led by Senators Pressler and John Glenn (D-Ohio), who were staunch nonproliferation advocates, and by supporters of better U.S.-India relations, such as Senators Daniel Patrick Moynihan

(D-N.Y.), Paul Sarbanes (D-Md.), and Sander Levin (D-Mich.). The fight took on a larger dimension after India, on the recommendation of Ambassador Siddhartha Shankar Ray, unwisely entered the lists to campaign against the amendment. Sparked by the Indian embassy, the million-strong Indian-American ethnic community lobbied vigorously, if inaccurately, that passage of the amendment would upset the strategic balance in South Asia. In fact, Pakistan's acquisition of the stranded arms and equipment would have only a marginal impact on the arms balance between the two countries. The smaller but more homogenous Pakistani-American ethnic lobby supported the amendment's passage with equal vigor and greater effectiveness. In the end, Brown carried the day, largely, he believed, on the basis of "fairness." The Senate approved the amendment by a 55-45 margin on September 21, 1995, and the president signed it into law after the joint House-Senate committee reconciled the provision later in the year.[39]

Islamabad hailed passage of the Brown amendment as a major victory; New Delhi blasted it as a severe setback. More-thoughtful Pakistanis, however, soon realized that the action provided largely symbolic relief. The Brown amendment left intact the heart of the Pressler sanctions: the ban on U.S. military assistance and government-to-government arms transfers. Pakistani officialdom, nonetheless, was satisfied. In its view, the Clinton administration had acknowledged the inherent unfairness of the Pressler amendment and tried to make amends.[40] In effect, Pakistanis agreed with what Assistant Secretary of State Raphel told a Senate hearing: "The key impact of sanctions relief is not military or financial. The effect would be primarily in the political realm, creating a sense of faith restored and an unfairness rectified with a country and a people who have been loyal friends of the United States over the decades."[41]

Although the Brown amendment removed the bar to economic assistance, the Clinton administration chose not to re-establish a bilateral aid program and gave only modest grants to Pakistani nongovernmental organizations, amounting to $2 million a year. Benazir Bhutto recalled that when she met Agency for International Development administrator Brian Atwood during her April 1995 visit to Washington, he told her that there were insufficient funds to restart a bilateral program.[42] In fact, had the Clinton administration wished to do so, it could have provided Pakistan's shaky economy with limited but symbolically important help. Although "enlarging democracy" constituted—rhetorically at least—a key element of the Clinton foreign policy, the administration failed to provide significant support for Pakistan's still-unsteady system of democratic governance.

Ring Magnets, M-11s, and Drugs

The Brown amendment did not entirely lift sanctions against countries that received help for an unsafeguarded uranium-enrichment facility, such as that at Kahuta, but limited their application to transactions that occurred after 1994. A major problem, therefore, arose when U.S. intelligence concluded that the China Nuclear Energy Industry Corporation had sold some five thousand custom-made ring magnets to the Kahuta uranium-enrichment facility in 1995.

Although the transactions involved only $70 thousand, the ring magnets were made to specification and provided a vital component for the high-speed centrifuges that produced Pakistan's enriched uranium. Since the sale occurred in 1995, a year after the cutoff date, the ring magnet transaction jeopardized the implementation of the Brown amendment and had the potential of further exacerbating bilateral troubles with China. Under the 1994 nuclear nonproliferation act, the sale could have resulted in the suspension of all Export-Import Bank lending, if the U.S. government concluded that the Beijing authorities had "willfully" approved the ring magnet transfer. Alternatively, a milder sanction barring U.S. dealings with the two enterprises involved in the sale was possible, if Washington concluded that senior Chinese authorities were unaware of the transaction.

As the Clinton administration was wrestling with ring magnets, it had to face yet another nuclear problem with the Pakistanis. Contrary to what Benazir Bhutto had indicated during her April 1995 visit to Washington, U.S. intelligence received indications that Islamabad had resumed production of weapons-grade uranium. To emphasize the administration's concern about the issue, Deputy National Security Adviser Samuel Berger made an unusual and rapid trip to Pakistan in January 1996. He warned the prime minister that the Clinton administration would have trouble in implementing the Brown amendment if these difficulties continued.[43]

The U.S. authorities waited for two months to gauge Pakistan's response and to discuss the ring magnet issue further with the Chinese. By March 1996, Washington felt sufficiently comfortable with the situation that it moved ahead to implement a major element of the Brown amendment: the release of $368 million of Pakistan-owned military equipment frozen by the Pressler amendment and the refund of $120 million for items paid for but not produced before the 1990 sanctions took effect.[44] Steering clear of a serious trade and political ruckus with China, the Clinton administration also concluded that the Beijing authorities had not knowingly approved the ring magnet transaction. This enabled the U.S. government to limit sanctions to blacklisting the entities directly involved. For their part, the Chinese reportedly told the Americans that they would not sell Pakistan this type of specialized nuclear equipment in the future.[45]

In the summer of 1996, China's dealings with Pakistan stirred fresh difficulties. The U.S. intelligence community concluded with "high confidence" that complete Chinese M-11 missiles were stored in crates near the Pakistani air force base at Sarghoda in Punjab and could be deployed in a matter of days. Another credible report indicated that China was assisting Pakistan in setting up a factory, just a few miles from the capital city of Islamabad, to manufacture the missiles.[46] The intelligence information put the Clinton administration in an awkward position, since it suggested that the Chinese were not keeping their word to abide by MTCR guidelines on missile exports to Pakistan. If Washington accepted this assessment, it would have to impose drastic sanctions that would cost American companies billions of dollars in sales to China. In the end, Clinton administration policy makers finessed the problem, taking no action on the grounds that the intelligence was insufficiently conclusive to justify the imposition of severe sanctions.[47]

During 1996, narcotics became yet another bilateral point of friction. Even though U.S. antinarcotics officials had become accustomed to having Islamabad's promises exceed its achievements, the State Department had dutifully certified throughout the 1980s and early 1990s—as required by U.S. law—that Pakistan was cooperating in the fight against the narcotics trade. But in 1996, after Washington found Benazir Bhutto's government singularly sluggish in pursuing well-known drug lords, U.S. authorities decided to send a stiffer warning. For the first time, the State Department refused to certify Pakistan. Sanctions were avoided, however, when President Clinton issued a waiver on the grounds that punishing Pakistan was not in the national interest.[48] Unlike nuclear legislation, antinarcotics laws provided the president with flexibility through the inclusion of broad waiver authority.

The possible sale of the F-16s to a third country to generate funds to reimburse Pakistan also ran into difficulty. For a time, it looked as if Indonesia would purchase nine of the stranded aircraft. But as the 1996 presidential election campaign began to heat up, so did congressional criticism of Indonesia's crackdown on political dissidents. As a result, the Clinton administration decided to avoid stirring trouble by putting the F-16 transaction with Indonesia on the shelf until after the new Congress convened in January 1997.[49] This time it was the Pakistanis, not the Americans, who were upset.

Afghanistan and the Taliban

In one sensitive foreign policy area—Afghanistan—Islamabad in the mid-1990s unexpectedly advanced toward its goal: a friendly regime in Kabul, led by the Pashtuns. Pakistan's chosen instrument was no longer mujahideen commander Hekmatyar, but rather the fundamentalist Taliban (literally, "students") movement that emerged suddenly in the summer of 1994 around Kandahar, the major city in southern Afghanistan. The Taliban were mainly Pashtun refugees who had been educated in religious schools (*madrassas*) in Pakistan's Baluchistan province. These schools were run by the fundamentalist Deobandi sect of Sunni Islam and its conservative political party offshoot, the Jamiat-e-Ulema Islam.[50] In a sense, the Taliban were the most prominent product of Zia's policy of promoting Islamic schools. In the two decades since Zia initiated the pro-*madrassa* policy in the late 1970s, the religious schools had spread widely, in the process spawning a vast subculture of youth lettered in the Koran but little else and inculcated with religious fanaticism: in essence, they produced cannon fodder for the Taliban's military campaigns. The success of the Taliban in suppressing unruly mujahideen commanders and imposing peace in and around Kandahar came to the attention of Nasrullah Babar, the interior minister in the Benazir Bhutto government, who had been close to Zulfikar Bhutto and remained close to his daughter. Deciding to take the Taliban under his wing, Babar arranged for ISI personnel to provide transportation, fuel, communications equipment, and advice to the movement. To coordinate assistance to the Taliban, Babar established an Afghan cell in the Interior Ministry.[51]

With the backing and support of Islamabad, the Taliban spread beyond the Kandahar area in the fall of 1995 to become the masters of western as well as southern Afghanistan. As they swept aside local mujahideen commanders, the Taliban ranks expanded to some ten thousand fighters. Defectors from different mujahideen groups, former members of the communist Afghan military, and fresh trainees joined the movement. Although the Taliban suffered a setback in an overambitious attempt to seize Kabul in midyear, they won a major victory in September 1955 by capturing Herat, the principal city in the west of the country. A populace tired of the excesses and harassment of unruly mujahideen commanders and their constant fighting welcomed the peace that the Taliban imposed. The fact that they also imposed the rigid and puritanical rules of the Deobandi version of Sunni Islam was not in itself upsetting in the religiously conservative Afghan villages and countryside.[52]

To promote his own and Benazir Bhutto's pet project of establishing overland trade links through Afghanistan to the Central Asian republics, Babar personally led a convoy of trucks in October 1995 from Quetta to Turkmenistan, passing through Kandahar and Herat. Several foreign envoys, including U.S. ambassador John Monjo, were in the party. When roadblocks mounted by local mujahideen commanders to shake down travelers and traders slowed the caravan's progress, Babar and the others were impressed by the ease with which the Taliban swept the mujahideen aside.[53]

By this time, relations had soured between Islamabad and Kabul, where the government of Afghanistan was still led by Rabbani, whose main support was the military force led by fellow Tajik Ahmed Shah Masood. Rabbani had especially upset the Pakistanis by establishing close links with the Indians. The day after the fall of Herat to the Taliban, an Afghan government-sponsored mob sacked the Pakistani embassy in Kabul, an event that triggered a major crisis in Pakistan-Afghan relations. Following a lull in fighting during the winter and spring of 1996, the Taliban resumed their military offensive. After taking Jalalabad on September 11, 1996, the Taliban forces advanced swiftly toward Kabul. As the Taliban swept forward, they brushed aside fellow Pashtun Hekmatyar, the ISI's longtime favorite. Casualties were minimal, as many of Hekmatyar's fighters defected to the Taliban.

On September 26, 1996, the Taliban capped their stunning two-year rise to power by capturing the capital city, Kabul. They faced little resistance as Masood withdrew his weary troops to the north. Masood's inability to control his fighters had made them unpopular in the Afghan capital and helped pave the way for an initially positive reception to the Taliban. One of their first acts was to hang Afghanistan's former communist ruler, Najibullah Khan, who had been living in asylum inside the UN office in Kabul ever since his fall from power in 1992.[54]

In their sweep to the Afghan capital, the Taliban used more-sophisticated, more-aggressive, and better-coordinated tactics than the cowboy-and-Indian fighting style of the mujahideen. Guidance received from ISI advisers and the significant role played in the movement by former members of the communist Afghan army were also significant factors in the Taliban victory. Although Pakistan routinely denied that it was helping the Taliban—as it had denied providing help for the insurgency against the Soviets in Afghanistan—Islamabad's support was a similarly open secret.[55]

What set the Taliban apart from other Afghan groups was the fervor and puritanical character of their Sunni religious beliefs. Barnett Rubin, a U.S. specialist on Afghanistan, described the Taliban as "fire and brimstone, backwoods preachers with an AK-47."[56] After capturing Kabul, they quickly made clear that women should remain at home, men should grow beards, videos were banned, and any deviation from their strict interpretation of the Koran would be sternly punished. The top Taliban leader, Mullah Mohammed Omar, a one-eyed war veteran, proclaimed that his country would become a "completely Islamic state" where a "complete Islamic system will be enforced."[57]

The U.S. government's initial reaction to the capture of Kabul by the Taliban was positive. The United States, the State Department spokesperson declared, could see "nothing objectionable" in the steps the Taliban had taken to impose Islamic law in the areas under their control and called on the Taliban to "move quickly to restore order" and to form "a representative interim government."[58] But the State Department rapidly changed its tune after nature of Taliban policies toward women became better known. "The last thing we wanted to do was fuel this total misperception that we were recognizing and embracing the Taliban," a senior official told the *New York Times* in an effort to rewrite history.[59]

Several factors explained the State Department's initial reaction. U.S. officials anticipated that the Taliban victory would end the civil war and at last permit reconstruction to begin. Among other things, peace in Afghanistan would greatly improve the prospects for a large gas-pipeline project involving a consortium led by Unocal, a major American oil company that hoped to transport natural gas from the vast fields of Turkmenistan across Afghanistan to energy-short India and Pakistan. Washington also hoped that the Taliban would make good on assurances they offered U.S. officials that, under their rule, Afghanistan would cease to be a breeding ground for terrorism and narcotics trafficking. Finally, frictions that had developed between the Sunni Taliban and Shi'a Iran were regarded positively in Washington against the background of continuing U.S. hostility toward Tehran.[60] The initial positive response to the Taliban victory, however, was a mistake that caused many to conclude—including, not unsurprisingly, the Iranians—that the United States, like Pakistan, actively supported the Taliban. Even though U.S. officials insisted that this was not the case—and the author found no reason to believe the contrary—the impression that Washington stood behind the Taliban lingered on in a region fueled by a variety of conspiracy theories.

Benazir Bhutto Out; Nawaz Sharif In

Benazir Bhutto did not have much time to savor the triumph of Pakistan's Afghan policy. In her second term as prime minister, Bhutto again was proving a poor manager of the economy, resorting to large-scale short-term borrowing to fill a widening gap between revenues and expenditures. Indeed, outlays for defense and debt service left few funds for education, health, and other development programs. Corruption and political cronyism were more than ever said to be the order of the day. Leading the pack was her husband, Asif Zardari, who became minister for investment in July 1996. It was widely believed that government contracts routinely included payoffs for Zardari.

Despite overall lackluster performance in the energy and power sector, Benazir Bhutto implemented an ambitious program to overcome the chronic shortage of electricity. To attract foreign investment, her government offered favorable terms for projects to install new electric-power generating capacity. After an impressed U.S. energy secretary Hazel O'Leary led an American business delegation to Pakistan, a number of U.S. companies signed contracts for major power and energy projects valued at $4 billion.[61] This development stirred hopes that private-sector investment would provide an important new element in the U.S.-Pakistan relationship.

Another serious problem facing Bhutto was the government's seeming inability to cope with the rise of Islamic extremist groups and the breakdown of law and order in many parts of the country. In the Punjab, the outbreak of serious sectarian violence between militant Sunni and Shi'a groups was an especially worrying development. It was widely assumed that the Iranians were funding the Shi'a groups and the Saudis the Sunni militants. Even though Islamic fundamentalist parties continued to score poorly at the polls, they had, nonetheless, managed to become a significant domestic political factor. The seeds that Zia had planted in the late 1970s had taken root. Participation in the "freedom struggle" in Afghanistan and Kashmir, as well as unofficial links with the ISI, lent added legitimacy to Islamic radical groups, as did the presence in the Pakistani government of the Jamiat-e-Ulema Islam, one faction of which was the intellectual forebear of the Taliban.

In spite of the fact that violence in Karachi continued at a high level, the authorities, led by Babar, responded with vigor—but acquired a reputation for shooting suspects first and asking questions later. On September 20, 1996, Benazir Bhutto's own brother, Murtaza, died in a shootout after his vehicle allegedly ran a police roadblock. Since Murtaza was at political odds with his sister and on bad terms with her husband, rumors spread that Zardari had something to do with his killing.

Notwithstanding Bhutto's difficulties, her position seemed relatively secure. President Leghari was her handpicked choice and a longtime PPP supporter. The highly professional chief of army staff, Gen. Jehangir Karamat, was disinclined to interfere in the political process. By the fall of 1996, however, relations between Leghari and Benazir Bhutto began to deteriorate. Upset by the prime minister's refusal to heed court orders restricting her ability to nominate judges, Leghari issued several pointed warnings. When the prime minister disregarded his admonitions, their falling-out worsened.

Finally, on November 5, 1996, the president invoked his constitutional authority to dismiss Bhutto on the familiar grounds of corruption, mismanagement, and inability to control lawlessness. This marked the fourth time in eight years that a president of Pakistan had removed a prime minister backed by a parliamentary majority. Leghari also dissolved the National Assembly, called for fresh elections in February 1997, and named octogenarian politician Malik Meraj Khalid, known for his honesty but not for his leadership skills, as temporary prime minister.[62]

With Benazir Bhutto discredited, Sharif was expected to sweep the polls. But the political and military elite had little confidence in his willingness or ability to tackle the hard problems facing the country. As a consequence, pressure developed for Leghari to postpone elections in order to provide time for a caretaker government to address Pakistan's underlying weaknesses. The army was reportedly willing to go along with this action. European Community ambassadors supposedly indicated understanding, provided constitutional norms were followed. The Americans, however, demurred. When approached by Najam Sethi, publisher of the influential Lahore newsweekly, the *Friday Times,* U.S. ambassador Thomas Simons, Jr., responded, "The answer for bad democracy is more democracy." In the end, Leghari decided not to delay the elections.[63]

The balloting on February 4, 1997, as anticipated, returned Sharif to power in a landslide—less a vote of confidence in him than one of no confidence in Benazir Bhutto. Sharif's Pakistan Muslim League and its allies won more than the two-thirds majority of National Assembly seats needed to amend the constitution. Shortly after taking office, the new prime minister was able to strengthen his political position when the assembly unanimously voted to repeal the eighth amendment to the constitution. This action stripped the president of the power to dismiss governments at will. For the first time since Zia ousted Zulfikar Bhutto in July 1977, the prime minister became the most powerful political figure in Pakistan—although the chief of army staff remained the ultimate arbiter of power.

Pakistan's Fiftieth Birthday

Sharif's return to office coincided with the beginning of Bill Clinton's second term after his sweeping victory in the November 1996 elections. Clinton named former U.S. representative to the UN Madeleine Albright to replace Christopher as secretary of state.[64] To serve as undersecretary of state for political affairs, he appointed top career diplomat and former ambassador to India Thomas Pickering. Karl Inderfurth, a senior member of Albright's team at the United Nations and a National Security Council staff member during the Carter presidency, succeeded Raphel as assistant secretary of state for South Asia.

The new foreign policy team made an early decision to try to broaden relations with India and Pakistan and to place less emphasis on nonproliferation matters.[65] To demonstrate increased interest in the subcontinent, a series of high-level trips was planned to culminate with the first presidential journey since Jimmy Carter's visit to India nearly two decades before. As Pickering put it, "We want to show that we don't consider South Asia the backside of the diplomatic globe."[66]

Despite chronic friction in the bilateral relationship, Sharif still hoped for better days with the Americans. One sign was his cooperation in the arrest of Mir Aimal Kansi, a Pakistani national charged with the fatal 1993 shooting of two Central Intelligence Agency employees outside the agency's headquarters in Langley, Virginia. After U.S. and Pakistani law-enforcement officials captured Kansi on June 14, 1997, in Dera Gazi Khan, a city on the Indus River in western Punjab, Sharif allowed the Americans to fly Kansi back to the United States to stand trial for murder without having to go through the normal extradition process. The action stirred domestic criticism in Pakistan, especially as the United States had refused to bypass its extradition procedures in the case of a Pakistani air force officer being held in a U.S. jail on drug charges. As a writer for the *Nation* (Islamabad) asserted, Washington "rarely acts to circumvent its own laws, but expects others to waive and ignore theirs."[67]

Two months later, on August 14, 1997, Pakistan celebrated the fiftieth anniversary of its independence in a subdued manner. Although the country had registered significant economic advances, its poor record in meeting basic human needs, its chronic political instability, and the appalling state of law and order in the country deprived the occasion of much joy. Sharif defensively told the *New York Times,* "In 50 years we've had our ups and downs like any other nation in the world. We've been off track, but we're on track now. . . . Of course, the enemies of Pakistan try to present it as a failed state. But it's not a failed state."[68]

Despite high-flown anniversary rhetoric, Islamabad judged that the Clinton administration had only marginal interest in better relations and mainly was interested in improving U.S.-India ties. Notwithstanding the passage of the Brown amendment, Washington had yet to repay Pakistan for the undelivered F-16 aircraft. The Pressler arms embargo remained intact. The U.S. government had done little to assist Pakistan's faltering economy, was becoming increasingly unhappy about Islamabad's support for the fundamentalist Taliban in Afghanistan, and was privately critical of Pakistan's involvement with the insurgents in Kashmir.[69]

In the nine years since the death of Zia, Pakistan had become more hawkish in dealing with its two most pressing national security issues: India and Afghanistan. The U.S.-Soviet Cold War may have ended, but South Asia's cold war continued unabated. In fact, India-Pakistan tensions had intensified during the 1990s as a result of Islamabad's backing for the Kashmiri insurgency. Efforts to broaden ties with India—through expanded trade, for example—were frustrated. The mantra pushed by hard-liners in Islamabad was that nothing could be done to improve relations until the Kashmir problem was solved. Given New Delhi's far greater strength and unwillingness to yield on the issue, the stance had little prospect of success, but still had widespread and highly emotional support in Pakistan.

In the case of Afghanistan, Pakistan's ISI continued its close support for the Taliban's effort to gain total control. Seemingly oblivious to growing criticism from abroad of its policy, Pakistan's approach was driven by its desire to see a friendly regime in power in Kabul, thereby supposedly ensuring "strategic depth" vis-à-vis India. After the unhappy dealings with the Tajik-dominated Rabbani government, Islamabad judged this outcome was possible only if the Pashtuns, the tribal siblings of Pakistan's Pathans, won out over the other Afghan ethnic groups. Even if the Taliban were Sunni extremists and at odds with most of the international community over their treatment of women, the fact that they were Pashtuns seemed to matter most in Islamabad. The frictions that the pro-Taliban stance caused in Pakistan's relations with the United States, Iran, the Central Asian states, and even to some extent with China, seemed to have little impact on Afghan policy.

Top-Level Exchanges

In September 1997, Clinton met Sharif for the first time during the UN General Assembly session in New York. The president spoke of his desire to enhance bilateral relations, urged renewed India-Pakistan dialogue, and reiterated his interest in visiting South Asia. The prime minister echoed hopes for improved bilateral relations, urged a more active U.S. role in the Kashmir dispute, and assured Clinton of a warm welcome when he visited Pakistan.[70]

Two months later, in November 1997, Secretary of State Albright traveled to the subcontinent to show "after a long absence, the United States at the highest levels is getting back in the South Asia game."[71]

Just a week before her arrival, the shooting in Karachi of five employees, four American and one Pakistani, of Union Texas Petroleum revived concerns about the safety of U.S. citizens in Pakistan and underlined the country's precarious security situation.[72]

Albright's visit was startlingly different from George Shultz's trip in 1983, reflecting the souring of bilateral relations during the fourteen-year interval. Shultz's stay, at the peak of the Afghan war partnership, had been described as a "love in." Albright's visit was all business. Nuclear weapons, Afghanistan, Kashmir, and drugs provided a full substantive agenda. Although the secretary asserted that Pakistan "will be able to count on the continuing friendship of the United States," she offered few specifics and little in the way of economic assistance.[73]

The high point of Albright's visit—like that of George Shultz's—was her meeting with Afghan refugees in Peshawar. In 1983, an emotional Shultz had offered his support for the mujahideen's struggle against the Soviets. In 1998, Albright voiced her emotional opposition to the policies of the Taliban. Talking with Afghan women refugees, the secretary of state declared, "We're opposed to their approach on human rights. We're opposed to their despicable treatment of women and children and their lack of respect for human dignity."[74]

At the very moment Albright was in Pakistan, the country was passing through yet another political crisis. What began as a dispute between Chief Justice Sajjad Ali Shah and Sharif over the appointment of judges developed into a full-fledged regime crisis, pitting the prime minister against the president and the chief justice. When the chief of army staff, General Karamat, refused to intervene to back Leghari, the prime minister won out. The president resigned and the chief justice retired.

Power Projects, Drugs, F-16s, and Missiles

By February 1998, Nawaz Sharif had been back in office for a year. Even though his political position seemed impregnable, the prime minister appeared strangely insecure and more interested in acquiring a monopoly of power than in tackling Pakistan's myriad problems. Even if there was less talk of corruption than during his first term, Sharif did little to address the country's basic economic woes. His administration moved aggressively, however, against a number of electricity projects that foreign investors, including Americans, had concluded with the

Benazir Bhutto government. Since power-project contracts were backed by a sovereign guarantee, his action further damaged the already poor climate for foreign investment.

As if there were not already sufficient bilateral problems, new difficulties developed. In 1998, for the third year running, Clinton had to issue a waiver to avoid the imposition of sanctions for Pakistan's lack of cooperation in the antinarcotics effort. During the previous year, a bitter dispute had arisen over the arrest of a Pakistani national, Ayyaz Baluch. An employee of the U.S. Drug Enforcement Agency's Islamabad office, Baluch had been involved in an effort to entrap a Pakistani air force officer suspected of drug smuggling. Not informed beforehand, the Pakistani authorities were indignant and embarrassed when the air force officer was arrested in the United States. They retaliated by jailing Baluch for "seducing" the air force officer to commit a crime. Intense "and sometimes angry" diplomatic pressure was needed before Baluch was pardoned and permitted to emigrate with his family to the United States.[75]

In April 1998, Pakistan's missile imports once more caused trouble. This time, North Korea, not China, was the culprit. Early in the year, the U.S. intelligence community concluded that Pakistan had imported North Korean technology to develop a medium-range missile, which—to highly emotional domestic acclaim—was successfully fired over a range of nine hundred kilometers on April 6, 1998. The Pakistanis claimed that the missile, provocatively named the Ghauri, after the ninth-century Muslim conqueror of India, gave them an edge over their neighbor. Islamabad denied the U.S. assertion that the missile was a modified version of the North Korean Nodong—itself a variant of the Soviet Scud—and declared that Pakistani scientists had developed the Ghauri on their own. Rejecting the Pakistani position, the U.S. government proceeded to impose sanctions against North Korea and Khan Research Laboratories, where the missile was produced. These sanctions had only symbolic effect, however, since earlier sanctions already barred dealings with the United States.[76]

Indian and Pakistani Nuclear Tests

In March 1998, India turned a new political page. Atul Behari Vajpayee, the leader of the Hindu nationalist Bharata Janata Party (BJP), was able to form a government after winning a plurality of parliamentary seats in general elections. The BJP traditionally had taken a hard line on Pakistan, advocated that India develop nuclear weapons, and believed Hinduism rather than secularism should be the country's guiding principle. After the Vajpayee government spoke of "induction" of nuclear weapons, Sharif warned Clinton about Indian intentions in an April 3, 1998, letter. Lulled by soothing comments in New Delhi, U.S. officials thought that the letter was an example of Pakistan's crying "wolf" regarding India and were confident that the BJP would not act precipitously.[77]

But Washington was unaware that, immediately after entering office, Vajpayee had given the green light for nuclear tests.[78] By concealing preparations at the Pokharan test site in Rajasthan, Indian scientists were able to avoid detection by U.S. satellites. As a result, when India exploded a series of underground devices on May 11, 1998, the United States was caught embarrassingly off guard. India's five nuclear tests were jarringly out of step with the world community's substantial progress in recent years on the nonproliferation front: the renunciation of nuclear weapons by Ukraine, Kazakhstan, and Belarus; U.S.-Russian nuclear weapons reductions; destruction of South Africa's covert capability; the decisions of Brazil and Argentina to join the nuclear Nonproliferation Treaty (NPT); the unconditional renewal of the NPT itself; and the successful negotiation of the Comprehensive Test Ban Treaty (CTBT). Although both India and, in its wake, Pakistan, had refused to adhere to the CTBT, the treaty won overwhelming backing from the international community.

The Indian tests once more put the nuclear issue on the center stage of South Asia policy. Calling them "a terrible mistake," an angry Clinton stated, "I want to make it very, very clear that I am deeply disturbed."[79] He promptly imposed wide-reaching sanctions against India mandated by the 1994 nonproliferation act: the United States cut off all aid, voted against loans by the World Bank and the Asian Development Bank, and urged other states to follow suit. Major industrial nations joined in strongly criticizing the tests. World Bank and Asian Development Bank loans were held up, but only Japan imposed sanctions as drastic as those of the United States.

Clinton's attention shifted to Pakistan. In the hope of persuading Sharif not to follow India's example, the president dispatched Deputy Secretary of State Talbott to Islamabad. The envoy dangled delivery of the F-16s and resumption of economic and military aid, argued that Pakistan would gain the moral high ground internationally by not testing—thereby focusing global disapproval on India—and added that from a technical standpoint Pakistan—unlike India—did not need to test to show that its nuclear device would work. (It was widely assumed that China had given Pakistan a proven bomb design during the 1980s.)[80]

To underscore Talbott's entreaties, President Clinton spoke with Sharif four times by telephone. The prime minister responded that he had not taken a decision but was under great domestic political pressure to show that Pakistan could match India. Publicly, he declared, "It is up to the international community" to address Pakistan's legitimate security concerns in the wake of India's nuclear tests.[81]

Most of all, the Pakistanis wanted the harshest possible punishment of India. "Invoking mandatory sanctions under U.S. laws against India hardly constitutes an effective response," Gauhar Ayub Khan, Pakistan's hawkish foreign minister and the son of former president Ayub Khan, declared.[82] At their annual meeting May 17–18, 1998, in Birmingham in the United Kingdom, the group of the world's eight leading economic powers (G-8) criticized India, agreed to oppose multilateral lending, but refused more draconian measures. Judging the G-8 response inadequate, the Pakistani foreign minister declared, "It's a matter of when, not if, Pakistan will test." Another source of pressure was the gloating tone of statements from New Delhi. In one, Home Minister L. K. Advani called on Pakistan to accept the new realities imposed by the tests. It was as if the Indians, eager to have company in the international doghouse, were egging the Pakistanis on. In spite of this, Clinton remained publicly hopeful "that the Prime Minister and the Pakistani government would not go through with a nuclear test. And I believe we can . . . work with them in a way which meets their security needs without the test."[83]

Sharif faced a difficult choice. If Pakistan tested, the economic cost would be high. Islamabad would automatically face the same severe sanctions imposed on India—sanctions that the nearly bankrupt Pakistani economy might not be able to withstand. Pakistan would also forego the opportunity for a major change in U.S. policy, one that Islamabad had been seeking ever since the Pressler axe fell in 1990. But after their past difficulties with the Americans, Pakistani officials had little faith in Clinton's words and were skeptical whether Congress would agree to lift sanctions and approve a substantial economic and conventional arms assistance package.[84]

On the other hand, if Sharif heeded Clinton's entreaties not to test, he would pay a heavy domestic political price. Not only the opposition PPP and pro-Islamic religious parties, but many in his own Pakistan Muslim League were vociferously clamoring for Pakistan to match India. In a meeting with newspaper editors, the prime minister reportedly was told bluntly by Arif Nizami, editor of the widely read and influential Urdu daily *Nawai-i-Waqt,* "There is going to be an explosion soon. It will either be a Pakistani nuclear test or your being blown out of office!"[85]

In the end, Sharif told Clinton that he needed a U.S. security guarantee against India to hold off from testing. The president said that he could not give this but reiterated his intention "to cut through the knot" of laws blocking aid and give Pakistan "the tools you need to defend your country." This was not good enough for the prime minister, who gave the green light for the tests. On May 28, 1998, Pakistan exploded five underground nuclear devices in Baluchistan.[86]

The Pakistani public celebrated wildly. People danced in city streets, shouting, "We have done it. We are India's equal." A proud Sharif declared, "Today we have settled a score. . . . Our hand was forced by the present Indian leadership's reckless actions."[87] A poll by the Pakistan Institute for Public Opinion showed that 97 percent of the respondents favored the tests.

In Washington, President Clinton commented sadly, "By failing to exercise restraint in responding to the Indian test, Pakistan lost a truly priceless opportunity to strengthen its own security, to improve its political standing in the eyes of the world." At the same time, the White House made clear that Clinton remained angrier at India. "Prime Minister Nawaz Sharif was honest and straightforward in the description of the decision he was wrestling with," presidential press secretary Michael McCurry declared, "and India manifestly was not."[88]

The next day, the UN Security Council "deplored" Pakistan's tests and urged both countries to show restraint. Nonetheless, on May 31, 1998, Pakistan detonated a sixth device, one more than India had exploded, before announcing the end of its test series. Meeting in Geneva on June 4, 1998, the foreign ministers of the five declared nuclear weapon states—also the permanent members of the UN Security Council—urged India and Pakistan to take steps to reduce the danger of nuclear war: to sign the CTBT; to join in talks about banning fissile material production; to strengthen nuclear export controls; and to show restraint in missile testing and deployment.[89]

Even as the Clinton administration was announcing the details of sanctions, efforts to water them down were under way. One impulse was commercial self-interest. If implemented fully, the sanctions, which barred agricultural export credits, would cost farmers in the U.S. Pacific Northwest, already hard hit by falling grain prices, a possible sale of 350,000 tons of wheat to Pakistan, or one-third of the area's production. In mid-July 1999, just two months after the tests, the Senate voted 98-0 and the House of Representatives followed suit to exempt agricultural credits from the sanctions. Recognizing that the rigidity of the 1994 legislation deprived the president of any flexibility in trying to deal diplomatically with India and Pakistan, Congress voted in a separate action to give the chief executive authority to waive all sanctions, including those imposed by the Pressler amendment.[90]

Deciding to launch a diplomatic effort to influence Indian and Pakistani nuclear policies, Clinton sent Talbott back to South Asia. Taking as his agenda the June 4, 1998, Geneva declaration by the five UN Security Council members, Talbott had seven rounds of separate talks with India and Pakistan during the remainder of 1998. These discussions, held in the United States, Europe, and South Asia, marked by far the most extended high-level U.S. engagement since John Kennedy and Lyndon Johnson were in the White House during the 1960s.[91]

Fears that sanctions might sink Pakistan's shaky economy were not misplaced. At the time Islamabad tested, the country had a foreign debt of over $30 billion and foreign exchange reserves of only $600 million. Pakistan would be unable to meet upcoming debt service payments unless it received fresh financial help from the International Monetary Fund (IMF). When the panicky government froze foreign-currency bank accounts immediately after the tests, the action created havoc for foreign companies working in Pakistan. The country's already terrible credit rating sagged even further.[92]

As U.S. officials grew increasingly concerned about Pakistan's possible financial collapse, they decided to provide Islamabad with some breathing room. The United States announced that it would no longer oppose IMF financial assistance.[93] After lengthy negotiations, the Pakistanis and the IMF agreed on an economic program—more of a bandage to prevent Pakistan from going under than a comprehensive attack on the country's fiscal ills. Given Islamabad's poor record of implementing previous accords with the IMF, observers adopted a "wait and see" attitude about the utility of the new agreement.

The Taliban and Osama bin Laden

In August 1998, Washington policy makers' attention turned once more to Afghanistan. The Taliban, who already controlled most of the country, suddenly appeared to be close to total victory over their foes, a ramshackle coalition of Uzbek, Hazara, and Tajik opponents called the Northern Alliance. Taliban troops captured Mazar-i-Sharif, the principal ethnically Uzbek city in Afghanistan, and Bamyan, the stronghold of the Shi'a Hazaras. Only Tajik leader Masood, who retreated into his native Panjshir Valley north of Kabul, blocked complete Taliban control. Supported by Iran, Tajikistan, and, ironically, Russia, whose soldiers Masood had bitterly battled in the 1980s, the Panjshir Valley warrior was the last holdout. Recognized by Pakistan, Saudi Arabia, and the United Arab Emirates—but by no one else—the Taliban had managed to acquire near-pariah status, especially in the United States, by their harsh treatment of women, their tolerance of the drug trade, and their willingness to provide a haven for Islamic extremists and terrorists.[94]

The ISI's support for the Taliban—which Pakistan continued to deny—had by this time become a significant source of friction with the United States. There was also growing concern that a Taliban-like movement, presumably supported by pro-Islamic political parties and fundamentalist elements in the ISI and the military, would have increasing appeal to a Pakistani public weary and frustrated after a decade of economic mismanagement, political feuding, and chronic lawlessness under Nawaz Sharif and Benazir Bhutto.

In mid-August 1998, Afghanistan loomed even larger on the Washington radar screen after the intelligence community concluded that terrorist attacks on U.S. embassies in Nairobi, Kenya, and Dar es Salaam, Tanzania, that took more than two hundred lives were organized by Osama bin Laden, a wealthy Saudi Arabian living in exile under Taliban protection. Like thousands of other young Islamic radicals, bin Laden had joined the Afghan mujahideen to fight against the Soviets during the 1980s. After returning home to Saudi Arabia, he bitterly opposed his country's close ties with the United States and was forced into exile. Bin Laden first went to Sudan and then found a haven near Jalalabad in Afghanistan. After the Taliban gained power, they continued to allow bin Laden to use their territory as a base for organizing terrorist activities.[95]

On August 21, 1998, the United States struck back. U.S. Navy warships launched cruise missiles against bin Laden's training camps in Afghanistan and also targeted a factory in Sudan supposedly linked to the Saudi terrorist. Although Washington did not inform Pakistan beforehand of the attacks, Gen. Joseph Ralston, vice chairman of the Joint Chiefs of Staff, was conveniently visiting Islamabad and was able to assure General Karamat that the missiles flying through Pakistani airspace were American, not Indian, and were aimed at Afghanistan.[96]

The U.S. missile strikes drew sharp criticism, nonetheless, not only from pro-Islamic groups but from across the political spectrum, as an infringement of Pakistan's sovereignty. Sharif even telephoned Clinton to complain about the U.S. action in the mistaken belief that a missile had struck a Pakistani village. To Islamabad's embarrassment, the strikes killed at least eleven Pakistanis, who were being trained for guerrilla warfare in a camp run by the Harkat al-Ansar, a Pakistani group active in the Kashmiri insurgency that was on the U.S. list of terrorist organizations.[97]

When American officials urged the Pakistanis to press the Taliban to hand over bin Laden, Islamabad said that it would do what it could but claimed that fiercely held Afghan customs regarding hospitality would render its efforts fruitless. Much as the Pakistanis would have liked to gain favor in Washington by arranging for the capture or departure of bin Laden, the action would have cost Sharif dearly both at home, where the Saudi had become an anti-U.S. cult hero, and in Afghanistan, where the Taliban would have been outraged.

Sharif Visits Washington; F-16 Issue Solved

In the fall of 1998, Clinton met again with Sharif at the UN General Assembly. On this occasion, in part to provide a psychological boost, Clinton invited the prime minister to pay an official visit to Washington. By then, the president had put off his trip to South Asia, first because of the Indian elections and then due to the nuclear explosions.[98] Even so, the Talbott talks had registered some progress. India and Pakistan had both indicated their qualified willingness to sign the CTBT, which both countries had previously spurned. They had agreed to join in multilateral negotiations looking toward a ban on the production of fissile material, although they refused to accept an immediate moratorium. Finally, they had expressed willingness in principle to strengthen their controls over exports of nuclear-related items.

On December 2, 1998, Sharif arrived in Washington for his first official visit to the United States as prime minister. The Pakistanis hoped that Clinton would further ease sanctions, press the IMF to relax its lending terms, clear up the still-unresolved F-16 problem, and apply greater pressure on India to negotiate over Kashmir. Although U.S. officials had cautioned Islamabad not to expect too much, the mere fact of the visit, especially since a parallel invitation had not been extended to the Indian prime minister, satisfied the Pakistanis.[99]

When the president greeted Pakistan's prime minister at the White House the next day, Clinton had a pleasant surprise: a concrete proposal to solve the F-16 issue. After the Pakistanis formally moved to initiate legal action against the U.S. government as a last hope to recover their money, the Justice Department concluded that Pakistan was likely to

President Bill Clinton and Prime Minister Nawaz Sharif confer at the White House, December 1998. (Courtesy of the White House Photo Office.)

win in court. This enabled the Clinton administration to tap a special fund used to pay judgments against the U.S. government. Since the Justice Department had assessed the chances of losing at 70 percent, the administration could tap the special fund for this percentage of the $470 million that was owed to Pakistan for the F-16s. To cover the remaining amount, the president accepted a Pakistani suggestion that the U.S. government make a "best effort" to provide $140 million of wheat and other commodities on a grant basis over the coming two years.[100] Even though the prime minister hardly sparkled in his public appearances in Washington—a lackluster speech at an Asia Society dinner and a number of fumbled questions at a press conference—the trip nonetheless marked a significant triumph. Eight years after the Pressler amendment was first invoked, the nettlesome F-16 issue was finally resolved in a manner that was satisfactory to Pakistan.

At the start of 1999, Talbott traveled to South Asia once more for his eighth round of nuclear discussions with India and Pakistan. This time the talks in Islamabad proved disappointing. Talbott's team had proposed a scenario under which the United States would seek the lifting of all sanctions against Pakistan, including the Pressler amendment, if Islamabad would sign the CTBT, stop its missile cooperation with North Korea, agree to participate in the multilateral negotiations to ban the production of fissile material, and put in place a comprehensive nuclear export-control regime. After preliminary discussions, the Americans were optimistic. Their hopes were dashed, however, during a working lunch with Sharif. Rather than reaching a separate bargain, the Pakistani reverted to a "me-too" stance, insisting that India had to take the lead in adopting the U.S. proposals before Pakistan would do so.[101]

The Spirit of Lahore, and Kargil

Washington was unambiguous in its delight over the highly successful visit by Prime Minister Vajpayee to Lahore in mid-February 1999 to mark the resumption of bus service between India and Pakistan. This was the first time an Indian prime minister had traveled to Pakistan since Rajiv Gandhi in 1988. The Lahore talks raised hopes that the two enemies, sobered by the dangerous implications of their decision to become overt nuclear weapons powers, might at last begin a serious effort to reduce tensions.[102]

Chances for early progress were set back, however, when the BJP government fell in April 1999 after losing a parliamentary vote of confidence by a single vote. Until new general elections in the fall of 1999, the Vajpayee government would remain in office in a caretaker status—as such, unable to carry forward either the nuclear talks with Talbott or the discussions with Pakistan envisaged by the Lahore agreement.

A far more devastating blow to the spirit of Lahore was New Delhi's realization in May 1999 that a large number of insurgents with Pakistani support had crossed the line of control in the far north of Kashmir to occupy 15,000-foot positions near the town of Kargil, overlooking the sole road link between Srinagar, the state's capital city, and Ladakh, the state's northernmost area. Given the high altitude and difficult terrain, the intruders held nearly impregnable positions. A difficult and costly assault would be required to prevent them from cutting off Ladakh.

The bold Kargil operation was qualitatively different from the guerrilla tactics that the Kashmiri insurgents had previously followed. Tactically clever, the strike hit the Indians where they had enormous difficulty in responding. But the move boomeranged and resulted in a major political setback for Sharif. In India, the government was doubly embarrassed. Caught napping, Indian intelligence became aware of the large-scale intrusion only after the invaders were entrenched on the heights. Since planning the Kargil operation had to have started many months earlier, well before Vajpayee's visit to Lahore, the prime minister and other Indians also felt that they had been duped by Sharif.

New Delhi reacted forcefully, employing air power for the first time in Kashmir and mounting a substantial counterattack, which made slow and costly progress against the insurgents dug in on the heights. Fear that India would broaden the conflict by striking across the line of control in an effort to cut off the intruders intensified worries in Washington that the fighting could widen and possibly spin out of control, raising the nightmare scenario of war between two states armed with nuclear weapons.[103]

Taken aback and dismayed by the Kargil adventure, the U.S. government responded vigorously—far more so than the Johnson administration had reacted during the early stages of the 1965 Kashmir war. President Clinton telephoned Sharif to urge him to have the forces withdrawn and sent Gen. Anthony Zinni to Islamabad to second this message directly with the prime minister and with Gen. Pervez Musharraf, who had replaced Karamat as chief of army staff.[104] Brushing aside

Pakistan's claim that it was not directly involved in the Kargil operation and lacked control over the mujahideen, the U.S. general urged Islamabad to see to it that the intruders pulled back across the Kashmir line of control.[105] When not even the Chinese, let alone the Americans, were willing to support the Pakistani position, Islamabad found itself internationally isolated. As the Indian counterattack continued to grind slowly ahead on the ground, Sharif realized that his gambit had failed and decided to cut Pakistan's losses.

Desperate to find a way out, the prime minister pressed for an early meeting with Clinton. After U.S. officials made clear that they expected Pakistan to accept a pullback, the president agreed in a July 3, 1999, phone conversation to receive Sharif the very next day—on the 223rd anniversary of the signing of the Declaration of Independence. By chance, Clinton had a free schedule until late afternoon for the July 4 holiday and thus had the time for extended talks with the Pakistani leader.[106] At first, according to a participant in the talks, "Nawaz Sharif seemed like a drowning man looking for a miracle, hoping that somehow the United States would bail him out." After the discussion dragged on inconclusively, the Americans tabled two draft statements. One spelled out the agreement that Sharif eventually accepted; the other indicated that Pakistan had turned down the U.S. suggestions. After mulling matters over, the prime minister agreed to the first statement, which indicated that he would "urge" the mujahideen to withdraw across the line of control and restart the stalled Lahore process with India. In turn, Clinton promised that he would take an active interest in efforts to address the Kashmir problem.[107]

The reaction in Pakistan to the Washington agreement was sour. Public opinion derided attempts by the government to portray events as a Pakistani victory. Supporters of the mujahideen denounced the accord as a sellout to the Americans. Others criticized Sharif for having approved a dangerous military operation without having fully thought through the consequences. Implicitly also, the Pakistani army came under criticism for having developed the ill-fated Kargil plan.[108] Rumbles of friction between the army and the prime minister over the Kargil episode began to be heard, especially after Sharif supporters tried to pin responsibility on the military for the operation. Clinton soon followed up on the July 4 accord, asking Sharif to send an envoy to Washington for confidential talks on Kashmir. After a considerable delay, and to the surprise of the Americans, who anticipated a low-key representative, the prime minister dispatched his high-profile brother, Shahbaz Sharif, the chief minister of Punjab and a close confidant.[109] By the time Shahbaz arrived, his main concern was not Kashmir but the threat of an army coup. After he pressed for a U.S. warning against a military takeover, the State Department issued such a warning. Even though the statement included an admonition against the heavy-handed repression of antiregime demonstrators by the government, the action upset the military and may have emboldened Sharif to think he had American support in the event of a showdown.[110]

Tensions nonetheless appeared to subside when the prime minister appointed General Musharraf as chairman of the joint chiefs, concurrent with his assignment as chief of army staff. But the calm was deceptive. On October 12, 1999, as Musharraf was returning to Karachi on a Pakistan International Airlines (PIA) commercial flight after a visit to Sri Lanka, the government announced his dismissal. The Karachi airport control tower was instructed not to allow the plane carrying Musharraf to land but to divert the aircraft elsewhere, even though it was dangerously low on fuel. After the military became aware of events, they reacted swiftly, arresting Sharif and his senior associates. By the time the PIA flight finally landed at Karachi, Musharraf had become his nation's leader. The military was in charge of Pakistan for the fourth time in the country's fifty-two years of independence.

The fact that the army seized power surprised few observers against the background of the increasingly serious domestic woes and of post-Kargil friction. The manner in which the takeover occurred, however, was surprising. The coup was, in effect, a Pakistani version of a "shoot out in the OK Corral." After Sharif fired first at Musharraf and missed, the general shot back and hit his target.

There was scant regret in Pakistan about the departure of Sharif and qualified hope that the military would put the country back on the rails. The reaction abroad to the coup, in Washington and elsewhere, was negative. Even if the Americans were well aware of Sharif's failings, a military takeover flew in the face of U.S. support for democracies. Publicly, the Clinton administration response was more nuanced than those of the European Union states or the countries of the post-Soviet Commonwealth of Independent States: Washington imposed additional sanctions that were legally required in the case of the overthrow of a democratically elected government. These had little immediate impact, however, since Pakistan was already under severe sanctions because of the Pressler amendment and the 1998 nuclear tests.

The new regime tried to dampen foreign criticism by playing down the military label, stressing its interest in reform, and emphasizing its interim character. Rather than becoming president or chief martial law administrator like Ayub Khan, Yahya Khan, or Zia had, Musharraf assumed the more benign title of "chief executive." He did not impose martial law, did not ban political parties, and did not institute press censorship. Although pleased with these steps, the Clinton administration was less happy with Musharraf's reluctance to offer a timetable for the return to democracy. The trial and ultimately conviction of Sharif for attempted murder also raised concerns, as did the regime's firing of roughly 10 percent of judges who refused to take an oath of allegiance to Musharraf—including the chief justice of Pakistan.

Washington was also worried because of the rise in India-Pakistan tensions after the coup. New Delhi took an instant dislike to Musharraf as the author of the Kargil operation and also blamed him for a post-Kargil upsurge of violence in Kashmir. Indeed, Pakistan's new leader seemed bent on pursuing a hard-line policy toward Kashmir, virtually acknowledging Pakistan's direct support for the Kashmir insurgents. He called support for their cause as just as support for the mujahideen against the Soviet occupation of Afghanistan.

Events reached near-fever pitch at year's end after the hijacking of an Indian Airlines jet en route from Kathmandu, Nepal, to New Delhi. When the aircraft ended up in Kandahar, Afghanistan, an embarrassed Indian government found it necessary to deal with the Taliban and to release several jailed Kashmiri extremists in return for the freedom of the passengers. The fact that one of those released was soon preaching jihad against India (and initially also against the United States) before cheering crowds in Pakistan stirred even more intense Indian anger. The Vajpayee government, which had returned to power after winning the fall 1999 elections, blamed the Pakistanis for the hijacking and ruled out a resumption of dialogue until Islamabad stopped its support for the Kashmiri insurgency.

At the end of January 2000, with India-Pakistan relations near their low point and widespread concern regarding possible Indian military retaliation across the line of control in Kashmir, Clinton announced that he would undertake his twice-postponed trip to South Asia two months later, in March. The original plan was to spend five days in India sandwiched between shorter stays in Bangladesh and Pakistan, but the announcement indicated that no decision had been made regarding a stop in Pakistan.

Whether the president should go to Pakistan became a source of contention within the U.S. government. There were serious security concerns because of the threat posed by anti-American terrorist groups—in November 1999, unknown assailants had fired rockets at the American Cultural Center in Islamabad—not to speak of the presence of Osama bin Laden and others of his ilk in neighboring Afghanistan. Washington was also wary that the visit might put the presidential stamp of approval on the Musharraf regime. It was further disappointed that Islamabad backed away from signing the CTBT rather than face the ire of Islamic parties who opposed the move. Those arguing in favor of a stop in Pakistan stressed the importance of keeping lines of communication open with Musharraf if the United States wanted to exert any influence on his policies. In the end, gravely concerned about the dangers of India-Pakistan tensions, Clinton decided to visit Pakistan briefly at the end of the trip.[111]

The Clinton Visit

Clinton arrived in Islamabad on March 25, 2000, the first time a president had been to Pakistan in more than thirty years, since Richard Nixon spent August 1, 1969, in Lahore. The Pakistanis were wondering what to expect after the president's highly successful visit to India. There, the presidential party had reacted strongly to the murder of thirty-five Sikhs in Kashmir and stressed that violence was not the way to solve the dispute, called for respect for the line of control, and in a strong rebuke, alleged that some elements in the Pakistani government were supporting the insurgency.[112] This warning to Pakistan contrasted with the positive glow during Clinton's five days in India. His well-crafted address to the Indian parliament was enthusiastically received by the legislators; in meetings and events in New Delhi, Agra, Rajasthan, Hyderabad, and Mumbai, the president charmed the public at large. Notwithstanding New Delhi's refusal to sign the CTBT, the president had been intent on a successful trip "in order to start a new chapter" in Indo-U.S. relations. And he achieved a considerable measure of success.[113]

His short stop in Pakistan was very different. To foil possible assassination plots, a decoy plane arrived first at the Islamabad-Rawalpindi airport carrying a presidential double. The president himself landed in an unmarked aircraft and then, shielded from the press and television cameras, quickly drove off to the seat of government fifteen miles away. The presidential motorcade sped along an eerily empty highway. The public was kept away and the only Pakistanis the president saw were soldiers, special forces personnel, and police who lined the roadway. Every few hundred yards, however, banners urging U.S. action on Kashmir reminded the president of Pakistan's single-minded focus on this issue.

Two hours of official talks and then lunch at the head of government's residence in Islamabad were cordial and relaxed. Musharraf proved an engaging conversationalist who, like most senior Pakistanis, knew how to receive American visitors in a friendly and seemingly open manner. For his part, Clinton exuded much empathy toward Pakistan and its problems. Although the substance of his message was blunt, he neither lectured nor scolded Musharraf. Stressing that he had come trying to help a friend in difficulty, the president outlined U.S. concerns about the direction in which Pakistan was heading in a frank but conciliatory manner. He argued that Pakistan would benefit by lowering the temperature on Kashmir, by reining in terrorist groups, by pressing the Taliban to be more forthcoming on bin Laden and on peace talks, and by undertaking nonproliferation measures.[114]

In discussing Kashmir, Clinton made clear that the United States, although prepared to help, could not mediate and that Pakistan had to deal directly with India. Pakistan's chief executive responded with his own, harder-line construct on Kashmir. "Musharraf obviously has a strong and passionate view" on this issue, National Security Adviser Berger later told the press.[115] Although the general indicated willingness to de-escalate on Kashmir, he stressed that Pakistan would not act unilaterally. On the Taliban, Musharraf said that he wanted to be helpful but stressed how difficult it was to deal with "people who believe that God is on their side."

When Musharraf elaborated on his plans to move Pakistan back toward democracy, Clinton asked when national elections would take place. Musharraf responded that he could not give a precise timetable. Once he fixed the election date, he feared, he would lose effectiveness, as opponents to reform would simply wait him out.[116] The two sides did not agree during the talk on many issues—nor did the president expect this. He came to Islamabad, Berger told the press, to discuss U.S. concerns about Pakistan's future—whether it would be "preoccupied with a nuclear weapons program and conflict over Kashmir" or whether it would address "the really serious problems with the economy and governance of Pakistan."[117]

After the lunch ended, the president made an unprecedented fifteen-minute television address to the people of Pakistan. In this well-drafted speech, Clinton repeated the themes he had stressed in his private discussion with Musharraf while making warm references to the country's founder, Mohammed Ali Jinnah, and to American friendship for Pakistan. In closing, the president pointedly warned of the "danger that Pakistan may grow even more isolated, draining even more resources away from the needs of the people, moving even closer to a conflict no one can win." Clinton then struck a more positive note, saying, "If you do meet these challenges, our full economic and political partnership can be restored for the benefit of the people of Pakistan."[118]

Omitting the usual departure remarks and picture-taking with Musharraf, Clinton drove directly back to the airport along the empty, troop-lined highway after finishing his television address. Slightly more than five hours after landing, he was in the air heading for Oman and then Geneva for a meeting the next day with President Hafez al-Assad of Syria.

Pakistanis were pleased that Clinton had not skipped their country altogether, but, as one person watching the president on television in Islamabad told the *New York Times,* "This is a very painful thing for us, only five hours in Pakistan and five days in India."[119] The reaction to the president's message was mixed: some Pakistanis thought he had given the country thoughtful and helpful advice; others either disagreed with the policy prescription or saw his words as further indication that the United States had chosen India and was once more dumping Pakistan.

Although U.S. officials hoped that the situation would improve after the visit, they feared that it might worsen. "A sick Pakistan," one official commented, "would make Afghanistan look like a kindergarten."[120] However events play out, this first presidential stop in Pakistan in more than three decades marked a major bilateral benchmark; it also marks the end of this narrative.

13

An Unstable Partnership

The preceding twelve chapters have traced the history of the complex interaction between the United States and Pakistan. At the outset, when Pakistan gained its independence in August 1947, few observers would have predicted the course of this relationship, which has veered between alliance intimacy and cordiality and times of friction and tension, but has also seen periods of standoffishness and indifference. As an impoverished new nation, Pakistan was struggling to get on its feet after the trauma of partition. Its future, even its survival, was far from secure. In contrast, the United States had emerged from World War II as the world's strongest and most prosperous country and by the summer of 1947 had become the leader of the anticommunist bloc in the Cold War. Washington showed only modest interest in the new state, and it expected to have closer ties with larger and more important India than with Pakistan.

Yet after New Delhi chose a neutralist path, Pakistan became attractive as a potential partner in security arrangements for containing Soviet expansion in the Middle East. The U.S.-Pakistan alliance partnership that followed in 1954–55, however, proved unstable. It came apart in the 1960s during the Kennedy and Johnson presidencies, came together again with Nixon in the White House, but fractured once more with Jimmy Carter as president. During the 1980s, the struggle against the Soviet presence in Afghanistan provided new glue to bind the two countries together. Since the departure of the Red Army and the end of the Cold War, relations once more have been plagued by differences.

How to Explain the Many Ups and Downs?

How can one explain the roller-coaster character of the U.S.-Pakistan relationship, marked by so many ups and downs? Pakistanis tend to attribute this to American inconstancy and fickleness. In turn, Americans often assert the frequent twists and turns stem from Pakistani wrong-headedness, especially its fixation on with India. But neither view explains satisfactorily why the two countries have failed to sustain stable relations after becoming allies in 1954–55. The reason, in the author's view, lies in the fact that over the years U.S. and Pakistani interests and related security policies have been at odds almost as often as they have been in phase. The United States and Pakistan were, broadly speaking, on the same wavelength during the Eisenhower, Nixon, and Reagan presidencies. During the Kennedy, Johnson, Carter, Bush, and Clinton administrations, however, policy differences have been significant.

Given these realities, the volatility of the relationship should not be surprising. Absent a greater and more continuous congruence of security goals, U.S.-Pakistan ties have lacked a solid underpinning of shared national interests. Major differences and consequent disputes were probably inevitable. The partnership was likely to prove a fragile structure. The tendency of Americans and Pakistanis to gloss over this basic problem has only served to sharpen the sense of frustration and disappointment about the actions of the other.

The core fact of Pakistan's national security policy has been its hostility toward India, especially over Kashmir. This antipathy has led to two parallel imperatives: first, heavier military expenditures than Pakistan's underdeveloped economy could afford, ever since the country's first budget in 1948; and second, the pursuit of external partners, especially the United States, to offset India's preponderance of strength. This preoccupation with India caused Pakistan to upset the Americans on numerous occasions, first by cozying up to China in the 1960s, then by going to war over Kashmir in 1965, next by launching a clandestine nuclear program in the mid-1970s and by pressing ahead with that program in 1990, more recently by supporting the anti-Indian jihad in Kashmir during the 1990s, and finally by matching their neighbor's nuclear tests in May 1998. For its part, the United States never shared Pakistan's perception of India as an enemy, even though Washington and New Delhi were often estranged. Except for Nixon's "tilt" during the 1971 Bangladesh crisis, U.S. administrations have been unwilling to side with Pakistan against its larger neighbor.

From the late 1940s until the Iron Curtain disintegrated in 1989, the main determinant of U.S. policy was the struggle with what Ronald Reagan picturesquely called the "evil empire." The American superpower expected allies such as Pakistan to be cooperative members of the Cold War team. When one of the junior partners refused to play the game of geopolitics according to Washington's rules—as Pakistan did in the 1960s over China—trouble ensued.

Furthermore, although unrelated to the Cold War, conflicting U.S. and Pakistani policies over who should and should not have nuclear weapons has been a major source of friction since the mid-1970s. Congressionally mandated sanctions severely hamstrung the ability of the White House to manage the nuclear problem with Pakistan through diplomacy. The inflexibility of sanctions, and their broad scope, also substantially increased the damage to relations when sanctions were imposed. Indeed, few supposed U.S. friends, let alone allies, have been on the receiving end of as many sanctions as has Pakistan.

"A Union of Unequals"

Gen. Mohammed Zia ul-Haq, a shrewd if undemocratic leader, told Secretary of State George Shultz in December 1982 that the United States and Pakistan formed "a union of unequals" and were "incompatible" in terms of culture, geography, and national power.[1] Zia was right. The United States was a global power with global interests and the world's most economically advanced country. And later, after the collapse of the Soviet Union, it became the sole remaining superpower. For its part, although an important Muslim state, Pakistan was an economically poor regional power whose security interests did not extend much beyond its neighbors—India, Afghanistan, Iran, and China.

In the bilateral relationship, the United States was clearly the senior and Pakistan the junior partner. Indeed, except for the Afghan war years, Pakistan rarely has been near the top of U.S. priorities. One indicator is that American presidents have traveled to Pakistan just four times in fifty-three years; only Eisenhower in 1959 and Nixon ten years later paid state visits. Johnson touched down briefly at Karachi airport in December 1967, and Clinton spent just a little over five hours in

Islamabad during his March 2000 South Asia trip. In contrast, Pakistani leaders have traveled to Washington twenty-one times, twelve of these for state or official visits.[2]

The Pakistanis have also made a special effort to cultivate U.S. political leaders and government officials. Although on the whole quite successful in dealing with Americans, they have made some serious mistakes. Two, in particular, produced major negative consequences for Pakistan. Gen. Ayub Khan charmed Washington in the 1950s with his straight talk. Yet, in the 1960s—reacting to U.S. military aid to India—Ayub first jeopardized Pakistan's economic development progress, largely dependent on American assistance, by moving closer to the Chinese than Lyndon Johnson found acceptable. Then, in 1965, Ayub lost U.S. military help and, for a while, economic assistance as well by allowing himself to be swayed by hawks like Zulfikar Ali Bhutto into plunging Pakistan into war with India over Kashmir.

During the Carter administration in the late 1970s, bilateral troubles were perhaps unavoidable. This was not the case for the events that triggered the imposition of Pressler amendment sanctions in 1990. Among the troika that ruled Pakistan after Zia died, only Prime Minister Benazir Bhutto was adept in handling Americans. But she did not have a decisive voice in nuclear policy—which lay with the other two troika members, Army chief Gen. Mirza Aslam Beg and President Ghulam Ishaq Khan. Neither of these men was skilled in dealing with Washington and they ignored Bush administration warnings that Pressler amendment sanctions would be imposed if the nuclear program advanced. By not heeding these cautions, Pakistan lost its chance to enjoy the continued flow of American military and economic aid while maintaining its unacknowledged nuclear weapons capability.

Theoretically, the close links with the United States ruptured in 1990 by the imposition of Pressler sanctions could have been restored in 1998 if Nawaz Sharif had desisted from matching India's nuclear tests. Given the lack of U.S. credibility and the highly emotional public opinion in then-democratic Pakistan in favor of testing, it would have taken a far shrewder and tougher leader than Sharif to have refrained from following India's example by conducting Pakistan's own tests.

These instances are only some examples of the United States's limited ability to influence Pakistan's policies. Time and again Washington has been shown to have no clothes in dealing with its erstwhile ally, unable to translate superior military, political, and economic strength into effective policy leverage with Islamabad. Even though pressed hard by Kennedy and Johnson after 1962, Ayub went his own way with China; then Zulfikar Bhutto, Zia, and their successors moved ahead with the nuclear program against all kinds of U.S. pressure. In more recent years, Pakistan has rebuffed repeated U.S. urgings to reduce its not-so-covert support for Kashmiri insurgents, to rein in Islamic extremists linked to terrorism, and to take a harder line with the Afghan Taliban.

This inability to sway Pakistan's policies should not be put down to a failure of diplomacy. It stems more from the fact that American and Pakistani perceptions of what is best for Pakistan and its national security have not been the same, especially where India is concerned. As then–secretary of state Dean Rusk wrote after his May 1963 South Asia trip, "fear, distrust, and hatred of India" mean "we cannot rely on Pakistan to act rationally and in what we think would be in its own interest."[3] That remains as true nearly four decades later as it was in 1963. When pushed to the wall, Pakistan has pursued its interests as it, not the United States, has seen them, even if though this has meant the costly loss of American military and economic assistance.

Impact on Pakistan of U.S. Security Engagement

Notwithstanding the failures noted above and the consequent ups and downs—and varied intensity—of U.S. security engagement with Pakistan, that involvement has had a profound impact on the sometime American ally. In the 1950s, early in the life of the new state, U.S. military aid reinforced the position of the army, which eventually seized power in 1958. The Pakistani military has ruled the country for half its existence and, after the October 1999 coup, is back in power for the fourth time. Yet, it would be wrong to conclude that the alliance with the United States was to blame for the failure of democracy to take hold in Pakistan in the 1950s. The weakness of the Muslim League after the deaths of Mohammed Ali Jinnah and Liaquat Ali Khan and the antidemocratic leanings of the West Pakistani elite were more important factors in explaining the collapse of civilian rule. It is hard to see that events in Karachi would have unfolded very differently if the Eisenhower administration had decided against extending military aid in 1954.

It is also true, however, that American arms assistance greatly bolstered the confidence and prowess of the professional military, enabling Pakistan to develop a larger and more capable defense force than the country could have afforded on its own. Along with India's poor showing in the 1962 border war with China and in the 1965 Rann of Kutch encounter with Pakistan, the enhanced military strength contributed to the overconfidence that led the usually cautious Ayub to blunder into the 1965 war with India.

Although Washington soon eased the resultant arms embargo, it was not until a decade and a half later, after the Red Army entered Afghanistan, that large-scale aid was resumed. The renewed flow improved Pakistan's military posture, even though Zia failed to take advantage of the opportunity to build up indigenous defense production capabilities. The cutoff of government-to-government arms transfers through the application of Pressler amendment sanctions in 1990 was costly, especially when coupled with the parallel loss of U.S. development assistance. The negative impact was amplified when new sanctions imposed after the 1998 nuclear tests went a step further and barred commercial arms purchases.

On the security front, a second significant area of U.S. engagement that has had mixed results was covert aid for the Afghan resistance. Even though the partnership between the Central Intelligence Agency and the Inter-Services Intelligence Directorate (ISI) proved highly successful in combating the Soviets and ultimately ousting them from Afghanistan, the unintended consequences—apart from the tremendous burden imposed by several million refugees—have caused great harm to Pakistan and nurtured a new breed of terrorists, the best known of whom is Osama bin Laden. The enormous inflow of arms into the region under the covert program was also an important cause of the violence and lawlessness that wracked Pakistan during the 1990s. Covert aid, in addition, strengthened the hand of the ISI, Pakistan's main intelligence agency, which has continued to fan the flames of Islamic extremism since the Soviets pulled out of Afghanistan.

U.S. acquiescence in the ISI's channeling of most arms aid to fundamentalist resistance fighters was perhaps understandable during the struggle against the Soviet occupation. Once the Red Army pulled out, however, the Bush administration erred in walking away from Afghanistan. The United States was remiss in failing to press harder for a peace settlement and in not opposing more emphatically continued

ISI backing for Islamic extremists. More vigorous U.S. engagement might not have averted the tragic civil war that spawned the Taliban and provided a haven for bin Laden. Nevertheless, given previous deep U.S. involvement and the threat ultimately posed to U.S. national interests and regional stability, Washington made a bad mistake in not trying much more energetically to stabilize Afghanistan after the Soviets left.

Pakistani and U.S. Perceptions

From the Pakistani perspective, the legacy of past dealings with the Americans has been negative. A sense of resentment and distrust of the United States pervades Islamabad. Many Pakistanis sincerely believe that their country has been unfairly and unjustly treated. Three main complaints were repeatedly pointed out to this author: first, Washington's refusal to help Pakistan during the 1965 war with India; second, the United States's discarding of Pakistan "like a used Kleenex" when it was no longer needed after the Afghan war; and, third, the discriminatory nature of U.S. nuclear sanctions, which—until the May 1998 nuclear tests—hit only Pakistan and did not affect India.

Paradoxically, in spite of this disenchantment and the absence of bilateral security and economic assistance programs for nearly a decade, the sole remaining superpower casts a long shadow over Islamabad. There is a popular saying among Pakistanis, only half in jest, that their country's fate is determined by three As: Allah, the army, and America. The fact is that this wobbly developing country, still insecure after more than half a century of independence, continues to yearn for a closer relationship with the United States.

The resulting ambivalence plays itself out graphically in the contrasting attitudes of different social groups. A desire for the American connection remains especially strong among the English-speaking elite who run the country: senior military and civil service officials, rural landlords, and urban business executives. They have strong personal ties to the United States through educational, official, and commercial contacts, through family links with the burgeoning Pakistani-American community (Gen. Pervez Musharraf's brother is a U.S. citizen), and through the shared use of English. Members of these upper reaches of Pakistani society may sincerely bemoan in public and in private U.S. policy toward their country. Yet, they send their children to American colleges and graduate schools, prefer business and investment ties with the United States, and, as possible, promote enhanced political and military liaison with Washington.

The situation is quite different with most non-English speakers, the large majority of Pakistanis. If literate, they read the harder-line Urdu-language press, not the more moderate English-language media. They also hold a more negative view of the United States as unfriendly, even hostile, toward Pakistan and toward the Muslim world in general. Even though foreign policy has largely been the domain of the elite, the views of the "man in the street" in Karachi, Lahore, Rawalpindi, Peshawar, and Quetta have importance, particularly as Pakistan's society has grown more open in the past decade.

In contrast, the proverbial American "man in the street" hardly puts Pakistan high on his list of overseas concerns. Nonetheless, there have been extensive contacts over the years between the two countries' peoples, in different spheres and at various levels, especially between the military, intelligence, economic development, and business communities. These encounters have generally been positive—in contrast with the often more difficult and prickly dealings between Americans and Indians. Until recent years, in spite of the wide swings in the bilateral relationship, Pakistan's image remained positive on Capitol Hill and with the U.S. media. Of late, however, these good feelings about "our old ally" have been increasingly tarnished by growing concerns about an erratically led and unstable Pakistan chronically given to military rule, armed with nuclear weapons—and possibly drifting toward Islamic fundamentalism.

As the Twenty-first Century Begins

From the American perspective, relations with Pakistan have come full circle from half a century ago. When Pakistan gained its independence in 1947, the United States wished it well but perceived few compelling positive interests. The main policy concerns were negative: fear that renewed fighting with India over Kashmir would result in further large-scale human suffering and that this would cause instability in another major region of Asia.

As the new century gets under way, the United States similarly wishes Pakistan well but similarly perceives few compelling positive interests. The main concerns, as in 1947, are negative. The United

States fears that renewed conflict with India—over Kashmir again—could trigger the first use of atomic weapons since 1945 and cause a South Asian nuclear holocaust with incalculable consequences. The United States worries that an economically weak Pakistan might export nuclear technology. Washington is troubled by the failure of democracy, the return of military rule, and the threat of Islamic extremism.

For Pakistan, there are fewer parallels with 1947. The hope then that the United States would serve as a stable source of security and economic help has vanished in the many twists and turns of the bilateral relationship. The bright promise on which Pakistan was founded has also vanished in the country's disappointing and often sad first half-century. Chronic political instability, failure to realize economic potential, a poor record in meeting basic human needs, and the continuing fixation on India have left Pakistan teetering on the edge of national failure.

So, what of the future for these allies of yesteryear? After the wide swings of the past half-century, predicting what will happen next is hazardous. What we can note are certain constants that will remain influential. Geography continues to give Pakistan strategic importance as the junction of western, southern, and central Asia. It is a large Muslim state with a population of nearly 150 million. The coming to power of an extremist Islamic regime in Pakistan, as has happened in Afghanistan, would have a profoundly negative impact not only on the subcontinent, but throughout the Islamic world. Helping to avoid such a development is clearly an important U.S. interest.

Now that Pakistan and its traditional enemy, India, have declared themselves to be nuclear weapons states, their chronic tensions have assumed a vastly more dangerous significance. How Islamabad and New Delhi manage their nuclear rivalry will have an impact far beyond the subcontinent. Indeed, averting a nuclear holocaust on the subcontinent has become a key U.S. policy goal, one that ensures that the United States will remain engaged with Pakistan in the years to come.

When President Clinton met General Musharraf in March 2000, the two leaders—and their governments' policies—differed over major issues: how best to deal with the Kashmir dispute with India, with the Taliban and other Islamic extremists, and with the nuclear question. If Washington and Islamabad are unable to narrow these differences, the bilateral frictions of recent years are likely to continue and perhaps even worsen. Should Islamabad temper its obsession with India and

Notes

Chapter 1. The United States and the Pakistan Movement

1. Consulate Karachi dispatch to State Department, August 8, 1947, 845F.00/8-847, Department of State Records (DSR), National Archives (NA), College Park, Maryland.

2. Ibid.

3. Phillips Talbot letter to Institute of Current World Affairs (ICWA), New York City, August 19, 1947.

4. Mildred Talbot letter to ICWA, August 27, 1947.

5. Ibid.

6. Embassy Karachi telegram to State Department, August 14, 1947, 845F.00/8-1447, DSR, NA.

7. Mildred Talbot letter to ICWA, August 27, 1947.

8. Stanley Wolpert, *Jinnah of Pakistan* (New York: Oxford University Press, 1984), 342.

9. Embassy Karachi dispatch to State Department, August 15, 1947, 845F.00/8-1547, DSR, NA.

10. Phillips Talbot letter to ICWA, August 19, 1947.

11. *Time,* August 25, 1947, 31–32.

12. Betty Miller Unterberger, "American Views of Mohammed Ali Jinnah and the Pakistan Liberation Movement," *Diplomatic History* 5 (1981), 313–14; and Iftikhar H. Malik, *U.S.–South Asian Relations, 1940–47: American Attitudes towards the Pakistan Movement* (London: Macmillan, 1991), 238–39.

13. *New York Times,* October 6, November 5, 6, 7, 8, December 9 and 14, 1939.

14. John Gunther, *Inside Asia* (New York: Harper and Brothers, 1939), 466.

15. Consulate General Calcutta dispatches to State Department, April 5, 1940, 845.00/1174, and April 5, 1941, 845.00/1226, DSR, NA.

16. See Dennis Kux, *India and the United States: Estranged Democracies, 1941–91* (Washington, D.C.: National Defense University Press, 1993), 12–21, for discussion of the Cripps mission and the considerable, if unsuccessful, U.S. involvement.

17. Roosevelt to Churchill, April 11, 1942, *Foreign Relations of the United States [FRUS], 1942,* Vol. 1, 633–34.

18. Gary Hess, *America Meets India* (Baltimore: Johns Hopkins University Press, 1979), 82.

19. *New York Times,* October 4, 1942. See also *New York Times* articles by Herbert Matthews on September 9, 1942, and February 7, April 25 and 26, and May 7 and 8, 1943.

20. Sir Ronald Campbell to Alexander Cadogan, August 5, 1942, quoted in Nicholas Mansergh, ed., *The Transfer of Power* (London: Her Majesty's Stationery Office, 1970–83), Vol. 1, 576–77.

21. William Phillips, *Ventures in Diplomacy* (Boston: Beacon, 1952), 373.

22. Ibid., 359.

23. *FRUS, 1942,* Vol. 1, 720–21.

24. Reports of Davies conversations with Jinnah, May 22, 1942, 845.00/1357, and February 18, 1943, 845.00/1852, enclosures to Mission New Delhi dispatches to State Department, DSR, NA.

25. Press statement by Acting Secretary Joseph Grew, January 29, 1945, *FRUS, 1945,* Vol. 6, 249.

26. State Department telegram to Embassy London, May 17, 1945, 845.00/5-1745, DSR, NA.

27. Office of Near Eastern and African Affairs memorandum to Undersecretary of State Acheson, March 27, 1946, 845.00/5-2746, DSR, NA.

28. Ibid.

29. *Time,* April 22, 1946, 28–31.

30. Mission New Delhi telegram to State Department, May 1, 1946, 845.00/5-146, DRS, NA.

31. Mission New Delhi dispatch to State Department, June 7, 1946, 845.00/6-746, DSR, NA.

32. Consulate General Calcutta airmail report to State Department, August 19, 1946, 845.00/8-2246; and Embassy London telegram to State Department, 845.00/8-2246, DSR, NA.

33. State Department press statement, August 27, 1946, DSR, NA.

34. Acheson memorandum to President Truman, August 30, 1946, 845.00/9-346, DSR, NA.

35. Memorandum of conversation between Acheson, Loy Henderson, Begum Shah Nawaz, and M. A. H. Ispahani, November 14, 1946, 845.00/11-1446, DSR, NA.

36. M. A. H. Ispahani, *Quaid-e-Azam Jinnah as I Knew Him* (Karachi: Royal Book Company, 1976), 240–41.

37. Z. H. Zaidi, ed., *M. A. Jinnah–Ispahani Correspondence, 1936–1948* (Karachi: Forward Publications Trust, 1976), 503.

38. Henderson memorandum to Acheson, November 26, 1946, 845.00/11-1246, DSR, NA.

39. State Department telegram to Embassy London, November 30, 1946, *FRUS, 1946,* Vol. 5, 97–98.

40. Secretary of State to Embassy London, December 3, 1946, *FRUS, 1946,* Vol. 5, 99–100.

41. Embassy London telegram to State Department, December 12, 1946, *FRUS, 1946,* Vol. 5, 104.

42. State Department telegram to Embassy New Delhi, December 19, 1946, *FRUS, 1946,* Vol. 5, 106.

43. Embassy Delhi telegrams to State Department, December 27 and 29, 1946, *FRUS, 1946,* Vol. 5, 106–9 and 109–12.

44. Embassy New Delhi cable to State Department, January 4, 1947, *FRUS, 1947,* Vol. 3, 136–37.

45. Consulate Karachi cable to State Department, January 6, 1947, *FRUS, 1947,* Vol. 3, 137–38.

46. Memorandum of conversation between Secretary of State and British ambassador, February 20, 1947, *FRUS, 1947,* Vol. 3, 143–44.

47. State Department press release, February 25, 1947, text reprinted in *Department of State Bulletin,* March 7, 1947, 450.

48. Embassy New Delhi cable to State Department, May 2, 1947, *FRUS, 1947,* Vol. 3, 154–55.

49. Ibid.

50. State Department press release, June 10, 1947, text reprinted in *Department of State Bulletin,* June 22, 1947, 1249–50.

51. Embassy New Delhi cable to State Department, July 2, 1947, 845.00/7-247, DSR, NA.

52. Consulate Karachi cable to State Department, June 21, 1947, 845.00/6-2147, DSR, NA.

53. Embassy New Delhi cable to State Department, July 2, 1947, *FRUS, 1947,* Vol. 3, 158.

54. State Department telegram to Embassy New Dehli, July 7, 1947, 159–60.

55. Embassy New Delhi cable to State Department, July 11, 1947, *FRUS, 1947,* Vol. 3, 161–62; and unpublished memoirs of Henry Grady, Harry S. Truman Library, Independence, Missouri.

56. Embassy New Delhi dispatch to State Department, April 22, 1947, 845.00/4-2247, DSR, NA.

Chapter 2. Truman: Friends, Not Allies

1. Interview with Agha Hilaly, Karachi, January 31, 1996; and Embassy Karachi to State Department, February 26, 1948, 845F.00/2-2648, DSR, NA.

2. Consulate General Lahore cable to State Department, October 2, 1947, 845F.00/10-247, DSR, NA.

3. Embassy Karachi dispatch to State Department, October 27, 1947, 845F.00/10-2747, DSR, NA.

4. Ibid.

5. Embassy Karachi to State Department, September 16, 1947, 845F.00/9-1647, DSR, NA.

6. Embassy Karachi dispatch to State Department, October 27, 1947, 845F.00/10-2747, DSR, NA.

7. Embassy Karachi dispatch to State Department, March 6, 1948, 845F.00/3-648, DSR, NA. Simons's son, Thomas W. Simons, Jr., served as U.S. ambassador to Pakistan in 1995–98.

8. Embassy Kabul to State Department, August 26, 1947, 890H51/8-2647, DSR, NA.

9. Minutes of meeting of the Emergency Committee of the Cabinet, September 11, 1947, 67/CF/47, National Documentation Centre (NDC), Islamabad.

10. Minutes of cabinet discussion, September 9, 1947, 67/CF/47, NDC.

11. Embassy Karachi to State Department, September 2, 1947, 845F.00/9-247, DSR, NA.

12. Minutes of meeting of the Emergency Committee of the Cabinet, September 11, 1947.

13. Pakistani Embassy memorandum to Assistant Secretary of State for Economic Affairs Willard Thorp, November 28, 1947, Pakistan Request for Economic Assistance, SOA Lot File, DSR, NA. In 1947, $2 billion was an enormous sum. During the five years of the Marshall Plan, U.S. aid to Western Europe totaled only $11.5 billion.

14. Memorandum from Acting Secretary of State to Ambassador Ispahani, December 17, 1947, *Foreign Relations of the United States [FRUS], 1947,* Vol. 3, 172–74.

15. Embassy Karachi to State Department, January 2, 1948, 845F.00/1-248, DSR, NA.

16. Embassy New Delhi to State Department, December 29, 1947, 845F.00/12-2947, DSR, NA.

17. Foreign Office to British diplomatic missions, January 2, 1948, DO 22/3162, Public Record Office (PRO), London.

18. Embassy New Delhi to State Department, December 29, 1947, 845F.00/12-2749, DSR, NA.

19. British Mission to the UN to Foreign Office, January 13, 1948, FO 371/69706, PRO.

20. Memorandum of conversation of meeting with Acting Secretary Lovett, January 10, 1948, *FRUS, 1948,* Vol. 5, pt. 1, 276–78.

21. U.S. Mission to United Nations (USUN) to State Department, January 28, 1948, *FRUS, 1948,* Vol. 5, pt. 1, 291–92.

22. Embassy Karachi to State Department, March 1, 1948, 845F.00/3-148, DSR, NA.

23. Embassy Karachi to State Department, April 10, 1948, *FRUS, 1948,* Vol. 5, pt. 1, 328–30.

24. State Department to Embassies New Delhi and Karachi, April 10 and 17, 1948, *FRUS, 1948,* Vol. 5, pt. 1, 330, 334–35.

25. Embassy Karachi to State Department, April 17, 1948, *FRUS, 1948,* Vol. 5, pt. 1, 335–36.

26. David Newsom letter to his mother, February 26, 1948, copy provided to author by Newsom. Newsom had recently arrived in Karachi for his first assignment. Three decades later, during the Carter administration, he would become undersecretary of state for political affairs, the top position normally held by career foreign service officers.

27. Ibid.

28. Embassy Karachi to State Department, March 22, 1948, 845F.00/3-2247, DSR, NA.

29. Ibid.

30. Interviews with Harold Josef and David Newsom, Washington, D.C., January 11 and February 17, 1995.

31. Embassy Karachi to State Department, August 17, 1948, 845F.00/8-1748, DSR, NA.

32. Stanley Wolpert, *Jinnah of Pakistan* (New York: Oxford University Press, 1984), 366–70; and interview with Brigadier Noor Hussain, Rawalpindi, November 26,

1995. Hussein, the military aide to Jinnah in 1947–48, had traveled with him on the last journey to Karachi.

33. Embassy Karachi to State Department, September 24, 1948, 845F.00/9-2448, DSR, NA.

34. *Time,* September 27, 1948, 36–39.

35. "A Year of Independence" (editorial), *New York Times,* August 17, 1948.

36. Embassy Karachi to State Department, September 27, 1948, 845F.00/9-2748, DSR, NA.

37. Embassy Karachi (Huddle) to State Department, July 15 and August 10, 1948, and Embassy New Delhi (Huddle) to State Department, July 19, 21, 27, and August 16, 1948, *FRUS, 1948,* Vol. 5, pt. 1, 349–53, 358, 362–65.

38. Embassy New Delhi (Huddle) to State Department, August 23 and September 10, 1948, and Embassy Karachi (Huddle) to State Department, August 31 and September 6, 1948, *FRUS, 1948,* Vol. 5, pt. 1, 366–67, 371–72, 376–79.

39. Embassy Karachi to State Department, September 10 and 24, 1948, *FRUS, 1948,* Vol. 5, pt. 1, 379–84, 405–10.

40. Embassy Paris (Marshall) to State Department, October 29, 1948, *FRUS, 1948,* Vol. 5, pt. 1, 435–36.

41. Memorandum of conversation between Secretary Marshall and Sir Alexander Cadogan, Paris, November 10, 1948, *FRUS, 1948,* Vol. 5, pt. 1, 445–48.

42. Embassy Paris (USUN) to State Department, November 23, 1948, *FRUS, 1948,* Vol. 5, pt. 1, 459–60.

43. U.S. Rep to UNCIP (Paris) to State Department, November 30, 1948, *FRUS, 1948,* Vol. 5, pt. 1, 466–67.

44. U.S. Rep to UNCIP (Paris) to State Department, December 12, 1948, *FRUS, 1948,* Vol. 5, pt. 1, 475–76, 479.

45. Embassy Karachi to State Department, September 23, 1948, 845F.00/9-2348, and September 24, 1948, 845F.00/9-2448, DSR, NA.

46. The reorganization, which reflected the vastly increased U.S. global role in the postwar years, created four regional bureaus to manage political dealings: Europe; the Far East; the Middle East, South Asia, and Africa; and Latin America.

47. Interview with George McGhee, Middlebury, Va., March 2, 1995.

48. State Department to Embassy London, forwarding message to Foreign Secretary Bevin from Acheson, July 30, 1949, *FRUS, 1949,* Vol. 6, 1728–29.

49. State Department to Embassy Karachi, August 25, 1949, *FRUS, 1949,* Vol. 6, 1733–34.

50. Embassy Karachi to State Department, September 8, 1949, *FRUS, 1949,* Vol. 6, 1740–41.

51. Embassy New Delhi to State Department, September 8, 1949, *FRUS, 1949,* Vol. 6, 1736–38; and interview with McGhee.

52. Memorandum of conversation between Acheson and Zafrullah Khan, September 15, 1949, *FRUS, 1949,* Vol. 6, 1744–45.

53. Interview with Howard Meyers, Washington, D.C., June 7, 1995. According to Meyers, the Kashmir issue was entirely handled within the State Department. Neither the Defense Department, nor the Central Intelligence Agency, nor the National Security Council staff played any role. Secretary Acheson personally handled coordination with President Truman.

54. Interview with McGhee.

55. British Deputy High Commission Lahore to Commonwealth Relations Office (CRO), June 13, 1949, FO 371/76093, PRO.

56. Discussion of the Liaquat "non-trip" to the Soviet Union is based on interviews with Ambassador Sajjad Hyder, Lahore, April 23, 1996, and Ambassador Tanvir Ahmed Khan, Islamabad, May 5, 1998; Sajjad Hyder, "The Visit That Never Was," *The Muslim* (Islamabad), October 30, 1982; Tanvir Ahmed Khan, "An Aborted Moscow Interlude," *The News* (Islamabad), June 11, 1994; Hasan Zaheer, *The Rawalpindi Conspiracy, 1951* (Karachi: Oxford University Press, 1998), 227–33; and documents available in the British and U.S. diplomatic archives. For the more traditional view of the episode, see Hafeez Malik, *Soviet-Pakistan Relations and Post-Soviet Dynamics, 1947–92* (London: Macmillan, 1994), 40–44.

57. British High Commission Karachi to CRO, June 10, 1949; and CRO circular telegram of June 24, 1950, FO 371/76093, PRO.

58. Quoted in Farooq Naseem Bajwa, *Pakistan and the West: The First Decade, 1947–1957* (Karachi: Oxford University Press, 1996), 22.

59. Memoranda from Assistant Secretary McGhee to the Secretary, September 12, 1949, and to Undersecretary Dean Rusk, October 18, 1949, Bureau of Near Eastern, South Asian, and African Affairs (NEA), Assistant Secretary Files, George McGhee Files, Pakistan, DSR, NA; memorandum from Secretary Acheson to President Truman, November 4, 1949, President's Secretary's Files (PSF), Pakistan; and note regarding November 17, 1949, discussion with President Truman about the Liaquat invitation, memoranda of conversation, Acheson Papers, Harry S Truman Library (HSTL), Independence, Missouri. See also George McGhee, *Envoy to the Middle World* (New York, Harper and Row, 1983), 88–93.

60. Many Pakistanis regard (in the author's view incorrectly) the aborted Liaquat trip to Moscow as a major milestone in Pakistan's foreign policy shift toward the West. See, for example, Ayesha Jalal, *The State of Martial Rule* (Lahore: Vanguard, 1991), 110–11; and S. M. Burke and Lawrence Ziring, *Pakistan's Foreign Policy: An Historical Analysis* (Karachi: Oxford University Press, 1990), 99–101.

61. Zaheer, *Rawalpindi Conspiracy,* 228–30.

62. U.K. High Commission Karachi to CRO, October 24, 1949, FO 371 76094, PRO.

63. One can only speculate what lay behind Moscow's action until the Soviet archives are opened.

64. Note regarding phone call from President Truman, March 31, 1950, memoranda of conversation, Acheson Papers, HSTL.

65. State Department background memoranda on the visit to the United States of Liaquat Ali Khan, April 14, 1950, President's Secretary's File, HSTL. It is interesting to contrast this forty-one-page paper with the voluminous briefing books prepared today for state visits.

66. Interview with McGhee.

67. British CRO Note on the Liaquat Visit, June 30, 1950, PREM 1216, PRO.

68. Interview with State Department officer David Newsom, who handled press relations during the Liaquat visit; letter about the trip from Newsom to U.S. Ambassador to Pakistan Avra Warren, May 27, 1950, Liaquat Trip File, SOA Office File, DSR, NA; and British Embassy Washington to Foreign Office, June 1, 1950, DO 35/2981, PRO.

69. Joseph A. Loftus, "Liaquat Ali Seeks Arms for Pakistan," *New York Times,* May 5, 1950; and British Embassy Washington to Foreign Office, June 26, 1950, DO 35/2981, PRO.

70. Richard H. Parke, "Jersey Blast Toll 4 Dead, 22 Missing; Loss Is in Millions," *New York Times,* May 21, 1950; and "Disaster: The Last Shipment," *Time,* May 29, 1950, 20–21.

71. CRO note regarding the Liaquat visit, June 30, 1950, PREM 1216, PRO.

72. Interview with McGhee, Washington, D.C., August 14, 1991.

73. Ibid., and McGhee, *Envoy to the Middle World,* 98–107, 290–98.

74. Hanson Baldwin, "Liaquat Ali Off for U.S.," *New York Times,* May 3, 1950.

75. British Embassy Washington letter to Foreign Office, June 1, 1950, DO 35/2981, PRO.

76. State Department to Embassy Karachi, July 1, 1950, *FRUS, 1950,* Vol. 7, 274–75; and memorandum of conversation between Secretary Acheson and Ambassador Ispahani, July 5, 1950, Acheson Papers, HSTL.

77. Memorandum of conversation between Ghulam Mohammed and Ambassador Phillip Jessup, July 17, 1950, NEA, George McGhee Files, Pakistan, DSR, NA; and State Department to Embassy Karachi, May 11, 1951, and Embassy Karachi to State Department, May 15, 1951, *FRUS, 1951,* Vol. 6, pt. 2, 2203–5.

78. Truman had chosen Merle Cochran to replace Alling, but Cochran's arrival in Pakistan was delayed after he became involved in trying to settle the dispute over independence for the Dutch East Indies. Eventually, Truman named Warren, who had earlier served in India and been Ambassador to Finland.

79. State Department to Embassy Karachi, May 14, 1951, *FRUS, 1951,* Vol. 6, pt. 2, 2505–6.

80. Interview with Agha Hilaly, Karachi, January 31, 1996. At the time, Hilaly was serving in a senior post in the Foreign Ministry.

81. Embassy Karachi to State Department, August 13 and 15, 1950, and Embassy New Delhi to State Department, August 11, 1950, *FRUS, 1950,* Vol. 5, 1420–23. The messages reported briefings by Dixon on his talks.

82. Embassy Karachi to State Department, August 21, 1950, *FRUS, 1950,* Vol. 5, 1423–25.

83. Embassy New Delhi to State Department, August 28, 1950, and Embassy Karachi to State Department, August 30, 1950, *FRUS, 1950,* Vol. 6, pt. 2, 1427–31.

84. Interview with Meyers.

85. Embassy New Delhi to State Department, September 5, 1951, FRUS, 1951, Vol. 6, pt. 2, 1830–31.

86. Memorandum for the President from Dean Acheson, October 22, 1951, PSF, Pakistan, HSTL.

87. USUN to State Department, October 19, 1951, memorandum on Kashmir from McGhee to Acheson, November 7, 1951, and USUN (Paris) to State Department, December 10, 1951, *FRUS, 1951,* Vol. 6, pt. 2, 1886–92, 1897–98, and 1911.

88. USUN cable to State Department, January 17, 1952, *FRUS, 1952–54,* Vol. 9, 1172–73.

89. Embassy Karachi to State Department, April 28, 1952, *FRUS, 1952–54,* Vol. 9, 1240–41.

90. Memorandum of conversation between Admiral Nimitz and Acting Secretary Bruce, May 28, 1952, *FRUS, 1952–54,* Vol. 9, 1251.

91. Embassies New Delhi and Karachi to State Department, June 26, 1952, *FRUS, 1952–54,* Vol. 9, 1263–64.

92. State Department to Karachi, July 4, 1952, *FRUS, 1952–54,* Vol. 9, 1269.

93. Embassy Karachi to State Department, July 12, 1952, *FRUS, 1952–54,* Vol. 9, 1279.

94. State Department to Embassy New Delhi, November 20, 1952, *FRUS, 1952–54,* Vol. 9, 1304–6.

95. Embassy Karachi to State Department, December 31, 1947, 845F/12-3147, and January 9, 1948, 845F.00/1-1248, DSR, NA.

96. State Department to Embassies Karachi and Kabul, November 2, 1950, *FRUS, 1952–54,* Vol. 9, 1455.

97. State Department to Embassy Karachi, November 28, 1950, *FRUS, 1952–54,* Vol. 9, 1457–58.

98. Memorandum of conversation between Assistant Secretary McGhee, Chaudhri Mohammed Ali, and Ambassador Ispahani, January 21, 1951, *FRUS, 1951,* Vol. 6, pt. 2, 1934–36.

99. Embassy Karachi to State Department, January 30, 1951, memorandum from McGhee to Acheson, February 1, 1951, State Department to Embassy Karachi, February 2, 1951, and memorandum of conversation between Secretary Acheson, Foreign Minister Zafrullah Khan, and Chaudhri Mohammed Ali, February 13, 1951, *FRUS, 1951,* Vol. 6, pt. 2, 1941–43.

100. Memorandum of conversation between Afghan Minister of Foreign Affairs, Mr. Ludin, Assistant Secretary McGhee, and Chargé Jandrey, Kabul, March 12, 1951, *FRUS, 1951,* Vol. 6, pt. 2, 1949.

101. Memorandum of conversation between Liaquat, McGhee, and Warren, Karachi, March 16, 1951, *FRUS, 1951,* Vol. 6, pt. 2, 1952.

102. State Department to Embassy Karachi, April 6, 1951, and Embassy Karachi to State Department, April 9, 12, 1951, *FRUS, 1951,* Vol. 6, pt. 2, 1954–57.

103. State Department to Embassy Kabul, September 27, 1951, *FRUS, 1951,* Vol. 6, pt. 2, 1190–91.

104. Memorandum for President Truman from Secretary Marshall, March 11, 1948, *FRUS, 1948,* Vol. 5, 496–97.

105. Embassy Karachi (from the military attaché) to the State Department, April 24, 1948, 845F.00/4-2448, DSR, NA.

106. Diplomatic Note from Pakistan Embassy to State Department, October 19, 1948, 845F.00/10-1948 DSR, NA.

107. Memorandum from George McGhee to MAP Coordinator Berkner, July 13, 1949, NEA, George McGhee Files, Pakistan, DSR, NA.

108. Caroe argued in his influential book, *The Wells of Power* (London: Macmillan, 1951), for defending the oil of the Persian Gulf from the northern-tier states—Turkey, Iraq, Iran, and Pakistan—rather than from the Suez Canal, the conventional wisdom at the time.

109. Foreign Office to Embassy Washington, October 13, 1951, FO 371/92875, PRO.

110. Memoranda reporting U.S.-UK Talks in London, February 14, 1951, *FRUS, 1951,* Vol. 6, pt. 2, 1653–64.

111. Interview with McGhee; Minutes and conclusions of South Asia Regional Conference, Nuwara Eliya, Ceylon, March 20, 1951, and State Department Policy Statement for Pakistan, July 1, 1951, *FRUS, 1951,* Vol. 6, pt. 2, 1664, 1666–69, and 2212.

112. U.S.-UK Talks at the Foreign Office with George McGhee, April 3, 1951, FO 371/92875, PRO.

113. Letter from B. A. B. Burrows, British Embassy Washington, to J. D. Murray, Foreign Office, May 2, 1951, FO 371/92875, PRO.

114. McGhee, *Envoy to the Middle World,* 18–24.

115. Memorandum of conversation between M. Ikramullah and Assistant Secretary George McGhee, October 18, 1951, *FRUS, 1951,* Vol. 6, pt. 2, 2220–21.

116. Memorandum of conversation between Ikramullah, Donald Kennedy, and Tom Weil, October 18, 1951, *FRUS, 1951,* Vol. 6, pt. 2, 2222–23.

117. Memorandum of conversation between Secretary Acheson and Ikramullah, October 19, 1951, *FRUS, 1951,* Vol. 6, pt. 2, 2225–26.

118. Memorandum of conversation between Zafrullah Khan and Dean Acheson, November 17, 1951, *FRUS, 1951,* Vol. 6, pt. 2, 2227–28.

119. Interview with Henry Byroade, Bethesda, Maryland, May 3, 1990; and Byroade oral history, Dwight D. Eisenhower Library (DDEL), Abilene, Kansas.

120. Interview with Byroade.

121. Ibid.

122. State Department minutes of DOS-JCS meeting, June 18, 1952, *FRUS, 1952–54,* Vol. 9, pt. 1, 237–38.

123. Briefing memorandum from Byroade to Secretary Acheson, July 17, 1952, 790D.5-MSP/7-17552, DSR; Nazimuddin letter to Acheson, June 23, 1952, 790D.5-MSP/6-2352; memorandum of conversation between Secretary Acheson and Mir Laik Ali, July 18, 1952, 790D.56/7-1852, DSR; and memorandum of conversation between Mir Laik Ali and Secretary of Defense Robert Lovett, July 23, 1952, Record Group 330, CD 092 (Pakistan), Records of Admin. Sec. Office of the Secretary of Defense, NA.

124. Memorandum of conversation between Byroade and Mir Laik Ali, July 31, 1952, 790D.56/7-3152; State Department telegram to Embassy Karachi, August 2, 1952, 790D.5-MSP/8-252, DSR; and interview with Lee Metcalf, Arlington, Va., May 30, 1995. Metcalf was the State Department's Pakistan desk officer at the time.

125. "Pakistan and the Middle East Defence Organisation," Foreign Office paper, August 1952; and CRO London circular telegram to British High Commissioners, November 3, 1952, DO 35/6650, PRO.

126. Foreign Office to Embassy Washington, November 4, 1952, DO 35/6650, PRO.

127. Embassy Washington to Foreign Office, November 15, 1952, DO 35/6650, PRO; and State Department to Embassies Karachi, London, and New Delhi, November 13, 1952, *FRUS, 1952–54,* Vol. 9, pt. 1, 315–17.

128. British Embassy Ankara to Foreign Office, November 21, 1952, and Embassy Paris to Foreign Office, November 7, 1952, DO 35/6650, PRO.

129. Minutes of discussion between CRO Secretary Liesching and Pakistan Foreign Secretary Baig, December 17, 1952, DO 35/6650, PRO; and Embassy New Delhi to State Department, November 20, 1952, *FRUS, 1952–54,* Vol. 9, pt. 1, 318–19.

130. State Department to Embassy New Delhi, November 28, 1952, *FRUS, 1952–54,* Vol. 9, pt. 1, 319.

131. British Embassy Washington (Burrows) letter to Southeast Asia Department, Foreign Office, December 2, 1952, DO 35/6650, PRO.

132. Minutes of November 28, 1952, State/Defense meeting, *FRUS, 1952–54,* Vol. 9, pt. 1, 323–24.

133. State Department to Embassy New Delhi, January 16, 1953, *FRUS, 1952–54,* Vol. 9, pt. 1, 343.

134. Selig S. Harrison, "Pakistan and the United States," *New Republic,* August 10, 1959, 14.

Chapter 3. Eisenhower I: America's Most Allied Ally in Asia

1. Kurt Stiegler, "John Foster Dulles and the 1954 United States–Pakistan Mutual Defense Agreement," Ph.D. diss., Texas A&M University, 1989, 62.

2. January 17, 1947, National Publishers' Association speech, Box 32, Dulles Papers, Harvey Mudd Library, Princeton, New Jersey.

3. Stiegler, "Dulles," 68–69.

4. Dennis Kux, *Estranged Democracies, India and the United States, 1941–1991* (Washington, D.C.: National Defense University Press, 1993), 71.

5. S. M. Burke and Lawrence Ziring, *Pakistan's Foreign Policy: An Historical Analysis* (Karachi: Oxford University Press, 1990), 133–35; and Stiegler, "Dulles," 76–80.

6. Thomas J. Hamilton, "Dulles Will Visit India and Pakistan for Defense Talks," *New York Times,* January 12, 1953.

7. "Mr. Dulles to Asia" (editorial), *New York Times,* January 13, 1953. Syed Amjad Ali, at various times in the 1950s and 1960s Pakistan's finance minister, ambassador to the United States, and representative at the United Nations, told the author that he had made a sustained and successful effort to cultivate the *Times*'s editorial board. Interview with Syed Amjad Ali, Lahore, January 21, 1996.

8. Memorandum of conversation of meeting between Foreign Minister Zafrullah Khan, Ambassador Mohammed Ali Bogra, and John M. Ohley, Office of the Director for Mutual Security, January 28, 1953, *Foreign Relations of the United States (FRUS), 1952–54,* Vol. 11, pt. 2, 1822–24.

9. Memorandum from Assistant Secretary Byroade to Secretary Dulles, March 25, 1953, *FRUS, 1952–54,* Vol. 11, pt. 2, 1825.

10. Undated memorandum to the President from Dulles and Foreign Operations Administrator Harold Stassen, International Series, Whitman File (WF), Dwight D. Eisenhower Library (DDEL), Abilene, Kansas.

11. When Nazimuddin asked the British queen to overturn Ghulam Mohammed's action, the British government quickly decided that the governor-general had not overstepped his authority. Commonwealth Relations Office (CRO) to UK High Commission, Karachi, April 17, 1953, PREM 11/1519, Public Record Office (PRO), London.

12. Embassy Karachi telegrams to the State Department, April 16, 18, 19, and 20, 1953, 790D.00/4-1653, 790D.00/4-1853, 790D.00/4-1953, and 790D.00/4-2053, Department of State Records (DSR), National Archives (NA), College Park, Md.

13. The attacks against the Ahmadiyah sect, which many Muslims considered heretical, prompted the imposition of martial law in Lahore on March 6, 1953. After Nazimuddin floundered about how to respond, Defense Secretary Iskander Mirza, on his own authority, ordered the army to impose martial law. Memorandum of conversation with Zafrullah Khan and Chargé d'Affaires John K. Emmerson, April 7, 1953, transmitted to the State Department as a top secret dispatch on April 10, 1953, 790D.00/4-1653, DSR, NA.

14. American Consulate General Lahore dispatch to State Department, April 28, 1953, 790D.00/4-2853, DSR, NA.

15. Memorandum from State Department Pakistan Desk Officer Lee Metcalf to South Asian Affairs Office Director Don Kennedy, April 21, 1953, Pakistan 1953 folder, SOA Office Files, DSR, NA.

16. Karachi Embassy telegrams to State Department, April 18 and 20, 1953, 790D.00/4-1853 and 790D.00/4-2053, DSR, NA.

17. Dulles's report of his May 22, 1953, meeting with Nehru, *FRUS, 1952–54,* Vol. 9, pt. 2, 119–21.

18. "Assessment of the Soviet Threat to Pakistan and the Armed Forces Needed to Meet This Threat," memorandum dated December 1952, presented to Dulles by Ayub Khan, May 23, 1953, Pakistan 1953 folder, SOA Office Files, DSR, NA.

19. Memorandum of May 23, 1953, meeting between Dulles and Gen. Ayub Khan, *FRUS, 1952–54,* Vol. 9, pt. 1, 132–34.

20. Memorandum of conversation of Lt. Col. Stephen Meade with Governor-General Ghulam Mohammed, May 23, 1953, *FRUS, 1952–54,* Vol. 9, pt. 1, 130–31.

21. Telegram from Dulles to the State Department sent by the Consulate General in Istanbul, May 26, 1953, *FRUS, 1952–54,* Vol. 9, pt. 1, 147.

22. Minutes of June 1, 1953, meeting of National Security Council (NSC), *FRUS, 1952–54,* Vol. 9, pt. 1, 379–83.

23. See *Department of State Bulletin,* June 15, 1953, 835, for text of Dulles's June 1, 1953, radio and television address.

24. Interview with Henry Byroade, June 5, 1990.

25. Dulles testimony, June 2, 1953, U.S. House Committee on Foreign Affairs, *Selected Executive Session Hearings,* 10, 96.

26. "Report by Secretary of State," June 3, 1953, *Executive Session Hearings of the Senate Foreign Relations Committee,* 5, 342.

27. Minutes of July 9, 1953, meeting of the NSC, *FRUS, 1952–54,* Vol. 9, pt. 1, 395–96.

28. Ibid., 403.

29. Interview with Byroade.

30. Ibid.

31. Memorandum of conversation between Dulles and General Ayub at the State Department, September 30, 1953, 790D.5-MSP/9-3053, DSR, NA.

32. Memorandum from Byroade to Assistant Secretary of Defense Frank Nash, October 15, 1953, *FRUS, 1952–54,* Vol. 9, pt. 1, 421.

33. Interview with Byroade.

34. John P. Callahan, "US-Pakistan Talks on Arms Awaited," *New York Times,* November 2, 1953.

35. Briefing memorandum for the President from Dulles, November 11, 1953, International Series, Pakistan, WF, DDEL; memorandum for the record of Ghulam Mohammed's meeting with Secretary Wilson, November 12, 1953, RG 330, 091, 112 Pakistan, ISA, OSD, and memorandum of conversation between Ghulam Mohammed with President Eisenhower, November 12, 1953, 790D.11/11-1353, DSR, NA.

36. Sarvepalli Gopal, *Jawaharlal Nehru: A Biography,* Vol. 2 (London: Jonathan Cape, 1979), 184.

37. Letter of December 1, 1953, Jawaharlal Nehru, *Letters to Chief Ministers,* Vol. 3 (New Delhi: Nehru Memorial Fund, 1984), 454.

38. UK High Commission (New Delhi) telegram to Commonwealth Relations Office (CRO), January 4, 1954, PREM 11/1520, PRO.

39. Eisenhower note to Dulles and Dulles reply, November 16, 1953, JFD Chronological File, Dulles papers, DDEL.

40. Transcript of Eisenhower's November 18 press conference, *New York Times,* November 19, 1953.

41. C. L. Sulzberger, *A Long Row of Candles* (New York: Macmillan, 1969), 920–21.

42. Memorandum of conversation between Secretary Dulles and Afghan Ambassador Ludin, January 5, 1954, *FRUS, 1952–54,* Vol. 11, pt. 2, 1408–9; and State Department telegram to Embassy Kabul, January 11, 1954, 790D.5 MSP/1-1154, DSR, NA.

43. Memorandum of conversation between Anthony Eden and Secretary Dulles, Bermuda, December 7, 1953, FO 371/106937, PRO.

44. Richard M. Nixon, *RN: The Memoirs of Richard Nixon* (New York: Grosset and Dunlap, 1978), 132.

45. Memorandum of conversation between Vice President Nixon, Ghulam Mohammed, and Ambassador Horace Hildreth, Karachi, December 7, 1953, *FRUS, 1952–54,* Vol. 11, pt. 2, 1831–32.

46. Embassy Karachi telegram to State Department, December 8, 1953, *FRUS, 1952–54,* Vol. 11, pt. 2, 1833–35.

47. Minutes of December 24, 1953, NSC meeting, NSC Series, WF, DDEL.

48. "Military Aid to Pakistan," memorandum from Dulles to the President, January 4, 1954, 790D.6/1-454, DSR, NA; and Dulles memorandum of January 5, 1954, meeting, White House Memoranda Series, Dulles Papers, DDEL.

49. Memorandum of January 14, 1954, meeting with the President, *FRUS, 1952–54,* Vol. 9, 453–54.

50. Dana Adams Schmidt, "Pakistan To Get Arms," *New York Times,* February 14, 1954.

51. British Mission Berlin telegram to Foreign Office, January 24, 1954, reporting Dulles-Eden conversation, PREM 11/250, PRO.

52. Interview with Byroade.

53. Stiegler, "Dulles," 101–9.

54. Interview with Byroade.

55. See *New York Times,* February 26, 1954, for the texts of Eisenhower's letter to Nehru and the U.S. government statement on arms aid to Pakistan.

56. Editorial, *New York Times,* December 11, 1953. The *Times* ran further editorials on December 18 and 22, 1953, and January 4, 1954.

57. Text of Bogra statement in UK High Commission Karachi telegram to CRO, February 26, 1954, PREM 11/1320, PRO.

58. Ibid.

59. Memorandum from Byroade and Hickerson to Secretary Dulles, March 14, 1953, and memorandum from Dulles to the President, March 24, 1953, *FRUS, 1952–54,* Vol. 11, pt. 2, 1314, 1316.

60. Memorandum from Eisenhower to Dulles, March 25, 1953, *FRUS, 1952–54,* Vol. 11, pt. 2, 1316.

61. Telegrams from Embassy New Delhi to State Department, April 17 and 23, 1953, and Hoffman letter to Secretary Dulles, April 28, 1953, *FRUS, 1952–54,* Vol. 11, pt. 2, 1316–21.

62. Report of meeting between Nehru and Dulles, May 22, 1953, *FRUS, 1952–54,* Vol. 9, pt. 1, 119–21.

63. Report of meeting between Dulles and Prime Minister Bogra, May 23, 1953, *FRUS, 1952–54,* Vol. 9, pt. 1, 122–23.

64. Memorandum of conversation between Dulles and Zafrullah Khan, Karachi, May 23, 1953, *FRUS, 1952–54,* Vol. 9, pt. 1, 127–29.

65. *US News and World Report,* January 15, 1954; Gopal, *Jawaharlal Nehru,* Vol. 2, 182; and Kux, *Estranged Democracies,* 117.

66. James F. Callahan, "East Pakistan Desires Freedom," *New York Times,* May 23, 1954.

67. Embassy Karachi to State Department, April 9, 1954, *FRUS, 1952–54,* Vol. 9, pt. 1, 493–94.

68. State Department telegram to Embassy Karachi, April 16, 1954, *FRUS, 1952–54,* Vol. 9, pt. 1, 495–97.

69. Letter to Ambassador Hildreth from Deputy Assistant Secretary Jernegan, April 22, 1954, *FRUS, 1952–54,* Vol. 9, pt. 1, 500–502.

70. Robert J. McMahon, *The Cold War on the Periphery: The United States, India, and Pakistan* (New York: Columbia University Press, 1994), 191.

71. Memorandum of conversation between Jernegan and Amjad Ali, August 6, 1954, *FRUS, 1952–54,* Vol. 11, pt. 2, 1860.

72. Embassy Karachi telegram to State Department, August 17, 1954, *FRUS, 1952–54,* Vol. 11, pt. 2, 1864.

73. Memorandum of meeting between Foreign Operations Administrator Stassen, Zafrullah Khan, and Ambassador Amjad Ali, June 22, 1954, *FRUS, 1952–54,* Vol. 11, pt. 2, 1849–50.

74. Report of the Heinz Mission to Pakistan, SOA Director's files, Regional Conference and Country Files, 1951–54, DSR, NA.

75. Memorandum of meeting between Dulles, Mohammed Ali Bogra, Amjad Ali, Henry Byroade, and Nicholas Thacher, October 18, 1954, *FRUS, 1952–54,* Vol. 11, pt. 2, 1868–69.

76. Letter from Ambassador Makins to Foreign Secretary Eden regarding Prime Minister Bogra's U.S. visit, October 1954, FO 371/112307, PRO.

77. State Department aide-mémoire regarding military supply to Pakistan, discussions, October 21, 1954, *Declassified Documents Catalogue,* State Department Library; briefing memorandum from Acting Secretary Herbert Hoover, Jr., to the President for his meeting with Prime Minister Bogra, October 15, 1954, Whitman File, DDEL; and State Department telegram to Embassy Karachi, October 22, 1954, *FRUS, 1952–54,* Vol. 11, pt. 2, 1869–71.

78. Memoranda of conversations between Secretary Dulles, Foreign Minister Naim, and Assistant Secretary Byroade, October 8, 1954, *FRUS, 1952–54,* Vol. 11, pt. 2, 1420–22.

79. Memorandum of conversation between Dulles and Ambassador Ludin, December 28, 1954, *FRUS, 1952–54,* Vol. 11, pt. 2, 1442–43.

80. Memorandum from Byroade to Dulles, July 26, 1954, 689.90D/7-2654, and State Department telegram to Embassy Kabul, July 28, 1954, 689.90D/7-2854, DSR, NA.

81. Robert Trumbell, "Asia Chiefs Split on Liberty Perils," *New York Times,* April 30, 1954.

82. George M. Kahin, *The Asian-African Conference* (Port Washington, N.Y.: Kennikat Press, 1956), 18–20, 57–58.

83. Gary Hess, "The American Search for Stability in Southeast Asia: The SEATO Structure of Containment," in Warren Cohen and Akira Iriye, eds., *The Great Powers in East Asia, 1953–1960* (New York: Columbia University Press, 1990), 283–84.

84. State Department telegram to Embassy Karachi, July 24, 1954, *FRUS, 1952–54,* Vol. 12, pt. 1, 671–72.

85. Report of conversation between Amjad Ali and Jernegan, July 27, 1954, *FRUS, 1952–54,* Vol. 12, pt. 1, 677.

86. Minutes of meeting on SEATO at the State Department, August 5, 1954, *FRUS, 1952–54,* Vol. 12, pt. 1, 707.

87. Interview with Agha Hilaly, Karachi, January 30, 1996.

88. Dulles reiterated his unwillingness to broaden the SEATO shield when he saw Bogra in Washington in October 1954. He made the point again in a December 21, 1954 letter to Bogra in December 1954. *FRUS, 1952–54,* Vol. 11, pt. 2, 1868–69; and *FRUS, 1952–54,* Vol. 11, pt. 1, 1055–56.

89. Foreign Office to British Embassy in Washington, D 1074/541, FO 371/111884, PRO; and Burke and Ziring, *Pakistan's Foreign Policy,* 167.

90. Interview with Hilaly.

91. Ronald Steel, *Walter Lippmann and the American Century* (New York: Random House, 1981), 503–4.

92. Anthony Eden, *Full Circle: The Memoirs of Anthony Eden* (London: Cassell, 1960), 243.

93. Urie Dann, "The Foreign Office, the Baghdad Pact, and Jordan," *Asian and African Studies* (Tel Aviv), November 1987, 247–48.

94. Farooq Naseem Bajwa, *Pakistan and the West: The First Decade, 1947–57* (Karachi: Oxford University Press, 1996), 140–42, 145–48.

95. State Department circular telegram to Embassy Karachi and other posts, October 29, 1955, 954.3124-8-231, cited in Bajwa, *Pakistan and the West,* 168.

96. Mohammed Ayub Khan, *Friends Not Masters* (London: Oxford University Press, 1967), 130.

97. Letter from UK High Commissioner in Karachi to CRO, November 9, 1954, DO 35 5405, and Letter from Acting UK High Commissioner in Karachi to Lord Swinton, CRO Secretary, December 10, 1954, DO 35 5406, PRO.

98. *Time,* November 8, 1954.

99. State Department telegram to Embassy Karachi, November 26, 1954, 611.90D/11-2654, DSR, NA.

100. State Department telegram to Embassy Karachi, March 5, 1955, *FRUS, 1955–57,* Vol. 8, 421–22.

101. Interview with Charles Burton Marshall, Arlington, Va., June 4, 1996.

102. According to Marshall, Mirza stressed "over and over" again in their conversations that Pakistan needed a dictatorship.

103. State Department telegram to Embassy Karachi, April 16, 1955, *FRUS, 1955–57,* Vol. 8, 173–74.

104. *Ibid.,* 188–90, State Department telegrams to Embassy Karachi, July 12 and 18, 1955, *FRUS, 1955–57,* Vol. 8, 188–90.

105. Editorial Note, *FRUS, 1955–57,* Vol. 8, 190–91.

106. Embassy Kabul telegram to State Department, December 21, 1955, *FRUS, 1955–57,* Vol. 8, 212.

107. Memorandum of conversation between Dulles, U.S. Ambassador to Pakistan Hildreth, Assistant Secretary Allen, and Pakistani Prime Minister Mohammed Ali, Karachi, March 7, 1956, *FRUS, 1955–57,* Vol. 8, 221–25.

108. Memorandum of conversation between Secretary Dulles, Ambassador Hildreth, and Governor General Mirza, Karachi, March 9, 1956, *FRUS, 1955–57,* Vol. 8, 226.

109. Embassies Kabul and Karachi telegrams to State Department, May 6 and 22, 1956, Joint State-International Cooperation Administration telegram to Karachi and Kabul, September 25, 1956, and Embassies Kabul and Karachi responses to the State Department, October 2, 1956, *FRUS, 1955–57,* Vol. 8, 240, 243–45.

110. Minutes of NSC Meeting, May 17, 1956, *FRUS, 1955–57,* Vol. 8, 235.

111. Report of a State-JCS staff meeting, January 14, 1955, *FRUS, 1955–57,* Vol. 8, 410–12.

112. Memorandum by Assistant Secretary of Defense H. Struve Hensel, February 17, 1955, *FRUS, 1955–57,* Vol. 8, 418–20.

113. Ibid.

114. Report of the Joint Strategic Plans Committee to JCS, March 24, 1955, cited in McMahon, *The Cold War on the Periphery,* 200–201.

115. Joint State-MAAG-FOA-USIS telegram to State Department, June 30, 1955, *FRUS, 1955–57,* Vol. 8, 430–32.

116. Embassy Karachi telegram to State Department, August 26, 1955, *FRUS, 1955–57,* Vol. 8, 435–37.

117. Embassy Karachi telegram to State Department, September 15, 1955, *FRUS, 1955–57,* Vol. 8, 437–39.

118. Memorandum for JCS Chairman Admiral Radford from Maj. Gen. Robert Cannon, Special Assistant to the Joint Chiefs for MDAP (military assistance programs), August 31, 1955, CJCS 091 Pakistan (31 August 55) Chairman's Files, JCS Records.

119. Consulate General Lahore to State Department, October 4, 1955, *FRUS, 1955–57,* Vol. 8, 445–46.

120. Karachi Embassy telegram to State Department and State Department telegram to Embassy Karachi, November 11, 1955, *FRUS, 1955–57,* Vol. 8, 449–50; Letter from Brig. Gen. Rothwell Brown, Chief of the Military Assistance Advisory Group (MAAG) in Pakistan to Brig. Gen. John K. Wilson, November 18, 1955, CJCS 091 Pakistan, (8-22-46) Chairman's Files, JCS Records.

121. Letter from Undersecretary of State Hoover to Assistant Secretary of Defense for International Security Affairs Gordon Gray, November 5, 1955, *FRUS, 1955–57,* Vol. 8, 446–48; McMahon, *The Cold War on the Periphery,* 204.

122. Gray to Hoover letter, December 5, 1955, and Embassy Karachi telegram to State Department, January 19, 1956, *FRUS, 1955–57,* Vol. 8, 450–52, 454–55.

123. Trip Report of Maj. Gen. R. M. Cannon of visit to the Middle and Far East, Joint Chiefs of Staff, February 10, 1955, *Declassified Documents Catalogue,* State Department Library.

124. Hildreth statement to the press of December 14, 1955, and editorial note regarding March 6–8, 1956, SEATO conference, *FRUS, 1955–57,* Vol. 8, 61, 65–66.

125. Carl McCardle oral history, 132–42, Dulles papers, Harvey Mudd Library, Princeton, New Jersey; and Abe Rosenthal, "U.S. Pledge Given India on Pakistan," *New York Times,* March 10, 1956.

126. Report of meetings between Dulles and Nehru, March 9 and 10, 1956, and Dulles telegram to President Eisenhower, sent from Colombo, March 11, 1956, *FRUS, 1955–57,* Vol. 8, 306–10.

127. Interview with Marshall.

128. Embassy Karachi telegram to State Department, September 24, 1956, *FRUS, 1955–57,* Vol. 8, 470–71.

129. For a participant's account of the episode, see Sir Morrice James, *Pakistan Chronicle* (Karachi: Oxford University Press, 1993), 34–51.

130. *London Daily Telegraph,* November 15, 1956, quoted in Burke and Ziring, *Pakistan's Foreign Policy,* 188.

131. National Intelligence Estimate No. 52–56, November 13, 1956, *FRUS, 1955–57,* Vol. 8, 473–75.

132. Interdepartmental Committee on Certain U.S. Aid Programs "Pakistan," June 19, 1956, NSC Series, Special Assistant for National Security Affairs Records, White House Office Files, DDEL.

133. Report of the January 3, 1957, NSC meeting, *FRUS, 1955–57,* Vol. 8, 25–26.

134. Ibid., 27.

Chapter 4. Eisenhower II: Ike Likes Ayub

1. Stephen E. Ambrose, *Eisenhower: The President* (New York: Simon and Schuster, 1984), 367–68, 377–81.

2. Interviews with Gen. Khalid Mahmud Arif, Lt. Gen. Syed Refaqat, Maj. Gen. Mujibur Rehman, Maj. Gen. Farman Ali, Lt. Gen. Nishat Ahmed, Lt. Gen. Kamal Matinuddin, Brig. Noor Hussain, and Air Marshals Nur Khan and Zulfikar Ali Khan (all retired), Islamabad, Rawalpindi, and Karachi, December 1995–April 1996 and February–May 1998.

3. See Shahid Javed Burki, *Pakistan: The Continuing Search for Nationhood,* 2nd ed. (Boulder, Colo.: Westview, 1991), 122–28, for fuller discussion. The Harvard advisory group was put together by Professor Edward Mason and included well-known economists such as David Bell, who later headed the Bureau of the Budget and the Agency for International Development.

4. Commonwealth Relations Office (CRO) Print, May 14, 1957, based on letter from UK High Commissioner in Karachi, DO 35/5408, Public Record Office (PRO), London.

5. Memorandum of conversation between H. S. Suhrawardy and Sir Gilbert Laithwaite, Commonwealth Relations Secretary, London, February 2, 1957, DO 35 8925, PRO; and interview with C. B. Marshall, June 4, 1996. See also Anwar H. Syed, *China and Pakistan: Diplomacy of an Entente Cordiale* (London: Oxford University Press, 1974) 65–70.

6. Embassy Karachi to State Department, January 2, 1957, *Foreign Relations of the United States (FRUS), 1955–57,* Vol. 8, 106–7.

7. US Mission to the UN (USUN) telegram to State Department, January 10, 1957, *FRUS, 1955–57,* Vol. 8, 107–10.

8. For Eisenhower's views, see Robert H. Ferrell, ed., *The Eisenhower Diaries* (New York: W.W. Norton, 1981), 300. With considerable justification, Suhrawardy told Laithwaite that Menon "was the best friend that Pakistan had in the world." Memorandum of Suhrawardy-Laithwaite conversation, February 2, 1957, CRO, DO 35 8925, PRO.

9. State Department telegram to USUN, January 7, 1956, *FRUS, 1955–57,* Vol. 8, 112.

10. UK High Commission Karachi telegram to CRO, February 23, 1957, DO 35/8925, PRO.

11. Ibid.

12. Macmillan's minutes of his meeting with Nehru and Suhrawardy, July 5, 1957. FO 371/129763, PRO.

13. Dulles memorandum for the president on the Suhrawardy visit, July 7, 1957, International Series, Pakistan, Whitman File, Dwight D. Eisenhower Library (DDEL), Abilene, Kansas.

14. Memorandum reporting meeting between Prime Minister Suhrawardy and Secretary Dulles, July 10, 1957, *FRUS, 1955–57,* Vol. 8, 482–84.

15. Memoranda reporting Suhrawardy's discussions about India-Pakistan relations with Secretary Dulles, July 10 and 12, 1957, *FRUS, 1955–57,* Vol. 8, 138–41.

16. Memorandum reporting Suhrawardy's discussion of Pak-Afghan relations with Secretary Dulles, July 10, 1957, *FRUS, 1955–57,* Vol. 8, 256–57.

17. C. B. Marshall recalled hearing from a senior CIA officer that Suhrawardy had given the green light for the intelligence facility during his meeting with Eisenhower. Similarly, Amjad Ali, Pakistan's ambassador in Washington at the time, wrote in his memoirs that Suhrawardy's personal assistant had advised the embassy staff that the prime minister had agreed to the U.S. facility. Syed Amjad Ali, *Glimpses* (Lahore: Jang Publishers, 1992).

18. Editorial note, *FRUS, 1958–60,* Vol. 15, 615.

19. Macmillan memorandum of conversation with Suhrawardy, July 29, 1957, PREM 11/1025, PRO.

20. Interview with Jules Bassin, Washington, D.C., July 16, 1996. The author also served in Karachi during Langley's tour, but was too junior to gain much insight into the ambassador's views.

21. Letter from Langley to Rountree, December 27, 1957, *FRUS, 1955–57,* Vol. 8, 487–88.

22. Ibid.

23. Embassy Karachi telegrams to State Department, January 2 and 11, 1958, *FRUS, 1958–60,* Vol. 15, 617–18.

24. "Pakistani Leader Berates the West," *New York Times,* March 9, 1958.

25. Embassy Karachi telegram to State Department, April 14, 1958, *FRUS, 1958–60,* Vol. 15, 635.

26. Memorandum reporting discussion of India-Pakistan relations during a meeting between Dulles, Amjad Ali, and General Ayub Khan, April 30, 1958, South Asian Affairs (SOA), General Subject Files, 1957–59, Pakistan 1958, Department of State Records (DSR), National Archives (NA), College Park, Md.

27. Memorandum of conversation at State Department between Finance Minister Amjad Ali and Assistant Secretary Rountree, April 29, 1958, *FRUS, 1958–60,* Vol. 15, 635–41.

28. Memorandum reporting meeting at Pentagon between Ayub, Asghar Khan, and Sprague, April 29, 1958, and meeting between Deputy Assistant Secretary Frank Shruff and Asghar Khan, May 7, 1958, *FRUS, 1958–60,* Vol. 15, 641–45.

29. Mohammed Ayub Khan, *Friends Not Masters* (London: Oxford University Press, 1967), 59; and Altaf Gauhar, *Ayub Khan: Pakistan's First Military Ruler* (Lahore: Sang-e-Meel, 1993), 116–23.

30. Memorandum from Rountree to Secretary Dulles outlining the agreed package plan proposal, April 10, 1958, *FRUS, 1958–60,* Vol. 15, 75–81.

31. Minutes of State-Defense meeting, January 10, 1958, *FRUS, 1958–60,* Vol. 15, 48–49.

32. Letter from Assistant Secretary of Defense Mansfield Sprague to Assistant Secretary of State William Rountree, January 17, 1958, *FRUS, 1958–60,* Vol. 15, 49–51.

33. Dulles's memorandum to Eisenhower is dated April 17, 1958. The president's handwritten response was sent April 21, 1958. *FRUS, 1958–60,* Vol. 15, 81–82.

34. Embassy Karachi telegram to State Department, May 16, 1958, *FRUS, 1958–60,* Vol. 15, 106.

35. Dennis Kux, *India and the United States: Estranged Democracies, 1941–91* (Washington, D.C.: National Defense University Press, 1993), 159.

36. Letter from Nehru to Eisenhower, June 7, 1958, *FRUS, 1958–60,* Vol. 15, 107.

37. Embassy Karachi telegram to State Department, January 31, 1958, and State Department telegram to Embassy Karachi, February 4, 1958, *FRUS, 1958–60,* Vol. 15, 619–22.

38. State Department telegram to Embassy Karachi, May 21, 1958, *FRUS, 1958–60,* Vol. 15, 648.

39. Memorandum of phone call from Dulles to Eisenhower, July 28, 1958, Telephone Call Series, Dulles Papers, DDEL.

40. *Department of State Bulletin,* Vol. 39 (1958), 272–73, for text of London declaration.

41. M. Rafique Afzal, *Political Parties in Pakistan, Vol. 1: 1947–1958* (Islamabad: National Institute of Historical and Cultural Research, 1986), 216–18.

42. Ibid., 208–12.

43. Embassy Karachi telegram to State Department, October 4, 1958, *FRUS, 1958–60,* Vol. 15, 664.

44. Embassy Karachi telegram to State Department, October 5, 1958, *FRUS, 1958–60,* Vol. 15, 664.

45. State Department telegram to Embassy Karachi, October 6, 1958, *FRUS, 1958–60,* Vol. 15, 666–67.

46. Ibid.

47. UK High Commission Karachi telegram to CRO, October 8, 1958, PREM 11/3902, PRO.

48. Eisenhower letter to Mirza, October 11, 1958, and Dulles letter to Mirza, October 17, 1958, *FRUS, 1958–60,* Vol. 15, 673–74 and 677.

49. CRO Print of December 19, 1958, based on UK High Commission report of December 6, 1958, PREM 11/2902, and Karachi High Commission telegram conveying report from "reliable source" who talked with Ayub, DO 35/8955, PRO.

50. M. Rafique Afzal, *Political Parties in Pakistan, Vol. 2: 1958–69* (Islamabad: National Institute of Historical and Cultural Research, 1987), 3–9, for discussion of Ayub Khan's reform program. See also Ayub, *Friends Not Masters,* 85–93 and 98–107.

51. Ayub, *Friends Not Masters,* 207–16, elaborates Ayub's views.

52. Embassy Karachi telegram to State Department, October 31, 1958, *FRUS, 1958–60,* Vol. 15, 681–82.

53. Embassy Karachi telegram to State Department, January 14, 1959, *FRUS, 1958–60,* Vol. 15, 693–95.

54. Embassy Karachi telegram to State Department, January 16, 1959, *FRUS, 1958–60,* Vol. 15, 695.

55. See *Department of State Bulletin,* Vol. 40 (1959), 416–17, for the text of identical bilateral agreements of cooperation between the United States and Turkey, Iran, and Pakistan, signed March 5, 1959.

56. Ayub, *Friends Not Masters,* 126–27.

57. Quoted in *Dawn* (Karachi), May 5, 1959.

58. Elie Abel, "Nehru Sees Risk of Pakistan War," *New York Times,* November 8, 1958.

59. National Intelligence Estimate no. 52–59, "The Outlook for Pakistan," May 5, 1959, *FRUS, 1958–60,* Vol. 15, 709–11.

60. Memorandum from Rountree to Dillon regarding Indus Waters talks, April 28, 1960, and Record of April 30, 1959, NSC meeting, *FRUS, 1958–60,* Vol. 15, 163–64 and 166.. See also Kux, *Estranged Democracies,* 150–51.

61. Memorandum of meeting at the White House between the president, Dillon, and Maj. John Eisenhower, August 11, 1959, and Memorandum for the president, authorizing disbursement of $517 million for the Indus Water agreement, from Dillon, Secretary of the Treasury Robert B. Anderson, and Budget Bureau Director Maurice Stans, *FRUS, 1958–60,* Vol. 15, 178–82.

62. Embassy Karachi telegram to State Department, May 5, 1959, *FRUS, 1958–60,* Vol. 15, 726.

63. Memorandum of conversation between Rountree and Ambassador Aziz Ahmed, May 8, 1959, *FRUS, 1958–60,* Vol. 15, 726–29.

64. Embassy Karachi telegram to State Department, June 22, 1959, *FRUS, 1958–60,* Vol. 15, 734, fn. 2.

65. Embassy Karachi telegram to State Department, June 23, 1959, *FRUS, 1958–60,* Vol. 15, 736.

66. Memorandum of conversation between Ambassador Langley and Undersecretary Dillon, September 17, 1958, *FRUS, 1958–60,* Vol. 15, 660–61.

67. Memorandum of briefing session for Ambassador-designate Rountree, July 30, 1959, *FRUS, 1958–60,* Vol. 15, 747.

68. Memorandum from Assistant Secretary Rountree to Undersecretary Dillon, July 2, 1959, *FRUS, 1958–60,* Vol. 15, 736–40.

69. Talking paper for use by Ambassador-designate Rountree in Pakistan, July 30, 1959, *FRUS, 1958–60,* Vol. 15, 752.

70. Memorandum of conversation between Acting Secretary Dillon and Pakistan Ambassador Aziz Ahmed, July 31, 1959, *FRUS, 1958–60,* Vol. 15, 752–56.

71. Ibid.

72. Dwight D. Eisenhower, *The White House Years: Waging Peace, 1956–61* (Garden City, N.Y.: Doubleday, 1965), 487.

73. Ulysses S. Grant was the first president to visit South Asia, but he did so after he left the White House, during his 1878–79 trip around the world.

74. Russell Baker and Paul Grimes, "Eisenhower Gets a Warm Welcome from Pakistanis," *New York Times,* December 8, 1959.

75. Memorandum of conversation at President Ayub's residence, Karachi, December 8, 1959, *FRUS, 1958–60,* Vol. 15, 781–84. The president, Undersecretary Robert Murphy, Ambassador Rountree, and Gen. Andrew Goodpaster were on the U.S. side; the Pakistani participants were President Ayub, Foreign Minister Qadir, Finance Minister Shoaib, and Foreign Secretary Ikramullah.

76. Ibid., 785–87.

77. Ibid., 787–90. By the time Ayub wrote his autobiography in the late 1960s, he had quite a different view of CENTO, the Chinese, and the Americans.

78. Eisenhower, *Waging Peace,* 495.

79. Memorandum of conversation, December 8, 1959, *FRUS, 1958–60,* Vol. 15, 788–92.

80. Baker and Grimes, "Eisenhower Gets Warm Welcome."

81. Embassy New Delhi telegram to State Department commenting on the Kabul stop, December 10, 1960, *FRUS, 1958–60,* Vol. 15, 325–26.

82. Memorandum of Eisenhower conversation with Franco, December 22, 1959, *FRUS, 1958–60,* Vol. 15, 327.

83. Report of January 11, 1960, meeting with congressional leaders, *FRUS, 1958–60,* Vol. 15, 327.

84. Embassy Athens telegram from Eisenhower to Secretary Herter, December 14, 1959, and State Department telegrams to Embassies Karachi and New Delhi, December 16, 1959, *FRUS, 1958–60,* Vol. 15, 195–97.

85. Embassy Karachi telegram to the State Department, December 23, 1959, *FRUS, 1958–60,* Vol. 15, 197–201.

86. Memorandum of conversation between President Eisenhower and General Franco, Madrid, December 22, 1959, *FRUS, 1958–60,* Vol. 15, 794–95.

87. Eisenhower, *Waging Peace,* 496.

88. State Department telegrams to Embassy Karachi, January 26 and February 19, 1960, *FRUS, 1958–60,* Vol. 15, 796 and 798–99.

89. Interview with William Spengler, Chevy Chase, Md., June 11, 1996.

90. State Department telegram to Embassy Karachi, March 3, 1960, *FRUS, 1958–60,* Vol. 15, 800.

91. Embassy Karachi telegram to the State Department, March 5, 1960, *FRUS, 1958–60,* Vol. 15, 801.

92. Quoted in Michael Beschloss, *Mayday: Eisenhower, Khrushchev and the U-2 Affair,* (New York: Harper and Row, 1986), 60.

93. Report of meeting between Secretary of State Herter and Pakistani Foreign Minister Manzur Qadir, June 2, 1960, *FRUS, 1958–60,* Vol. 15, 812.

94. Beschloss, *Mayday,* 256.

95. Interview with a senior CIA official who dealt with the U-2 question in 1960.

96. Beschloss, *Mayday,* 267–68.

97. *Dawn,* May 18, 1960.

98. Paul Grimes, "Ayub Doubts U.S. Can Act Swiftly," *New York Times,* June 27, 1960.

99. Ayub, *Friends Not Masters,* 161–62; and interview with Agha Shahi, Islamabad, December 31, 1995.

100. Text of Eisenhower statement at September 7, 1960 press conference, *FRUS, 1958–60,* Vol. 15, 212.

Chapter 5. Kennedy: Alliance Troubles

1. John F. Kennedy, "A Democrat Looks at Foreign Policy," *Foreign Affairs,* October 1957, 44–59; *Congressional Record,* U.S. Senate, 85th Congress, 2nd sess., March 25, 1958, 104, 5246–55.

2. State of the Union Message, January 30, 1961, *Public Papers of the Presidents of the United States, 1961* (Washington, D.C.: U.S. Government Printing Office, 1962), 19.

3. Talbot, who was in South Asia almost continuously from 1939 until 1947 as an exchange student, naval officer, and newspaper correspondent, believed he was named the region's assistant secretary of state to emphasize the administration's interest in South Asia and because he had not been previously associated with the Arab-Israeli dispute. Talbot knew Rusk from their World War II service in India, had met but was not close to Bowles, and had never met Kennedy. Interview with Phillips Talbot, New York, February 8, 1995.

4. Robert Komer oral history, Lyndon Baines Johnson Library (LBJL), Austin, Texas.

5. Interviews with Talbot and with James P. Grant, New York, June 25, 1990. Grant, who had previously served in the Eisenhower administration's foreign aid agency, later headed the U.S. Agency for International Development's mission in Turkey and became the director-general of the UN Children's Emergency Fund.

6. Embassy Karachi telegram to State Department, February 16, 1961, *Foreign Relations of the United States (FRUS), 1961–63,* Vol. 19, 8–10.

7. Letter from President Ayub to Kennedy, February 16, 1961, *FRUS, 1961–63,* Vol. 19, 11.

8. Memorandum of conversation between President Kennedy and Finance Minister Shoaib, March 7, 1961, *FRUS, 1961–63,* Vol. 19, 16–20.

9. Embassy Karachi telegram to State Department, March 22, 1961, *FRUS, 1961–63,* Vol. 19, 26–30.

10. Iqbal Akhund, *Memoirs of a Bystander* (Karachi: Oxford University Press, 1997), 294–96.

11. In the annual tussle over Chinese representation in the United Nations, Pakistan's practice had been to try to have it both ways, by first voting with the U.S. that the question required a two-thirds majority but then voting in favor of seating communist China. Bhutto argued successfully that this was illogical and Pakistan should vote that the seating question require only a simple majority. Interview with Agha Shahi, Islamabad, January 29, 1996.

12. Interview with L. Bruce Laingen, Washington, D.C., April 29, 1997.

13. Memorandum of conversation between Vice President Johnson and President Ayub and advisers, Karachi, May 20, 1961, *FRUS, 1961–63,* Vol. 19, 45–50.

14. Embassy Karachi telegrams to State Department, May 21 and 22, 1961, Vice President's Security File, National Security File (NSF), International Meetings and Travel, VP's Far East Trip, LBJL; and Embassy Karachi dispatch to State Department, June 9, 1961, 033.1100-JO/6-961, Department of State Records (DSR), National Archives (NA), College Park, Md.

15. Memorandum from the vice president to President Kennedy, "The Mission to Southeast Asia, India and Pakistan," May 23, 1961, VP Security File, NSF, VP Far East trip, LBJL.

16. Memorandum of conversation between Finance Minister Shoaib and Undersecretary Ball, June 8, 1961, *FRUS, 1961–63,* Vol. 19, 54–57.

17. Jim Becker, "Ayub Says U.S. Policy Perils Asia," *Washington Post,* July 7, 1961.

18. Record of conversation between Ayub and Harold Macmillan, July 10, 1961, PREM 11/3457, Public Record Office (PRO), London.

19. Calvin Coolidge had given a tea for Queen Marie of Romania at Mount Vernon in 1926, but there had never been a state dinner there.

20. Interview with Talbot.

21. See Mohammed Ayub Khan, *Friends Not Masters* (London: Oxford University Press, 1967), 136–39, for his account of the visit.

22. Excerpts from Ayub's Address to the Congress, *New York Times,* July 13, 1961; Ayub Khan, *Friends Not Masters,* 137.

23. Memorandum of conversation between Presidents Kennedy and Ayub, July 11, 1961, *FRUS, 1961–63,* Vol. 19, 68–71.

24. Ibid., 74.

25. Ibid.

26. Memorandum of conversation between Presidents Ayub and Kennedy, July 13, 1961, National Security Files (NSF), Country Series, Pakistan, John F. Kennedy Library (JFKL), Boston, Massachusetts.

27. Ibid.

28. British embassy Washington report to Foreign Office, July 14, 1961, PREM 11/3457, PRO.

29. Interview with Talbot.

30. See Dennis Kux, *India and the United States: Estranged Democracies, 1941–91* (Washington, D.C.: National Defense University Press, 1993), 191–98, for fuller discussion.

31. Ayub Khan, *Friends Not Masters,* 139.

32. Memorandum reporting July 11, 1961, meeting between Ayub and Kennedy, and NSC memorandum from Komer to Bundy and Walt W. Rostow, the chairman of the State Department's Policy Planning Council, "Pak/Afghan Impasse—The Need for Action," September 12, 1961, NSF, Country Series, Afghanistan, JFKL.

33. Memorandum from Komer to President Kennedy, September 2, 1961, and memorandum from Talbot to Secretary Rusk, September 6, 1961, *FRUS, 1961–63,* Vol. 19, 87–88 and 90–92.

34. Kennedy messages to King Zahir and Ayub cabled on September 17, 1961, and Embassy Kabul telegram to State Department, September 20, 1961, *FRUS, 1961–63,* Vol. 19, 101–6.

35. Memorandum of conversation between President Kennedy and Livingston Merchant, October 16, 1961, *FRUS, 1961–63,* Vol. 19, 114–15.

36. Embassy Karachi telegram to State Department, October 27, 1961, and Komer memorandum regarding Merchant's mission, October 26, 1961, *FRUS, 1961–63,* Vol. 19, 116–20.

37. For further details regarding the 1962 constitution and revival of the Muslim League, see Ayub Khan, *Friends Not Masters,* 204–26; Altaf Gauhar, *Ayub Khan: Pakistan's First Military Ruler* (Lahore: Sang-e-Meel Publications, 1993), 161–92; and M. Rafique Afzal, *Political Parties in Pakistan, Vol. 2: 1958–1969,* Vol. 2 (Islamabad: National Institute of Historical and Cultural Research, 1987), 22–37 and 54–72.

38. Stanley Wolpert, *Zulfi Bhutto of Pakistan* (New York: Oxford University Press, 1993), 60.

39. Komer memo to McGeorge Bundy, January 12, 1962, *FRUS, 1961–63,* Vol. 19, 190–91.

40. State Department telegram to Embassies Karachi and New Delhi, January 15, 1962; Embassy Karachi telegram to State Department conveying Ayub's response, January 18, 1961; Embassy New Delhi telegram to State Department conveying Nehru's response, January 29, 1962; State Department telegram to New Dehli, January 31, 1962, *FRUS, 1961–63,* Vol. 19, 194–95, 201–3, and 211–13.

41. Memorandum from Assistant Secretary of State for International Organization Affairs Harlan Cleveland to Rusk, June 22, 1962, *FRUS, 1961–63,* Vol. 19, 287–91.

42. Ayub Khan, *Friends Not Masters,* 161–64.

43. Memorandum for the record of President Kennedy's meeting with Ambassador McConaughy, Undersecretary McGhee, Acting Assistant Secretary Grant, McGeorge Bundy, and Robert Komer, June 19, 1962, *FRUS, 1961–63,* Vol. 19, 278–79.

44. Memorandum of conversation of Kennedy-Ayub talks (India-Pakistan issues), September 24, 1962, NSF, Country Series, Pakistan, JFKL.

45. Memorandum of conversation between Presidents Kennedy and Ayub, Pakistan and Afghanistan, September 24, 1962, *FRUS, 1961–63,* Vol. 19, 327, 328.

46. Ibid., 329–31.

47. E. W. Kenworthy, "Pakistan to Get $945 Million Loan," *New York Times,* January 26, 1962.

48. Interview with Talbot.

49. *The Statesman* (Calcutta), October 13, 1962.

50. Memorandum from Robert Komer to Assistant Secretary Talbot, October 24, 1962, NSF, India, Memos and Misc., LBJL.

51. Memo from Kaysen to Kennedy, October 26, 1962, *FRUS, 1961–63,* Vol. 19, 351–52.

52. Embassy Karachi telegram to State Department, October 27, 1962, *FRUS, 1961–63,* Vol. 19, 353–55.

53. Interview with Altaf Gauhar, Islamabad, November 19, 1995.

54. State Department telegram to Embassy Karachi, October 28, 1962, transmitting the text of letter from Kennedy to Ayub, *FRUS, 1961–63,* Vol. 19, 358–59.

55. Charles Naas, then the State Department's Pakistan desk officer, recalled his surprise when he learned that the decision to offer military aid to India was taken without consulting Ayub. In the crisis atmosphere prevailing at the time, senior officials dealing with South Asia simply overlooked Kennedy's commitment to do so. Interview with Charles Naas, Bethesda, Maryland, July 15, 1996.

56. Statement by McConaughy quoted in Sir Morrice James, *Pakistan Chronicle* (Karachi: Oxford University Press, 1993), 81–82.

57. Embassy Karachi telegram to State Department, November 5, 1962, *FRUS, 1961–63,* Vol. 19, 369–70.

58. Embassy Karachi telegram to State Department, November 5, 1962, *FRUS, 1961–63,* Vol. 19, 370.

59. Footnote 6 for text of the aide-mémoire, transmitted to State Department as an enclosure to Karachi's airgram 883, February 23, 1963, *FRUS, 1961–63,* Vol. 19, 372.

60. See *Department of State Bulletin,* December 3, 1962, 837–38, for the text of the November 17, 1962, statement.

61. State Department telegram to Embassy Karachi, November 13, 1962, transmitting the text of Ayub letter to Kennedy, *FRUS, 1961–63,* Vol. 19, 377–80.

62. State Department telegram to Embassy Karachi, November 12, 1962, *FRUS, 1961–63,* Vol. 19, 376–77.

63. Komer memorandum to the president, November 12, 1962, *FRUS, 1961–63,* Vol. 19, 375.

64. State Department telegram to Embassy New Delhi, November 19, 1962, conveying the text of the Nehru-Kennedy letter. The message was declassified in 1998 in response to the author's request under the Freedom of Information Act.

65. "Ayub Is Said to Support a Shift toward Neutralism by Pakistan," *New York Times,* November 22, 1962.

66. State Department telegram to Embassy New Delhi, for Kennedy-Harriman message, November 25, 1962, *FRUS, 1961–63,* Vol. 19, 405–8.

67. Memorandum of conversation between Ayub, Duncan Sandys, and Harriman, November 28, 1962, *FRUS, 1961–63,* Vol. 19, 409–12.

68. Harriman's memorandum of his November 29, 1962, conversation with Ayub Khan, *FRUS, 1961–63,* Vol. 19, 413–14.

69. John Kenneth Galbraith, *Ambassador's Journal* (Boston: Houghton Mifflin, 1969), 436–37.

70. "Report of the Harriman Mission," 5–8, S/S Files, NSC Subcommittee on South Asia, DSR, NA.

71. Record of meeting of the NSC Executive Committee, December 3, 1962, *FRUS, 1961–63,* Vol. 19, 418.

72. Interview with Talbot.

73. Letter from Ayub to Kennedy, December 17, 1962, *FRUS, 1961–63,* Vol. 19, 441.

74. Embassy New Delhi telegram to State Department, December 10, 1962, *FRUS, 1961–63,* Vol. 19, 423.

75. Memorandum of conversation of Kennedy-Macmillan South Asia talks, 3 P.M., December 20, 1962, Nassau, Bermuda, *FRUS, 1961–63,* Vol. 19, 452.

76. Memorandum of conversation of Kennedy-Macmillan South Asia talks, 6 P.M., December 20, 1962, Nassau, Bermuda, *FRUS, 1961–63,* Vol. 19, 455–56.

77. State Department telegram to Embassy Karachi, December 22, 1962, transmitting text of Kennedy-Ayub letter, *FRUS, 1961–63,* Vol. 19, 458.

78. Embassy Office Murree telegram to State Department, December 27, 1962, *FRUS, 1961–63,* Vol. 19, 461–62.

79. Embassy Karachi telegram to State Department, January 11, 1963, transmitting text of Ayub letter to Kennedy, *FRUS, 1961–63,* Vol. 19, 466.

80. Interview with Shahi.

81. Ibid.

82. Embassy Office Murree telegram to State Department, December 28, 1962, DSR, NA; James, *Pakistan Chronicle,* 90.

83. State Department telegram to Embassy Karachi, January 4, 1963, 690D.91/1-463, DSR, NA.

84. Embassy Karachi telegram to State Department, January 14, 1963, 791.56/1-1463, DSR, NA.

85. James, *Pakistan Chronicle,* 93; Embassy New Delhi telegram to State Department, January 19, 1963, 690D.91/1963, DSR, NA.

86. Embassy Karachi telegram to State Department, February 3, 1963, POL 32-1 India-Pak, DSR, NA.

87. Embassy Karachi telegram to State Department, February 2, 1963, POL 32-1 India-Pak, DSR, NA.

88. Embassy New Delhi telegrams to State Department, February 7, 1963, POL 32-1, India-Pak, DSR, NA.

89. Embassy Karachi telegrams to State Department, February 7, 1963, POL 32-1 India-Pak, DSR, NA; James, *Pakistan Chronicle,* 94.

90. James, *Pakistan Chronicle,* 94–96; Embassy Karachi telegrams to State Department, February 9–11, 1963, POL 32-1 India-Pak, DSR, NA.

91. Informal notes regarding President Kennedy's February 21, 1963, meeting on Kashmir prepared by David T. Schneider, officer-in-charge of India in the State Department, *FRUS, 1961–63,* Vol. 19, 508.

92. Memorandum of conversation between Dean Rusk and Aziz Ahmed, Pakistan and Afghanistan, February 23, 1963, *FRUS, 1961–63,* Vol. 19, 510.

93. State Department telegram to American Consulate General in Dacca, March 9, 1963, transmitting letter from Kennedy to Ayub, *FRUS, 1961–63,* Vol. 19, 518–19.

94. Consulate General Dacca telegram to State Department, March 11, 1963, POL 32-1 India-Pak, DSR, NA.

95. James, *Pakistan Chronicle,* 96–97.

96. "Kashmir: Tactics for Fifth Round," memorandum from Rusk to Kennedy, March 31, 1963, and "Elements of a Settlement," attachment to that memorandum, *FRUS, 1961–63,* Vol. 19, 529–34.

97. Embassy New Delhi telegrams to State Department, April 15 and 20, 1963, POL 32-1 India-Pak, DSR, NA.

98. Komer memorandum to Kennedy, April 14, 1963, *FRUS, 1961–63,* Vol. 19, 553.

99. Sarvepalli Gopal, *Jawaharlal Nehru: A Biography,* Vol. 3 (London: Jonathan Cape, 1984), 259.

100. Embassy New Delhi telegram to State Department, April 22, 1963, POL 32-1 India-Pak, DSR, NA.

101. State Department telegram to Embassy Tehran, April 20, 1963, POL 32-1 India-Pak, DSR, NA; James, *Pakistan Chronicle,* 99.

102. Report on Kennedy's meeting with advisers on South Asia, April 25, 1963, *FRUS, 1961–63,* Vol. 19, 561–64.

103. Memorandum reporting Kennedy's May 20, 1963 meeting with T. T. Krishnamachari, *FRUS, 1961–63,* Vol. 19, 602.

104. Report of June 3, 1963, meeting between Presidents Kennedy and Radhakrishnan, *FRUS, 1961–63,* Vol. 19, 610.

105. Telegram from Secretary Rusk to State Department, May 2, 1963, *FRUS, 1961–63,* Vol. 19, 567.

106. Notes by Dean Rusk on his South Asia trip, *FRUS, 1961–63,* Vol. 19, 575–77.

107. James, *Pakistan Chronicle,* 99–100.

108. Embassy Delhi telegrams to State Department, May 2 and 3, 1963; State Department telegram to Embassy Office Murree, May 15, 1963; Embassy Karachi telegram to State Department, May 17, 1963; and State Department telegram to Embassy Karachi, August 26, 1963, POL 32-1 India-Pak, DSR, NA.

109. State Department telegram to Embassy Karachi, July 11, 1963, *FRUS, 1961–63,* Vol. 19, 617–19.

110. Ibid.

111. "Pakistani Hints of Red China Aid," *New York Times,* July 18, 1963.

112. Interview with Air Marshal Nur Khan, Karachi, January 31, 1996.

113. "Delay Is Ordered on Pakistan Loan," and "Pakistanis Plan a U.S. Showdown," *New York Times,* August 30 and September 1, 1963.

114. Summary of July 31, 1963, NSC meeting, *FRUS, 1961–63,* Vol. 19, 627, 628.

115. Report of meeting with President Kennedy on Ball's trip to Pakistan, August 12, 1963, *FRUS, 1961–63,* Vol. 19, 635–39.

116. Ibid., 638.

117. Embassy Tehran telegram to State Department, September 5, 1963, *FRUS, 1961–63,* Vol. 19, 661–68.

118. Embassy Lisbon telegram to State Department, "Eyes Only for the President and Secretaries of State and Defense from Ball," September 6, 1963, *FRUS, 1961–63,* Vol. 19, 671–74.

119. Report of Undersecretary Ball's September 9, 1963, meeting with President Kennedy, *FRUS, 1961–63,* Vol. 19, 676–77.

120. Text of Kennedy's press conference remarks in *New York Times,* September 13, 1963.

121. State Department telegram to Embassy Karachi, October 10, 1963, *FRUS, 1961–63,* Vol. 19, 679.

Chapter 6. Johnson: The Alliance Unravels

1. Interview with Altaf Gauhar, Islamabad, February 6, 2000.

2. State Department memorandum of conversation between President Johnson and Foreign Minister Bhutto, November 5, 1963, National Security File (NSF), Pakistan, Memos, Lyndon Baines Johnson Library (LBJL), Austin, Texas.

3. George Ball, *The Past Has Another Pattern* (New York: W. W. Norton, 1982), 282, 315.

4. State Department telegram to Embassy Karachi, December 2, 1963, *Foreign Relations of the United States (FRUS), 1961–63,* Vol. 19, 694–96.

5. Ball, *The Past Has Another Pattern,* 314; and interview with Phillips Talbot, New York, February 8, 1995.

6. Robert Komer oral history, 68–69, LBJL.

7. Komer memo to Bundy, November 23, 1963, NSF, NSC Histories, South Asia, LBJL.

8. From Ayub Khan's personal papers, quoted in Altaf Gauhar, *Ayub Khan: Pakistan's First Military Ruler* (Lahore: Sang-e-Meel, 1993), 247.

9. Ibid., 248–50.

10. Memorandum of conversation between General Taylor and President Ayub and memorandum for the record, December 20, 1963, *FRUS, 1961–63,* Vol. 19, 709–19.

11. Ibid.

12. Memorandum from General Taylor to secretary of defense, "Next Steps on Military Aid to India and Pakistan," December 23, 1963, NSF, Int. Meetings and Travel, Taylor Trip, LBJL.

13. Memorandum to the president from Dean Rusk, "Military Assistance to India and Pakistan: General Taylor's Report," January 16, 1964, NSF, Int. Meetings and

Travel, Taylor Trip, and National Security Action Memorandum (NSAM) 279, "Military Assistance to India and Pakistan," February 8, 1964, NSF, NSC Histories, South Asia, LBJL.

14. Sir Morrice James, *Pakistan Chronicle* (Karachi: Oxford University Press, 1993), 112–13. See also *New York Times,* February 19, 20, 21, 22, 23, 24, 25, 26, and 27, 1964.

15. "Pakistan Accepts Loan From China," *New York Times,* August 1, 1964.

16. Embassy Karachi telegram to State Department, June 24, 1964, NSF, Pakistan, LBJL.

17. Embassy Karachi telegram to State Department, June 23, 1964, NSF, Pakistan, LBJL.

18. Memorandum of conversation between President Johnson and Ambassador G. Ahmed, July 7, 1964, U.S. Military Assistance to India, LBJL.

19. Memorandum of conversation between Johnson and Ahmed, July 7, 1964, Bashir Ahmed, LBJL. Because of Johnson's interest, the U.S. embassy in Karachi had taken Bashir Ahmed under its wing, arranging for his purchase of a truck and then contracting for its use.

20. State Department telegram to Embassy Karachi, July 29, 1964, NSF, NSC Histories, South Asia, LBJL.

21. Interview with Altaf Gauhar, Islamabad, November 19, 1995.

22. State Department telegram to Embassy Karachi, December 31, 1964, and "Pakistani Transgressions of U.S. Friendship," NSF, Pakistan, LBJL.

23. Ayub Khan, *Friends Not Masters* (London: Oxford University Press, 1967), 119.

24. CIA intelligence cable report, April 26, 1965, NSF, Pakistan, LBJL.

25. Altaf Gauhar, *Ayub Khan,* 290; "Peking Gives Ayub Warm Welcome," *New York Times,* March 4, 1965.

26. "Ayub in China, Asks Talks on Vietnam," and "China Silent as Ayub Asks Talks on Vietnam," *New York Times,* March 5 and 8, 1965.

27. "Chen Tells of Step for Tie with Turkey," *New York Times,* March 29, 1965.

28. Altaf Gauhar, *Ayub Khan,* 299–300; and interview with Altaf Gauhar, November 19, 1995.

29. State Department telegram to Embassy Karachi, April 14, 1965, NSF, NSC Histories, South Asia, LBJL.

30. Interview with Robert Komer, Washington, D.C., August 5, 1990.

31. Altaf Gauhar, *Ayub Khan,* 302.

32. Komer memorandum to Bundy, April 21, 1965, NSF, NSC Histories, South Asia, LBJL.

33. *Keesing's Contemporary Archives* (Bristol, U.K.), August 28–September 4, 1965, 20927.

34. Lt. Gen. Gul Hassan Khan, *Memoirs of Lt. Gen Gul Hassan Khan* (Karachi: Oxford University Press, 1993), 163–66.

35. James, *Pakistan Chronicle,* 123–26. In the end, the arbitration panel basically upheld Pakistan's claim.

36. State Department memorandum of conversation between Dean Rusk, Indian Ambassador B. K. Nehru, Deputy Assistant Secretary of State William Handley, and India Country Director David T. Schneider, May 8, 1965, NSF, India, Memos and Misc., LBJL.

37. "India's Food Crisis, 1966–67," NSF, NSC Histories, South Asia, LBJL.

38. Agency for International Development, *Statistical Fact Book, Pakistan, 1968* (Washington, D.C.: U.S. AID, 1968).

39. "Our Pakistan affairs," memorandum from Komer to President Johnson, April 22, 1965, NSF, NSC Histories, South Asia, LBJL.

40. Memoranda for the president from Komer, June 8, 1965, NSF, Komer Files; and "Listing of decisions on Pakistan," September 9, 1965, NSF, NSC Histories, South Asia, LBJL.

41. Memorandum to president from Bell, June 8, 1965, and memorandum for Rusk, McNamara, and Bell from Bundy, "Presidential Decisions on Aid to India/ Pakistan," June 9, 1965, NSF, NSC Histories, South Asia, LBJL.

42. Interview with Sartaj Aziz, Islamabad, February 6, 1996. Sartaj Aziz served as Shoaib's aide during the trip.

43. "Pakistan: Effective Economic Development," NSF, NSC Histories, South Asia, 5–7, LBJL.

44. Interview with Sartaj Aziz.

45. State Department telegram to Embassy Karachi, June 30, 1965. The message, drafted and approved by Undersecretary Mann, was personally cleared by President Johnson, NSF, Pakistan, cables, LBJL.

46. Harold H. Saunders, "Narrative and Guide to the Documents," 6, NSF, NSC Histories, South Asia, LBJL.

47. Ibid.

48. "Pakistan's Response to the Postponement of the Consortium Meeting," State Department Bureau of Intelligence and Research memorandum RNA-35, July 28, 1965, Department of State Records (DSR), National Archives (NA), College Park, Md.

49. Komer to the President, July 30, 1965, Confidential Files, CO 230, LBJL.

50. Memorandum from Bell to Rusk, July 29, 1965, NSF, NSC Histories, South Asia, LBJL.

51. Altaf Gauhar, *Ayub Khan,* 318–19; Gul Hassan Khan, *Memoirs,* 115–17.

52. Quoted in James, *Pakistan Chronicle,* 128.

53. Altaf Gauhar, *Ayub Khan,* 320–21. The ISI, which drew on the three military services, had responsibility for external intelligence collection and covert operations, much like the CIA. In the 1970s, Zulfikar Bhutto also authorized the ISI to engage in domestic intelligence activities.

54. Ibid., 321–22.

55. Ibid., 328.

56. Komer memorandum to President Johnson, August 31, 1965, NSF, NSC Histories, South Asia, LBJL.

57. State Department telegram to Embassies Karachi and New Delhi, September 2, 1965, NSF, Pakistan, cables, LBJL.

58. State Department telegram to Embassy Karachi, September 4, 1965, NSF, NSC Histories, South Asia, LBJL.

59. Text of Embassy Office Rawalpindi telegram to State Department, September 6, 1965, cited in Roedad Khan, *The American Papers* (Karachi: Oxford University Press, 1999), 9–27; and Embassy Office Rawalpindi telegram to State Department, September 6, 1965, NSF, Pakistan, cables, LBJL. Altaf Gauhar, *Ayub Khan,* 336–37, provides a Pakistani version of the meeting.

60. Embassy Office Rawalpindi telegram to State Department, September 6, 1965, NSF, Pakistan, cables, LBJL.

61. Embassy Karachi telegram to State Department repeated to White House, September 7, 1965, NSF, Pakistan, LBJL.

62. State Department telegram to Embassies New Delhi and Karachi, September 8, 1965, NSF, NSC Histories, South Asia, LBJL.

63. The Pakistani version of the Bhutto-McConaughy meeting can be found in Farhat Mahmud, *A History of U.S.-Pakistan Relations* (Lahore: Vanguard, 1991), 282–291; for the U.S. report of the meeting, see Roedad Khan, *The American Papers,* 45–49.

64. Text of Embassy Office Rawalpindi telegram to State Department, September 10, 1965, cited in Roedad Khan, *The American Papers,* 55–57.

65. James, *Pakistan Chronicle,* 140.

66. Altaf Gauhar, *Ayub Khan,* 343.

67. CIA situation report telegram to White House Situation Room, September 13, 1965, NSF, Pakistan, LBJL.

68. Embassy Office Rawalpindi telegram to State Department, September 15, 1965, NSF, Pakistan, LBJL.

69. Excerpts from September 17, 1965, meeting in White House Cabinet Room, Office of the President File, Valenti Meeting Notes, LBJL.

70. Altaf Gauhar, *Ayub Khan,* 351–53.

71. Ibid., 353. Professor G. M. Choudhury, in his *India, Pakistan, Bangladesh and the Major Powers* (New York: Free Press, 1975), 190–91, also wrote that Ayub secretly visited China before announcing Pakistan's acceptance of the cease-fire. His account is substantively similar to Altaf Gauhar's version. Although Sir Morrice James, the British high commissioner in Islamabad at the time, doubted Choudhury's version, his comments in *Pakistan Chronicle* predate the publication of Altaf Gauhar's book. Moreover, James concedes that the Beijing trip was feasible.

72. State Department telegrams to U.S. Mission to the UN and Embassy Karachi, September 21, 1965, NSF, Pakistan, cables, LBJL.

73. "Pakistan Agrees to a Cease-Fire," *New York Times,* September 23, 1965; and interviews with Iqbal Akhund, Montpellier, September 12, 1998, and Agha Shahi, Islamabad, December 31, 1995.

74. Altaf Gauhar, *Ayub Khan,* 357–59.

75. Ibid., 359.

76. Memorandum from Komer to president, October 1, 1965, NSF, Komer Files, Memos, LBJL.

77. Department of State Intelligence and Research memorandum, "Attitudes toward the USSR, the US and the UK," RNA-65, December 10, 1965, obtained through Freedom of Information Act (FOIA) request.

78. Dean Rusk oral history, 36, LBJL.

79. White House talking points for Bill Moyers press backgrounder, November 27, 1965, LBJL.

80. Memorandum of President Johnson's meeting with Ayub and advisers, Cabinet Room, 1 P.M., December 15, 1965, NSF, Pakistan, LBJL.

81. Altaf Gauhar, *Ayub Khan,* 373–75.

82. Memorandum of Johnson's meeting with Ayub and advisers, December 15, 1965.

83. Memorandum reporting President Johnson's second private meeting with Ayub, 4:30–5:30 P.M., December 15, 1965, Howard Wriggins Files, India-Pakistan Military Assistance, LBJL.

84. Memorandum of meeting between Presidents Johnson and Ayub attended by their advisers, White House, December 15, 1965, NSF, NSC Histories, South Asia, LBJL.

85. Ibid.

86. Altaf Gauhar, *Ayub Khan,* 376.

87. Ibid., 377.

88. Memorandum of the Johnson-Ayub meeting, 4:30–5:30 P.M., December 15, 1965, Howard Wriggins Files, India-Pakistan Military Assistance, LBJL.

89. Komer memorandum to President Johnson, January 12, 1966, Komer Files, Memos, LBJL.

90. Memorandum of conversation of Vice President's meeting with Ayub, Karachi, February 15, 1966, NSF, Pakistan, LBJL. (Most of Humphrey's but almost none of Ayub's remarks have been declassified.)

91. Copy of Embassy Karachi telegram to President Johnson, March 26, 1965, Komer Files, India, LBJL; "Pakistan Goes All Out to Greet China's Liu," *Washington Post,* March 27, 1966; and Warren Unna, "Liu Gives Aid Pledge to Pakistan," *Washington Post,* March 28, 1966.

92. Memorandum of conversation between Finance Minister Shoaib and Walt Rostow, April 19, 1966, NSF, Pakistan, LBJL.

93. "An Aid Deal for Pakistan," memorandum from Rusk to the president, April 27, 1966, and memorandum for the record of talk between the President, Rusk, and Rostow, April 27, 1966, NSF, Pakistan, LBJL. Ultimately, after further foot-dragging, the United States backed out of the steel-mill project, which the Soviets, with much political flourish, then undertook. The steel mill has turned out to be a consistent money-loser.

94. State Department telegram to Embassies Karachi and New Delhi, February 12, 1966, NSF, Pakistan, LBJL.

95. James W. Spain, *In Those Days: A Diplomat Remembers* (Kent, Ohio: Kent State University Press, 1998), 96. Spain was in charge of Pakistan at the time in the State Department.

96. Rostow briefing memo for President Johnson for his meeting with Ambassador Locke, July 25, 1966, NSF, Pakistan, Memos, LBJL.

97. Embassy Saigon telegram to State Department, August 11, 1966, NSF, Pakistan, cables, LBJL.

98. Undated message from Locke to White House aide Marvin Watson, read by President Johnson, and September 1966 handwritten letter from Locke to Johnson, NSF, Pakistan, LBJL.

99. Embassy Rawalpindi telegram to State Department (for Johnson, McNamara, and Rusk), September 27, 1966, and Rostow memorandum to the president, September 28, 1966, NSF, Pakistan, LBJL.

100. Warren Unna, "U.S. Envoy Known as 'Junior Lyndon,'" *Washington Post,* March 17, 1967.

101. John W. Finney, "U.S. to Renew Arms Sales to India and Pakistan" and "U.S. Won't Renew Arms Aid to India and Pakistan," *New York Times,* April 12, 13, 1967; "Military Supply Policy toward India and Pakistan," memorandum from Rusk to the

president, March 17, 1967; and State Department telegram to Embassies Rawalpindi and New Delhi, April 6, 1967, NSF, Pakistan, LBJL.

102. "U.S. Rejects Pleas for Sale of Arms," "Indians Voice Anger Over U.S. Arms Aid to Pakistan," and "India Says U.S. Shift May Help Pakistan Get Arms," *New York Times,* April 16, 17 and 18, 1967.

103. Memorandum of conversation between Johnson and Ayub, Karachi, December 22, 1967, NSF, Pakistan, Memos, LBJL.

104. Spain, *In Those Days,* 97–98; memorandum for the president from Nicholas Katzenbach, October 22, 1968, and memoranda for Johnson from Rostow, October 25 and 29, 1968, NSF, Pakistan, LBJL; and Warren Unna, "U.S. Seeks Tanks for Pakistan," *Washington Post,* October 18, 1968.

105. Altaf Gauhar, *Ayub Khan,* 416–18; Warren Unna, "Moscow Is Sending Troopcopters to Pakistan in Policy Switch on India," *Washington Post,* August 6, 1967; and Joseph Lelyveld, "Kosygin Pledges More Economic Aid for Pakistan" and "Kosygin Brings Smiles But No Concessions," *New York Times,* April 19, and 21, 1968.

106. Warren Unna, "U.S. May Lose Base in Pakistan," *Washington Post,* May 15, 1968; and "Pakistan Bids U.S. Close Base in 1969," *New York Times,* May 21, 1968.

107. Memorandum from Katzenbach to the president, August 6, 1968, NSF, Pakistan, LBJL.

108. "Pakistani Neutralism: The Czech Case," State Department Intelligence Note 706, September 6, 1968, POL 27-1, Com Bloc-Czech, DSR, NA.

109. Interview with Altaf Gauhar, Islamabad, February 6, 2000.

Chapter 7. Nixon: The Tilt

1. See *New York Times,* January 18, 21, 22, 23, 25, and 29 and February 2, 1969, for articles on the political disturbances and unrest that undermined the Ayub regime.

2. See *New York Times,* February 22, 23, and 27 and March 5, 9, 14, and 15, 1969.

3. Text of Ayub's resignation speech reprinted in *New York Times,* March 26, 1969.

4. Henry Brandon, *The Retreat of American Power* (Garden City, N.Y.: Doubleday, 1973), 252.

5. Letter from President-elect Nixon to President Ayub, January 10, 1969, Nixon Presidential Materials Project (NPMP), National Archives (NA), College Park, Md.

6. Henry A. Kissinger, *White House Years* (Boston: Little, Brown, 1979), 848.

7. Tilman Durdin, "Rogers Reassures Pakistan on Arms," *New York Times,* May 25, 1969.

8. Golam Wahid Choudhury, *The Last Days of United Pakistan* (Karachi: Oxford University Press, 1993), 61–66.

9. Sultan Mohammed Khan, *Memories and Reflections of a Pakistani Diplomat* (London: London Centre for Pakistan Studies, 1998), 233.

10. Ibid., 233–34; and Golam Wahid Choudhury, *India, Pakistan, Bangladesh and the Major Powers* (New York: Free Press, 1975), 63–65.

11. S. M. Khan, *Memories and Reflections,* 234.

12. Choudhury, *India, Pakistan, Bangladesh,* 67–68.

13. Tilman Durdin, "Nixon Ends Tour of Asia with Hope for Era of Peace," *New York Times,* August 2, 1969.

14. Kissinger, *White House Years,* 180–81.

15. Interview with Agha Hilaly, Karachi, January 30, 1996. As Pakistan's ambassador in Washington, Hilaly took part in the Nixon visit to Lahore and later played an important role in the arrangements for the secret Kissinger trip to China.

16. Richard Nixon, "Annual Report to the Congress on United States Foreign Policy in the 1970s," *Public Papers of the Presidents of the United States: Richard Nixon, 1970* (Washington, D.C.: U.S. Government Printing Office, 1971), 143–44; and Nixon, "Annual Report to the Congress on United States Foreign Policy," *Public Papers of the Presidents of the United States: Richard Nixon, 1971* (Washington, D.C.: U.S. Government Printing Office, 1972), 279–81. Quotation is from the latter.

17. Kissinger, *White House Years,* 703–4.

18. "U.S. to Resume Arms Sales to Pakistan" and "U.S. Aides in India Concerned over Sale of Arms to Pakistan," *New York Times,* October 9 and 11, 1970.

19. Tad Szulc, "Foreign Leaders Meet with Nixon," *New York Times,* October 26, 1970.

20. Kissinger, *White House Years,* 698–700.

21. Interview by telephone with Joseph Farland, April 24, 2000.

22. Kissinger, *White House Years,* 850.

23. Ibid., 700–701.

24. Interview with Hilaly.

25. For a more detailed description of events from December 1970 until March 25, 1971, see Robert Jackson, *South Asian Crisis: India, Pakistan, and Bangladesh* (New York: Praeger, 1975), 26–32; Choudhury, *Last Days,* 144–79; and Leo E. Rose and Richard Sisson, *War and Secession: Pakistan, India, and the Creation of Bangladesh* (Berkeley: University of California Press, 1990), 91–133. "US Policy in the Indian-Pakistani Crisis," State Department Historical Office Research Project No. 1033, March 1973, 5–10, NCS Files, Indo-Pak War, Nixon Presidential Materials Project (NPMP), NA, provides an account of events based on State Department telegrams.

26. Choudhury, *Last Days,* 161.

27. "US Policy in the Indian-Pakistani Crisis," 10, NSC Files, Indo-Pak War, NPMP, NA.

28. Ibid., 11.

29. Grace Lichtenstein, "Army Expels 35 Foreign Newsmen from Pakistan," *New York Times,* March 28, 1971.

30. See, for example, Sydney B. Schanberg, "Heavy Fighting, Raids Reported in East Pakistan," *New York Times,* March 28, 1971.

31. "US Policy in the Indian-Pakistani Crisis," 11, NSC Files, Indo-Pak War, NPMP, NA.

32. Ibid., 11–13.

33. At the time, the author was acting political counselor in the Islamabad embassy and assisted Farland in negotiating the arrangement for the evacuation with the government of Pakistan.

34. Benjamin Welles, "Pakistan Offers Airliners to Evacuate Americans," *New York Times,* April 3, 1971.

35. Sydney Schanberg, "Foreign Evacuees from East Pakistan Tell of Grim Fight," and "Bloodbath in Bengal" (editorial), *New York Times,* April 7, 1971.

36. After unhappiness among U.S. officials about the Vietnam War had led to frequent media leaks, the State Department had established a special "dissent channel"

so employees could air differences about policy within the system without feeling the need to go public. The Dacca staff used this channel to voice their complaint.

37. The author was with Farland when he read the telegram.

38. See Kissinger, *White House Years,* 853–54.

39. Ibid., 713–14.

40. Ibid., 724.

41. S. M. Khan, *Memories and Reflections,* 250–52.

42. Interview with the CIA chief of station who worked out the arrangements for Kissinger's trip.

43. Kissinger, *White House Years,* 853.

44. "An Internal Matter?" (editorial), *New York Times,* April 21, 1971.

45. Jackson, *South Asian Crisis,* 40–42; and Rose and Sisson, *War and Secession,* 250–51.

46. Rose and Sisson, *War and Secession,* 240–41; and Jackson, *South Asian Crisis,* 39–40.

47. S. M. Khan, *Memories and Reflections,* 301–8.

48. Benjamin Welles, "U.S. Acknowledges Sales of Ammunition to Pakistan," *New York Times,* April 14, 1971.

49. Christopher Van Hollen, "The Tilt Revisited: Kissinger-Nixon Geopolitics and South Asia," *Asian Survey* (April 1980), 339–61. In 1971, Van Hollen was deputy assistant secretary of state for South Asia. His analysis differed radically from Kissinger's seventy-five-page account of the crisis in *White House Years.* The author finds Van Hollen's version the more persuasive of the two.

50. See *New York Times,* June 22, 23, 24, 25, 27, and 30, 1971; and Dennis Kux, *India and the United States: Estranged Democracies, 1941–91* (Washington, D.C., National Defense University Press, 1993), 293–94.

51. Van Hollen, "The Tilt Revisited," 344.

52. Kissinger, *White House Years,* 856.

53. Kathleen Teltsch, "Yahya Tells Thant Relief Aid Is Not Needed Now," *New York Times,* May 13, 1971.

54. Jackson, *South Asian Crisis,* 46.

55. Memorandum of conversation between President Nixon and M. M. Ahmed, May 10, 1971, Kissinger Pakistan Chronology, NSC Files, Indo-Pak War, NPMP, NA.

56. Tad Szulc, "U.S. Says It Will Continue Aid to Pakistan Despite Cutoff Urged by Other Nations," Szulc, "Deep Dents in the Nixon Doctrine," and "Why Aid Pakistan?" (editorial), *New York Times,* June 29 and July 11 and 14, 1971. See also Jackson, *South Asian Crisis,* 62–64.

57. Henry Tanner, "House Group Bids U.S. Stop Aiding Greece, Pakistan," *New York Times,* July 16, 1971. Administration policy is outlined in an August 3, 1971, memorandum from Kissinger to the president, NSC Files, Indo-Pak War, NPMP, NA.

58. Sultan Khan's account of the trip can be found in *Memories and Reflections,* 260–67.

59. Kissinger, *White House Years,* 861–62.

60. Interview with Sultan Mohammed Khan, Bethesda, Maryland, July 6, 1995.

61. S. M. Khan, *Memories and Reflections,* 269–70.

62. Kissinger, *White House Years,* 863.

63. Sisson and Rose, *War and Secession,* 146–48.

64. Memorandum for the president's file on meeting with Ambassador Farland, July 18, 1971, President's Office File, NPMP, NA.

65. Informal notes, Senior Review Group meeting, July 31, 1971, quoted in Van Hollen, "The Tilt Revisited," 347.

66. Grace Lichtenstein, "40,000 Cheer 2 Beatles in Dual Benefit for Pakistanis," *New York Times,* August 2, 1971.

67. Text of President Nixon's press conference remarks, reprinted in the *New York Times,* August 5, 1971.

68. The author obtained a copy of the Nixon-Yahya letter dated August 7, 1991, from Lt. Gen. (Rtd.) Kamal Matinuddin, who received it from Yahya Khan's son. A copy is also available in the Policy Planning Staff, Director Files (Winston Lord), DSR, NA.

69. Nixon-Yahya and Kissinger-Yahya July 26, 1971, letters, President's Office File, NPMP, NA.

70. Kissinger, *White House Years,* 866–67.

71. Rose and Sisson, *War and Secession,* 242–45.

72. Memorandum for the record of President Nixon's August 11, 1971, meeting with Pakistan Senior Review Group, Kissinger Pakistan Chronology, NSC Files, Indo-Pak War, NPMP, NA.

73. Ibid.

74. "Yahya Schedules a Secret Trial of Separatist Chief Tomorrow," *New York Times,* August 10, 1971.

75. Memorandum for President Nixon from Kissinger, August 18, 1971, NSC Files, Indo-Pak War, NA.

76. Embassy Islamabad telegram to State Department, August 20, 1971, Kissinger Chronology, NSC Files, Indo-Pak War, NPMP, NA; and Maurice Williams oral history, Association of Diplomatic Studies and Training (ADST), Arlington, Va.

77. Williams oral history, ADST.

78. Memorandum, "A.I.D. Deputy Administrator's Report on Pakistan," November 5, 1971, NSC Files, Indo-Pak War, NPMP, NA.

79. Rose and Sisson, *War and Secession,* 173–74 and 193–94.

80. Interview with S. M. Khan. In *Memories and Reflections* (337–41), Khan also wrote that Yahya responded in this way to a suggestion from Soviet president Podgorny when they met at Persepolis in Iran.

81. Embassy Islamabad telegrams to State Department, November 29 and December 3, 1971, NSC Files, Indo-Pak War, Kissinger Pakistan Chronology, NPMP, NA; and interview with Farland.

82. Van Hollen, "The Tilt Revisited," 430.

83. See Kux, *Estranged Democracies,* 297–302, for fuller discussion of the Gandhi-Nixon talks. Kissinger's account of the visit can be found in *White House Years,* 878–82.

84. S. M. Khan, *Memories and Reflections,* 350–51.

85. "The Smell of War" (editorial), and Sydney H. Schanberg, "Soviet Official Leaves; India Hints New Arms Aid," *New York Times,* October 20 and 28, 1971.

86. Memo from Kissinger to Nixon, November 22, 1971, and Embassy Islamabad telegram to State Department, November 23, 1971, NSC Files, Indo-Pak War, NPMP, NA. See also Rose and Sisson, *War and Secession,* 213.

87. Memorandum of conversation between Kissinger and Huang Hua, November 23, 1971, and memo from Kissinger to Secretary Rogers conveying November 22, 1971, message from the Chinese, Policy Planning Staff, Director's Files, DSR, NA.

88. Manekshaw stated this when interviewed for *Dynasty*, a BBC television documentary about India's first fifty years that was shown in 1998 on PBS in the United States.

89. Stung by private criticism from Bhutto, hurt by the Western press ridicule of Pakistan's leaders as "nitwits" and "idiots," and disappointed when the international community failed to react to India's more aggressive tactics, Yahya and his colleagues decided to attack militarily in the West. Rose and Sisson, *War and Secession,* 227–230, and S. M. Khan, *Memories and Reflections,* 360–61.

90. Rose and Sisson, *War and Secession,* 215.

91. S. M. Khan, *Memories and Reflections,* 368–69.

92. "U.S. Policy in the Indian-Pakistani Crisis," 38, NSC Files, Indo-Pak War, NPMP, NA.

93. Henry Tanner, "Russian Vote in U.N. Kills Troop-Pullback Proposal," *New York Times,* December 6, 1971.

94. Bernard Gwertzman, "Calling India Aggressor, Washington Cuts Loans," *New York Times,* December 7, 1971; and "U.S. Policy in the Indian-Pakistani Crisis," 39, NSC Files, Indo-Pak War, NPMP, NA. State Department spokesperson Charles Bray announced the decision to suspend aid in the December 6, 1971, daily press briefing.

95. Transcript of White House Henry Kissinger December 7, 1971, press backgrounder, and "U.S. Policy in the Indian-Pakistani crisis," 39–40, NSC Files, Indo-Pak War, NPMP, NA.

96. Kissinger, *White House Years,* 900–901.

97. Memorandum of conversation between President Nixon and Soviet Minister of Agriculture Vladimir Matskevich, December 9, 1971, President's Office File, NPMP, NA.

98. State Department telegram to New Delhi, December 10, 1971, NSC Files, Indo-Pak War, NPMP, NA.

99. Richard Nixon, *RN: The Memoirs of Richard Nixon* (New York: Grosset and Dunlap, 1978), 526–28.

100. Kissinger, *White House Years,* 905. In his *On Watch: A Memoir* (New York: Quadrangle/New York Times Book Co., 1976), 367–69, then-chief of naval operations Adm. Elmo Zumwalt commented that the evacuation was completed two days before the task force entered the Indian Ocean. Zumwalt wrote that he never knew the true mission of the task force group.

101. Memorandum of conversation between Henry Kissinger and Chinese UN Representative Huang Hua, New York, December 10, 1971, Policy Planning Staff Director's Files, DSR, NA.

102. Ibid.

103. S. M. Khan, *Memories and Reflections,* 375–76.

104. Kissinger, *White House Years,* 909–10.

105. Ibid., 910–11.

106. Memorandum of conversation between Chinese UN Ambassador Huang and Brig. Gen. Haig, December 12, 1971, Policy Planning Staff, Director's Files, DSR, NA.

107. See S. M. Khan, *Memories and Reflections,* 343–48, for his account of the China visit.

108. See Kux, *Estranged Democracies,* 303.

109. Memorandum of conversation between Nixon, Kissinger, and Pompidou, the Azores, December 13, 1972, White House Special Files, President's Office Files, NPMP, NA.

110. Ibid.

111. Ibid.

112. "US Policy in the Indian-Pakistani Crisis," 67–72, NSC Files, Indo-Pak War, NPMP, NA.

113. U.S. Mission to the UN telegram to State Department, December 15, 1971, NSC Files, Indo-Pak War, NPMP, NA; interview with Agha Shahi, January 30, 1996; and Henry Tanner, "Bhutto Denounces Council and Walks Out in Tears," *New York Times,* December 16, 1971.

114. Memorandum of conversation of Nixon-Bhutto meeting, December 18, 1971, President's Office Files, NPMP, NA.

115. Interview with L. Bruce Laingen, Washington, D.C., April 29, 1997.

116. Jack Anderson (with George Clifford), *The Anderson Papers* (New York: Random House, 1972), 253, 256.

117. Walter Isaacson, *Kissinger: A Biography* (New York: Simon and Schuster, 1992), 380–85; and Zumwalt, *On Watch,* 369–76.

118. *Public Papers of the Presidents: Richard Nixon, 1972* (Washington, D.C.: U.S. Government Printing Office, 1974), 295–304.

119. Nixon, *RN,* 530.

120. Kissinger, *White House Years,* 913–15.

121. Williams oral history.

122. Interviews with Shahi, Hilaly, and S. M. Khan.

123. *National Herald* (New Delhi), April 5, 1971.

124. Raymond L. Garthoff, *Detente and Confrontation: American-Soviet Relations from Nixon to Reagan* (Washington, D.C: Brookings Institution, 1985), 315.

125. See S. M. Khan, *Memories and Reflections,* 414–19, for his account of the Middle East trip.

126. "Pakistan, Strengthening Friendly Ties, Recognizes North Korea," *New York Times,* November 10, 1972.

127. S. M. Khan, *Memories and Reflections,* 434.

128. "Pakistan: Bhutto's Problems," News of the Week in Review, *New York Times,* March 19, 1972.

129. James P. Sterba, "U.S. Will Resume Aid to Pakistan," *New York Times,* June 20, 1972.

130. C. L. Sulzberger, "Bhutto Wants a Defense Pact with U.S." *New York Times,* February 13, 1972.

131. Interviews with Abdul Sattar, Islamabad, December 14, 1995, and Ashok Chib, New Delhi, February 6, 2000. Both Sattar and Chib were members of their country's teams at Simla. What Bhutto did or did not tell Indira Gandhi when they met alone has generated considerable debate. Since there is no language to this effect in the joint statement or even in the negotiating records, it is irrelevant in terms of committing Pakistan to such a course.

132. See the *Washington Post,* July 2, 3, and 4, 1972, for reporting on the Simla conference.

133. "Indo-Pakistani Pact Welcomed by the U.S." *Washington Post,* July 4, 1972.

134. Embassy Tehran telegram (in eight parts) to State Department, July 8, 1972, obtained through Freedom of Information Act (FOIA) request.

135. Embassy Islamabad telegram to State Department, July 6, 1972, obtained through FOIA.

136. Murray Marder, "U.S. Eases Pakistan Arms Ban," *Washington Post,* March 15, 1973.

137. Although Sober reported that his action was limited to expressing the hope that the Pakistanis "would be able to arrive at a Constitution acceptable to all the major political elements," both the government and opposition thought his comments helped bring about the compromise. Sober memorandum for the record, April 17, 1973.

138. Briefing memorandum to President Nixon from Kissinger, White House Special Files, President's Office Files, NPMP, NA.

139. Memorandum of conversation between Zhou Enlai and Henry Kissinger, November 14, 1973, Policy Planning Staff, Director's Files, DSR, NA.

140. State Department telegram to Embassy Islamabad, September 24, 1973, obtained through FOIA; and Dan Morgan, "U.S. Arms Are Sought by Bhutto," Morgan, "Bhutto Apparently Failed to Get U.S. Arms Commitment," and "Mr. Bhutto's Visit" (editorial), *Washington Post,* September 19, 20, and 22, 1973.

141. Henry Byroade oral history, Harry S. Truman Library, Independence, Mo.

142. Undated memorandum of conversation of Kissinger-Bhutto meeting, November 1973, obtained through FOIA; and Kissinger telegram to the President, November 10, 1973, NSC Files, Kissinger Office Files, NPMP, NA.

143. Lewis M. Simons, "Irony Marks Mujib's Trip to Pakistan," and "Sadat Sees Altered U.S. Israel Policy," *Washington Post,* February 24 and 25, 1974.

144. "Pakistan Bars Blackmail," David Binder, "Pakistan Sees India as Nuclear Threat," and Kathleen Teltsch, "Pakistan Disputes India on A-Arms," *New York Times,* May 20, 21, and June 8, 1974.

145. Steve Weissman and Herbert Krosney, *The Islamic Bomb* (New York: Times Books, 1981), 43–48.

146. Patrick Keatley, "The Brown Bomb," *Guardian* (Manchester), March 11, 1965.

147. Iqbal Akhund, *Memoirs of a Bystander: A Life in Diplomacy* (Karachi: Oxford University Press, 1997), 262–64.

148. Zulfikar Ali Bhutto, *The Myth of Independence* (London: Oxford University Press, 1969), 153; and interview with Abdul Sattar, Islamabad, November 6, 1995.

149. Interview with Munir Ahmed Khan, Islamabad, May 4, 1998.

150. "Ford Assures Pakistan," *New York Times,* August 11, 1974.

151. Choudhury, *India, Pakistan, Bangladesh,* 142. Choudhury's source was Yahya Khan.

Chapter 8. Ford: Enter the Nuclear Issue

1. Lewis W. Simons, "Bhutto, Citing Sikkim, Seeks Arms," *Washington Post,* September 11, 1974.

2. Bernard Weinraub, "Pakistani Presses U.S. for Arms," *New York Times,* October 14, 1974.

3. Embassy Islamabad telegram to State Department, "The Secretary's Visit: View from Pakistan," September 21, 1974, obtained through Freedom of Information Act (FOIA) request.

4. Lewis W. Simons, "U.S. Seen Weighing Arms for Pakistan," *Washington Post,* September 25, 1974.

5. "U.S. Officials Debate Possible Arms Sales to Pakistan," *New York Times,* October 17, 1974.

6. See Dennis Kux, *India and the United States: Estranged Democracies, 1941–91* (Washington, D.C.: National Defense University Press, 1993), 327–28, for discussion of the Kissinger visit to India.

7. State Department checklist for Secretary Kissinger's use in Islamabad, undated, but presumably October 30–31, 1974, obtained through FOIA.

8. Embassy Tehran telegram to State Department, November 2, 1974, obtained through FOIA.

9. Bernard Gwertzman, "Kissinger Pledges U.S. Support to Bhutto," *New York Times,* November 1, 1974.

10. Embassy Islamabad telegrams to State Department, October 10 and 17, 1974, and Embassy Riyadh telegram from Secretary Kissinger to Embassy Islamabad, October 13, 1974, obtained through FOIA.

11. Murray Marder, "U.S. Arms Are Sought by Bhutto," *Washington Post,* February 5, 1975; and "Ford Sees Bhutto and Hints U.S. May Ease Pakistan Arms Curb," *New York Times,* February 6, 1975.

12. National Security Decision Memorandum 289, "U.S. Military Supply Policy Toward India and Pakistan," March 25, 1975, *Declassified Documents Catalogue,* State Department library.

13. "Arms Supplier" (editorial), *New York Times,* February 26, 1975; and "South Asian Prospect" (editorial), *Washington Post,* February 27, 1975.

14. Iqbal Akhund, *Memoirs of a Bystander: A Life in Diplomacy* (Karachi: Oxford University Press, 1997), 264.

15. State Department briefing paper for Secretary Kissinger's February 5 meeting with Prime Minister Bhutto, January 31, 1975, obtained through FOIA.

16. Undated briefing memorandum regarding the Bhutto visit from Secretary Kissinger to President Ford, obtained through FOIA.

17. Interview with Peter Constable, Washington, D.C., July 13, 1997; and undated talking points for President Ford's meeting with Prime Minister Bhutto on the nuclear issue, obtained through FOIA.

18. Akhund, *Memoirs of a Bystander,* 264. Akhund was Pakistan's ambassador to France in the late 1970s.

19. Interview with Nasrullah Babar, Islamabad, April 18, 1998.

20. Robert G. Wirsing, *Pakistan's Security under Zia, 1977–1988* (New York: St. Martin's, 1991), 38–39.

21. William Borders, "Pakistan, Under Bhutto's Strong Rule, Shows Signs of Progress," *New York Times,* January 29, 1976.

22. State Department memorandum from Assistant Secretary of State Atherton to Secretary Kissinger, August 2, 1976, obtained through FOIA.

23. Zulfikar Ali Bhutto, "Bilateralism: New Directions," *Pakistan Horizon,* Vol. 29, no. 4 (1976), 3–59.

24. State Department briefing paper for President Ford's meeting with Prime Minister Bhutto, February 2, 1975, obtained through FOIA. A former chairman of Pakistan's Atomic Energy Commission, Munir Ahmed Khan, asserted that because of international safeguards the reprocessing plant was not directly intended as part of the weapons program but as a way to gain technical knowledge that indirectly would help Pakistan's efforts. Interview with Munir Ahmed Khan, Islamabad, May 8, 1998.

25. State Department telegram to USDEL secretary, May 5, 1976, obtained through FOIA.

26. Memorandum to Kissinger from Undersecretary of State Joseph Sisco, February 12, 1976, and State Department telegram to U.S. Mission to the International Atomic Energy Agency (IAEA), April 9, 1976, reprinted in *U.S. Nuclear Non-Proliferation Policy, 1945–1991* (Washington, D.C.: National Security Archive, 1991).

27. State Department memorandum to Secretary Kissinger, May 11, 1976, reprinted in *U.S. Nuclear Non-Proliferation Policy.*

28. Bernard Gwertzman, "Kissinger Meets Pakistani Leader on Nuclear Issue," *New York Times,* August 9, 1976.

29. Interview with Brent Scowcroft, Washington, D.C., May 4, 1999. Scowcroft was Ford's national security adviser and, later, George Bush's.

30. Briefing paper for Secretary Kissinger's visit to Pakistan from Assistant Secretary Atherton, August 2, 1976, obtained through FOIA.

31. Gwertzman, "Kissinger Meets Pakistani Leader."

32. Memorandum of conversation between Bhutto and Kissinger, August 9, 1976, obtained through FOIA. Among the attendees were National Security Council staff member Robert Oakley (who would serve as U.S. ambassador to Pakistan in 1988–91) and Bhutto's diplomatic assistant Riaz Khokar (who would be Pakistan's ambassador to the United States in 1997–99).

33. Ibid.

34. Interview with Robert Oakley, Washington, D.C., June 14, 1995.

35. Ibid.; and Steve Weissman and Herbert Krosney, *The Islamic Bomb* (New York: Times Books, 1981), 163.

36. Interviews with Agha Shahi, Islamabad, January 29, 1996, and Air Marshal Zulfikar Ali Khan, Islamabad, December 6, 1995. Both took part in the meeting during which Bhutto discussed Kissinger's proposal.

37. Interview with Oakley, Washington, D.C., April 2, 1999.

38. Weissman and Krosney, *Islamic Bomb,* 175.

39. Interview with Munir Ahmed Khan, Islamabad, May 5, 1998.

Chapter 9. Carter: The Low Point

1. William Borders, "Pakistan Wonders Whether Ties to U.S. Will Erode under Carter," *New York Times,* December 26, 1977.

2. Peter Constable oral history, Association for Diplomatic Studies and Training (ADST), Arlington, Virginia.

3. William Borders, "Bhutto Faces Strong Challenge in Elections," *New York Times,* February 27, 1977. For more detailed discussion of the election campaign, see Shahid Javed Burki, *Pakistan under Bhutto, 1971–1977,* 2nd ed. (Boulder: Westview,

1991), 171–221; and Marvin Weinbaum, "Where Everyone Lost," *Asian Survey,* July 1977, 599–618.

4. Emma Duncan, *Breaking the Curfew* (London: Joseph, 1989), 68–69.

5. Quoted in Stanley Wolpert, *Zulfi Bhutto of Pakistan* (New York: Oxford University Press, 1993), 278–79.

6. "Opposition Demonstrations in Pakistani Cities Heighten Crisis Mood," "Pakistani Police Wound 21 in Riots over Arrest of Opposition Leaders," and "Part of Karachi under Army Rule," *New York Times,* March 15, 19, and 20, 1977.

7. Wolpert, *Zulfi Bhutto,* 262–63.

8. Khalid Mahmud Arif, *Working with Zia* (Karachi: Oxford University Press, 1995), 70–73.

9. Memorandum from Assistant Secretary Alfred Atherton to Secretary of State Cyrus Vance, April 22, 1977, obtained through Freedom of Information Act request (FOIA).

10. Ibid. The decision to revoke the license was taken by the Bureau for Near East and South Asian Affairs after a *Washington Post* reporter asked the Pakistan desk whether exporting tear gas to Pakistan was consistent with Carter's emphasis on human rights. Secretary of State Vance and the top level of the State Department became aware of the action only after the fact.

11. Lewis M. Simons, "Pakistan, Spurred by Tear Gas Decision, Seen Reconsidering Ties to U.S." *Washington Post,* April 27, 1977.

12. U.S. diplomats serving in Pakistan assumed that the Pakistani intelligence services routinely tapped their telephone conversations.

13. Interview with Howard Schaffer, Washington, D.C., October 27, 1995, and Constable oral history.

14. Lewis W. Simons, "Bhutto Alleges U.S. Plot," *Washington Post,* April 29, 1997; and James M. Markham, "Pakistan Mediation by Arabs Reported," *New York Times,* April 29, 1997.

15. Constable oral history; James Markham, "Bhutto Presses Political Attack as Clashes Continue," *New York Times,* May 1, 1977; and "U.S. Responds to Bhutto," *Washington Post,* May 4, 1977.

16. Constable oral history. Constable had become the chargé after Byroade completed his assignment and left Pakistan, and served in that capacity until the new ambassador arrived in July 1977.

17. Ibid.

18. Arif, *Working with Zia,* 77–78. Agha Shahi, the foreign secretary at the time, told the author that when the foreign minister discussed charges of U.S. interference with Foreign Ministry officials, he was never able to provide any specifics. Interview with Agha Shahi, Islamabad, December 31, 1995.

19. Memorandum of conversation between Secretary of State Cyrus Vance and Foreign Minister Aziz Ahmed, May 31, 1977, obtained through FOIA.

20. Lewis W. Simons, "Charges of U.S. Conspiracy Win Bhutto Vital Army Support," *Washington Post,* May 8, 1977.

21. Memorandum from Assistant Secretary of State Atherton to Secretary Vance, "Denial of A-7 Sales to Pakistan," June 3, 1977, obtained through FOIA; and Bernard Weinraub, "U.S. Withholds Sale of Jets to Pakistan," *New York Times,* June 3, 1977.

22. Embassy Islamabad telegram to State Department, June 4, 1977, obtained through FOIA.

23. Wolpert, *Zulfi Bhutto,* 290.

24. Ibid., 299. Reflecting his suspicions about the United States, as well as his increasingly desperate situation, Bhutto reportedly told the Soviet ambassador on June 15, 1977, that he was ready to withdraw from CENTO if the Soviets agreed to support Pakistan. Ibid., 277–79.

25. Arif, *Working with Zia,* 79–81.

26. Interview with Arthur Hummel, Chevy Chase, Md., July 15, 1995.

27. Ibid.

28. Interviews with Peter Constable, Washington, D.C., March 15, 1997, and with Schaffer.

29. Arif, *Working with Zia,* 93–94.

30. Wolpert, *Zulfi Bhutto,* 302.

31. Ibid., 308.

32. Arif, *Working with Zia,* 113.

33. "Bhutto, Released from Detention, Assails Martial Law in Pakistan," *New York Times,* July 30, 1977.

34. See Wolpert, *Zulfi Bhutto,* 304–15; and Arif, *Working with Zia,* 99–115 and 135–47, for accounts of events that followed the July 5, 1977, coup.

35. Embassy Islamabad telegram to State Department, September 3, 1977, obtained through FOIA.

36. After the term of office of President Fazal Elahi Chaudhry expired in September 1978, Zia assumed the position. Under the 1973 constitution, the president had been a titular head of state, with real power residing with the prime minister.

37. See Dennis Kux, *India and the United States: Estranged Democracies, 1941–91* (Washington, D.C.: National Defense University Press, 1993), 352–55, for fuller discussion of the Carter visit to India.

38. The original Glenn amendment to the foreign assistance act barred aid to countries that had not signed the NPT and that imported nuclear fuel reprocessing equipment, technology, or materials. The Symington amendment barred aid to non-NPT signatories that imported uranium-enrichment equipment, technology, or materials. Because of legislative language, a subsequent amendment by Senator Glenn covered both reprocessing and enrichment transfers. To avoid confusion, the entire package is often referred to as the Glenn-Symington amendment. Usually, however, the Glenn amendment is cited when discussing fuel reprocessing, and the Symington amendment is invoked when discussing uranium enrichment.

39. Steve Weissman and Herbert Krosney, *The Islamic Bomb* (New York: Times Books, 1981), 165.

40. "Pakistan: France Must Hold to Nuclear Deal," *Washington Post,* January 12, 1978.

41. Weissman and Krosney, *The Islamic Bomb,* 169–71. See Shirin R. Tahir-Kheli, *The United States and Pakistan: The Evolution of an Influence Relationship* (New York: Praeger, 1982), 128–31, for a useful discussion of the dealings with the French regarding the reprocessing plant. Iqbal Akhund's *Memoirs of a Bystander: A Life in Diplomacy* (Karachi: Oxford University Press, 1997), 272–80, presents an illuminating account of French-Pakistani dealings. Akhund was Pakistan's ambassador in Paris at the time.

42. "U.S. to Renew Aid to Pakistan," *Washington Post,* August 25, 1978.

43. Interview with Jane Coon, Washington, D.C., September 15, 1995.

44. Weissman and Krosney, *The Islamic Bomb,* 172.

45. See Don Oberdorfer, "Pakistan: The Quest for an Atomic Bomb," *Washington Post,* August 27, 1979, for a detailed report on Pakistan's secret nuclear program and the U.S. government's response.

46. Interview with Hummel.

47. State Department telegrams to Embassy Islamabad, March 21 and 22, 1978, obtained through FOIA.

48. Embassy Islamabad telegram to State Department, April 3, 1978, obtained through FOIA.

49. Embassy Islamabad telegram to State Department, December 19, 1978, obtained through FOIA.

50. Interview with Shahi.

51. "Pakistan Quits CENTO: Calls Alliance Irrelevant," *New York Times,* March 13, 1979.

52. Interview with Shahi.

53. Islamabad Embassy telegram to State Department, February 6, 1979, obtained through FOIA.

54. Embassy Islamabad telegram to State Department, March 2, 1979, obtained through FOIA.

55. See Arif, *Working with Zia,* 189–220, for an account of Bhutto's final days.

56. Interview with Hummel. Despite explicit U.S. government denials, many Pakistanis, including Bhutto's daughter, Benazir, continue to see a U.S. hand behind Bhutto's overthrow. Interview with Benazir Bhutto, Karachi, April 14, 1998. For example, Iqbal Akhund, Pakistan's UN representative at the time, concluded that the United States was in some fashion involved in Bhutto's overthrow despite explicit denials he received from U.S. envoy to the United Nations Andrew Young and former Central Intelligence Agency Director George Bush. Akhund, *Memoirs of a Bystander,* 319–24 and 327.

57. Sir Morrice James, *Pakistan Chronicle* (Karachi: Oxford University Press, 1993), 75.

58. Richard Burt, "U.S. Aid to Pakistan Cut after Evidence of Atom Arms Plan" and "Pakistan Is Offered a Choice on A-Arms," *New York Times,* April 7 and 17, 1979; and interview with Coon.

59. Thomas P. Thornton, "Between the Stools?: U.S. Policy towards Pakistan During the Carter Administration," *Asian Survey,* October 1982, 967; and Simon Winchester, "Pakistan Shows Pique at Criticism in Bhutto Case," and Richard Weinraub, "U.S. Expressed Concern over Sentence for Bhutto," *Washington Post,* April 7, 1979.

60. Robert Trumbell, "Pakistan Denies It Plans A-Bomb; Denounces Washington Aid Cutoff," *New York Times,* April 9, 1979.

61. Interview with senior Pakistani official.

62. Embassy Islamabad telegram to State Department, August 17, 1979, reprinted in *U.S. Nuclear Non-Proliferation Policy, 1945–1990* (Washington, D.C.: National Security Archives, 1991).

63. Seymour Topping, "Zia Denies Pakistan Builds Nuclear Bomb and Urges U.S. to Resume Aid," *New York Times,* September 23, 1979.

64. Richard Burt, "U.S. Will Press Pakistan to Halt A-Arms Project," and "Pakistan Protests to U.S. Envoy on Nuclear Report," *New York Times,* August 12 and 15, 1979; and Don Oberdorfer, "Arms Sales to Pakistan Urged to Stave Off A-Bomb There,"

"U.S. Denies Covert Plans in Pakistan," and "Pakistan: The Quest for an Atomic Bomb," *Washington Post,* August 6, 15, and 27, 1979.

65. Embassy Islamabad telegram to State Department, June 28, 1979, reprinted in *Documents from the U.S. Espionage: U.S. Intervention in Islamic Countries, Pakistan,* Vol. 1 (Tehran: Iranian Revolutionary Authorities, 1979–91), 76–77.

66. Interview with Shahi, Islamabad, January 26, 1996.

67. Don Oberdorfer, "Uranium Parley with Pakistanis Is Inconclusive," and "Effort to Block Pakistan from A-Bomb Faltering," *Washington Post,* October 18 and 20, 1979; and "U.S.-Pakistan Talks Inconclusive," *New York Times,* October 19, 1979.

68. Interview with Shahi, January 26, 1996.

69. Ibid.

70. Interview with Hummel. See also Diego Cordovez and Selig Harrison, *Out of Afghanistan* (New York: Oxford University Press, 1995), 33–34.

71. Interview with Nasrullah Babar, Islamabad, April 18, 1998.

72. Robert M. Gates, *From the Shadows* (New York: Simon and Schuster, 1996), 144–47, describes Carter administration deliberations about the Afghan covert program. Congressional reforms passed in 1975 required an explicit presidential authorization, called a "finding," before the CIA could undertake a covert action program.

73. Herbert G. Hagerty's "Attack on the U.S. Embassy in Islamabad, 1979," in Joseph G. Sullivan, ed., *Embassies under Siege* (Washington, D.C.: Brassey's, 1995), 71–89, provides a detailed, eyewitness report of the incident: Hagerty was one of the 137 people trapped inside the communications vault in the embassy. The account presented here also draws on interviews with Hummel, Shahi, Gen. K. M. Arif (Rawalpindi, December 10, 1995), Maj. Gen. Mujibur Rehman (Islamabad, March 6, 1996), an oral history by Deputy Chief of Mission Barrington King (ADST), and a telephone conversation with *Time* correspondent Marcia Gauger (June 4, 1998). All were present in Islamabad or Rawalpindi at the time of the attack on the embassy.

74. Michael Kaufman, "Body of 2d American Is Found in Islamabad Embassy," *New York Times,* November 23, 1979.

75. Interview with Hummel.

76. Interview with Thomas P. Thornton, Washington, D.C., September 28, 1995.

77. Thornton, "Between the Stools," 969.

78. Interview with Thornton.

79. Interview with Shahi, December 31, 1995.

80. Interview with Arif.

81. Interview with Shahi.

82. Interviews with Arif and with Shahi, December 31, 1995.

83. Interview with Arif, Rawalpindi, March 29, 1998.

84. Interview with Arif, December 10, 1995.

85. Interview with Shahi, Islamabad, January 29, 1996.

86. Terence Smith, "Carter Embargoes Technology for Soviets and Curtails Fishing and Grain," *New York Times,* January 5, 1980.

87. Memorandum from Assistant Secretary Harold Saunders to Secretary of State Cyrus Vance, "NSC Discussion of Support for Pakistan," January 1, 1980, obtained through FOIA.

88. Interviews with Coon and Thornton.

89. Stuart Auerbach, "Pakistan Is Reluctant to Accept Limited U.S. Arms Pledge," *Washington Post,* January 6, 1980.

90. State Department Scope Paper for Shahi visit, undated but presumably January 8 or 9, 1980, obtained through FOIA.

91. Memorandum from Assistant Secretary of State Harold H. Saunders to Secretary Vance, "Agha Shahi Visit to Washington," January 8, 1980, obtained through FOIA.

92. State Department Talking Points for Secretary Vance's meetings with Agha Shahi, January 12, 1980, obtained through FOIA.

93. Stuart Auerbach, "Pakistan Ties Arms Aid to Economic Assistance," *Washington Post,* January 14, 1980.

94. Don Oberdorfer, "Pakistan Offered $400 Million Aid," *Washington Post,* January 15, 1980.

95. William Borders, "Pakistani Dismisses $400 Million in Aid Offered by U.S. as 'Peanuts,'" *New York Times,* January 19, 1980; and Stuart Auerbach, "Pakistan Seeking U.S. Guarantees in Formal Treaty," *Washington Post,* January 18, 1980.

96. William Branigan, "Pakistan Seeks Billions in U.S. Aid," *Washington Post,* January 23, 1980.

97. Zbigniew Brzezinski, *Power and Principle: Memoirs of the National Security Adviser, 1977–1981* (New York: Farrar, Straus, Giroux, 1983), 448; State Department telegram to Embassy Islamabad, January 18, 1980, obtained through FOIA; and John M. Goshko, "U.S. Forging Ahead on Pakistan," *Washington Post,* January 19, 1980.

98. Terence Smith, "Carter Proposes Taking Olympics Away from Moscow," *New York Times,* January 21, 1980.

99. "State of the Union Message," January 21, 1980, *Presidential Papers of the Presidents of the United States: Jimmy Carter, 1980* (Washington, D.C.: U.S. Government Printing Office, 1981), 172.

100. Undated Department of State Scope Paper for Brzezinski-Christopher visit to Pakistan, obtained through FOIA.

101. Interview with Coon. The reference refers to Poland's refusal to accept Nazi pressures in 1939 and Czechoslovakia's earlier buckling under to Hitler.

102. Interview with Arif.

103. Thornton interview, Washington, D.C., November 13, 1998.

104. Interview with Arif; and Brzezinski, *Power and Principle,* 449.

105. Interviews with Shahi and Arif.

106. Interviews with Coon and Thornton.

107. Embassy Islamabad telegram to State Department, March 6, 1980, obtained through FOIA; and Dusko Doder, "Pakistan Uninterested in U.S. Aid Offer," *Washington Post,* March 6, 1980.

108. "Pakistani Foreign Minister Rejects $400 Million U.S. Aid as Harmful," *New York Times,* March 6, 1980.

109. Embassy Islamabad telegram to State Department, March 9, 1980, obtained through FOIA.

110. Memorandum to Secretary of State Edmund Muskie from Acting Assistant Secretary of State Peter Constable, "Assistance to Pakistan," May 22, 1980, obtained through FOIA; Embassy Islamabad telegram to State Department, June 11, 1980, obtained thorough FOIA; and Thornton, "Between the Stools," 972–73.

111. Charles G. Cogan, "Partners in Time: The CIA and Afghanistan since 1979," *World Policy Journal,* Vol. 10, no. 2 (Summer 1993). At the time of the Afghan assistance, Cogan was the Near East division chief of the CIA's Directorate of Operations.

112. Gates, *From the Shadows,* 148.

113. Ibid., 149; and interviews with Arif and senior U.S. intelligence officers.

114. Interviews with senior U.S. intelligence officers.

115. "Pakistani Foreign Minister Rejects $400 Million U.S. Aid."

116. Interviews with Arif, a senior U.S. intelligence officer, and Eliza Van Hollen, McLean, Va., May 3, 1999. Van Hollen was the Afghan specialist in the State Department's Bureau of Intelligence and Research.

117. Don Oberdorfer, "U.S. Urged to Keep Out of Iran-Iraq War," *Washington Post,* October 4, 1980.

118. Thornton, "Between the Stools," 973.

119. Interview with K. M. Arif, Villanova, Penn., October 27, 1997.

Chapter 10. Reagan: Partners Again

1. Interview with Najmuddin Sheikh, Islamabad, April 27, 1998.

2. Interview with Arthur Hummel, Chevy Chase, Md., June 15, 1995.

3. State Department memorandum from Assistant Secretary–Designate Nicholas Veliotes to Deputy Secretary of State William Clark, March 7, 1981, obtained through Freedom of Information Act request (FOIA).

4. Interviews with Agha Shahi, Islamabad, December 31, 1995, and January 29, 1996, and K. M. Arif, Rawalpindi, December 10, 1995.

5. Interviews with Alexander Haig, Washington, D.C., July 28, 1998, Shahi, and Arif.

6. Interview with Jane Coon, Washington, D.C., September 15, 1995.

7. Interviews with Haig and Arif.

8. Interview with senior U.S. intelligence officer.

9. Interview with Arif.

10. "Pakistan Reports U.S. Has Offered 5-Year Aid Deal," *New York Times,* April 22, 1981.

11. Don Oberdorfer, "U.S., Pakistan Progressing on New Aid Plan," *Washington Post,* April 22, 1981.

12. Interviews with Robert McFarlane, Washington, D.C., October 20, 1996, and Shahi.

13. Interviews with Shahi, Arif, and Coon.

14. Interviews with Shahi, Coon, and Thomas Thornton, Washington, D.C., September 28, 1995.

15. Interview with Robert Peck, Charleston, W.V., May 15, 1991; and Barbara Slavin and Milt Freudenheim, "The World: Pakistan Takes Aid on Its Terms," *New York Times,* September 20, 1981.

16. Judith Miller, "Pakistan Is Being Offered the F-16 as Part of a U.S. Military Aid Plan," and Juan de Onis, "Agreement on Pakistan Aid," *New York Times,* June 13 and 16, 1981; "Silent Buckley Leaves Pakistan," Bernard Gwertzman, "Pakistan Agrees to U.S. Aid Plan and F-16 Delivery Schedule," *New York Times,* September 10 and 16, 1981; Edward Gargan, "U.S. Aide Defends Sale of F-16s to Pakistan," *New York Times,* November 9, 1981; Stuart Auerbach, "Delay on F-16s Hurts U.S. Ties with Pakistan," and "U.S. to Speed F-16s as Pakistan Approves Aid," *Washington Post,* August 14 and September 16, 1981; and Don Oberdorfer, "Hill Panels Back F-16s for Pakistan," *Washington Post,* November 18, 1981.

17. Interviews with Arif and Lt. Gen. Ejaz Azim, Islamabad, November 30, 1995.

18. Interview with Ronald Spiers, South Londonderry, Vt., December 1, 1997.

19. Interview with Arif.

20. Ronald Spiers oral history, Association for Diplomatic Studies and Training, Arlington, Va.

21. Interview with William Barnds, former staff director of the House Foreign Affairs Committee Asia Subcommittee, Washington, D.C., June 22, 1998.

22. State Department telegram to Embassy Islamabad, April 27, 1981, obtained through FOIA.

23. James Buckley, letter to the editor, *New York Times,* August 5, 1981.

24. Interview with Spiers; and Spiers oral history.

25. Ibid.

26. Interview with senior U.S. intelligence officer involved with the Afghan program.

27. Interview with concerned CIA chief of station.

28. Interviews with CIA officer, Arif, and Robert M. Gates, *From the Shadows* (New York: Simon and Schuster, 1996), 252.

29. Interviews with knowledgeable U.S. intelligence officers and Spiers.

30. Charles C. Cogan, "Partners in Time, the CIA and Afghanistan," *World Policy Journal,* Summer 1993, 79; and interview with Spiers. See Gates, *In the Shadows,* 251–52, for his description of Zia's "red triangle" briefing for Casey.

31. A useful source about the management of the Afghan program is Mohammed Yousaf and Mark Adkin, *The Bear Trap* (Lahore: Jang Publishers, 1992). A former ISI logistics chief for the program, Brigadier Yousaf provides a good account of the mechanics of the Afghan program. The book, however, suffers badly when Yousaf strays from his area of expertise. See also Steve Coll, "The Anatomy of a Victory: CIA's Covert War in Afghanistan," *Washington Post,* July 20, 1992.

32. Interviews with U.S. intelligence officers.

33. Don Oberdorfer, "U.S. and Pakistan Progressing on New Aid Plan," *Washington Post,* April 22, 1981.

34. Arnaut van Lynden, "High Pakistani Aide Expects U.S. Congress to Approve Assistance," *Washington Post,* May 3, 1981.

35. This discussion of the Afghan peace negotiations draws heavily on two excellent ringside accounts: Riaz Mohammed Khan, *Untying the Afghan Knot: Negotiating the Soviet Withdrawal* (Durham: Duke University Press, 1991); and Diego Cordovez and Selig Harrison, *Out of Afghanistan* (New York: Oxford University Press, 1995). Cordovez focuses on the negotiations while Harrison provides the background for the talks. Riaz Khan provides the Pakistani perspective as a member of his country's negotiating team.

36. Interview with Shahi, December 12, 1995.

37. According to Howard Schaffer, deputy assistant secretary of state for South Asia in 1981–1984 and 1987–89, Yaqub greatly impressed George Shultz and other senior U.S. officials. Interview with Schaffer, October 27, 1995.

38. Interview with Sahibzada Yaqub Khan, Islamabad, December 30, 1995.

39. Interviews with Yaqub, Arif, and Niaz Naik, Islamabad, December 13, 1995.

40. Interviews with Richard Murphy, New York, June 30, 1999, and other concerned State Department and CIA officials.

41. Interview with Spiers.

42. Interview with Schaffer.

43. State Department briefing memorandum and talking notes for Secretary Shultz's meeting with Zia ul-Haq, December 6, 1982, obtained through FOIA.

44. State Department memorandum of conversation between President Zia and Secretary Shultz, December 6, 1982, obtained through FOIA.

45. Memorandum of conversation between Presidents Reagan and Zia and aides, Washington, D.C., December 7, 1982, obtained through FOIA.

46. William K. Stevens, "Zia Sees Pakistan as the Front Line," *New York Times,* December 8, 1982.

47. Memorandum of conversation between Presidents Reagan and Zia and aides, December 7, 1982.

48. William Claiborne, "Zia Says U.S.-Pakistani Ties Based on Strategic Concerns," *Washington Post,* December 3, 1982.

49. Bernard Weinraub, "Zia Sees No Quick Solution to Soviet Role in Afghanistan," *New York Times,* December 9, 1982.

50. Riaz Khan, *Untying the Afghan Knot,* 113–18.

51. Interview with Yaqub, Islamabad, February 29, 1996.

52. Cordovez and Harrison, *Out of Afghanistan,* 97–98.

53. "U.N. Reports Progress in Talks on Afghanistan," *New York Times,* April 23, 1983.

54. *Pakistan Times* (Lahore), May 12, 1983.

55. Bernard Weinraub, "Pakistanis Tell of Soviet Hint on Afghanistan," "Soviet Said to Seek Afghan Peace," and "An Opening on Afghanistan?" *New York Times,* May 27, June 2 and 5, 1983.

56. Riaz Khan, *Untying the Afghan Knot,* 118–20; and Cordovez and Harrison, *Out of Afghanistan,* 131–32.

57. Interview with Yaqub; and Riaz Khan, *Untying the Afghan Knot,* 120–22.

58. Interviews with Yaqub.

59. Cordovez and Harrison, *Out of Afghanistan,* 102–7.

60. Riaz Khan, *Untying the Afghan Knot,* 125–26.

61. Interview with Yaqub, Islamabad, March 20, 1996.

62. Ibid.

63. Telegram from USDEL (U.S. delegation) Secretary in Islamabad to State Department, July 4, 1983, obtained through FOIA.

64. Interview with Nicholas Veliotes, Arlington, Va., October 20, 1997.

65. Telegram from USDEL Secretary to the White House, July 4, 1983, obtained through FOIA.

66. Philip Taubman, "Afghan Refugees Hear Shultz Vow 'We Are With You'," *New York Times,* July 4, 1983.

67. Interview with Veliotes.

68. Richard Halloran, "Weinberger Meets Zia and Afghan Refugees," *New York Times,* October 2, 1983.

69. Fred Hiatt, "Weinberger, in Pakistan, Calls Riots Internal Problem," *Washington Post,* October 1, 1983.

70. State Department briefing papers for Vice President George Bush's visit to Pakistan, May 1984, obtained through FOIA.

71. William Claiborne, "Bush at Khyber Pass: Whiff of War and Fine-Tuned Welcome," *Washington Post,* May 18, 1984.

72. Embassy Islamabad telegram to White House, May 17, 1984, obtained through FOIA.

73. Embassy Islamabad telegram to State Department, May 26, 1984, obtained through FOIA.

74. Interview with U.S. intelligence officer.

75. Interview with Veliotes.

76. Interview with U.S. intelligence officer.

77. Background paper on Afghanistan in State Department briefing book for the May 1984 Pakistan trip of Vice President George Bush, obtained through FOIA.

78. Telegram from USDEL Secretary in New York to State Department, October 1, 1984, obtained through FOIA.

79. Interview with U.S. intelligence officer.

80. Interviews with U.S. intelligence officers.

81. Interview with Spiers.

82. Interviews with U.S. intelligence officers.

83. Interview with Eliza Van Hollen, McLean, Va., January 15, 1998. Van Hollen, who followed Afghanistan for the State Department's Bureau of Intelligence and Research, argued strongly that the CIA should have taken a tougher line on arms distribution with the Pakistanis.

84. Cited in Zahid Malik, *Dr. A. Q. Khan and the Islamic Bomb* (Islamabad: Hurmat Publications, 1992), 116.

85. "Cranston Says Pakistan Can Make A-Bomb," *New York Times,* June 21, 1984.

86. Rick Atkinson, "Nuclear Parts Sought by Pakistan," and Alan Cranston, "The China Treaty: Don't Blame Israel," *Washington Post,* July 21 and August 7, 1984. Credible intelligence that China was providing assistance for Pakistan's nuclear program caused further difficulties that ultimately led the Reagan administration not to implement a nuclear agreement that had been reached with Beijing.

87. Letter from President Reagan to Zia ul-Haq, September 12, 1984. The sanitized text, obtained under the Freedom of Information Act, deletes the reference to the 5 percent enrichment limit. This limit was, however, cited in an October 26, 1984, *Washington Post* article.

88. Interview with Pakistani Foreign Ministry official who participated in drafting the response, Islamabad, February 20, 1998.

89. George P. Shultz, *Turmoil and Triumph: My Years as Secretary of State* (New York: Scribner's, 1993), 493–94.

90. Letter from John Glenn to fellow Senators, March 27, 1984.

91. Interview with Leonard Weiss, Senate Government Operations Committee chief of staff and aide to Senator John Glenn, November 28, 1998. An active promoter of nonproliferation, Weiss negotiated the amendment on behalf of Senator Glenn.

92. Interviews with Azim, Abdul Sattar, and Lt. Gen. Syed Refaqat, Rawalpindi, February 16, 1996.

93. Interview with Stephen Solarz, Washington, D.C., February 13, 1997; and Robert Pear, "Legislators Move on Atom Exports," *New York Times,* March 27, 1985.

94. Letter from Shirin Tahir-Kheli to author, July 1999. In 1985, Tahir-Kheli was responsible for South Asia on the National Security Council staff.

95. Interviews with Azim and McFarlane. The account of the Zia-McFarlane meeting was provided by Azim, who was briefed by Zia. McFarlane described it as accurate.

96. Interviews with Yaqub, Arif, and Refaqat, April 17, 1996.

97. Interview with senior U.S. intelligence official.

98. A friendly foreign intelligence service had purloined the blueprint from the hotel room of A. Q. Khan.

99. Interview with U.S. intelligence officer.

100. Interview with Munir Ahmed Khan, Islamabad, April 16, 1998.

101. See Khalid Mahmud Arif, *Working with Zia* (Karachi: Oxford University Press, 1995), 225–33, for further background.

102. William Claiborne, "Vote Puts Pakistan Nearer Democracy but Zia Faces Risks, U.S. Envoy Says," *Washington Post,* February 27, 1985.

103. Steven R. Weisman, "How Much Democracy Will Zia Accept?" "Shurocracy in Pakistan" (editorial), and "Pakistan's Parliament Reopens after 8 Years," *New York Times,* March 3, 9, and 24, 1985; Steven R. Weisman, "Pakistan's President Agrees to Ease His Grip," *New York Times,* November 10, 1985; and "For Zia, Much of Power Remains" and "Pakistan Ruler Ends Martial Law," *New York Times,* December 29 and 31, 1985.

104. Riaz Khan, *Untying the Afghan Knot,* 89; and Cordovez and Harrison, *Out of Afghanistan,* 187–89.

105. Cordovez and Harrison, *Out of Afghanistan,* 191 and 219.

106. Ibid., 190–94; Riaz Khan, *Untying the Afghan Knot,* 140; and interview with former undersecretary of state Michael Armacost, Washington, D.C., January 5, 1998.

107. Cordovez and Harrison, *Out of Afghanistan,* 226.

108. Ibid., 227.

109. See ibid., 194–98, for a detailed account of the decision to provide the Stinger missile.

110. Michael Armacost said that he agreed to the Stinger proposal on the strong recommendation of Morton Abromowitz, then head of the State Department's Intelligence and Research Bureau. Interview with Armacost.

111. Peter W. Rodman, *More Precious than Peace* (New York: Scribner's, 1994), 339–40.

112. Interview with senior U.S. intelligence officer.

113. A senior CIA official estimated that only about forty thousand Afghans were actually fighting at any one time, or one-tenth of the number for whom arms were provided.

114. Cordovez and Harrison, *Untying the Afghan Knot,* 274–75.

115. Ibid., 282.

116. Interview with Yaqub.

117. Letter from Shirin Tahir-Kheli to author, July 1999.

118. State Department briefing papers for Junejo's meetings with former president Nixon and Henry Kissinger, July 18, 1986, obtained through FOIA.

119. Stuart Auerbach, "U.S. Eyes Technology Agreement," and Don Oberdorfer, "Pakistani Spurns Soviets' Pullout Plan," *Washington Post,* July 17 and 18, 1986.

120. Robert Woodward, "Pakistan Reported Near Atom Arms Production," *Washington Post,* November 4, 1986.

121. Interview with Armacost.

122. Sanjoy Hazarika, "A Tense India Seeks Talks with Pakistan and Sees No Attack," and Steven R. Weisman, "Pakistan Appeals to India on Crisis," *New York Times,* January 25 and 26, 1987; and "India-Pakistan Troop Tensions Ease" and "Pakistani to

Visit India," February 5 and 18, 1987. Kanti Bajpai et al., *Brasstacks and Beyond: Perception and the Management of Crisis in South Asia* (New Delhi: Manohar, 1995), provides a comprehensive study of the episode. See also Devin T. Hagerty, *The Consequences of Nuclear Proliferation: Lessons from South Asia* (Cambridge: MIT Press, 1998), 96–115.

123. Mitchell Reiss, *Bridled Ambition: Why Countries Constrain Their Nuclear Capabilities* (Washington, D.C.: Woodrow Wilson Center Press, 1995), 218.

124. *Observer* (London), and Steven R. Weisman, "Report of Pakistani A-Bomb Causes a Stir in the Region," *New York Times,* March 1, 1987.

125. *Financial Times,* March 2, 1987.

126. Interviews with Refaqat, Munir Ahmed Khan, and Maleeha Lodhi, Islamabad, April 20, 1998. Lodhi replaced Mushahid Hussain as editor of *The Muslim.*

127. *Time,* March 30, 1987, 42.

128. Interview with Jamshed Marker, New York, November 20, 1998.

129. Elaine Sciolono, "Afghan Air Raids against Pakistan Are Said to Kill 85," *New York Times,* March 25, 1987. Hinton told the author that he had given the essence of the nuclear speech several months earlier before a military audience and decided that it was time to repeat the warning in a public forum. Telephone interview with Deane Hinton, September 15, 1999.

130. Michael R. Gordon, "Pakistani Seized by U.S. in a Plot on A-Arms Alloy," *New York Times,* July 15, 1987.

131. An article by Hedrick Smith in the March 6, 1988, *New York Times Magazine* provides a detailed account of the Pervez episode and the overall Pakistani nuclear saga.

132. For further coverage of the Pervez affair, see articles in the *New York Times,* July 16, 17, 18, 19, 22, 23, 26, and 29, 1987. See Michael Gordon, "U.S. Indicts 3 in the Export of Equipment to Pakistan," *New York Times,* July 18, 1987, regarding arrest of the trio in Hong Kong.

133. Elaine Sciolino, "U.S. to Seek Pakistani Aid in Atom Case," and Michael Gordon, "Pakistan Rejects Atomic Inspection," *New York Times,* August 2 and 6, 1988.

134. Interview with Marker.

135. Letter from President Reagan to House Speaker Jim Wright, December 17, 1987, obtained through FOIA. Earlier in 1987, State Department legal adviser Abraham Sofaer had found that a country could "possess" a nuclear device even if it had not assembled all the elements.

136. Michael R. Gordon, "Congress Delays New Pakistan Aid Amid Nuclear Rift," and "Businessman Convicted in Pakistan Nuclear Plot," *New York Times,* September 30 and December 18, 1987; and David K. Shipler, "Pakistan Tied to Atom Shipping Plot," and "Man Gets Prison Term in Bid to Send Metals to Pakistan," *New York Times,* January 14 and February 11, 1988.

137. Presidential Determination No. 88-5, January 15, 1988, *Federal Register,* Vol. 53, February 5, 1988, 3325.

138. Testimony of Deputy Assistant Secretary of State Robert A. Peck before the House Foreign Affairs Asia and Pacific Subcommittee, February 18, 1988.

139. Rodman, *More Precious than Peace,* 344.

140. Interview with Armacost.

141. Quoted in Cordovez and Harrison, *Out of Afghanistan,* 259.

142. Riaz Khan, *Untying the Afghan Knot,* 227; and interview with Refaqat.

143. Interviews with Yaqub and Refaqat.

144. Riaz Khan, *Untying the Afghan Knot,* 254–57; and interviews with Refaqat and Sattar.

145. Elaine Sciolino, "Shultz Said to Back Pakistan on Afghan Coalition Regime," *New York Times,* February 23, 1988.

146. Richard Weintraub, "Pakistani Leaders Urge Afghan Accord," *Washington Post,* March 7, 1988.

147. Riaz Khan, *Untying the Afghan Knot,* 261–62.

148. Interview with Refaqat, who commented that Zia used Hammer as a personal back-channel in his dealings with Moscow as well as Kabul.

149. Riaz Khan, *Untying the Afghan Knot,* 248–53. See also Robert G. Wirsing, *Pakistan's Security under Zia, 1977–1988* (New York: St. Martin's, 1991), 66–71, for a useful discussion of the episode.

150. David K. Shipler, "Pakistan's Afghan Moves Perplex U.S.," *New York Times,* January 15, 1988.

151. Quoted in Rodman, *More Precious than Peace,* 345.

152. Interview with Robert Oakley, Washington, D.C., July 14, 1995; and Rodman, *More Precious than Peace,* 345–47.

153. Shultz, *Turmoil and Triumph,* 1091.

154. Interview with Robert Oakley, Washington, D.C., July 15, 1998.

155. "Pentagon Sends Team to Help Pakistanis," Henry Kamm, "Blast in Pakistan at Weapons Depot Kills at Least 75," and "Pakistan Chief Hints Sabotage in Arms Blasts," *New York Times,* April 10, 11, and 12, 1988.

156. "Pakistani Leader Says Blast at Arms Depot Was Sabotage," *New York Times,* April 15, 1988.

157. Interviews with Refaqat and Arif.

158. Interviews with Sattar and senior U.S. intelligence officers.

159. Interviews with Marker and a senior U.S. intelligence officer.

160. Riaz Khan, *Untying the Afghan Knot,* 284.

161. Interview with Refaqat.

162. Interviews with Refaqat, Marker, and Sattar.

163. Interview with Oakley, Washington, D.C., June 14, 1995.

164. Interviews with Refaqat, Lodhi, and Marker.

165. In addition to media reports and the summary of the investigation, the account of the C-130 crash draws on interviews with Oakley; Al Eastham, Islamabad, March 2, 1998; Robert Boggs, Washington, D.C., May 20, 1999; and Refaqat. Eastham was an aide to Undersecretary Armacost and Boggs was the State Department Pakistan desk officer at the time of the crash.

166. Oakley took credit for keeping the FBI out of the joint inquiry. He told the author that he was worried about the FBI's prematurely leaking information. When FBI officials missed the flight bringing the U.S. team to Pakistan, he was able to block their involvement. Interview with Oakley.

167. Interviews with Murphy; Richard Armitage, Arlington, Va., May 5, 1999; and Oakley, Washington, D.C., April 1, 1999.

168. David Ottoway, "Pakistan May Lose U.S. Aid," *Washington Post,* January 28, 1989.

Chapter 11. Bush: The Partnership Collapses

1. Interview with State Department official.

2. Interviews with U.S. intelligence officers dealing with Afghanistan, and with Teresita Schaffer, Washington, D.C., December 4, 1998; Robert Oakley, Washington, D.C., June 14, 1995; and Eliza Van Hollen, McLean, Va., March 13, 1999.

3. Iqbal Akhund, *Trial and Error: The Rise and Eclipse of Benazir Bhutto* (Karachi: Oxford University Press, 2000), 193.

4. Interviews with Yaqub Khan, Islamabad, January 16, 1996; and Schaffer.

5. Interview with Eliza Van Hollen.

6. Interview with Benazir Bhutto, Karachi, April 6, 1998; and Akhund, *Trial and Error*, 160–61.

7. Interview with Lt. Gen. Hamid Gul, Rawalpindi, April 17, 1998.

8. Interview with Lt. Gen. Brent Scowcroft, Washington, D.C., June 5, 1999.

9. "Afghan Factions to Hold Assembly"; Barbara Crossette, "Shevardnadze Extends His Talks in Pakistan," and "Shevardnadze Ends Pakistan Trip with Little Gain"; and Stephen Lohr, "Top Afghan Rebels Select Centrist as Interim Leader," *New York Times,* February 5, 6, 7, and 24, 1989.

10. Interviews with Yaqub, February 29, 1996; and Oakley, July 15, 1998.

11. Akhund, *Trials and Error,* 175.

12. Interviews with Benazir Bhutto; Iqbal Akhund, Montpellier, September 15, 1998; Hamid Gul; Yaqub; and Oakley; and Akhund, *Trial and Error,* 176–77. See also Henry Kamm, "Pakistan Officials Tell of Ordering Afghan Rebel Push," *New York Times,* April 23, 1989.

13. Interview with Hamid Gul; John F. Burns, "Kabul Offers Rebels Local Power," *New York Times,* March 31, 1989; and Akhund, *Trial and Error,* 175–77.

14. George Bush and Brent Scowcroft, *A World Transformed* (New York: Knopf, 1998), 134–35.

15. Interview with a senior U.S. intelligence officer.

16. Interview with Richard Armitage, Arlington, Va., May 5, 1999.

17. Interview with Benazir Bhutto.

18. Interview with Scowcroft.

19. Ibid.

20. Interview with Oakley.

21. Interview with Benazir Bhutto.

22. Interviews with Gen. Mirza Aslam Beg, Rawalpindi, February 6, 1996; and Benazir Bhutto.

23. John Kifner, "Bhutto Moves to Strengthen Hold on Pakistan," *New York Times,* June 1, 1989.

24. Interviews with Benazir Bhutto and Oakley.

25. David Ottaway, "Addressing Congress, Bhutto Formally Renounces Nuclear Arms," *Washington Post,* June 8, 1989.

26. Interview with Benazir Bhutto.

27. Interviews with Richard Haass, Washington, D.C., April 23, 1997.

28. Lally Weymouth, "Pakistan's Imperiled Prime Minister," *Washington Post,* October 8, 1989; and John F. Burns, "Bhutto Survives Nearly a Year in Office, but a New Era Proves Elusive," *New York Times,* November 8, 1989.

29. Benazir Bhutto's autobiography, *Daughter of the East: Benazir Bhutto* (London: Mandarin, 1989), provides details of her experiences under the Zia regime.

30. Interview with Benazir Bhutto.

31. Interview with Oakley.

32. Ibid.

33. Interview with Oakley and Teresita Schaffer, Washington, D.C., December 4, 1998.

34. John F. Burns, "Afghan Rebels Losing Against the Enemy Within" and "Pakistan Wearies of Afghan Burden," *New York Times,* August 30 and December 15, 1989; Barbara Crossette, "State Dept. Team Finds Nations in Afghan Conflict Flexible on Future Rule," *New York Times,* January 20, 1990; and interview with Schaffer.

35. See Sumit Ganguly, *The Crisis in Kashmir: Portents of War, Hopes of Peace* (Cambridge: Cambridge University Press; Washington, D.C.: Woodrow Wilson Center Press, 1997), 80–102; Ajit Bhattacharjea, *Kashmir: The Unhappy Valley* (New Delhi: UBSPD, 1994), 241–71; and Sten Widmalm, "The Rise and Fall of Democracy in Kashmir," *Asian Survey,* November 1997, 109–23, for background on the Kashmir uprising.

36. Interview with Oakley.

37. Al Kamen, "Tension over Kashmir Called Strongest in Decade," *Washington Post,* April 21, 1990; and Barbara Crossette, "India and Pakistan Make the Most of Hard Feelings," *New York Times,* April 22, 1990.

38. John Goshko, "Bush Sending Envoy to India, Pakistan," *Washington Post,* May 16, 1990.

39. Interview with Oakley.

40. Interview with Haass.

41. *Conflict Prevention and Confidence-Building in South Asia: The 1990 Crisis* (Washington, D.C.: Stimson Center, 1994) provides the transcript of a February 1994 Stimson Center conference regarding the 1990 crisis. The participants included Ambassadors Oakley and Clark, their defense attachés, and other Americans, Indians, and Pakistanis knowledgeable about the 1990 crisis. None of the attendees thought Hersh was correct in claiming that Pakistan was preparing for a nuclear strike.

42. Interview with Haass.

43. Interviews with Oakley, a top-level Pakistani official who wished to remain anonymous, and other knowledgeable U.S. officials. See also Mitchell Reiss, *Bridled Ambition: Why Countries Constrain Their Nuclear Capabilities* (Washington, D.C.: Woodrow Wilson Center Press, 1995), 188; and Rodney W. Jones and Mark G. McDonough, *Tracking Nuclear Proliferation* (Washington, D.C.: Carnegie Endowment for International Peace, 1998), 132.

44. Interview with Oakley.

45. Interview with Yaqub.

46. Benazir denied that she was trying to avoid meeting Gates and said her schedule had been mishandled by a Pakistani diplomat in the Persian Gulf. Interview with Benazir Bhutto. Then–foreign secretary Tanvir Ahmed Khan and journalist Najam Sethi, who were traveling with Bhutto at the time, confirmed that this was the case. Interviews with Tanvir Ahmed Khan, Islamabad, May 5, 1998; and Najam Sethi, Lahore, February 5, 2000.

47. Interview with Oakley.

48. Barbara Crossette, "Bhutto Is Dismissed in Pakistan after 20 Months," *New York Times,* August 7, 1990.

49. Barbara Crossette, "Bhutto Blames Army for Her Ouster," *New York Times,* August 8, 1990.

50. Interview with Beg.

51. Interview with Scowcroft.

52. Interview with Oakley.

53. Interview with Ejaiz Naik, who was in charge of Pakistan's foreign assistance dealings during much of the 1980s, Islamabad, February 7, 1996.

54. Paul Leventhal, "Cut Off Aid to Pakistan," and R. Jeffrey Smith, "Administration Unable to Win Support for Continued Aid to Pakistan," *Washington Post,* October 8 and 10, 1990; and interviews with Leonard Weiss (from Senator Glenn's staff), Washington, D.C., January 15, 1997, Schaffer, and Oakley.

55. Interviews with Yaqub, Oakley, and Schaffer.

56. Views like this were voiced frequently during the author's November 1995–April 1996 stay in Pakistan.

57. Interviews with knowledgeable U.S. officials and Reiss, *Bridled Ambition,* 188.

58. Benazir Bhutto provided the author with another possible explanation. After returning to office in 1993, she said that Pakistani nuclear specialists told her the program was not relaunched in 1990 but that some "degraded" sensitive material had been "refurbished." Knowledgeable U.S. officials said that this explanation was not implausible and conceded, as Benazir Bhutto stated, that the Pakistanis may have only maintained, not added to, their existing capability. Nonetheless, U.S. sources were insistent that Pakistan had machined enriched uranium into bomb cores in 1990.

59. Interview with Benazir Bhutto.

60. Interview with Beg.

61. Interview with Scowcroft.

62. Barbara Crossette, "U.S. Aid Judgment Upsets Pakistanis," *New York Times,* October 16, 1990; and Steve Coll, "Rifts Appear in U.S.-Pakistani Alliance," *Washington Post,* October 22, 1990.

63. Barbara Crossette, "Bhutto Foes Win a Strong Majority," and "New Pakistani Prime Minister Is Sworn In," *New York Times,* October 26 and November 7, 1990; and interview with Oakley.

64. Interview with Shahryar Khan, Islamabad, April 29, 1998.

65. Barbara Crossette, "In Pakistan, War Stirs Emotions and Politics," *New York Times,* February 1, 1991; and Steve Coll, "Pakistan Seeking New Identity as Alliance with U.S. Falters," *Washington Post,* February 8, 1991.

66. Beg told the author that he believed that the Saudis had panicked and that the enormous size of the Allied force indicated the West wanted to destroy Iraq, not just defeat Saddam. Interview with Beg.

67. Interview with Lt. Gen. Nishat Ahmed, Islamabad, April 29, 1998.

68. Barbara Crossette, "War in the Gulf: The Muslims, Islamic Asians Solidly Back Hussein," *New York Times,* January 27, 1991.

69. Interview with a knowledgeable senior Pakistani official who wishes to remain anonymous.

70. Interview with Oakley.

71. Interviews with several knowledgeable but anonymous U.S. officials, Oakley, and Abdul Sattar, who served as foreign minister when the Pakistani government decided to end the F-16 payments.

72. Interview with Akram Zaki, Islamabad, March 10, 1996; and Maleeha Lodhi, *The External Dimension* (Lahore: Jang Publishers, 1994), 111–21.

73. Interview with Zaki; and Steve Coll, "Pakistan Seeks Talks on Nuclear Weapons," Coll, "India Rejects Pakistani Bid for Talks on Nuclear Ban," and David Hoffman, "Pakistani Says Arms Plan Well-Received," *Washington Post,* June 7, 8, and 14, 1991.

74. Interviews with Shahryar and Abida Hussein, Islamabad, March 11, 1996. Abida Hussein was present at the meeting before taking up her assignment as Pakistan's ambassador to the United States.

75. Interview with Abida Hussein.

76. Interview with Shahryar.

77. Quoted in Lodhi, *External Dimension,* 95. Lodhi succeeded Abida Hussein as Pakistan's ambassador in Washington after Benazir Bhutto returned to power in 1993.

78. R. Jeffrey Smith, "Pakistani Official Affirms Capacity for Nuclear Device," *Washington Post,* February 7, 1992. According to Shahryar, Sharif personally approved this important change in Pakistan's public stance on the nuclear program.

79. Interview with Abida Hussein.

80. Ibid.

81. Interview with Nicholas Platt, New York, February 9, 1995.

82. Interviews with Shahryar, Lt. Gen. Asad Durrani, Islamabad, April 25, 1998, and Platt.

83. Lodhi, *External Dimension,* 107.

84. Interview with John Holzman, Islamabad, December 10, 1995.

85. "The Last Cat's-Paw War," *New York Times,* April 18, 1992.

86. Edward A. Gargan, "The Chastened Pakistanis: Peace with U.S. Is Aim," and "Pakistan Crushes Militants' Attempts to Storm Kashmir's Dividing Line," *New York Times,* February 19 and March 31, 1992; and interview with Shahryar.

87. Steve Coll and David Hoffman, "Shipments to Pakistan Questioned," and Hoffman, "Sales to Pakistan Survive in U.S. Policy Rift," *Washington Post,* March 7 and April 13, 1992; and "U.S. Reportedly Let Pakistan Buy Arms from Private Sellers," and Stephen Greenhouse, "Senators Seek Full Cutoff of Arms to Pakistan," *New York Times,* March 7 and 8, 1992.

88. James Mann, *About Face: A History of America's Curious Relationship with China* (New York: Knopf, 1999), 250; and Keith Brasier, "Baker Warns China against Selling New Missiles," and Nicholas D. Kristoff, "For China, a Summer of Diplomatic Triumphs," *New York Times,* June 13 and August 22, 1991.

89. Mann, *About Face,* 251–52; Elaine Sciolino, "U.S. Lifts Its Sanctions on China over High Technology," *New York Times,* February 22, 1992; and R. Jeffrey Smith, "U.S. Lifts Sanctions against Chinese Firms," *Washington Post,* February 22, 1992.

90. R. Jeffrey Smith, "China Said to Sell Arms to Pakistan," *Washington Post,* December 4, 1992; Elaine Sciolino, "Sale of Computer to China Delayed," *New York Times,* December 5, 1992; and Mann, *About Face,* 271.

Chapter 12. Clinton: Living with a Nuclear Pakistan

1. *U.S. Department of State Dispatch,* January 25, 1993, 49.
2. A separate bureau was originally proposed to Henry Kissinger by T. N. Kaul, the

Indian ambassador in Washington in the mid-1970s. The idea had languished because the State Department disliked further organizational fragmentation.

3. Raphel was the ex-wife of former ambassador to Pakistan Arnold Raphel, who died in the plane crash that killed President Zia ul-Haq. She had become acquainted with Clinton when both were graduate students at Oxford.

4. Douglas Jehl, "Pakistan Is Facing Terrorist Listing," *New York Times,* April 25, 1993; and interview with senior State Department official.

5. Edward Gargan, "Radical Arabs Use Pakistan as Base for Holy War," *New York Times,* April 8, 1993.

6. Reuters, "Six Libyan Terrorist Suspects Arrested by Pakistan Police," *New York Times,* March 29, 1993; James Rupert, "Pakistan Sets Crackdown on Islamic Extremists," *Washington Post,* April 2, 1993; and Edward Gargan, "Radical Arabs Use Pakistan as Base for Holy War," *New York Times,* April 2, 1993.

7. Douglas Jehl, "Pakistan Is Facing Terrorist Listing," *New York Times,* April 25, 1993; and Thomas W. Lippman and R. Jeffrey Smith, "Pakistan Avoids U.S. Listing as Nation Supporting Terrorism," *Washington Post,* July 15, 1993.

8. Interview with senior U.S. official.

9. Molly Moore and John Ward Anderson, "After Cold War, U.S.-Pakistani Ties Are Turning Sour," *Washington Post,* April 21, 1993.

10. Maleeha Lodhi, "Removing the Noose of Terror," *News* (Islamabad), May 15, 1993.

11. Interviews with State Department officials.

12. U.S. Department of State, "International Narcotics Strategy Report," March 1993, April 1994, and March 1995.

13. John Ward Anderson and Molly Moore, "Pervasive Heroin Traffic Putting Pakistan at Risk," *Washington Post,* April 29, 1993. See also the annual narcotics reports of the U.S. Department of State (cited in the preceding endnote) for more detailed discussion of the Pakistani drug problem.

14. Mushahid Hussain, "Emerging Political Scenario," *Nation* (Islamabad), April 4, 1993.

15. Edward Gargan, "President of Pakistan Dismisses Premier and Dissolves Parliament," "Pakistan's Chiefs Dismissal Is Overturned," and "Pakistan Government Collapses," *New York Times,* April 19, May 27, and July 19, 1993. See also Mushahid Hussain, "Dissolution: An Act of Desperation," "Caretakers: The Credibility Gap," "The Political Weakening of GIK," and "Politics Enters a New Phase," *Nation,* April 20 and 29, May 13, 1 and July 22, 1993.

16. Edward Gargan, "After a Year of Tumult, Pakistanis Will Vote" and "Following a Tough Act; Bhutto Gets Another Chance to Get It Right," *New York Times,* October 6 and 24, 1993; and interview with Abdul Sattar, Islamabad, November 6, 1995.

17. Douglas Jehl, "China Breaking Missile Pledge, U.S. Aides Say," *New York Times,* May 6, 1993; and Ann Denny and R. Jeffrey Smith, "U.S. Evidence 'Suggests' China Breaks Arms Pact," *Washington Post,* May 18, 1993.

18. John Goshko and William Branigan, "U.S. Warns China of Sanctions for Missile Exports to Pakistan," *Washington Post,* July 26, 1993; Elaine Sciolino, "U.S. May Threaten China with Sanctions for Reported Arms Sales," *New York Times,* July 20, 1993; and Stephen A. Holmes, "China Denies Violating Act by Selling Arms to Pakistan," *New York Times,* July 20, 1993.

19. James Mann, *About Face* (New York: Knopf, 1998), 285–87.

20. Maleeha Lodhi, "Pakistan Entangled in Sino-U.S. Missile Row," *News,* August 24, 1993.

21. Stephen A. Holmes, "U.S. Determines China Violated Pact on Missiles," *New York Times,* August 25, 1993; Stephen Greenhouse, "$1 Billion in Sales of High-Tech Items to China Blocked," *New York Times,* August 26, 1993; Stephen A. Holmes, "High Tech Exports Cutoff; Washington Penalizes China for Missile Technology Sales," *New York Times,* August 29, 1993; and Daniel Williams, "U.S. Punishes China over Missiles Sales," *Washington Post,* August 26, 1993.

22. "Pakistan Holding Firm to Nuclear Plans," *New York Times,* November 21, 1993.

23. Eric Schmitt, "Lifting Aid Ban Is Proposed to Control Pakistan's Arms," *New York Times,* March 13 1994; Michael Gordon, "South Asian Lands Pressed on Arms," *New York Times,* March 23, 1994; R. Jeffrey Smith, "U.S. Proposes Sale of F-16s to Pakistan," *Washington Post,* March 23, 1994; and interviews with concerned U.S. officials.

24. George Perkovich, *The Indian Bomb* (Berkeley: University of California Press, 1999), 342.

25. Mushahid Hussain, "Army and the Nuclear Issue," *Nation.* April 3, 1994.

26. John Ward Anderson, "Pakistan Rebuffs U.S. on A-Bomb," *Washington Post,* April 8, 1994.

27. Dana Priest, "U.S., Pakistan to Renew Talks," *Washington Post,* January 11, 1995.

28. "Pakistan's Premier Asks for Planes or a Refund," *New York Times,* January 11, 1995.

29. Interview with Senator Hank Brown, Washington, D.C., July 11, 1996.

30. Ibid.

31. David Johnston, "Fugitive in Trade Center Blast Is Caught and Returned to U.S." *New York Times,* February 9, 1995; Richard Bernstein, "Behind Arrest of Bomb Fugitive, Informer's Tip, Then Fast Action," *New York Times,* February 10, 1995; and John F. Burns, "Pakistan Officials Hope to Repair Ties with the U.S." *New York Times,* February 13, 1995.

32. John F. Burns, "Two Americans Shot to Death in Pakistan," *New York Times,* March 8, 1995.

33. Interview with Robin Raphel, Washington, D.C., April 25, 1997.

34. Quoted in Todd S. Purdum, "Bhutto Renews Demands for Delivery of Jet Fighters or a Refund," *New York Times,* April 11, 1995.

35. Thomas Lippman, "Bhutto Receives Clinton Promise of Aid," *Washington Post,* April 12, 1995.

36. Interview with Maleeha Lodhi, Islamabad, April 1, 1998. Bhutto named Lodhi Pakistan's ambassador in Washington.

37. The package included 3 P-3C antisubmarine aircraft, 28 Harpoon surface-to-surface missiles, 360 Sidewinder air-to-air missiles, and a variety of artillery pieces, spare parts, and explosives.

38. Thomas W. Lippman, "Compromised Proposed on Fighter Sale to Pakistan," *Washington Post,* May 24, 1995.

39. Interview with Brown. See also Thomas Lippman and Dan Morgan, "With Clinton Approval, Senate Votes to End Ban on Arms Shipment to Pakistan," *Washington Post,* September 22, 1995; and Elaine Sciolino, "Despite Nuclear Fears, Senate Acts to Lift Pakistan Curbs," *New York Times,* September 22, 1995.

40. Interview with a senior Pakistani official.

41. Raphel statement at Senate Foreign Relations Near East and South Asia Subcommittee hearing, September 14, 1995.

42. Interview with Benazir Bhutto, Karachi, April 6, 1998.

43. R. Jeffrey Smith, "China Aids Pakistan Nuclear Program; Parts Shipment Reported by CIA Could Jeopardize U.S. Trade Deals," "U.S. May Waive Sanctions on China for Sale Related to Nuclear Arms," and "Proliferation Concerns May Delay U.S. Arms Shipment to Pakistan," *Washington Post,* February 7, 8, and 15, 1996; and Tim Weiner, "China Sold Parts for Nuclear Arms, U.S. Officials Say" *New York Times,* February 8, 1996.

44. R. Jeffrey Smith, "U.S. Decides to Transfer Weapons that Pakistan Had Paid For," *Washington Post,* March 20, 1996; and "U.S. Waiving Ban, Will Send Weapons to Pakistan," *New York Times,* March 21, 1996.

45. R. Jeffrey Smith, "U.S. Relents on Chinese Sanctions" and "China Silent on Nuclear Export Plans; Deal That Averted Penalties Draws Criticism in Congress," *Washington Post,* May 11 and 14, 1996.

46. R. Jeffrey Smith, "China Linked to Pakistani Missile Plant; Secret Project Could Renew Sanctions Issue," *Washington Post,* August 25, 1996; and Tim Weiner, "U.S. Says It Suspects China Is Helping Pakistan with Missiles," *New York Times,* August 26, 1996.

47. Stephen Erlanger, "U.S. Wary of Punishing China for Missile Help to Pakistan," *New York Times,* August 27, 1996.

48. Presidential Determination 96-13, March 1, 1996.

49. Steven Lee Myers, "Sale of Fighter Jets to Indonesia Is Postponed," *New York Times,* September 6, 1996.

50. Ahmed Rashid's *Taliban* (New Haven: Yale University Press, 2000) provides an excellent study of the movement and its broader implications. Another useful account can be found in William Maley, ed., *Fundamentalism Reborn? Afghanistan and the Taliban* (New York: New York University Press, 1998).

51. Interview with Nasrullah Babar, Islamabad, April 18, 1998.

52. Rashid, *Taliban,* 31–40; and Malley, ed., *Fundamentalism Reborn?* 53–55.

53. Interview with Babar.

54. Rashid, *Taliban,* 41–50.

55. John F. Burns and Steve Levine, "Roots of Repression, A Special Report: How the Afghan Rulers Took Hold," *New York Times,* December 31, 1996; Malley, *Fundamentalism Reborn?* 45–50 and 63–71; Rashid, *Taliban,* 31–40; and Babar interview.

56. Quoted in Kenneth J. Cooper, "Kabul Tests Islamic Limits," *Washington Post,* October 6, 1996.

57. Barbara Crossette, "Kabul Falls to Islamic Militia; Afghans Accuse Pakistan," and "Afghan Fundamentalists Sweep into Kabul," *New York Times,* September 26 and 27, 1996.

58. Michael Dobbs, "Analysts Feel Militia Could End Anarchy," *Washington Post,* September 28, 1996.

59. Anonymous official quoted in Elaine Sciolino, "State Dept. Becomes Cooler to the New Rulers of Kabul," *New York Times,* October 23, 1996.

60. Conversations with U.S. government officials; and Rashid, *Taliban,* 157–80.

61. Shirin Tahir-Kheli, *India, Pakistan, and the United States: Breaking with the Past* (New York: Council on Foreign Relations Press, 1997), 122–23.

62. Peter Waldman, "Pakistan's Bhutto Is Driven from Office" and "Pakistan's Bhutto Under Guard; Interim Prime Minister Sworn In," *Wall Street Journal,* November 5 and 6, 1996.

63. Interview with Najam Sethi, Lahore, April 15, 1998. Ambassador Simons told the author that Sethi's account was accurate. Interview with Thomas Simons, Jr., Islamabad, May 2, 1998.

64. Albright's father, Czechoslovak diplomat Josef Korbel, had worked on Kashmir in 1948 as a member of the UN Commission on India and Pakistan and later authored *Danger in Kashmir* (Princeton: Princeton University Press, 1954), which for many years was a standard work on the dispute.

65. Interview with a senior U.S. government official.

66. Conversation with Thomas Pickering, Washington, D.C., June 2, 1997.

67. Quoted in John F. Burns, "Spiriting Off of Fugitive by U.S. Irks Pakistanis," *New York Times,* June 23, 1997.

68. John F. Burns, "Premier Says Pakistan Is at Last on Track," *New York Times,* August 15, 1947.

69. Interviews with senior Pakistani officials.

70. Barbara Crossette, "Pakistan Asks India to Open No-War Talks," *New York Times,* September 23, 1997; and interview with U.S. government official.

71. Thomas Lippman, "U.S. Plans More Active S. Asia Role; Albright's Trip Signals New Interest in the Region," *Washington Post,* November 19, 1997.

72. The Union Texas Petroleum employees were gunned down as they left their hotel to go to work. Since the murder occurred two days after Kansi had been sentenced to death by a U.S. court, there was speculation that the killings were revenge for the Kansi sentencing. Kenneth J. Cooper, "4 Americans Shot Dead in Pakistan; Oil Company Workers Gunned Down 2 Days after Kansi Sentenced," *Washington Post,* November 12, 1997, and "Anti-U.S. Sentiment in Pakistan Dates to One of the Cold War's Final Chapters," *Washington Post,* November 15, 1997.

73. Thomas Lippman, "Albright's Trip Signals New Interest in Region," *Washington Post,* November 19, 1997.

74. Stephen Erlanger, "Albright Hammers Taliban," *New York Times,* November 19, 1997.

75. Tim Golden, "In Drug War, America Barks, but Fear of Bite Fades" and "Pakistan Frees Drug Enforcement Employee," *New York Times,* March 1 and April 18, 1998.

76. "Pakistan Tests Missile with 900-mile Range," *New York Times,* April 7, 1998; and Tim Weiner, "U.S. Says North Korea Helped Develop New Pakistani Missile," *New York Times,* April 11, 1998.

77. Nora Boustany, "Pakistan Sees Worries about India Vindicated Now," *Washington Post,* May 13, 1998; Steven Mufson, "Pakistan Weighs Response to India," *Washington Post,* May 15, 1998; and interview with senior U.S. official.

78. See Perkovich, *India's Nuclear Bomb,* 404–43, for detailed discussion and analysis of the May 1998 tests.

79. Stephen Lee Myers, "Clinton Imposes Penalties on India over Atomic Tests," *New York Times,* May 13, 1998; James Bennet, "Clinton Calls Tests a 'Terrible Mistake' and Announces Sanctions against India," *New York Times,* May 14, 1998; and Steven Mufson, "Pakistan Rules Out Tit for Tat," *Washington Post,* May 16, 1998.

80. Interviews with U.S. officials. A senior Pakistani official told the author that Abdul Qadeer Khan, Pakistan's nuclear expert, advised him that Pakistan did not need to test for technical reasons, since it already possessed a bomb of proven reliability.

81. Stephen Kinzer, "Next Door Neighbor Demands World Powers Shun India," *New York Times,* May 14, 1998; James Bennett, "Clinton Calls Tests a Terrible Mistake," *New York Times,* May 14, 1998; and Steven Mufson, "The Pressure on the Finger on the Nuclear Test Button," *Washington Post,* May 17, 1998.

82. Kinzer, "Next Door Neighbor"; and Steven Mufson, "Pakistan Weighs Response to India," *Washington Post,* May 15, 1998.

83. Dan Balz, "U.S. Urges Pakistan to Forgo Tests," *Washington Post,* May 18, 1998.

84. Interview with senior Pakistani officials.

85. Telephone conversation with Abdul Sattar, Washington, D.C., June 10, 1998.

86. Tim Weiner, "After an Anguished Phone Call, Clinton Penalizes the Pakistanis," *New York Times,* May 29, 1998; and interviews with U.S. officials. Just hours before the tests, Islamabad accused New Delhi of planning a pre-emptive strike on Pakistan's test sites. U.S. officials believed the charges were false and cooked up by Pakistani intelligence.

87. John Ward Anderson, "Pakistan Sets Off Nuclear Blasts; 'Today, We Have Settled a Score,' Premier Says," *Washington Post,* May 29, 1998.

88. John F. Burns, "Pakistan, Answering India, Carries Out Nuclear Tests; Clinton's Appeal Rejected," *New York Times,* May 29, 1998; John Kifner, "Complex Pressures, Dominated by Islam, Led to Testing," *New York Times,* June 1, 1998; and Jonathan Karp, Anne Robbins, and Hugh Pope, "Pakistan Economy Faces Fallout of Bomb Test; Nuclear Move Prompts U.S. to Punish Islamabad," *Wall Street Journal,* May 29, 1998.

89. Robert S. Greenberger, "Nuclear Freeze Is Urged for Pakistan and India," *Wall Street Journal,* June 5, 1998.

90. Robert Hathaway, "Confrontation and Retreat: The U.S. Congress and South Asia Nuclear Sanctions," *Arms Control Today,* Vol. 30, no. 1 (January–February 2000), 7–14. See also Thomas Lippman, "Senators Seek to Ease Nuclear Test Sanctions," *Washington Post,* July 3, 1998; "House Passes Bill to Lift Nuclear Sanctions on Food for India and Pakistan," *New York Times,* July 15, 1998; Eric Schmitt, "Senate Votes to Lift Most Remaining India-Pakistan Penalties," *New York Times,* July 16, 1998; and Dave Rogers, "Senate Exempts Farm Products from Sanctions," *Wall Street Journal,* July 10, 1998.

91. Interviews with knowledgeable U.S. officials.

92. John Kifner, "Pakistan, Facing Sanctions, Urges Citizens to Cut Back," *New York Times,* June 12, 1998.

93. John F. Burns, "U.S. and India Meet on Standoff over Nuclear Tests," *New York Times,* July 21, 1998; and David E. Sanger, "Despite A-Test, U.S. Won't Bar Pakistan Bailout," *New York Times,* July 22, 1998.

94. Rashid, *Taliban,* 67–79.

95. Ibid., 128–40, provides useful background on bin Laden and his relationship with the Taliban.

96. Interview with knowledgeable U.S. official.

97. Kamran Khan and Pamela Constable, "Pakistanis Reportedly Killed in Raids," *Washington Post,* August 22, 1998; Raymond Bonner, "Muted Criticism and Marches

in Pakistan," *New York Times,* August 22, 1998; and Pamela Constable, "U.S. Strike Is Blow to Pakistan's Rulers," *Washington Post,* August 26, 1998.

98. Carol Giacomo, "S. Asian Nuclear Programs May Delay Clinton Trip," *Washington Post,* September 19, 1998; and David Stout, "Clinton Putting Off Visits to India and Pakistan," *New York Times,* October 1, 1998.

99. Interviews with U.S. and Pakistani officials who participated in the Sharif-Clinton talks.

100. Ibid.

101. Interview with knowledgeable U.S. officials.

102. K. K. Katyal, "Symbolism and More," *Hindu,* March 1, 1999; V. R. Raghavan, "The Lahore Declaration and Security," *Hindu,* March 3, 1999; and Tanvir Ahmed Khan, "The Lahore Summit," *Dawn,* February 23, 1999.

103. Stephen Kinzer, "The World Takes Notice: Kashmir Gets Scarier," *New York Times,* June 20, 1999; Francoise Chipaux, "Au Pakistan, les préparatifs s'intensifient pour une guerre avec l'Inde," *Le Monde,* June 18, 1999; and "Ever More Dangerous in Kashmir," *Economist,* June 19, 1999, 66–67.

104. Sridhar Krishnaswamy, "Pull Back Forces, Clinton Tells Sharif," *Hindu,* June 126, 1999. In a development that underscored the strength of Sharif's political position, General Karamat had resigned a few months before the end of his term after the prime minister was unhappy about some critical remarks Karamat had made regarding the domestic situation in the country.

105. Amit Baruah, "U.S. Asks Pak. to Pull Out Intruders," *Hindu,* June 25, 1999.

106. Interview with senior U.S. officials.

107. Ibid.

108. See Maleeha Lodhi, "The Kargil Crisis," *Newsline* (Karachi), July 1999; and Irfan Hussain, "The Cost of Kargil," *Dawn,* August 14, 1999, for comprehensive critiques of the government's handling of the Kargil crisis.

109. Interview with senior U.S. official.

110. Interview with senior Pakistani official.

111. Interview with senior U.S. officials.

112. Transcript of Clinton interview with Peter Jennings on ABC News, March 21, 2000.

113. Celia W. Dugger, "In Charmed India, Clinton Wooed, and Maybe Won," *New York Times,* March 31, 2000; C. Raja Mohan, "Respect for the LOC Must for Dialogue, Says Clinton," *Hindu,* March 22, 2000; and Dileep Padagaonkar, "A Star-Spangled Manner," *Economic Times* (Mumbai), March 28, 2000.

114. Interviews with senior U.S. and Pakistani officials.

115. Text of briefing aboard Air Force One by Samuel Berger, March 25, 2000, released by White House press office.

116. Interview with senior U.S. official.

117. Text of briefing by Samuel Berger, March 25, 2000.

118. Text of President Clinton's television remarks to the people of Pakistan, March 25, 2000, released by the White House press office.

119. Barry Bearak, "A Little Shop in Pakistan Tunes in to Clinton on TV," *New York Times,* March 26, 2000.

120. Interview with senior U.S. official.

Chapter 13. An Unstable Partnership

1. Memorandum of conversation between President Zia and Secretary Shultz, December 6, 1982, obtained through a Freedom of Information Act request.

2. State or official visits were made by Liaquat Ali Khan (1950), Mohammed Ali Bogra (1954), H. S. Suhrawardy (1957), Ayub (1961 and 1965), Zulfikar Ali Bhutto (1973 and 1975), Zia (1982), Mohammed Khan Junejo (1986), Benazir Bhutto (1989 and 1994), and Nawaz Sharif (1998).

3. Notes by Rusk on his South Asia trip, *Foreign Relations of the United States, 1961–63,* Vol. 19, 575–77.

Bibliography

Memoirs

Akhund, Iqbal. *Memoirs of a Bystander: A Life in Diplomacy.* Karachi: Oxford University Press, 1997.

———. *Trial and Error: The Advent and Eclipse of Benazir Bhutto.* Karachi: Oxford University Press, 2000.

Ali, Syed Amjad. *Glimpses.* Lahore: Jang Publishers, 1992.

Arif, Khalid Mahmud. *Working with Zia.* Karachi: Oxford University Press, 1995.

Ball, George W. *The Past Has Another Pattern.* New York: W. W. Norton, 1982.

Bhutto, Benazir. *Daughter of the East: Benazir Bhutto.* London: Mandarin, 1989.

Bhutto, Zulfikar Ali. *If I Am Assassinated.* Lahore: Classic, 1994.

Brzezinski, Zbigniew. *Power and Principle: Memoirs of the National Security Adviser, 1977–1981.* New York: Farrar, Straus, Giroux, 1983.

Bush, George, and Brent Scowcroft. *A World Transformed.* New York: Knopf, 1999.

Eisenhower, Dwight D. *The White House Years: Waging Peace, 1956–1961.* Garden City, N.Y.: Doubleday, 1965.

Gates, Robert M. *From the Shadows.* New York: Simon and Schuster, 1996.

Hyder, Sajjad. *Foreign Policy of Pakistan: Reflections of an Ambassador.* Lahore: Progressive Publishers, 1987.

Khan, Air Marshal M. Asghar. *The First Round: Indo-Pakistan War 1965.* New Delhi: Vikas, 1979.

Khan, Lt. Gen. Gul Hassan. *Memoirs of Lt. Gen. Gul Hassan Khan.* Karachi: Oxford University Press, 1993.

Khan, Mohammed Ayub. *Friends Not Masters.* London: Oxford University Press, 1967.

Khan, Sultan Mohammed. *Memories and Reflections of a Pakistani Diplomat.* London: London Centre for Pakistan Studies, 1998.

Khan, Sir Muhammed Zafrullah. *The Forgotten Years.* Lahore: Vanguard, 1991.
Kissinger, Henry A. *White House Years.* Boston: Little, Brown, 1979.
Musa, Gen. Mohammed. *My Version: India-Pakistan War 1965.* Lahore: Wajidalis, 1980.
Nixon, Richard M. *RN: The Memoirs of Richard Nixon.* New York: Grosset and Dunlap, 1978.
Noon, Firoz Khan. *From Memory.* Lahore: Ferozsons, 1966.
Shultz, George P. *Triumph and Turmoil: My Years as Secretary of State.* New York: Scribner's, 1993.
Sulzberger, C. L. *The Last of the Giants.* New York: Macmillan, 1971.
Zumwalt, Elmo R. *On Watch: A Memoir.* New York: Quadrangle/New York Times Book Co., 1976.

Secondary Works

Afzal, M. Rafique. *Political Parties in Pakistan.* 2 vols. Islamabad: National Institute of Historical and Cultural Research, 1986–87.
Ali, Chaudhri Muhammed. *The Emergence of Pakistan.* New York: Columbia University Press, 1967.
Anderson, Jack, with George Clifford. *The Anderson Papers.* New York: Random House, 1973.
Bajpai, Kanti, P. R. Chari, Pervaiz Iqbal Cheema, Stephen Cohen, and Sumit Ganguly. *Brasstacks and Beyond: Perception and the Management of Crisis in South Asia.* New Delhi: Manohar, 1995.
Bajwa, Farooq Naseem. *Pakistan and the West: The First Decade, 1947–1957.* Karachi: Oxford University Press, 1996.
Barnds, William J. *India, Pakistan and the Great Powers.* New York: Praeger, 1972.
Baxter, Craig, ed. *Zia's Pakistan: Politics and Stability in a Frontline State.* Boulder: Westview, 1985.
Beschloss, Michael R. *Mayday: Eisenhower, Khrushchev and the U-2 Affair.* New York: Harper and Row, 1986.
Bhatty, Maqbool Ahmed. *Great Powers and South Asia.* Islamabad: Institute of Regional Studies, 1996.
Bhutto, Zulfikar Ali. *The Myth of Independence.* London: Oxford University Press, 1969.
Brines, Russell. *The Indo-Pakistani Conflict.* London: Pall Mall, 1968.
Bundy, William. *A Tangled Web: The Making of Foreign Policy in the Nixon Presidency.* New York: Hill and Wang, 1998.
Burke, S. M., and Lawrence Ziring. *Pakistan's Foreign Policy: An Historical Analysis.* Karachi: Oxford University Press, 1990.
Burki, Shahid Javed. *Pakistan: The Continuing Search for Nationhood,* 2nd ed. Boulder: Westview, 1991.
———. *Pakistan under Bhutto, 1971–1977.* London: Macmillan, 1980.

Burrows, William E., and Windrem, Robert. *Critical Mass: The Dangerous Race for Superweapons in a Fragmenting World.* New York: Simon and Schuster, 1994.

Callard, Keith. *Pakistan: A Political Study.* London: George Allen and Unwin, 1957.

Chari, P. R. *Indo-Pak Nuclear Standoff: The Role of the United States.* New Delhi: Manohar, 1995.

Cheema, Pervaiz Iqbal. *Pakistan's Defense Policy, 1947–58.* New York: St. Martin's, 1990.

Choudhury, Golam Wahid. *India, Pakistan, Bangladesh and the Major Powers.* New York: Free Press, 1975.

———. *The Last Days of United Pakistan.* Karachi: Oxford University Press, 1993.

Clymer, Kenton J. *Quest for Freedom: The United States and India's Independence.* New York: Columbia University Press, 1995.

Cohen, Stephen P. *The Pakistan Army.* Berkeley: University of California Press, 1984.

Cohen, Stephen P., ed. *The Security of South Asia.* Urbana: University of Illinois Press, 1987.

Cooley, John K. *Unholy War: Afghanistan, America, and International Terrorism.* London: Pluto Press, 1999.

Cordovez, Diego, and Selig Harrison. *Out of Afghanistan.* New York: Oxford University Press, 1995.

Duncan, Emma. *Breaking the Curfew.* London: Joseph, 1989.

Embree, Ainslie T., ed. *Pakistan's Western Borderlands.* Karachi: Royal Book, 1979.

Ganguly, Sumit. *The Origins of War in South Asia,* 2nd ed. Boulder, Colo.: Westview, 1994.

———. *The Crisis in Kashmir: Portents of War, Hopes of Peace.* Cambridge: Cambridge University Press; Washington, D.C: Woodrow Wilson Center Press, 1997.

Garthoff, Raymond L. *Detente and Confrontation: American-Soviet Relations from Nixon to Reagan.* Washington, D.C.: Brookings Institution, 1985.

Gauhar, Altaf. *Ayub Khan: Pakistan's First Military Ruler.* Lahore: Sang-e-Meel Publications, 1993.

Gopal, Sarvepalli. *Jawaharlal Nehru: A Biography.* 3 vols. London: Jonathan Cape, 1975–84.

Gupta, Sisir. *Kashmir: A Study in India-Pakistan Relations.* Bombay: Asia Publishing House, 1966.

Hagerty, Devin T. *The Consequences of Nuclear Proliferation: Lessons from South Asia.* Cambridge: MIT Press, 1998.

Hersh, Seymour. *The Price of Power: Kissinger in the Nixon White House.* New York: Summit Books, 1983.

Hussain, Mushahid. *Pakistan's Politics: The Zia Years.* Lahore: Progressive Publishers, 1990.

Jackson, Robert. *South Asian Crisis: India, Pakistan and Bangladesh.* New York: Praeger, 1975.

Jalal, Ayesha. *The State of Martial Rule.* Lahore: Vanguard, 1991.

———. *The Sole Spokesman: Jinnah and the Demand for Pakistan.* Lahore: Sang-e-Meel Publications, 1992.

James, Sir Morrice. *Pakistan Chronicle.* Karachi: Oxford University Press, 1993.

Kadian, Rajesh. *The Kashmir Tangle: Issues and Options.* Boulder: Westview, 1993.

Kapur, Ashok. *Pakistan's Nuclear Development.* New York: Croom Helm, 1987.

Khan, Riaz Mohammed. *Untying the Afghan Knot: Negotiating the Soviet Withdrawal.* Durham: Duke University Press, 1991.

Korbel, Josef. *Danger in Kashmir.* Princeton: Princeton University Press, 1954.

Krepon, Michael, and Mishi Faruqee, eds. *Conflict Prevention and Confidence-Building Measures in South Asia: The 1990 Crisis.* Washington, D.C.: Stimson Center, 1994.

Kux, Dennis. *India and the United States: Estranged Democracies, 1941–91.* Washington, D.C.: National Defense University Press, 1993.

Lamb, Alistair. *Crisis in Kashmir, 1947–66.* London: Routledge and Kegan Paul, 1966.

———. *Kashmir: A Disputed Legacy, 1846–1990.* Hertingfordbury: Roxford Books, 1991.

———. *Birth of a Tragedy: Kashmir 1947.* Karachi: Oxford University Press, 1994.

Lamb, Christina. *Waiting for Allah: Pakistan's Struggle for Democracy.* New Delhi: Viking, 1991.

Lodhi, Maleeha. *The External Dimension.* Lahore: Jang, 1994.

———. *Pakistan's Encounter with Democracy.* Lahore: Vanguard, 1994.

Mahmud, Farhat. *A History of U.S.-Pakistan Relations.* Lahore: Vanguard, 1991.

Maley, William, ed. *Fundamentalism Reborn? Afghanistan and the Taliban.* New York: New York University Press, 1998.

Malik, Hafeez. *Soviet-Pakistan Relations and Post-Soviet Dynamics.* London: Macmillan, 1994.

Malik, Iftikhar H. *U.S.–South Asian Relations, 1940–47: American Attitudes towards the Pakistan Movement.* London: Macmillan, 1991.

Malik, Zahid. *Dr. A. Q. Khan and the Islamic Bomb.* Islamabad: Hurmat Publications, 1992.

Matinuddin, Kamal. *Tragedy of Errors: East Pakistan Crisis, 1968–71.* Lahore: Wajidalis, 1994.

McMahon, Robert J. *The Cold War on the Periphery: The United States, India and Pakistan.* New York: Columbia University Press, 1994.

Moshaver, Ziba. *Nuclear Weapons Proliferation in the Indian Subcontinent.* New York: St. Martin's, 1991.

Newberg, Paula R. *Double Betrayal: Repression and Insurgency in Kashmir.* Washington, D.C.: Carnegie Endowment for International Peace, 1995.

Noman, Omar. *Pakistan: Political and Economic History since 1947.* London: KPI, 1990.

———. *Why Pakistan Did Not Become a Tiger: Economic and Social Change in Asia.* Karachi: Oxford University Press, 1997.

Oberdorfer, Don. *The Turn: From the Cold War to a New Era.* New York: Poseidon Press, 1991.

Palit, D. K., and P. K. S. Namboodiri. *Pakistan's Islamic Bomb.* New Delhi: Vikas, 1979.

Rais, Rasul Bakhsh. *War Without Winners.* Karachi: Oxford University Press, 1994.

Rashid, Ahmed. *Taliban.* New Haven: Yale University Press, 2000.

Raza, Rafi. *Zulfikar Ali Bhutto and Pakistan, 1967–1977.* Karachi: Oxford University Press, 1997.

Reeves, Richard. *Passage to Peshawar.* New York: Simon and Schuster, 1984.

Reiss, Mitchell. *Bridled Ambition: Why Countries Constrain Their Nuclear Capabilities.* Washington, D.C.: Woodrow Wilson Center Press, 1995.

Rizvi, Hasan-Askari. *The Military and Politics in Pakistan, 1947–86.* New Delhi: Konark, 1988.

———. *Pakistan and the Geostrategic Environment.* New York: St. Martin's, 1993.

Rodman, Peter W. *More Precious than Peace.* New York: Scribner's, 1994.

Rose, Leo, ed. *United States–Pakistan Relations.* Berkeley: University of California Press, 1987.

Sayeed, Khalid bin. *Pakistan: The Formative Phase.* Karachi: Pakistan Publishing House, 1960.

———. *The Political System of Pakistan.* Karachi: Oxford University Press, 1967.

Shafqat, Saeed. *Civil-Military Relations in Pakistan.* Boulder, Colo.: Westview, 1997.

Shahi, Agha. *Pakistan's Security and Foreign Policy.* Lahore: Progressive Printers, 1988.

Singh, Anita Inder. *The Limits of British Influence: South Asia and the Anglo-American Relationship, 1947–56.* New York: St. Martin's, 1993.

Sisson, Richard, and Leo E. Rose. *War and Secession: Pakistan, India, and the Creation of Bangladesh.* Berkeley: University of California Press, 1990.

Spector, Leonard S. *Nuclear Proliferation Today.* Cambridge: Ballinger, 1984.

Spector, Leonard S., with Jacqueline R. Smith. *Nuclear Ambitions.* Boulder, Colo.: Westview, 1991.

Stephens, Ian. *Pakistan.* Harmondsworth: Penguin, 1964.

Syed, Anwar H. *China and Pakistan: Diplomacy of an Entente Cordiale.* London: Oxford University Press, 1974.

Tahir-Kheli, Shirin R. *The United States and Pakistan: The Evolution of an Influence Relationship.* New York: Praeger, 1982.

———. *India, Pakistan, and the United States: Breaking with the Past.* New York: Council on Foreign Relations Press, 1997.

Thornton, Thomas P. *Pakistan: Internal Developments and the U.S. Interest.* Washington, D.C.: Foreign Policy Institute, 1987.

Venkataramani, M. S. *The American Role in Pakistan, 1947–1958.* Lahore: Vanguard Books, 1984.

Weinbaum, Marvin G. *Pakistan and Afghanistan: Resistance and Reconstruction.* Boulder, Colo.: Westview, 1994.

Weisman, Steve, and Herbert Krosney. *The Islamic Bomb.* New York: Times Books, 1981.

Wirsing, Robert G. *Pakistan's Security under Zia, 1977–1988.* New York: St. Martin's, 1991.

———. *India, Pakistan, and the Kashmir Dispute.* Calcutta: Rupa, 1995.

Wolf, Charles Jr. *Foreign Aid: Theory and Practice in Southern Asia.* Princeton: Princeton University Press, 1960.

Wolpert, Stanley. *Roots of Confrontation in South Asia: Afghanistan, Pakistan, India and the Superpowers.* New York: Oxford University Press, 1982.

———. *Jinnah of Pakistan.* New York: Oxford University Press, 1984.

———. *Zulfi Bhutto of Pakistan.* New York: Oxford University Press, 1993.

Yousaf, Mohammed, and Mark Adkin. *The Bear Trap.* Lahore: Jang Publishers, 1992.

Zaheer, Hasan. *The Rawalpindi Conspiracy, 1951.* Karachi: Oxford University Press, 1998.

Ziring, Lawrence. *Pakistan in the Twentieth Century.* Karachi: Oxford University Press, 1997.

Ziring, Lawrence, Ralph Braibanti, and W. Howard Wriggins, eds. *Pakistan: The Long View.* Durham: Duke University Press, 1977.

Journal Articles and Book Chapters

Abdullah, Sheikh Mohammed. "Kashmir, India and Pakistan." *Foreign Affairs,* April 1965, 528–35.

Bhaskar, C. Uday. "The May 1990 Nuclear Crisis: An Indian Perspective." *Studies in Conflict and Terrorism,* 1997, 317–32.

Bhatty, Maqbool Ahmed. "Changing U.S. Perceptions on South Asia." *Spotlight on Regional Affairs* 112, December 1992 (Institute of Regional Studies, Islamabad).

———. "The Great Powers and South Asia." *Regional Studies* (Islamabad), 13, no. 4, Autumn 1995.

Blank, Jonah. "Kashmir: Fundamentalism Takes Root." *Foreign Affairs,* November/December 1999, 36–53.

Cogan, Charles C. "Partners in Time: The CIA and Afghanistan." *World Policy Journal,* Summer 1993, 73–82.

———. "Shawl of Lead: From Holy War to Civil War in Afghanistan." *Conflict* 10, 1993, 189–204.

Critchfield, Richard. "Background to Conflict." *The Reporter,* November 4, 1965, 28–30.

Dobell, W. M. "Ramifications of the China-Pakistan Border Treaty." *Pacific Affairs,* Autumn 1964, 283–95.

Fukuyama, Francis. "The Security of Pakistan: A Trip Report." *Rand Note* (N-1584-RC), 1980.

Hagerty, Devin T. "The Development of American Defense Policy toward Pakistan, 1947–1954." *Fletcher Forum,* Summer 1986, 218–42.

———. "Pakistan's Foreign Policy under Z. A. Bhutto." *Journal of South Asian and Middle Eastern Studies,* Summer 1991, 55–70.

———. "Nuclear Deterrence in South Asia: The 1990 Indo-Pakistani Crisis." *International Security,* Winter 1995–96, 79–114.

Hagerty, Herbert G. "Attack on the U.S. Embassy in Pakistan." *Embassies under Siege,* ed. Joseph Sullivan. Washington, D.C.: Brassey's, 1995, 71–87.

Harrison, Selig S. "Pakistan and the United States." *New Republic,* August 1959.

———. "Baluch Nationalism and Superpower Rivalry." *International Security,* Winter 1980–81, 152–163.

Hersh, Seymour M. "On the Nuclear Edge." *New Yorker,* March 29, 1993, 56–73.

James, Morrice (Lord Saint Brides). "New Perspectives South of the Hindu Kush." *International Security,* Winter 1980–81, 164–170.

Joeck, Neil. "Pakistani Security and Nuclear Proliferation in South Asia." *Strategic Consequences on Nuclear Proliferation in South Asia,* ed. Neil Joeck. London: Frank Cass, 1987.

Jones, Rodney W. "Old Quarrels and New Realities: Security in Southern Asia after the Cold War." *Washington Quarterly,* Winter 1992, 105–128.

Khan, Sultan Mohammed. "Pakistani Geopolitics: The Diplomatic Perspective." *International Security,* Summer 1980, 26–36.

Kreisberg, Paul. "The United States, South Asia, and American Interests." *Journal of International Affairs,* Summer–Fall 1989, 83–96.

Kux, Dennis. "Pakistan." *Economic Sanctions and American Diplomacy,* ed. Richard Haass. New York: Council on Foreign Relations Press, 1998, 157–76.

Lerski, George. "The Pakistan-American Alliance: A Reevaluation of the Past Decade." *Asian Survey,* April 1980, 400–14.

Perkovich, George. "A Nuclear Third Way in South Asia." *Foreign Policy,* Summer 1993, 85–105.

Rashid, Ahmed. "The Taliban: Exporting Extremism." *Foreign Affairs,* November/December 1999, 22–35.

Reeves, Richard. "A Reporter at Large: Journey to Pakistan." *New Yorker,* November 14, 1986, 39–106.

Richter, William L., and Eric Gustafson. "Pakistan 1979: Back to Square One." *Asian Survey,* February 1980, 188–96.

Sattar, Abdul. "Foreign Policy." *Pakistan in Perspective, 1947–1997,* ed. Rafi Raza. Karachi: Oxford University Press, 1997, 61–173.

Spain, James W. "Middle East Defense: A New Approach." *Middle East Journal* 8, Summer 1954, 251–66.

———. "Military Assistance for Pakistan." *American Political Science Review* 48, September 1954, 738–51.

Thornton, Thomas P. "Between Two Stools?: U.S. Policy Towards Pakistan in the Carter Administration." *Asian Survey,* October 1982, 959–77.

———. "The New Phase in U.S.-Pakistani Relations." *Foreign Affairs,* Summer 1989, 142–59.

———. "Pakistan Foreign Policy: Fifty Years of Insecurity." *India and Pakistan: The First Fifty Years,* ed. Selig Harrison, Paul Kreisberg, and Dennis Kux. Cambridge: Cambridge University Press; Washington, D.C.: Woodrow Wilson Center Press, 1998, 170–88.

Van Hollen, Christopher. "Leaning on Pakistan." *Foreign Policy* 38, Spring 1980, 35–50.

———. "The Tilt Revisited: Nixon-Kissinger Geopolitics and South Asia." *Asian Survey,* April 1980, 339–61.

Weaver, Mary Anne. "Letter from Pakistan." *New Yorker,* November 14, 1988, 97–114.

Weinbaum, Marvin G. "The March 1977 Elections in Pakistan: Where Everyone Lost." *Asian Survey,* July 1977, 599–618.

———. "War and Peace in Afghanistan: The Pakistani Role." *Middle East Journal,* Winter 1991, 71–85.

Weinbaum, Marvin G., and Gautam Sen. "Pakistan Enters the Middle East." *Orbis,* Fall 1978, 595–612.

Widmalm, Sten. "The Rise and Fall of Democracy in Jammu and Kashmir." *Asian Survey,* November 1997, 1005–29.

Interviews and Oral Histories

Interviews

Pakistanis

Khurshid Ahmed. Vice President, Jamaat-i-Islami, 1982–.

Lt. Gen. (Rtd.) Nishat Ahmed. Commandant, National Defense College, 1980–84; Inspector General, Ministry of Foreign Affairs, 1988–93.

Iqbal Akhund. Ambassador to the UN, 1973–76; National Security Adviser, 1988–90.

Zamir Akram. Deputy Chief of Mission, Washington, D.C., 1993–98 and 2000–.

Maj. Gen. (Rtd.) Farman Ali. Political Adviser in East Pakistan, 1971.

Saiyid Amjad Ali. Ambassador to the United States, 1953–55; Minister of Finance, 1956–58.

Gen. (Rtd.) Khalid Mahmud Arif. Senior aide to President Muhammed Zia ul-Haq, 1977–84; Deputy Chief of Army Staff, 1984–87.

Lt. Gen. (Rtd.) Ejaz Azim. Ambassador to the United States, 1981–85.

Sartaj Aziz. Aide to Finance Minister Mohammed Shoaib, 1965; Minister of Finance and Foreign Affairs, 1997–99.

Maj. Gen. (Rtd.) Nasrullah Babar. Minister of Interior, 1988–90 and 1993–96.

Gen. (Rtd.) Mirza Aslam Beg. Chief of Army Staff, 1988–91.

Maqbul Ahmed Bhatty. Ambassador to China, 1985–88.

Benazir Bhutto. Prime Minister, 1988–90 and 1993–96.

H. K. Burki. Journalist, 1950s–1980s.

Lt. Gen. (Rtd.) Assad Durrani. Director-General, Inter-Services Intelligence Directorate, 1990–91.

Altaf Gauhar. Information Secretary and close associate of President Ayub Khan, 1963–68.

Lt. Gen. (Rtd.) Hamid Gul. Director-General, Inter-Services Intelligence Directorate, 1987–89.

Mahmud Haroon. Interior Minister and Governor of Sindh under President Zia ul-Haq.

Lt. Gen. (Rtd.) Gul Hassan. Chief of Army Staff, 1972–73.

Agha Hilaly. Ambassador to the United States, 1967–72.

Zafar Hilaly. Foreign policy adviser to Prime Minister Benazir Bhutto, 1993–96.

Mushahid Hussain. Journalist; Minister of Information, 1997–99.

Brig. (Rtd.) Noor Hussein. Military aide to Governor-General Mohammed Ali Jinnah, 1947–48.

Syeda Abida Hussein. Ambassador to the United States, 1991–92.

Sajjad Hyder. Diplomat and author.

Salim Abbas Jilani. Defense Secretary, 1990–95.

Sadiq Kanju. Minister of State for Foreign Affairs, 1991–93 and 1997–99.

Munir Ahmed Khan. Chairman of Pakistan Atomic Energy Commission, 1972–91.

Air Marshal (Rtd.) Nur Khan. Director-General, Pakistan International Airlines, 1962–65; Air Force Commander-in-Chief in the 1965 war with India.

Roedad Khan. Senior civil servant and close associate of President Ghulam Ishaq Khan.

Sahibzada Yaqub Khan. Ambassador to the United States, 1972–75; Foreign Minister, 1982–87, 1988–90, 1996.

Shahryar Khan. Foreign Secretary, 1991–94.

Sultan Mohammed Khan. Foreign Secretary, 1970–72; Ambassador to the United States, 1972–74 and 1978–81.

Tanvir Ahmed Khan. Foreign Secretary, 1990–91.

Air Marshal (Rtd.) Zulfikar Ali Khan. Chief of Air Staff, 1975–78; Ambassador to the United States, 1989–90.

Riaz Khokar. Ambassador to the United States, 1997–99.

Maleeha Lodhi. Journalist; Ambassador to the United States, 1993–96 and 2000–.

Jamshed Marker. Ambassador to the United States, 1985–88.

Lt. Gen. (Rtd.) Talat Masood. Head of defense production under President Zia ul-Haq.

Lt. Gen. (Rtd.) Kamal Matinuddin. Director-General, Joint Staff, 1979–81.

Ejaz Niak. Senior civil servant, coordinator for foreign aid during 1980s.

Niaz Naik. Foreign Secretary, 1982–85.

Majid Nizami. Editor, *Nawai-i-Waqt.*

Hanif Ramey. Chief Minister, Punjab, 1973–75.

Ahmed Rashid. Journalist.

Lt. Gen. (Rtd.) Syed Refaqat. Senior aide to President Zia ul-Haq, 1985–88.

Maj. Gen. (Rtd.) Mujibur Rehman. Information Secretary, 1979–85.

Abdul Sattar. Foreign Secretary, 1986–88; Foreign Minister, 1993 and 1999–.

Najam Sethi. Editor, *Friday Times.*

Agha Shahi. Deputy Chief of Mission, Washington, D.C., 1955–57; Ambassador to the UN, 1967–72; Foreign Secretary, 1973–77; Foreign Minister, 1977–82.

Nawaz Sharif. Prime Minister, 1991–93 and 1997–99.
Najmuddin Sheikh. Deputy Chief of Mission, Washington, D.C., 1978–82; Ambassador to the United States, 1990–93; Foreign Secretary, 1993–97.
Maj. Gen. (Rtd.) Mohammed Umar. Adviser to President Yahya Khan, 1969–71.
Akram Zaki. Secretary-General of the Foreign Ministry, 1990–93.

Americans

Michael Armacost. Undersecretary of State for Political Affairs, 1984–89.
Richard Armitage. Assistant Secretary of Defense, 1983–89.
Jules Bassin. Political-Military Affairs Officer, Karachi, 1956–58.
William Boggs. Pakistan Desk Officer, Department of State, 1988.
Hank Brown. Senator (R-Colo.), 1991–97.
Henry Byroade. Assistant Secretary of State for Near Eastern, South Asian, and African Affairs, 1952–54; Ambassador to Pakistan, 1973–77.
Peter Constable. Pakistan Desk Officer and Country Director, Department of State, 1970–71 and 1972–76; Deputy Chief of Mission, Islamabad, 1976–79; Senior Deputy Assistant Secretary of State for Near Eastern and South Asian Affairs, 1979–81.
Jane Coon. Political Officer, Karachi, 1956–58; Pakistan Country Director, Department of State, 1977–78; Deputy Assistant Secretary of State for Near Eastern and South Asian Affairs, 1979–81.
Matthew Daley. Deputy Chief of Mission, New Delhi, 1993–97; Senior Adviser, Bureau of South Asian Affairs, Department of State, 1998–2000; Policy Planning Staff member, Department of State, 2000–.
Alan Eastham. Special Assistant for South Asia to Undersecretary of State for Political Affairs, 1987–89; Deputy Chief of Mission, Islamabad, 1997–99; Deputy Assistant Secretary of State for South Asian Affairs, 1999–.
Robert Einhorn. Deputy Assistant Secretary of State for Political-Military Affairs, 1993–98; Assistant Secretary of State for Nonproliferation, 1999–.
Joseph Farland. Ambassador to Pakistan, 1969–72 (interviewed by telephone).
Richard Haass. National Security Council staff member, 1989–92.
Herbert Hagerty. Political Counselor, Islamabad, 1977–81; Pakistan Country Director, Department of State, 1983–85.
Alexander Haig. Deputy to National Security Adviser Henry Kissinger, 1969–73; National Security Adviser, 1973–75; Secretary of State, 1981–82.
Deane Hinton. Ambassador to Pakistan, 1984–87 (interviewed by telephone).
John Holzman. Pakistan Country Director, Department of State, 1992–94; Deputy Chief of Mission, Islamabad, 1994–96.
Arthur Hummel. Ambassador to Pakistan, 1977–81.
Karl Inderfurth. Assistant Secretary of State for South Asian Affairs, 1997–.
Harold Josef. Political Officer, Karachi, 1948–50.
Richard Kennedy. Ambassador to the International Atomic Energy Agency, 1984–92.

Robert Komer. National Security Council staff member, 1961–66.

L. Bruce Laingen. Political Officer, Karachi, 1961–64; Pakistan Country Director, Department of State, 1969–72; Deputy Assistant Secretary of State for Near Eastern and South Asian Affairs, 1973–75.

Charles Burton Marshall. Adviser to government of Pakistan, 1955–57.

Robert McFarlane. Counselor, Department of State, 1981–83; National Security Adviser, 1984–86.

George McGhee. Assistant Secretary of State for Near Eastern, South Asian, and African Affairs, 1949–51; Undersecretary of State for Political Affairs, 1961–63.

Lee Metcalf. Pakistan Desk Officer, Department of State, 1952–54.

Howard Meyers. Bureau of UN Affairs, Department of State, 1949–51.

William Milam. Ambassador to Pakistan, 1998–.

John Monjo. Ambassador to Pakistan, 1993–95.

Richard Murphy. Assistant Secretary of State for Near Eastern and South Asian Affairs, 1984–89.

Charles Naas. Pakistan Desk Officer, Department of State, 1960–63.

David Newsom. Information Officer, Karachi, 1948–50; Undersecretary of State for Political Affairs, 1978–81.

Robert Oakley. National Security Council staff member, 1975–77 and 1986–88; Ambassador to Pakistan, 1988–91.

Robert Peck. Deputy Assistant Secretary of State for Near Eastern and South Asian Affairs, 1984–87.

Nicholas Platt. Ambassador to Pakistan, 1991–92.

Robin Raphel. Assistant Secretary of State for South Asian Affairs, 1993–97.

Bruce Reidel. National Security Council staff member, 1997–.

Randy Rydell. Staff member, Senate Committee on Governmental Affairs, 1987–98.

Harold Saunders. National Security Council staff member, 1961–74; Assistant Secretary of State for Near Eastern and South Asian Affairs, 1978–81.

Howard Schaffer. Political Counselor, Islamabad, 1975–77; Deputy Assistant Secretary of State for Near Eastern and South Asian Affairs, 1982–84 and 1988–89.

Teresita Schaffer. Deputy Assistant Secretary of State for Near Eastern and South Asian Affairs, 1989–92.

Brent Scowcroft. National Security Adviser, 1974–77 and 1989–93.

Thomas W. Simons, Jr. Ambassador to Pakistan, 1995–98.

Sidney Sober. Deputy Chief of Mission and Chargé d'Affaires, Islamabad, 1969–73; Senior Deputy Assistant Secretary of State for Near Eastern and South Asian Affairs, 1974–76.

Stephen Solarz. Member, House of Representatives (D-N.Y.), 1975–93.

James Spain. Pakistan Country Director, Department of State, 1965–68; Chargé d'Affaires, Islamabad, 1969.

William Spengler. Pakistan Desk Officer, Department of State, 1958–60.

Ronald Spiers. Ambassador to Pakistan, 1981–84.

Phillips Talbot. Correspondent for South Asia, *Chicago Daily News,* 1946–48; Assistant Secretary of State for Near Eastern and South Asian Affairs, 1961–65.

Strobe Talbott. Deputy Secretary of State, 1994–.

Thomas P. Thornton. Chief South Asia analyst, Bureau of Intelligence and Research, Department of State, 1963–69; Policy Planning Council member, Department of State, 1973–76; National Security Council staff member, 1977–81.

Christopher Van Hollen. Political Officer, Karachi, 1958–59; Officer-in-Charge, Murree Office, 1960–61; Deputy Assistant Secretary of State for Near Eastern and South Asian Affairs, 1969–72.

Eliza Van Hollen. Afghanistan analyst, Bureau of Intelligence and Research, Department of State, 1978–82, 1986–88; Chief, South Asia Division, Bureau of Intelligence and Research, Department of State, 1989–94.

Nicholas Veliotes. Assistant Secretary of State for Near Eastern and South Asian Affairs, 1981–84.

Leonard Weiss. Staff Director, Senate Committee on Governmental Affairs, 1976–99.

Charles Wilson. Member, U.S. House of Representatives (D-Texas), 1966–96.

W. Howard Wriggins. Policy Planning Council member, Department of State, 1961–65; National Security Council staff member, 1966–67.

Oral Histories

(Unless otherwise noted, oral histories are from the archive of the Association for Diplomatic Studies and Training, Arlington, Virginia. Those listed are U.S. officials, unless noted otherwise.)

J. Wesley Adams. Mission to the UN, 1948–50; Political Officer, New Delhi, 1952–54 (Harry S Truman Library).

Archer K. Blood. Consul General, Dacca, 1969–71.

Henry Byroade. Assistant Secretary of State for Near Eastern, South Asian, and African Affairs, 1952–54; Ambassador to Pakistan, 1974–77 (Harry S. Truman Library).

Peter Constable. Pakistan Desk Officer and Country Director, Department of State, 1970–71 and 1972–76; Deputy Chief of Mission, Islamabad, 1976–79; Senior Deputy Assistant Secretary of State for Near Eastern and South Asian Affairs, 1979–81.

Raymond Hare. Officer-in-Charge, South Asia, Department of State, 1947–49.

Mohammed Zafrullah Khan. Foreign Minister of Pakistan, 1947–54 (John F. Kennedy Library).

Barrington King. Deputy Chief of Mission, Islamabad, 1979–83.

Ridgway Knight. Deputy Chief of Mission, Karachi, 1957–59.

William Kontos. Pakistan Deputy Director, Agency for International Development, 1966–69.

Edward Masters. Political Officer, Karachi, 1953–55.

John McCarthy. Deputy Chief of Mission, Islamabad, 1984–88.

Armin Meyer. Deputy Chief of Mission, Kabul, 1954–56.

Sidney Sober. Deputy Chief of Mission and Chargé d'Affaires, Islamabad, 1969–73; Senior Deputy Assistant Secretary of State for Near Eastern and South Asian Affairs, 1974–76.

Ronald Spiers. Ambassador to Pakistan, 1981–84.

Christopher Van Hollen. Political Officer, Karachi, 1958–59; Officer-in-Charge, Murree Office, 1960–61; and Deputy Assistant Secretary of State for Near Eastern and South Asian PAffairs, 1969–72.

Maurice Williams. Pakistan Director, Agency for International Development, 1966–69; Deputy Administrator, Agency for International Development, 1970–73.

Index